DAVID LLOYD GEORGE
a political life

David Lloyd George

a political life

Organizer of Victory
1912–1916

Bentley Brinkerhoff Gilbert

Ohio State University Press. Columbus

Jacket design by Paul Wood

Type set in Hong Kong by Graphicraft Typesetters Ltd.

Printed by Mackays of Chatham, Great Britain

The paper in this book meets the guidelines for permanence and durability of
the Committee on Production Guidelines for Book Longevity of the Council on
Library Resources.∞

9 8 7 6 5 4 3 2 1

Contents

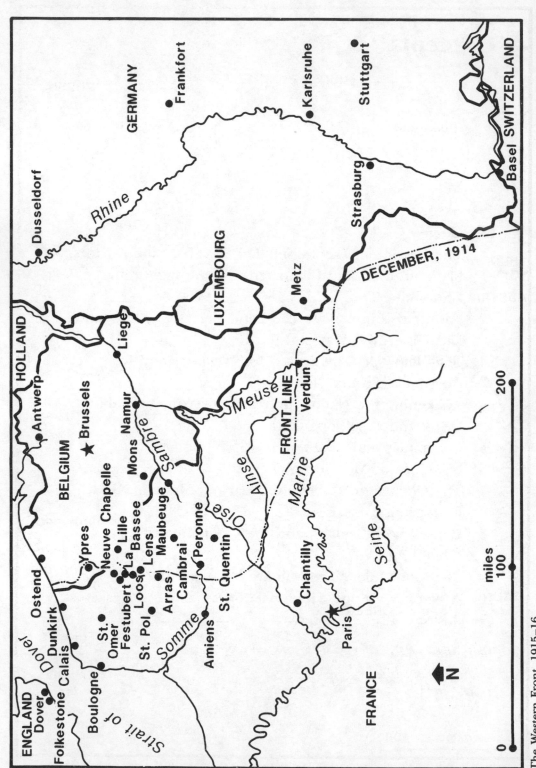

The Western Front, 1915–16

AUSTRIA-
HUNGARY

RUSSIA

Budapest

TRANSYLVANIA

Danube

HUNGARY

ROMANIA

AUSTRIA-

Belgrade

Bucharest

Constanza

River

SERBIA

Nish

Black
Sea

MONTENEGRO

Vardar

Sofia

Adriatic Sea

MACEDONIA

BULGARIA

Monastir

River

Salonika

Constantinople

ALBANIA

ITALY

Sea of
Marmara

Dardanelles

GREECE

LEMNOS

Ionian Sea

Aegean Sea

TURKEY

Smyrna

N

Athens

0   miles   100

The Balkans

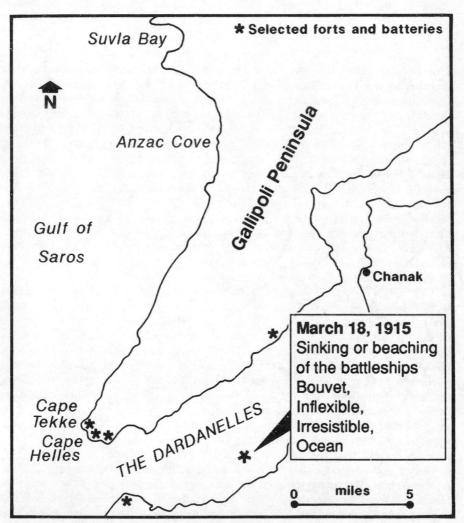

The Dardanelles and the Gallipoli peninsula

Preface

This volume takes its title from the sobriquet awarded Lazare Carnot, a member of the Committee of Public Safety under the French Revolutionary Convention, who helped to frame the decree for the *levée en masse*, who rebuilt the republican army which carried the French Revolution to Europe, and who in 1796 gave the young colonel Napoleon Bonaparte his first independent command. Soon Carnot faded quietly into private life as he saw the decay of the republican institutions to which he was devoted. Clearly he was not a Lloyd George. Yet one senses that without him his nation would not have survived. Perhaps the same may be said of Lloyd George.

For Carnot, the *levée en masse* was not simply a requirement of military service for unmarried men, although that was certainly a part of it, but a call literally for a popular rising, a mobilization of the totality of France's power. Everyone, in one way or another, was to participate in the nation's military effort. The *levée* demanded not only the commitment of the body, but also of the spirit. Lloyd George would have understood.

After 1911 the creative phase of Lloyd George's parliamentary work as a legislation craftsman, the architect of change, was behind him. Indeed if there is a theme to his political life in the last two years before the war it is of failure and near disaster. The Marconi episode and the budget of 1914 both threatened to end his career. The land campaign attracted no support. His good advice on Irish Home Rule was not taken, until it was too late.

However biography is not quite the same thing as history. For the life of the nation, bills that do not pass, institutions that fail to come into existence, political contests that are lost, are usually, although not always, of little interest. But for the story of a man, his mistakes, the roads not taken, are as significant and perhaps more instructive than his successes. The biographer may be certain that his subject ponders them at length.

Only a word need be said here about the account of Lloyd George's ascent to the Prime Ministership after the war began: It is as much the story of Herbert Asquith's decline in vigor and leadership — indeed one has the feeling that somehow the Prime Minister lost interest in the war — as it is of the thrust of Lloyd George's ambition. Of course Lloyd George wanted to be Prime Minister; there is no need to take seriously his repeated protestations that he did not. After his work at the Ministry of Munitions, the reversion of the post would have been his in any case when Asquith retired at the end of the war. But the deterioration of the genuinely cordial relationship between the two men proceeded from differences over the conduct of the war, organization of industry and, specifically, the management of the army, not place seeking.

There are a substantial number of long quotations in this volume. I justify them, first, because evidence so far as possible should be allowed to tell its own story. Second, while Lloyd George reproduced in his *War Memoirs* a great many of his Cabinet papers, most of which are of great importance, he is never exact about what is left out. The deletions are usually, almost always, interesting.

Third, most important, since the composition of the first volume of this work in 1985, the complete diaries of George, Lord Riddell have been made available by the British Library. These comprise an immense set of fourteen volumes of manuscript and nearly as many volumes because of additions, of typescript. The unpublished material amounts to perhaps three times the text of the three rather slim volumes of the extracts Riddell published in the early 1930's. They are in no sense a diary of Lord Riddell. Rather they are an almost day by day account of Riddell's conversations with Lloyd George, conversations with others, both friends and enemies, about Lloyd George, and, perhaps most enlightening of all, of his reflections, which hardly appear in the published diaries, about Lloyd George's position in politics and about his successes and failures. These ruminations, by an immensely well-informed and intelligent contemporary, who had no political ambitions of his own, a man by no means uncritical but who wished Lloyd George well, constitute a treasure house for the biographer. John McEwen has done historians a service by producing a beautifully annotated, but alas far too short, edition of some of the unpublished diaries, although this writer wishes he had devoted himself entirely to hitherto unpublished material rather than to correcting the many mistakes in Riddell's own volumes. (John M. McEwen, ed., *The Riddell Diaries, 1908–1923*, London, 1986.) In any case, a huge amount of information remains hidden in the British Library Manuscripts Room. Stories hitherto guessed at, or known only by an obscure reference, become clear: Lloyd George's break with Churchill, the political murder of C.F.G. Masterman (it was a suicide), above all the transcending importance of the ghostly figure in early Georgian Liberal politics, Reginald McKenna, and of Pamela McKenna, his wife.

Another source of quotations is Lucy Masterman's typescript diary, for the use of which I am indebted to Mr. Neville Masterman. Mrs. Masterman's record is neither as full nor as perceptive as Riddell's. Unlike Riddell she had no independent sources of information beyond her husband. Nonetheless, until the summer of 1914, her husband, Charles Masterman, was Lloyd George's closest political lieutenant. On the Chancellor's trials and difficulties in the last years of peace, the struggle with the doctors over health insurance and the painful Marconi episode, her diary, now at the University of Birmingham, is of enormous value, with all its fuzziness on dates.

Finally I must express my gratitude to Professor David Woodward for allowing me to see the typescript of his collection of the military correspondence of Field Marshal Sir William Robertson, published in 1989 by The Bodley Head for the Army Records Society. This really excellent book deserves a wide circulation. It provides, with careful annotations, both sides of Robertson's correspondence, not half of which have been printed before, with all the major figures of the war. Robertson has had no biographers except an admiring but cursory volume by Victor Bonham-Carter (*Soldier True: The Life*

and Times of Field Marshal Sir William Robertson, 1860–1933, London, 1963).
Beyond his own memoirs and his account of his battles with Lloyd George
in *Soldiers and Statesmen*, his story remains to be told. Prof. Woodward has
made a much needed beginning.

I thank the editors of the *Historical Journal*, the *Journal of British Studies* and
Historical Research for allowing me to reprint parts of articles that appeared
first in those journals. Similarly I must acknowledge the support of the John
Simon Guggenheim Memorial Foundation and the University of Illinois
Institute for the Humanities which enabled me to begin, and largely to
complete, the basic research for this study in Britain and Northern Ireland.

Among those to whom this volume is indebted I must mention the forty-
odd members of the Department of History of the University of Illinois at
Chicago for their patience with their Chairman during its composition. Several
however were kind enough to read the typescript and comment, and criticize, at length. Particularly, I want to thank my colleagues in British history,
Professors James Sack and Carolyn Edie, who uncovered many obscurities,
mistakes and sheer stupidities. I take credit myself for those that remain.

Several stylistic conventions have been continued from the first volume. I
have followed *The Times Gazetteer* in the spelling of place names. Again, I have
used the term 'Unionist' when referring to the combined Conservative and
Liberal Unionist parties because the party headed by Andrew Bonar Law
continued to use that title, even though after 1912 the Liberal Unionist
interest, for practical purposes, had disappeared.

In dealing with quotations, I have tried to continue the practice of citing
the most readily available source. Hence, for example, if a Lloyd George
letter has been subsequently printed the citation will refer to the printed
version. However if the printed version has been altered, or is incomplete,
the reference will be to the letter collection with a note that part of the item
appears also in a published work.

At last, I must express my deepest gratitude for the skill, historical
knowledge, and above all patience, of Katharine Stohrer, who can hear and
transcribe inaudible tapes, decipher indecipherable notes, and make a word
processor beg for mercy. She has made this book.

Chicago, Illinois   Bentley Brinkerhoff Gilbert
December, 1990

Introduction

In the first month of 1912, on 17 January, David Lloyd George entered his fiftieth year. Between that time and the last month of 1916 he traveled from one pinnacle of success to an even greater one. In 1911 he had been a Minister of the Crown for six years and Herbert Asquith's Chancellor of the Exchequer for nearly four. He had laid the foundation of the welfare state with the National Insurance Act and had seen to the final destruction of the House of Lords' veto. By doing so he had rescued Liberalism from the slow suffocation that awaits a political party which has outlived its mission. Almost exactly five years later he became Prime Minister because the political, and indeed, many of the military, leaders of Britain, including a large number who distrusted him personally and abhorred the politics he stood for, believed that he and he alone could save the British nation from defeat in war.

Nonetheless, as in the earlier period of Lloyd George's political life, there was no inevitability, no inexorable progression, about his elevation to higher office. At least twice in the years covered by this book he appeared to be on the edge of career-shattering disaster. In the Marconi scandal, when he neglected to tell the truth, at least the whole truth, to the House of Commons — the difference between complete honesty and the omission of small, inconvenient, but pertinent, facts was never clear to him — he was saved by Prime Minister Asquith who put the weight of his own enormous prestige into his defense. Just a year later in the summer of 1914 he achieved the unexampled distinction of having his budget for the coming fiscal year, a measure that he saw as the successor to the great People's Budget of 1909, declared out of order by the Speaker of the House of Commons. This was accompanied by a revolt against Lloyd George within the Liberal party. Faced also by civil war in Ireland, the Prime Minister was eager to resign. In the projected election the Liberals, as Asquith himself believed, would have been slaughtered. It is hard to imagine Lloyd George returning to the Exchequer in any subsequent Liberal administration. But again he was saved, as was indeed the Liberal government, by the outbreak of war. The fatal dissolution did not occur.

The war made Lloyd George Prime Minister as surely as it ruined Asquith. More than that, one is left with the sense of a cause and effect relationship, almost as if the two men were attached to the ends of a rope over a pulley. As the Prime Minister descended, he pulled up Lloyd George.

Lloyd George himself believed, as he told his confidante Sir George Riddell, after his appointment to that office, that he would never win the Premiership. He would, he thought, be deprived of it by party jealousy and intrigue.

Without the war, in a single party Liberal government, one must believe he was correct. The Marconi episode and the rebellion over the 1914 budget demonstrated, if nothing else, the depth of the distrust particularly among senior Liberals for Lloyd George and his schemes.

To be sure, when the war began he had a cadre of followers, one could style them disciples, among the survivors of the 1906 generation of radicals in the House of Commons who gave him considerable political power. The men were represented by Charles Masterman and Christopher Addison within his immediate entourage. But these men were distrusted by the main body of old line Liberals nearly as much as was Lloyd George himself. In any case nearly all of them were driven away in the conscription debates of 1915 and 1916.

Compulsory military service, and for Lloyd George its larger expression, national service, which would have included direction of labor, became the core of the dispute between Lloyd George and his old radical semi-socialist and pacifist constituency. Yet for him military conscription was only a part of the linked efforts of national mobilization and inter-Allied cooperation, without which Britain would lose the fight against Germany. Cooperation involved the search for alternative fronts, the integration of Allied military commands with the coordination of Allied military planning, and the destruction of British military exclusiveness and secrecy, all of which would insure that his nation's armed power and diplomatic policies would provide support for each other. He was aware of the helplessness of the amateur political planner in the face of the military professional. And he was sure that the professional soldier, if not controlled, would lead the nation not to victory but to defeat. The military commanders could not be trusted when speaking to their political superiors, he was convinced. Generals always spoke in generalities, he observed.

All of this, then, became the theme of a series of papers submitted to the Cabinet and the Prime Minister, beginning in January 1915. Repeatedly he called for centralization — the military command should not be permitted to operate as an independent, almost hostile, estate. There should be continuous planning, examination of options and centralized consultation within a small body of politicians with access to continuing and reliable military advice. 'Pre-vision' he termed it. The nation should understand that everyone must work or fight. It was an engineer's war as much as it was a soldier's. Above all there should be total organization, as he believed there was in Germany. Here was a flat contradiction of everything Liberalism stood for. Lloyd George's opponents in the Cabinet, led by Reginald McKenna, insisted that Germany would not be defeated by the Prussianization of Great Britain.

Lloyd George was unhappy about his estrangement from radical Liberalism, which began in the autumn of 1915 and which was associated in the minds of newspaper editors with a plot to overthrow Asquith. In effect, the Liberal papers argued, Lloyd George had been captured by the Tories and by Lord Northcliffe, proprietor of *The Times* and the *Daily Mail.* His support for conscription proved it. Afterwards Lloyd George described this period, during which he was totally occupied as Minister of Munitions, as the hardest time of his life. No doubt his feeling of isolation accounts for his continual and determined courtship of Sir William Robertson Nicoll, the powerful editor and publisher of the non-conformist *British Weekly*, who had supported Lloyd George since the days of the education revolt and who offered at least a dependable channel of communication to his old constituency.

Lloyd George's emergence as the proponent of the knockout blow, at so much cost both to his peace of mind and to his political position, is traced in the chapters that follow. It may be taken that his statement to the American journalist Roy Howard on 28 September 1916 represented his debut as an unforgiving hard liner on victory in the war, as the Queen's Hall speech of 19 September 1914 had been his personal declaration of war. To be sure the Howard statement was also a warning to the United States not to 'butt in,' and try to compromise a war that Britain was determined to win. But he intended to convey no less a challenge to the growing peace party in his own country, a challenge that was recognized by Lord Lansdowne in a Cabinet memorandum six weeks later.

One may question whether the breach in the Liberal party that appeared with the fall of Asquith was the fault of Lloyd George or of the Prime Minister. The antipathy for Lloyd George among the Liberals, both within the radicals in the House of Commons, who were his traditional following, and among the members of the ministry, who were almost uniformly devoted to Asquith, certified to those around the Prime Minister that nearly all Lloyd George's ministerial and parliamentary support would come from Unionists. (By December 1916 the Unionists possessed a somewhat larger delegation in the House of Commons than the Liberals.) Such an unstable combination could not last, Asquith's friends, of whom McKenna was the leader, uniformly assumed. Asquith would soon return. Here lies the key to the Prime Minister's intransigence in the last days of the fatal week of Friday, 1 December to Thursday, 7 December 1916. Even after it became clear that Lloyd George could form a government, Asquith's advisors were convinced that the artificial marriage would quickly dissolve. Therefore Asquith had, they argued, no reason to compromise. He should keep his army intact and prepare to fight another day. Accordingly Asquith declined the Lord Chancellorship. He would support the war effort to be sure, but he certainly would not strive officiously to keep Lloyd George's government in office. The historian is left with the sense that Liberalism died at this time, done in by a man who for perfectly honest reasons expected to use the weapons of the party machinery in the country, which he still controlled, and the undying loyalty of the Liberal party's talent and leadership, to overthrow the King's government as soon as possible.

An important theme of this volume, then, concerns the decay of the genuinely warm relationship between Lloyd George and Asquith. The two men were never social friends, but the Prime Minister trusted Lloyd George and supported him, sometimes almost alone, in his projects, and leaned upon him for political intelligence and advice. Lloyd George, for his part, honestly liked Asquith, admired his astute and impartial judgment in administrative matters, and sincerely regretted the Prime Minister's growing indolence, selfishness, and his obvious physical deterioration which became apparent during the second year of the war.

A similar evolution occurred in Lloyd George's relationships with C.F.G. Masterman, with Churchill, and with Reginald McKenna. The first man saw his political career destroyed by National Health Insurance and his friendship with Lloyd George died little more than six months later under circumstances painful to Masterman, although not, apparently, to Lloyd George. Churchill's story was more complicated. Churchill's career as a Liberal had begun on 31 May 1904 when, after a characteristically dramatic pause at the Bar of the House, he had turned to the right instead of the left and had taken a seat next to Lloyd George on the second bench below the gangway. For the next seven and a half years, he had delighted in antagonizing the party of his father by posing as an undiluted, anti-Chamberlainite, social reforming, radical. In the process he built a warm personal friendship with Lloyd George even though the personalities of the two men could not have been more different. This phase of Churchill's career ended as abruptly as it had begun in the autumn of 1911 in the aftermath of the sinister Agadir crisis when Asquith, at Lloyd George's urging, had proposed Churchill to replace Reginald McKenna as First Lord of the Admiralty. Churchill's appointment was announced on 23 October 1911.

For the new First Lord, social reform, welfare legislation, lower taxes, and land reform upon which Lloyd George had hoped to build a new Liberalism, evaporated as causes. To him they counted for nothing in the face of the imperious demands of naval competition with Germany. His personal friendship with Lloyd George declined more slowly. But it died quickly in the first six months of the war, partly as a result of Lloyd George's impatience, shared with everyone, at Churchill's war-time behavior in the Admiralty. The final breach between the two derived from Churchill's fury over his loss of the Admiralty in May 1915. He was completely oblivious to the widespread dislike of his arrogance and to the nearly universal mistrust of his judgment on both sides of the House. Instead he blamed Lloyd George for his enforced resignation. Although Churchill's early rage — hysteria would not be too strong a word — eventually dissipated and after a time the two men saw each other with some regularity, the old easy intimacy was gone. Still Lloyd George continued to admire Churchill's undoubted intelligence and industry in office and in December 1916 he was desperate to find any senior Liberal who would take office in his Cabinet. But he seems to have made no attempt to challenge the Unionists' absolute prohibition on any post for Churchill in his new government. Yet after becoming Prime Minister Lloyd George did not forget Churchill.

For Lloyd George, Churchill was a personal although hardly a political problem. His unpopularity left him powerless. On the other hand, in the years covered by this study Reginald McKenna remained continually both a frustration and a danger. Since 1895 McKenna, a nominal Congregationalist, had been Member of Parliament for Monmouthshire North and in his first ten years in the House was as dependable a supporter of non-conformist causes as Lloyd George himself. The two men had been close colleagues if not friends in the protracted battle over A.J. Balfour's Education Act of 1902. However, in the spring of 1908, in the process of the formation of Asquith's government, McKenna believed with some reason that the incoming Prime Minister wished to appoint him Chancellor of the Exchequer and had failed to do so because of the intervention of Lloyd George who insisted upon the post for himself. McKenna was consoled with the Admiralty. Subsequently, after the Cabinet had been chosen but before it was announced, McKenna told Asquith that Lloyd George had been responsible for an article in the *Daily Chronicle* listing quite accurately the members of the still-secret government. Lloyd George of course denied the accusation, but his suspicion of McKenna began and did not abate.

In the summer of 1908 McKenna married the handsome, accomplished, and wealthy Pamela Jekyll, a young woman whom Asquith had long admired. During the next half dozen years, despite McKenna's painful loss of the Admiralty to Churchill in 1911 (for which he blamed Lloyd George as well as Churchill), the Prime Minister was a frequent visitor at the house of the 'McKennae' for dinners and evenings of bridge. Then in May 1915, to the political world's utter astonishment, McKenna, who was regarded as a diminishing or dying public figure, succeeded Lloyd George at the Exchequer. Asquith, as will be recounted, still loyally supported Lloyd George at the Ministry of Munitions in his battles to take weapons design, manufacture, testing and delivery from the army. But the former Chancellor's collegial intimacy with the Prime Minister, the short chats each morning about things in general, which Asquith seems to have enjoyed, ended. McKenna, whose understanding of Treasury business was excellent but whose political instincts were as innocent and egocentric as Churchill's, took Lloyd George's place as Asquith's political chaplain and confessor. In the end, Asquith became neither the first nor the last great political leader to be destroyed by loyal men around him whom he trusted, but who did not trust each other.

Among the figures who had appeared in Lloyd George's life earlier and who now must be introduced was Frances Louise Stevenson. In August 1911 Miss Stevenson came to Criccieth to serve as the summer tutor for Lloyd George's youngest daughter, Megan. She had graduated from the Royal Holloway College and earlier had attended Clapham High School at the same time as Lloyd George's eldest daughter, Mair Eluned. In 1907 Mair Eluned had died of appendicitis while a student there. Miss Stevenson was a tall, pretty young woman, 23 years old, very nice but 'slightly bitten by suffragettism, about which George never fails to rag her', observed Charles Masterman's wife, Lucy. She was in every way, in solid suburban background, exceptional education, advanced political opinions, and handsome appearance, the incarnation of H.G. Wells' Ann Veronica Stanley. (But see the testimony of Lloyd George's second daughter, Lady Olwen Carey Evans, on Miss Stevenson. While conceding her good looks, Lady Olwen found Frances Stevenson 'as hard as nails' and 'possessive and avaricious beyond words.')[1] In 1911 Miss Stevenson was teaching at Allenswood, a girls' school in Wimbledon in which Olwen was a student and where Megan was enrolled for the following autumn.

Lloyd George returned to London in the middle of September 1911. Miss Stevenson quickly followed. Megan's place as a student at Allenswood necessitated visits to the school and meetings with Miss Stevenson even during Lloyd George's busy autumn of 1911. He invited her to the House of Commons to observe him in action and she allowed him to take her to Gatti's for dinner. A warm friendship developed. In January 1913 she became Lloyd George's mistress and in 1943 his wife.

Miss Stevenson's place in Lloyd George's life, the fact that she was only two years older than his adored, dead, Mair Eluned, has occasioned a certain amount of psychological speculation among writers. Lloyd George indeed contributed these neo-Freudian bubbles, as Frances Stevenson recorded on the second anniversary of their 'marriage,' by recording that he had confessed she had 'taken the place somewhat of Mair, "my little girl whom I lost."'[2] Yet in fact Miss Stevenson's relationship with Lloyd George was more nearly that of an intelligent, efficient and trusted confidential employee of whom he was also very fond. She could oversee both political and domestic arrangements, be commissioned to conduct correspondence, translate into and out of French, give orders in his name, and under certain circumstances, act as his hostess. Arnold Bennett's Sam Raingo's first encounter with Miss Stevenson ('Miss Parker') at one of Lloyd George's ('Andrew Clyth') famous business breakfasts at No. 10 in April 1918 provides a fair summary of the impression Frances Stevenson evidently made upon many men.

> She was bright as the morning, efficiently and continuously bright, bright when she spoke and bright when she listened or reflected. And her glance and carriage indicated that unlike many personal secretaries dedicated to the comfort and convenience of great men, she was not suffering from any suppressed desires. She had the air of being familiar with every variety of human character and experience and knowledge, and of mysteriously hiding a thousand secrets and a thousand personal opinions.[3]

That Miss Stevenson was important and useful to Lloyd George cannot be questioned. Nor can there be any doubt that he was the absolute focus of her life. Her diary, in which the first entry records that Lloyd George told her to keep it, displays nothing but total affection. His causes were hers. He was always right, always victorious in Cabinet battles. Yet there is no evidence that he read her manuscript or even saw it. Many details are incorrect: for example, the dates of Cabinet meetings before he was Prime Minister. Matters he might have wished to alter, such as his declared opinions on political issues, which of course frequently changed, or his repeated announcements that he would resign over one matter or another, are recorded faithfully.

Miss Stevenson is remarkably candid in her diary about the several opportunities for marriage that came her way and equally realistic about the fact that Lloyd George would never leave his wife. Yet her determination not to be separated from him, at least during the years of his Prime Ministership, appears never to have wavered. For his part Lloyd George, disorderly as he frequently was in personal affairs, remained constantly attentive to Miss Stevenson. Although his letters to his wife diminished in number, he wrote to Miss Stevenson constantly when away and passed surreptitious notes to her when the two were together. He made time to be alone with her on weekends. He delighted her with imitations of his Cabinet colleagues and repeated, not always accurately, Cabinet secrets. She was a refreshment and a restorative. As she loved him, he needed her.

Frances Stevenson's presence completed, rather than caused, the destabilization of Lloyd George's family arrangements. This is a complicated topic, but an important one that helps to account for the singular rootlessness that characterized the remaining years of his life. She did not cut him off from

Wales. This estrangement had begun long before and in any case the sojourns there during the Whitsun parliamentary recess continued. Moreover he never gave up his care for Welsh, especially Caernarvonshire, political interests, or for Welsh patronage, although these were managed from London. He remained until his death an Alderman of the Caernarvonshire County Council, his first political office.

Rather for Lloyd George, his family was atomized, if the word may be used in this sense. Those who accepted Miss Stevenson's place, Megan for example, he saw frequently. When the whole world gathered in Paris after the war, with Lloyd George at the pinnacle of his international prestige, Megan and Miss Stevenson accompanied him, not Margaret his wife. When Sir George Riddell provided him with a house on Walton Heath in Surrey in 1913, Frances Stevenson was usually the hostess and when Margaret visited, Frances Stevenson had of course to disappear. After he became Prime Minister, Margaret seems to have visited London somewhat more frequently. She insisted that Lloyd George move into No. 10, even though he would have been content to remain in No. 11. No. 10 he thought was too expensive. Bonar Law, who had plenty of money, could live in No. 10. But Lloyd George would leave Margaret in Downing Street to visit Walton Heath and Frances Stevenson on week-ends.

Lloyd George, then, was not separated from the members of his family, but from the family as a unit. They were now individuals. Olwen, later Megan, and particularly his elder son, Richard, bitterly resented Frances Stevenson and in the process he clearly lost some intimacy with some of his children. He continued to see them, but the corporate family disappeared. The summers at Criccieth with guests from London, walks in the fields, the picnics, and the evenings of song, were things of the past.

Withal he continued to love his children, and his wife, as even Frances Stevenson admitted, allowing them, as she saw it, to intrude endlessly upon his time and leisure. Indeed, perhaps understandably, Lady Olwen Carey Evans and Miss Stevenson each say remarkably similar things about the ill nature and carelessness of the opposite side of Lloyd George's double menage, remarking particularly upon the shabby selfishness with which he was treated. What Lloyd George thought of this arrangement is hard to say but he allowed it to continue for thirty years.

In conclusion, one must describe Lloyd George's tangled political position at the end of the year 1911. Paradoxically, even as he savored his triumph in the year-long battle over the National Insurance Act, Lloyd George's overwhelming public popularity had begun to decline, a fact that would become painfully evident to his colleagues and to himself as the year 1912 progressed. The problem lay in the provisions of the national health insurance scheme for beneficiary contributions, which were set to begin on 15 July 1912.

This matter requires a brief explanation chiefly because health insurance, notwithstanding its prodigious importance as a pattern for Britain's future welfare state, constituted for the Liberals, at least until the war, a political burden, instead of the expected trophy. It helped to drain the party of energy and resolution. It destroyed Liberal candidates at by-elections, costing among others Lloyd George's valued and expert political lieutenant Charles Masterman his parliamentary career. It isolated Lloyd George from his colleagues, provided fuel for the doctors' resistance to the insurance program, and clearly retarded the land campaign of 1913–14.

That a four pence per week (three pence in the case of women) workers' contribution toward the support of what would prove to be on the whole an excellent and useful, if limited, program for medical care should have generated such widespread discontent would seem to constitute an outrage without an aggravation. It should be noted that Lloyd George himself was surprised and depressed at the public's reaction. Yet it must be remembered that in the years before the war, as indeed had been the case for centuries, for the ordinary British citizen, government was local. The income tax, beginning at £160 per year, did not touch the worker. He was hardly aware of customs and excise. 'Tax' meant the household rate that went to support the county and borough, to pay for schools and for poor law relief. The national health insurance contributions were not heavy even in pre-war working class terms, but they represented an unprecedented intrusion from a far-away government in London. There were many stories. The money would be used to pay the salaries for Members of Parliament, who began to receive £400 per year in 1911. It was to be wasted on public housing for the poor or it would pay for government propaganda, or indeed it somehow would become part of Lloyd George's personal fortune. (The contribution was popularly called 'the Lloyd George'.) This automatic but unfocused popular resentment of the insurance contribution as a tax innovation was given ideological respectability by some trade union leaders and socialist thinkers who argued that the entire cost of health insurance should be borne either by the employer or by the government. In truth, as it stood the contribution was simply a regressive income tax.

To be sure most of the opposition to health insurance disappeared in the explosion of state activity that came with the war. The imposition of a four pence national tax by a government that could take for itself power to force men to serve in the army was obviously a minor matter. And in the inter-war period health insurance was decently popular. Yet equally, by this time Lloyd George's place in its founding was of course forgotten. Unlike for example the general acceptance of William Beveridge as the father of the post-war welfare state, Lloyd George never received popular acknowledgement for his greatest legislative achievement.

1 The Decline of Liberalism: The Revolt of the Doctors, Marconi, the Land Campaigns, the struggle with Churchill

For the Liberals and for Lloyd George the years of achievement passed with the end of 1911. Although no one except perhaps H.W. Massingham understood it yet, the heroic age of the new Liberalism was over.[1] The great measures that had revived a drooping and dispirited Liberal party after the humiliations over education and licensing: the People's Budget, the Parliament Act, health and unemployment insurance, were now on the statute books but their consequences had to be faced. Health insurance, the jewel of Lloyd George's reforms, was not only unpopular with the medical profession which had to operate it but was actively disliked by the working population who were supposed to be its beneficiaries. The Parliament Act meant that Irish Home Rule was no longer a fictitious issue. The elections of 1910 destroyed the Liberals' immense majority of 1906 and gave the Irish Nationalist party in the House of Commons the leverage to force action upon Home Rule from the Asquith government. Henceforth the claims of Ireland again would dominate politics as they had done when Lloyd George entered the House of Commons.

Abroad, the sinister anger in Germany, which Lloyd George's Mansion House speech the previous July had done so much to arouse, continued to boil. Through the autumn of 1911 there had been warnings to the government, both public and private, that the result would be a large increase in German naval construction in 1912. The official notification of this in the form of a draft copy of a new German Navy Law reached the Cabinet at one of its first meetings in 1912. So died Lloyd George's old dream, pursued since 1908, of a naval understanding with the Kaiser's empire.

At the same time, in the spring of 1912, appeared, as in the year before, the dangerous malaise of labor discontent which exploded in a series of national strikes. Organized labor could indeed, as one leader boasted, paralyze the nation. The Cabinet sensed its failing grip on the course of events and repeatedly in the next years, discussed resignation.

For Lloyd George as well, the magic that accomplished so much, that had put new heart into the party after the trough of despair in 1908, seemed to have dissipated. He was, of course, easily able to outwit the British Medical Association and preside over the beginning of health insurance benefits in

January 1913, but he failed, and failed disastrously, to establish his cherished land program. Welsh disestablishment was not achieved. Nor could he find an escape for the Liberals from their commitment to Home Rule for all of Ireland. Finally as the result of sheer bad luck, compounded by one of his most characteristic, but in this case innocent, personal frailties, the tendency to tell some but not all of the truth, he became enmeshed in the terrifying web of the Marconi scandal.

In the early months of 1912 Lloyd George was depressed and restless.[2] He disliked the Cabinet's intransigence over the question of a minimum wage for miners which boiled up in January after the miners' union had voted to call its first nationwide strike, involving one million men. He was not, pointedly, invited to take single charge of negotiations with the miners' union, although he had been a member of the ministerial team that met unsuccessfully with the workers and employers before the strike began on 1 March.[3] He was conscious that the Cabinet saw health insurance as an electoral disadvantage, as by-elections were demonstrating.[4]

Part of his unhappiness was the result of the cooling of his friendship with Winston Churchill exacerbated by differences of opinion between the two over the coal strike.[5] Churchill thought Lloyd George a 'waning force' F.E. Smith reported.[6] The alliance between the two men seemed to have broken up, said Charles Masterman to George Riddell in April 1912. They were still friendly, but did not concert action as before.[7] Herbert Lewis was more precise. 'So long as the L.G. chip was on the crest of the wave the Churchill chip was there too,' he wrote on 26 March, 'but now that the L.G. chip is in the trough the Churchill chip seems to be sheering off.'[8]

Lloyd George's marvelous sensory antennae, the actor's empathy that enabled him to explore other men's minds, made all too real to him his decline in his party's estimation. A public manifestation of this was the fact that the Unionists were finding it profitable, as it had not been three years earlier, to attack him by name on the public platform before a general audience. Walter Long, who was traveling in the North and West estimating the state of the Liberals in the cities that provided the government's margin of victory in December 1910, wrote cheerfully from Newcastle to the new party leader, Andrew Bonar Law, that the Insurance Act was unpopular everywhere. 'The moderate Liberal is beginning to be alarmed,' he reported,

> and I am told by a gentleman who lately lunched at the local Liberal club that he was surprised to see how Lloyd George had lost popularity with the business Liberals...'Mr. Lloyd George is moving too quickly for us...' The Socialist legislation of the Government are the main assets at the present moment of the Unionist party. The radicals have undoubtedly lost a great deal of their popularity.

The better class Liberal, Long concluded, was also 'sick and tired of Lloyd George finance and the "people's budget" is beginning to be felt.'[9] 'They make me wonder whether I am a Liberal at all,' Lloyd George complained to Lucy Masterman.[10]

Lloyd George and Bonar Law were, in fact, friends of six years standing and intimate in a way the Chancellor never could have been with Arthur Balfour whom he also admired, although from a distance. The Unionist leader shared with Lloyd George the alien nonconformist background, the lost parent, and the lack of a university education. Neither cared for the ceremonies of London society nor country week-ends, and while Lloyd George's public charm was legendary, beyond politics he was, like Bonar Law, whose wife had died in 1908, a solitary figure. Above all the two shared the conviction that politics was a serious twenty-four hour a day business, not a gentleman's game or an aristocratic duty. Bonar Law was essentially a pugnacious tactician and party manager, a fighter, who was troubled no more than Lloyd George by a sense of delicacy or fitness in the achievement of party goals. He lacked Lloyd George's vision of a better society, but he was quite as willing as the Chancellor of the Exchequer to use any means within, or without, the political world to embarrass his opponents and thwart the will of the government. His accession meant an escalation in the level of party confrontation and a renewal of demagogic Toryism.[11]

When Bonar Law succeeded to the Unionist leadership Lloyd George had written him a wry congratulation observing that 'had the Unionist party always shown the same wisdom in their decisions, I should not have been writing this letter in the Chancellor of the Exchequer's room in the House of Commons.'[12] However, Bonar Law's and the Unionists' realization that health insurance was an electoral liability insured that the opening of the next session would see a concerted attack upon its sponsor uninhibited by any claims of friendship. On 26 January at the Albert Hall Bonar Law, in what was in a sense his inaugural address as leader, announced the new style of opposition in a withering attack upon Lloyd George and health insurance for wasteful finance and corruption on the American scale: 'Revolutionary governments are always corrupt governments.' The new style in the debate that followed it, was recognized and widely commented upon.[13] Lloyd George replied immediately, for him an unusual tactic, in a singularly ill-tempered speech at the City Liberal Club on 3 February comparing Bonar Law's intellect unfavorably with Balfour's and denying in a swirling fog of figures that the insurance program was either wasteful or corrupt. The force of his speech was lessened by the necessity of explaining away a near loss the day before in the solidly Liberal seat of Edinburgh East.[14]

I

Political rhetoric aside, health insurance was in trouble. The Royal Assent on 16 December did not mean the end of problems, but the beginning of new ones. Early in the autumn Lloyd George had asked Charles Masterman to become its House of Commons spokesman, a post that after the division of the administration among the four British nationalities would carry the title of Chairman of the Joint Insurance Committee. Masterman accepted, and in November, to the political world's astonishment, he recommended the appointment of the infamous R.L. Morant as insurance's civil service head.[15] Morant was an administrator of genius, but since March of 1911 he had been an outcast in Whitehall for putting his name to a private Board of Education report, the so called 'Holmes Circular', which was critical of the level of scholarship and culture found among local authority education administrators and teachers. This misstep brought down upon him the full wrath of the nonconformist education establishment, who regarded Morant, in any case, as the secret eminence behind Balfour's education act and were happy now to take their revenge.[16] In political terms he was a marked man. It must be emphasized that Lloyd George, sensitive as he was to the feelings of his free church constituency and certainly aware that he was taking a risk, bore no grudge of this sort. In 1909, he had asked Morant to take over the Development Commission with a thousand pound increase in salary. Morant had refused.[17] But now this talented executive was under sentence. He had to take health insurance or retire. With the callousness that was as much a part of his nature as his charm, the Chancellor allowed W.J. Braithwaite, who was the designer of health insurance and who confidently expected the post, to be passed over.

On his way to Cap Martin for Christmas, Lloyd George paused in London to attend the first meeting of the Joint Insurance Committee.[18] At this time, apparently, the committee decided to begin a national propaganda campaign with hundreds of paid speakers employed to expound the virtues of health insurance, all to be supported by party funds. This unprecedented step was itself a risky proposition and provided a topic for Bonar Law and many other Unionist speakers. (Although Lloyd George always denied it, Bonar Law had evidence from excellent sources that the speakers' bureau was also supported by Treasury funds.)[19] Nonetheless, the campaign, using as speakers chiefly industrial insurance agents, was moderately effective although insurance remained a political liability.

Through the whole of 1912 and into 1913, the most visible manifestation of popular discontent with insurance was not chronic working class resentment at the compulsory four penny deduction from wages, which came to be known as 'the Lloyd George', but the unhappiness of the leadership of the British medical profession.[20] Lloyd George had not mollified the doctors in his speech to the British Medical Association on 1 June 1911 as he had at first believed. But even after it became clear that he had failed, the profession's alliance with industrial insurance had secured a number of amendments to the insurance bill which provided all but two of the 'Six Cardinal Points' which had been passed at the meeting he had addressed. However, of these two, one, 'adequate' compensation (i.e. a capitation fee in the neighborhood of 8s 6d per head without counting the cost of drugs), the profession deemed of supreme importance. Out of the question of medical remuneration grew the famous 'revolt of the doctors'.

In the late summer of 1911, the Medical Secretary of the British Medical Association, Dr. James Smith Whitaker, had begun to solicit signatures from the membership on a pledge not to accept work under health insurance unless all six points were achieved. By the time the bill left the Commons the association was claiming over 27,000 affirmative replies which would have represented about eighty percent of the professionally active names on the medical register. Then at the end of November, at the same time Morant was appointed, Lloyd George offered the post of Deputy Commissioner of the English Insurance Commission, in effect chief medical officer of the insurance administration, to Dr. Smith Whitaker. After consulting the B.M.A. council he accepted. The appointment of the B.M.A.'s highly competent professional director immensely strengthened the national insurance executive, but it caused a whirlwind of outrage among doctors and drew endless abuse upon Lloyd George and upon Smith Whitaker himself, who felt it keenly for the rest of his life.[21] The appointments of Smith Whitaker and Morant were surely clever and useful acts, but they poisoned what little good will remained for health insurance. At the beginning of 1912, after a special meeting of delegates, the B.M.A. broke off all negotiations with the health insurance administration and called upon all doctors in government service to resign. If the medical profession would only stand together, wrote the president of the B.M.A., Sir James Barr, an Ulsterman and strong Unionist, 'Mr. Lloyd George could retire with his act to the obscurity from which he never should have emerged. I quite agree with the *Standard* that it is nothing short of a national calamity that such a man should hold any office in any government.'[22]

In the face of this bombast, and much more like it, Lloyd George was unconcerned. For some time he had held a low opinion of the leaders of the British Medical Association as indeed he did all trade union grandees who claimed to speak for the working man. 'It is difficult to ascertain the true feelings of doctors as a whole on any proposal affecting them,' he had observed during the Brighton conference on 18 February 1911, 'since a Deputation of Doctors is always a Deputation of Swell Doctors: it is impossible to get a Deputation of poor Doctors or of slum Doctors.'[23] He was sure that he knew the condition of the medical rank and file better than did their own leaders. When the time came for the medical service to begin, which for the doctors was 15 January 1913, he would reach them. Thus, while Masterman, Morant and a team of civil servants struggled to put together an administrative structure to collect insurance contributions, due to begin on 15 July 1912, Lloyd George waited. The government and the B.M.A. did not meet again until 7 June 1912.[24]

At this meeting the Chancellor pointed out that four of the six cardinal points had already been granted fully and that distinct concessions had been made on the fifth, a £2 maximum income limit for the insured for purposes of the medical benefit, and that all that separated the two sides was the size of the capitation fee. The government had in mind 6s per year per contributor. The B.M.A. demanded 8s 6d. However both sides agreed that very little was known about how much doctors earned in the United Kingdom. The result of these discussions was the appointment, both sides agreeing, of the well-known accountant, Sir William Plender, who had worked for Lloyd George before, to make a systematic survey of doctors' remuneration. Plender did his work quickly and reported on 11 July.[25] Sir William's findings so staggered the medical profession that the historian must wonder whether Lloyd George had not made some prior survey which anticipated the result — he hinted in October that he had done so — and had thus invited the doctors to destroy their own case. Plender calculated that in the six representative towns he visited, the two hundred sixty-five practitioners surveyed earned an average from all patients of all classes, not the 8s 6d per head that the British Medical Association demanded, nor the 6s the government offered, but a net of 4s 5d per person per year. Lucy Masterman and Dr. Alfred Cox, by now Medical Secretary of the B.M.A., both agree that Plender's report ruined the profession's credibility and turned general practitioners as well as public opinion against the Association.[26]

Although the B.M.A. responded by breaking off negotiations a second time, the Plender report was a dazzling victory for Lloyd George. Equally it disheartened the Unionists, especially as its publication coincided with the uneventful beginning of the collection of contributions, a tribute to the energy and skill of Morant and Masterman. The Unionist strategy through the first six months of the session had been to try to delay the starting of insurance fearing that once the machinery was in place and contributions were flowing in, vested interests, the provident societies and industrial insurance, the 'approved societies', would make any useful amendment impossible.[27] There was also some discussion among the opposition leadership of an attempt to organize passive resistance to the payment of contributions.[28] Finally, the Unionists discovered that the doctors, in trying to match wits with Lloyd George, were such unsophisticated boobs that they embarrassed their allies. When negotiations resumed in November, the Unionist party chairman, A. Steel Maitland, discounted the chances of gains for the British Medical Association: 'It is. . .more likely that Lloyd George will be more than a match for a Committee of this kind and may outwit them. I think therefore that if. . .you do not want the doctors outwitted, it would be a good precaution for you' to send along a politician.[29]

The general result was a relaxation, virtually a cessation, of official Conservative opposition to health insurance (although not an end to hostile sniping), much to Lloyd George's relief. 'Insurance news continues good,' he informed his wife, Margaret ('Maggie'), in mid August, 'I dreaded a holiday abroad this year as I pictured the *Daily Mail* and *Telegraph* everyday full of letters and articles on the "insurance muddle". Instead they barely mention it.'[30] At the same time he began to consolidate the position won in July with an offer of compromise combined, however, with sinister warnings of what would happen should the doctors undertake a boycott of the act. In a signed article in the *Nation* on 3 August, Lloyd George remarked that for some time he had been pressed 'from very influential quarters' to consider unspecified changes in the administration of the medical benefit, but so far he had resisted because of his concern for the happiness and comfort of the medical profession. The approved societies would of course like to see medical control restored to themselves but there were also other alternatives. Even though the Plender report had shown the generosity of the government offer for the doctors, if a case could be made for a still higher capitation fee he would be glad to recommend it to the House of Commons.[31] Should some of the more obtuse doctors miss the lightly veiled threats of the article, Lloyd George followed it the next week with a letter in the *Nation* signed ominously 'X' in which the nation's medical readers were asked whether they understood that the Chancellor had been referring to a salaried state medical service as an alternative. It would save money and would surely come if there were a strike. The approved societies could easily administer it. They had the experience.[32]

Lloyd George was serious about his offer to negotiate a higher capitation fee. If the average doctor earned less than four and one half shillings per year per patient, it would be easy to destroy the solidarity of the medical profession. On 22 October, with less than three months until the medical service under the act was scheduled to begin, he obtained from the Cabinet permission to ask for a supplementary grant from parliament to raise the capitation fee from the proposed 6s to 7s 6d with an extra 1s 6d for the provision of drugs.[33] The next day he announced the new pay scales before a large, but private, meeting that included approved society leaders, officials, and many doctors.[34]

For the next two months it seemed that the threat of a medical boycott had passed. The B.M.A. began to make temperate inquiries about contracts and conditions of service and the health insurance administration set about drawing up regulations. Then on 21 December 1912, after acrimonious debate, another special meeting of B.M.A. delegates voted by a majority of four to one to refuse the government's terms and called upon all doctors to reaffirm their pledge to deny service under the act. This was folly. 'On the morning of the meeting,' recalled Dr. Cox sadly, 'I had in my possession scores of letters from our local secretaries which showed that in some areas a majority of men had already joined the panel [the body of doctors in a locality available for health insurance work], in spite of the fact that nearly one hundred percent had signed the pledge that they would not do so until released by the Association. More telegrams to the same effect came in during the meeting. Doctors in the poorest areas found that their income would double under health insurance.'[35]

By now Lloyd George was totally unconcerned. The doctors were 'hopelessly divided' he wrote a few days later to the Prime Minister who had inquired what the Chancellor would think of a dissolution in April 1913.[36] Indeed to Riddell, who had remarked that the doctors should have accepted the Chancellor's last proposal and claimed victory, he commented that he had been frightened that they would indeed accept. Now the public would believe he had defeated them.[37] Nonetheless he took care to publicize the government's plan for a salaried service in areas where an inadequate number of medical men joined panels. For example, he announced in a speech early in the year, fifty doctors, at £500 each, could easily handle the one hundred thousand contributors in Bradford. They would receive in addition a monopoly of care, on a private basis, of the insured's family.[38]

Soon after the first of the year the dimensions of Lloyd George's victory were clear. On 11 January the *National Insurance Gazette* reported that 11,000 doctors had already joined panels and that others were scrambling to put in applications.[39] At the end of the first week of the new year Herbert Lewis, Lloyd George's oldest and most loyal supporter among Welsh MPs, called at No. 11 and, after passing an agitated physician cowering in the hall, found Lloyd George in the highest of spirits. Resistance was collapsing everywhere he crowed. He was allowing the man at the door to wait before he provided an answer as to whether there was still space on panels in Surrey. Lloyd George and Lewis spent the evening singing Welsh hymns.[40]

On 15 January, the day the medical benefit began, far more than the required fifteen thousand doctors had applied. The B.M.A. was smashed and humiliated. A meeting on 17 January released all doctors from their pledges. The organization did not recover either its membership or its financial health until after the war.

However, it does not follow that Lloyd George's personal triumph indicated a reversal of public opinion on contributory insurance. This hostility remained a burden to the Liberals and more important a danger to Liberal candidates. Curiously, in the country at large, as opposed to Westminster, Lloyd George retained a devoted cult of followers, making him by far the most popular public man in the nation, even if by now he was detested by many.[41] And although his name was still usually cheered at radical Liberal meetings, wrote Sir Edward Russell, the venerable editor of the *Liverpool Post and Mercury*, insurance was not. It divided the country and hurt Liberalism more than Home Rule.[42] The Unionists believe the same thing.[43] The sufferers were the men associated with insurance and with Lloyd George, who were always liable to political retaliation both from the Unionists and from Labour. Two of his best and most loyal supporters, Charles Masterman and G.P. Gooch, were lost in the next eighteen months. Almost certainly the need to revive the declining popularity of reform became a major cause of the Chancellor's precipitous and badly handled campaign to reconstruct British land holding. Writing in the fall of 1913, just as the public portion of the land campaign was beginning, A.G. Gardiner of the *Daily News* reflected on the Lloyd George phenomenon. He attracted either adoration or hatred. The more polite the circle the more bitter the hostility. Some regarded him simply as one of the afflictions of the country. 'Sometimes it was the Black Death, sometimes the small-pox, now it was Mr. Lloyd George.' The feeling was that Lloyd George was not, like Gladstone, 'one of us,' mused Gardiner. He was not a fallen angel. He had been an outsider from the beginning.[44]

II

When Herbert Lewis visited Lloyd George on 5 January 1913 and found him rejoicing at the defeat of the British Medical Association he would have been astonished to know that his friend had learned only in the last few days that evidence had been uncovered suggesting his involvement in what was already styled the 'Marconi scandal'. Not only his political programs but his career, he believed, were in jeopardy, as indeed was true.

The story of the General Post Office contract with the Marconi Wireless Telegraph Company, and what followed from it, has been told well, if not completely, by Frances Donaldson. References to it appear in nearly every history of pre-war Britain.[45] Yet Lloyd George's place in the affair is always misunderstood.[46] Lloyd George had had no connection with the Marconi contract, which until the early months of 1913 was the center of the uproar. Nor had he invested in English Marconi company stock. Nor, indeed, was he seriously suspected of wrongdoing until the private warning that evidently came to him about Christmastime of 1912. For Lloyd George the entire affair constituted a travesty of ill-fortune compounded by the singular lack of parliamentary skills on the part of the Postmaster General, Herbert Samuel. But even though his participation in the affair was peripheral, on balance one must conclude that the potential of danger to Lloyd George in the Marconi scandal was greater than that of any other man involved. He was the most visible, and therefore the most vulnerable, member of the government. He had secured almost as if by magic the extinction of his valuable Unionist weapon of the Lords' veto and he had given his party new courage. But he had also lowered the dignity of parliament by appealing over its head to the crowd. Most of all, Lloyd George always waved aloft the banner of moral outrage, injecting an ethical dimension into perfectly adjudicable political issues. The comparisons with Caesar's wife during the Kynoch debate with Joseph Chamberlain had not been forgotten. Inevitably there were many, Liberals as well as Unionists, who regarded Lloyd George as a cheap hypocrite, with much to hide, who deserved to be found out and brought down. Even before Marconi the new vigor of the opposition that followed Bonar Law's accession to leadership clearly had heightened interest on both sides of the House in this sort of political warfare.[47]

The Marconi Wireless Telegraph Company had been chartered in Britain in 1898 by the inventor of the wireless, Commander Guglielmo Marconi, as a limited stock company. Although Marconi dazzled the world by sending a signal across the Atlantic in 1901 and spent much of the company's money on research and development, as a commercial venture the firm was not profitable and had never paid a dividend. In 1910 Marconi chose to retire from active management and return to research. In August 1910 he appointed Godfrey Isaacs, the brother of the then Solicitor General, Rufus Isaacs, as Managing Director. Godfrey Isaacs knew nothing of radio but a great deal about finance and business. One of his first acts, spurred by the knowledge that Telefunken of Germany was considering an international wireless communications network, was to write to the Colonial Office proposing that Marconi establish, at its own expense, an eighteen station system throughout the British empire. As things happened in those days, he received no reply. He wrote again and was put off. Finally after a third letter in January 1911, citing the German competition, the Colonial Office referred the proposal to the Cable (Landing Rights) Committee of the House of Commons. The committee quickly approved the idea of an imperial wireless network but suggested that it be government owned although built by Marconi and that the work be started as soon as possible. There was no proposal for competitive bidding as the only serious alternative contender for so large a project would have been Telefunken. Negotiations on a contract began in the autumn of 1911 with the government represented by a committee of the Post Office under the chairmanship of Herbert Samuel, the Postmaster General. A formal tender was submitted by the Marconi Company on 13 February 1912 and, after a review by the Contracts Department of the Post Office, it was accepted on 7 March. The Marconi Company immediately issued a statement of its terms to its stockholders, which appeared in the financial papers.[48]

The tender now approved provided for the construction of an initial six stations at £60,000 each to be paid by the government. It gave the company also a royalty of ten percent of the gross earnings of the network for the next twenty-eight years. According to standing orders a contract of this size, even though accepted by the Post Office, could not bind the government unless it was approved by parliament. This requirement was stipulated in the tender, which was in fact only the framework upon which the subsequent contract would be drawn.

The chronology of the Marconi tender has been recited in some detail because it was initially over the terms of this document and subsequently over the men involved in the negotiations that led to it, that the storm first erupted. Part of the difficulty proceeded from dallying by the Post Office partly by Samuel's remarkable unwillingness to discuss in parliament matters that were already public knowledge and the subject of comment in newspapers. The House of Commons had no opportunity to debate the tender. Samuel would not answer questions about it. The draft contract itself, a much longer document, was not tabled until 19 July. Meanwhile Marconi shares had gone up over one hundred percent. This was not surprising. Marconi had given much publicity to its dealings with the government. Long suffering shareholders were at last to be rewarded for their loyalty. Then on 15 April the news arrived of the collision of the liner *Titanic* with an iceberg in which accident the Marconi operator appeared as a hero. This caused the value of Marconi shares to leap up another fifty percent. In defense of the Marconi contract, the historian must say that it illustrates perfectly the problem of buying hardware in an area of exploding technology. It would be pointed out many times that Marconi's master patent had only three years to run yet the company would receive royalties for twenty-eight years. But the government, as the tender stipulated, was being paid not only for present inventions but for future developments that would be incorporated into its transmitters and receivers. This is difficult to explain today. It was even more difficult in 1912.

To be noted at this point is the fact that newspaper comment in the spring of 1912 often referred not only to the singular demand for English Marconi shares but to the demand, both in London and New York, for shares in the American Marconi company.[49] As the purchase of American equities became eventually the center of the Marconi affair, the position of the American company must be described. Like the English company until the advent of Godfrey Isaacs, it had done little business, having been established apparently to protect Marconi patents in the United States. However, in March 1912, while it was engaged in an infringement suit against the failing United Wireless Telegraph Company of America, Godfrey Isaacs, a director of the American company also and in the United States to give evidence, discovered that with the assets of United Wireless, most of which it could acquire with a successful judgment, the company would control all the radio business in North America. He learned further that the mammoth Western Union Telegraph Company and the Great Northwestern Telegraph Company of Canada were willing to negotiate an agreement to accept and distribute his overseas messages through their 25,000 offices. But all this required a large increase in the capital of the American company to buy the remaining assets of United Wireless and to expand the Marconi system. Involved was a new issue of 1,400,000 shares with a par value of $5 or £1.16. Commander Marconi was unwilling to obligate the English company, itself burdened by huge new expenses as a result of the government contract, to absorb the new issue. He agreed to take 900,000 shares if Isaacs himself would undertake to place the remaining 500,000. A secret contract with Western Union was signed on 14 April. The directors of the American company would meet on 18 April to authorize the new issue.[50]

Meanwhile, on 8 April, Godfrey Isaacs had returned to London having placed all but 100,000 shares with American and English brokers.[51] After his return, in conversations with his brothers Rufus and Harry Isaacs, he expounded the approaching profitability of the American Marconi Company. This was a perfectly legitimate expectation. The company now had a monopoly of overseas transmissions to and from the United States and Canada with

Western Union as its distribution agent. The American *Financial World*, which was reporting every week on the absorption of the United Wireless, stated that American Marconi that year for the first time had earned a profit, albeit small, and predicted a bright future for the company. The contract with Western Union was still secret, but rumors evidently were circulating and the stock was rising in price.[52]

On 17 April Rufus Isaacs determined to purchase 10,000 shares of American Marconi from his brother although he refused to accept them at the jobbing price of 21s, which his brother offered, and paid instead the London market price of 40s. That evening he saw Lloyd George and Alexander Murray, the Chief Whip, who was living temporarily at No. 11, and offered each 1,000 shares. According to his son, Isaacs assured them, quite truthfully, that there was no connection between the English and the American companies. The Marconi tender to the Post Office had now been public for nearly six weeks. The English company might profit from the prosperity of the American company, but the reverse would not be true. In any case an equity investment in the American company was perfectly justifiable in its own right.[53] Each man took 1,000 shares at 40s, financed by Isaacs.[54]

As usual Lloyd George was full of enthusiasm for the new stock venture. It was of the sort upon which he frequently had embarked in the past and in which, equally frequently, he had lost money. Isaacs had told him of the opportunity in American Marconi a few days before the purchase on 17 April, for on 12 April he wrote to his wife, Margaret, in the man-of-the-world tones he customarily employed on these occasions.[55] 'Would you like to try another little "spec"? You will make a hundred or two out of it.' Margaret replied saying she had only £50. 'Very well I will invest that for you,' he wrote on 15 April. 'Sorry you have no more available as I think it is quite a good thing I have got.'

'Well your "spec" came off and. . .made another £100,' he wrote on 19 April when trading in the new American Marconi shares opened for the first time at 65s and closed the day at 80s. 'I also made a few hundred out of it so we are all a little better off than at the beginning of the week.'[56]

When he appeared before the select committee appointed to examine the Marconi contract, Lloyd George was hazy about the date of his stock sales, as he had been with his purchases. Attempting to show that he regarded the American Marconi ventures as an investment rather than as a speculation, he asserted that he had not made his first sale, of 500 shares, until 20 April although he admitted that his broker had telegraphed him on 19 April urging him to sell.[57] His letter to Margaret shows that he sold on the 19th. Sixteen days later, on 5 May, Isaacs sold in a considerably weaker market 357 more of Lloyd George's remaining 500 shares as well as a proportionate share of Murray's and his own. By that date Lloyd George had a profit of £743 plus ownership of 143 of the original 1,000 shares.[58] But then, ill advisedly, on 22 May he and Alec Murray each bought 1,500 more shares at about 43s, little more than the original price of 17 April. What neither Lloyd George nor anyone else knew in the summer of 1912, was that Murray, as Chief Liberal Whip, on 18 April and 14 May foolishly had put £9,000 of Liberal party funds into the purchase of 3,000 American Marconi shares at full market prices. Murray's purchase remained undetected in the account of a City broker, Montmorency and Company, until the beginning of June 1913. The discovery of this transaction was the sensation of the affair and very nearly ended the careers of Lloyd George and Isaacs.

One has to conclude that although the English Marconi stock price reflected a genuine demand, because the quotation remained strong and relatively stable at 100s for a number of weeks, someone, perhaps the American directors of whom Godfrey Isaacs was one, had been able to effect a corner on the American company stock in New York when it began to trade on 18 April. Only they knew that well over half the new American issue would be taken up by the English company, that there would be, in fact, relatively few shares available for public sale. The *Insider's Index* did not exist in those days. Certainly most of the American public, who simply placed orders through brokers, were able to buy only a portion of the shares requested and those at a high premium. There were rumors of a ring.[59] The London market, a secondary market for American Marconis and a day behind, simply followed New York up and down. In this movement Lloyd George and Alec Murray were caught. The question is who knew about it. Perhaps Rufus Isaacs did. His brother might have told him and Lloyd George's broker may have suspected it. Hence the broker's earnest appeal to Lloyd George to sell on 19 April coupled with Isaacs' sale of two-thirds of the syndicate's (i.e., Isaacs, Lloyd George and Murray) remaining holdings on 3 May. But even if Isaacs knew, and this itself is speculation, he did not tell Lloyd George and Murray for the two bought in again on 21 May, after the bubble had burst, this time heavily and with disastrous results. Here one sees the ordinary suburban Juggins who, having made a small amount in a rising market and being dazzled by the prospect of unlimited riches, buys again in a falling market only to see his holdings fall further and his profits disappear. The stockholders who made money in New York were, first of all, the English Marconi company which owned at the beginning more than half the American subsidiary and, one suspects, Godfrey Isaacs.

The purpose of this review has been to show that in purely financial terms Lloyd George was the victim, not the beneficiary, of private information and that at the end of what may be identified as the first phase of the Marconi affair, the charge against him is only that of greed combined with ignorance, one that can be made against many men.

Through May, June and much of July the Marconi contract lay, not so much unremarked, as undiscussed. Herbert Samuel showed a genius for political clumsiness in refusing to answer questions in the House of Commons on the grounds that the terms of the contract were under discussion. Whether or not this attitude caused suspicion, it clearly gave rise to irritation when at last the draft contract was laid before the House on 19 July.

Reaction was immediate and hostile. From the House of Commons Major Martin Archer-Shee wrote to *The Times* on 26 July condemning the agreement as unfavorable to the British government. There had been no competitive tender solicited, yet the government had tied itself up for years. The transmitters Marconi was obligated to provide already were out of date; they could send a signal only 2,100 miles while similar equipment available in the United States could transmit 3,000 miles.[60] Major Archer-Shee would remain a principal antagonist in the Marconi affair until the end. While his charges, in common with those of most others in what may be identified as the respectable wing of Marconi opposition, were centered on the contract and not on individuals, it must be noticed that he had a personal interest which may or may not have been important. Archer-Shee was the half brother of George Archer-Shee (the 'Winslow boy' in Terence Rattigan's play) who had been dismissed from Osborne in October 1908 for stealing 5s and who took the government to court for breach of contract. The Solicitor General at first, before the facts were heard, had attempted to stonewall the case on a point of law: a Petition of Right could not be used to bring a civil suit such as breach of contract, only to have the ruling reversed on appeal. When the facts finally came out in court, he withdrew the government's case. The ungracious Solicitor General defending for the government was Rufus Isaacs.

Outside parliament the attack proceeded at first from a single journalist, Wilfred R. Lawson, who wrote a weekly financial column in the *Outlook*. Lawson was a fairly well-known business writer, a member of the Stock Exchange, and a strong tariff reformer as was the owner of the *Outlook*, Walter Guinness, who was also a Unionist Member of Parliament. There was nothing surprising in Lawson's attacks on the Marconi contract. For weeks he had been denouncing Lloyd George and national insurance in similar terms. Marconi for him was simply another dangerous and ill-founded Liberal scheme.[61] Although Lawson noted on 31 August that much of the stock in the Marconi company that was not in bearer form was held by people with Jewish names, his attacks generally were not racial; they were centered upon the unbusinesslike manner in which the contract had been handled, Samuel's silence, and the failure to investigate other wireless systems. He credited himself with forcing the announcement, made on 6 August, that a select committee would look into the contract after the recess.[62] By and large he echoed what was being said by Members of Parliament.

The 'disreputable,' in effect personal, opposition to the Marconi contract appeared in *Eye-Witness* magazine only on 8 August as parliament rose, more than two weeks after Lawson's original article and Major Archer-Shee's first letter. The article's tardiness and the fact that the new critics never appeared to know very much about wireless telegraphy, the terms of the Marconi contract or commercial enterprise in general, suggests a strong element of opportunism.

Lawson at least knew what he was talking about. The unhealthy speculation both in English and American Marconis troubled him, as it worried *The Times* and a number of other serious commentators. In contrast, *Eye-Witness* was a curious magazine combining a strong, rather nostalgic, social conscience with contempt for the trade unions as co-conspirators in the oligarchy of largely Jewish financial powers that it felt dominated British political and public life. Long before Marconi it had been attacking Lloyd George, Isaacs, and Samuel, among many others, nearly every week for a variety of sins: Isaacs for excessive fees for a watching brief on the *Titanic* enquiry, Samuel for laying out far too much for the purchase of British National Telephone, and Lloyd George for having made £80,000 in the purchase of the London dock companies.[63] On 8 August in an article entitled 'The Marconi Scandal', and in a second on 15 August, the magazine charged by implication Samuel, Rufus and Godfrey Isaacs with a corrupt conspiracy to defraud the government.

In fact the articles offered nothing that was new. The details, so far as any were provided, came from Lawson's article in the *Outlook*, and the charge of corruption proceeded from Samuel's place as Postmaster General. Samuel had the power to award contracts and Rufus Isaacs to review them. Therefore a large sum of taxpayers' money would go to Godfrey Isaacs.[64] The *Eye-Witness* articles did not imply that the writer had evidence of corrupt intent. Rather the criminal act would occur because elective government was first of all a system for making money. And all were Jews. Lloyd George was not mentioned.

Scurrilous as this was, the *Eye-Witness* charges were thin and unsubstantiated, printed in a journal of tiny circulation and indeed without friends except for the *Daily Herald*, which advertised for subscribers in its pages. It would have had no impact on the Marconi affair had not Herbert Samuel seen a copy of the 8 August issue on a newsstand in King's Cross Station and sent it to Isaacs who sent it on to Asquith, telling the Prime Minister at the same time of his, but not Lloyd George's or Murray's, ownership of American Marconis.[65]

All in all, contrary to the conventional story of Marconi, there was no rising clamor in the newspapers, no public outrage demanding that the government appoint a committee of investigation, above all, except for the *Eye-Witness*, no charges of corruption, only incompetence, and most of these were aimed at the unworldly, fidgety, painfully sensitive, Herbert Samuel. (Asquith privately always referred to Samuel as 'The Infant'.) Through August and September, the case was kept alive by Wilfred Lawson's articles in *Outlook* and, beginning in October, in the *National Review*, and by occasional letters about the technicalities of the contract from Members of Parliament. None of the national quality press, of either party, mentioned the subject except for an intervention in September by the *Spectator* to comment in mild terms upon a short article by Major Archer-Shee in the *National Review*.[66] By the time parliament reassembled in the first week of October, even though there was some excitement among the opposition that the Post Office at last would have to defend the unfavorable contract it had so far refused to discuss, the issue was ready to die. No new information had appeared and even Lawson's investigations had gone clearly astray. In *Outlook* on 12 October he reported that 'the man behind the scenes' in Marconi stock speculation 'is a well-known Kaffir [South African gold mining millionaire] magnate.'[67] A select committee would be appointed, the bewildering rival claims of the Paulson, Lodge-Muirhead and Marconi wireless systems could be looked into quietly and the political world could pass on to something else.

On 11 October, on the motion for a select committee, Lloyd George made a mistake that in the end nearly cost him his political life. Through the autumn, it must be emphasized, he had not figured in the debate over the contract, although he was a favorite target for both *Eye-Witness* and *Outlook* on other issues. To be sure, there were hints, as he admitted to the select committee on 28 March, that he possessed a great fortune, a villa in the south of France and so on.[68] In his mind he appears to have connected these charges with the secret of the American Marconi stock purchases. Even though he always insisted that he cared nothing for what was said about him in the papers, on personal, as opposed to party, issues precisely the opposite was true. Speculation about his private life, his relations with women for example, drove him into self-righteous rage, especially if there was some basis in fact. Inevitably he looked for someone to sue. These characteristics made him extremely vulnerable in the Marconi affair. Although leading the House on 11 October because of Asquith's illness, he had sat silent as the contract was debated. Until the intervention of George Lansbury, which brought Lloyd George to his feet, the opponents of the Marconi agreement without exception had disassociated themselves from any charges of corruption.[69] Generally their complaints were the familiar ones of lack of information and the failure of the Post Office to investigate other wireless systems or even to appoint a technical committee. Finally George Lansbury, in a rambling, hesitant speech, brought up the rumors of speculation in Marconi shares. The select committee should investigate these also, he suggested, and there should be 'no shrinking'.[70] Instantly Lloyd George shouted: 'I hope that there will be no shrinking on the part of those who make the allegations.' Lansbury was evidently surprised and a little taken aback by the violence of this interjection. All he had said, he repeated, was that gambling had been heavy in Marconi shares, as everyone knew, and that some people had made money who should not have done so. 'I am entitled to say that without interruption.'

Mr. Lloyd George made a remark which was inaudible [evidently along the lines of 'I am not one who made money'].

Mr. Lansbury: I do not think you are. I never mentioned the Rt. Hon. Gentleman. Why should he be so eager to rise in his place and speak as he has done, I do not know.

Mr. Lloyd George: The Hon. Member said something about the Government and has talked about 'rumours'. I want to know what those rumours are. If the Hon. Gentleman has any charge to make against the Government as a whole or against individual Members of it, I think it ought to be stated openly. The reason why the Government wanted a frank discussion before going to Committee was because we wanted to bring here the rumours, those sinister rumours, that have passed from one foul lip to another behind the backs of the House.[71]

Lansbury asked, a little plaintively, why Lloyd George was so angry at him and not at the others who had spoken. Lloyd George replied that no one else had talked that way and no one else was making charges of corruption. Other Members who had spoken immediately shouted agreement. After saying again that no one but Lansbury had mentioned corruption, Lloyd George sat down.

But this was not the end. Lloyd George had made a fatal mistake in drawing attention to himself. He had not been mentioned in the controversy until now and had made no comment upon it. What then was the cause of his anger? Did he too have something to hide? This suspicion was compounded a few minutes later when Isaacs, after admitting that it would be an affectation to pretend that he was not the subject of rumor, took the opportunity, in words that would become in fact the subject of the real Marconi scandal, to deny any culpability. He had not even known of the tender, he said, until a few days before it was signed. To the suggestion that he had profited from it:

I desire to say frankly, on behalf of myself, that it is absolutely untrue. Never from the beginning, when the shares were 14s or £9 have I had one single transaction with the shares of that company. I am not only speaking for myself but I am speaking on behalf, I know, of both my Rt. Hon. friend the Postmaster General and the Chancellor of the Exchequer who in some way or other, in some articles, have been brought into this matter.[72]

Lloyd George's outburst evoked little comment at the time and indeed historians of the affair have hardly noticed it.[73] Both *Eye-Witness* and Wilfred Lawson, now writing for the *National Review* as well as *Outlook*, turned their attention to the inadequacies of the select committee, a view that seemed well justified as hearings on the tangled mysteries of wireless telegraphy began at the end of the month. The topic virtually disappeared from the papers.

Yet some men understood that something had happened. Hilaire Belloc, himself an editor of *Eye-Witness* until June of 1912, wrote to Maurice Baring on 26 October, and made one of the first direct references to stock market speculation that this researcher has found. On the rise of English Marconi shares from 14s to £5 and on Isaacs's statement that he had not heard of the tender until a few days before it was signed Belloc commented:

To the truth of this Sir Rufus has himself testified amid the cheers of the House of Commons. . .unfortunately foul tongues are at it again and suggesting that Mr. Lloyd George, our popular Welsh Chancellor, though sprung from the people, has fallen into the aristocratic vice of fluttering and, having inside knowledge, had made no small profit on the difference between 14s. and 100s. No one, I am assured, gives credence to this vile tale with the exception of a couple hundred gossiping bankers in the City and some eight or ten thousand in the West End.[74]

Most dangerous for Lloyd George was the interest now being taken in Marconi by Leopold Maxse, proprietor of the *National Review*, a Tory enragé and tariff reformer and the man who had driven A.J. Balfour from the Unionist leadership only a year before. In September Maxse had hired Lawson to write a regular article on Marconi which he supplemented with his own caustic, sometimes violent, comments in the 'Episodes of the Month'. In the first issue after the select committee debate Maxse pointed out precisely what would become by the following June the core of the Marconi affair: that while Isaacs had disclaimed any interest in English Marconis, Lloyd George 'had failed to deny' similar ownership. Had he something to hide? Was he himself truly, as he had demanded of Joseph Chamberlain in the Kynoch debates, like Caesar's wife, above suspicion?[75] Maxse soon received a letter from his friend Leopold Amery, a Unionist member of the select committee, asking whether he knew something that he wished to place before the body. He replied on 19 November, rather lamely, saying he had 'no special knowledge as to financial transactions in which members of the Government may or may not be concerned. . .I am merely in the position of a person who found the topic almost completely boycotted by the press and called attention to it through the most authoritative writer who has taken the matter up [i.e. Lawson].'[76]

In the next two months, Marconi seemed to disappear from public notice. The *National Review*, in its issue of 1 January 1913, carried virtually nothing on the affair and on 25 January, after the incompetent performance of Wilfred Lawson before the select committee, the *Westminster Gazette* proclaimed the 'ignoble collapse' of the 'unscrupulous campaign' against the government.

Yet something was afoot. At some time toward the end of December Lloyd George received word that certain people knew that although he did not own shares in the English Marconi company he had gambled rather heavily in stock of the American one. The date on which this occurred can be set roughly from the memoirs of his then secretary (and later his mistress and wife), Frances Stevenson. In the summer of 1912 Lloyd George had asked Miss Stevenson, who was still at Allenwood, to come and work for him, as he put it, 'on his own terms'.[77] Miss Stevenson needed time to think about this and at the end of the summer she went off to Scotland. She remained there through the autumn of 1912 and returned toward the end of the year because of a letter from Lloyd George saying that he was in desperate trouble and needed her at once. She recorded that she returned to London 'soon after Christmas'.[78] The two became lovers on 21 January 1913.[79] Where Lloyd George's information came from remains a mystery. He had many connections in journalism, but the sequence of events in the next month suggests that he may have received a warning letter from Leo Maxse of the *National Review* which told him that word of the American Marconi shares was abroad.

Lloyd George's first act, either early in the new year or still in 1912, was to go with Isaacs to the Prime Minister, tell him of the share purchases, and offer to resign.[80] Asquith scoffed at this proposal and apparently reassured the two men. He wrote to Venetia Stanley on 7 January referring, as if he had just heard of it, to 'certain follies' committed by Isaacs and Lloyd George.[81] In the next day's Cabinet the mood of crisis was apparent. J.A. Pease noted in his diary that all Cabinet members clearly were aware of the matter although nothing was said.[82]

For a time Lloyd George obviously hoped that the story of the American Marconis would go no further than rumor. Equally clearly, Leo Maxse intended that it should come into the open. Although the January issue of *National Review* carried for the first time in five months very little on Marconi with the next issue, in February, the second phase of the Marconi scandal began. In the 'Episodes of the Month' Maxse noted that Liberal papers were saying that the campaign against the Marconi 'contract' had collapsed. The select committee had uncovered nothing. Whether this was true, Maxse continued, the reader could judge after he had himself given his evidence to the select committee. 'Not the least amazing feature of an amazing affair' wrote Maxse

is the conduct of certain of His Majesty's Ministers, from whom passionate protestations of ignorance and innocence concerning the great Marconi gamble were made in the House of Commons so long ago as October 11. The unsophisticated might have imagined that men in their positions would have insisted on being heard by the Committee at the outset in order that they might dissipate the atmosphere of suspicion and clear their own fair fame.

41

The committee could not have refused the demand of 'say the Chancellor of the Exchequer to come [before them] with his passbooks, his bankers and his brokers. . .' The reader would recall, concluded Maxse, that Lloyd George had made no denial on 11 October and had preferred instead to pick a quarrel with Lansbury.[83]

Lucy Masterman records in her typescript diary that her husband told her that he had heard of Lloyd George's purchases early in February. One may speculate that Lloyd George himself told Charles Masterman the facts after seeing the article in the *National Review*. 'George thought he could keep on concealing it,' wrote Mrs. Masterman. 'Charles pointed out that they would have to state on oath in the Committee that they held nothing in the Marconis or any dependent company. It was then decided that the facts should be brought out in the course of the "*Matin*" case'.[84] Leo Maxse's testimony to the select committee, advertised in his magazine at the beginning of February, occurred on 12 February; an article commenting upon it in the French paper *Le Matin* appeared on 14 February. The *Matin* article constituted perhaps the only piece of good luck enjoyed by the unfortunate Liberal ministers during the Marconi affair.

Maxse's select committee testimony, so well advertised by himself, produced only small bits of new information. He did give some clues, as presumably he intended to do. He called attention to the fact that Lloyd George, on 11 October, had 'omitted to deny that he owned any Marconi shares, although Isaacs and Samuel had disclaimed any interest in the English company.' Toward the end of his presentation, after repeating his bewilderment that ministers had not been asked to testify before the committee, he produced the key detail.

> One might have conceived that they would have appeared at the
> first sitting clamouring to state in the most categorical and emphatic
> manner that neither directly nor indirectly, in their own names or
> other people's names, have they had any transactions whatsoever, either
> in London, Dublin, New York, Brussels, Amsterdam, Paris or any other
> financial centres in any shares in any Marconi company throughout the
> negotiations with the government.[85]

Pressed for the sources of his information, Maxse declined to give them. (Asquith refused the request of the committee chairman, Albert Spicer, for power to compel Maxse to divulge his evidence.)

Although he had not provided much beyond his original intimations in the February *National Review*, Maxse's evidence caused a 'sensation', observed St. Loe Strachey in the *Spectator* later that week.[86] Nevertheless, Leo Maxse's part in the affair has all the appearances of a journalistic stunt. Through the autumn of 1912 he had kept the Marconi affair alive in his journal with the regular articles of Wilfred Lawson and his own comments. All of this had been carried forward entirely on speculation. As he had admitted to Leo Amery on 19 November he had no special knowledge. By the Christmas recess the matter seemed to have died. Then, one may imagine, Maxse suddenly uncovered a gold mine. In place of the corrupt Jewish conspiracy he had expected, he found, not an indictable crime to be sure, but an abuse of Cabinet honor and parliamentary privilege, in a matter all the graver for being less easily defined. In doing so Maxse won for himself in the next few months the most desirable of all public positions for a newsman: that of creating the news himself. He had first called attention to the startling facts he intended to lay before the select committee, then, when he appeared, he had heightened the suspense by saying that he had documents saying that some ministers were interested in some Marconi companies, after which he declined to name the ministers, the correspondents, or to produce the letters. The *National Review* in its March issue reprinted Maxse's testimony with the key phrase '*any* Marconi company' in italics.

But two days later, on 14 February, Leo Maxse's initiative was snatched away from him by the French newspaper *Le Matin*, which published a short and inaccurate article saying that Leo Maxse had testified that Godfrey and Rufus Isaacs and Herbert Samuel had bought shares in the English company and had sold them at a large profit.

Until Maxse's testimony Lloyd George's instinctive strategy, reinforced by Asquith's recommendation, had been to keep silent in the well founded hope that the public would tire of Marconi as had nearly occurred twice. With Maxse's evidence, whatever it was, such tactics were now impossible. The editor would reveal his evidence, no doubt a letter at a time, and the sensation would build, not diminish. But the garbled *Matin* story, even though quickly retracted, provided an opportunity for a libel action, during which the tale of the American Marconis could be brought out and Maxse's attack preempted. It was a strategy that could misfire but the chance was worth taking. Isaacs obtained a writ against *Matin*. Trial was set for 19 March. On that day Sir George Riddell wrote in his diary: 'for some days I have known that something serious was about to take place. What I did not exactly know.' However that morning Charles Masterman had told him of the American shares and said that Sir Edward Carson, Isaacs and Lloyd George's attorney, would make a disclosure in the *Matin* trial.

> He also said that this transaction had worried LG terribly and that LG had offered his resignation to Asquith who had ridiculed the idea. He said that LG wanted to write (yesterday) a long letter to the press explaining the transaction but he (Masterman) had persuaded him from doing so saying that the case had better speak for itself. I said, 'Why did not Rufus and LG make a disclosure immediately after the Marconi attack began?' I said 'The long silence coupled with their emphatic disclaimers of any interest in the Marconi company gives a bad appearance to the transaction.' Masterman said this was his opinion and that he had not known the facts until a few months ago. . .Masterman said the Prime Minister had counseled silence and was chiefly responsible for the course which had been pursued. . . Masterman said that the press had been arranged with. Northcliffe had promised that 'The Times' and the 'Daily Mail' would not be objectionable and Harry Lawson had agreed to refrain from attacks in the 'Telegraph.' Massingham had been very nasty and they feared an attack in the Nation'. Gardiner of the 'Daily News' and Donald of the 'Chronicle' were both friendly. Masterman said that the thing has been

like a black cloud hanging over the Ministry and that at one time he feared Lloyd George would break down (I am bound to say he has shown no signs of doing so).[87]

There were two problems in the *Matin* case. First, as the case was undefended Carson was unsure whether the judge would allow the unrelated matter of the American Marconi shares to be brought in. But worse, Lloyd George had not been named in the *Matin* story and so was not even a party to the case. However, as it turned out Carson was not interrupted and was able to blurt out the fateful words. After explaining how Isaacs had come to hold 10,000 shares of American Marconi, Carson continued:

> He [Isaacs] sold some of the shares, and amongst others 1,000 to Mr. Lloyd George and another 1,000 to the Master of Elibank, who is now Lord Murray. They were intimate friends of his though at the time neither of them knew of the shares and probably never would have heard of them, it is right to say he offered them the shares believing them to be a good investment, having nothing whatever to do with the shares of the English Company. They were offered and bought 1,000 each of these shares, and I am afraid it also turned out to be a loss for them.[88]

For the moment these revelations caused less of a furor than might have been expected. The major London newspapers had pledged silence. The *Spectator,* which followed the *National Review* as the most active serious journal directing attention to the Marconi affair remarked only that the miscreants should have seen Asquith before purchasing the stock and that what had been done, while not corrupt, was not in accord with the high standards of public life.[89] Even the opposition seemed satisfied. Lloyd George reported to Riddell that he had spoken a few days later with the Unionist leader Andrew Bonar Law 'in a most friendly and manly way regarding Marconis [and] he had said', Lloyd George reported, 'that he was quite sure that there had been no moral wrong on LG's part but that he would have to raise the question in the House.' There would be no need for Lloyd George to produce evidence.[90]

After this Lloyd George's interview with the select committee on 28 and 31 March was merely an anticlimax except for the fact that he was still unclear in his mind about the details of his stock transactions. As he had bought stock that did not exist with money he did not have and had, nevertheless, for a short time made some money, he was completely bewildered about what he had done although he was aware that he was paying interest on a broker's loan. Isaacs had to explain matters to him. 'I have never seen Rufus so nearly lose his temper', observed Mrs. Masterman.[91]

Before the select committee Lloyd George was modest and humble, a poor man living on his ministerial salary with a £2,000 house in Wales and investments that produced £400 per year. He admitted he still owned 1,643 shares of American Marconi stock which were listed in his own name on the books of his broker, Smith Rice & Co. He pointed out, reasonably enough, that what he had done quite innocently in April had only been made an issue by the subsequent questions about the propriety of the English contract, over which he had no control whatever.[92]

Neither the *National Review* nor the *Spectator* could make much of Lloyd George's testimony. Even though Maxse devoted the entire issue of his journal to the topic in May, the escalation of the Marconi scandal perceptibly slowed. Lloyd George himself was much relieved after his appearance and thought he had done well in every way. Riddell recorded that Churchill had heard from Northcliffe that if Lloyd George had been clever the whole thing could have been cleared up in October with a short political note in *The Times.* Nonetheless, concluded Churchill, 'all's well that ends well'.[93]

But the arsenal of bad luck was not yet exhausted. The mystery figure in the affair until the end of May was the former Whip Alec Murray, now Lord Elibank. Although he had bought stock with Lloyd George in April 1912 he had not figured in any of the rumors until he was named by Carson at the *Matin* trial of 19 March. Even Leo Maxse admitted that he had been unaware of Murray's involvement until that time.[94] Murray had taken a post with Lord Cowdray and had left England for South America in January 1913 so he was out of the country during the spring. Now there were demands in the press and elsewhere that he return to testify. The friction over Murray kept Marconi alive.

Then in the first week of June, through a series of gradually more explicit newspaper articles, it became evident that Murray was further implicated. It was announced in the press on Tuesday, 5 June, that he had bought not only 1,000 American Marconi shares from Isaacs for himself on 17 April 1912, but a further 2,500 the next day from a broker and a few weeks later another 500, all for the account of the Liberal party. This news was a 'bombshell' as George Riddell termed it. No one in the Liberal administration had known of the party shares. Of all the unfortunate coincidences of the Marconi scandal this was the most bizarre and the most enjoyed by the Unionists. Lucy Masterman heard from John Seely the story of how Murray's Liberal party shares were uncovered. Seely related that J.F. Remnant, a Unionist, had been asked by another member of his party whether it was true that Murray had put Liberal party funds into American Marconis.

> '"Yes it is true," said Remnant. "How did it ever come out?" "The oddest way in the world. A stockbroker defaulted and it was found upon his books." The Tory clasped his hands together. "Now I am beginning to believe there really is a God."'[95]

The stockbroker, Charles Fenner, had been hammered on the Stock Exchange at the end of April 1913 and his firm, Montmorency and Company, had been declared bankrupt early the next month.[96] The sensational news became public only a month later and with it the third phase of the Marconi scandal began. (The Unionists had known of Murray's Liberal Marconis for some weeks and had tried and failed to introduce the evidence in a suit Isaacs had brought for libel against Cecil Chesterton, which began on 27 May. Only when the judge refused to admit it did they give it to the newspapers.)[97] Most dangerous for Lloyd George was the anger of the newspaper editors who earlier had been cooperatively silent after assurances that since the *Matin* trial there was nothing new to reveal.[98]

June, then, saw the climax and the real crisis of the Marconi affair. Stories of absconding stockbrokers, the whereabouts of Alec Murray, and of deliberate concealment of stock transactions by Isaacs and Lloyd George which they nevertheless insisted were innocent, filled newspapers to the near exclusion of everything else. 'The whole thing is just too horrible for words', lamented Masterman.[99] Meanwhile, nearly forgotten, in the middle of May the select committee had begun to consider reports. Its chairman, Albert Spicer, an old colleague of Lloyd George in the Cymru Fydd agitation, presented a draft for the majority on 28 May, indeed a week before the news about Murray had appeared. As there was little possibility of an agreed report even before that event Lloyd George evidently attempted to influence the chairman's report. He pushed in the direction of a majority declaration of innocence for himself and Isaacs. Among the very few letters on Marconi in his papers there exists a note, not in fact mentioning Marconi, from his private secretary at the Treasury, Horace Hamilton, to the Chancellor at Criccieth saying that he, Hamilton, had talked with 'F' (Albert Falconer, the most openly Liberal partisan member of the select committee). Falconer had interviewed 'A.S.' (Albert Spicer) on the 'A' (American) transactions, pointing out that those were outside the committee's terms of reference. Spicer declined to say what he had intended to do, but Falconer had told Hamilton that he believed all that could be done to direct Spicer had been done and no further attempts should be made.[100] As it turned out Spicer wrote what was clearly intended to be a moderate but reasonably balanced report dwelling at some length on the American transactions and pointing out justly that if Lloyd George and Isaacs had been candid in the House of Commons on the debate of 11 October the result would have 'tended to avert much misunderstanding and to lessen. . .the labours' of the committee. But all this was lost in the tumult surrounding the revelation of the Liberal party Marconi shares. As a result, the committee finally provided three reports. A second, written by Albert Falconer, completely exonerated the men, although it made no recommendation, as was later remarked, upon the contract which had been the committee's original charge. Finally Lord Robert Cecil, certainly the strongest member of a weak committee, retaliated with a long and highly detailed attack upon the original contract concluding in a skillful dialectical exercise, the basis for many Unionist speeches in the House of Commons, which argued that the terms under which Lloyd George, Isaacs and Murray had obtained the American shares implied an obligation to Godfrey Isaacs. Thus even if the American Marconi transactions were not corrupt in themselves, they contained the potential for corruption. Moreover the ministers understood this themselves as their failure to admit their holdings on 11 October proved.[101] The whole 'edifice of calumny' would have tumbled down, muttered John Burns to Almeric Fitzroy, if Lloyd George had only stood up last October 'with a tear in his throat' and said that he acted unwisely but not dishonestly. After a short attack by Bonar Law the whole thing would have been over.[102]

The official committee report, essentially Falconer's, was adopted by the committee in an 8 to 6 party line vote and published on 13 June. Given the construction of the committee there was never much chance that the accused ministers could be found guilty of corruption, but the unblinking refusal of the majority even to admit a suspicion of misjudgment brought widespread expressions of contempt, not only upon the clumsy document, but upon the committee itself, and by implication upon the entire Liberal party. An inept investigation by an inept committee had produced, not surprisingly, an inept report. But the effect now was to transfer the Marconi case from the select committee to the House of Commons. Here the potential for damage was immense. Marconi was no longer the property of a few military specialists and telegraphic engineers. Rather the whole Unionist party was out for the kill. Lloyd George and Isaacs now had to win their case by themselves, in public, before their colleagues. They could not take refuge behind the whitewashing report of a discredited committee.[103]

Prime Minister Asquith understood this quite well. During the past year he had made no public comment upon the case but now he took action. The greatest danger was Lloyd George's own combative temperament. This fear was well founded. Riddell records that Lloyd George had told him on 21 May, albeit before the Liberal party share disclosures, that he intended to make a fighting speech revealing similar Tory behavior: Selborne and the P. & O., Balfour and the Whitaker Wright shares. 'LG and Rufus never admit they have done anything,' Riddell wrote on 9 June. The opposition was always unscrupulous. They never will agree that they have 'brought the attacks on themselves or that they acted unwisely.'[104] But Asquith was determined that Lloyd George would have to express regret for what he had done. A self-righteous speech, his normal response to attack, would bring disaster. In the Cabinet of 7 June, devoted solely to the Marconi affair, J.A. Pease noted that while Isaacs was morose and dejected, Lloyd George 'had fire in his eye'.[105]

The critical debate on the select committee recommendation was scheduled for 18 and 19 June. The opposition gave notice of a resolution to be moved by George Cave that: 'the House regrets the transactions of certain of His Majesty's Ministers...and the want of frankness' in the debate of 11 October. If that resolution passed, or indeed if it failed by fewer than 50 votes, Charles Masterman explained to his wife, Lloyd George and Isaacs would have to resign from the government and also from the House of Commons.[106] (That weekend, Mrs. Masterman noted, Lloyd George invited Robert Donald, editor of the *Daily Chronicle*, to play golf at Walton Heath knowing that Donald would not be able to attack him in his paper after a golf game the Saturday before.)[107] If the government failed to defeat the Cave resolution by more than 30–40 votes the entire Cabinet would have to resign, thought *The Times* on the eve of the debate.[108]

That the ministers did not resign, that the Cave resolution was defeated by 78 votes on 19 June, was the result, almost entirely, of the work of H.H. Asquith. On 16 June he sent nearly identical letters to his erring colleagues, explaining that he had consulted the Foreign Secretary Sir Edward Grey and that he hoped each would apologize for want of candor, saying also that were the occasion to arise again each would behave differently, not because the share purchases were wrong, but because they were open to misinterpretation.[109] Neither man should make a fighting speech, that would come from himself.[110] Asquith's task was difficult. He had to make clear to the Liberal party in the House of Commons that he wanted the two men excused. The Cave resolution could not be a matter of formal confidence in the government and there were many on both sides who for various reasons would have been glad in the absence of a whip to vote against Lloyd George and Isaacs.

Asquith had to show by a vigorous defense that those who supported his leadership would divide against the Cave resolution.

Hence the debate of 18 and 19 June became the real point of the Marconi scandal. The select committee report was forgotten; the Marconi contract was forgotten; the charges of gambling in English Marconi shares were forgotten. The issues were the American Marconi purchases and above all the failure of Lloyd George and Isaacs to admit them on 11 October. The culprits, Asquith decided, would speak and withdraw. He would take charge of the battle after they had gone.

Isaacs spoke first and was followed by Lloyd George. Neither man admitted any sense of guilt for the transactions although both assured the House they would not repeat their action. Lloyd George's conclusion provides the tone of the defense.

> I am conscious of having done nothing which will bring a stain
> upon the honour of a Minister of the Crown. If you will, I acted
> thoughtlessly, I acted carelessly, I acted mistakenly, but I acted
> innocently, I acted openly and I acted honestly. That is why I, with
> confidence, place myself in the hands, not merely of my political
> friends, but of the Members of all parts of this great assembly.[111]

Neither man had said at any time that he 'regretted' his action.

Although Lucy Masterman records that during Lloyd George's speech her husband, Churchill, and even Asquith, were crying, there seems to have been little in either address to evoke such sympathetic emotion.[112] John Burns' estimate may be a little closer to the truth. 'Rufus good but not generous. Too legal, not human enough. Too long and differentiating at least in his mind as to what was legal, proper and expedient. Chancellor too long, and had he made a short simple apology for what he had done the suspicions and prejudices would have been blown away.'[113]

All of this made Asquith's task more difficult when he spoke the next day, 19 June. Now he offered a list of six rules of conduct for ministers and after defining each he carefully asserted that neither Lloyd George nor Isaacs had broken any of them.[114] He made clear that the Cave resolution as it stood amounted to a vote of censure which would cause the men to leave public life. But more importantly, addressing his own party not the opposition, he covered the accused men with the shield of his own honor and judgment. Alec Murray had told him, he said, of the purchases by the three ministers the previous July or in early August in a letter that the Prime Minister unfortunately no longer possessed.[115] He had told him also that there was no connection between the American and English companies and that the American transactions occurred after the English contract had been made public. He recalled that he had thought nothing of it. Further, Asquith said that he was ill during the sitting of 11 October but he had read the debate and saw nothing in it of importance. He put himself, in effect, among the accused. He was asserting that what they had done was neither wrong nor even important. The Liberal party was to understand that to censure Lloyd George and Isaacs would be to censure its leader. That Asquith may have not known all the facts at the time he suggested he did, does not detract from the magnanimity of his performance.

The Prime Minister concluded with an offer of compromise. 'They have on the floor of this House, with perfect manliness, expressed their regret.' Let the House, he urged, accept that admission of regret as expressed in the amendment put down yesterday. Immediately the Prime Minister was overwhelmed with cries of 'No'.[116] Asquith had, it would seem through inadvertence, nearly given his strategy away. No amendment had been put down. After Lloyd George and Isaacs had spoken, Stanley Buckmaster had indeed tabled an amendment to the Cave resolution proposing that the two men be totally exonerated, but nothing resembling what Asquith referred to was before the House. After some interval, Ryland Adkins hurried in with an amendment to Buckmaster's providing the required text: 'that this House. . .accept the expressions of regret that such purchases were made and that they were not mentioned in the debate of October 11.'[117]

Balfour followed Asquith with a speech of distinct moderation in which he denied wanting to see Lloyd George and Isaacs driven from politics, but in which he pointed out what must have been clear to every Member of the House, that despite the Prime Minister's affirmation, neither minister had expressed anything like regret for his actions.[118] *The Times* also pointed out the next day the absence of 'regret'.[119]

Nevertheless, 'regret', to be precise *who* would regret, became the key issue in the Marconi debate. The government offered an amendment to the Cave resolution proposing in place of the words 'that this House regrets' the Marconi transactions, a formula saying 'that this House. . .accepts the expressions of regret' of Lloyd George and Isaacs. There was a narrow line, Charles Masterman explained to his wife, between the House regretting an action and allowing the ministers to do the same, which, nonetheless, made all the difference in the world.[120] If the House 'regretted' they would have to go. If it allowed them to 'regret' they were saved. Asquith had put into his ministers' mouths the words which made it possible to save them. There was a certain amount of negotiation between the two parties over this formula. Bonar Law was willing to amend the Cave resolution to include a statement acquitting the ministers of charges of corruption but containing nevertheless the fatal words 'this House regrets. . .' Balfour's pressure for an expression of regret from the House, even though coupled with a sympathetic speech, caused Masterman to conclude he was playing a double game. Masterman thought it impossible to believe that the former Prime Minister did not know that a recorded resolution of regret by the House would cause the ministers' resignation.[121]

In the end the negotiations came to nothing and the matter had to be settled by a straight party line vote. The Cave resolution was defeated 346 to 268, a majority of 78 or about 15 votes fewer than the government's normal majority in 1913. The O'Brienite Irish and the Labour party radicals abstained as did F.E. Smith and Edward Carson, the attorneys in the *Matin* case, but three Liberals voted with the Unionists.[122]

There is no evidence that Churchill went back and forth between Bonar Law and Lloyd George to see what sort of censure the latter would accept, as Bruce Lockhart recalls being told by Randolph Churchill in 1934. They were said to have agreed upon the word 'indiscretion' which in fact does not appear in either resolution.[123] Nor did the Unionists forbear because of stupidity or kindliness to bring Lloyd George down as Randolph Churchill records having heard from his father.[124] Bonar Law was in earnest.[125] The opposition mustered nearly every vote they controlled for the Cave resolution. The abstentions and absences were on the government's side.

Asquith had held the party together in support of two of its most visible and controversial figures. His biographer and friend, J.A. Spender, states in his account of the affair that 'to the end of his days he regarded this as the most difficult and painful personal incident that he had had to deal with in the course of his public life.'[126] Certainly a number of Liberals, including, one suspects, several members of the Cabinet, felt that the two men should be allowed to go and certainly he himself was more than impatient with their conduct. Spender argues that Asquith was impelled by a sense of justice, although one must add that he was too clear a thinker not to remember that to an extent he had implicated himself as a result of his insistence upon secrecy after the revelations of January 1913. There was, moreover, the danger that too severe a condemnation of the men, or too small a majority against the Cave resolution, could have brought down the government, as *The Times* had pointed out. Yet there exists a letter from his wife Margot Asquith to Isaacs, incredible even from someone with a talent for indiscretion, that must be noted. Writing some years later, certainly after 7 December 1916, Margot wished Isaacs to know how much she and her husband cared for him. 'H saved LG over Marconi, Why? — because LlG was young [50?] and he loved *you* had it not been for *you* he wd have let LlG go.' To show how much the couple esteemed Isaacs she told him of a letter from Isaacs's wife sent to 10 Downing Street after the Asquiths had been 'turned out' saying 'this was what we always wanted.' Alice Isaacs had forgotten, Mrs. Asquith explained, that although Lloyd George was now Prime Minister the Asquiths continued to occupy No. 10. She and her husband were terribly hurt but continued to love Isaacs.[127] The involvement of Isaacs, then, had saved Lloyd George.

During the Marconi attacks Lloyd George had moved through his usual public poses: from bewildered innocence, to self-righteous indignation, to fury. But by the conclusion of the matter on 19 June his anger and his realization of danger were genuine enough. On the one hand he felt, as always, unjustly accused, but he came soon to understand that he had had a very narrow escape. Despite a certain attitude of cocksureness displayed during his speech, Lucy Masterman recalled seeing him after the debate with his hair on end, his face flushed, unable to sit still, 'almost hysterical' with relief.[128] 'I thought LG looked very old in so short a time,' John Burns recorded in his diary early in July.[129]

In conclusion, then, there was in reality no 'Marconi scandal'. Such questions as there were about the unfavorable contract disappeared when the select committee began to sit, or at least after Lawson's disappointing testimony in January 1913. The belief in a conspiracy of ministerial speculators resided, if at all, only in the minds of men connected with *Eye-Witness* magazine and perhaps with Leo Maxse. Many men, from Bonar Law to Northcliffe to St. Loe Strachey, editor of the *Spectator*, had affirmed in the spring of 1913, after the American purchases were public, that there was no foundation for a charge of corruption. Nonetheless the burden of historical writing to the present has been to find a connection between the American shares and the English ones and to establish a causal relationship where only a casual one exists. Lloyd George's mistake was not the purchase of the American Marconis, itself only another case of bad luck or bad timing, but the failure to tell the truth about it.

Thus, there was instead of a Marconi scandal in fact a Lloyd George-and-Rufus Isaacs-parliamentary-privilege scandal in which the catalyst was the Liberal party Marconi shares and the issue the prevarication of 11 October 1912. The catalyst, the Liberal party shares, could not have been avoided; the collapse of Montmorency and Company was an entirely unrelated matter that would have occurred anyway. But without the tumult over Marconi the American shares would have made no political difference. The fact that no one could have confessed to knowledge of them, because no one knew, was by this time irrelevant.[130]

At the most elementary level of the Marconi affair Murray was perhaps most culpable. But he was a secondary figure, gone beyond the reach of the House of Commons. However, Lloyd George was genuinely in great danger. Many people wanted to destroy him for other reasons. In politics motives and the means available seldom coincide. One stick is as good as another to break a back.

At the more complex level, much of the animosity was of course personal, especially for the figures of Leopold Maxse and Wilfred Lawson, who carried the burden of the attack for most of the nine months. But neither Lloyd George nor Isaacs was a popular figure in the close world of Westminster political society. Lloyd George already was regarded as a charlatan genius, free with the truth, too willing to attack the motivations of others. Men like Lord Robert Cecil admired him, yet hated themselves for doing so. For the same men, Isaacs was simply an ambitious, and extremely clever, Jew.

Marconi is also a lesson, if another is needed, in the power of the British political press. The critical event in the affair was the discovery of the Liberal party shares. This should have made no difference to Lloyd George and Isaacs; they had nothing more to confess. They possessed no more than anyone else knowledge of these purchases. But an enraged press, which had behaved responsibly before, now insisted upon punishment. As a result, the lack of candor on 11 October, known at least since mid-March, became an issue in mid-June and Lloyd George and Isaacs, not to mention perhaps the Liberal administration, nearly suffered political execution.

For Lloyd George the effects of Marconi soon wore off. Unlike Isaacs, for whom the Marconi episode left a permanent wound, kept open by vicious attacks years later, Lloyd George was soon back in fighting trim.[131] On 29 June at the National Liberal Club he denounced his critics in a speech so full of wounded sensibilities and moral outrage that one might be excused for not remembering that he had in fact done certain things that caused the Marconi scandal. This address, which may be taken as the end of the Marconi affair, basically attacked the Unionists for raising the issue in the first place. He had received many letters from friends among the opposition, he said, apologizing for their party's behavior. Having lost the political war over the House of Lords they were now resorting to underhanded trickery.

It is the shabbiest chapter in the history of any party. Hitting a man when he is down, hitting a man when his hands are tied behind his back — that is the Tory notion of fair play. There is one kind of martyrdom which I have always thought was the least endurable of all, and that was where the victim has his hands tied and arrows were sped into his body from all quarters and he could neither protect himself, nor tear them out, nor fling them back. I quite understand something of that now, for months every dastardly and cowardly journalist of the Tory party shooting his poison darts into your body, knowing that your hands were tied behind your back by the principles of honourable loyalty to the House of Commons. . .A downright, honest, one-sided fellow I will take my hat off to, but the other is just a hungry humbug, steeped in smugness and self-righteousness. I wanted to say that.[132]

This speech evoked a jeering rejoinder in an article from L.S. Amery entitled 'St. Sebastian of Limehouse', but essentially the Marconi affair was over.[133] Leo Maxse's enmity for the Chancellor would continue and he attempted to use Alec Murray to disrupt the land campaign, now in full swing, but Lloyd George was now beyond harm, on this charge at least.

In the midst of the Marconi scandal, indeed five days after the *Matin* libel, a house for Lloyd George paid for by George Riddell under construction on Walton Heath was partially blown up by suffragettes. Two aspects of this potentially lethal event deserve comment. The first, briefly, concerns Lloyd George's relationship with Sir George Riddell.

Riddell was an elusive figure who throughout his life remained at pains to keep details of his career unavailable both to his contemporaries and to posterity. Indeed his famous diary, twenty-two volumes of typescript and not a diary at all but a daily chronicle of the life of Lloyd George, essentially between 1912 and 1922, remained securely under lock and key in the British Library until 1985. The three published volumes that appeared in 1933 and 1934, although extremely valuable, delete nearly all unfavorable comment about living people and contain far less than half the original text, tell nothing of the writer.[134] The long-hidden typescript tells little more about Riddell but it is a gold-mine of Lloyd George information, far more useful than Frances Stevenson's diary. Lloyd George frequently did not tell Miss Stevenson the whole truth and usually, almost always, embroidered his stories to increase their dramatic effect. Riddell had his own excellent connections in Whitehall and Fleet Street. Thus, while Lloyd George certainly did not tell him every-thing, for example about meetings with Lord Northcliffe of which Riddell disapproved, the publisher was well aware of them and reflected on their danger in his diary.

Riddell, trained as a solicitor, was in 1913 proprietor of the immensely profitable Sunday paper, the *News of the World,* as well as of *Country Life* and some smaller magazines. Lloyd George apparently came to know him soon after his appointment to the Board of Trade in 1905 for Riddell remarks in his diary about visiting the Lloyd George house in Routh Road, Wandsworth. In any case by 1908 Lloyd George and Riddell, with Churchill and Masterman, were frequently together. Riddell's attractions for Lloyd George, besides wealth, were an inexhaustible supply of usually accurate Whitehall and newspaper gossip and candid advice upon political matters.[135] He did not lecture about the True Principles of Liberalism as Scott and Massingham tended to do. Indeed it is difficult to extract from his diaries any political point of view although Riddell records in his typescript diary a joking assertion by Lloyd George that Riddell was a socialist. Perhaps because of his candor the Riddell association lasted until the end of the premiership despite some quarrels over diplomatic issues after the Paris Peace Conference. Riddell was distrusted by many people who feared his influence over Lloyd George. Frances Stevenson, who in fact liked him, saw his darker side — he could be hard and mean. She worried about Lloyd George's dependence upon him both as an advisor and a friend.[136] W. Watkin Davies, writing while Lloyd George was still alive and from the point of view of a detached acquaintanceship, found his influence almost wholly bad. He was a schemer, like Lloyd George, and Lloyd George did not need more partners in conspiracy.[137]

Perhaps the worst to be said of Riddell is that his interest in Lloyd George proceeded solely from his wish to be near the seat of power. He did not retail stories to newspapers, his own, or others. He helped to flatter the vanity of Robertson Nicoll and was instrumental in obtaining the *British Weekly* editor's much coveted knighthood. He was patient, helpful, and well-informed. He served as an intermediary for Lloyd George in delicate personal affairs. But when Lloyd George was ejected from office he promptly transferred his allegiance to Bonar Law and the two men rarely saw each other after that. However Riddell left Lloyd George £1,000 when he died in 1934.[138]

Among other favors such as an automobile in 1912, Riddell was preparing to give Lloyd George the lease to the five bedroom house near the Walton Heath golf course in Surrey (with a similar one for Masterman).[139] The course itself was a new one, founded only in 1904, and Riddell apparently had a speculative interest in property adjoining it. (Robert Donald, editor of the *Daily Chronicle* also bought a house there.) The location catered to the Chancellor's love of the sport and the house itself provided a private refuge for meetings with Frances Stevenson. (Before Walton Heath became available his retreat was a villa in Brighton, lent by Lord Rendel.) The attack upon it on 19 February 1913 demonstrated, as did the Marconi affair, the political danger associated with Lloyd George's position as the party spokesman on domestic reform. He was to blame for the government's failure to grant voting rights to women.

In fact Lloyd George supported the principle of universal franchise. But he foresaw endless peril in the divisiveness of the process of franchise legislation. On one side the Liberals were under attack by the Labour party, and radicals in their own ranks, who demanded a large, comprehensive measure providing broadbased electoral reform. Yet on the other side were the Irish who had no interest in the matter, who were jealous of any issue that diverted attention from Home Rule and who were well aware that 'reform' might include a reduction in Ireland's gross over-representation in the House of Commons.[140] The party and even the Cabinet were divided on the matter. Asquith, and especially Churchill, strongly opposed concessions to women, the latter to the point where he threatened to break with Lloyd George although publicly he supported a referendum on the issue.[141] Lloyd George himself felt the uncertainties within the party meant that any bill would be simply a gift to the opposition. Either the party should go forward with a measure giving votes to all women and to all men while also abolishing plural voting, or drop the idea altogether. As his most important point, he argued that to give suffrage only to spinsters and widows who controlled property, as men possessed it under existing household franchise, would be to hand over several hundred thousand votes to the Tories.[142]

In July 1912, after a year and a half of dithering over voting measures put down by private members, the government brought forward its own franchise reform bill aimed at ending plural voting and university representation while also simplifying registration. The Prime Minister had announced at the time that the government was prepared to accept an amendment for women's suffrage. The division on the matter would be left to a free vote in the House of Commons. This weak compromise fell to pieces on 27 January 1913 when Speaker Lowther ruled that an amendment of this nature would so change the bill before the House as to make it an entirely new measure. Hence it should be presented as a separate bill. Although the Prime Minister insisted that the Speaker's ruling came as a surprise, in reality he had received much notice of it and the Cabinet had considered its response two days before. Privately Asquith was greatly relieved even though he admitted to Venetia Stanley that the result would be a renewed outbreak of suffragette violence.[143]

The violence began as expected and an immediate target, a little more than three weeks after the Speaker's ruling was Lloyd George's still unfinished house. As the attack was against a private residence, rather than public property, it was received with some outrage — the *Nation*, although it supported the women's vote, referred to the culprits as 'perverts' — which was heightened by Lloyd George's announcement that had the carpenters arrived on time that morning they would have been killed.[144] This elicited a letter, six months later, from one of the bombers denouncing the Chancellor for suggesting that they wished to harm anyone but himself. The women had intended to cause the explosion sometime between 5:00 and 5:30 in the morning but had failed to pile enough shavings around the candles used as fuses.[145] Hence the explosion was about an hour late.

Lloyd George continued to be a major target for suffragette violence in the intensified campaign that embarrassed the government until the outbreak of the war. Yet the evidence is clear that he suffered only because of his visibility within the ranks of political figures. His private relations with individual leaders within the suffrage movement continued to be generally good. Catherine Marshall, the handsome parliamentary secretary of the Fawcett organization, the non-violent suffrage society, corresponded with him frequently in amiable almost intimate terms, and visited him at No. 11 for the conference breakfasts which had become a regular part of his working schedule. By the summer of 1914 on the eve of the war, he had offered the Women's Social and Political Union, the more militant society, another opportunity to move a women's suffrage amendment in the new voting reform bill the government was preparing. Meanwhile he intervened with Reginald McKenna the Home Secretary on behalf of Sylvia Pankhurst, recently released from prison, who, he said, was about to give up violence.[146] It should be noted that the W.S.P.U. was unenthusiastic about the opportunity for another free vote, demanding instead a clear government commitment of support for women's suffrage.[147]

III

Lloyd George's last independent initiative as Chancellor of the Exchequer, potentially his largest public project, was the so-called 'Land Campaign' of 1912 to 1914. Its collapse on the eve of the war accompanied by forced revision of his 1914 budget marked his first important defeat and may have signaled also the end of the new Liberalism, while causing a potentially serious setback for his own career.

Because his program of land reform never developed, much of what it might have become remains a matter of conjecture. Like all Lloyd George initiatives it was grand in conception and meager in detail. Again, as with the 1909 budget or health insurance, the initial legislation would have been only a beginning. Indeed it was itself, in reality, only a continuation of the earlier projects. The land valuation inserted so awkwardly into the People's Budget was for Lloyd George the starting point of land reform.

But in a larger sense, the attack on the British system of real property holding had been at the core of Lloyd George's political conscience through most of his adult life. Rating appeals, rent collecting, conveyancing, had been the stuff of his legal apprenticeship at Breeze, Jones and Casson. He had watched and pondered Gladstone's struggle to deal with the land problems in Ireland through land courts. Within months after its publication in England he had read Henry George's *Progress and Poverty*, indeed purchasing his copy in January 1884 with money he had saved to pay his subscription to the Portmadoc Law Library. His comments on the book, recorded at the time in his diary, manifested as much the influence of Herbert Spencer as Henry George. They may be as close to a real philosophy of land reform as his empirical mind could achieve.

11 January 1884 I don't believe in his scheme — appropriation of rent is nothing but aimless plunder. The great object is to get control of the *land itself* into the hands of those whose interests are so vitally affected by it — and it strikes me that now most every argument applicable to such confiscation is also an argument for State appropriation of personal property. My own idea is the devolution to the State of deceased owners' properties, so that all alike may have an equal chance of starting life.[148]

Behind the sensible perception that the property problem was a question of land use rather than a problem of wealth lay, nevertheless, a real, not simulated, anger. Landlords were evil because they were indolent, wasteful and selfish, not because they were rich. 'Idle land in the hands of idle men,' was Lloyd George's repeated slogan after 1912. Those who owned the land, and coal and slate deposits, did not work. Those who worked the land owned nothing and were even without a right to a roof over their heads. His hatred of the landlords was broadly focused to include his other enemies. The Dukes were first of all landlords. The vicar and the voluntary schoolmaster were the landlords' clients. The laws of England provided privileges for land accorded no other form of property. Occupiers not groundrent owners paid the rates. Agricultural property was specially relieved. The echelons of estate office functionaries, stewards, tithe bailiffs, colliery managers and quarry contractors, protected the land owner from the wrath of the anonymous laborer, quarryman or coal miner whom the landlord defrauded. The poachers and trespassers Lloyd George had defended in county courts in Pwllheli and Portmadoc were not criminals, he had argued, but Robin Hood-like figures who defied a vicious system.

Two qualifications must be made. First Lloyd George's sympathy for the land worker was less intense than the antipathy for his exploiter. Moreover it was usually expressed in personal rather than class or doctrinaire socialist terms. Lloyd George, as has been seen, thought of working men's sufferings almost entirely in terms of his life and experience in North Wales, of tenants who were turned out of cottages for voting Liberal, quarrymen killed in explosions or slides, farmers distrained for refusing to pay the tithe. He seldom employed the rhetoric of even Welsh organized labor and found most union representatives whom he knew, from William Abraham to Keir Hardie, either stupid or eccentric. 'I would rather see a Conservative get in than a Labour man,' he declared to J.E.B. Seely, in Riddell's hearing in the summer of 1912 on the eve of the Hanley by-election.[149]

On the other hand landowners anywhere, Welsh, English or Scot were equally the enemy. Second, it scarcely need be reiterated that he enjoyed and solicited the company of wealthy businessmen and the conveniences, motor cars, villas on the Riviera, and yachts, they could provide. As his tale of the Duke of Westminster's treatment of Frederick Gorringe illustrated, he felt that capitalists too suffered at the hands of the land monopolist. The self-made man — Alfred Thomas, Hudson Kearley, or for that matter Bonar Law — had nothing to be ashamed of. In all this Lloyd George separated himself absolutely from the ideological orthodoxy of the Liberal radicals of the 1906 generation in the House of Commons, many of whom, it should be remarked, were far wealthier than he.

The single-minded antagonism for the landlord in all his guises that Lloyd George had brought with him from Wales had informed his political life from the beginning. His first act in elective office, in the Caernarvonshire County Council, was to move a petition to parliament for leasehold enfranchisement. Few of his major public speeches after that time avoided some reference to the matter. Rating reform, old age pensions, Church schools, protection, all issues could be adapted to it. The 1909 budget as first drafted had included not only land valuation but also a site value tax to be based upon it. The failure of the Cabinet to accept the site value tax made necessary the inclusion of the nuisance land taxes in order to justify the provision for valuation in a money bill.[150] But it should be recalled that land valuation was not the sole property of Lloyd George. The issue had been a staple of the King's speeches since the Liberals came to power; a large body of opinion among House of Commons radicals, organized since 1903 by the United Committee for the Taxation of Land Values, supported the principle of a uniform national valuation of land separated from improvements. Bills toward this end for Scotland had passed the House of Commons both in 1907 and 1908 only to be promptly killed by the House of Lords.

Lloyd George, however, saw far more in land reform than the simple wealth redistribution function of site value taxation with which the radicals were enamored. As the practical failure of John Burns's Housing and Town Planning Act of 1909 became apparent, he grew interested in working class housing. Section 39 of the National Insurance Act specified that health insurance reserve funds could be invested in public housing and the land valuation, when it was complete, would facilitate the acquisition of land by local authorities for this purpose.

Similarly health insurance, even though it represented a giant step forward in primary health care for workers, afforded no specialist or institutional treatment and did nothing for dependents. Even before the bill was passed it had come under criticism from more doctrinaire health reformers for its narrow application. Local authorities, it was argued, should be put to work providing treatment for needs not covered by the insurance scheme: deficiencies uncovered in school medical inspection, more frequent and better school meals, and clinics for expectant mothers which might provide also facilities for consulting physicians. The list was long and grew further after the evidence, provided by health insurance claims in the spring of 1913, of widespread chronic ill-health among working class wives and mothers. All of this, by inference, was part of the land program because the proposals for a vast expansion of local authority duties required new sources of revenue which a site value tax, or rate, would supply. The growing financial requirements of the local authorities determined the shape of what was supposed to be the first installment of land reform, the ill-fated 1914 budget. Early evidence that the Chancellor's thoughts were moving in the direction of tying local authority reform to land taxation appeared with his appointment in November 1911 of a strong departmental committee under the Treasury Controller, Sir John Kempe, including also his trusty lieutenant from Cardiff, Alderman T.J. Hughes, to study local taxation and to look into ways of equalizing the wide discrepancies in the financial health of local governments.[151]

The conclusion then must be that land reform was to represent not only the achievement of Lloyd George's oldest and most personal aim in politics but also the culmination, or a joining together, of all previous Liberal reforms. Freeing the land, a healthier nation, and the imposition of the cost of these achievements on the sterile wealth frozen in real property, all projected in the budget speech of 1909, would finally be accomplished. Lloyd George reminded the party of this in a speech to the National Liberal Federation at Bath on 24 November 1911 while the National Insurance Bill was still before parliament. After noting that health insurance was nearly through the House of Commons, he announced that 'The most urgent need of Britain today is the regeneration of rural Britain. You will not do that without a complete reform of the land laws.' 'Millions' of robust countrymen were being driven off the land to the debilitating climes of the cities. National vigor was declining in urban slums. Insurance alone could not rebuild the British race.[152]

A little more than a month later H.W. Massingham, in his important article 'The Position of Mr. Lloyd George', reiterated for his readers the widespread belief among the politicians that the budget of 1909 would have a sequel. 'That sequel is the transformation of British agriculture through the three roads of reform of the land laws and land taxation, the further reform of housing and state control of the railway system. . .'[153]

The early months of 1912, as has been seen, were a period of Liberal malaise, and of particular unhappiness for Lloyd George similar to the last months of 1908, except that now disappointment over the unpopularity of health insurance and over labor problems were added to the sense of political impotence. For Lloyd George frustration meant action. The immediate impulse for the new program which became the land campaign seems to have been a modest, privately printed, seven-page pamphlet dated 20 May 1912, entitled 'Labour Unrest and Liberal Policy', and signed by a number of important advanced Liberal publicists and thinkers including B. Seebohm Rowntree.[154] The pamphlet stated at the beginning that the undersigned felt that the Cabinet committee on Labour Unrest (of which Lloyd George was a member) 'might care to hear their views'. In very sketchy terms there followed the outline of a reform program that might have occupied the Liberals for a generation: minimum wages for every worker beginning with agriculture and transport, railway nationalization and the extension of trade boards to these industries, relief and reform of local taxation, and finally, 'connected with this are the problems of housing and the acquisition of land'. The writers hoped to do a report on this. This pamphlet evoked a response from Lloyd George. Although he did not know B.S. Rowntree well at this time, he certainly had heard of him and for years had mined his survey of living conditions in York, published in 1901, for gloomy statistics on working class life. Now the Chancellor wrote to Rowntree saying that he had already decided on a big campaign 'to regenerate rural England'. He invited the signers of the pamphlet to a breakfast at No. 11.[155]

As he frequently did, Lloyd George began immediately to work out his ideas in discussion with Riddell. At first he was concerned mostly with the plight of the agricultural laborer. His position was worse than that of any other worker in the kingdom. The government would establish land courts, similar to the tribunals in Ireland, but which would set both farmers' rents and laborers' wages. Rent would be reduced to a sum bearing a relation to the real productivity of the land, but the money thus saved by the farmer would be passed through to the laborer. In effect a higher wage in agriculture would come from the pocket of the landowner, not the tenant. 'I am convinced that the land question is the real issue,' Lloyd George exclaimed to Riddell on 27 May. 'You must break down the remnants of the feudal system. . .There are times when radicalism needs a greater stimulus — when the Radical cause has fallen into the abyss of respectability and conventionality. Something must be done to put fresh life into dry bones. I feel that the land and the agricultural labourer are at the root of the whole social evil.'[156] Working out his figures on the back of an envelope, he declared that a £100 reduction in rent on a 500 acre farm would result in a 2s per week increase in the laborer's wage, although he admitted that he was unsure how many workers a farm of that size would employ. Riddell wondered to himself how many other great matters of state were decided in this way.[157]

'The land scheme is a shrewd political move,' mused Riddell a few weeks later after a dinner, including C.F.G. Masterman and Robertson Nicoll, editor of the *British Weekly*, when Lloyd George reported that he had received Asquith's assent to move ahead. 'While it deals with present day economic troubles, it is framed to appeal to the Liberal politician who is not prepared to attack the commercial classes, but will rejoice in attacking the pockets and privileges of his traditional bugbears and enemies, the squires and the ground landlords.'[158]

The breakfast that in fact began the land campaign evidently occurred soon after the dinner with Riddell, Nicoll and Masterman. Included were most of the men who would be involved in the public portion of the campaign, Seebohm Rowntree, A.H.D. Acland, and Charles Roden Buxton among others, together with C.P. Scott and several of Lloyd George's political cronies, Isaacs, Murray, and Masterman and some other Liberal Members of Parliament. At the breakfast Lloyd George announced that he would like an intensive investigation of conditions on the land. There would be a committee, which became the 'Land Enquiry Committee', for which he proposed Rowntree as honorary secretary.[159] Rowntree declined this distinction, nominating Buxton, although as it turned out Rowntree did most of the work of the investigation. Other members of the committee were Rowntree's lawyer Richard Cross and Baron Maurice DeForest the enormously rich illegitimate son of Baron Hirsch. J.St.G.C. Heath became paid secretary.[159] Indeed Lloyd George himself took little part in the inquiry which was really only the public, and least important, part of a very much larger project.

Lloyd George described his proposals to the Cabinet, evidently on 15 June, in grand but general terms and assured them he was not a single taxer.[160] At the end of the session, as Wilfred Lawson's first articles on the Marconi contract began to appear in *Outlook*, he left England for Marienbad with Isaacs and T.P. O'Connor. While there, as Isaacs was hearing from Samuel of the libelous article in *Eye-Witness*, he received regular reports on the progress of the committee while at the same time stirring up, apparently deliberately, rumors of a large and important Liberal agricultural program to come.[161]

The Unionists understood quickly what Lloyd George was up to. Less than a month after the original breakfast Lord Hugh Cecil wrote to Bonar Law comparing the 1909 budget and what the Chancellor now proposed. There was little difference, he thought, between taxing the real value of a site at the time of its transfer and taxing it each year. But in doing so the Chancellor was probably outrunning a large section of his party in the country and no doubt in the Cabinet. 'The situation is not unlike that of 1903,' Cecil remarked cheerfully, with Lloyd George playing the part of Chamberlain. 'We all remember how damaging discussions were in those circumstances for the government.' There was much potential advantage here, concluded Cecil. The Liberals could be forced into defending policies upon which they were not agreed. Some sort of resolution ought to be put down.[162]

Cecil's estimate of the Liberal reaction to the land program, and indeed of its end, was perfectly correct. It is hard to say whether Lloyd George's proposals or his working methods irritated his colleagues more. But it is clear that throughout its life as an active political project the land campaign was dogged both by ministerial and public unpopularity. In effect Lloyd George became a danger to the Liberals. Land reform was not the doctrine of the ministry, nor of the party, nor of a majority of Liberals in the country, although as has been pointed out it had its adherents among the radicals in the House of Commons. As an expedient in 1909 to counter the appeal of tariff reform among working class voters, land valuation and the land taxes had been a useful weapon, but as Cecil correctly inferred, there were a good many well-to-do Liberals who saw land reform and site value rating as a surrender to a group of economic cranks and a potential disaster for the party. By the middle of August there were signs of unhappiness about the program particularly among well-established northern Liberals.[163]

Many of the Land Enquiry Committee's problems were of its own making. For reasons of strategy Lloyd George wanted the investigation to be kept quiet until the report was ready, while the Cabinet insisted that the entire project remain unofficial. Consequently during the first year everything seemed to go wrong. There were private complaints within the party about tinkering with the tax system and the consequent effect on property values. These were paralleled by public and parliamentary speculation about mystery surrounding the goals of the land investigation, its official status, its finance, its personnel, even its questionnaire, which was eventually uncovered by *The Times* and published on 23 September. (The campaign's official stationery named only Buxton and Heath and placed the headquarters at 170 Palace Chambers, Bridge Street, Westminster.) Eventually, on 15 October 1912 just four days after the disastrous Marconi debate, the House debated the land investigation on a motion to adjourn. Lloyd George was reminded that secrecy caused rumor and there were jeering references to whispers about the survey passing 'from one foul mouth to another'.[164] On this occasion, however, he kept his temper and was able to force Austen Chamberlain to admit that what his party really wanted were the names of tenants who were telling stories about their landlords to interviewers.

On the whole Lloyd George felt pleased with the results. In his usual letter of self-congratulation to his wife he told of the cheers in the House (which he was leading during Asquith's illness), but he provided also evidence of the importance he assigned to the land campaign in assisting a Liberal revival.

> Had a glorious row last night. Austen rushed on to the point of a cloaked sword. Our followers were delighted. They rose and cheered as I left the House. But it definitely raised the land question and it gave the House a glimpse of the savage passion that will be rowsed [sic] by the Campaign when it is well on. Home Rule and all else will be swept aside.[165]

Many of the committee's early difficulties were financial. By the spring of 1914 Lloyd George was forced to call upon Sir William Lever and Joseph Fels and Riddell for money. At the beginning it had been expected that money for the support of the committee would come from DeForest. But it soon became clear that DeForest was incapable of carrying out the simplest administrative tasks and as his place in committee affairs diminished so did his financial help. Rowntree called upon his father. DeForest was a peculiar and unstable colleague. (When contesting Southport in January 1910 he had offered to buy all of the land in the constituency.) By the spring of 1913 he was denouncing members of the committee for an insufficient commitment to land nationalization and later threatened to publish correspondence with Lloyd George and others.[166] His final estrangement from the committee in the late summer of 1913 made money problems even more acute, and his outrageous behavior seriously embarrassed Lloyd George, already distracted by the Marconi scandal.[167]

Through the winter of 1912–13 Lloyd George was beset by the struggles with the B.M.A. and the Marconi affair. He paid little attention to the land inquiry except to write an occasional letter soliciting money. As he explained to C.P. Scott on 16 January 1913, he did not intend to begin his campaign until he had at least £50,000 to enable him to flood the country with pamphlets getting out relevant facts. He expected the campaign to last two years. So far he had no scheme of reform, he told Scott, although the general lines were fixed. The agricultural laborers' wages must be raised and their housing must be improved. 'At present [the] three dominant objects of [the] landlord class were first Power, then Amenity, last, profitable use of the land in the public interest. The order must be reversed.' He jeered at R.B. Haldane's attempts in a recent speech to intervene in land reform. Haldane, he said, was 'a barrel of tallow' which when set afire would produce any amount of smoke but no illumination.[168]

Meanwhile the report on rural conditions was being completed and in March was ready for printing. After seeing it rejected by Sir Frederick Macmillan, 'A Bitter Tory', who said 'he would not publish it for £1,000', Robertson Nicoll was able to place it with Hodder and Stoughton.[169] Lloyd George had not yet bothered to read it. Only after the speech at the National Liberal Club, his revenge for Marconi, did he begin, now characteristically with some haste, and with the advice of Riddell, Nicoll and Masterman, to pull together the threads of a plan he hoped to present to the country in October.[170]

The beginnings of the scheme which would eventually be embodied in the 1914 budget appeared first in a highly tentative, unsigned, memorandum entitled 'Land', dated 21 August 1913, which Lloyd George appears to have ordered prepared for himself during the autumn parliamentary recess.[171] The memorandum did not in fact offer any plan. Rather it was concerned with arguments for the preparation of a plan for regulating rural wages, suggesting that the land boards' wage fixing powers could be based upon the precedent of trade boards and the Coal Mines Act of 1912. However, at the end of the memorandum, after discussing the familiar reasons for bettering the condition of agricultural laborers at the expense of the Dukes, the memorandum also noted that the powers of the land boards might be increased to exempt property improvements from rating. This might be better, the paper concluded, than 'a more ambitious scheme' of site value rating. These diffident suggestions were expanded slightly in the direction of solving urban problems in a second memorandum, again prepared evidently for Lloyd George alone, by Charles Hobhouse early in October. The land boards, thought Hobhouse, besides setting wages and rents, and assessing improvements, could grant extensions on the leases to urban tenants and approve the compulsory purchase of land by municipalities for slum clearance.[172]

Although parliament was still in recess, Lloyd George was now in a great hurry. He still talked of the land program mainly in terms of the countryside, but it had long been clear that there was no logical, nor indeed legal, way to separate the economic distress and squalid living conditions of the rural laborer from the equally deplorable conditions of the city laborer. The Land

Enquiry Committee had determined months earlier that the rural report should be followed by a second on urban conditions. Nonetheless Lloyd George remained at heart a countryman. His imagery and the examples in speeches and in his conversations with his colleagues, dealt almost entirely with conditions in the countryside. Part of the reason for the failure of the land campaign must be assigned to this unwillingness, or inability, to come to terms, until it was too late, with landlordism in the cities.

There were other problems. Most pressing was the clear indication that the government and the party, paralyzed by the leverage of the Irish Nationalists, the growing budget, women's suffrage and the unpopularity of national insurance, had nearly run out of steam. An election could not be far off. Some ministers might welcome a defeat. Asquith continually canvassed the Cabinet on sentiment for a dissolution. If land reform was to be part of the Liberal program in an election a plan would have to be produced soon.

Most of Lloyd George's projects began as a short list of excellent but unspecific goals buttressed by a large emotional statement of needs. However the land reforms that he struggled to prepare in the last weeks of September and early October of 1913 contained more than the usual share of hasty improvisations. Nothing was ready. He had no plan to present to the Cabinet and indeed there had been no Cabinet since the first weeks of August. To be sure, he had finally begun to read the rural land inquiry report in mid-August and wrote on 25 August asking Rowntree 'to select a few parishes where the wages of the Agricultural Labourer are low and his housing bad, but where the landlord lives in a fine house and keeps up a great style.' He suggested that Rowntree pick a few great houses from the pages of *Country Life* and then go and investigate the neighborhood. He needed material for speeches.[173] But no matter how much sensational ammunition for the denunciation of Dukes the land report provided, it was not a program and Lloyd George did not intend that it should be. Nevertheless land agitation had to begin, with or without a plan. Accordingly, on 11 October, at Bedford, without anything but the most elementary scheme for land boards and the derating of improvements in mind, and with no official approval except the personal and apparently rather offhand acquiescence of the Prime Minister, for which Lloyd George had journeyed to Arran, he began his second war with Britain's landlords.

At the last Cabinet in August the Prime Minister had asked his colleagues not to mention land during the parliamentary recess. When Lloyd George objected that he could hardly refrain from referring to the land program Asquith assented, provided that no policy was enunciated.[174] Later, when Lloyd George saw him at Arran the Prime Minister again urged caution. In Bedford Lloyd George amply observed the Prime Minister's injunction not to be too specific. Essentially the address was a denunciation of rich landowners — 'one third of the land of England belongs to the House of Lords' — with some kind words for the oppressed agricultural laborer. His wages were less in purchasing power than in the days of Henry VIII. His very existence was at the whim of the landowner. From his house in Wales, said Lloyd George, he could see three cottages whose tenants had been turned out in 1868 for voting Liberal.[175] Land was bought for status and pleasure, not cultivation — there were 23,000 gamekeepers in Scotland. Laborers were forced to stand by and watch their crops destroyed by game kept for sport. One farmer had told him that in his field of mangolds, only one in a dozen had not been destroyed by pheasants. Yet landowners were not controlled like factory owners or even mine owners. And still the present system of rating, said Lloyd George, urging his audience to listen very carefully, discouraged improvements and rewarded the individual who declined to put his land to the best use.[176]

The Bedford speech was important not because of what the Chancellor told his audience — he said very little and outlined no program — but because Lloyd George himself believed it was important, because he had worked hard at it for a number of days, and because contemporaries in both parties saw in it the inauguration of another campaign of violence and denunciation like the one conducted in the autumn of 1909.[177] He worried about interruptions from suffragettes and took great pains to arrange advance publicity and line up newspaper support.[178]

As a public event the results were undoubtedly sensational even for Lloyd George, whose every public act, by this time, was news. Riddell himself wrote the leader for the *British Weekly* and other Liberal newspapers were equally ecstatic.[179] Volume I of the land inquiry report was published just four days later and Hodder and Stoughton wrote to report that while they had experienced 'extraordinary difficulty' in getting the trade to advance order before the speech — W.H. Smith had asked for only three hundred — the Bedford speech had changed everything. Smith had sent in a new order for one thousand and they expected to have distributed 15,000 copies by the end of the day.[180] The speech brought also a check for £5,000 from W.H. Lever who was at that time visiting in Vancouver, British Columbia.[181]

Before the speech, Unionist apprehension equalled that of Lloyd George. The opposition, under the urging of Leo Maxse, had attempted to upstage Lloyd George with a rally of their own featuring George Cave at the Bedford Corn Exchange on 9 October which was intended to express national outrage at the villainies of Alec Murray who had at last returned to Britain.[182] This competition seriously upset Lloyd George, causing a letter of complaint to F.E. Smith with whom usually he was quite friendly.[183]

Yet beneath the well-managed public acclaim there were disquieting private reflections. The Cabinet as yet had never considered land reform. Asquith had firmly refused to talk about it at Arran.[184] Both Lucy Masterman, a friendly critic and John Burns, an unfriendly one, found the speech uneven and empty, 'Ragtime statesmanship', Burns had termed it. And both felt, Mrs. Masterman no doubt with the instruction from her husband, that it was an attempt, in the style of Joseph Chamberlain, to stampede the Cabinet into a policy upon which it was seriously divided.[185]

Even more than was customary with Lloyd George the Bedford speech had been a work of imagination. Unfortunately he had little more to say before the Cabinets of 14 and 16 October when his colleagues gave the land proposals the only discussion they would ever have, except briefly six months later in connection with the 1914 budget. He was virtually unprepared, thought J.A. Pease. The only document that he could furnish was a highly tentative memorandum of one and a half pages by Arthur Thring, the Cabinet's draftsman of legislation, suggesting in the briefest skeletal form the powers that possibly could be transferred to a proposed 'ministry of land and forests'.

Asquith himself was forced to take charge of the discussion and to remind the Chancellor, as he had done many times before, that the protection he was suggesting for agricultural workers would have to be available also to city laborers.[186]

When, after reviewing the growing crisis in Ireland, the Cabinet returned to the subject on the 16th, the discussion did not go much further; it dealt still with ends rather than with means. Summarizing the two meetings for the king on 18 October, Asquith wrote with some clear exasperation that a consideration of the land question evidently involved 'particularly the remuneration and housing of laborers, the protection of tenant farmers against capricious eviction (especially in change of ownership), increase in garden allotments and small holdings, and the rating of agricultural land.' The general conclusion was that 'all these matters (except the last) could only be effectively dealt with by the appointment of a control commission under the Board of Agriculture or a Land Ministry.' The Chancellor was to draw up a paper about the land commission.[187]

For Lloyd George the order to draw up a plan amounted to the same thing as the approval of his policy. Indeed he told Riddell the next day, in high glee, that everything was settled.[188] Accordingly, on 22 October at Swindon, he described the ministry of land and its proposed activities as if all were about to come into existence. Essentially the Swindon speech was a recitation of the outline plan that Thring had drawn up for the Cabinet of 14 October, except that its meagre details were now presented as decisions of the government. There would be a ministry of land and under it a board of land commissioners. The latter would handle the national valuation incorporated in the budget of 1909 which, Lloyd George said, was about two-thirds complete and should be finished by March 1915, a new Domesday Book. There would be more security for the leaseholder, fair rent, a living wage for laborers and new houses built with money borrowed from national health insurance reserves.[189]

The momentum built up by the Bedford and Swindon proclamations was almost immediately interrupted by a sharp political defeat at Reading on 8 November. (Until Reading, the Liberal by-election record in 1913, in contrast to 1912, had been relatively good. The party had won two seats, one from the Unionists and one from Labour, and had lost one to the Unionists.) In Reading, a seat held by the Liberals since 1900, albeit with small margins, and vacated by Rufus Isaacs upon his elevation to the lord chief justiceship, was captured by the Unionists in a large turnover of votes. Most distressing was the clear indication that many Liberal voters had defected to Labour rather than to the Unionists, even though the Liberal candidate, G.P. Gooch, a solid radical, had campaigned exclusively on the Lloyd George platform of national health insurance and land reform.[190] Again it had been shown that the land campaign had no appeal in the city. Lloyd George had been warned of this innumerable times and had acknowledged it. But somehow his speeches, as at Bedford and Swindon, suggested an exclusively rural interest. In some way the cities would have to be made part of the program; but this would complicate everything immensely and now there was no time.

The origins of the 1914 budget disaster lie in the incredibly confused and crowded months of December and January of 1913 and 1914. The overriding fact was that there would be a general election fairly soon. On 12 November, four days after the Reading by-election, Asquith, Crewe, Grey, Haldane and Lloyd George held a long discussion over dinner at No. 11 on the program of the coming session. Haldane spoke persuasively for a massive reform in education but there was much sentiment in the group, led by Grey and strongly supported by Asquith, which Lloyd George alone is recorded as having resisted, for a dissolution during the coming summer.[191]

For Lloyd George a summer election could throw everything into jeopardy. He could not possibly put together a bill for the coming session, even the relatively simple land commission supervising laborers' wages and farmers' rent that he had first envisaged. And if he tried to create a full-blown ministry of land, covering country and town, dealing with valuation and valuation appeals, compensation for improvements, leasehold enfranchisement (a particularly Welsh grievance which he added in a speech at Holloway on 4 December), investigation, arbitration and enforcement of land disputes and agreements, two years would not be enough.[192] An election with land reform as the major issue would be excellent, but not until some legislation was on the table. Still worse, a major land bill, after being passed by the House of Commons, would surely be held up by the Lords for another two years, well beyond the specified end of the present parliament. These factors, the need to do something for the cities, the need for haste, and the need to circumvent the House of Lords, clear enough not even to merit discussion, rather than any pressure from the United Committee for the Taxation of Land Values, account for the dramatic change in the strategy of the land campaign at the end of 1913 and for the Chancellor's ill-considered and hasty insertion of site value rating and relief of improvements in the budget of 1914.

He had of course been receiving letters from land value groups in the week after the Reading by-election reminding him of their disappointment that there had been no commitment to site value taxation.[193] But Lloyd George could hardly feel that he needed to make a pledge on the taxation of land separated from improvements. His intentions on this had been explicit since the 1909 budget when he had tried, as has been seen, to push site taxation as well as land valuation and had been frustrated by the Cabinet. The increment value tax had been only a substitute. There is no evidence that he yielded to 'pressure' and finally 'accepted' the argument that land reform should include rating reform.[194] A full year earlier in November 1912, he had written to Sir John Kempe, the chairman of the Departmental Committee on Local Taxation, asking him specifically to look into the question of site value rating and local authority reform as a way of equalizing the wide variation in the wealth and revenue of local governments.[195] The sudden concentration upon site value taxation or rating proposals proceeded then from the exigencies of Westminster politics, the crowded parliamentary schedule, the Lords' vote, the burden of the demands of Ireland, and Asquith's constant murmuring about an early dissolution, all of which left the budget as the only vehicle available for the affirmation of the Liberal commitments to land reform.

By December, Lloyd George had virtually given up work on the ministry of land and was calling for information on site value taxation and rating, even though the valuation initiated in the 1910 Finance Act (i.e., in the 1909 budget) was still only two-thirds complete and the critical part of it, the valuation of the centers of large towns, was progressing very slowly. There were other impediments. The relative merits of a site value rate and a tax were by no means clear although it was certain that whichever was chosen, the land valuation now being so painfully completed, because it was keyed to a one-time value for a tax on the increment, would have to be extensively revised.[196] Hence, although Lloyd George wrote to P.W. Raffin on 1 January 1914 saying that the government had decided to use the valuation 'now being put through at great expense' to compel those site owners who are not bearing their share of local taxation to do so, he was careful not to declare himself either for a tax, which the reformers wanted, or a rate, and he was silent as to when it would come.[197]

In this letter Lloyd George wrote, as he always did, with the utmost confidence, a captain whose ship was ready to sail at a moment's notice. In fact, work on land reform had stopped in the middle of December. For most of the next six weeks he was almost continually occupied by a fierce battle with Churchill over naval estimates. When this ended with a victory for Churchill at the Cabinet of 11 February, nearly two months had been lost. Despite his oblique hint to Raffin that a levy on site values would be coming soon, the Chancellor made no public announcement of the change in direction of his land reforms and during January received many letters (apparently unanswered) warning him that he must broaden the appeal of his program. Worse, the opposition appeared to be moving into the field. On 17 January, Walter Long made a speech at Holloway announcing a Conservative plan for compensation for improvements, extended leases, and a land court to be made up of 'practical men' not officials.[198] The interruption caused by the naval estimates crisis represented only one of several diversions encountered by Lloyd George in his struggle to put the Liberal government on record for land reform, but those six weeks may have been critical. In June, Lloyd George was defeated less by party opposition than by simple lack of time.

IV

The story of the controversy with Churchill over money for the Navy estimates in the 1914–15 budget must be kept within the framework of the land campaign. It was clearly, and was so perceived by the other participants, a battle Lloyd George did not wish to fight, and in the event, one he could not win. His ordinary weapon of threat of resignation would not be taken seriously if, as the world knew, his departure would mean a dissolution, the one thing at that point he hoped to avoid. Nonetheless in the account of Lloyd George's career, this battle with his friend is of much importance, illuminating the temperament and character of both antagonists. For Churchill the only goal always was to win. But in this stubborn determination also lay his weakness. His stubborn unwillingness to accept defeat made him, in the intimate fraternity of the Cabinet, a difficult, and disliked, colleague. As the world came to know, Churchill could lead and inspire great loyalty. His military instincts taught him to obey orders from above. But he could not and never learned how to cooperate with equals. Finally, his bitterness was heightened because he felt, with much justice, that Lloyd George had given, and broken, a commitment to support the Navy estimates. In contrast, Lloyd George, at least until he became Prime Minister, thought always in terms of movement. Every issue needed to be weighed against the claims of others. No setback was ever final, but for that matter no victory was ever complete and no threat of resignation ever serious.

Like virtually everything else that occurred in British defence and diplomatic policy in the last years before the war, the estimates crisis and the expansion of the Navy that caused it flowed from Agadir. The result of Lloyd George's pugnacity at the Mansion House was not only a two-month war scare but a real determination in Germany not to be intimidated again by Great Britain and its Navy. As a result, the German government prepared an amendment to the basic Navy Law of 1900, finished by the end of January 1912, increasing substantially the rate of dreadnought construction and, more dangerously from the British point of view, making provision for keeping a large proportion of its most modern ships in full commission at all times. This program, when complete, would give the Germans a striking force of twenty-five dreadnoughts against which the British, according to the formula of a sixty percent preponderance insisted upon by the Admiralty, should possess in home waters forty or forty-one ships of equal quality.[199] But Britain had only twenty-two battleships in full commission available for the North Sea.

The Cabinet tried first, on Lloyd George's, Churchill's, and Grey's initiative, to persuade Germany to alter its naval plans; R.B. Haldane, still Secretary of State for War, was sent to Germany in February 1912 for a personal interview with Kaiser William II. When this failed a general reorganization of fleet dispositions was planned and finally announced on 1 May 1912. These involved basically stripping the Mediterranean of heavy units, except for four battle cruisers based upon Malta and a small group of older battleships at Gibraltar, which was in any case three and one half days of steaming and one day of coaling away from any participation in the defense of Great Britain. The rest would be brought to England and consolidated into the newly created Home Fleet.

At that same time, in the summer of 1912, a number of other occurrences converged to affect the critical margin in the North Sea. First, it had become clear that by 1914 at the latest, Italy would have six and Austria four new dreadnoughts in the Mediterranean. Although Italy was never an implacable enemy of Great Britain and her loyalty to the Triple Alliance always more than uncertain, the Austrian dreadnoughts, built, Churchill believed, at German suggestion, powered by Parsons turbines with Yarrow boilers, were formidable vessels carrying more gun power and heavier armor than any but the latest British battleships. Alone, they were more than a match for the British forces that would remain in the area.[200]

But second, the French, also aware of the growth of potentially hostile naval forces beyond their southern coast, began pressing for the resumption of the naval conversations with Great Britain which had been suspended, officially, since the Cabinet revolt of November 1911. Then, in September 1912 with the transfer of the Brest squadron to Toulon, France began the concentration of its entire fleet in the Mediterranean so leaving unprotected its Channel and Atlantic coast. To some extent this movement made good the loss of British power along the southern life line, but it evoked complaints from true blue Saxons who found reliance on the decadent French repugnant and, more ominously for the future, caused predictions that the defenselessness of the French Atlantic coastline created an obligation for British naval support in case of a war between France and Germany. Churchill, in the summer of 1912, attempted to argue that this was not the case. Concentration to face one's principal antagonist was proper for both nations. These dispositions would have been made even if the other nations did not exist.[201] But, as Asquith observed ruefully after the war, even though there were no 'compacts. . .France undoubtedly felt that she could calculate [in the case of war] upon our vetoing any attack by sea on her Northern and Western coasts. . .'[202] These dispositions in the autumn of 1912 were of crucial importance two years later.

Finally, if Britain continued her annual dreadnought building schedule, the so-called 'Cawdor Programme', of four and occasionally five battleships a year, she would just maintain her sixty percent superiority in capital ships over Germany. But, Churchill argued, a dramatic increase in British building would stimulate the Germans to greater activity. How then, the question arose, could Britain build the extra ships necessary to end her vulnerability in the Mediterranean and so to end the dependence on the French, without causing the Germans to encroach upon the sixty percent margin in the North Sea. The Canadian election of September 1911, ending the long Liberal administration of Sir Wilfred Laurier, seemed to provide the answer.

At the Committee of Imperial Defence meeting on 11 July 1912, apparently for the first time before his colleagues but in terms that suggested previous private conversations, Churchill proposed to the new Canadian Prime Minister, Robert Borden, who was present, that the dominion furnish three dreadnoughts for imperial defense to be laid down immediately. This he explained would not upset the balance in the North Sea because it could be justified to the Germans simply as a Canadian recognition of its duty to the empire.[203] Borden clearly was prepared for Churchill's proposal. (The election the previous September that had brought the Conservatives to power in Canada involved as a major issue the alternatives of a Canadian contribution to the Royal Navy, supported by the Conservatives, or a self-contained dominion naval force.) The First Lord was able to announce in the Cabinet five days later that Borden had 'undertaken to help us with dreadnoughts' but could not announce the decision until his return to his Canadian colleagues.[204] After seeing Lloyd George privately Borden returned to Ottawa.[205] The speech from the throne in the Canadian parliament, on 5 December 1912 announced that an appropriation of $35,000,000 would be sought to provide a Canadian contribution to an 'Imperial squadron'. Borden did not emphasize that the ships were chiefly for the Mediterranean, but he justified this extraordinary expenditure with a British promise that the ships would be *in addition* to Britain's already announced construction program. The appropriation bill passed the Canadian House of Commons, on 15 May 1913, 99 to 66. But on 28 May it was killed, 51 to 27 by the Canadian Senate, whose members, appointed for life, were largely Liberals. 'Eighty-seven old men', the spryest of whom 'is just able to descend from his limousine without the aid of his chauffeur', snorted Stephen Leacock in the *National Review* in July. What did they know? But inevitably some would soon expire and Churchill would get his dreadnoughts.[206] In politics, as it has been said, where there is death there is hope.

Borden's immediate reaction to this defeat was to propose to Churchill that Britain build the ships anyway. Canada would then buy them when he got his way with the Senate which he expected would take about three years. Although Churchill was enthusiastic for this course he was overruled by the Cabinet.[207] However, as an alternative, the Cabinet approved the acceleration of three ships of the 1913–14 program. These would be laid down immediately instead of at the end of the fiscal year in March 1914.[208] This decision, which was expected to cost about £500,000 and would be made good by Supplementary Estimates, began in effect the budget crisis of 1914. (Construction of capital ships usually was delayed until the very end of the fiscal year in which they were authorized so causing a negligible expenditure in the first year's budget.) These unexpected obligations, together with similar amounts for oil and naval aviation, were before the Cabinet in the fall of 1913 just as Lloyd George had begun to plan for large new expenditures in aid of local authorities as part of the first installment of the land program. By beginning the three battleships earlier the most expensive part of their construction would appear now in the 1914–15 budget to be combined with the scheduled construction of four for the new fiscal year, i.e., a total of seven battleships. Moreover, even though the accelerated battleships were part of the 1913–14 budget and their cost had been authorized in that fiscal year, the tax money to pay the contractors would be raised as part of the 1914–15 budget.[209]

At the first Cabinet after the autumn recess the Chancellor noted that everyone wanted money in the coming fiscal year. (He had, at a Cabinet dinner less than a week before on 12 November, warned also about increasing taxation. Both Asquith and Grey wanted a dissolution in 1914. It would not be good to increase taxation just before an election.) Increased departmental requests — local government, education, as well as the Navy — were likely to be £10,000,000, but the yield from existing taxation would grow at most £6,500,000.[210] Churchill was not intimidated. His estimates for the coming fiscal year were discussed in the Cabinet on 8 and 11 December.[211] Although nominally amounting to £50,694,800 in total, Churchill had counted the supplementary estimate for the accelerated battleships, oil supplies, and aviation, as a part of the budget of the previous year. Thus 1914–15 showed an increase over 1913–14 of less than £3,000,000. But to repeat, this money, already authorized and spent, would have to be found from 1914–15 taxation. Lloyd George's copy of the estimates shows the figure for the increase over the previous year, £2,985,500, angrily scratched out and the figure £5,200,000 underlined and inserted in the margin. In Churchill's defense it should be noted that the increases were by no means entirely the result of new construction. New designs requiring oil reserves and larger crews, the decision to maintain a number of ships in full commission, and finally a rise in prices which Churchill reckoned at twelve percent since McKenna's tenure, were also involved.[212]

Nonetheless, criticism from the Cabinet radicals, rising quickly to denunciation, centered on the demand for four new superdreadnoughts, costing over their two years' construction nearly £3,000,000 each. Could not this figure be reduced to two?[213] For nearly ten days Lloyd George was remarkably silent. Churchill had already shown him the preliminary figures, evidently in

September and again in October, probably after the Bedford speech announcing the land campaign.[214] Even though he well understood that the young radicals in the Cabinet and the House of Commons would be astonished should he fail to oppose the First Lord's increases in the estimates, he agreed, indeed it would seem he proposed, to support them in return for Churchill's support in land reform. For Lloyd George it was a straightforward and characteristic political contract. Each man would lay aside scruple and principle in order to forward important matters of state. '*I have made a bargain with Winston*,' he told George Riddell at the beginning of November.

> *He has agreed to support my land policy with which he is not in sympathy and I have agreed to give him more money for the Navy. You may call this a bribe, but I have nothing to gain personally. I am only endeavouring to carry out my scheme of social reform which I believe is for the good of the people. I am not at all sure that the bargain will meet with the approval of some members of our party. Indeed I already see signs that it will not.*[215]

Opposition in the Cabinet was led by Herbert Samuel, supported by Simon, Beauchamp, Hobhouse, Buxton, the Beagles as Asquith called them, and indeed by McKenna. This was accompanied by a chorus of protests in the House of Commons and in the advanced Liberal press. In the middle of December, radicals in the House of Commons, the 'Suicide Club' as the Tory press styled them, began to gather signatures, eventually numbering about one hundred, on a petition to drop two battleships in the coming year. This was more than Lloyd George could bear. On 16 December he joined in the protests. Churchill was enraged. 'I consider that you are going back on your word: in trying to drive me out after we had settled, and you promised to support the Estimates' he wrote on a slip of paper which he pushed across the table.

Lloyd George replied: 'I agreed to the figure for this year & I have stood by it & *carried it* much to the disappointment of my economical friends. But I told you distinctly I would press for the reduction of a new programme with a view to 1915 & I think quite respectfully you are unnecessarily stubborn. It is only a question of 6 months' postponement of laying down. That cannot endanger our safety.' 'No. You said you would *support the Estimates*.' Churchill retorted.[216]

Before the discussion was over, noted the delighted Hobhouse, Churchill 'protested his inability to carry on and went off characteristically *banging* the dispatch box and the door as he went out as loud as he could.'

> An interesting feature of these discussions was Ll.G.'s repudiation of the bargain which had evidently been come to between Churchill and himself, as soon as he saw the others were prepared to fight Churchill: the PM's equally unblushing agreement with Lloyd George as to the construction of some words which had passed between Ll.G. and Churchill; and his desertion of the latter as soon as the Cabinet were seen to be adverse [sic] to him. This is the third important occasion on which the so-called minor members of the Cabinet have beaten the more prominent ones since I have been there.[217]

On the other hand Burns, also a pacifist, was nervous and worried, although as usual he misread the situation:

Cabinet a serious meeting in some respects the most serious since 1906. PM behaved with great dignity reserve and indulgent forbearance under provoking circumstances. When the parachute [sic gondola] parts from the Balloon what will happen to both?

Economy has at last been seized on with a vengeance. For 8 years I have preached and preached it but never with the sudden zeal of belated converts. There was hardly any reason for taking a hand the reinforced rakes and repentant spendthrifts were sufficient.[218]

Of course the critical figure was Asquith. He loathed quarrels in the Cabinet, as Lloyd George well knew. He loved office, it has been observed, but hated politics. His response was to adjourn discussion of the estimates until after the holidays as he had done during the 1909 naval scare. One may speculate Lloyd George anticipated exactly this response. Churchill wrote to Asquith on 18 December saying that it would be 'impossible' for him to compromise on the dreadnought construction program.[219]

Even though Churchill frequently staged tantrums in Cabinet meetings, his anger on this occasion was genuine. He knew that many of the younger men disliked him and clearly suspected that the opposition to the building program was organized as a means of driving him from office. He could not believe that Lloyd George would join such a cabal. In fact, Lloyd George had told Riddell in mid-November: 'Some of our people would like to see him go over to the Tories.' Lloyd George opposed this. Churchill was less dangerous within the Cabinet.[220] But an element of the old friendship may have been present still. Much as he disliked the estimates he said to Riddell a month later as the revolt of the Beagles was growing, 'I shall be no party to driving Winston out of the Cabinet. I do not agree with some of my colleagues.'[221] In the end Lloyd George would save Churchill from resignation and, not for the last time, from political extinction.

But for Lloyd George there were other complications. The economizers in the Cabinet and in the House of Commons were also supporters of the land campaign. Worse, if Churchill were driven to resignation, he might be supported by Grey. The result would be a dissolution and the end of the land campaign and as well, probably, of Churchill himself. 'Samuel, Simon, Runciman & co. are doing their utmost to "down Winston,"' Lloyd George told Riddell on the day the Cabinet broke up. He had promised earlier he would join no attempt to drive the First Lord from the Cabinet, although he admitted on 18 December that there were times when one could not be influenced by personal considerations. 'Lloyd George did a fatal thing for Winston,' observed Charles Masterman to Riddell on the same day, 'when he persuaded the P.M. to send him to the Admiralty, and since he has been there he has lost all touch with Liberalism and has become a man of one idea.'[222]

After the Cabinet separated, Lloyd George spent the next week composing an elaborate memorandum showing that Britain's sixty percent margin in the North Sea would be maintained even if two battleships were dropped from the 1914–15 program. Because British superdreadnoughts were far superior to the German both in the weight of their broadside (13.5" and 15" main batteries as against 12" for the German) and in their greater speed, national security was assured even at a lower ratio. The burden of

71

his argument was the clever thesis that technical superiority was even more expensive than numerical superiority but that Britain did not need, nor could afford, both.[223] If Britain were to cut back, liberal forces within other European nations would mobilize to require similar reductions. 'France and Germany are both faced with financial difficulties which would make them very glad to seize an opportunity of reducing expenditure without reducing either the number of ships provided for by their respective navy laws or their relative strength in comparison with Great Britain or with one another.' To continue extravagant armament expenditure was to invite disaster.

> To commit the country to new expenditure of millions, unless it is
> abundantly clear that it is necessary in order to maintain the security
> of our shores, would be a proceeding that would lay the Government
> open to a serious charge of extravagant folly, and to do so now, when
> trade is on the decline, when we are confronted by a political crisis of
> the gravest possible character, and when there is widespread revolt not
> merely in this country, but throughout the whole of Europe, against
> the grievous burden imposed by increased armaments, would be
> not merely to invite but to deserve disaster for the party and the
> government responsible for such a proceeding.[224]

Churchill immediately responded with a longer memorandum laying stress on the Austrian threat in the Mediterranean and the obligations to Prime Minister Borden. The Cabinet, he argued, had agreed that Borden and the Canadian parliament should understand that the dominion gift was *outside* the sixty percent margin and would serve for imperial defense. (Borden of course knew privately that this meant the rehabilitation of Mediterranean strength against the Austrians, who were, after all, also outside the sixty percent margin.) In no other way could the dependence upon France be ended.[225] But above all, to accept a huge and magnificent gift from Canada while reducing one's own efforts at home was a breach of faith.

Churchill's memorandum was completed on 29 December, although not printed until 10 January. In the interval, on 31 December Churchill received a devastating telegram from Borden. The aged Liberal Senators still clung obstinately to life and 'in the absence of any assurance as to Senate's favorable action we [must] declare it undesirable on imperial consideration to submit measure to irresponsible Senate for further rejection, but that we are firm in determination to provide ships as soon as Senate majority are in accord with popular will.'[226] This was confirmed on 11 January by a second telegram from Borden saying that he did not intend to mention the topic in the King's speech in 1914. However, he added, it was 'just possible' that the Conservatives would have a majority in the Senate before the end of the session.[227] Perhaps some of the Liberal Senators were failing.

'Borden's telegram is a heavy blow,' wrote Churchill to his private secretary, James Masterton-Smith on 3 January,

> and I am surprised you did not appreciate its unpleasant significance.
> It will in all probability necessitate further alterations in the last
> memorandum I prepared [i.e. 'Naval Estimates, 1914–15', the answer to
> Lloyd George, not yet circulated] however the argument can be turned
> either way. If Borden starts out on his 3 ships we are bound to honor

not to compromise his position. If he fails to make any effort for his 3 ships, all the more reason for our going forward with our 4...The Chancellor of the Exchequer's interview in the *Daily Chronicle* is a fine illustration of his methods, and I should imagine it would deeply vex the Prime Minister...Impress all concerned the need for secrecy at this juncture. That there is a row everyone will know after the Chancellor's interview, but whether it is about 2 ships or 4 ships or 7 ships should remain for the present in obscurity.[228]

The *Daily Chronicle* interview which appeared on 1 January 1914, did indeed vex the Prime Minister. More than that, as Asquith wrote to Venetia Stanley a few days later it 'set all Europe (not to mention the poor Liberal Party here at home) by the ears.'[229] But, in fact, a careful reading of the entire statement, which filled the front page of the paper, shows that the Chancellor's remarks were less about relations with Germany and the Navy than about finance and social reform. To the horror of the Cabinet, of the Unionists, and of the King, Lloyd George did assert that huge expenditures on weapons were less important than formerly because relations with Germany were improving as a result of the diplomacy of Sir Edward Grey. (This was in fact true. In the early months of 1914 Grey's compromises with Germany over that country's presence in the Turkish empire, and over the disposition of Portuguese colonies, had brought the two nations so close that the French were becoming alarmed.)[230] Both Britain and her North Sea neighbor seemed to realize the futility of quarreling. Recalling, as indeed Churchill had done in his Cabinet paper a few days earlier, the nightmare of the 1911 crisis, the Chancellor asserted: 'The Agadir incident served a very useful purpose in bringing home to the two great countries the perils involved in the atmosphere of suspicion which had been created by the politicians, the Press, and certain interests.' Neither nation wanted to take a risk like that again.

But for Lloyd George, parting company with the bulk of the radical and pacifist movement in the House of Commons and the nation, the objection to battleships was not that they were evil but that they were expensive. Rates in towns were too high and were going higher. The land campaign, which he discussed at length, would alter the incidence of local taxes, but substantial government help would be necessary to pay for improved local services. All of this was difficult because of the competitive burden of armament expenditure. Fortunately this was being recognized both at home and in Europe he said, reiterating his statements in the earlier Cabinet paper, not only by the working class, but in financial circles as well. He had received many letters about it.[231]

Nothing in the *Daily Chronicle* interview was really new, or inconsistent with Lloyd George's previous positions on Germany. He had said much the same thing in his Mansion House addresses in 1912 and 1913.[232] Nor had he reversed the position taken at the Mansion House in 1911 — Germany then was threatening, now she was not. He had joined the pacifists in resisting battleships, but for his own reasons, not theirs. He needed their support for the land campaign. They were being made use of, not he. Balfour, who could penetrate other men's minds as easily as Lloyd George, was nearly correct in his comments to Lord Selborne on 7 January.

I think this move on L.G.'s part is purely political. I do not mean to say that, as Chancellor of the Exchequer and a taxpayer, he is not seriously alarmed at the growth of expenditure. I have no doubt he is...What I do suppose is that he wants an election cry which will rally what remains of the old Radical Nonconformist Party, the new semi-Socialist-Radical, and the Labour Party. A campaign against armaments is admirably suited for the purpose. He also, of course, wants the public mind to be, as far as possible, distracted from the question of Ulster, and he perhaps doubts whether his Land Campaign will be sufficient to attain this end...[also] there may be, and probably are, private and personal ambitions [in the Cabinet] which would be served by pressing these divisions to [the] breaking point over a subject like military and naval retrenchment...[233]

Balfour of course was right. The men quickest to applaud the *Daily Chronicle* interview were the idealistic Liberal land reformers.[234]

The *Daily Chronicle* statement should be considered in tandem with Lloyd George's speeches at the Mansion House on 17 July 1914 and at the third reading of his abused and mutilated Finance Bill on 23 July, the day, as it happened, that Austria presented her ten point ultimatum to Serbia. On each occasion, in nearly identical words, he called upon the businessmen of the world to bring their weight to bear to arrest the slide into uncontrolled expenditure on weapons. 'It is a sad reflection', he told the bankers, 'and I believe I have said before that I do not believe this creeping catastrophe which is coming upon us will be arrested until finance takes the matter in hand and saves the world from disaster.'[235] In the House of Commons on 23 July he was more explicit. At the beginning of the debate, Austen Chamberlain had asserted that taxes were too high, the financial requirements of defense intractable, and the tax base too narrow. The solution, of course, was import duties.[236] In his reply Lloyd George separated himself sharply from the pacifist and collectivist doctrines of the radicals in and around his own party who were already arguing that the demand for armaments came from the industrialists and capitalists. He agreed that the cost of arms was too high but denied that it would be lowered by 'political criticism or calls for humanity. I am firmly of the opinion that they will only be arrested when the giant financial interests of the world begin to realize what a menace they are to prosperity, to industry, to the prosperity of the world, and I think they are beginning to realize it.' He noted again that the relations between Britain and Germany were improving; the press of each nation no longer snarled at the other. One day, he concluded, disputes among states would be settled by orderly processes, as they are among individuals. Then there would be a better way of raising money for social reform.[237]

The tragic irony of the fact that within two weeks after this speech Britain was at war with Germany obscures the fact that at the moment he delivered it, Lloyd George was reaffirming, and enlarging upon, the position he had taken at the beginning of the year, a position which, in fact, had been his at least since his clumsy and homemade attempt at negotiations with Germany in the summer of 1908.[238] International anarchy and domestic social disharmony, Lloyd George always felt, were twins. Equally, peace at home depended upon peace abroad. This had nothing to do with the socialist doctrine or the class struggle. Leadership for peace would come not from humanitarians or politicians but from international businessmen. (As the European crisis developed at the end of July, Lloyd George continually reminded the Cabinet that the men most appalled by the approaching conflict were the City bankers that he was at that time seeing every day.) But finally, the *Daily Chronicle* statement is another example of a Lloyd George parliamentary tactic which invariably drove his colleagues into a screaming rage, but was entirely typical of the new style of politics he represented: the appeal to public opinion at large for adjudication of private Cabinet disputes. By taking his case, good or bad, to the people in this way Lloyd George had undoubtedly personalized and cheapened a highly complex issue. Did the Liberals in the country want battleships and higher taxes, he asked, or social reform and lower taxes and, in a reference to Randolph Churchill's departure from the Salisbury Cabinet in 1886 over naval estimates, did the nation desire that he resign?

But if Lloyd George had turned an honest disagreement within the Cabinet into an unseemly public row, matching his threat of resignation against Churchill's, he had done it with clear provocation. No doubt he joined the attackers in the Cabinet on 16 December in order to guard his left flank as the leading Cabinet radical — certainly many of the younger men suspected opportunism — but in the *Chronicle* interview he was sincere. His methods were not those of classical English political behavior. They were all his own. But neither did Churchill negotiate honestly. It will be remembered that in the estimate submitted to the Cabinet on 8 December, which Lloyd George, to be sure, had seen and approved earlier, he had included a supplementary estimate, already noted, of £1,400,000 which would be, de facto, a part of the 1914–15 budget. However, after the Cabinet had separated, the First Lord wrote Lloyd George a stiff, formal note that he was notifying the Treasury 'officially' that the supplementary estimate would not be the figure 'which you mentioned to me [sic] but instead 'about' £3,000,000.'[239] Although this note is dated 18 December, by accident, or possibly by design, Lloyd George does not appear to have received it until the middle of January, after his return from Algiers on 13 January. By which time the Admiralty's £3,000,000 in unfunded outstanding obligations had become £3,500,000. Churchill, according to Hobhouse, had concealed from both the Cabinet and the Treasury the sums he had held back from Admiralty contractors (which resulted in unspent surpluses in one fiscal year but deficits in the next) and the costs of his acceleration of construction.[240] It is possible that Lloyd George learned of these Admiralty secrets from T.J. Macnamara, Parliamentary and Financial Secretary to the Admiralty, a solid radical and his old ally from the days of the education revolt. Macnamara, who was also deeply involved in driving Morant from the Board of Education, was with Lloyd George privately the evening after the Chancellor had returned, earlier than he had intended, from Africa. The next day, 15 January, Lloyd George saw Churchill and wrote to his wife he was prepared to resign to get his way. 'As you may imagine', he wrote to Maggie, 'I am very fully occupied with the Navy tangle.'

It is serious and may involve a smash up of the Ministry. Last night I had Macnamara with me till midnight. Winston gave me two hours today. Up to the present I cannot see the light. Tonight I am with John

Simon who is entirely with me and will go with me. I wish you were here. Asquith is returning Monday [19 January] then I must take an all important decision — the same decision as Gladstone & Bright had to take.[241]

Lloyd George saw Macnamara again privately, at the latter's initiative, on 17 January.[242]

Probably because he had told Lloyd George privately of the Canadian default — 'you shd see this correspondence with Borden. I do not propose to read letters to the Cabinet except *in extremis*.' — the conversation with Churchill on Friday, 15 January, referred to in the letter to Maggie, produced the elements of the compromise upon which the crisis would finally be resolved.[243] Lloyd George gave up his insistence on a reduction in the 1914–15 construction program — Churchill could have his four dreadnoughts — but in return the First Lord would have to promise to keep 1915–16 estimates under £50,000,000.[244] But Churchill remained less than candid. Clearly he told no one else but the Prime Minister about Borden's 'default' as he described it, nor did he make it clear that as a result of it he intended to accelerate two dreadnoughts of the 1914–15 construction thus insuring 'most intractable arrears for the next fiscal year. My relations with him [Lloyd George],' he told Asquith are 'civil and somber'.[245]

In conceding four ships on 15 January Lloyd George evidently believed he had elicited some promise from Churchill about the following year and indeed Churchill's draft letter of 18 January, which probably Lloyd George never saw, elaborating the difficulties of naval cost projections, suggests that there had been a step toward compromise. But the next day the First Lord thought better of it, and no doubt had consulted with the Sea Lords. In any case he wrote to the Chancellor saying that he would not, and could not, anticipate costs twenty-seven months ahead. Lloyd George, at last, took the matter to Asquith, who asked the two men to come to see him.[246]

The meeting with the Prime Minister took place on 20 January and lasted five hours. Lloyd George's account of it the next day, at breakfast with C.P. Scott, makes clear what transpired, but leaves the impression, as usual, that the Chancellor had won. The talk, Scott recorded Lloyd George as saying, was 'polite but deadly'. He had dared Churchill to resign. 'What will you resign upon? Everything has been conceded to you. You have your four ships; your estimates are up to over £53 millions. You are not satisfied. You want more. And you will go out of office on top of that and expect the country to support you.' There was a strong impression among important people, Lloyd George said, reminding Scott that the two men were in the presence of the Prime Minister,

> and not those merely Churchill's opponents on question of naval armaments, that if he did not resign on that he would resign on the Irish question and therefore it was useless to make concessions to him, and Lloyd George challenged him to say if this were so or not. Churchill greatly confused and taken aback.

Finally Churchill began to mumble about possible reductions for next year. Lloyd George reported that he had demanded a pledge from the Prime Minister not from Churchill. '"Why?" asked Churchill. "Because I do not trust you." "I had your promise for this year and you have broken it; my whole Budget was based on your estimate and now it has proved wholly delusive." This ended the interview.'[247]

In fact Asquith had won. In the middle of the conference he declared, according to Lloyd George's account to Scott, that if the Chancellor resigned he would dissolve within a week, although in a letter to his wife Asquith suggested he intended to take this course if either man resigned.[248] Suddenly the stakes had been raised beyond Lloyd George's reach. If Churchill resigned no doubt his career would end, but little else would change. The German threat would still exist. The next First Lord, probably a Unionist if Asquith carried out his threat, would not ask for smaller estimates. If Lloyd George resigned he would become the hero of the Liberal-Socialist doctrinaires, which might mean something in ten years, but he would have lost the land program.[249] In addition, as he confessed to Masterman, who appears to have been the only person taken into his confidence, he had been much affected by the mass of letters sent both to himself and Maggie, expressing fear that his resignation would mean the end of Welsh disestablishment.[250]

Asquith had achieved what he needed. He had postponed the problem, although he had given Churchill a victory in 1914–15 while Lloyd George received only an unfillable promise for the next year. And in the end, as Churchill observed in the *World Crisis*, 'when the time came, I was not pressed to redeem this understanding.'[251]

Lloyd George's sense of political tactics told him of course that he had been defeated. Yet for the next two weeks he kept up in rather elaborate detail the pretense of continuing to fight. However, as Scott noticed on a visit to Walton Heath on 25 January, the spirit had gone out of him.[252] Asquith, also, quickly sensed the change. 'I think we shall get through our little troubles over the Navy without much more ado,' he wrote cheerfully to his wife on 23 January. 'Ll.G. squeezing in one direction, and Winston in the other. Neither of them wants to go and in an odd sort of way they are really fond of one another. Even small crises reveal people's qualities.'[253] However, Simon, Samuel, Hobhouse, McKenna, and Runciman were determined, Lloyd George knew, to use the estimates and Churchill's dependable bad temper to drive the First Lord from the Cabinet and, with any luck, from politics.[254] Hence, Lloyd George began what clearly appears to have been a charade, first to save the Liberal government from a damaging resignation and second to save Churchill from himself. Immediately he called together the rebels and told them everything was settled. Churchill had promised drastic reductions in the next year's estimates. This was received, understandably, with much skepticism and both Hobhouse and Simon wrote the Chancellor letters repudiating his leadership.[255] At the same time he continued to urge economy almost daily upon Churchill who evidently did not realize that he had won and lived in a mood of profound despondency.[256] In this context, the frequently quoted letter Lloyd George wrote to Churchill on 27 January, taking care that the rebels saw it, appears to be a bit of stage management.[257] 'My Dear Winston, I have striven hard for a friendly and honourable settlement without the slightest regard for the effect upon my personal position, but your letter has driven me to despair, and I must decline further negotiations, leaving the issue to be decided by the Prime Minister and the Cabinet. [This was in response to a letter from the First Lord the previous day in which Churchill reiterated that he could make no promises about the 1915–16 estimates.]

> I have laboured these last few days — not to favour you or to save myself — but to rescue Liberalism from the greatest tragedy which has yet befallen it. I have a deep and abiding attachment for Liberal causes, and for the old Party and the prospect of wrecking them afflicts me with deep distress. That is why I have been prepared to risk the confidence of my friends and to face the jibes and sneers from friend and foe alike with which I foresaw the publication of the figures would be greeted. I know too well that every paper would gloat over my humiliation. That I did not mind if the ship and its precious cargo could be saved. You decreed otherwise, and the responsibility is yours and yours alone.[258]

The above paragraph, concluding the letter, although written in Lloyd George's usual tone of injured innocence, was true enough.

However, in the Cabinet the same afternoon the economizers realized that they were alone.

> . . .it soon became evident that a reconciliation had been effected. Lloyd George began with a lecture on the desirability of economy, to which Winston replied with a dissertation on National Security, and we examined in detail some fresh papers circulated by the Admiralty put forward to show that his expenditure had been preannounced and was inevitable. McKenna took him to task over details, but he got no effective help from Ll.G. and practically our entire sitting was taken up with a real attack on the Admiralty by McKenna, Simon and myself, with occasional interventions from Runciman and Beauchamp.[259]

That evening at a dinner given by the new Chief Whip, Percy Illingworth, Lloyd George tried again to break up the opposition block in the Cabinet. 'We had an interesting discussion on poetry', wrote Hobhouse

> in which Ll.G. revealed a much greater knowledge of English literature than I had credited him with. He made himself vastly agreeable in explaining the system of Welsh poetry which seems to depend for its rhythm on a double or even triple system of alliterative effect. After dinner we got back to the old subject. Ll.G. tried to wean us and Simon in particular from the view of our group but we went home unseparated and unconvinced.[260]

McKenna, the only senior member of the group and the only man among them with the information and the skill to deal with Churchill on naval affairs, intimated to Scott that he believed the Chancellor was acting as a 'bellwether to bring the stalwarts into the Churchill fold.'[261] McKenna liked neither Lloyd George nor Churchill, but in these imputations of duplicity he was certainly correct.

The official end of the dispute was reached at the Cabinet of 11 February with the acceptance of slightly reduced estimates. Churchill offered some savings in aviation, the rate of accumulation of the oil reserve, and in small vessel construction while promising to do as much as he could to hold down the following year's expenditure. McKenna's boast to Riddell that the rebels had forced the substitution of a test mobilization for the usual summer maneuvers is an uncharacteristic mistake.[262] This change was included in the original draft of the estimates on 5 December 1913. However, the result was that when Britain declared war on 4 August the fleet was already fully manned. But Churchill had his four superdreadnoughts, no one had resigned, and Lloyd George would have to raise taxes.[263]

What might have been the effect of the unpleasantness on the Cabinet fraternity in the future, had not the Liberal administration encountered the overwhelming pressures of the Home Rule and European crises in the next six months, no one can say. The already cooling friendship between Lloyd George and Churchill survived, although with less intensity on Lloyd George's part. Churchill, in contrast, particularly during a convivial evening, could still exclaim in the most sentimental terms of his intimacy with Lloyd George. At a dinner at Morley's in early March, as Asquith wrote to Venetia Stanley, Churchill 'in a rather maudlin mood said to Lloyd George "a wonderful thing our friendship. For ten years there has hardly been a day when we haven't had an hour's talk together," to which Birrell rejoined in his most ironic way asking whether the two were not bored with each other by this time.'[264] Churchill was the only person, it has been noted, who addressed the Chancellor as 'David' although the world called the First Lord 'Winston'. Certainly he was aware before long that Lloyd George had saved him from the political wilderness where his own impetuous combativeness would have driven him. Perhaps he sensed that his friend would need to do so again.

In his memoirs Lloyd George does not mention the 1914–15 estimates issue but he had his own story of the surrender which was, as always, simplistic and lighthearted. Maggie had convinced him. 'You know my dear,' he told Churchill she had said,

I never interfere in politics; but they say you are having an argument with that nice Mr. Churchill about building dreadnoughts. Of course I don't understand these things but I should have thought it would be better to have too many than too few.[265]

2 From Crisis into War: The Land Campaign, Home Rule and Ulster, The War and The City

The struggle with Churchill diverted Lloyd George from critical work on the land campaign for a full six weeks. This time lost turned out to be disastrous when the 1914 budget was presented in May. On 4 February in Glasgow he made his first public statement on land reform in nearly two months, an appearance, it should be noted, he had originally scheduled for early in December. The government, he said, was preparing to allow local authorities to rate the unimproved value of land. Hitherto he had always put off questions by saying he could make no declaration on the subject until the Departmental Committee on Local Taxation had reported. In fact when he spoke at Glasgow the committee still had not reported and when it did report on 3 March 1914 the majority advised against a site value levy pointing out, quite properly, that the land valuation currently underway was not adapted to it.[1] However, a minority recommended such a rate as a local option and Lloyd George had evidently seen an advance copy of their draft. It was in terms of this recommendation that he made his announcement at Glasgow.

In general the Glasgow address was a typical Lloyd George blunderbuss charge of denunciations of landlords (this time, however, generally Scottish landlords), but with a few kernels of fact.[2] The important declaration, that the government had decided upon a levy on ground values, that it would be a rate — there was not mention of a national site value tax — and that it would be added to, and not in place of, other rates appeared without fanfare just after a story about the Duke of Bedford and before one about the Marquess of Tullibardine. Lloyd George described the government's plans unclearly, implying that they were founded upon the departmental committee report, and suggesting that nothing he said was new. In terms of what was to come, perhaps the most specific part of the announcement was that the land valuation 'would be ready next year, so at any rate when our proposals are submitted to Parliament you will have saved five years in the matter of valuation. . .' The most that can be gleaned from this muddy sentence is that he was still thinking in terms of 1915 for beginning his program, but not for the legislation establishing it. In any case he had done nothing yet at the Treasury. The speech from the throne on 10 February mentioned only measures for housing 'the industrial and agricultural population', a matter on which Lloyd George was under heavy pressure from Rowntree.[3]

Almost immediately he was diverted again from the land campaign by the growing crisis in Ireland. Not surprisingly, in the next few weeks he was asked continually in the House of Commons to elaborate upon the Glasgow announcements. Had the government in fact decided on a policy of site value rating? When would it be described? After the matter was raised on adjournment on 27 February, Lloyd George took refuge in a statement by Asquith of February 1908 in favor of site value rating to show that the government had always supported his proposals and that the Glasgow speech was nothing new.[4]

Work on land reform and on the budget which would embody its first items did not proceed again until the middle of April. Asquith saw some preliminary figures brought him by Edwin Montagu, Lloyd George's new financial secretary, on 10 April and a week later spent an hour with the Chancellor himself. 'We played about with millions and tens of millions with good humour & even gaiety,' he wrote to Venetia Stanley. 'No one can hop with greater agility from one twig (or even one tree or forest) to another. Meanwhile the land campaign, housing, repeopling the deserted glens, getting fair play from the ground landlord for Gorringes & C — all these have receded into a dim background, & are for the moment as though they had never been.'[5]

No one but Asquith had seen Lloyd George's proposals until 23 April when at a morning conference and again at a dinner that evening Lloyd George outlined his budget to the Cabinet Finance Committee. It would 'throw out of gear the whole Tory line of battle,' he wrote to William George. 'This view of it commended it to my colleagues who approve. As it has formed part of my general policy for improving conditions of life for the people I am delighted with the opportunity for advancing them. It's an ill wind that blows nobody any good.'[6]

Privately, others at the dinner on 23 April were less impressed with the Chancellor's proposals than he was himself. Lloyd George had not consulted them soon enough, complained J.A. Pease. Too much money was being raised. But now it was too late to do anything.[7] Certainly Lloyd George understood also that the pressure of time had stilled criticism. The last two weeks of March and the first week of April had been occupied with the Curragh Mutiny, which probably accounts for his remark to his brother about the 'ill wind'. His elation was tempered the next day when, on 24 April, Herbert Samuel, in a public speech, forecast large subventions to local authorities in the coming budget. The Chancellor furiously described his colleague to George Riddell, as an 'ambitious Jew'.[8]

The full Cabinet finally examined the budget on three successive days, 28, 29 and 30 April.[9] The deficit carried forward from the 1913–14 fiscal year, now ended, would be £6,850,000 Lloyd George estimated, of which £5,250,000 was the responsibility of the navy. To finance expenditures which were for the first time in Britain's history over £200,000,000 he proposed, among other adjustments, to lower the threshold of the super tax to £3,000 and to put 2d on the income tax. The large items in the budget for the new year were, in addition to the navy, a tremendous program, £11,095,000 on an annual basis (approximately the total cost of four superdreadnoughts which would have been, in any case, spread over nearly three years), for the relief of local authority rates.[10]

The budget was a 'thing of shreds and patches', thought John Burns.[11] For once he was right. Lloyd George's presentation to his colleagues exploded with ideas and plans, but he had no program. Nothing was ready. His budget received none of the line by line analysis given his 1909 production. And in four days, after having bluffed the Cabinet, he would have to bluff the House of Commons.

Neither a finance bill nor a revenue bill was ready when he rose in the House of Commons on 4 May to give his budget statement.[12] It was typical of his working methods in these days that before a long speech at three in the afternoon, for which he was woefully unprepared, Lloyd George invited C.P. Scott to lunch to ask the *Guardian* editor whether he thought that the old proposal of Home Rule All Round would offer a solution to the problem of Ireland.[13] Like the 1909 budget, of which it was the successor, the 1914 budget represented a long step toward breaking the traditional limit imposed upon government expenditure by the stable revenue of customs and excise. It threw over forever the notion that income from permanent duties payable by all ought about to balance 'extraordinary' revenue taken from the rich by income tax, super tax, and death duties. Lloyd George announced with pride that whereas the two sources had been of equal value when the Liberals came to power, indirect taxes now would provide less than forty percent of the total revenue.[14]

The core of the 1914 budget statement, indeed nearly all of it except for the bare announcement about tax increases (there was virtually nothing on battleships), was devoted to land and rating reform. Lloyd George began his speech with a long and rather sophisticated discussion of the inequities of the present rating system — the poor paid a far higher percentage of their income in rates than the rich — and on the resulting financial hardships suffered by many local authorities. All of this was preface to the declaration that the government intended to use the national valuation of land separate from premises as the basis for a complete overhaul of rating. It would be very easy, said Lloyd George in a characteristic burst of the thoughtless mendacity that always put him into trouble; the machinery was all set up.[15] The two parts of the reform were first, as soon as possible, the partial derating of improvements, and second, for the future, a rate on site value. Land would be brought into the market by making it more expensive to hold, while construction would be encouraged by partly exempting it from rates. Reaching back to his first parliamentary battle over land reform in 1896 Lloyd George announced that the Exchequer grant to compensate local authorities for the derating of agricultural land would be abolished.[16] To effect all this the government proposed a large new system of grants to local governments, partly to compensate them for the loss of income resulting from the derating of improvements when it began, and partly to take care of increased expenses that would result from their new duties in education, health, poor relief and police.

But, and here began the chain of difficulties, derating could not begin until the valuation was complete. Hence compensatory grants could not start at least until the next fiscal year, 1915–16. But because many local authorities were already nearly bankrupt, the Chancellor proposed for the current year, a program of 'provisional grants'. These were for four months only, to begin on 1 December 1914 and end on 31 March 1915 and were tied solely to the new local authority responsibilities. However, Lloyd George also tied them firmly but needlessly, and as it turned out disastrously, to the derating powers, with which they were not in fact connected, by pledging in his speech that the provisional grants could not begin until legislation was passed giving local authorities power to derate improvements, even though the authorities could not in fact take action under this power until the valuation was complete. Nonetheless, and this was most important, the two penny increase in the income tax, about half of which was to pay for the provisional grants, would commence immediately. In effect then, beginning at that moment, the government would be raising money through the income tax which it could not spend until a revenue bill incorporating the derating powers, not yet drawn up let alone introduced, was passed. (Revenue bills, although not new, had become a regular feature of the House of Commons procedure since 1911. They were not 'money bills' within the terms of the Parliament Act but were supposed to cover financial business — for instance the imposition of new taxes that required extensive debate and could not properly be dealt with in the tightly scheduled finance bill which included only changes in customs and excise and the renewal of income tax. They were a response to the crippling provisions of the Parliament Act. With the obligation of the Speaker to certify that a finance bill was purely a money bill, a separate measure to handle the administrative side of tax raising had become legally necessary. Additional pressure was added with the passage in 1913 of the Provisional Collection of Taxes Act. This had been made necessary by a judicial decision in a case brought by Lloyd George's old friend, Mr. Gibson Bowles, holding that the collection of taxes after the veto of the 1909 budget had been illegal. The act authorized the imposition of taxes immediately after the budget statement, but required that the finance bill become law by a specific date, in 1914, 5 August.)

Lloyd George's budget speeches were never among his most finished performances, but in 1914 he reached a new pinnacle of ineptitude. He read his address in an inaudible monotone and clearly lost his place at least once.[17] As a result the opposition was almost totally bewildered during the discussion of the budget statement. 'The budget debate collapsed,' the Prime Minister wrote to Venetia Stanley the next day, 'as Ll.G. landed the House in a well (or luckily) contrived morass of obscurity in which for the moment everyone was bogged. Even today people seem to be in two minds what it is all about.'[18] Even after the debate on the financial resolutions began most speakers were forced to confine themselves to the one solid and terrifying fact they could grasp: that the income tax was to be raised to 1s 4d in the pound, a level never achieved before even during the Boer War when, in addition, there was no super tax. Hence it was not until the second day of debate on the budget resolutions that a speaker for the Unionists defined what was the central weakness of the budget, a weakness that in the end would destroy the entire plan and effectively bring an end to the land campaign. What the Chancellor had done, said Captain Ernest Pretyman on 7 May, was to ask the House to vote for large increases in taxes to pay for grants that could only be distributed after authorization for new forms of rating and valuation had passed into law. But it was now clear from the press, said Captain Pretyman, that there would be no autumn session and it was demonstrably impossible to get the necessary bills through before the August recess. In effect therefore, concluded Captain Pretyman, the Chancellor of the Exchequer 'has told us definitely that, in an event that is bound to arise, the money will not be devoted to the purpose to which he desires to apply it.' It was an 'unprecedented position'. And so, he asked Lloyd George, who was sulking on the opposite bench, can the Chancellor give 'a simple straight answer: would the money go for the grants irrespective of whether the [revenue] bills are passed? Can he say yes or no to that?' Lloyd George unhelpfully answered in a single word: 'No'.[19] A few minutes later Lloyd George intervened angrily to say that he was not responsible for what might be in the newspapers and the government intentions were unchanged.[20] The fact was that the entire plan depended upon an autumn session. Lloyd George was virtually alone in the Liberal party in wanting one. Meanwhile the press was beginning to speculate about an election as soon as parliament rose.[21]

Lloyd George had made a disastrous parliamentary error and in attempting to rectify it in the next few weeks he blundered into new entanglements. He had originally intended to put the provisional local authority grants and the derating power that would legalize them into a single revenue bill. But the distractions since the beginning of the year had delayed action and neither a revenue bill nor the finance bill was nearly ready at the time the Chancellor made his budget statement. As in 1909, he had thrown everything into the budget statement (for instance land development,) while leaving the final embodiment of his programs for separate pieces of legislation. He had obtained a ruling from the Speaker, for which he was immediately attacked, that as local authority grants were not to be part of the Finance Bill, any discussion of them during the debate on the Ways and Means Resolutions following the budget statement was out of order. Accordingly he declined to answer questions on the principles upon which the money he demanded would be distributed. And because he expected a separate revenue bill he had not included in the Ways and Means Resolutions, disastrously as it turned out, any references to the local authority grants. Thus what came out of the Ways and Means Committee was the power for government to raise revenue that it had promised not to spend without additional legislation which could not be discussed.

The last two weeks of May and first two weeks of June of 1914 were hectic and unhappy times for Lloyd George. In addition to hints even in the friendly press that it would have been well to postpone his rating reform until the next year's budget, the public portion of the land campaign was in a muddle.[22] Rowntree and G. Wallace Carter, the General Secretary of the Central Land and Housing Committee, reported that there was enthusiasm in rural areas but much less in towns and that London was 'unmoved'.[23] The leaders of the land campaign were as puzzled by the budget statement as had been the House of Commons. Rowntree wrote in mid-May pleading with Lloyd George for several hours' discussion on a number of questions, some simple, some basic. Where were the first houses to be built? What were the main lines of rating reform? Would leasehold enfranchisement apply to churches? 'I know how anxious you are that the Land Campaign should succeed, and I can assure you its success is being seriously interfered with for want of a more clearly defined policy with regard to the above and other matters. . .Very sorry to be such a plague,' he concluded with some asperity, 'but it's your own doing! You asked me to make the Campaign go, and I am trying to!'[24] At the end of the month, having heard the now widespread rumors of an election, Rowntree wrote again almost in desperation. 'What of the political situation?' The campaign was presently aiming at an election in 1915. 'Do you want us "to slow down or hurry up?"' Frances Stevenson apparently replied that the Chancellor certainly did not want the campaign to slow down for Rowntree wrote to her on 28 May saying that he had not intended to slow down and that he thought there might be an earlier general election.[25]

In the midst of the conflict over the budget, on 23 May Lloyd George received a blow, both personal and political, that would affect his fortunes for years to come: the defeat of Charles Masterman in a by-election at Ipswich. At the Chancellor's insistence, Masterman, the chief executive for national health insurance, had been brought into the Cabinet in February as Chancellor of the Duchy of Lancaster, succeeding Hobhouse in that post. In those days an appointee to the Cabinet was required by law to vacate his seat in the House of Commons and stand for re-election. In his seat in Bethnal Green on 19 February, Masterman was defeated by a Unionist 2,824 to 2,804, a margin of twenty votes in a three cornered poll in which an Independent Labour candidate, John Scurr, attracted 316. This defeat made his second attempt at Ipswich a national event. There, as in February, he was attacked by both the left and the right. Mr. Scurr, somehow liberally supplied with money, reappeared to siphon off working-class voters who opposed national health insurance contributions while the Unionist candidate with money, banners, and sidings from Tory newspapers and supported by Sir Edward Carson denounced Home Rule in a strongly nonconformist community. (The previous Member in Ipswich was the free church leader and Lloyd George's associate in the education revolt, the Reverend Sylvester Horne, whose death on 3 May caused the vacancy.) As if determined to lose, Masterman, the devout High Churchman, always wore a large gold cross on his waistcoat. He was heavily defeated in Ipswich, 6,406 to 5,874, a larger margin than Scurr received, although Masterman himself believed that many workmen had voted for the Unionists.[26]

For the Liberals, Masterman's repeated losses were a disaster from every point of view, '. . .quite the worst we have had and a smasher for poor Masterman,' wrote Asquith to Venetia Stanley.[27] Asquith felt no votes were lost on Home Rule. However, the Unionist press declared the opposite.[28] Besides the humiliation of a brilliant, if eccentric, young minister, the two defeats showed that neither the old nor the new Liberalism was popular. Masterman blamed Lloyd George for making him go to Ipswich. Lloyd George retaliated with a lecture on self-pity.[29] The nonconformists of Ipswich opposed Home Rule and the workers in Bethnal Green were not attracted by contributory health issues. Lloyd George's appearance for Masterman at Ipswich had done nothing to revive the Liberal-Labour alliance. It showed only that Masterman, high minded and reflective, but somehow vulnerable and soft, was a safer target for the opposition than the more robust Chancellor of the Exchequer he represented. Conversely, of course, the Unionists were hugely elated.[30]

Lloyd George rarely looked back on defeats, but Ipswich worried him. Although by polling day he expected Masterman to be defeated, he had hoped at the beginning that the popularity of his program would pull Masterman through.[31] 'LG is jumpy, irritable, overworked, and unhappy,' wrote Masterman to Arthur Ponsonby on 30 May,

> Disturbed at the unpopularity of Insurance, at the failure of the land campaign to pack up a great emotional wave (though I believe it is going well in the country districts): now at the failure of his budget to command any measure of enthusiasm. Also he is very disturbed about the Irish question where his sympathies are necessarily with Protestant Ulster.[32]

Masterman had agreed to contest Ipswich only with a promise that he could continue in the Cabinet, whether he was successful or not.[33] Hence he remained Chancellor of the Duchy of Lancaster, until February 1915. But without a seat in the House of Commons his power declined; he became querulous and fearful and his relationship with Lloyd George deteriorated rapidly. Clearly he was approaching some sort of breakdown. He was neglecting his work, 'drinking more than is good for him' and looking very unkempt and untidy, Lloyd George complained to Riddell. Would Riddell speak to him? Lloyd George said he himself already had done so without effect.[34]

As could be imagined, the impending eclipse of the Chancellor's chief lieutenant was quickly remarked upon at Westminster. Almost immediately after the election Lloyd George received a letter from Violet Mond asking why should he 'not let Alfred manage insurance for the next few months? At least you know it will be well done...There will be no by-election in Swansea.' He was a 'businessman'. 'Keep this letter *strictly* private.'[35]

However, it would appear Lloyd George had already identified Masterman's replacement. Among the many difficulties revealed by Ipswich was a moribund Liberal organization. Within a few days he had consulted Alec Murray, now in London hovering about the fringes of the Westminster world, who proposed a second whip to look after the Liberal party organizations in the constituencies, a system the Conservatives already used. On 5 June Lloyd George wrote to Asquith urging the creation of the new office and suggesting that it be filled by Arthur Ponsonby or Christopher Addison. All of this, he said, should be put delicately to the incumbent Chief Whip Percy Illingworth, with assurances that the changes would not reduce his authority. Nor should he be told that Murray had been consulted.[36] Asquith promptly sent this confidential message to Venetia Stanley with the remark that it was probably the longest letter the Chancellor had ever written with his own hand.[37] But he replied approving the idea.[38] Predictably, the Chief Whip, when informed, resisted the proposal for a second whip but with the Chancellor's help, Addison became Parliamentary Secretary at the Board of Education under Pease when the government was reconstructed at the outbreak of the war and then went to the Ministry of Munitions with Lloyd George in May 1915.[39]

For the immediate future Ipswich illuminated starkly the unpleasant conclusion that Lloyd George clearly was trying to thrust from his mind: that in terms of public popularity the land campaign was not reviving the party as the 1909 budget had done. The Chancellor, without delay, must find a way to bridge the city-country gap in the land campaign, wrote G. Ward Humphrey to Lloyd George a few days after the Ipswich election, reporting for the Land and Housing Council. The question is always asked: are low wages and poor housing only a country problem? 'It needs to be made clear *officially*, if such be the fact, that the principle of a living wage, Urban as well as Rural, is a basic principle of the whole scheme!' The urban land problem and the rural land problem must not be separated, concluded the report, even though the urban solution will be more difficult politically because it is more complicated, 'has more experts, and does not lend itself so easily to legitimate sentimental appeal.'[40]

As usual, Lloyd George rested at Criccieth during the Whitsun recess, although this summer his buoyant nervous energy and his good humor were nearly exhausted. While there, at bay, trying to hold together a legislative program disliked even by his own colleagues, Lloyd George characteristically took the fight to the public platform. He derided the notion that a general election was coming soon and promised that the revenue bill in preparation would provide for building houses in Criccieth.[41]

Lloyd George was fighting recklessly and dangerously. The Finance Bill, and the revenue bill upon which rating depended, still were not ready although the budget statement was now a month old and both measures had been promised time and again before recess. Worse still, he was adding new freight, the promise of cottages in Wales for instance, while the deadline of 5 August, when the provisional collection of income tax would cease, was creeping up. Then, sometime between his return from Criccieth on the first day of June and the publication of the Finance Bill the following week, he changed the structure of both measures. As there would be no time in the two remaining months to put through both bills, the revenue bill would have to be lightened or possibly put off. Only the vital Finance Bill would be proceeded with. The party had to be committed to local authority grants in case of a general election and it would be even more desirable to have them on the statute books if the Unionists won. Accordingly, at the last minute, and clearly without much thought, Lloyd George grafted the entire scheme of local authority grants, which he had originally intended for a revenue bill, onto the Finance Bill although as a result the Finance Bill was not congruent with the financial resolutions of the Ways and Means Committee by authority of which it had to be introduced. He incorporated also the proviso first announced in the budget statement: that local authority grants, even though enacted by the Finance Bill, could not begin until authority for separate rating of site and premises had become law. Thus Captain Pretyman's charge, that parliament was raising more money than it legally could spend, still stood, but there was now added a parliamentary tangle — that the Finance Bill might not only be unconstitutional but worse, out of order.[42]

Parliament reconvened on Tuesday, 9 June, and a rumble of complaint about the Finance Bill began immediately on both sides of the House. By the end of the week Lloyd George had heard the backbench resistance to the budget which crystallized rapidly. At noon on Monday, 15 June, a group of between thirty and forty 'influential' Liberal backbenchers met Asquith who was attended by Montagu, Samuel, Simon and Illingworth, with Lloyd George conspicuously absent, to complain about the budget. This Liberal 'cave', as it was immediately styled (after the Liberal opponents of Gladstone's 1866 Franchise Bill who had, as John Bright put it, retired to the 'Cave of Adullam') was a group Asquith could not ignore although he was reported by *The Times* the next day to have given them an 'uncompromising' reply. Their leaders, John Holt, John Jardine, Frederick Cawley, Charles Nicholson, Percy Molteno, and significantly two former supporters of Lloyd George who were alike only in the fact that each was Jewish, extremely wealthy, and each already had a reason to dislike the Chancellor, Alfred Mond and Maurice DeForest. In general the men of the cave represented either wealth, usually of imperial or shipping origin, or the old public and civil service. But above all, except for DeForest and Mond, they were a remnant of the nineteenth-century Liberal manufacturing and intellectual establishment whose money and leadership had sustained the party since the days of Palmerston and whose numbers now were rapidly diminishing. They were neither Whig nor radical. They were by no means reactionary. Their fathers had built the modern Liberal party, which now was slipping into other hands.

The report of the Monday meeting had indicated that the Liberal malcontents would make no statement after their unsuccessful interview with Asquith, but the next day they drew up a long letter explaining their position. The Chief Whip, Percy Illingworth, attempted to suppress the letter but failed and it appeared in *The Times* on Thursday, 18 June. It is worth some attention, for while it literally destroyed the Lloyd George budget, the letter represents also possibly the last enunciation of the serious Gladstonian principles of House of Commons fiscal control in a nation where the welfare state had already begun to grow.

The letter essentially restated the objections to the budget that have been outlined previously in this study: that a large new burden was to be laid upon the income tax payer to support local authority grants which were themselves dependent upon problematical and highly controversial future legislation. Yet even if the enabling legislation were passed and the provisional grants begun, the future system of grants (i.e. the application of the grants to the derating of improvements) could not start until the valuation was complete. This would be many months in the future and in the interval there must surely be a general election which the Unionists could well win. If they did the local authority grants, unattached to any new form of rating, would become simply a gift to local landlords.

These were political objections, but they were constitutional arguments as well. The revenue bill (still unpublished when the letter was written), authorizing the separate rating of improvements and allowing the grants to be made, would almost certainly be held up by the House of Lords and so for the coming year parliament would have on its hands a large sum of money which it could not legally spend. As a result 'either some new means of expending the money will be hastily devised and rushed through Parliament or it will pass to the Sinking Fund. In either case it will have been diverted to uses that the House of Commons did not intend when voting the Budget, and for purposes to which the House might never have agreed. . .We think it vitally important,' the writers concluded, 'in the interests of representative government that money should not be asked by a Government until Parliament has first approved the scheme which it is intended to finance, until machinery for expending it in a manner acceptable to Parliament has been provided, and until its expenditure is no longer dependent upon contingencies.'[43]

The letter of 18 June profoundly impressed the one man who had supported Lloyd George firmly, if reluctantly, and who was the single person without whose help the Chancellor could not proceed — the Prime Minister. It manifested precisely the kind of ironclad logic, proceeding from principle to conclusion, that he often used himself with great effect, earning him the name, 'The Hammer'. 'It is (I think) a very able document,' he wrote to Venetia Stanley on 18 June,

> and to most of its arguments there is no real answer. If we could put off the last stage of the Finance Bill (as we thought we could) till Sept., we shd. have time to do something; but as it has to be passed by Aug. 5th it is quite impossible to get both it & the Revenue Bill by that date, and we should be in the absurd position of having imposed a lot of unnecessary taxes, with the chance (if there is an election & it goes wrong) of the Tories coming in & spending the money. (Is this clear, I wonder?)
>
> The rational course is to drop the whole thing — except so much as is necessary to pay for the Navy &c. this year. Simon & McKenna both agree about this, but of course it would be very nauseous & even humiliating to Ll.G., who attributes all his trouble to the 'Radical millionaires,' i.e. Mond, Molteno, deForest & Co. He will probably threaten to resign, tho' your friend at the Home Office [McKenna] — with whom I had a talk this morning — thinks (as he says) that he (Ll.G.) will not 'adhere' to it. We are going to have a Cabinet on Monday after the 'trooping' to deal with the situation, which is quite as embrangled as in the early days of the year when the Beagles were in full cry. [The Navy estimates.][44]

Asquith clearly had made up his mind on Thursday that the inauguration of the land program would have to be postponed for at least a year even at the risk of losing his Chancellor of the Exchequer. The government's parliamentary position on the budget was not only uncomfortable, it was untenable. If any further pressure was needed it came on the same day, 18 June, when the Liberal cave, whose numbers now were estimated at between forty and fifty, announced they intended to put down a reasoned amendment against the budget. 'The Liberal revolters apparently mean business,' remarked *The Times*. If they proceeded with their threat it could mean a government defeat. *The Times* noted also that the Revenue Bill which finally had appeared on that day, did not after all authorize site value rating and the derating of improvements, but stated only that Inland Revenue could collect information 'with a view' to these reforms. In legal terms, said the paper, it was 'a fishing inquiry'. There evidently had been some desperate 'blue penciling' in the bill at the last minute.[45]

Although Lloyd George doggedly defended his budget in speeches over the weekend, on Monday morning, after a long discussion of the Irish situation, the Cabinet agreed to drop Part IV of the Finance Bill, the local authority grants.[46] *The Times* parliamentary correspondent felt that the decision was entirely the Prime Minister's. But despite his offhand statements about it to

Venetia Stanley, Asquith clearly had not made up his mind easily. Morley reported to Almeric Fitzroy the next day that the Prime Minister was 'writhing with humiliation' at having his government take back half its budget.[47] As a result of the reduced expenditure the proposed income tax would be decreased from 1s 4d in the pound to 1s 3d.

In Asquith's mind the paramount objection was obviously his Chancellor's contravention of the ordinary rules of parliamentary financial control, the political furor stirred up by the cave, and the impolicy of raising taxes before an election. Nevertheless, for the younger members of the Cabinet, 'the Beagles', the issue appears to have been simply the lack of parliamentary time. Hobhouse recorded the conversation in the 22 June Cabinet. 'Ll.G.,' Hobhouse wrote, 'said he had "a little doubt" as to the time necessary for his Finance Bill, to which the P.M. rejoined that he had "none" — then Ll.G. suggested that an adjournment for Sept. would enable us to get the measure in Oct. I said I would retire from Office and the H. of C., the others joined in, and an autumn session was stillborn.'[48]

Lloyd George had lost. No autumn session meant no Revenue Bill. Without a Revenue Bill there could be no site value rating. And until site value rating was legal there was no way to authorize the local authority grants, the taxes to pay for which were already piling up in the Treasury. The Chancellor's agony was not yet over. At 3:30 on Monday afternoon, as soon as the Clerk of the House had read the motion for leave to read the Finance Bill a second time, Mr. Felix Cassel, Unionist MP for St. Pancras West, rose on a point of order to say that the bill before the House contained provisions not covered in the budget resolutions passed five weeks earlier and that as such it was out of order. An extended argument followed at the end of which the Speaker stated that as it stood the Finance Bill with the newly included local authority grants did indeed exceed the resolutions but that this situation could be 'cured' by amending the resolutions or by amending the bill. However, when eventually Herbert Samuel began his speech to move the second reading, he announced that the offending local authority grants, embodied in Part IV of the bill, had already been deleted and the proposed income tax rate had been reduced by one penny. So the bill was in order after all. But Samuel did not say whether the changes in the bill were a result of the Speaker's ruling or of the Liberal revolt. Consequently many journalists in the next few days gave Mr. Cassel's motion more importance than it really deserved.[49]

As if the Liberals were not in enough disarray, the reduction of the income tax caused a second revolt, this time among the Liberal radicals and the Labour party. At the vote for the second reading of the Finance Bill on 26 June most of Labour and a number of Liberals abstained, and one Liberal, Luke White, voted against the government so that the ministry's normal majority of about ninety-five fell to thirty-eight. The budget provided another demonstration that the government was tired and losing control of the party. Asquith's speech on the last day of the debate on the Finance Bill had been full of optimism and promises that everything would be taken care of in the next session, but many commentators doubted this and looked forward to a dissolution. Lloyd George's budget had been a 'noble effort' remarked the *New Statesman* two days later in a lead article entitled 'The Coming General Election', but 'as is not unusual with him, he had not got all his bills ready.'[50]

The *Nation*, whose sentiments echoed the *New Statesman*, noted on the same day that there was now a real danger that the Revenue Bill would be held up by the House of Lords. The *Saturday Review* added that it would have been impossible for the Speaker to certify the Finance Bill as a money bill had Part IV remained a part of it.[51]

Lloyd George's 1914 budget, which should have been a campaign asset, had become a liability. 'The whole business is extremely damaging to the prestige of the government and especially to that of the Chancellor of the Exchequer,' declared *The Times* on 23 July. He had pleased no one. The wealthy Liberals had denounced him for putting the income tax rise in and the radicals damned him for taking it out. Although it was not yet clear, land reform had died, killed by party uncertainty, governmental inefficiency, lack of preparation, and the unsolvable problem of Ireland which drained the Liberals of resolution and vitality.

With some obvious pleasure, if inaccurately, Walter Runciman described to Robert Chalmers, who until 1913 had been Permanent Secretary to the Treasury and was now Governor of Ceylon, what had happened. Lloyd George, he said

> is taxing heavily in order to meet the claims of his friends at the Admiralty and he aimed at gilding the pill by a heavy set of subsidies to local authorities. The subsidies are even yet undefined. Some of the financial purists on our side. . .declared that they would not vote taxation for undefined objects: they said in private very freely that they refused to trust the Treasury with any money except what was clearly earmarked & voted by the House. Publically they laid their case down in a manifesto which on constitutional grounds was unanswerable. The P.M. insisted on L-G respecting it and the infant [Samuel] had to come down to the House. . .to announce on L-G's behalf that. . .that part of the budget is dropped & one d less is now to be raised in Income tax. . .You can imagine the blow this had been to L-G — and the dreadful muddle which we are now let in for. Banks and local authorities and electioneering Radicals are all enraged; our programme and legislation are horribly upset. . .We are indeed in a precarious plight, and but for the follies of Bonar and his Orange and Tariff Reform colleagues we should be easily displaced.[52]

'Ll.G. has had a bad week,' recorded George Riddell on 12 July, 'his stock stands low in the Party. The Budget has been a fiasco. Nonetheless he seems in excellent spirits and is full of fight.'[53] Lloyd George was never downcast for long, and characteristically blamed everyone but himself for the budget disaster. Meanwhile he pushed ahead with the land campaign as if nothing had occurred. On 25 June he bravely produced the final Cabinet paper on land reform and during July discussed with his new advisor, Christopher Addison, plans for a revenue bill in 1915.[54] However on 13 July the Cabinet voted to end the current session 'as soon as may be' and to meet again in November or December.[55]

Despite these optimistic plans for the future it cannot be denied that but for the war, the budget of 1914 would have hurt Lloyd George's career seriously and perhaps permanently. His reputation for magic was destroyed. Ignoring the warnings of the unpopularity of land reform among the Liberals, he had been too reckless in attempting to repeat the miracle of 1909. He had tried to accomplish too much. He had stretched parliamentary rules too far. For the first time he had been outmaneuvered and humiliated, less by the opposition than by dissidents within his own party. Instead of rallying the Liberals he had divided them. Instead of diverting popular interest from Ulster resistance, as the 1909 budget had turned attention from tariff reform, he had delayed his land initiative too long, bringing it forward when public preoccupation with competing matters could not be overcome. Worst of all, luck, which in politics is no doubt only the instinct for timing, had deserted him. Finally the very small team that had driven Liberal reform forward, that had put together the budget of 1909, health and unemployment insurance, had broken up. Churchill was lost. Masterman was dead politically. Lloyd George's commitment to land reform was too advanced for the backbench stalwarts of his party, while its young radicals demanded something less personal and more anti-capitalist. Perhaps the budget debacle of 1914 marked the end of the new Liberalism.

II

Among all the burdens of Asquith's Liberal administration, none was more exhausting and interminable than the matter of Irish Home Rule. Since January 1910 no question occupied more Cabinet and House of Commons time, provided the subject for more speeches, and filled more newspaper space than did the commitment for a Dublin parliament. No one felt this more keenly than the Chancellor of the Exchequer. Since his fights with Gladstone in 1893, Ireland had blocked the way. The nation's preoccupation with the subject was a large factor in the failure of the land campaign to generate enthusiasm. Asquith's nervousness about armed rebellion in Ulster caused him to ponder continually a dissolution. But, except as a problem to be solved, or pushed aside as quickly as possible, Lloyd George had no concern for Home Rule unless, as he had made clear many times, it was a part of a larger scheme of national devolution within the United Kingdom.

All of this meant that his place in the Home Rule struggle, even after the bill was introduced in April 1912, was that of negotiator. Compromise or postpone the difficulties whatever they may be, he urged, but bring the battle to an end as soon as possible. He approached the problem of legislation for the Irish as he approached all legislative problems: do not begin with an ideal scheme and then water it down to meet difficulties, rather define what were the attainable goals and then search for a parliamentary path to arrive at them. In Ireland the problem was the Protestant minority concentrated largely in four counties of the northeast who had announced in a representative convention in 1911 that Ulster would resist by force any exercise of authority by a parliament in Dublin. He saw from the beginning that jurisdiction in the end would have to be enforced by the army and he doubted whether the army could be trusted. He realized before anyone else that the simple alternatives for Ulster were exclusion or coercion.

Lloyd George put this intractable logic to the Cabinet of 6 February 1912 — which also authorized Haldane's visit to the German Emperor — when he proposed that the bill under consideration should allow any Irish county, by referendum, to contract out of the Home Rule settlement.[56] 'What will we do

93

about Ulster if it rebels?' he told Herbert Lewis later he had asked his colleagues. 'Can we order the soldiers in? If they go will they actually fire?' 'Wait and see' was the answer. When he suggested cutting out Ulster he was told that Redmond and Dillon would never agree. Afterwards, he said, he went to see Dillon and was told that, speaking for himself alone, there would be no trouble although it might cost the Treasury another half million a year.[57] One must comment here that it is likely Lloyd George did not propose to Dillon the outright exclusion of Ulster that he had suggested in the Cabinet, but some special privileges for the North within the Dublin framework. Dillon's biographer refers to no such meeting.

Nonetheless one can say that the failure to adopt at this time Lloyd George's motion for some form of Ulster exclusion constituted one of the most disastrous mistakes of modern British, not to mention Irish, history. What was passed off on 6 February with a short discussion as a bow to the convenience of the Irish Secretary, Augustine Birrell, and to the moral convictions of the Lord Chancellor, Loreburn, was in fact conceded in the summer of 1914, by which time the compromise was impossible. This needs to be stressed. For one moment, in the spring of 1912, separation was possible, and three quarters of a century of Irish civil war might have been avoided. 'If Ulster, or rather any county, had a right to remain outside the Irish Parliament,' Bonar Law told Riddell less than a month later, 'for my part my objectives would be met.'[58] If Ulster had been excluded 'it would have been impossible to prevent the bill from being passed into law,' wrote Walter Long, one of the most powerful English opponents of Home Rule. 'To this day I marvel that the Government did not take some step in this direction.'[59] These were the possibilities in the spring of 1912. The chance, once lost, never came again.

Asquith introduced the Home Rule Bill on 11 April 1912. It provided for a Parliament at Dublin with power over virtually all domestic affairs except religion and with jurisdiction over all thirty-two counties. 'Went off quite well, but no enthusiasm', Lloyd George wrote Maggie that day. 'It is much too soon to form any estimate of its effect on our party.' And he added ominously: 'my opinion — [in Welsh] between you and me — is that the Liberal party will by and by be looking in the direction of the Welsh hills for another man to extricate them out of their troubles.'[60]

Much of the debate in the ensuing twenty-nine months, as the Home Rule Bill wound its way back and forth between the House of Commons and the House of Lords under the Parliament Act, dealt with the ethical question of the freedom of the Protestant counties of Ulster from Catholic oppression. Nonetheless Lloyd George was convinced that the governing sentiment among many senior Unionists was not directed towards safeguards for northern Protestantism within a Home Rule framework, but rather at using Ulster to defeat Home Rule altogether. This conviction did not apply to the Ulster leader, Sir Edward Carson, nor to Bonar Law, a middle-class nonconformist from Glasgow. But the rest of the party spokesmen, Balfour, or the Cecils, or Walter Long, and above all, the 'diehards', the great Irish landlords such as Lansdowne or Midleton, or Londonderry, cared nothing, Lloyd George reasoned, for the industrial workers of Belfast who in September 1911 had followed their parsons in tens of thousands to sign the covenant of resistance. If the soldiers of Carson's volunteer army could break up the movement toward Home Rule, they would be useful. They would save not only Ulster but the rest of Anglo-Ireland and, by implication, would discredit the Parliament Act.[61]

That Ulster's demand for freedom gave the anti-Home Rule cause the moral dimension it otherwise lacked, Lloyd George understood perfectly well and he was the first of the Liberal leaders to recognize its depth and sincerity. Later in the summer of 1912, when he was with Mark Lockwood at the Hotel Stern in Marienbad, a meeting already mentioned in connection with the land campaign, T.P. O'Connor, Irish Nationalist MP for the Scotland Division of Liverpool, who was also there, exerted himself to convince the two men that the claim of Ulster rights had no popular foundation and would disappear once Home Rule was passed. Lloyd George disagreed. When O'Connor left them Lloyd George declared, as Lockwood reported to Bonar Law:

'Mark, I knew you were right when you told T.P. how real the movement was, and how deep, but what can we do with a man like that (i.e., T.P. and Devlin, who is of course the real leader) [Joseph Devlin, Nationalist Chairman in Ulster and MP for West Belfast] we want to leave Ulster out — it would put you fellows in a hole, for a certainty, but they are too much for us.'

Lloyd George concluded his conversation with Lockwood with an attack on Birrell who '"makes a mess of everything."'[62]

This important conversation with Colonel Lockwood was no doubt a political gambit. Probably it was an attempt by Lloyd George to send a signal on Home Rule as well as land reform to Bonar Law who had announced at Blenheim on 27 July what amounted to unequivocal support for Ulster violence. Nevertheless, during the first passage of the Home Rule Bill through the House of Commons, to the time of its first rejection by the House of Lords at the end of January 1913, other Liberals, above all the Prime Minister, remained unaccountably blind to the danger toward which they were drifting. The Liberal leadership allowed to slip away the opportunity to negotiate about Ulster while the bill was still in the House of Commons where it could be amended while remaining under the protection of the Parliament Act. (Unhappily the delusion that the Ulster revolt was a bluff happened to be re-enforced on 30 January 1913, the day of the House of Lords' first rejection of the bill, by a Liberal Home Rule victory in the shrine of Ulster loyalism, Londonderry City.) For the next two years the Liberals were bound by the terms of their own measure limiting the power of the House of Lords.

In order to circumvent a second chamber veto, a bill under the Parliament Act had to remain in the identical form to that in which it first passed the House of Commons. Not a comma could be changed. After the first passage, amendments could be inserted only by the Lords themselves, although the Act provided that the Commons could 'suggest' amendments for the Lords to take up. Politically, after the beginning of January 1913, this meant that concessions to Ulster could no longer be only the minimum necessary to satisfy Carson and his followers. They now would have to overcome the opposition of the entire Unionist establishment, above all the Unionist leader in the House of Lords, Lord Lansdowne, a great Kerry landlord who was far more concerned about Dublin than about Belfast and who accordingly did not wish to see Ulster satisfied in any regard. For such men Ulster discontent, the 'Orange Card', would defeat the entire bill. By 1913 Bonar Law was aware he could only partially control and probably could not defeat the diehard network in his party, and had to alter the position he had made clear to Riddell in April 1912: that concessions to Ulster would be enough.[63] After approval in the House of Commons, concessions to Carson were useless without consideration of the South. Only coercion remained and by the spring of 1914 that too was impossible.

After it was too late, in the summer of 1913, Asquith began to show interest in compromise. Even though he had mildly supported Lloyd George in the Cabinet of 6 February 1912 when the Chancellor had proposed Ulster exclusion and had written to the King afterwards saying that the Irish Nationalists would be told that the government was free to make provision for Ulster counties by amendment later, he had resisted a number of amendments providing for the exclusion of some or all Ulster counties during the critical first passage of the Home Rule Bill through the House of Commons.[64] But as the end of the 1913 session approached, prompted by the King whom he saw on 11 August, the Prime Minister began to search, through Lloyd George, for an avenue toward the settlement of the Ulster question.[65] 'Had an important chat on the political situation with PM this morning,' Lloyd George reported to Maggie on 12 August. 'He told me things that he has not yet informed his colleagues as to serious talk with the King on Home Rule etc.'[66]

Lloyd George quickly opened a line to the Unionists using as he customarily did an intermediary, this time F. Harcourt Kitchin, the editor of the *Glasgow Herald* and a friend of Bonar Law. He put 'all his cards on the table' yesterday in a two and one half hour meeting, reported Kitchin to Bonar Law on 30 September. He was very worried about Ireland. Ulster should not be coerced, there would be bloodshed, nor should there be a general election. He would let Ulster vote itself out. He would propose a conference if the Unionists would introduce an amendment for exclusion in the House of Lords. Finally, he had added, the Unionists ought to support the land campaign.[67]

Through the next few months there were negotiations between Asquith and Bonar Law for a conference to explore the question of Ulster exclusion. The two men met, with elaborate secrecy, at Cherkley Court, Max Aitken's house just outside Leatherhead in Surrey, on 14 October, again on 6 November, and again on 10 December. Bonar Law received immediately after the first meeting a note from Lansdowne deploring the idea of a conference which could lead to compromise, although he expressed hope that the Nationalists, not he (Lansdowne) would prevent it.[68]

Nonetheless at the second meeting with the opposition leader on 6 November, Asquith proposed in the vaguest 'hypothetical' terms, in his own words, the exclusion of the six plantation counties of Ulster 'for a period of years, say ten, and then a plebiscite', Bonar Law reported to Balfour. The Prime Minister agreed to put it to the Cabinet without suggesting that Bonar Law had agreed to it.[69] The Prime Minister, Bonar Law reported, believed he could impose this concession on the Nationalists. Bonar Law wrote the following day to Walter Long, 'Redmond and the "Old Guard" realize that this is their last chance, and they must choose between such a settlement or nothing.'[70]

Evidently Asquith soon thought better of putting this plan to his colleagues himself and asked the Chancellor to put it forward as his own proposal. Whether Lloyd George knew that the Prime Minister had already offered this concession to Bonar Law is uncertain, but in any case he made the proposal at a private dinner at No. 11 Downing Street on 12 November. This dinner is usually connected with the Home Rule struggle, however Lloyd George had other reasons, already mentioned, for summoning it. Churchill's estimates, which Lloyd George had already seen, were about to come before the Cabinet. There were the usual mutterings that the easy way out of the government's troubles was dissolution, which Lloyd George hoped to avoid. These factors, as well as a desire to compromise on Ireland, may have determined the guest list which included Asquith, Grey, Crewe and Haldane. None of the Beagles, nor Birrell, the Irish Secretary, nor, significantly, Churchill was present. The men invited were Asquith's friends not his. Most of the early talk concerned the Navy and politics. The cost of dreadnoughts would raise taxes which was undesirable before an election. 'Grey strongly in favour of a July 1914 election. Prime Minister clearly leaning toward a 1914 dissolution,' wrote Lloyd George in his notes of the conversation.

> I urged that it was a question of tactics, that could not be determined so many months in advance — that it was too much like a general deciding that he would fight a battle this day twelvemonth — that strategical and tactical situations at the time must necessarily determine the advisability or otherwise for fighting an action.
>
> The Prime Minister assented.

After dinner the party moved upstairs to the drawing room. 'Here,' recorded Lloyd George, 'Prime Minister raised question of Ulster but offered no suggestion as to outlet.'

> Grey said something about Home Rule [for Ulster] within Home Rule. I then expressed opinion that it would be impossible to propose anything acceptable to the Nationalists which the Unionists would accept, and that no scheme which the Unionists would openly assent to could possibly be supported by the Nationalists. We therefore ought to propose a scheme which would knock all the moral props from under Carson's rebellion, and make it impossible for Ulster to take up arms, or if they did, put us in a strong position with British public opinion when we came to suppress it. Therefore suggested temporary exclusion of Ulster with an automatic inclusion at the end of the term. Proposed we should if possible put it forward as a suggestion in the House of Commons.
>
> This scheme met with general approval — no objections raised to it. Haldane told me afterwards the PM in driving away with him expressed satisfaction.[71]

'My dinner on Wednesday,' Lloyd George told Riddell a few days later, 'was one of the most important gatherings I have attended. We came to some important decisions, so important that I made a note of what took place, a thing I have never done before. It was a historic occasion.'[72] This was more than the customary Lloyd George hyperbole. Now that it was too late, temporary exclusion became Liberal policy on Home Rule.

The day after the Downing Street conclave Lloyd George brought the plan before the full Cabinet, proposing that Ulster be excluded for a period of six years after which it would automatically return to the jurisdiction of the Dublin parliament unless the Westminster parliament decreed otherwise. This period, he explained, would allow two general elections on the subject. Either the Liberal position would be confirmed or the Unionists would return to reverse the process. Meanwhile it would break up Carson's support. He could not hold his volunteers together to resist something that would not happen for six years. 'This suggestion', Asquith concluded in his letter to the King, 'met with a good deal of support and it was agreed that the Prime Minister should discuss it with Mr. Redmond whom he is to see privately on Monday.'[73]

Asquith duly conferred with Redmond on Monday morning, 17 November, and on the same day Lloyd George saw Dillon twice, in the afternoon and the evening. Asquith's meeting was less than a success but Lloyd George found Dillon, usually stiff and harsh, willing to listen to what was now referred to as the 'Lloyd George plan'. The Irish leader emphasized that he must be able to say publicly that he knew nothing of the plan and that Devlin and the Ulster Nationalists would resist, but that the party might help to carry it in Ireland once it was proposed.[74] However, in the next few weeks what had seemed to be some progress toward a compromise on North Ireland came to an end. The rank and file of the Nationalist party, stirred by rumors of an accommodation, protested. Particularly the Ulster section, led by Joseph Devlin, scoffed at the Liberals' timidity in the face of what they considered a much exaggerated Protestant threat. (Devlin, MP for West Belfast, was an important figure in negotiations on Ulster in this period. Unlike the more austere Redmond and Dillon, he was a short, attractive, and witty man, whose talent for popular oratory nearly equalled that of Lloyd George, the 'vest-pocket Demosthenes'.) On 24 November Asquith read to the Cabinet a long memorandum from Redmond saying that although he was prepared for an autonomous Ulster, the party felt otherwise and at present negotiations were unthinkable.[75] Lloyd George himself saw Redmond the next day, 25 November, and sought to apply more pressure. The Ulster threat was real. Birrell had announced in Cabinet the previous day the passage from Liverpool to North Ireland of 1,500 rifles, with over sixty ball cartridges for each. Moreover, if coercion were to begin without an offer of exclusion first, Churchill, Grey, Haldane, and probably he himself, would resign.[76]

Finally, shortly before Christmas, and even though Asquith had seen Bonar Law a third time on 10 December only to have temporary exclusion soundly rejected, Lloyd George met T.P. O'Connor and Devlin. This time, with the Cabinet already seething over the Navy estimates, the government's manifest weakness provided the Chancellor's most powerful weapon. O'Connor reported Lloyd George's conversation to Dillon. 'Winston had stated openly in the Cabinet,' Lloyd George had said, that if coercion were applied to Ulster without her having received any reasonable offer, he would have to resign. In addition, L.G. repeated to me a conversation with Winston, the details of which I need not go into; it amounted to this, that Churchill was seriously thinking of the possibility of his having to go back to the Tories and had been laying his plans for the purpose. I heard from another source that Churchill had declared in a public room in a Tory club that the mistake of his life was to have left the Tory party; Churchill does speak with this startling imprudence. L.G. thinks it would be a great mistake to allow Churchill to leave just now, characteristically saying that to keep him was worth a million, a million, of course he meant, on the Navy Estimates. Others of the Cabinet, I gathered, would be quite ready to shed Churchill; but L.G. insisted he was worth keeping, for the moment; though, as you see, he has no illusions about him.[77]

Making allowances for Lloyd George's habitual exaggeration, and the conversion of rumor and speculation into fact, this statement, on the eve of Lloyd George's return to Criccieth where he would give the *Daily Chronicle* interview, tells much about the crisis within the Liberal Cabinet and more about the deteriorating relationship between the Chancellor and the First Lord. Everyone knew Churchill was a genius, although there was much disagreement about the form of this genius. But there was no disagreement that he had the temperament of a spoiled baby, insolent when he was not insufferable, a 'man child', snorted Siegfried Sassoon who was acquainted with Churchill through Edward Marsh.[78] Still his departure could kill Home Rule.

Lloyd George, almost alone in the Cabinet, was ready to make sacrifices to keep him, as he would do again over the naval estimates within the next few weeks. Surely he knew that Churchill's return to the Unionists was not a real possibility. Despite his friendship with the Cecils, F.E. Smith, and Austen Chamberlain, the First Lord was even more unpopular among the opposition than was the Chancellor himself, as his dismissal from the Admiralty in May 1915 would prove.

The attempts at compromise over Ulster, stalemated by a diehard Irish minority in each party, had provoked some agitation among partisans of another measure, the fourth Welsh Disestablishment Bill, that was making its way toward the statute book in tandem with Home Rule under the ponderous machinery of the Parliament Act. Lloyd George had little to do with the preparation of the bill which was McKenna's task, and he had long since ceased to occupy himself with Welsh parliamentary affairs, but this issue, as part of his early political life, he could not ignore. He made a rousing speech during the second reading on 25 April 1912, two days after McKenna's introduction of the measure, pounding Welsh Churchmen William Ormsby-Gore and Arthur Griffith Boscawen for betraying Wales and denouncing the Cecil brothers for allowing their ancestors to plunder Church property. There were many interruptions and shouts of 'Limehouse'. The old Welsh radical had returned.[79]

In neither England nor Wales did Church and chapel affairs carry the moment of twenty years earlier. Nonetheless Lloyd George was able to fill Caernarvon Pavilion for a great rally during the Whitsun recess where the aged patriarch Evan Jones warned him, as he had been doing for a quarter century, not to compromise for the sake of passage of the bill. 'Rather than submit to that, sir, we will wreck the Government.'[80]

Inevitably emotion surrounding Home Rule and disestablishment became intertwined. Even if the feelings about the latter among ordinary voters were less intense, there were a large number of Unionist Members of Parliament who took disestablishment very seriously indeed and most of them were diehards on Home Rule. 'It is my belief,' Bonar Law told Asquith in their first meeting on 15 October 1913, 'that a very much larger number of our members would, if they had to choose, prefer Home Rule rather than disestablish the Church.'[81] This estimate, from a man who had no personal, as opposed to political, prejudices about either issue, represented exactly the reverse of the Liberal position. Within Lloyd George's party few beyond a handful of Welsh MPs, emphatically not the Chancellor himself, were much concerned with the ancient demands of nineteenth-century religious fundamentalism. Indeed to relieve the burden of managing two controversial and incredibly complex measures at the same time, the government had considered dropping disestablishment when it was first rejected by the peers early in 1913 and were only dissuaded by McKenna's threat to resign.[82]

Then at the end of October, as Bonar Law looked for an avenue of agreement on Home Rule, a rumor began to circulate that Welsh disestablishment offered a valuable opportunity to Unionists for detaching Welsh and English nonconformity from the Liberals. Wales was not radical, only the chapel counted. It did not support health insurance, or the land campaign, or Home Rule. The Unionists would be well advised to put aside their devotion to the Church and let disestablishment pass in order to concentrate on the other issue, in effect they should sell out the Welsh Church for compromise on Home Rule.[83] The Welsh episcopacy clearly had heard the same rumors interpreted, however, differently. If the Liberals compromised on Home Rule they would be bound to push for a harsh settlement in Wales. 'The situation is obscure', wrote St. Asaph to Bishop Owen of St. Davids on 3 November. 'High pressure is being put forth to arrive at a settlement upon the basis of excluding Ulster and this solution has within the Cabinet the powerful support of Winston Churchill and Lloyd George and, with certain limitations, of Sir Edward Grey. Such a solution would be detrimental if not disastrous to our own particular cause.'[84] The government could not compromise on both measures.

In the end the Disestablishment Bill, unchanged, became law under the terms of the Parliament Act, only to have its operation suspended because of the outbreak of the war, much to the anger of Welsh nonconformists who denounced Lloyd George for allowing this to happen.[85]

Lloyd George had long since given up Welsh battles, but Wales, as the disestablishment tangle would prove again and again, claimed him still. Welsh nonconformity looked for a political solution for every religious discontent, and demanded that Lloyd George provide it. An anonymous pamphlet, widely circulated at the time, expressed what must have been almost precisely the Chancellor's own opinions about his fellow countrymen. In Wales, it said, nonconformity had become flaccid and lazy. Its ministers depended only on politics, had no courage, and had given up preaching.

Ministers of religion had better give up praising Lloyd George and the *London Daily News* and study the Sermon on the Mount. Mr. Lloyd George has better friends and sincerer admirers in Wales than the parasites who serenade him, who pray for him by name from the pulpit, who whisper every gossip into his ear, simply from selfish motives, and who pretend to speak with his authority. He has some favours to bestow, just now, and in his honour be it said he will never forget his countrymen.

But he would not last forever. Welsh free churchmen should learn to stand by themselves.[86]

Lloyd George surely understood this. As the Welsh chapels' dependence upon him increased, the more he came to despise them. Here, one suspects, are the origins of the extraordinarily generous settlement he made with the Welsh Church after the war.

At the first of the year of 1914, after speaking to the *Daily Chronicle* reporter and with Home Rule apparently at an impasse, Lloyd George took his holiday in Algiers, accompanied by T.P. O'Connor. He talked little of Ireland except to say that a resignation by Churchill over Home Rule, rather than the Navy, would be serious for the government and also for Ireland.[87]

At the end of the previous year, Redmond and Dillon, after some initial reflection, had, as has been seen, refused the 'Lloyd George plan' for the temporary exclusion of Ulster. But in early February, as the naval estimates crisis subsided, Asquith, after several conferences with the King and with news from Ulster of increasing activity among Carson's volunteers, determined to push ahead with this measure, whatever the Nationalists' attitude. Increasingly he leaned upon Lloyd George for negotiation. 'The P.M.'s trouble is that he hates anything unpleasant or in the nature of a row' Lloyd George told Riddell a few weeks later. 'He hates an unpleasant interview. He said to me, "I think you had better have a preliminary conversation with the Irish!" He thought it would be an unpleasant and troublesome task!'[88] It may be significant that Carson told Lloyd George, probably during the war when they cooperated in unseating Asquith, that he knew he would win over Ulster. For years he had held a low opinion of the Prime Minister as a barrister. He never fought his cases hard enough, particularly when there was anything disagreeable. He would leave this work to juniors.[89]

In the middle of February, 1914, the Chancellor drew up a proposal for a plebiscite in any Irish county on the question of exclusion, the plebiscite to be in response to a petition signed by perhaps ten percent of the parliamentary electors. The exclusion would last for an unspecified number of years and at the end the county would come under the jurisdiction of the Dublin parliament, unless in the interval Westminster had acted to prevent it.

The core of Lloyd George's argument in this proposal, slightly changed in emphasis from that made in the Cabinet in November, was that by offering this amendment the government was not admitting that the bill before parliament was defective. On the contrary the Liberals were conceding the point made many times by both Bonar Law and Carson: that the dismissal of the Protestant counties of Ulster from the protection of the Westminster parliament should be submitted to the judgment of the electorate. As the next election would have to occur before December 1915, even a short period of exclusion would include a general election. If the Unionists were returned they could solve the problem as they chose.[90]

Lloyd George's paper evidently was submitted to Devlin who replied with a counter offer, first put forth in a letter to *The Times* on 10 February by Horace Plunkett, which permitted Ulster counties to vote themselves out after ten years under the Dublin parliament.[91] To this Lloyd George responded on 23 February saying that admirable as the Plunkett plan was, it had one fatal defect: it would never be accepted by the Unionists. He continued with a remarkable forecast of the melancholy events that have led Irish Catholic and Protestant affairs to their present state.

> If the Ulster Unionists state that the moment they are forced in
> even temporarily they will take up arms, and riots as a matter of fact
> will ensue, a blood feud will have been set up between the Irish
> Parliament and the Ulster Protestants. Ten years count as nothing in a
> bloodstained quarrel of this kind, and at the end of that experimental
> period the defeated Protestants and their sympathizers would certainly,
> under any circumstances, vote the exclusion of Ulster. The submission
> of an offer of that kind is therefore essentially dependent upon the
> complete and *bona fide* acceptance of it by the Unionist leaders, and
> a practical guarantee that resistance would be withdrawn and the
> experiment fairly tried. . .That risk might be worth taking for a
> settlement entered into in good faith by all parties. This I feel
> confident we cannot hope for.[92]

Two days later, after a long Cabinet meeting, Lloyd George and Birrell were commissioned to state and to sell to Redmond and Dillon the new exclusion scheme. The attitude of the government was this:

> . . .it was necessary to make concessions to legitimate fears in England
> and Ireland, which were thought quite groundless but recognized
> as sincere; that permanent exclusion of any part of Ireland was
> undesirable in itself and undesired by any part in England or Ireland;
> that temporary exclusion of the four north-eastern counties either
> singly or *en bloc* would be considered by the Opposition, an acceptance
> which for political reasons they would probably not concur in. . .Beyond
> that we were not ourselves prepared to go and should not ask them to
> yield further.[93]

Lloyd George, with Birrell in tow, met Redmond, Dillon and Devlin at the Treasury on 27 February and again, on 2 March, at 10 Downing Street with Asquith and O'Connor also in attendance. (This highly secret meeting was of course reported by the Prime Minister to Miss Stanley even before it occurred. He was, he wrote, 'going to dine with Lloyd George (a very unusual adventure) to talk "shop" with one or two choice colleagues,' not any of Miss Stanley's favorites. 'Irish business.' (This extract does not appear in the published Venetia Stanley letters.) The substance of these two meetings was an agreement, confirmed by Redmond in a letter to the Cabinet after the second meeting, by which the Irish accepted reluctantly the principle of exclusion by plebiscite of any Ulster county for three years only. The Irish leader insisted that the changes be presented to the House of Commons in such a way that his party would not be required to vote for them and that the Cabinet agree that these concessions represented the 'last word' of the government, in effect there were to be no further changes in the bill.[94] Redmond's fear, his reason for insisting on no further changes, turned out to be a remarkably accurate forecast of events. He expected, he told Lloyd George at the first meeting, that after the exclusion amendment was introduced in the Lords the upper chamber would broaden its provisions and 'at the last moment the Government might present us with the alternative of accepting this enlarged proposal or of dropping the Bill.'[95]

Asquith read the Irish leader's letter to the Cabinet two days later on 4 March. His statement to the King makes clear that he recommended it, although he did not report Cabinet approval.[96] Lloyd George, on the other hand, told his brother that the problem was solved. 'Settled with the Irish and carried my plan through the Cabinet today. Next step is to submit it to the other side which the P.M. will do Monday.'[97]

The next day the whole of the Cabinet plan appeared in the *Daily News* giving Unionists warning of the concession to Ulster they were supposed to approve. The reaction to the plan as well as the discontent of the King, coupled with the fact that Lloyd George had originally suggested a five or six year term for exclusion, caused Asquith to determine over the week-end of 7–8 March that, despite his promise about a 'last word', the proposal that the House of Commons would see must be for six years.

Asquith placed the exclusion plan before the House on 9 March in the form of a White Paper. It was promptly rejected by Carson in the stinging phrase 'a sentence of death with a six year stay of execution.'[98] However the Unionists had no wish to appear as blind opponents of any compromise and so negotiations between Bonar Law and Asquith continued for the next two weeks until they were interrupted by the so-called Curragh Mutiny.

The news that some fifty-eight officers of Brigadier General Hubert Gough's Third Cavalry Brigade, stationed at the Curragh Barracks southwest of Dublin, had refused duty in Ulster arrived in London on 21 March. The mistakes, misunderstandings, and sheer stupidity that caused this lamentable incident are not a part of the life of Lloyd George, but its effect upon the government's Ulster policy the Chancellor recognized immediately. The option of coercion, if ever it had existed, was now gone.

The 'mutiny' itself, the request by some officers for dismissal from the army to avoid obedience to orders to move north to protect military installations in Ulster (although the purpose of the move had not been made clear), could hardly have been a surprise. Lloyd George had questioned the army's loyalty at the time of his original proposal for Ulster exclusion on 6 February 1912 and for at least the previous six months military officers, and indeed the King, men not inaccessible to Cabinet members, had been talking about growing discontent in the army at the prospect of being employed against Ulster loyalists.[99] Nonetheless, the government's handling of the original protest at Curragh, its apparent desire to obscure the discontent rather than to restore discipline, and its final badly worded statement which seemed to forgive the indiscipline by a promise that the Army would not be used to suppress political opponents in Ulster, all combined to provide evidence of a sense little short of panic. Thus, the initiative in Ulster passed to the Unionists.

After Curragh, Bonar Law and Carson were in a position to dictate the Ulster settlement. No amending bill, nor any amendment to the Home Rule Bill opposed by them, could pass the House of Lords. Yet if a Dublin parliament with jurisdiction over the North were established the result would be violence which the government would be powerless to control. In Ulster the power of civil authority would lie in the streets.

Lloyd George was quickly convinced that the only feasible policy was surrender. The permanent exclusion of a redefined Ulster was all that was left, he told the King in the middle of May. 'Limited exclusion is already gone; all the fight will be over area.' The Lords, he continued, should put permanent exclusion in the amending bill (with which the government intended to introduce limited exclusion) and when the measure reached the House of Commons the Cabinet would be ready to force Redmond's hand.[100] But despite the tough minded assertions about the government's willingness to coerce Redmond, in fact the will of the Cabinet seemed broken. Within a few days of the time the Chancellor spoke to the King, Hobhouse recorded sadly in his diary:

> I tried to induce the Cabinet to consider what actual steps should be taken if the Ulster provisional government was actually set up. But no one felt inclined to move until the trouble actually arrived. History, if it concerns itself with us at all, will write us down as either the most patient, wise, farseeing Govt. this or any country ever had, or else as the [most] inept, blind, and cowardly crew that ever disgraced Downing Street. No middle judgement is possible.[101]

Early in May, over the protests of Lloyd George and others, Asquith had determined not to attempt to amend the Home Rule Bill but to introduce instead a separate Amending Bill in the House of Lords that would allow a plebiscite on a six year exclusion. On all sides it was argued this was no longer an issue. Nothing less than permanent exclusion was possible. Not surprisingly, therefore, when the Amending Bill was finally introduced in the upper chamber by Crewe the measure was promptly amended to require the permanent exclusion of all nine counties of Ulster without a plebiscite. (There were solid Protestant majorities in only four Ulster counties.) The question, as Lloyd George had foreseen, was no longer whether some part of Ulster would be excluded, but simply how much.

Out of this stalemate began the movement toward what became in the third week of July, the Buckingham Palace or 'Speaker's' Conference. This began at the end of June with a proposal by Alec Murray to Carson and Redmond, as well as to Asquith and Lloyd George, for another attempt at a negotiated settlement. Murray extracted from the Unionists an assent to the permanent exclusion of the four Protestant counties with parts of two others, all of which would vote as a unit.[102] In the next few weeks there was a round of private conferences among the principals on all sides, although Lloyd George, still occupied with the budget, was only peripherally involved. From these, it became clear that the point of contention between the two sides was County Tyrone. Only forty-four percent of its population was Protestant, but they held the county's wealth and property. Carson could no more allow them to pass under Home Rule than Redmond could allow them to escape.[103] (It should be noted, as it was at the time although usually forgotten since, that as Ulster paid nearly four-fifths of Ireland's income taxes, exclusion of nine counties would have left a Dublin government in a desperate financial position.) Meanwhile the Lords' Amending Bill, excluding all nine counties immediately and permanently, had passed the upper house and was scheduled for debate in the House of Commons. Either the government would have to accept it and admit the practical defeat of Home Rule or reject it and invite the proclamation of Carson's provisional government which it would be unable to control. Henry Wilson, the Director of Military Operations, who had been intriguing eagerly with the Unionists for months, recorded in his diary on 3 July that unless Asquith accepted the Lords' amendments, which he did not expect, Carson, whom he saw regularly, would soon establish his provisional government. 'What would the Army do?' asked Lord Milner. 'If the Army were ordered to attack Belfast City Hall, with Carson sitting in it', replied the general, 'we would not go.' He noted that he talked it over with his colleagues afterwards and they all agreed.[104]

Fortified by this news Milner's was a powerful voice against all concession and opposed any conference. 'Generally speaking I don't see why we should give way any further,' he wrote to Carson, who valued his opinions, on 21 July as the meeting was about to convene. 'The Government are in a weak position. They can't fight because they can't rely on the Army, and they daren't face an election, because they know they would be beaten. If we stick our toes in the ground, I don't see what else they can do but give way to us or else go blindly to destruction.'[105]

Why Asquith believed a formal conference would succeed after private consultation had failed is not clear. Debate on the Amending Bill in the House of Commons would harden divisions, he told the King, but divisions hardly could have hardened further.[106] No doubt he hoped for further delay. He always did, although playing for time without a solution in view would seem to be a dubious exercise. At least the Commons' debate on the Amending Bill could be postponed. He saw the King, who for months had been pleading for a conference, on 17 July, suggesting that he would write a memorandum advising a conference to which the King would reply with an invitation. The attendance was worked out on the spot. Each of the four sides would send two delegates. For the Liberals Asquith of course was one and 'as between Crewe and Ll.G.,' he told Venetia Stanley, 'the K. was (with me) in favour of the latter.'[107] Lloyd George received his invitation immediately.[108]

The conference, under the chairmanship of the Speaker, met at Buckingham Palace on 21 July and continued until 24 July, when it collapsed as it had begun, over the issue of Tyrone. Neither Carson nor Redmond could give up the county nor would they divide it. Redmond, the Prime Minister reported, had said there were 53,000 Catholics to 40,000 Protestants; Carson replied that three quarters of the rates where paid by those 40,000. Neither could give way.[109] Bonar Law, Asquith said after the talks collapsed, refused any settlement except six county permanent exclusion and Lansdowne (the other Unionist delegate) never tried to settle at all.[110]

In the afternoon of 24 July, Asquith, Lloyd George, Birrell, Redmond and Dillon met at No. 10. Now Asquith announced that he intended to go on with the Amending Bill without a time limit. Dillon and Redmond, the Prime

Minister wrote, 'after a good deal of demur reluctantly agreed to try & persuade their party to assent.'[111] The Cabinet met immediately afterwards, at 3:15 p.m., and agreed to permit the Ulster counties to renew their exclusion by plebiscite at the end of a six year period. Exclusion thus would be permanent.[112] So the Liberals, at the end, had retreated to the point at which Lloyd George had urged them to start when the bill was drawn up.

Carson had won, as he always expected he would do. But this was not quite the conclusion. The measured acquiescence in a renewal of exclusion that Asquith thought he had obtained from Redmond and Dillon disappeared almost immediately. On 26 July the Irish Volunteers, the Catholic counterpart of Carson's army the Ulster Volunteers, attempted to land a large shipment of arms at Howth on the north side of Dublin Bay. In this they were attempting to repeat the almost unopposed landing of a much larger shipment to the Ulster Volunteers on the night of 24–25 April at Larne in County Antrim. The landing itself was successful but as the Volunteers, with their arms and accompanied by a large crowd, returned to Dublin they were met by troops and police. Although most of the armed men slipped away, a dispute broke out between the mob and the soldiers which ended with shooting. The soldiers killed three and wounded thirty-eight. To Irishmen the inequality between Catholic and Protestant was clear. After Larne in Ulster the government had declined even to prosecute the smugglers, although they were well-known. Now, in Batchelor's Walk in Dublin, men were murdered. It was the 'general conviction in Ireland that the government were deliberately dealing out different measures to Ulster and the rest of Ireland,' wrote C.P. Scott the next day after a conversation with Dillon. 'Position as to Amending Bill difficult before, now impossible. Nationalists could not vote for it.'[113] Asquith's response was to postpone the Amending Bill again. He had not much hope for it in any case, he told Venetia Stanley, but he expected the King to require a dissolution as the price of royal approval of the Home Rule Bill. 'A general election under such circumstances,' he wrote, 'would be one of the worst things that cd. happen to the country, or (I suspect) to the Liberal party.'[114]

All the avenues of escape from the impending crisis now were closed. The Liberals faced either a vote by the Irish against their amendments to the Amending Bill which could put them out of office, or they could drop the Amending Bill, push on with the Home Rule Bill alone and cause an election which, punctuated by outbreaks of violence in Ireland, they would surely lose. Then suddenly the horror disappeared, reduced to only a remembered nightmare, swept away by the clangor of alarm from Europe.

III

As the Cabinet of 24 July was about to separate, having pondered miserably the failure of the Buckingham Palace conference, Grey called the ministers back to say that he needed to inform them of an approaching grave confrontation in the Balkans. Austria's ultimatum to Serbia, Asquith reported to the King, 'may be a prelude to war in which at least four of the great powers might be involved.'[115]

Lloyd George's behavior in the crucial eleven days between Grey's announcement and Britain's declaration of war on Germany has commanded much scholarship and more speculation. While every member of the Cabinet, including the Chancellor himself, has left records of the agonizing week and a half, Lloyd George's part remains unclear. There is the legend he himself composed, that he opposed any British declaration until he heard of the German invasion of Belgium. In his *War Memoirs* his suspense becomes a cliffhanging melodrama. 'The Germans had signed a treaty not merely to respect, but to protect the neutrality of Belgium,' wrote Lloyd George. 'Would they honour their bond? Great Britain was a party to that compact. If anyone broke its terms, Britain was bound to throw her might against the invader. Would the faith of Prussia strengthened by fear of Britain prevail? If the treaty stood the situation might yet be saved.'[116]

This, in historiographical terms, may be designated the 'official' story. It puts Lloyd George within the mainstream of British Liberal radicals, most of whom opposed intervention at the outset of the crisis but who supported the war more or less reluctantly after the flagrant German violation of Belgian neutrality became clear on 3 August. However to be logically tenable it must be assumed that the individuals opposed to the war had no foreknowledge of German plans, as Lloyd George suggests he did not in the passage quoted. Certainly after the crisis he took great care to associate himself with those who expressed horror and shock at the violation of the London Treaty of 1839 while declaring that, but for this dastardly and unexpected crime, he would have resigned rather than support a declaration of war. Such a story provided also the neat halo that Lloyd George always liked to see hovering over his decisions.

Yet there are facts to indicate that all of this was instead a pantomime in which Lloyd George engaged, first to prevent a breakup of the Cabinet and resignations from a divided party, and second to maintain contact with his usual constituency, most of whom were against the war. The aftermath of Agadir was not so far in the past that he could forget the attacks upon himself and Grey in the fall and winter of 1911.

Most important, he had known since the Committee of Imperial Defence meeting of August 1911 that the Germans would attack through Belgium. Other senior Cabinet members knew it, the Army expected it, British battle plans were based upon this assumption; McKenna, A.K. Wilson and the whole blue water naval strategy had been sacrificed to these anticipations.[117] He believed also that without British support the French could not withstand the Germans and that a second German conquest of France within little more than a generation would be a disaster for Britain. He had made his opinions amply clear at the time of Agadir. On the other hand, he rarely mentioned, as Grey invariably did, the commitment of British honor to France, nor was he concerned about the secret military and naval conversations, which were continuing despite the Cabinet resolutions of November 1911. However, he did admit the existence of a British obligation to defend the French channel coast as a result of the movement to the Mediterranean of the French fleet. But his concern was mainly for British national security.

Nothing here should be read to mean that Lloyd George welcomed the war, as Churchill seems to have done, or that the agonies of decision he described in letters to his wife were less than genuine, always making allowance for a modicum of dramatic flair. War harmed the nation; it was wasteful, like industrial disputes or absentee landlords. It represented the breakdown of the processes of mediation and compromise that to him were the engine of progress.

Nonetheless, the prospect of armed conflict aroused also his pugnacity, the resistance to the bully. Both Esher and Hobhouse state flatly in their journals, unfortunately without dates, that Lloyd George's first reaction to the warnings of the crisis in July 1914 had been hostility toward Germany. But when it became apparent that his usual followers in the party and the press were overwhelmingly against intervention, he withdrew his belligerent statements and fell silent.[118] But most telling is the statement by Frances Stevenson in her memoirs. Miss Stevenson records that she spent the entire weekend of 31 July–3 August at No. 11 and observed the Chancellor's unhappiness. He knew, she said, that Britain was not prepared for war, and his instincts were against it. Still he trusted the judgment of Asquith and Grey far more than the opinion of the younger anti-war radicals in the Cabinet, 'the beagles'. 'My own opinion' concluded Miss Stevenson, 'is that L.G.'s mind was really made up from the first, that he knew we would have to go in, and that the invasion of Belgium was, to be cynical, a heaven-sent excuse for supporting a declaration of war.'[119]

Although there are many mistakes in Frances Stevenson's memoirs, this seems to be a fair assessment. It is consonant with what Lloyd George knew through his regular attendance at the Committee of Imperial Defence of the continuing conspiracy between the military leaders of the two nations and of the growing dependence of France upon British support. Lord Esher's statement to C.P. Scott on 6 May 1914 must be quoted here. In August 1911, Esher had told the editor, Britain had 'come within an ace of war with Germany,' Everything, he continued, had been handled 'by a small junta of Cabinet members of the Committee [of Imperial Defence].'

> It consisted in fact of the Prime Minister, Lloyd George, Churchill, Grey, General French and Lieutenant General Ewart and two Admirals, I think Admiral Seymour and Prince Louis of Battenburg [sic]. But he admitted that it was known to the Defence Committee that intimate communications were going on between Army and Navy chiefs of France and England with a view to possible war with Germany, and he added they are still going on, in spite of the tremendous row in the Cabinet and of the pledge that nothing of the kind should happen again without the Cabinet's knowledge — strange he should speak so freely about these matters unless he knew that I already knew, as I did, which he may have inferred from the tone of conversation. What was new to me was that in his view the pledge given was worthless.[120]

After his initial outbursts against the Germans, Lloyd George had said nothing publicly, although he assured C.P. Scott in confidence on 27 July that at the moment there 'could be no question of our taking part in any way in the first instance. Knew of no minister who would be in favor of it. . .' Although he 'admitted that a difficult question would arise if the German fleet were attacking French towns on the other side of the channel. . .'[121]

In the next few days the Liberal press, responding to a series of strongly pro-French leaders in *The Times*, awoke to the danger that Russia might support

Serbia thus inviting war with Germany which would inevitably cause war between Germany and France. The *Manchester Guardian*, the *Daily News*, the *Nation*, the *Liverpool Post*, and for Lloyd George most important, the *British Weekly*, began to declare that continental tensions were not Britain's affair. This sentiment was echoed in the House of Commons. On 30 July, 22 Liberal pacifist MPs sent Asquith a manifesto demanding that Britain remain neutral even if Belgium were invaded. And as late as 2 August, Asquith wrote to Venetia Stanley that he believed three-quarters of his party in the House of Commons were 'for absolute non-intervention at any price'.[122] At the same time Lloyd George was receiving a flood of messages demanding that he speak out for peace. His letters, even to his wife, while affirming a perfectly justified horror of war, give no hint of his position.[123]

Historians have made much of which, and how many, British politicians knew in the week before the war that official military planning was based absolutely on the assumption that the Germans would attack France through Belgium.[124] In fact many radicals simply refused to believe the obvious. Grey, like statesmen in every generation, was continually faced with the invincible ignorance of enthusiasts who believed their earnest faith would control events. He recalled meeting a dedicated young Liberal pacifist in the lobby of the House of Commons who informed him loftily that under no circumstances should Britain intervene. '"Not even if Germany invades Belgium?" He for a moment looked as if he had collided with a brick wall. "She won't do it." "I don't say she will, but supposing she does." "She won't do it," he repeated confidently, and with that assurance he left me.'[125]

However, the consideration of pacifist attitudes obscures the far more important fact that Sir Edward Grey was determined to intervene on behalf of France whether or not the Germans invaded Belgium. The Foreign Secretary made this clear in the Cabinet on 2 August. The country might not be bound to France in legal terms, Masterman reported Grey saying with great emotion but he, personally, was bound in honor. 'We have led France to rely on us,' he said, 'and unless we support her in her agony I cannot continue at the Foreign Office.'[126] It was very likely at this point that Louis Harcourt tossed Lloyd George the note showing what leadership could have been his: 'Speak for us. Grey wishes to go to war without the violation of Belgium.'[127]

In fact, as Lord Morley points out in his *Memorandum on Resignation*, most of the talk in the Cabinet was not on Belgium but, as in 1911, over the nature of Britain's obligations to France and what should be done, or not done, to fulfill them. The pacifists, none of whom had attended the Committee of Imperial Defence meeting of 23 August 1911, could refuse to believe, if they chose, that the invasion of Belgium, calling into operation the Guarantee Treaty of 1839, was imminent. As late as the evening of Sunday, 2 August, indeed after the German ultimatum to Belgium had been delivered, Herbert Samuel could write to his wife: 'I still have hopes that Germany will neither send her fleet down the Channel nor invade Belgium and that we shall be able to keep England at peace. . .'[128] Samuel is as responsible as anyone for the myths that have grown up around the Cabinet action in these last days of peace. Asked by the *Manchester Guardian* in 1928 after the publication of Morley's *Memorandum* to comment upon it, he contradicted the letter cited above: 'The information which was before us was categorical that the German strategic plan did involve the invasion of Belgium and that there was no like-lihood that it would be changed in any circumstances or on any conditions.'[129]

It would appear that Lloyd George used his junior colleagues' frightened perplexity to hold the Cabinet together, that he indeed encouraged the self-delusion about Belgium by suggesting perhaps that the Germans would cross only the southwest tip of the country. He was the only man who could have led a revolt. But he saw also that the violation of Belgian integrity could provide the ethical umbrella under which the junior ministers could safely and honorably return to obedience.

For Britain's entrance into the war, two dates were decisive. The first was 1 August 1914 when Germany declared war upon Russia. Even without exact knowledge of the Schlieffen Plan, all British leaders assumed that in a war against France and Russia together, the Germans would attack France first and that the trigger of the German assault would be Russian mobilization. Asquith and William Tyrrel, Grey's Private Secretary, understood this well enough to rouse George V from his Buckingham Palace bed at about 1:30 a.m. on 1 August and there to dictate to the sleepy king, clad in a brown bathrobe over a long nightshirt, a telegram to Czar Nicholas II pleading with him not to order mobilization.[130] Nonetheless the Imperial *Ukase* for general mobilization was posted in every village in the Czar's empire before daylight that morning and in the afternoon Germany declared war. By the following morning, 2 August, visitors to Germany were reporting that the roads through the Rhineland had become rivers of men in field gray all marching west.

Therefore, Sunday, 2 August, brought the time of decision for Britain. About three quarters of an hour before the first Cabinet of the day, set to convene at 11:00 a.m., Lloyd George called together at No. 11 Downing Street most of his younger non-interventionist Cabinet colleagues. Out of this conclave came a resolution, at whose motion is unknown but one may surmise that the Chancellor inspired it, that all were 'agreed we were not prepared to go to war now, but that in certain events we might reconsider position, such as the invasion wholesale of Belgium.'[131] In the Cabinet Samuel, according to his letter to his wife, repeated the substance of this resolution: 'That we should be justified in joining the war either for the protection of the northern coast of France, which we could not afford to see bombarded by the German fleet and occupied by the German army, or for the maintenance of the independence of Belgium, which we were bound by treaty to protect and which again we could not afford to see subordinated to Germany. But I held we were not [obliged?] to carry England into war for the sake of our good will from France or for the sake of maintaining the strength of France and Russia against that of Germany and Austria. This opinion is shared by a majority of the Cabinet. . .'[132] After the first Cabinet of that day which recessed at about 1:00 p.m., and at which Grey was author-ized to tell the French that the Royal Navy would not allow the Germans to enter the Channel and bombard the French coast, causing John Burns to say he would resign, the same group, with Lloyd George and Morley, met at Lord Beauchamp's for lunch. Morley by now suspected what Lloyd George was up to, indeed his prescience provides some of the best evidence of the Chancellor's game. Suddenly there was much talk of Belgium where there had been little before. 'The general voice was loud and clear [presumably

Lloyd George participating] that "Burns was right..." Lloyd George and Simon [who believed, incredibly, that he could influence Lloyd George] were energetically decided at the end, as they had been at the beginning, to resist at all costs bellicose interferences from the Entente.'[133] And yet Morley felt that the end would be war. Belgium, he believed, was simply a trap.

> The German line on Belgian neutrality might be met in two ways. One, we might make a *casus belli*; the other we might protest with direct energy, as the British protested on the Russian repudiation in 1870 of the Black Sea article of the Treaty of Paris, and push on diplomatizing. What was the difficulty about the second course? Why, our supposed entanglement with France, and nothing else. The precipitate and peremptory blaze about Belgium was due less to the indignation at the violation of a Treaty than to the natural perception of the plea that it would furnish for intervention on behalf of France, for expeditionary force, and all the rest of it. Belgium was to take the place that had been taken before, as pleas for war, by Morocco and Agadir.

The Cabinet met again that Sunday at 6:30 p.m. While it sat the Germans delivered their ultimatum to Belgium: free passage, or war in twelve hours. Although the Cabinet did not hear of this, it would have made no difference. The inevitable hardly could be a surprise. Churchill, on his own initiative, already had ordered the fleet to remain mobilized and the Director of Military Operations had begun, on Asquith's order, to turn the pages of the war book.[134]

That evening Lloyd George with Charles Masterman, Simon, and Ramsay MacDonald dined with Riddell. Lloyd George told Riddell that the Cabinet that day had agreed to tell Germany that Britain would remain neutral if the German fleet did not enter the Channel, a mirror image of the truth. He said, bowing to the presence of two well-known pacifists, that if the Germans observed this and the neutrality of Belgium, he would resign rather than support the war. When Riddell remarked, and Masterman agreed, that Britain had to prevent the violation of France under any circumstances, Lloyd George responded by calling them 'jingoes'.[135] Ramsay MacDonald was suspicious of the Chancellor's histrionics. 'Lloyd George harped on the exposed French coast and Belgium' he recorded afterwards, 'but I gathered that an excuse was being searched for.'[136]

Later in the evening the game came to an end. Riddell received a telephone call from Field Marshal Sir John French, appointed a few days earlier Commander in Chief of the British Expeditionary Force: 'He said, "Can you tell me, old chap, whether we are going to be in this war?"' Riddell, holding his hand over the mouthpiece, consulted Lloyd George. 'Lloyd George says: "Be at Downing Street tomorrow at ten o'clock sharp."' Thus, with a joke, Lloyd George announced the war.[137]

As always Lloyd George was concerned not to move too abruptly from his newspaper friends, of which the most important was W. Robertson Nicoll of the *British Weekly*. Nicoll, he had told Riddell, was 'the greatest living journalist from a polemical point of view. It is a pity he is too old to edit a daily paper. He would make it an enormous power.'[138]

Accordingly, early the next morning Riddell visited Nicoll whose paper the previous Thursday, noting the Austrian declaration of war, had insisted: 'the quarrel in no way concerns us and we are fortunately unbound by any engagements that would require us to intervene.'[139] 'I now explained the situation to him fully,' wrote Riddell. 'Before I left he told me that he thought we had no alternative but to support France, and we must all stand together and sink differences of opinion. I wrote a note to Masterman saying what Nicoll had told me and suggested he show it to L.G., which he did. I think L.G. attached considerable importance to Nicoll's decision.'[140]

As the Cabinet sat that morning, Monday, 3 August, a telegram arrived from King Albert of the Belgians appealing for British assistance and in the early afternoon Edward Grey gave the House of Commons, and the world, the story of British commitments to France while reminding the Members that no legal obligations existed except for the protection of Belgium. On the following day, Tuesday, 4 August, Germany received the British ultimatum. Britain declared war on Germany at 11 p.m. that evening.

In the end only Morley and Burns resigned. The Liberal government remained intact. Britain entered the conflagration united and in good spirits. Lloyd George lost no time in establishing his place among the vanguard of the pacifists who had been reluctantly driven to war. 'I am moving through a nightmare world these days' he wrote his wife on 3 August. 'I have fought hard for peace and succeeded so far in keeping the Cabinet out of it but I am driven to the conclusion that if the small nationality of Belgium is attacked by Germany all my traditions and even prejudices will be engaged on the side of war. I am filled with horror at the prospect.'[141] He lunched with Samuel before Grey's speech and drove with him to the House of Commons. The Chancellor 'was warmly cheered by the [excited?] people waving little union jacks', Samuel wrote to his wife. '"This is not my crowd," he [Lloyd George] said. "I never want to be cheered by a war crowd."'[142]

On the same day Lloyd George telegraphed C.P. Scott, like Nicoll a hugely influential newspaper ally, and asked him to come and see him. Scott arrived on Tuesday. 'Up to last Sunday,' he told Scott, 'only two Members of the Cabinet had been in favor of our intervention in war,'

> but the violation of *Belgian territory* had completely altered the situation. Apart from that it would have been impossible to draw us into war now. (He had gone so far, however, as to urge that if Germany would consent to limit her occupation of Belgium — the sort of nose land running out by Luxemburg — he would resign rather than make this a *casus belli*.) Presumably therefore some such offer was made to Germany and declined.
>
> At the same time he said we could not have tolerated attacks on the French coast of the Channel and had the Government done so public opinion would have swept them out of power in a week. He had done his utmost for peace but events had been too strong for him.[143]

Viewed in perspective it seems nearly impossible to believe that Britain could have remained neutral in the First World War. Even leaving aside the obligations within the Entente, the destruction of France was too great a risk. Rather the questions were whether Britain would enter the war immediately or later, and whether the government would have united popular and political support. This last was Lloyd George's to give or withhold. The evidence is that he never questioned that Britain's fate was bound with France and that also he personally liked the French as he disliked the Prussians. Nor did he doubt that the Germans would invade Belgium. Indeed his correspondence with Churchill in 1911 shows that the two men were far more accurate in their anticipations of German strategy than the military planners.

But unlike 1911, in 1914 Lloyd George kept all he knew to himself. For this there would appear to be two reasons. One was personal. He did not wish to become involved in a storm such as had blown up over the secret commitment to France that had raged around the figure of Edward Grey in the autumn and winter of 1911. The second reason was grounded simply in practical patriotism. Assuming as he did, and as was clear by 1 August, that the war would come and that Britain would be carried into it, the most useful service he could provide was to hold the Cabinet together. So he consorted with pacifists and paraded the moral question of Belgian integrity in place of the diplomatic-military issue of French security. As he knew Belgium would be invaded and the pacifists did not, or could not bring themselves to believe it, he could secure agreement on what was to the dissidents a hypothetical event and then wait for it to occur. Then he could make the rights of small nations the bridge by which the dissidents could return to the Cabinet and support the war while holding tight to their principles. Morley understood what he was doing, but was too weak to expose the trick. So did MacDonald. Riddell glimpsed it also, but approved and helped him to square Robertson Nicoll.

So the anti-war movement, which could have torn Britain apart in 1914, was nipped before it could flower. Burns and Morley left the Cabinet as isolated figures. The Liberal government survived. The war did not become a party issue as would have occurred had the government resigned. Not for the last time in his career, Lloyd George saved the nation.

During the last anxious days before the declaration of war, while fully occupied with Cabinet politics, Lloyd George had to deal as well with a City financial crisis that was as sharp and dangerous as it was unexpected. His resourcefulness and courage in this affair, turning on matters about which he knew very little and in which there were no precedents even to guide experts in any case, won him praise in financial circles which were not usually remarkable for warm feelings toward the Chancellor. His 'saving of the City', as he termed it modestly in his *War Memoirs*, signalled the beginning of a new surge in his public popularity that began with the war, which grew during his tenure at the Ministry of Munitions in 1915 and 1916, and which catapulted him from near isolation in his party after the rejected budget of 1914 into the prime ministership a little more than two years later.

Specifically the City crisis resulted from the failure of the remittance system by which London banks, the stock market, and the City bill brokering and acceptance houses, collected money due them from abroad. The crisis began with the closing of all continental stock exchanges by Thursday, 30 July. Only London and New York remained open. Large holdings of stock owned by German and Austrian nationals were sold in New York in the next few days, forcing down prices in London. At the same time London banks found themselves unable to collect extra margin money from European stock purchasers. Thus brokers were forced to sell out European accounts at large losses. The result, even before war was declared, was a threat to English bank liquidity.[144]

Worse was to follow. In July 1914, London financial institutions held bills of exchange (promises to pay for goods or services at some future date, 30, 60 or 90 days), worth about £350,000,000, a sum amounting to one-half the national debt in 1914 and many times the liquid resources of the banks and discount houses which owned them.[145] If the bills could not be collected when they fell due many ancient financial institutions would be bankrupt. A second problem was that the bills had been 'accepted' (i.e. guaranteed or insured) by 'acceptance houses', which were usually banks. Acceptance in effect authenticated, for a fee, the debtor's reliability and thus made the bill marketable. The primary claim by the holder of an overdue bill would be against its acceptor. But with the coming of the war many of those owing money on bills held in London, the financial capital of the world, were now the King's enemies. Hence the first English casualties of the war would be in the City of London.

The crisis began even before it was clear that Britain would be involved in the war. After the Austrian declaration of war on Serbia, European depositors in Britain's banks began withdrawing gold and simultaneously British banks began calling in gold from the Bank of England.[146] On 31 July, the Bank raised the discount rate from four to eight percent and on the same day, Friday, the governor, Walter Cunliffe, asked Lloyd George, as he was bound to do under the Bank Charter Act of 1844, to suspend gold payments entirely.[147] This necessitated a further rise in the discount rate to ten percent. That evening Lloyd George, Asquith, and the Bank's directors conferred, and dined at No. 10 Downing Street.[148]

By this time the crisis in the London discount market was apparent. Foreign creditors were selling bills due them in London and withdrawing the proceeds from Britain while delaying by every means, the payment of debts owed. Fortunately, the weekend of 1 to 3 August was the Bank Holiday. On Sunday, 2 August, after meeting with Reading, John Bradbury, and Sir George Paish, the editor of the *Statist*, the Chancellor was convinced that the City could be saved only by a moratorium on all debt payments, which was proclaimed that evening. The moratorium was made legal by a one clause measure, the Postponement of Payments Act, giving the Chancellor the power to declare a month's moratorium on the payment of all outstanding bills, which passed through all its stages in the House of Commons just before Grey's historic speech on the afternoon of 3 August.[149] Lloyd George spent most of the rest of the day of 3 August closeted in the Treasury making preparations for the moratorium. On Monday also, Lloyd George confirmed the announcement, made the night before, that the Bank Holiday would continue until Friday, 7 August, although for banks only, not other businesses.

On Wednesday, 5 August, before the banks reopened, during the debate on the first war credit, Lloyd George announced the details of the system of the modified gold exchange standard which he proposed to institute on Friday, and which indeed governed British specie circulation until the restoration of full convertibility in 1925. Banks would redeem paper currency in gold only at their own discretion, which, for practical purposes, meant that they would not redeem it at all. In order to replace this contraction of the circulating medium and to replace the now disappearing gold sovereign, he announced, also, the creation of new £1 and 10s notes, issued not by the Bank of England, but by the Treasury, and signed therefore not by the Governor of the Bank but by John Bradbury, Secretary to the Treasury. (The smallest bank note was for £5.) These, although fully legal tender, were ugly little bits of paper, printed on one side only and were immediately christened 'Bradburys'. They were, in fact, technically exchangeable for gold, but only by a personal appearance in the lobby of the Bank of England as agent for the Treasury. As the submarine menace soon made insurance for the private export of gold prohibitively expensive, to this extent Lloyd George, although he insisted otherwise, had taken Britain effectively, if not legally, off the gold standard.[150] When the banks reopened the next day the discount rate was reduced to five percent. Ten percent had never been necessary. Enquiries to the large clearing banks on Friday, 7 August, produced reports that business was back to normal.[151] 'My arrangements to save a financial panic have been a complete success,' Lloyd George wrote to Maggie that evening, '— a real triumph — the first great British victory of the war.'[152]

Thus in the first week of August British banks had been secured from the panic of their depositors and the London acceptance houses from the collapse of the bill collection system. But much of the machinery of international trade financing, the City's life blood, had been brought to a halt. The problem now was to start it again as quickly as possible. One difficulty derived from the fact that the merchant banks were themselves large owners of bills of exchange, having, at J.M. Keynes's estimate, as much as £125,000,000, or fifteen percent of their assets, tied up in these instruments which now were unmarketable because of the moratorium.[153] The first step to re-establish bank liquidity, announced after parliament recessed (parliament recessed from 10 to 25 August), came on 12 August. It allowed the Bank of England, with contingent support from the Treasury, to rediscount, in effect to buy, any pre-moratorium accepted bill. The Bank would discount at bank rate and would allow the acceptor to postpone payment on unredeemed bills for an interest charge of two percent over bank rate.[154] The possible losses could not be estimated, but it might save the whole trade of the country, wrote J.A. Pease in amazement after Lloyd George announced it to the Cabinet.[155] Thus the banks and discount houses were relieved of their frozen assets, but the accepting houses, after their flirtation with catastrophe, were reluctant to underwrite new business. Hence the final step, on 5 September, lay in permitting the Bank of England to guarantee funds to a select group of acceptors for paying off post-moratorium bills unredeemed at maturity.[156] The final accounting would be postponed until after the war. This, of course, involved the Bank, and ultimately the state, in a financial commitment of unknown size for an indefinite term. Asquith's nervousness was evident in his letter to the King when the plan was approved in Cabinet. 'It was, after much discussion, agreed to approve, in principle, a scheme under which the Bank of England (backed by the credit of the State) and the joint stock banks [as opposed to private or "merchant" banks] (secured by the State up to the extent of fifty percent of their advances) would discount all foreign bills drawn upon and accepted by an approved list of financial houses.'[157] The final stages of this plan Lloyd George considered peculiarly his own and indeed it is difficult to imagine any of his predecessors, certainly not Asquith, persuading the Bank of England to enter, on a regular basis as opposed to an emergency basis, the wholesale bill discount market.

The saving of the City may have been in fact one of Lloyd George's greater wartime achievements. Walter Runciman, not usually one of Lloyd George's warmest friends, told the Cabinet on 21 August when Lloyd George was absent with a cold, that the Chancellor's quick mastery of international finance was little short of marvelous.

> He knew nothing originally of commerce and trade, bills of lading or of exchange, holders, drawers, acceptors, had no meaning for him. Not withstanding all of this he has mastered these problems and captivated the bankers and the measures taken have been wise, prudent and far seeing.[158]

Lloyd George's own pride was evident in a letter to William on the day that the Bank of England discount program began. 'I have launched my great scheme,' he wrote

> — the boldest financial experiment any Government ever launched. Harold Webb helped. I went to Walton so as to think over it alone in that exhilarating air. Just received a letter signed by the Rothschilds congratulating me on the way I tackled the greatest difficulty that has ever occurred in the finances of this country. Then they go on 'You surveyed the situation with a masterly eye, you solved the same with a masterly hand, so pray accept our warmest congratulations.' PM told me it was the greatest success that Government had yet scored.[159]

Maynard Keynes himself roundly applauded the 'sense' of the Treasury and the 'courage' of the Bank, which he may have overestimated. But the payments crisis, he said, was genuine and very serious. 'The Minister and his civil servants stood alone,' he concluded, 'and had the courage that the country required.'[160] By the end of October the emergency had receded. The Government (War Obligations) Act, at the end of November, legalized the high-handed but necessary actions of the Chancellor of the Exchequer, and the Bank, in fact, lost little money on the bills it rediscounted.

During these weeks Lloyd George had been closeted almost continually with Treasury officials and bankers. Neither the general public nor, indeed, his colleagues had seen much of him.[161] He had not attended the great War Councils on 5 and 6 August when Brigadier Sir Henry Wilson, against the advice both of the new Secretary of State for War, Herbert, Lord Kitchener, and the Commander in Chief of the British Expeditionary Force, Sir John French, bullied the government into adhering to the original plan he had outlined to the Committee on Imperial Defence on 23 August 1911. So the tiny British Army was ordered to deploy before Maubeuge and thus was thrown, not neatly on the right flank of a German force advancing toward Paris, but directly into the path of two entire German armies.

The Chancellor corresponded with Redmond, Dillon and O'Connor who pleaded with him to insure that the government allow the Home Rule to go on the statute books even if its effect was suspended for the duration of the war.[162] On 25 August, to the Cabinet's consternation, Churchill proposed the institution of military conscription. After a half hour's speech on the subject, he was squelched by Asquith and, surely to his later regret, by Lloyd George, who argued jointly that there was no need for compulsory service at the moment.[163] So on the day the Belgian fortress of Namur fell, precipitating the British retreat from Mons, the Cabinet, with Lloyd George participating, passed off in less than an hour the opportunity to take early control of the most intractable problem of the war, the allocation of manpower. However, a few days later, after the Cabinet had wrestled for weeks with the question of press censorship and the maintenance of the news supply from the front, Lloyd George drew his colleagues' attention to the differences between military security and the need for a continuous supply of positive favorable news which would, as Asquith reported to the King, 'inform and influence public opinion abroad and...confute German mis-statements and sophistries.' Charles Masterman was assigned to look into the matter. So was founded what would become eventually the highly successful Ministry of Information.[164]

Meanwhile, Lloyd George was putting pressure on Kitchener to permit the organization of a Welsh army corps, in which he partly succeeded. However, he was in no hurry to see his sons, Richard and Gwilym, go to France.[165] Eventually Gwilym became an aide to Brigadier Ivor Philipps, Commander of the 38th (Welsh) Division, and Richard, who had begun to work for Lord Cowdray, went into the Royal Engineers.

The promotion of a Welsh army corps provided the occasion for one of Lloyd George's most famous and most important speeches, at Queen's Hall, which marked the end of the unusual silence he had maintained since the beginning of hostilities with Germany and which may be designated as his personal declaration of war. Riddell, who with Simon and Reading, dined at No. 11 on 19 August in the midst of the City crisis, had told Lloyd George that the time had come for him to make a major patriotic address telling the nation why it was at war. Lloyd George, who usually thought well of Riddell's opinions on publicity matters, grumbled that he did not feel like speaking.[166] Nonetheless, three weeks later, in the midst of the First Battle of the Marne, he reported to Maggie that he was working on 'a rattling good speech — at least I think so — for the Queen's Hall Saturday week.'[167] The speech was to be aimed specifically at the London Welsh community whom he hoped to inspire to enlist in large numbers in a Welsh brigade.[168] A strong response to his call for men would be proof to Kitchener that an appeal for Welsh recruits could be made on a national basis. He noted in a letter to Maggie, written on the day of the speech, that he was conferring with the Chairman of the meeting, Lord Plymouth, Lord Lieutenant of Glamorganshire, about a Welsh army contingent.[169]

The Queen's Hall speech, on Saturday afternoon, 19 September, therefore, was an important occasion for Lloyd George. He had to make an impression, but it would be a difficult audience. There would be many Englishmen present and many prosperous, satisfied, Anglicized Welshmen, 'layers of fat' he would have to talk through.[170] Although he was ordinarily tense before any public address, his nervousness on this occasion was pronounced and noticed. 'He said he was miserable and inert. His brain would not work,' wrote George Riddell on 18 September. 'He was terribly nervous, feeling, he said as if he were about to be executed,' said Riddell the next day as the two men waited at Riddell's house in Queen Anne's Gate for the three o'clock hour to come. 'It was a curious sight to see him lying on the sofa, yawning and stretching himself in a state of high nervous excitement.'[171]

Yet when the time came the speech was a blazing success. Lord Plymouth, who had heard only a few weeks before that his son had died of wounds on 26 August, read Kipling's charge to the nation:

> There is but one task for all —
> One life for each to give
> What stands if Freedom fall?
> Who dies if England live?[172]

The audience responded by standing to sing 'March of the Men of Harlech'. Lloyd George forwent his customary jokes at the opening of his address. Instead, leaning rather forward and speaking slowly and gravely, he began:

> There is no man who has always regarded the prospect of engaging in a great war with greater reluctance and greater repugnance than I have done through all my political life. There is no man more convinced that we could not have avoided it without national dishonour.

He repeated the now standard story of the violation of Belgium: without the German challenge of the invasion of Belgium, Britain would never have declared war. The sole cause was this assault upon her international honor.

> Why is our honour as a country involved in this war? Because we are bound by an honourable obligation to defend the independence, the liberty, the integrity of a small nation that has lived peaceably, but she could not have compelled us because she was weak. The man who declines to discharge his debt because his creditor is too poor to enforce it is a blackguard.

Germany, of course, had called the Guarantee Treaty of Belgium a scrap of paper.

> Have you any of those neat little Treasury £1 notes about you? If you have, burn them; they are only scraps of paper. What are they made of? Rags. What are they worth? The whole credit of the British Empire. The machinery of commerce is moved by Bills of Exchange. I have seen some of them — wretched, crinkled, scrawled over, blotched, frowsy — and yet these wretched little scraps of paper move great ships, laden with thousands of tons of precious cargo from one end of the world to the other. What was the motive power behind them? The honour of commercial men. Treaties are the currency of international statesmanship.

He insisted he would not say a single word in disparagement of the German people. They were a grand people and had great qualities of head, hand and heart, but they did not understand Britain. They could understand why France and Russia went to war, for territory, but not Britain. The Kaiser taught them that he was the vice regent of God. 'There has been nothing like it since Mahomet.' It was 'lunacy', Lloyd George exclaimed. (D.R. Daniel, in the audience and already beginning to sever his ties with Lloyd George, found this reference most offensive. 'I could hardly go on sitting in my seat,' he wrote, noting that the passage was cut out of the published versions of the speech.)[173] The Kaiser exemplified the Prussian Junker, 'the roadhog of Europe'.

> They think we cannot beat them. It will not be easy. It will be a long job; it will be a terrible war; but in the end we shall march through terror to triumph. We shall need all our qualities — every quality that is Britain and its people possess — prudence in council, daring in action, tenacity, in purpose, courage in defeat, moderation in victory; in all things faith. . .
>
> Wales must continue doing her duty. . .I should like to see a Welsh Army in the field. I should like to see the race that faced the Norman for hundreds of years in a struggle for freedom, the race that helped to win Crecy, the race that fought for a generation under Glendower against the greatest captain in Europe — I should like to see that race give a good taste of its quality in this struggle in Europe; and they going to do it.

Finally came the peroration, calling the democracy to duty, but containing also a hint of the theme that would become the staple of his speeches as the conflict moved toward its close: equality of sacrifice and a better world, the 'new patriotism'.

> I see a new recognition amongst all classes, high and low, shedding themselves of selfishness — a new recognition that the honour of the country does not depend merely on the maintenance of its glory in the stricken field, but also in protecting its homes from distress. It is a new patriotism which is bringing a new outlook over all classes. The great flood of luxury and sloth which had submerged the land is receding, and a new Britain is appearing. We can see for the first time the fundamental things that matter in life and that have been obscured from our vision by the tropical growth of prosperity.

> *   *   *   *

> May I tell you a simple parable what I think this war is doing for us? I know a valley in North Wales between the mountains and the sea. It is a beautiful valley, snug, comfortable, sheltered by mountains from all the bitter blasts. But it is enervating, and I remember how the boys were in the habit of climbing the hill above the village to have a glimpse of the great mountains in the distance, and to be stimulated and freshened by the breezes which came from the hilltops, and by the spectacle of their grandeur. We have been living in a sheltered valley for generations. We have been too comfortable and too indulgent — many, perhaps, too selfish — and the stern hand of fate has scourged us to an elevation where we can see the great everlasting things that matter for a nation — the great peaks we had forgotten, of Honour, Duty, Patriotism, and clad in glittering white, the great pinnacle of Sacrifice, pointing like a rugged finger to heaven. We shall descend into the valleys again; but as long as men and women of this generation last, they will carry in their hearts the image of those great mountain peaks whose foundations are not shaken, though Europe rock and sway in the convulsions of a great war.[174]

119

There was, of course, prolonged cheering, some attempts to begin a song, and more to the point, a movement toward enlistment stations which had been set up outside the hall. However, Lloyd George was depressed as he drove to Walton Heath with Frances Stevenson that evening.[175] He was disgusted with his speech and disgusted with the complaisant audience. But Sunday, the papers described it as a triumph. It was printed in pamphlet form, translated into many languages, and distributed throughout the world. It became Britain's first great propaganda success. Hodder Williams reported a month later they had distributed one half million copies in the British colonies alone, remarking also that they had hoped at this time to be giving instead a little dinner to celebrate the final volume of the land report.[176] Lloyd George was deluged with congratulations not only, as he noted cheerfully, from the usual people but from experienced journalists like J.A. Spender, Henry Lucy and Robertson Nicoll.[177] The Prime Minister noted the address in a letter to Venetia Stanley, a thing he rarely did except when a speech by one of his colleagues displeased him, which was often. Nonetheless Lloyd George determined that his future recruiting speeches in Wales must attract genuine Welsh audiences, quarrymen, agricultural laborers, the artisans of Caernarvonshire and Anglesey. He wanted a genuine Welsh atmosphere and warned he would not share a platform with an English speaker.[178]

The Queen's Hall address represents a genuine departure in Lloyd George's career. Beside announcing his now unequivocal and single minded support for the war, it showed he had emerged from the wilderness into which the land campaign had taken him and was again a national leader. Moreover, unlike the other major efforts of his political maturity, the Newcastle speech, Limehouse or Bedford, the previous fierce partisanship was gone.[179] He had, perhaps for the first time, addressed the nation. As for so many of his countrymen, 1914, the *anno belli*, opened a chasm across his career. This was clearly a new Lloyd George. Never, at least since the Mansion House address, observed *The Times* on 21 September, has he 'spoken so clearly for us all'.

3 The New War: The Search for Weapons and for Alternative Fronts

As it was bound to do, the war changed, effectively and permanently, the course of Lloyd George's career, and that of millions of other Britons. But whereas it destroyed hundreds of thousands of his fellow countrymen in body or spirit, the war carried Lloyd George to the highest office in the land. Similarly Herbert Asquith became a casualty as surely as did his adored son Raymond, who fell at the Somme. The war's immediate effect, already described, was to force Lloyd George out of the area of his experience as Chancellor of the Exchequer, first of all into the exotic field of international finance and bill brokering. Here of course he had astonished everyone with his facility for the quick comprehension of the principles, if not the details, of a very intricate business. But soon, by mid-September, after the crisis in the City was resolved, he began to worry about the broader aspects of the conduct of the conflict in France, the choice of theaters of operation and the supply of munitions, and in fact the treatment of Germany after her defeat.

This latter concern to which he would return more and more frequently until the Armistice in 1918 seems to have proceeded from the idealism expressed in the Queen's Hall speech. Toward the end of November, 1914 he remarked in Cabinet that he hoped Germany would not be stripped of all her colonies after the war, 'an issue', Charles Hobhouse recorded 'everyone avoided replying to.'[1] More elaborately he commissioned his patronage secretary, William Sutherland, to put together a memorandum on the state of politics at the end of the war. This document is of considerable interest although one cannot of course be sure of its effect upon Lloyd George. Nonetheless it contains a phrase which Lloyd George adopted virtually as a slogan four years later. The politicians, Sutherland wrote, must give the returning soldier 'a land that was worth fighting for'.[2]

More immediately the gigantic problems of munitions and strategy, of where the war would be fought and with what, form a continuing theme in the story of Lloyd George's life between 1914 and 1918. It is necessary to state here only that Lloyd George's involvement in the procurement of arms and ammunition began long before his appointment to the Ministry of Munitions in May of 1915. He seems to have perceived, sooner than anyone, certainly sooner than the War Office and its Master General of the Ordnance, Stanley Von Donop, that the war in which Britain was involved and the war that it was prepared to fight based upon the lessons of South Africa, were as different as was the mud of Flanders from the windswept high veldt of the Transvaal. Haldane's reforms between 1906 and 1912, meticulous as they had been, had left the British army desperately unready. The army therefore needed not only to be greatly expanded, but almost totally re-armed. To this end the Chancellor undertook, still in the autumn of 1914, to investigate the possibility of munitions purchases in the United States, beginning a connection of prodigious, and increasingly vexatious, importance. His concern for military strategy evolved from his realization very early in the war that the front in Belgium and France had stabilized, that battlefield tactics had descended to something resembling siege warfare, and that this situation was unlikely to change. For him the obvious conclusion was the mounting of an attack at some other point in the Central Powers citadel. These proposals, as will be discussed, were refined as the war progressed to include a centralized battlefield command, a generalissimo who would be charged with looking at the perimeter around the Central Powers as a whole and whose commission would be to probe for the weakest point, not only between the Swiss border and the English Channel but between Heligoland and the Persian Gulf. The logic of Lloyd George's argument, endlessly re-iterated in his war memoirs, was that the Allies, by abandoning the strategic initiative, threw away the priceless advantage of command of the seas. The Germans on the other hand had to win the war in France by defeating the French army and driving the French nation from the war, or by pushing the British into the sea, as German commanders, Generals Falkenhayn and Ludendorff, certainly understood. But the Allies did not need to conduct the war on terms dictated by the enemy, especially as the Germans, with interior lines of transport, and fighting on enemy territory had the option, which the Allies and particularly the French never possessed or were never willing to use, of tactical withdrawal from untenable positions.

All of this then became the burden of Lloyd George's endless conflict with the military hierarchy which began in 1914 and continued until the removal of Sir William Robertson as Chief of the Imperial General Staff (C.I.G.S.) in 1918. It is wrong to describe him as an 'Easterner' in strategy. A better term would be perhaps an 'Anti-Westerner', a seeker for the indirect approach. These opinions of course were instinctive in him and simply confirmed his usual behavior in politics. He displayed as the war progressed, greater and greater degrees of angry frustration after conversations with generals who seemed unable to grasp the logical clarity of his ideas and who insisted on concentrating every man and gun in northern France.

Finally, the strain and pressures of the war altered, in some cases per-manently, most of Lloyd George's old political associations and connections. The Welsh radical supporters of whom the most important were D.R. Daniel, W. Llewelyn Williams and Beriah Evans turned against him, although he continued to see occasionally Herbert Lewis, who became Parliamentary Secretary to the Board of Education in 1916 and Vincent Evans who became Sheriff of Merionethshire in 1919 and a Companion of Honour in 1922. Nonetheless, even with the Whitsun holidays in Criccieth, the Welsh connec-tion practically disappeared during the war. His home, as George Riddell's and Frances Stevenson's diaries show, was the house built for him on Walton Heath golf course in Surrey. Here he retreated on every possible occasion, to the point, after he became Prime Minister, of requiring Cabinet ministers and generals to journey through south London and the suburbs to confer with him.

At Westminster the change in mood and the decline of Cabinet collegiality were even more immediate and apparent. Some of this altered temper resulted from Churchill's already well-known headstrong determination to have his own way. To be engaged in a great war with the control of the navy in his hands intoxicated Churchill and his recklessness quickly brought trouble for the government. But for Lloyd George the greatest change from the peacetime milieu to which he was accustomed, bringing a clash of personalities with a man of a sort he had never known before, came from the appointment to the War Office on 5 August 1914 of Horatio Herbert, Earl Kitchener.

I

It would not be too much to say that for the next seventeen months, to the end of 1915 when his power was reduced, Kitchener, and the War Office and military effort he represented, were the center of Lloyd George's political activity and the focus of most of his anger and exasperation. However, the battle with the generals and its corollary the battle with the newspapers, which began with the appearance of Kitchener and continued unabated after the latter's death, provided a continuing story of British politics during the war.

In August 1914 Lord Kitchener was Britain's senior Field Marshal on active duty. The winner of the battle of Omdurman in 1898, which secured the Sudan for Britain, and for practical purposes the victor in the war against the Boers, he had served successively as Governor General of the Sudan, Commander in Chief in India, and since 1911 as the British agent and Consul General, in effect the Governor, in Egypt. To the public he was, as his appearance confirmed, the incarnation of the power, indeed the majesty, of the British Empire. But more than that, and in the end disastrously for the principles of civilian control of the military, Kitchener's appointment, immensely popular as it was, represented a specific admission of the infallibility of the military. It seemed to show that the war was a soldier's business only, and that the exercise of political control in the usual way constituted, as the newspapers soon styled it, interference.

Such was the long term result, but Kitchener brought more immediate problems. As a man of 64, already at the pinnacle of his profession, immensely popular but with no political ambitions whatever, in fact rather despising politicians, he was not simply a difficult Cabinet colleague; he was an impossible one. He declined to share information on the conduct of his office. He declined to participate in the highest function of Cabinet government: the coordination, or the blending, of the activities of one's own department with other ministries so that a coherent policy might emerge. Yet he could not be disciplined in the ordinary way by translation to a lesser office. He could resign and his resignation, he well understood, would cause more pain to the Liberal administration than to himself. By making Kitchener Secretary of State for War, Asquith, on his own initiative but with the enthusiastic support of everyone, had created a glittering political monster who neither could be controlled nor killed.

The problem was that this decorative exemplar of military arts, even had he been more amenable, was by no means the ideal man to preside over the unlimited expansion and re-equipping of the British Army. Kitchener was essentially a quartermaster as his friend for many decades, Lord Esher, makes clear.[3] He was steady and methodical. He loved rounding up stores, rolling stock and weapons, adding columns. Figures were living realities which told the truth, as opposed to politicians, who did not. In this way, by meticulous, elaborate and economical preparation, he had won the wars in the Sudan and South Africa. But he could not plan for a war in which the answer to all supply questions was the demand for immediate and unlimited amounts of everything.

Kitchener's greatest weakness, which indeed he understood himself, lay in his ignorance of the country whose martial virtues he so splendidly symbolized. He knew nothing of trade unions, non-conformity, or commerce. Indeed he really had very little knowledge of the British Army Haldane had created and despised what he knew.[4] This unworldliness, combined with a disinclination to confide in the Cabinet and an inability to delegate authority, made him, from Lloyd George's point of view, almost impossible to work with. Withal, when not angry or exasperated, Lloyd George rather liked him. He was almost pathetically eager to learn about England and could render decisions, and act upon them, in a moment.[5]

With his arrival in the Cabinet, evidently on 10 August 1914 at his second attendance, Kitchener set the course of Britain's participation in the war and committed the nation to the massive military effort over which Lloyd George eventually had to preside. As this decision was arguably the most important single determination in twentieth-century British history, it merits a brief discussion.[6] In all of the controversy that had raged since the Agadir crisis concerning the firmness and the extent of Britain's commitment to aid France, no one had questioned the size of the British Expeditionary Force. The BEF consisted of six infantry divisions and one cavalry division. The Territorials would remain at home to guard against invasion. All of this was based upon the assumption, which obtained both among the Allies and the Central Powers, that the war would be short, that it would be fought largely with resources available at its outbreak, and that its course would be a battle or a series of battles and then a peace. This had been the story of the Franco-Prussian and Russo-Japanese wars. Britain would have neither the time nor the need to raise a mass army on a continental scale. Kitchener, by what process of logic he never revealed, decided otherwise and announced at the Cabinet of 10 August that the war would last at least three years with many cataclysmic battles and that Britain must be engaged on a scale proportionate to her power.[7] He intended to begin by activating twenty-four divisions.[8]

The Cabinet sat in stunned but assenting silence. Clearly there was no discussion. Asquith does not mention this statement in his letter to the King sent after the next day's meeting.[9] So without a word the government overthrew two centuries of British military tradition and agreed to demand an unlimited mobilization of the nation and its resources. But for this there were no plans, nor at the moment even ideas. Kitchener himself clearly had none. The man who realized first the meaning of the new obligation and who set about trying to fulfill it was David Lloyd George.[10]

The fight for munitions, always with the parallel preoccupation of a search for an alternative strategy to concentration in France, would occupy Lloyd George at least until he became Prime Minister, by which time the quest for weapons became instead a struggle for manpower. The search for weapons began early in October, as an argument with Lord Kitchener in the Cabinet as to whether, unbelievably, a potential shortage of military supplies existed.[11] Through August and most of September Lloyd George, busy with the City financial crisis and toward the end of August ill with a cold, attended few Cabinets. By the time he returned Kitchener had settled into what would be his customary posture toward his colleagues: a gruff assertion that everything was well in hand, that he needed no advice, and that he would furnish no information. Kitchener was by this time, however, pressing Grey to procure Portugal's entrance into the war, not because he cared anything for Portuguese troops but because her army had a rather large amount of modern artillery that he hoped to appropriate. Portugal declared war on Germany on 27 November 1914.[12] Even though Britain was committed to a mass army and a three years war at his determination, Kitchener was remarkably short sighted.

'The W.O., K. seem unable to look forward more than six months in the matter of [munitions] requirements' wrote Charles Hobhouse on 8 October. 'They were only prepared to order 400 guns, and it was all LG's insistence alone which induced them to say 650 and this is not half enough. K. refused to take the extra 20,000 Canadians [soldiers], and is very unwilling to order any military supplies from America.'[13] 'K. is still very obdurate about the sufficiency of supplies,' wrote Hobhouse the next day. 'He is most difficult to persuade that they are now likely to be short next July, and then we will not be able to improvise. Ed. Gray [sic] and Ll.G., accordingly combined to force him to agree to an investigation.'[14]

The investigation here mentioned became a committee, finally appointed on 11 October, consisting of Kitchener, Churchill, Haldane and Lloyd George with some others, to look into munitions production. Lloyd George states in his war memoirs that he asked for a committee in September but after objections by Kitchener Asquith had refused one.[15] In any case during this period the Cabinet was entirely preoccupied by the fate of the B.E.F. in France and Lloyd George was rarely in attendance. As it turned out the committee met only six times between 12 October 1914 and the beginning of 1915, but Lloyd George's work here is of importance. With his membership on the committee he began to investigate sources for munitions supply in the United States, and, as always, wanting to see for himself, he made his first visit to the front, vastly changing his perspective of the war.

The trip to France officially was justified as an inspection of that nation's facilities for the production of munitions, but of the three days abroad, 17 through 19 October, only one was spent in Paris.[16] Lloyd George received his most impressive lesson in Amiens at the headquarters of General Edouard de Castelnau, commander of France's Northern Army. From General Castelnau Lloyd George appears to have first apprehended the true nature of modern battle. Instead of the Napoleonic war of movement, the Germans and French were locked in a great siege operation. Mobility, cavalry and the famous French 75mm cannon, counted for little. Lloyd George was clearly much impressed by Castelnau himself and by the general's information.[17] He told the Cabinet of him, and used what he had learned at length in an important lecture to the House of Commons in April 1915 on the realities of the new war.[18] Before 1914, he said, British strategy had been based upon a great navy and a small but efficient army. No party, some individuals but no party, suggested anything else. At that time no one ever proposed that the BEF should be more than six divisions. He noted, praising Lord Kitchener, that Britain now had six times as many men in the field adding, with some exaggeration, that they were all fully equipped.

But all of this was for another war. When he was in France, he continued, he had met a French general who told him that everything was completely changed. The general had said:

> The surprise of this War has been the amount of ammunition which we have had to expend. Artillery ammunition, I mean, not small arms ammunition. The ordinary ideas of strategy were that after three or four weeks of manoeuvering you would have a great battle and that battle might occupy a fortnight or three weeks, and, of course, there would be a very great expenditure of ammunition; and we thought that after that one or the other of the parties would have been defeated. There would have been a retreat, a reconstruction, and the other army would have advanced, and perhaps after another month's time, we would have another great fight. But for seventy-nine days and nights my men have been here fighting, and firing has gone on almost night and day by the great cannon.

'I have marched my men from Lorraine to Normandy and they have been fighting incessantly. . .and they are still fighting,' Castelnau had added as Lloyd George recorded in his memoirs.[19] 'In the recent two weeks around Neuve Chapelle almost as much artillery ammunition was used as in two and three quarter years of the Boer War,' Lloyd George concluded, 'and what was needed was not shrapnel but high explosive.'[20]

It must be emphasized that this conversation had occurred on 19 October 1914 when some men were still expecting the war to be over by Christmas and many, far more expert than Lloyd George, looked for a victory by the middle of 1915.[21] Lloyd George believed he now knew better and began immediately, and characteristically alone, a search for arms. Early in November he got in touch with Edward C. Grenfell, a City merchant banker and a partner in Morgan Grenfell, to propose that J.P. Morgan & Company act as an agent for the British government in the purchase of between 250,000 and 500,000 rifles in the United States. These would be manufactured by established United States firms, Remington or Winchester, or by others who would convert to the work, Singer Sewing Machine Company or International Harvester.[22]

Reaction from the War Office was immediate. On 12 November Lloyd George received a note from Major General Stanley Von Donop, Master General of the Ordnance, saying that he understood that Grenfell had received an order from Lloyd George to make enquiries about purchasing rifles in the United States and that he also understood that J.P. Morgan & Company was making enquiries. 'Some weeks ago', he continued, he had himself sent an officer to the United States to purchase rifles and was about to close a contract for 200,000, delivery to begin in July. Now there would be two separate British agencies competing. Should not Mr. Lloyd George tell Messrs. Morgan and Grenfell not to proceed and to turn everything over to the War Office?[23]

Von Donop's annoyance did not end with the note to Lloyd George. Simultaneously the War Office representative in New York, Lieutenant Bernard Smyth-Pigott, visited 23 Wall Street and there ordered the House of Morgan, evidently in somewhat peremptory terms, to end its interference with the war effort of the British Empire. Meanwhile E.C. Grenfell in London received a telephone call from Von Donop enjoining him to get out of the arms business. The result was a truly furious letter from Grenfell to Lloyd George saying that neither he nor J.P. Morgan in New York were accustomed to such treatment, that they had offered to help only at Lloyd George's request, and they would now withdraw.[24] Obviously this was not a happy beginning, and so on the day he received Grenfell's letter, 13 November, Lloyd George hastened to see Kitchener. To his credit, the Secretary of State for War saw Lloyd George's point, and admitted the War Office was absolutely mistaken and that Von Donop's interventions were unauthorized. The next day he personally apologized to Grenfell. But he reminded Lloyd George that 200,000 rifles already ordered would strain Remington's and Winchester's facilities to the limit and that if Lloyd George were to proceed he should get in touch with Morgan again to see what alternative facilities could be found.

Despite Kitchener's understanding help, the real powers in the War Office were as obstructive as ever. Von Donop had already written to Rufus Isaacs, now Lord Reading, urging him to press Lloyd George to return to financial matters. He needed no further rifles beyond May 1915. 'We should hold our hand about further orders.' Lloyd George responded to this nine days later asking the Master General of the Ordnance whether he understood what he was saying. Since the original order was placed, parliament had sanctioned the enlistment of another 100,000 men.[25]

Lloyd George evidently had already seen an American, an H.O. Berg, one of many American promoters who had descended upon London since August, all of whom claimed to have extensive American contacts, knew all about weapons manufacture, and who were ready, for a fee, to open American industrial power to the British government. This suggestion was communicated by Grenfell to Morgan's who replied they were willing to forget about the previous insults and would look into weapons supply, but who warned that the Chancellor should stay away from Berg who was a disreputable man.[26] Not much had been accomplished so far, but the connection with Morgan's was established and, as important, the first step had been taken to deprive the War Office of its control of munitions supply.

Early in December Henry P. Davison, a Morgan partner, arrived in London with some other members of the firm and on 16 December Davison met Lloyd George, Asquith and Montagu at the Naval and Military Club for lunch. Here emerged what may have been in Lloyd George's mind from the beginning: that Morgan's would not only contract for arms as the British government's agent, but, far more attractive for the bank, would arrange as well for the financing of purchases.[27]

Out of the Naval and Military Club meeting, and after some further conversations with the Army Council, came the great contract signed on 15

January 1915 naming Morgan's 'Commercial Agents' for His Majesty's Government. Morgan's would use their 'best endeavours' to obtain the best quality, prices, discounts, and rebates, for their employers in the purchase of arms. For this Morgan's would receive a two percent commission on the first £10 million of goods purchased and one percent thereafter.[28] This simple document of less than half a dozen pages which would not be sufficient today to buy a used automobile became the basis of a huge and increasingly complex financial and military relationship. Its terms show that at the beginning of 1915 no one foresaw the size of the American-British armament effort nor, more important, the effect on Britain after the war of the mortgaging of its vast financial holdings overseas. Lloyd George does not mention his initiative in establishing the connection with Morgan's in his *War Memoirs* although two long chapters of the first volume are devoted to 'the fight for munitions', meaning generally the fight with the War Office. Nor does he make it clear that his antagonist usually was Von Donop. Kitchener, in these early months, was frequently helpful.

Kitchener was willing to learn and his very genuine confidence in himself and his position made it easy for him to give way when he was proven wrong. But part of his weakness lay in the fact that his entire experience derived from a life of contact with professional soldiers only. He knew nothing of the background, motivations, or interests of the hundreds of thousands of young men whom patriotism, since the beginning of August, had brought under his command, men who had no desire to remain in the army and who thought of soldiering entirely in terms of fighting while being impatient about training and discipline. Nor did Kitchener realize that the expansion of the army into millions made its opinions a political force to which democratically elected politicians had to listen. Military-political views were no longer the preserve of a handful of retired colonels.

These factors resulted in a series of fierce Cabinet battles toward the end of October which brought Kitchener several times close to resignation before he had been in office three months. For the historian they have some importance, first because most of the time Lloyd George was the spokesman for the anti-Kitchener group, but second, because Churchill, through his own rash intemperance, had become so unpopular both with his colleagues and the world of politics generally, that there was a danger he would have to be removed. Thus Asquith's administration, at the beginning of a great war, would have lost both its war ministers. In fact, the first dispute with Kitchener was relatively mild and occurred immediately after Lloyd George's return to the Cabinet. It involved the appointment of non-conformist chaplains. Kitchener had not realized that such persons were necessary, however he acceded with good grace. Lloyd George reported that the Field Marshal had asked him to write down the names of these mysterious sects so that he could investigate them and he reported after a few days 'do you know, I've discovered a dozen new religions'.[29]

The second, really also a minor affair, was more dangerous. It concerned entertainments and diversions for troops in the evening, a matter becoming especially important as shelter for many men was still improvised and winter was coming on. J.A. Pease, President of the Board of Education, was assigned to chair a committee to look into this. Kitchener exploded that he did not need advice, whereupon Pease went to Asquith who wrote to Kitchener. Kitchener shouted in the Cabinet that he would brook no interference and would resign. The Prime Minister was appalled at his anger.[30] This small matter soon merged into a larger concern. Lloyd George had sought, as always, to use the war to emphasize Welsh identity. The Queen's Hall speech on 19 September was, for practical purposes, the beginning of the campaign to summon the Welsh to remember their obligations in the defense of small nations. In the next few weeks Lloyd George made several speeches in Wales and Welsh enlistments, handled by a committee under Lord Plymouth, who had been chairman at Queen's Hall, had indeed risen out of proportion to the rest of the United Kingdom. Immediately there were problems. Evidently in the third week of October he discovered that Welsh recruits had been forbidden to speak the language not only on duty but in their billets. This evoked an angry letter followed by a conciliatory reply from the Director General of the Territorial Forces. The culprit, apparently a single commanding officer, had been ordered to desist.[31]

Nonetheless, the necessary changes did not occur, for on 27 October Lloyd George wrote again, this time to Kitchener, not mentioning his previous letter, but saying that orders had been given in some camps forbidding Welsh *either* on parade or in billets. When he first heard of it, said Lloyd George, he 'thought it too incredibly foolish to be true'. But he found that it was true and he intended to raise it in the Cabinet. If this were done against Gaelic in the Highlands there would have been a mutiny.[32] The next day, 28 October, Lloyd George brought up in Cabinet, not the minor matter of the Welsh language, but the much larger question of general interference and discouragement by the War Office of his attempts to raise homogeneous Welsh divisions leading eventually to a Welsh Army Corps. Charles Hobhouse could hardly believe his ears.

> Lloyd George raised the recruitment of a Welsh Army Corps; the W.O. had only left Lord Plymouth and the committee raising it some 5,000 men out of 16,000 [in effect stealing the men after they had enlisted]. About 46,000 Welsh recruits enlisted before the W.A.C. was mooted, had been formed into 30 new units incorporated into other divisions, and the balance had been taken to maintain the three Welsh Regiments at the front. K. refused to form any of these units into the W.A.C. and was obstructive as possible. Ll.G. argued his case with skill and patience. K. saw no reason in grouping Welshmen together, etc. At long length Ll.G. told K. that he forgot he was not an autocrat but only one of a body of 20 equals, that his attitude showed his sterility of ideas and ignorance of British conditions and that he must expect and would get criticism of his doings. K. retorted that he was ready to be criticized and to retire if necessary, but he would tolerate no interference with his plan at the W.O. Everyone, even W.S.C. and Grey sided with Ll.G. and K. made us very angry by trying to laugh aside the argument. He got a great rebuff, which surprised and disgusted him, but did him good. The P.M. sat very silent.[33]

As may be surmised, through all this Asquith was in agony. He hated disputes in the Cabinet and even, as he remarked to Venetia Stanley, hostile questions in the House of Commons. He desired a quiet life, his bridge games every evening, his weekends at Walmer Castle, his May-September liaison with Miss Stanley, so long as he could remain Prime Minister. But now he had to take action. Kitchener, and one may imagine Lloyd George who used it as punctuation for his arguments, had threatened resignation. On 30 October he saw both the Secretary of State for War and the Chancellor and effected a compromise.[34] Lloyd George and Kitchener again were friends. That afternoon in the Cabinet J.A. Pease recorded in his diary that when Kitchener asked for extra money for kit expenses for officers' commissioned from the ranks, Lloyd George cheerfully agreed (perhaps suggested by Asquith). Kitchener, for his part agreed to a Welsh division.[35]

Later that day Lloyd George saw Kitchener. 'Look here!', Lloyd George declared to George Riddell, 'Kitchener is a big man. [Six days earlier he had described him to Riddell as a big figurehead, a good poster.] Nothing small or petty about him.'

> Yesterday he sent for me. He said, 'I have thought over what you said. There is a good deal of justification for those complaints. Tell me exactly what you want.' I said, 'That, that, that and that!' K. wrote an appropriate order against each item. He really acted extraordinarily well. (A favourite phrase with L.G.) Then he said, 'Whom would you like to place in command in North Wales?' I said, 'I really don't know, but I have a very clever Welsh officer with me now. He is outside. Colonel Owen Thomas.' Kitchener said, 'Have him in!' and rang the bell. Thomas came in. K. said, 'I remember you in South Africa. As from today you will be Brigadier-General Owen Thomas, but go and put on your uniform. Never let me see you in mufti again during the war!' 'Very dramatic!' added Lloyd George.[36]

Eventually a Welsh division, the 38th, came into existence, although General Owen Thomas did not command it at the front. The command eventually went to Major General Ivor Philipps, a Liberal Member of Parliament for Southampton since 1906, with Lieutenant Gwilym Lloyd George as his A.D.C.[37] (Remarkably Lloyd George recorded no interest in the activation of the Welsh regiment of the Brigade of Guards, which occurred at about the same time.)

For Lloyd George, the last five months of 1914 saw the final rupture of two important personal and political relationships, with Churchill and with Masterman. In both cases the breakdown in friendship was not entirely Lloyd George's responsibility, indeed these men eventually came to dislike Lloyd George far more than he disliked them. Yet he seems to have done little to try and mend the hostility, nor to warn either that their outrageous words and actions were turning the political world, not only Lloyd George, against them. Nonetheless the result, in the early months of 1915, was the apparent destruction of the political careers of two eccentric geniuses, each of whom had been for a time as close a friend as Lloyd George would ever have.

There is no evidence that he mourned the change. He rarely spoke of either man afterwards except to criticize, even when at considerable political risk he brought Churchill back into his government. But the change for Lloyd George was profound. He had no enduring senior allies among the

Liberals in the next two years, except paradoxically in Asquith himself. During the year at the Ministry of Munitions, he would continually lament that he was entirely alone. And his personal life became remarkably solitary. The visitors at Walton Heath were newspapermen whom he wanted to cultivate, low ranking MPs, frequently Conservative, for a short time the McKennas, who had a revival in the autumn of 1914 as Churchill declined, Reading, and Frances Stevenson and Sir George Riddell. Lloyd George's circle became during the war, and would remain until the end of his life, a collection of allies of convenience, those who worked for him, clients and cronies, but no comrades. 'There are', he was fond of saying, 'no friendships at the top.'

Of the two, the breach with Churchill was the more important although less dramatic. Lloyd George had known him for ten years. The two, equal in rank, both senior Cabinet members, seemed to be intimate friends. No one but Churchill, it should be repeated, called the Chancellor 'David'. Obviously during the budget struggle of 1914 relations between the two had cooled, but Lloyd George had refused to allow Churchill to be driven from the Cabinet and Churchill had loyally supported the Chancellor over Marconi when many Liberals would have been glad to see him go.

The war changed Churchill, or, perhaps more accurately, magnified hugely his egocentricity, his stubbornness, and his loquacity, characteristics that the Cabinet as a whole, including Lloyd George, had long found trying. Now he became intolerable. He gloried in his post as First Lord. He gloried in making history. He gloried in the war. It was a 'glorious delicious war', he told Margot Asquith.[38] The problem was that the navy's successes in the early months of the conflict — the safe passage of the army to France and the maintenance of trade — were undramatic. Its mistakes, the seizure on 1 August at Churchill's insistence of two battleships being built for Turkey by Vickers, which resulted immediately in strained relations, and the subsequent escape of the new and powerful German battle cruiser *Goeben* with attending small vessels into Turkish waters where the Turks allowed them to remain, were clear and visible.

Worse was Churchill's insensitivity and arrogance to his colleagues and to the political world in general.[39] Indeed Churchill's ordinary behavior, far more than any particular offensive act, seems to have turned Lloyd George, as well as others, against him. Of the man who had boasted only a few months earlier of his friendship with Lloyd George, Riddell records the Chancellor as saying that

> He cannot trust Winston — never knows what he may be up to and afraid to leave town for long for fear Winston may bring forward some dangerous plan. Does not approve Winston going to the fleet and says Admiralty Board very weak and too much under Winston's possessive thumb. I have seen a lot of McKenna lately. He hates Winston like poison and cannot conceal his feelings. He said to me the other day, 'He (Winston) is not really good. He is clever but not a man of action. He has made three bad mistakes lately (1) To seize the Turkish man of war (2) To let the *Goeben* slip through his fingers (3) Not to mine the German Coast immediately after our first ship was destroyed by German mines. He is an advertiser. I hate him. He treated me disgracefully. He fought my programme. He got my job and now without a word of

acknowledgement he is fighting with my ships — the very ships which would not have been built had he had his way.'[40]

Much of this of course was unfair. The escape of the *Goeben* from the Mediterranean to Constantinople in the first days of the war was only technically Churchill's fault. McKenna obviously had reasons of his own for hating the First Lord. Nonetheless in the anxious months of autumn of 1914, as the Cabinet struggled to adjust itself and the government to a war the dimensions of which it could not know, while buried in the reports of events it could scarcely follow, most of its members, including Lloyd George, who for years was one of his few Liberal friends, came to regard Churchill as a public menace.

The events of September were only a beginning. The trail of naval misfortune and Churchill's exuberant folly continued. On the day following the conversation recorded by Riddell quoted above, on 22 September, three armored cruisers, the *Aboukir, Hogue,* and *Cressy,* were sunk off the Dutch coast by a single submarine. The ships themselves were old, laid down at the turn of the century, but they carried 700 men each. Fourteen-hundred were lost.[41]

Less than two weeks later, on 3 October, Churchill disappeared to Antwerp. He was followed by some marines and two brigades of naval reservists armed as infantrymen, who were to stimulate the Belgians in the defense of their city. Although the strategic profit of an Allied retention of Antwerp would have been immense, Churchill's theatrical performance as an army commander caused true anger both inside and outside the Cabinet. Fewer than 60 were killed, but about 1500 were interned in the Netherlands for the duration of the war and 936 were taken prisoner by the Germans when the city fell on 9 October.

'Our greatest danger is incompetent English Junkers. Winston is becoming a great danger', said Lloyd George to Isaacs (now Lord Reading), Riddell and Mr. and Mrs. McKenna over tea at Walton Heath the next day.

McK: Yes the reports which came through of his doings at Antwerp were most flamboyant and evidently intended to create the impression that he was taking a prominent part in the proceedings. We suppress them at the [Press] Bureau.

Riddell: How did Winston come to go to Antwerp? Why did he take part in land operations? Was that not a matter for Kitchener?

LG: The decision was arrived at on Friday night [2 October]. The Cabinet could not be called together. Winston, Grey and Kitchener decided that Winston should go to Antwerp to endeavour to persuade the Belgians to defend the place.

R: But surely the Head of the Admiralty should remain at his post?

LG: Yes, he should. Owing to Winston's absence we might have lost the transports which were carrying the Seventh Division, one of the best in the Army. They were allowed to start notwithstanding the mine area. One actually went through it and was saved only by a miracle. Why it did not strike a mine we do not know. We have luckily been saved a most horrible disaster. There was no one to give orders. The Sea Lords are very weak and Prince Louis [of Battenburg, First Sea Lord] quite incompetent.[42]

McK: All Winston's great excursions have been most unfortunate. The Antwerp business is a repetition of Sydney Street.

LG: Yes, or the railway strike all over again. Winston then had a plan to shut the Welsh miners in their valleys by military cordon and starve them out. A mad plan! I shall never forget the remarkable scene which I witnessed at the Home Office. Winston with his generals and the plan of campaign. He is an extraordinary fellow — too wild and impulsive. He makes me very uneasy. His interference with land operations, or for that matter naval operations, is all wrong.

R: I hope Jellicoe [Admiral Sir John Jellicoe, Commander of the Grand Fleet] will not allow him to interfere.

McK: No, I think Jellicoe would not brook interference.

LG: I wonder whether Fisher ought not to return to the Board [of Admiralty].

McKenna, Riddell continued, did not think this advisable. Fisher was unpopular. He went on to blame Churchill again for the loss of the *Aboukir*, *Hogue* and *Cressy* which should not have been operating in the Narrow Sea.

Riddell asked why the Cabinet did not require the First Lord to remain in his office.

LG: Yes, but Winston is like a torpedo. The first you hear of his doings is when you hear the swish of the torpedo dashing through the water. He is very difficult to handle.

R: But why did not the Prime Minister object to the raising of Winston's army?

LG: I think he was amused.

R: The price is rather heavy even for the amusement of a Prime Minister. The stakes are too high.[43]

This conversation has been quoted at length as an illustration of the complete isolation of Churchill in the Cabinet by the beginning of the third month of the war. With Grey almost totally occupied in the Foreign Office, the two men with the most influence over Asquith on practical political matters were, in fact, Lloyd George and McKenna.

Meanwhile Asquith's amusement at Churchill's game of soldiering, if it had existed, had dissipated. On 13 October his third son, Arthur (Oc) who had been an officer in one of the naval brigade units at Antwerp, with three days of military experience behind him, came to London to explain to his father what had happened. 'Strictly between ourselves,' the Prime Minister wrote to Venetia Stanley who was a close friend of Clementine Hozier and indeed had been a bride's attendant at the Churchill's wedding, 'I can't tell you what I feel of the *wicked* folly of it all.'

> ...nothing can excuse Winston (who had all the facts) for sending in the two...Naval Brigades. I was assured that the recruits were all being

left behind and that the main body consisted of seasoned Naval Reserve men. As a matter of fact only about ¹/₄ were Reservists, and the rest were a callow crowd of the rawest tyros, most of whom had never fired off a rifle, while none of them had ever handled an entrenching tool. . .It was like sending sheep to the shambles.[44]

While he was at Antwerp Churchill pleaded with Asquith, twice and at length, to be allowed to leave the Admiralty for a major command in the field. He had, he told the Prime Minister, 'tasted blood'. It intoxicated him. 'His mouth waters at the sight of the thought of K's new army,' wrote Asquith.[45]

None of this should be understood to mean that Antwerp was not worth saving. Had it been rescued the Flanders coast would have remained in Allied hands and the course of the war both on land and sea decisively altered. Churchill, more quickly than the French and British commands, recognized this. It was well worth a determined effort by both the British and the French armies. Its loss was one of the great tactical failures of the war.

However, Churchill's belated and ill-organized excursion provoked little more than contempt, particularly in Lloyd George. His statements to Frances Stevenson and to C.P. Scott as well as the conversations with his colleagues and with Riddell already recorded betray a genuine personal aversion. There are repeated remarks about the First Lord's desire for glory, for self-promotion, of his high-handedness at the Admiralty which nonetheless resulted in a slack and 'muddled' administration. Churchill, Lloyd George told Riddell, was referred to as the 'Dundee Advertiser'.[46] Their battles in the Cabinet were violent.[47] But although usually they were reconciled, the upshot of it all was that when the government was reconstructed not a man among his former colleagues tried to save the First Lord. It was characteristic that he never seems to have understood, nor even apprehended, his unpopularity within the Cabinet.[48] Nonetheless it was not only the Conservatives who insisted upon Churchill's demotion although the man he blamed for his fall was Lloyd George.[49]

Lloyd George's breach with Charles Masterman was quick, tragic, final, and resulted in the complete destruction of Masterman's promising political career. Moreover even though Masterman attempted to mend his fences with Lloyd George afterwards, the Chancellor apparently never concerned himself about his former friend's well-being.[50] Masterman did not receive a coalition endorsement in the 1918 election and probably would have refused it. He was given no preferment in the next four years during which Lloyd George was Prime Minister. The two men had almost no contact with each other although Lloyd George attended Masterman's funeral after his premature death in 1927. In 1939, with Masterman gone more than a decade, Lloyd George denounced in the strongest terms to his secretary, A.J. Sylvester, the statement in W. Watkin Davies's newly published biography that Masterman had played a large part in the construction of national health insurance.[51]

Masterman's story must be told in some detail because the usual accounts, now that Masterman has become something of a hero for historians of the New Liberalism, usually depict his fall as simply another example of Lloyd George's faithlessness. Lloyd George could indeed be brutal to his friends, but Masterman's demise was not quite so simple and to a considerable extent was his own doing.

Masterman's strength and weakness was his pathological, almost physical, sensitivity to human misfortune. It made him the unique philosopher of the New Liberalism in that he not only undertook to define the task of the party in the reduction of economic adversity in books and in any number of brilliant essays — J.A. Hobson, L.T. Hobhouse, H.W. Massingham, and Harold and J.A. Spender and many others had done this — but that he alone had gone into active politics and reached Cabinet rank to carry the program forward. He and Morant had put together, and in the autumn of 1914 were managing, the gigantic and expensive machine of national health insurance while planning already for its expansion. He had given Lloyd George much expert help in the land clauses of the 1909 budget and in the planning of insurance. Earlier he had introduced his friend Winston Churchill to the Webbs and had presided over Churchill's brief engagement as a social reformer. He provided a solid link between Lloyd George and the frequently troublesome radical back bench of the 1906 generation of MPs. In effect the new Liberal program had benefited greatly from his presence. But he never learned, as Lloyd George never forgot, that the first task of a politician was to be elected. He could not manage a constituency. He was unseated on a petition in North West Ham after the December 1910 election on a charge not of fraud but of imperfectly kept financial records, in which expenses seemed, and only seemed, to have exceeded the legal limits because many checks had never been presented. This time a seat was quickly found for him in Bethnal Green where at the end of July 1911 he reduced a majority of 682 only seven months before, to 184 in a poll ten percent larger. Here as has been seen he was defeated on 19 February 1914 at a by-election after having been appointed to the Cabinet, and again three months later in a hotter contest, he was beaten more heavily at Ipswich. Since then he had remained in the Cabinet, but without a seat in the House of Commons.

Ipswich clearly crushed Masterman's self-confidence and spirit. An immediate result was the deterioration of his relationship with Lloyd George whom he blamed for the disaster. More important for the future, he developed a growing terror of electoral disappointments and a conviction that Lloyd George, the Liberal leadership, and the party at large, did not appreciate his talents. Worse he was unable to keep to himself this rather adolescent sense of persecution and insisted upon complaining about Lloyd George to anyone who would listen. As Lloyd George, Riddell and Masterman were at this time near neighbors on Walton Heath, Riddell's diary records the unhappy progression of events in some detail. With Lucy Masterman present, Charles Masterman poured out his frustration to Riddell over dinner on 1 November 1914.

LlG has great defects really. He really does not understand the working classes in the towns. He knows only the agricultural labourer. He thinks the mechanics want his insurance scheme. They don't. They hate it. Then again LlG is hated by the civil service. He works men to death then casts them aside. Look at Chalmers. [Sir Robert Chalmers became Permanent Secretary of the Treasury in 1911. In 1913 he resigned in disgust and was appointed Governor of Ceylon. He was succeeded by John Bradbury.] He was devoted to LlG and worked himself to death for him but LlG threw him over, humbled and disgraced him, because he had given decisions without LlG's sanction; decisions which he could not get LlG to make. He will never look at papers. Chalmers came to hate him. He used to call him 'that little Welsh cad'. The truth is the Welsh are a difference race from us. We might just as well try to be on friendly terms with a Red Indian. We cannot understand the Welsh. Now Winston is different. He is impulsive, dangerous, and unreliable, but he is a loyal friend. And so on, although Masterman described himself as Lloyd George's most intimate friend.

At a second dinner, a month later, again with Mrs. Masterman, Riddell wrote:

> Mr. and Mrs. Masterman say that LlG is not loyal to their friends if they are unsuccessful and instances Seely as a victim. Masterman says LlG is loyal only to the Welsh — to his own people. The truth is there are two points of view — the LlG point of view which insists upon efficiency before friendship and the Masterman, which places friendship first — a system which is productive of the most flagrant abuses of public life.[52]

Even if Masterman was a little drunk, most of the comments on both Lloyd George and Churchill are clearly accurate. The disorderliness of Lloyd George's work habits, his bad treatment of subordinates, his failure to make and keep friends, and his ignorance of the great urban working class of the nation were certainly quite true. Although one must believe that he understood well enough by the autumn of 1914 the unpopularity of contributory insurance. Even Riddell's comment that efficiency came before friendship, which really meant that Lloyd George kept people around him so long as they were useful, is both perceptive and important. These characteristics would become more pronounced as Lloyd George grew older. The biographer is not often given a statement of the dark side of a public man's character by his intimates, as opposed to opposition journalists' calendars of his misdeeds. Lloyd George was cruel and would remain so. He who could read other men's feelings and reactions so perfectly cannot have been unaware of the devastation he caused, yet he never seemed to care. The truth was that men Lloyd George could trust, the civil servants who worked for him, Braithwaite for example, and the junior politicians he kept at his elbow, Masterman, Addison, and later Arthur Lee, he tended to despise and showed it. Conversely the few men he admired, Churchill and Edward Carson, he did not trust.

However, Masterman, in his agony, by his intemperate language, was damaging more than his relationship with Lloyd George. After dinner with Lloyd George at Walton Heath on 6 December, Riddell wrote

> LlG said tonight that Masterman is the most unpopular man in the House of Commons, because he is unpopular with his own party as well as with the other. Mrs. LlG does not like him. She is a dear good woman but loves jobbing her Welsh proteges into positions [in national health insurance]. Masterman has not been amenable at the insurance office, but as he is not above a job on his own account, Mrs. LlG regards his purity as spurious.[53]

December of 1914 and January of 1915 saw the sudden death of Masterman's career not by Lloyd George's hand but by his own. Early in December the Liberal Chief Whip, Percy Illingworth, who had succeeded Alec Murray and who was one of the few Liberals who sympathized with Masterman, arranged for the appointment of David Brynmor Jones, MP for Swansea District since 1895 as Master in Lunacy. Lloyd George told Frances Stevenson he had not been involved in this maneuver, even though Jones was an old ally from the battles with D.A. Thomas and was in 1914 the official leader of the Welsh party.[54] The appointment appeared in *The Times* on 8 December. *The Times* noted that C.F.G. Masterman and a T. Jeremiah Williams, were 'possible Liberal candidates' for the vacancy.

Masterman's behavior in the next few weeks is nearly incomprehensible. Even though he had long objected to the use of Wales as a haven for English Liberal politicians who were unable to find seats elsewhere, at Masterman's, and probably Illingworth's, request Lloyd George wrote to the Swansea District Liberal Association citing the government's need for 'such a capable' man in the House of Commons and recommending the nomination of Masterman.[55] This caused a revolt in the South Wales Liberal party. Under the wartime electoral truce the two major parties had agreed not to contest by-elections. Hence nomination by the party holding the seat supposedly insured election. However in Swansea it quickly became clear that many Liberals opposed Masterman. Jeremiah Williams, a well known local barrister whose father had once represented Swansea District, claimed the seat for himself and threatened to run as an independent if Masterman were nominated.[56]

The prospect of opposition seems to have aroused Masterman's incurable depressive pessimism. Suddenly he no longer wanted the seat. He would look for another. 'Masterman will lose this seat if he is not careful,' Lloyd George announced on 20 December to Riddell, guest at a dinner of minced lamb and eggs, milk and plum pudding, fruit and coffee, typical fare at Lloyd George's table.

> I warned him today. He was very ill conditioned. I shall do no more for him in this matter. He is a bad candidate. He seems to think everyone should strive for him. I just left him. He said 'I shall see the Prime Minister'. Strange conduct after my letter. Unless he is careful he will become impossible as a candidate.

Riddell observed that the Conservatives regarded Masterman as a renegade Churchman with which Lloyd George agreed, adding again that he was the most unpopular man in either party.[57]

There was a complication beyond Masterman's reluctance to fight in Swansea: the Prime Minister did not want a contested election. The Conservatives, Asquith feared quite correctly, were already restive in the electoral truce. They would object to a contest between Liberals in a constituency they had agreed not to fight themselves.[58] The Liberal whips must induce Williams to withdraw, he told J.A. Pease, a junior whip on 22 December. (The Chief Whip, Percy Illingworth, was ill and soon to die.) If there was to be a fight, the Prime Minister wanted Williams, Pease informed Lloyd George on 1 January 1915. Pease reported that he had talked to some local Liberals although he feared to make the pressure too obvious, but if Masterman had boldly stepped forward and announced he wanted the seat, there would have been no trouble. 'As always' he was hesitant.[59]

Masterman's selection as the prospective candidate for Swansea had been announced on 24 December 1914 but by this time he appears to have been nearly hysterical with indecision and a sense of persecution and asked for some time before accepting.[60] Brynmor Jones's appointment had been arranged by Illingworth to create a vacancy, he told Riddell on 14 January, but the Whip's illness had caused the arrangement to break down. 'He [Masterman] does not like going to Wales,' thought Riddell 'and I doubt if he really likes LlG.'

> He said, 'LlG does not want me to go to Wales. The Welsh Party have to follow his orders. I might not be sufficiently compliant.' I said 'I think he just wants to see you back in the House. Just now the Welsh Party is not important.'

> Masterman: 'Yes, see me back to do his dirty work I suppose. He ought to help me get a safe seat. He was responsible for my going to Ipswich. That was a cruel thing.'[61]

By the middle of January Masterman had refused the Swansea nomination, possibly because of a vacancy at Shipley, the West Riding of Yorkshire, caused by the death of the Chief Whip on 3 January 1915.[62] The appointment of the new Chief Whip, John Gulland, made on 24 January and announced the next day, brought the end. Gulland told Asquith in the plainest terms that Masterman would have to go. There were in fact two vacancies, at Shipley and at Norwich. In neither place would the local Liberals accept Masterman.[63] Asquith immediately interviewed Lloyd George who did not recommend that Masterman be saved. Meanwhile Gulland spoke to Masterman saying that the Prime Minister wanted him to resign from the Cabinet. This would not have happened if Illingworth had been alive, said Masterman to Riddell. He blamed Lloyd George who was faithless and had no friends.[64] There followed a 'disagreeable' conversation between Masterman and Asquith at which Lloyd George was again denounced much to Asquith's annoyance.[65]

Masterman by this time had offended nearly every senior politician who might have been able to help him. His resignation was required. He was replaced at the Duchy of Lancaster by Edwin Montagu on 3 February 1915. Lloyd George reported to Riddell that Masterman had sent him a 'silly letter' evidently after his resignation offering 'to let bygones be bygones' but not apologizing.[66] He now passed from Lloyd George's life. He continued the work, in which he was in fact already engaged, in Wellington House, the embryonic Department of Propaganda which finally became the Ministry of Information in 1918. Nonetheless his family circumstances were much reduced. Riddell who clearly felt sorry for him, told Masterman that he could continue to live in the house on Walton Heath and pay rent later, an offer which was refused. Riddell also urged Robert Donald to find him a place on the *Chronicle*.[67] (Max Aitken, in 1916 Lord Beaverbrook, proprietor of the *Daily Express*, thought Masterman one of the two best journalists in England. The other was Winston Churchill.)

II

On 17 November Lloyd George presented his first war budget, the seventh of his own preparation.[68] As the creature of a man whose political stock in trade was fertility of imagination, brilliant innovation, and courage, the 1914 supplementary budget was a remarkably pedestrian effort and one to which he clearly had given only slight attention. (Reading warned him a few days later that the notes for a speech prepared for the Finance Bill debate were full of inaccuracies not only of 'understanding' but of fact. He would be wise to confine himself to generalities.)[69] The overriding fact of his speech was that Britain was spending nearly £1,000,000 a day above the amount budgeted for the fiscal year of 1915 and that the Treasury would have to find between 1 December 1914 and 31 March 1915, an additional £339,500,000 in new money, approaching twice the total, £200,000,000, of his summer budget and that for a period of only four months.

To accomplish some of this he proposed doubling the standard rates of income tax and super tax although not increasing their coverage. To extend the liability for income tax to the working class would be complicated and expensive; rather he would claim the working man's contribution through excises, chiefly beer, wine, spirits and tea.

But even with the new taxes, most of which would take effect on 1 December, he would still need to borrow £321,300,000 to accommodate the spending of the next four months and to redeem the soon expiring six month Treasury Bills with which the war hitherto had been entirely financed. This sum would be raised through a £350,000,000 $3\frac{1}{2}$% bond issue offered at 95% maturing on 1 March 1928. The bonds would be denominated in units of £100. Anything smaller, Lloyd George asserted, would deplete the savings banks.

All of this was fair for the City and fair for the government he insisted, but as a crowning inducement he announced that the Bank of England had agreed to accept until 1 March 1918 the bond as collateral at face value. In effect the Bank was underwriting the price of the entire issue.[70]

One need only note that of course the loan was quickly taken up.[71] Yet the first war budget remains an unadventurous affair, designed only not to fail, and leaning entirely upon Britain's well established capital market. The tax increases were minimal, although to be fair, they did not seem so at the time. But there was no attempt to tap the already growing prosperity of the working class. Apparently this was partly a result of the influence of Austen Chamberlain whom Lloyd George had consulted and who had advised against broadening the tax base.[72]

A week after his budget speech, on 24 November 1914, Lloyd George received a short note from the Prime Minister: he wished to have at noon the next day a small 'conclave on the Naval and Milty situation'. Beside Lloyd George only Grey, Kitchener, Churchill and, he hoped, A.J. Balfour would attend. 'But of course we must observe strict secrecy.'[73] At the meeting, on 25 November, attended also by John, Lord Fisher, recently reappointed First Sea Lord, and General Sir James Wolfe Murray, the Chief of the Imperial General Staff, occurred the first important general discussion of the implications of Turkish declaration of hostilities upon Britain on 29 October 1914. This meeting may be taken therefore as the beginning of the disastrous Gallipoli adventure.[74] Although Lloyd George was, as yet, only slightly concerned with the international dimensions of the war, the domestic consequences of Turkey's adherence to the Central Powers were so vast, and its impact upon his career so large, that it must be given some attention.

Turkey's entrance was fully anticipated. The welcome given to the *Goeben* and the anger at the British seizure of the Turkish battleships, all of which became part of the general political campaign against Churchill, had made clear that the Ottoman Empire's historic friendship for Britain was at an end. What should be Britain's response, specifically how would the nation defend the Suez Canal, had been a frequent Cabinet topic. The universal assumption, implicit in all conversations about the rising crisis in the eastern Mediterranean, including the discussions at the meeting on 25 November, was that Turkey's decision for Germany and Austria would inevitably bring in the Balkan states on the side of the Allies. The Greeks' hatred of the Turks represented a tradition centuries old; Romania's was hardly less so and her antagonism for the Central Powers was reinforced by her claims on Hungary's Transylvania. The problem was Bulgaria, the strongest Balkan military power. With a reasonably well trained army of 300,000 men, larger than any other Balkan army, Bulgaria was feared and distrusted by all its neighbors. Moreover, since its defeat in the Second Balkan War of 1913, the Bulgars reciprocated those sentiments completely. No nation could move unless the commitment of Bulgaria was assured.

Bulgaria then was the key and to Sir Edward Grey had been so since the beginning of the war.[75] In August the Greek Prime Minister Eleutherios Venizelos, anticipating a declaration of war on Britain by Turkey, or an attack on Greece or Serbia by Bulgaria with perhaps Turkish support, had proposed an alliance between Britain and Greece. With British help the Greeks would aid Serbia.[76] A base in the Balkans as a staging area for a war with Turkey or as a channel for help to Serbia would be a rare benefit. The Cabinet agreed to send a 'cordial acknowledgement' and urged Venizelos to proceed with attempts to form a Balkan federation.[77] Very soon the brothers Noel and Charles Roden Buxton, both radical Liberal MPs, were sent to Romania, ostensibly to attend King Carol's funeral, but in fact to enter Bulgaria as quickly as possible.[78] The two men arrived in Sofia on 10 December. Their task as Noel Buxton outlined in a letter to Grey, who evidently had given his instructions orally, was to 'secure Bulgarian good will' with the aim of: 1) avoiding a Bulgarian attack on Serbia, 2) allowing Romania to attack Austria, and 3) supporting the hostility of Bulgaria for Turkey, all the while insisting that they were on an unofficial mission. Buxton concluded that he thought war with Turkey would be popular in Bulgaria and no other war would be.[79]

The justifications for this excursion into Balkan diplomacy at the outbreak of the war are several. One can see here an emerging eastern Mediterranean policy which if pursued with sufficient energy could have saved Serbia, possibly forced Austria and Turkey from the war, and opened a warm water route to Russia, with, it might be added, incalculable results for twentieth-century history. Second, for the career of Lloyd George, a Balkan front based upon the reasoning outlined above became Lloyd George's war strategy at least until the end of 1916. The two Buxtons were already close associates of Lloyd George and Masterman. Noel Buxton had contributed a chapter to *The Heart of the Empire*, the bible of the new Liberalism, which Masterman had edited;

he was a member, with Masterman, of the Christian Social Union and a strong temperance advocate. Charles Roden Buxton was a member of the land inquiry committee. The Buxtons, principally Noel, were an important source of information for the Chancellor. The Lloyd George Papers contain a thick file of letters, advice, and information, which continue through most of the year 1915 when Lloyd George was pursuing, as his principal contribution to military strategy, the expedition to Salonika in Greece.[80]

In 1914 however the assumption in the Cabinet was that if Bulgaria could be neutralized the Balkan powers would attack Turkey on their own while Romania attacked Austria-Hungary. Britain ought to take 'vigorous action' to force such a combination, Asquith wrote to the King on 3 November remarking that the government was reversing a century of diplomatic tradition, that the time had come to 'forget about Ottoman integrity'.[81] He was more succinct to Venetia Stanley at the end of the year. The possibility appeared that Italy, despite her pacts with Germany and Austria, might also join the Allies. '. . .when the carcass is ready to be cut up each wants as big & juicy slice as it can get.'[82] At the meeting of 25 November however the concern was less on the future division of Turkish territory than about the immediate problem of defending Egypt and the Suez Canal. At the beginning of the discussion Churchill stated that the ideal method of defending Suez was by an attack on the Gallipoli peninsula. This would require, he immediately added, a very large force, with many transports, which Grey quickly pointed out were not presently available. The possibility of cooperation by Balkan armies was again discussed and the impediment of Bulgarian hostility to Serbia and Greece was re-explored. Nothing, Grey concluded, could be expected from Greece unless Bulgaria was bound to the Allies.[83]

For the story of Lloyd George's wartime career, the eastern strategy discussed in the last months of 1914 became of decisive importance. He had already concluded that the war in the west had assumed a character that promised nothing but useless slaughter. The intervention of Turkey had opened an exposed flank in the Balkans and the surprising ability of the Serbs to defend themselves against Austria provided an avenue through which the Central Powers could be attacked. Here, with the command of the sea, the Allies could take the initiative with very little risk. This realization came not only to Lloyd George. At almost the same time, in November 1914, Aristide Briand, Minister of Justice in the Viviani government in France, and a man whose association with Lloyd George would become of great importance in the next years, proposed that an army of 400,000 men be sent to Salonika in Greek Thrace. However, since the Battle of the Marne the real ruler of France was General Joseph Joffre, who refused to consider the idea.[84]

Lloyd George put his thoughts together in a long memorandum for the Cabinet dated 1 January 1915 entitled 'Suggestions as to the Military Position'. Although this document has been printed before, it summarizes so well Lloyd George's convictions about the conflict upon which his nation was engaged, and to which he would refer again and again in the next two years, and from which convictions indeed he would not depart during the war, that it must be quoted at length. Lloyd George began with an acute political observation about the new army: that it was to a large extent made up of middle class and upper working class men with ideas of their own, men who would not cut themselves off from civilian concerns and political interests as professional soldiers traditionally had done. He did not add, although certainly by now he knew, that this was a fact Britain's generals never seemed to apprehend. The Chancellor's point at this time however was that such a force would understand quickly if it were being wasted in a hopeless enterprise and 'the country will be uncontrollably indignant at the lack of prevision and intelligence shown in our plans. . .Good soldiers will face any dangers and endure any hardships which promise ultimate progress, but this intermittent flinging themselves against impregnable positions breaks the stoutest hearts in the end.' He referred again to what he had learned in France in October: 'I cannot pretend to have any military knowledge', he began in a section entitled 'Stalemate on the Western Front'

> But the little I saw in France as to the military position, coupled with such reading on the subject as I have been able to indulge in, convinces me that any attempts to force the carefully prepared German lines in the west would end in failure and in appalling loss of life and I expressed this view to my colleagues. . .Is it not therefore better that we should recognize the possibility of this particular tack, and try to think out some way by which the distinct numerical advantage which the Allies will have attained a few months hence [Britain would have over half a million men in the trenches by March] can be rendered effective?

To this end Lloyd George proposed two alternatives, an attack upon Austria either by landing on the Dalmatian coast or by a force operating from Salonika. The presence of a large British force here would keep the Bulgarians honestly neutral and so encourage the participation of the Greeks and Romanians, while the Austrians would have to transfer men from the Russian front. Thus Germany would need to reinforce her army in the east from France. Meanwhile Italy, seeing territory she desired herself being conquered by others, would be forced, in her own interest, to join the Allies.

His second proposal, less ambitious, was a landing in Syria should the Turks dispatch any substantial force south into Palestine to attack the Suez Canal. This force would cut the coastal railroad and could easily be supported by sea. The Turks, isolated in the Negev, would have to fight at a disadvantage or surrender.

Lloyd George concluded with an urgent plea for consultation, for planning. So far there had been nothing.

> We cannot allow things to drift. We ought to look well ahead and discuss every possible project for bringing the War to a successful conclusion. . .
>
> If a decision were to come in favour of some such plan as I have outlined, it will take weeks to make the necessary preparations for it. I cannot recollect that in our discussions at the C.I.D. such an operation was ever contemplated. The ground therefore has not been surveyed . . .All this must take time. Expeditions decided upon and organized with insufficient care and preparation generally end disastrously. And as similar considerations will probably apply to any alternative campaign, I urge the importance of our taking counsel and pressing it to a decision without delay.[85]

Asquith was impressed by Lloyd George's memorandum, as he remarked in a letter that day to Venetia Stanley. In the same letter, recording no reaction, he said that he had also received a memorandum from Churchill.[86] The First Lord also proposed an alternative strategy, the seizure of the German island of Borkum, for security reasons always called Sylt in his correspondence. The island would be made a submarine base which would allow the Royal Navy eventually to dominate the Baltic Sea. In the first War Council meetings of the new year, on 7 and 8 January 1915 the Baltic and the Mediterranean strategy competed for attention interrupted by offstage whispers from Sir John French claiming all available men for the western front. Kitchener in contrast generally supported an alternative strategy though he was reluctant to choose any particular plan.[87]

Then at the War Council on 13 January Churchill announced that he had been exchanging telegrams with Vice Admiral S.H. Carden about the possibility of an attack through the Straits of Dardanelles to Constantinople carried out by a naval force alone. It would involve the systematic reduction of the forts along both sides of the channel up to the Sea of Marmora and possibly a naval action with the German, now officially Turkish, battle cruiser the *Goeben*. Carden believed the enterprise possible.

This departure from the rather leisurely discussion of other alternatives was the result of an almost frantic telegram from the British ambassador in Petrograd, Sir George Buchanan, which arrived at the Foreign Office in the early hours of 2 January. He recounted an interview with the commander of the Russian armies, the Grand Duke Nicholas Nicholaevich, who pleaded for a western diversion to relieve Turkish pressure in the Caucasus. Sir George agreed action was necessary, and immediately. Carden's plan seemed to provide a means of helping the Russians while at the same time beginning a flanking strategy to separate Turkey from its allies without the use of troops, which all other alternatives required. The War Council meeting on the 13th ordered the Admiralty to prepare for a naval expedition to begin in February with the objective of Constantinople.[88]

In his memoirs, Lloyd George is at pains to show that he opposed the Dardanelles expedition strenuously and continued to press for a landing in the Balkans at Salonika or elsewhere. The first assertion is not altogether accurate. The minutes of the War Council show, on the contrary, that once the bombardment of the forts on Cape Hellas began, on 19 February, he fairly consistently supported Churchill in his battles with Kitchener for the dispatch of troops for the occupation of the Turkish capital after the ships broke through into the Sea of Marmora.[89] But neither did Lloyd George give up his campaign for a Balkan diversion.

Within a week after the War Council ordered preparation for an attack on the Dardanelles forts Lloyd George saw the Prime Minister and Kitchener privately.[90] Here he apparently expounded again the need for a clear British commitment in the Balkans, not only to isolate Turkey but to save Serbia by intimidating Bulgaria. Afterwards he saw an unnamed Greek official (evidently John Gennedius, Greek Minister to Britain, 1910–18) who promptly telegraphed Prime Minister Venizelos. He had just seen Lloyd George, he reported, 'after a conference' with Asquith and Kitchener. The Germans and Austrians were preparing a serious attack upon Serbia. The fall of Serbia would surely bring Bulgaria in on the side of the Central Powers. Lloyd George wanted to know, the minister inquired, what Greece and Romania would need from Britain to induce them to support Serbia. France also would be brought in. The message concluded by saying that Venizelos should make no mention of the present telegram in his reply but should simply say that Greece would support Serbia if Britain sent forces to assist.[91] Clearly Lloyd George and, apparently, Asquith, were negotiating with the Greeks behind the backs of their colleagues on the War Council.[92]

The next day Lloyd George pushed the Salonika excursion further in an interview at Kitchener's temporary London residence in Carlton Gardens with Alexandre Millerand, the French Minister of War. Here, supported by Grey, he pressed the minister for a French contribution for the Eastern Mediterranean. Millerand, wrote Lloyd George in his *War Memoirs,* 'was a sturdy and aggressive exponent of the views of the French Commander in Chief. . .General Joffre did not want to part with a single battalion from his French command. He was convinced that he could break through the German lines that year.'[93] At this time Lloyd George obviously did not appreciate that for his objects he was talking to the wrong man. The ruler in France in 1914, 15, and for most of 1916 was General Joseph Joffre, the hero of the Marne. His headquarters at Chantilly was in effect the national capitol, which made and unmade political careers, dictated policy, and received and sent ambassadors, of whom Millerand was one. At this time the French government had only recently returned from Bordeaux where Joffre had ordered it to go before the Battle of the Marne. Apparently he so enjoyed the independence thus acquired that he did not allow the ministers to return to Paris until December.[94] As Lloyd George discovered within a few weeks, Millerand did not even trouble to convey his argument to the French Cabinet.

For some days Lloyd George had projected an extended trip to Paris to meet his opposite numbers in the French and Russian governments, Alexandre Ribot and Peter Bark. Both governments, although particularly the Russian, desired access to the London credit market in order to purchase arms in the United States and, although each possessed large reserves of gold, both were finding it difficult to borrow for military purchases within their own countries.[95] In return the British government was anxious to promote a general Allied subsidy to the Belgian government; otherwise the Belgians might believe themselves abandoned and accept German occupation as their only alternative.[96] On 1 February, just as the unhappy Masterman episode was ending, Lloyd George left London in the company of Walter Cunliffe, Governor of the Bank of England, and Edwin Montagu, taking also his confidential secretary, J.T. Davies. The Chancellor had bought a new suit for the occasion.[97]

In Paris Lloyd George was indeed able to exact promises for the release of gold by Britain's allies, while allowing the Russians to enter Britain's capital market. On his return he received the usual congratulations, including a rare letter from Alec Murray, all of which he reported to Frances Stevenson.[98]

However, the underlying purpose of the trip was military, not financial, strategy. Lloyd George hoped to attract French and Russian support for his Balkan plans. Therefore, although he refused to admit it, he may have been overly generous in the terms by which the allies would be able to tap the reserves of the City, a matter of great importance for the future, first when the Allies became competitors for American munitions, bidding up prices with dollars bought in Britain and later as they accumulated huge post-war debts which were never paid. Over dinner at Walton Heath on 13 February Lloyd George bristled at a suggestion of this to Robert Donald, editor of the *Chronicle* who also had been in Paris in January.

'Donald says British made a bad bargain in Paris,' recorded George Riddell.

> LG does not like this, says question not entirely financial. His object had been to cement a compact between Britain and Russia, political, commercial and financial.[99]

Obviously an important part of the visit lay in conversations with French politicians. As Lloyd George wrote to Edward Grey on 7 February, the day after his return, he was shocked to discover that Millerand had never laid his proposal for an allied force in Salonika before the French Cabinet. 'They were astonished,' he wrote, 'and not a little annoyed that the matter had not been reported to them. I found that their attitude was much more friendly to the idea than was that of Millerand. Briand, who is much the ablest man in the Ministry, was strongly for it — in fact, he told me that he had been for some time urging some diversion of this kind upon General Joffre.' Briand would become an important association for Lloyd George in the next few years. Lord Esher wrote in 1916 that Briand thought Lloyd George possessed a clearer view of the war than any other French leader and clearly Lloyd George was enchanted by his French counterpart. Briand was a Breton and Lloyd George repeatedly commented upon the fact that both were Celts and hence had 'too much imagination'.[100]

'I met Briand at Sir Francis Bertie's [British Ambassador in Paris]' Lloyd George continued to Grey,

> and the three of us had a prolonged talk on the position. Briand told us that the Cabinet had considered the suggestion on Thursday [4 February]; that Millerand stood absolutely alone in his opposition to it, Delcassé hesitating a little, not knowing what the attitude of Russia would be towards it; the rest of the Cabinet being perfectly unanimously in favour of the principle of an expeditionary force of two divisions being sent to Salonika at the earliest practicable moment, preparations to be made at once, and the troops to be sent as soon as General Joffre and the French could be persuaded to spare them. The French wished for an expeditionary force in which the French army should be represented. They therefore suggested that one British and one French division be sent. The President of the Republic [Raymond Poincaré] was also present at the Council, and he approved of this course.

Lloyd George was as usual being a little over enthusiastic. Francis Bertie's report of the conversation to Grey, sent 3 February, was somewhat more cautious. President Poincaré, he wrote to Grey on 3 February, seemed to be moderately in favor of Salonika but Bertie was sure that Joffre was against. Joffre, he said, had been assured that German morale was cracking; and he was going to attack as soon as the weather improved. He expected great success. In contradiction to what Lloyd George had reported, Bertie stated, Joffre had no objection to the British carrying on alone.[101]

'The French are very anxious to be represented in the expeditionary force,' Lloyd George's letter to Grey continued.

> Briand thinks it desirable from the point of view of a final settlement that France and England should establish a right to a voice in the settlement of the Balkans by having a force there. He does not want Russia to feel that she alone is the arbiter of the fate of the Balkan peoples. Yesterday I saw Sir John French and General [William] Robertson, the new Chief of Staff. Every soldier I have met since the beginning of the War has placed Robertson in the forefront as the most conspicuous success among our generals, and he made a deep impression on the Governor of the Bank, Montagu, and myself yesterday. He is a shrewd, clear headed, strong man. No general except Kitchener made quite the same impression on my mind as Robertson did yesterday. French introduced the idea of an expedition, and at first he was hostile, not in principle, but on the ground he could not spare the troops. *However, he called Robertson in, and when I had explained to him exactly what the proposal was, he had no hesitation in saying that it was 'good strategy.' He maintained that view throughout the discussion.* This influenced French's attitude very considerably. I told him we were very anxious to carry his judgement along with ours in any scheme which affected the military operations for which he was responsible. Ultimately he agreed that if the Rumanians and the Greeks promised to march on our undertaking to send an expeditionary force to Salonika, he would spare at least a Division for the purpose. He is willing, and I think, anxious, to come over to discuss the project with the War Council. He suggested that he should be invited, and I hope that the Prime Minister and Kitchener can see their way to asking him to attend an early meeting of the War Council.

Lloyd George concluded:

> *Unless, therefore, we mean to allow the great possibilities of the Balkans to slip out of our hands, we ought not to dilly dally any longer. If we fail to take timely action here, our condemnation will be a terrible one.* As I read the sections I feel that even days count now. My experience yesterday shows that the generals, if properly taken in hand, can be persuaded. No general likes to have his troops taken away to another sphere of action. His mind is naturally concentrated on the trenches in front of him, unless he is a very big man indeed and a man, moreover, who has the responsibility, not merely for the success of the operation under his immediate control: and neither Joffre nor French are [sic] quite in this position.[102]

Obviously this letter is both enthusiastic and optimistic. But in fact, in Lloyd George's mind, even as he wrote it, the war was going badly. On 22 February he addressed a highly pessimistic paper to the War Cabinet which was stimulated, probably, by the thoughtless rejoicing in the press over the beginning of the bombardment of the outer forts at the Dardanelles on 19 February.[103]

The paper, entitled 'Some Further Considerations on the Conduct of the War' began:

I am anxious to put before my colleagues a few considerations on the general situation. It must be acknowledged to be one of utmost gravity, and one which, if not taken in hand at once firmly and boldly, may end in irretrievable disaster for the cause of the allies and for the future of the British Empire. . .

The Press and the Country have up to the moment treated the progress of the War as one of almost unbroken success. . .Every trivial military incident which turns to our advantage is magnified and elaborated in headlines which occupy half a column and descriptions which take a page. On the other hand, grave misfortunes such as those which have befallen the armies of our Russian Allies in the course of the last few days are relegated to a few lines of type, whilst they are explained away in columns of leaded matter.

He feared, continued Lloyd George, that many in authority with fuller command of the facts, followed the same mental processes, dwelling upon those facts which pleased them and forgetting the others. 'The only pathway to success is paved by reality. Unless we look facts, however unpleasant, in the face, we shall never grapple with them.'

The unhappy facts were that while not a yard of German territory was in Allied hands, the enemy occupied nearly the whole of Belgium and some of the richest provinces of France. Moreover, while holding the west easily, they had withdrawn reserves, and a gigantic disaster was building in the east. Russia at the moment was 'knocked out'. She had no guns nor shells, not even rifles.

So far Britain had not made the effort of which she was capable in either men or material. Lloyd George quickly added that he was not calling for conscription, but there was now an oppressive need for haste. The war would not be over soon; it might well go through the next year. Men and machines should be mobilized immediately. Perhaps a county by county quota could be set up for enlistments; local pressure and patriotism would take care of the rest. Keeping public houses closed until 11 a.m. might increase industrial production. Implicit in this was the horrible possibility that Russia might be driven from the war. The allies would then be at great disadvantage.

But what, he asked, of the immediate future? Unlike the Germans who had attacked the Russians promptly even before the German reserves were ready, with brilliant results, Britain had been hesitant to take risks. Was Britain ready now to do so?

The momentous step we have taken in attempting to force the Dardanelles must have a decisive effect one way or another in the Balkans. Are we prepared for either or for any event?

If this great movement succeeds — then, if we are prepared to take immediate advantage of it — its influence may be decisive as far as the Balkan States are concerned. This means that if we have a large force ready, not merely to occupy Gallipoli, but to take any other military action which may be necessary in order to establish our supremacy in that quarter, Rumania, Greece, and I think, very probably Bulgaria will declare for us.

All of this would provide a large army to throw against Austria, relieve pressure on Russia and indirectly on France, and give Russia time to recover. But then there followed a remarkable forecast of what in fact was to come.

Let us take the other contingency — the failure of the Dardanelles effort. Unless it is at once countered, such a failure will be disastrous in the Balkans, and might very well be disastrous throughout the east... not merely Bulgaria but Rumania and Italy have a good deal to gain by way of territory by throwing their lot with Germany. There is only one guarantee against a catastrophe being precipitated in that quarter as a result of a repulse in the Dardanelles. There must be a strong British force there available to support our friends. Is it quite out of the question that we should anticipate our April preparations by three or four weeks and thus follow the German example of taking risks so as to arrive in time?[104]

Lloyd George rarely put so many proposals into a single document and never into a speech. With the memorandum of 1 January, the two together manifested most of the Chancellor's convictions about the conduct of the struggle: a lessening concentration on the western front, the need for national mobilization, the danger to which the west would be exposed if Russia dropped out. There was even a mention of temperance, a point to which Lloyd George would turn his attention within two weeks. Finally, at a time when the Dardanelles operation seemed to be going well, he raised the possibility of the disastrous consequences of its failure and argued that either in victory or defeat Britain would need a strong land force in the eastern Mediterranean immediately. (The War Office was planning a leisurely concentration of men on the Island of Lemnos which could not be ready before April and included no trained men. Kitchener remained opposed to sending any experienced troops from Britain or the western front.)

Lloyd George received an enthusiastic note from Admiral Fisher agreeing in italics that the Dardanelles was futile without soldiers. He was accorded a longer, somewhat testy, reply from Kitchener saying as usual that everything that could be done was being done although he would be glad to see greater munitions production and no doubt a step in this direction would be taken if workers were not intoxicated when they arrived at the factory. However, there were no troops available 'at present' to fight on the Gallipoli peninsula.[105]

But apparently Lloyd George convinced the War Council. On 26 February, in a discussion of the Dardanelles in which Churchill reported that the outer forts were falling one by one, the Prime Minister stated, in Hankey's words,

that the immediate object of the Dardanelles operation was to open the sea road to the Black Sea, but the ultimate object was to bring in the Balkan States. Nearly every member of the War Council mentioned that as our ultimate aim. Some members went further and suggested that we might find scope in the Near East for the employment of the new armies. As Mr. Lloyd George has pointed out, the employment of British military forces in the Balkans is probably indispensible if we are to secure the adherence of the Balkan States to the cause of the Allies. Probably, therefore, the War Council will accept the view that the ultimate object of the operation now commenced is to open the way for military operations against Austria in which a British army will, it is hoped, co-operate with the armies of Roumania, Servia, and perhaps Greece.[106]

This paper was written by Maurice Hankey, evidently for Asquith, at a time of general confidence that the Dardanelles operation would succeed. Although these words do not appear in the available minutes of the War Council of Friday, 26 February, one may be sure that they were said. They express a general acceptance that the Balkans would become a major theater of war. For one brief moment Lloyd George seemed to have turned the attention of the government away from its concentration on the mud of Flanders. The Dardanelles operation, begun simply as an emergency measure to help Russia, was a means to this larger end.

Thus in the next few weeks everything changed. The Balkan project died and when proposals for an expedition to Salonika appeared again in the autumn, the initiative was French and the contingent emergencies against which Lloyd George had warned so urgently had occurred.

Lloyd George does not seem to have understood that although the Dardanelles represented only a subsidiary operation to the opening of a general Balkan front, for the Balkan states themselves Turkey counted for everything. To some extent he was undone by his own lack of knowledge. He could see into the hearts and minds of men with whom he was negotiating but the complex and traditional antagonisms of these far-away nations were outside his experience, even with the Buxtons at his elbow. Greece for example could offer, or seem to offer, her services to the allies for the aid of Serbia, but her real interest lay in Turkey's European territory, above all in Constantinople. This meant a successful naval penetration of the Dardanelles. If this were accomplished there would be allies clamoring to participate. Otherwise there would be no one.

The end came quickly. The bombardment of the outer forts at the western end of the straits began on 19 February and after a short recess because of bad weather continued on 25 February. By 2 March the outer defenses of the channel were destroyed and the allied fleets prepared to move into the narrow waters. This success brought the expected reaction. On 1 March Greek Premier Venizelos, whose response to Lloyd George and Asquith's approaches in January for aid to Serbia had been distinctly lukewarm, suddenly offered three Greek divisions for a march upon Constantinople.[107] Briefly even Bulgaria was interested. Greek King Constantine looked forward to entering the ancient center of the Greek Empire, from whose founder he took his name, in person at the head of his soldiers. 'It is far the most interesting moment of the war. . .' wrote Asquith to Venetia Stanley that night.[108] This elation ended within two days. On 3 March the Russian foreign minister, after a conference with the Czar, told the British Ambassador Sir George Buchanan that the Russian government 'could not consent' to Greek participation in the Dardanelles campaign. 'Grey's information', records G.M. Trevelyan, himself a Balkan expert and a friend of the Buxtons, 'was that a strong party there thought more of winning Constantinople than of beating the Central Powers. . .'[109] Within twenty-four hours the French government had heard the same. Constantinople would be Russian.

There was a good deal of anger in the Cabinet at Russia's assumption of the right to choose Britain's allies and Grey was ordered to search for a compromise.[110] Asquith's disappointment was palpable in his letter to Venetia Stanley. The Russians 'declined absolutely to allow Greece to take any part in the Dardanelles business' and the Greeks refused to fight anyone but the Turks or perhaps the Bulgarians. 'They won't raise a finger for Serbia.'[111] There were rumors saying that if the Russians were deprived of Constantinople they would leave the war. On 7 March Venizelos resigned.[112]

With a Salonika expedition out of the question, Lloyd George turned his attention to other matters. But a corner had been turned. For a moment it seemed he had convinced the Cabinet, certainly the Prime Minister, to reduce its concentration on France and Belgium and to consider an alternative strategy. British troops at Salonika to restrain the Bulgarians would allow Greece to deploy her army in support of a British naval expedition through the straits. With Turkey defeated or at least isolated, the Balkan states would join the Allies. Serbia would be saved and Russia relieved. But all of this had foundered on the rocks of Russian unwillingness to see anyone but themselves in Constantinople and of the generals', both French and British, refusal to release even a small force for Salonika. Therefore everything, the entire eastern strategy, depended upon the Royal Navy's success in pressing through to the Sea of Marmora. Suddenly on 18 March came frightening news. Four battleships of the attacking fleet, three British and one French, had been sunk or damaged by underwater or floating mines or torpedoes. Admiral de Robeck, who had replaced Carden, intended to break off the action. Although the fixed fortification within the Straits, at this point only about 10,000 yards wide, had been silenced, the Turks had mobile field guns on both sides of the channel. These weapons were not heavy enough to harm the armored battleships, but they were able to inflict great damage on minesweepers. As a result, sweeping had been hastily and inadequately accomplished. To secure the minesweepers against the field guns the shoreline of the Straits would have to be occupied. So an army was required after all. But now it was too late.[113]

4 Awakening the Nation, and the Government: Labor, Drink and Munitions

As Kitchener's reply to Lloyd George's memorandum of 22 February indicated, even as the bombardment of the Dardanelles fortresses began, some British war leaders were becoming aware of a singular new problem connected with munitions production, particularly of shipbuilding: that of drunkenness among workers. The immediate effect was absenteeism. The point is worth noting because the anti-drink campaign in which Lloyd George involved himself in March and April of 1915 is usually presented as an eccentric project of his own which came up at his insistence and was disregarded or opposed by the rest of the Cabinet as a diversion from the general question of industrial mobilization for war.[1] In fact J.A. Pease's diary and other sources report a general concern in the Cabinet about labor discontent in the North, falling production in shipyards and over the long turnaround time of incoming cargo ships. In the middle of February Lloyd George and Simon were instructed to prepare a second amendment bill to the Defence of the Realm Act to deal with the labor problems. The draft was laid before the Cabinet on 24 February.[2] In short, the anti-drink crusade was an integral part of the general munitions problem and not simply an echo of Lloyd George's past.[3]

For Lloyd George himself, the anti-drink campaign began only gradually, with a rather casual reference in a speech in Bangor on 28 February, nine days after the first bombardment of Cape Hellas. Historically the Bangor address belongs in the tradition of Queen's Hall. It was above all a call for sacrifice with the warning that a failure of British exertion would mean the Prussianization of Europe.

The immediate motivation for the Bangor speech was the outbreak in Glasgow on 16 February at G. and J. Weir of an unofficial strike over a demand for a two pence an hour increase in wages. The strike quickly spread. By 20 February over 10,000 men on the Clyde were refusing labor. Ominously, the strike was not sanctioned by the Amalgamated Society of Engineers to which most of the men belonged, but had been promoted within the shops by men of extreme left-wing political sympathies: James Messer, William Gallacher, David Kirkwood and Tom Clark who had organized themselves into the 'Labour Withholding Committee'. Eventually this committee became the Clyde Workers Committee, the so-called 'Shop Stewards Movement', with which Lloyd George would have to deal often in the future.[4]

At Bangor, after an elaborate apology for speaking on Sunday, Lloyd George made the pointed charge that the British, unlike the Germans or the French, did not yet know what the war meant. 'A few weeks ago I visited France,' he declared

> Paris is a changed city. Her gaiety, her vivacity are gone. You can see in the faces of every man there, and of every woman, that they know their country is in the grip of grim tragedy. They are resolved to overcome it, confident that they will overcome it, but only through a long agony.
>
> No visitor to our shores would realize that we are engaged in exactly the same conflict, and that on the stricken fields of the Continent and along the broads and narrows of the seas that encircle our islands is now being determined, not merely the fate of the British Empire, but the destiny of the human race for generations to come. We are conducting a war as if there is not war. I have never been doubtful about the result of the war, and I will give you my reasons by and by. Nor have I been doubtful, I am sorry to say, about the length of the war and its seriousness. In all wars nations are apt to minimize their dangers and their durations...I have been accounted a pessimist among my friends in thinking the war would not be over by Christmas.

All of this was an introduction to the subject of the speech: that Britons would have to do more. He returned to his invariable topic, the need for weapons.

> Much as I should like to talk about the need for more men, that is not the point of my special appeal today. We stand more in the need of equipment than we do of men. This is an engineers' war, and it will be won or lost owing to the efforts or shortcomings of engineers. Unless we are able to equip our armies, our predominance in men will avail us nothing. We need men but we need arms more than men, and delay in producing them is full of peril for this country.

He called for a mobilization of industry, what in later days would be styled total war.

> We must appeal for the cooperation of employers, workmen and the general public; the three must act and endure together, or we delay and may be imperil victory. We ought to requisition the aid of every man who can handle metal. It means that the needs of the community in many respects will suffer acutely. Vexatious and perhaps injurious delay; but I feel that the public are prepared to put up with this discomfort, loss and privation if thereby their country marches triumphantly out of this great struggle.
>
> If the absorption of all our engineering resources is demanded, no British citizen will grudge his share of inconvenience. But what of those more immediately concerned in that kind of work? I am now approaching something which it is very difficult to talk about. I must speak out quite plainly; nothing else is of the slightest use. For one reason or another we are not getting all the assistance we have a right to expect from our workers. Disputes, industrial disputes, are inevitable; and when you have a good deal of stress and strain, men's nerves are not at their best. I have no doubt that the spirit of unrest creeps into

relations between employers and workmen. Some differences of opinion are quite inevitable, but we cannot afford them now; and, above all, we cannot resort to the usual method of settling them.

I suppose I have settled more labour disputes than any man in this hall, and the thing you need most is patience...But you know, we cannot afford those leisurely methods now. Time is victory; and while employers and workmen on the Clyde have been spending time disputing over a fraction, and when a weekend, ten days, and a fortnight of work which is absolutely necessary for the country has been set aside, I can say here solemnly that it is intolerable that the life of Britain should be imperilled for the matter of a farthing an hour.

* * * *

There is a good deal to be said for, and a vast amount to be said against, compulsory arbitration, but during the war the Government ought to have the power to settle all those differences, and the work should go on. The workman ought to get more. Very well, let the Government find it out and give it to him. If he ought not, then he ought not to throw up his tools. The country cannot afford it. It is a disaster, and I do not believe the moment this comes home to the workmen and employers they will refuse to comply with the urgent demands of the Government. There must be no delay.

There is another aspect of the question which it is difficult and dangerous to tackle. There are all sorts of regulations restricting output. I will say nothing about the merits of this question. There are reasons why they have been built up. The conditions of employment and payment are mostly to blame for those restrictions. The workmen had to fight for them for their own protection, but in a period of war there is a suspension of ordinary law.

Output is everything in this war...There must be plenty of safeguards and the workman must get his equivalent, but I do hope he will help us to get as much out of those workshops as he can; for the life of the nation depends on it.

Then towards the end of the speech he passed to another delicate topic. Most workmen, he said, put forth every ounce of strength, but unfortunately not all of them did so.

I hear of workmen in armaments works who refuse to work a full week for the nation's need...What is the reason? Sometimes it is one thing, sometimes it is another, but let us be perfectly candid. It is mostly the lure of drink. They refuse to work full time and when they return their strength and efficiency are impaired by the way they spend their leisure. Drink is doing us more damage in the war than all the German submarines put together.

Except for remarking that the Russians, in their zest for efficiency, had imposed national prohibition at the beginning of the war and that the government had power under the Defence of the Realm Act to control drinking, these few sentences were all that Lloyd George said about the problem of alcohol in an address of one and one quarter hours. He closed with an old Welsh folk parable illustrating the point that even the physically handicapped could be of use in the great national endeavor of war.[5]

In terms of hard information conveyed, as opposed to his usual violent but unspecific denunciation of public abuses, the Bangor speech is one of the most important that Lloyd George would make during the war. He rarely said so much. In one way or another he had informed his audience of all his domestic initiatives for the rest of the year: drink, labor dilution, and the beginnings of industrial mobilization that would come with the Treasury agreement and the Munitions of War Act. Lloyd George in fact was bringing the country up to date on matters that the Cabinet had already under consideration. The speech and the phrase 'an engineers' war' were widely applauded although few commentators neglected to note the remarks about drink.[6]

As has been seen, industrial unrest in the North particularly in Scotland had been a worry for several weeks. For a time Lloyd George felt that its origins were treasonable. On 10 March G.R. Askwith wrote to the Prime Minister:

Lloyd George seemed to say today, on [Isaac Haig] Mitchell's [Trade Unionist and Labour Advisor to the Board of Trade] authority, that an anti-war sect exists in Glasgow and is at the bottom of the Clyde dispute. I understand this is a mistake, Mitchell says it is not correct that there is such a party. Churchill also suggested that Germans might be at the back of it. I do not think there is much in this theory; if the men suspected anyone they would tear them in pieces.[7]

In fact the causes of the discontent appear to have derived from the rising food and rent costs which were outstripping the increased wages earned by workers through overtime. But linked to the real economic pressure of lagging earnings was the clear perception in the minds of workers that employers with more orders than they could handle were making huge fortunes. The paradox of rigid wage rates compared to uncontrolled living costs and profits had become a staple of shop stewards' speeches and newspaper articles.[8]

The restlessness on the Clyde was beginning to subside by the time Lloyd George made his Bangor speech, but the Cabinet was well aware that the problem of war worker discontent would have to be addressed. The Defence of the Realm (Amendment Number 2) Bill already under consideration dealt with the core of the problem of the Clyde strikes and with the larger matters of bringing into war production the myriad of smaller firms not presently engaged in it. Many of these smaller firms were bound by contract to fulfill orders for civilian use, which were now pouring in with war-produced prosperity. And even if surplus capacity was available in the North, labor was not.

To a considerable extent the failure to enforce the conversion of civilian production to war work was the result of the almost sentimental affection of the army ordnance department, fully supported by Master General Von Donop and by Kitchener, for the traditional British armament companies. These, the so-called War Office list, with the Royal Ordnance factories, had supplied the junior service with weapons since the middle years of Victoria. The most important, the 'Big Five', were Vickers, Armstrong Whitworth, Cammell Laird, the Coventry Ordnance Works, and Beardmore. The army simply declined to deal with firms it did not know. Theoretically the members of this old boy network would subcontract for components of the huge orders they had received, but the final responsibility for quality, the Ordnance Department insisted, lay with them.[9] The inevitable result was the explosive growth in subcontractors' tenders, with the smaller firms frequently offering different bids to competing principals for the same work with the assurance that the desperation of the principal would insure his tender was accepted. It was at this level that the phrase 'war profiteer' had real meaning and it was in the elimination of the non-competitive subcontracting that the Ministry of Munitions would perform some of its most important work.

It is unlikely that anyone in the government fully understood in February 1915 the complicated logistics of ordnance subcontracting but all were acutely aware that performance on contracts already let was far behind schedule, and second, that the cost of work delivered was rising rapidly, and third, that thousands of firms in the United Kingdom were doing no war work at all. At this log jam the second Defence of the Realm Amendment Bill was directed.

The early drafts of the bill, discussed in the Cabinet on 24 and 26 February and clearly at a separate meeting with the civil service at No. 10 on 5 March, provided not only powers for the government to commandeer unused or underused facilities for war purposes, but also authority to prohibit strikes and lockouts and to require arbitration of industrial disputes.[10] Lloyd George records in his war memoirs that on 26 February he persuaded the Cabinet to delete the arbitration provisions so that he could make an attempt at a voluntary agreement.[11] However, the most important determination upon the Amendment Bill came, in fact, at a meeting with civil servants on 5 March which included, besides the Prime Minister, Lloyd George, McKenna, Crewe and Kitchener, Sir George Askwith of the Board of Trade, Sir George Gibb, now at the Board of Trade but the former Managing Director of the Northeastern Railway and a member of Askwith's Committee on Production at the Board of Trade, and Maurice Hankey as secretary. The consensus of the meeting was that the core of the production problem was housing for labor. There was, for example, idle machinery at the Vickers Works at Erith on the Thames, but there were no surplus engineers in London. There was available labor in South Wales, but the men could hardly be moved *en masse* and more important there were no available lodgings for them in the London suburbs.[12] It may be inferred that the powers in D.O.R.A. Amendment 2 to commandeer housing, proceeded from agreements at this meeting. However, for the life of Lloyd George, the 5 March meeting, to which Lloyd George himself attached much importance, was a part of the educational process that would prepare him for the Ministry of Munitions.[13] Further, the meeting, as Hankey's minutes show, and as Lloyd George reiterated in an acid letter to A.J. Balfour the following day, demonstrated for all, and especially for the Prime Minister, that the War Office was not only incapable of managing the supply of weapons, but even of keeping in touch with the army to which the weapons would go.[14] In the course of the discussion, which was generally about rifles and small arms ammunition and the impossibility at the present rate of production of supplying any weapons to Russia, Kitchener remarked that he was basing all his calculations on an army of 2,000,000 men. Lloyd George immediately interjected that the projected army was 3,000,000. Kitchener replied that this was 'a new figure' to him. Amid general astonishment Asquith confirmed that the House of Commons indeed had recently authorized the increase.[15] The War Office admitted they were short of all forms of ammunition and rifles and would be able to do nothing to aid the allies until 1916. Lloyd George angrily reported to Balfour: 'Nothing can remedy this state of things except the placing at the head of [a] new Executive of an energetic, fearless man who will not be cajoled and bamboozled by von Donop nor bullied by anyone else.'[16]

Three days after this letter Lloyd George introduced the Defence of the Realm Amendment Bill, doing it, he told Riddell later, because everyone else in the Cabinet was afraid of it. 'They thought there would be a terrible row in the House of Commons. It was not my job, but I agreed to do it.'[17] In fact the Bill passed easily in two days. The Unionists generally welcomed it asking only why it had not appeared before. Most of the questions, usually concerning interference with personal rights, came from the Labour party.

Basically the D.O.R.A. (Amendment Number 2) Bill, in all only one clause, gave the government power to order national industrial mobilization. It extended to any manufacturing establishment, not only existing armament manufacturers, which were already so controlled, the liability of government direction or indeed seizure, however for war production only. It did not nullify existing contracts between civilian agencies, but stipulated that government action would provide 'a good defence' against suits for breach of contract and it affirmed that workers' housing could also be requisitioned. In effect it took the British war effort in the direction Lloyd George had been saying since the middle of August that it must move. But laws, as he knew, and as he made clear in his speech, did not produce munitions. Men did. He emphasized that the great powers now assumed would be used only in consultation with manufacturers and indeed he was at the moment 'on the lookout for a strong businessman with some go in him who would be able to push the thing through. . .'[18] Thus was born 'the man of push and go', so much a part of the industrial miracle that was the Ministry of Munitions of War. Lloyd George gathered many such men around him between the summer of 1915 and the summer of 1916, but the quintessential man of push and go was Lloyd George himself.

The Defence of the Realm Act (Amendment Number 2) stipulated nothing about the control of labor. It had simply extended to firms not currently engaged in war work the powers that the government already possessed under D.O.R.A. Amendment Number 1 over armament firms. As has been noted, Lloyd George states in his *War Memoirs* that he was responsible for the omission of labor control. In fact, Asquith's letters to the king and J.A. Pease's diary show that the Cabinet as a whole was convinced that a policy on profit control should appear before labor was asked to forego its ordinary peacetime privileges and immunities. Lloyd George and Runciman were commissioned, with D.O.R.A. Number 2 enacted, to look into the control of labor, wrote Pease on 11 March. Workers would be asked, in effect, to agree to compulsory arbitration in return for control of profits. Again there was discussion of the problem of drinking.[19]

Three days later the Prime Minister reported to the King that Runciman was talking to Vickers and Armstrong about profit limitations (tentatively set at no more than 15% greater than 1914 and finally established at 20% more than the average of the previous two years) while Lloyd George and Runciman were to meet representatives of fifty-three unions to discuss arbitration and relaxation of rules.[20]

Despite what he tries to suggest in his memoirs, the burden of the evidence then is that in the spring of 1915 Lloyd George was less the originator than the executor of Cabinet policy.[21] This is not intended in any way to diminish his achievement. Lloyd George had understood earlier than most the true nature of the European conflict and the meaning of the unlimited British commitment to it. He had called constantly for a real mobilization of Britain's vast industrial resources. And now, in the first weeks of March, 1915, he had prevailed. The catalyst at the beginning, one may guess, was the shortage of rifles and small arms ammunition and the consequent inability to train the thousands of men enlisting. The same shortages made impossible aid to Russia whose plight hung like an evil cloud over all deliberations. And all problems were exacerbated by the Clydebank strikes of February and the reports of slackness and drinking of which apparently everyone, not only Lloyd George, had heard.[22] The question was what to do. The first response had been D.O.R.A. Amendment Number 2 but how would the government use the enormous powers it had given itself? Asquith, sitting alone in the Cabinet room on 18 March writing to Miss Stanley, understood the urgency and sought characteristically for a way to delegate the problem. '. . .all sorts of things are going on, and it's quite in the cards (this is most *secret*) that I may create a new office for Ll. George ('Director of War Contracts' or something of the kind) & relieve him of his present duties. I shan't do anything without consulting you. . .'[23] Virtually as he wrote, at 12:54 p.m. G.M.T., the naval attack upon the inner forts in the Straits of the Dardanelles collapsed when the French battleship *Bouvet* struck a mine. Britain's war effort moved toward its first crisis.

Asquith did in fact offer Lloyd George the post of Director of War Contracts with a separate department a few days later. As Lloyd George told Frances Stevenson, he was reluctant to accept as it would mean either leaving the Treasury or taking on more work than he could handle. But urged on by everyone, including A.J. Balfour, eventually he agreed to consider the idea. The proposed directorate, which could have become an embryonic Ministry of Munitions, died when Lord Kitchener announced that the War Office would have to control it. At this time, Miss Stevenson recorded, Lloyd George determined to turn his attention to the drink question.[24]

Between 17 and 19 March Lloyd George and Runciman were closeted with a large body of working men representing a score of trade unions in the board room of the Treasury, attempting to elicit a promise of relaxation of union work rules which would balance the concessions in profitability and the controls that the government intended to impose upon employers. This meeting, the so-called Treasury Conference, was clearly a public relations exercise designed to impress the working man with the gravity of the munitions problems. Besides Lloyd George and Runciman, A.J. Balfour, Edward Montagu, J. Wolfe ('Sheep') Murray, the powerless Chief of the Imperial General Staff, and Admiral F.D. Tudor, the Third Sea Lord, were present, together with a number of other martial figures in glittering uniform and a body of civil servants including H. Llewellyn Smith, Askwith and W.H. Beveridge.

The conference had opened on 17 March with a speech by Lloyd George. He began by announcing that Lord Kitchener apologized for his absence and continued with the customary explanation of the great need for ammunition. He cited the example of France in industrial mobilization, noting that women were already employed there in large numbers, and made his usual reference to 'excessive drinking among some workers in some districts'. He promised that profits among armament makers would be controlled. In return he asked for an end to strikes, an agreement on arbitration, the dropping of work rules and output restrictions, and the employment of women.[25] Later Balfour spoke to the assemblage, somewhat nervously Lloyd George told Riddell a few days later, and there were many questions, particularly on control of drink, with much discussion.[26]

There were unfortunate objections: the coal miners withdrew citing the existing controls in their industry under the Mines Act, and the Amalgamated Society of Engineers' representatives announced that they were not empowered to sign anything and so had to be dealt with separately a week later. Finally, on 19 March, an almost toothless document, drawn up principally by William Beveridge, was signed by Lloyd George, Runciman, and by Arthur Henderson and William Mosses as leader and secretary of the union representatives. The agreement promised that the trade union officials present 'will recommend' to their members arbitration of disputes and that workmen 'will take a favourable consideration for the relaxation of work restrictions'. The introduction of female and semi-skilled workers would not affect job rates.[27] As a step toward the achievement of industrial peace and the expansion of the work force, the Treasury Agreement meant nothing, although Lloyd George boasted of his accomplishment to Frances Stevenson and gave much space and proud attention to it in his *War Memoirs,* all of which has been reflected, with little evidence, in recent historical writing.[28] It was, however, a personal publicity triumph for Lloyd George on the order, if not so large, of his settlement of the railway dispute in 1907. It seemed to be connected in the public mind with the pacification of the Clyde dispute which was announced as the meetings were in progress. *The Times,* by now growing critical of the government, devoted a fulsome leader to his accomplishments. Mr. Lloyd George 'has shown a large grasp of the situation created by the war' and 'has much enhanced his reputation for statesmanship'. He had made an excellent beginning with his frankness, and so on.[29] However, it was not until the provisions of the Treasury Agreement were embedded in legislation in the Munitions of War Act in the summer of 1915, by which also the government made clear its intention to control profits, that the relaxation of work rules and the dilution of labor became possible.

I

Although Asquith could, without apology, spend a Tuesday afternoon at the Athenaeum reading a book on modern English essayists and would predict to Venetia Stanley on 30 March, twelve days after the collapse of the Dardanelles naval attack, that the war ought to be over in three months, for everyone else March, 1915 was a busy and, perceptibly, a critical month.[30] At the end of 1914, Kitchener had ordered General Charles Callwell to prepare a paper proving that the Central Powers would run out of men in months. This appeared on 6 January 1915.[31] It took no account of the mass of German civilians who had received no military training because of financial stringency in the years before the war, and argued that as Germany was fighting on two fronts, she was losing twice as many men.[32] Lloyd George saw clearly that the war was going badly, that the enthusiasm and sense of urgency of the autumn of 1914 had wilted. But for many Britons life had never been better. Such reflections had inspired the Bangor speech.

Into this feverish and unsettled period intruded a crisis with the Welsh party over church disestablishment, a ghost from Lloyd George's past. He himself was not involved in the quarrel. The minister responsible was Reginald McKenna, who had neglected to confer with the Welsh on a subject so close to their hearts, but Lloyd George was called upon to put it down, which in the event he was unable to accomplish. However for the mind of Lloyd George, even so far from Wales as he now was, any differences with the Principality were important.

The Welsh Church (Disestablishment and Disendowment) Bill of 1912 had become an act on 18 September 1914 under the terms of the Parliament Act at the same time as the Home Rule Bill and, like the latter, had been immediately suspended until the end of the war. But unlike Home Rule which was frozen completely, only the date for disestablishment was put back. The Church Commissioners, created by the bill to handle endowments and above all the tithe, which the Church would lose, were permitted to go about their very complex business. For most Churchmen disestablishment itself was far less important than the loss of revenue decreed by the act. Accordingly there was a good deal of complaint among leading Churchmen that the disorganization caused by the war left the Church in a weakened position to defend itself against the appropriation of its property, which was in fact going forward. On 16 February the Cabinet itself took note of the controversy and proposed a peace conference among the leaders on both sides.[33] Then early in March the Duke of Devonshire gave notice in the House of Lords of intent to put down a bill delaying disestablishment until a year after the war's end and prohibiting any action under its terms until that time. To avert this, on 9 March, the government introduced a bill in the Lords setting the date for action at six months after the end of the war and accompanied it by an agreement from Lansdowne that no government would undertake to alter its terms.[34] Immediately there was an uproar among the Welsh MPs with apparently fair support from back-bench Liberals and from Labour.[35] The Welsh complained they had not been consulted. They had talked to McKenna on 8 March in a casual way, but had not realized they were discussing the terms of the measure until the Lords' debate the next day.[36] There were deputations to the Prime Minister and angry editorials in the non-conformist press, generally making the point that during the six month delay after the war, pledge or no pledge, there would surely be a general election which the Conservatives might win. The whole thing was a plot to kill disestablishment.

Lloyd George, of course, had to speak. On 15 March he made a bitter speech, which in terms of his career as a Welshman is of some importance. The Welsh MPs, he said, were divisive, selfish, and petty, seeking to rob the Church while its members were away fighting a war. Particularly he denounced the apparent leader of the rebellion, Ellis Griffith, whom he had disliked since the days of the Edwards case twenty years before.[37] All the distilled anger and disgust with a generation of indecisive squabbling and futile intrigue came out. He was still shaking with anger half an hour later when he saw Frances Stevenson.[38] 'They [the Welsh MPs] are a poor lot of hounds,' he wrote to his wife that evening, and 'God help the little scabs' he fired off a few weeks later after Llewelyn Williams reported that protests were continuing.[39]

Lloyd George was not alone in his rage. After the debate Asquith, 'fortified', as he put it, by Lloyd George and McKenna, had seen the dissident Welshmen whose leaders beside Griffith were Ellis Davies and Walter Roch, in what was always for him a painful interview.[40] He burst out a few days later to J.A. Pease who was peacefully warming his back before the fire at No. 10 waiting for dinner, saying that he hated the Welsh and their trivial hatred. Then taking that back, he made an exception of Lloyd George but criticized McKenna, as he rarely did, for his handling of the bill.[41]

Asquith, Lloyd George reported to Frances Stevenson, had told him that his speech was the best he had ever made in the House and Lord Robert Cecil had called it the 'most courageous he had heard'.[42] Privately the Prime Minister said the same to Venetia Stanley.[43] Less routine were letters of praise from Church of England clergymen, the Bishop of Birmingham, the Church of England chaplain of the Highland Division, and most surprising of all, from a 'Bishop of Wales', almost certainly John Owen of St. Davids, who admitted that after differing from Lloyd George on the Welsh Church for many years he wrote now 'to thank you sincerely for your courageous and statesmanlike speech last Monday.'[44]

This was satisfying appreciation from unaccustomed sources but as he had been so careful to do at the outbreak of war, Lloyd George had to justify himself with his nonconformist constituency. The body of Welsh MPs could do him no harm, he was sure. He had simply told them what he had long felt privately and indeed, he continued to see Herbert Lewis, William Jones, and for a time Llewelyn Williams. But the nonconformist press was another matter. On the morning before the speech of 15 March he had breakfasted with C.P. Scott of the *Manchester Guardian* and had explained carefully that the bill placed each side in the disestablishment controversy in precisely the same position as if there had been no war. He made clear that he had had nothing to do with it and that the trouble with the Welsh was McKenna's fault.[45] To Robertson Nicoll, who had urged Riddell to convey his anger, he made approximately the same argument: that by obtaining Conservative agreement to the six months postponement of Welsh Church disestablishment the long quarrel was finally ended. Nonconformists should be pleased not bitter.[46] Nevertheless, after repeated promises to bring it forward, the Welsh Church (Postponement) Bill was withdrawn on 26 July 1915.

The disestablishment struggle was a troublesome matter, although obviously minor when measured against the gigantic political strains caused by the war. But, as has been seen, it carried within it causes to which Lloyd George personally was extremely sensitive. If he was willing to denounce certain Welsh MPs as scoundrels, he was by no means ready to give up his position as the tribune of reformist nonconformity even as he won unusual applause from Conservatives and Churchmen. He may have searched for a new issue with which to make amends with his customary friends. This suggestion is prompted by the fact that only four days after his speech on Welsh disestablishment, while the issue was still boiling, he brought up for the first time in the War Council the question of temperance.[47] The subject in the War Council was the recent Battle of Neuve Chapelle, which, Kitchener reported, was almost a victory. 'Owing to bad luck they had just missed this. He laid great stress on the very heavy expenditure of ammunition for field and heavy guns.' Although Lloyd George had been lecturing the Cabinet and War Council about this remarkable characteristic of modern warfare since the middle of October, Kitchener, the quartermaster, was appalled by it. He wanted French to be more sparing of arms and ammunition and he wanted the War Council to authorize him to say so.[48]

It was at this point that Lloyd George brought up the drink problem, pointing out, reasonably, that the cure for ammunition problems was not the slower firing of guns but greater production. Drink was a cause of low munitions production. He and Balfour had been interviewing employers who said that twenty to thirty percent of workers' time was lost from this problem. Vickers would like to see total prohibition in the North, but workmen insisted upon general restrictions throughout the country, not only in industrial areas.[49] There was some support for limiting pub hours from the Prime Minister and from Churchill, although the governments powers in this area were doubtful. Could Lloyd George 'arrange' for closing pubs except from 12–2 p.m. and from 7 to 9 p.m.?[50]

The presentation of the drink problem suggests Lloyd George had been waiting for an opportunity. He had obviously turned it over in his mind for some weeks, at least since the preparation of the Bangor speech, but it must be repeated drink was not his issue alone. Newspapers had been full of demands for temperance in one form or another since the beginning of March.[51]

Lloyd George had begun the systematic collection of data on the drinking problem about the middle of March, 1915 while occupied with the postponement bill and the Treasury conference. G.R. Askwith was asked to get into correspondence with armament firms and soon after his contribution on drink in the War Council the Chancellor had a file of satisfactorily horrible statistics.[52] With these in hand he organized a meeting of shipbuilders at the end of March to give momentum to his case.

Clearly Lloyd George hoped that the meeting, always referred to as a 'deputation', would appear to have been called at the shipbuilders' initiative. He refers in his *War Memoirs* to having 'received' a deputation from the National Shipbuilders' Federation and the report of the meeting to the Cabinet used this term. However, G.J. Carter, the chairman of Cammell Laird, in his opening statement reminded Lloyd George that he and his colleagues were there 'in response to your [Lloyd George's] wire'.[53]

Nevertheless Lloyd George received what he anticipated, unanimous complaint about drink. This did not imply drunkenness, but an impairment of efficiency or of unwillingness of men to work after drinking, although they were physically present at their jobs. There was much discussion of the Black Squads, the riveters, who worked as a group and divided the pay among themselves according to a hierarchy of skill. The aim was to achieve a decent average wage for all which used to take $4\frac{1}{2}$ to 5 days. But now with overtime the average could be earned in 3 to $3\frac{1}{2}$ days.

In his speech to the delegation, Lloyd George called for what seemed to be total prohibition of alcohol. 'Nothing but root and branch methods will be of the slightest avail in dealing with this evil. . .' he declared, and closed with the assertion soon to be amended into stronger language: 'If we are to settle German militarism we must first of all settle with drink.'[54]

The discussions at the conference were not made public but the stenographic transcript shows that there was much sentiment among ship-builders for total prohibition at least in dockyard areas.[55] Beyond his speech Lloyd George did not say much and promised that the problem would be studied. In statements afterwards to the press several members of the delegation affirmed, first of all, that the problem was real and, second, it was the result of higher wages the men were earning which were spent frequently on bottles of whisky. The result was not drunkenness, but an inability to settle into work. The restriction of pub hours by itself would produce 'absolutely no result'.[56] The first stage of the anti-drink campaign was the proposal of total prohibition of all alcoholic beverages. This Lloyd George reported to the Cabinet the next day was what the shipbuilders wanted.[57] The Cabinet agreed to consider a milder restriction involving the temporary prohibition of spirits and wine and a limitation on the hours of the sale of beer.[58] The most sensational item in the 30 March Cabinet was Lloyd George's production of a letter from the King's secretary Lord Stamfordham announcing that to provide an example to the nation the Royal Household was willing to give up 'All' alcohol for the duration of the war 'if it was deemed advisable' so that there would be no difference in the level of sacrifice between the rich and the poor.[59] The idea for a royal pledge seems to have originated with Riddell who records that he had suggested it on 13 March to Lloyd George, who was skeptical that it would have much effect.[60] Nonetheless Lloyd George spoke with the King for three quarters of an hour on the morning of 30 March before meeting the shipbuilders. Evidently he promised to send a report of the meeting and probably dropped a hint that some royal example would be useful.[61] Lloyd George mentioned the King's interest in the drink problem in his speech to the deputation. In any case, immediately after the meeting he sent a transcript of the proceedings and a strong letter, written in his own hand, to the King's secretary. After noting that he had promised to keep His Majesty informed, he wrote:

> It was a very powerful deputation and represented practically all the great firms engaged in turning out munitions of war and ships for the Admiralty. [The deputation had been at some pains to keeps its membership anonymous.] The statements they made were of a very sensational character and I enclose a transcript of their speeches, every word of which will bear his perusal. So far from working harder now than they did before the war, the men are giving less time and slacking is on the increase. The employers are in utter despair. Mere restriction of [pub] hours they regard as quite inadequate and they are firmly of the opinion that unless drink is pressed altogether for the period of the war they will be unable to perform their contracts.

There was not a teetotaler amongst them, but as they were of the opinion that it was most important that the workmen should not imagine that drink was to be forbidden them whilst the rich were still able to indulge in it, they proposed that rich and poor alike should be deprived of liquor during the war. It was altogether a most impressive but depressing deputation. They attributed the [munitions] shortage entirely to drink.[62]

Stamfordham's letter, laid before the Cabinet, arrived the next day. Lloyd George replied immediately saying royal leadership was 'essential'.[63]

The King's Pledge was duly celebrated in all the newspapers and seemed to have made a great impression.[64] Briefly Lloyd George was confident. It 'must now be followed', he wrote to Stamfordham on 1 April, 'by declarations from Judges, Cabinet Ministers, Clergy, the Medical Profession, and the great Manufacturers, and if possible the Trade Union leaders.' He was trying to find someone to take this on.[65] But this hope quickly died. Among governmental leaders only Kitchener followed the royal example.[66] It could be noted that Lloyd George's solicitation of the unheeded King's Pledge embittered his relations with Buckingham Palace for many months. In a conversation with Arthur Lee in July 1916 during the award of a K.C.B. His Majesty was most outspoken. Lloyd George has 'made a fool of him over drink'. The Chancellor had made 'an impassioned plea' to the King and he had agreed, but to no purpose.[67]

The first adverse reaction to the public momentum toward prohibition now being so skilfully generated, came, almost predictably, from the union whose workers were the target of most criticism, the Boilermakers' and Steel Shipbuilders' Society. On the day after the meeting of the employers' deputation the union executive council issued a long statement terming Lloyd George's speech to the deputation a libel, asserting that its own members did not drink excessively and that when there was a report of drunkenness the union investigated, finding eighty percent of the reports untrue. Finally the false reports of low production would give Germany 'real joy'.[68]

The hard opposition from the Boilermakers caused much concern and elicited an immediate reaction in the form of a covert investigation into the drinking habits of shipyard workers. After consultation between Lloyd George and McKenna, apparently on 31 March, the Home Office sent 33 experienced Special Branch men in plain clothes to shipbuilding areas, 17 to the Clyde, 6 to Newcastle, 4 to Barrow, and 2 each to Sunderland, Stockton, and West Hartlepool. They remained there from 1 to 3 of April and were in the words of McKenna's report to the Cabinet 'to visit the public houses, talk freely with the men, and report what comes within their personal observation'.[69] The center of the difficulty, as the employers themselves had emphasized, were the riveters, who worked in groups of six, one blacksmith, two riveters, one holder-on (bucker in the United States) and two boys.[70] The squad was paid as a whole and the money usually shared out in a local pub. If one man was absent the Black Gang did not work and worker fellowship as well as union rules prevented mixing gangs. The drinking was done on weekends, always whisky followed by beer (a 'boilermaker' in America), and the evil effects felt on Monday. Frequently the squad would bribe one member to stay away from the yard so that the rest would not have to work. Sunday work itself was so poor as to be of no value.

Everywhere the riveters insisted that the nature of their work was such that alcohol was a necessity. (One can sympathize. Bucking a rivet inside a boiler or a hollow ship's hull would be similar to spending one's working hours inside a bass drum.) In Scotland where pubs were closed on Sunday there were many private drinking clubs and many pubs sold bottles of whisky, lined up on the bar on Saturday night, for consumption the next day. In the northeast the drink was beer, but the pubs opened at 6 a.m. Uniformly the agents agreed that the root of the problem was wartime prosperity. Whatever might be said of Lloyd George's motives, the drink problem was real.[71]

So far Lloyd George had discussed control of drink solely in terms of national prohibition, either of all alcohol or of spirits and wine. This had been the substance of his proposal to the Cabinet on 30 March and was prompted by the invariable response from working men that any restrictions would have to be universal, not applied only to crucial areas. But already he was having doubts. In reality he was, as always, feeling his way. His goal after all was an increase in munitions production and not the imposition of any particular scheme for the control of alcohol. On 2 April George Riddell warned that he felt total prohibition would be 'very dangerous' and Lloyd George agreed.[72] Evidently he solicited C.P. Scott's opinion, for on 6 April he received the same response in almost precisely the same terms: it would provoke unrest and could not be enforced. Scott however suggested what was in fact the second and probably the central phase of the anti-drink campaign, one upon which Lloyd George was already at work, the nationalization of public houses.[73] This was by no means a new idea. Reform groups of all sorts, for example the Fabian Society, had been urging it for years.

One is inclined to wonder whether Lloyd George ever took total prohibition of all or even of some drink seriously. Rather it seems he was proceeding in his usual way, indirectly, allowing the opposition to waste their ammunition against a false target, after which the real one would be produced. Evidently, in early March he had commissioned his trusty accountant, Sir William Plender, to appraise the value of the brewing trade and the licensed houses, for Plender's first report was rendered on 30 March.[74] Lloyd George hinted that state purchase was his real plan to Riddell on 10 April after Riddell had remarked that the teetotalers, who were thunderously applauding the notion of national prohibition and so annoying labor, were hurting their own cause by their agitation. Lloyd George agreed, but added that when the prohibitionists saw his new plan they would attack it and so help him.[75] In any case he was by this time hard at work on a scheme for the nationalization of public houses and through Archibald Salvidge of Bent's Brewery in Liverpool was in contact with important English brewers as owners of licensed premises. He had seen Salvidge at breakfast at No. 11 sometime in March to ask about the political prospects and the possible cost of state purchase of pubs.[76] The rather important date of this interview unfortunately cannot be established because of Salvidge's failure to indicate days of the month in his letters to his wife. But it is clear that while talking about prohibition publicly for weeks, Lloyd George had been working toward a plan for state purchase. Salvidge was unfamiliar with Lloyd George's un-English habit of working breakfasts and had already eaten at the Constitutional Club, so he had to consume a second one. 'Lloyd George's son was with us, he was in uniform,' Salvidge wrote to his wife.

> In short, what he is after is nothing less than nationalization of the drink trade. There is to be some sort of Government control by Orders in Council, but state purchase is the real aim. He made no secret that with millions being chucked about like pence he can get things done now that would not be looked at in peace-time. He must have someone of political experience and public spirit who knows the trade from the inside. Was I prepared to come and help?[77]

Much of Lloyd George's political genius lay in his sense of the temper of the hour. There were times when the public could accept a change and times when it sought stability. The Liberal disaster with the Licensing Bill in 1908 could provide an example. Above all, he thought, during a war anything could be justified in terms of military necessity. This fairly obvious lesson, one could note, Churchill did not seem to understand after the Beveridge Report during the Second World War. Nationalization of public houses, it must be repeated, was a venerable cause of the nonconformist, social reformist radicals, such as C.P. Scott, who were Lloyd George's national constituency and whom he did not want to lose. This change would please them. It might also increase munitions production. Although he occasionally sipped champagne, Lloyd George had been a temperance advocate since his days at Breeze, Jones and Casson and it had helped his career, yet he was anything but a single minded eccentric idealogue. Now with cries for control of drink coming from all over the country, here again, with the war as an excuse, was the opportunity to lead a crusade.

Alderman Salvidge, although a leading Conservative in his city, was apparently mildly sympathetic with Lloyd George's plans and saw Lloyd George at Downing Street at least once again at the end of March and agreed to canvass quietly among important owners of tied (brewery owned) public houses.[78] Officially, it must be remembered, during these weeks Lloyd George was still proposing some form of prohibition. However in the middle of April newspapers, led by the *Daily Express*, began to carry reports that the Cabinet had given up prohibition and would consider instead state purchase of the trade. There were also warnings that there would be opposition not only from brewing interests but from the temperance reformers who believed that the state ought not to be associated with the 'unclean thing'.[79]

This was a blow. Despite all the publicity about prohibition, theoretically no one but the Cabinet realized that work was going ahead on a plan for purchase.[80] Lloyd George showed his dismay at the publication of his nationalization plan in a letter to St. Loe Strachey on 16 April. After thanking Strachey for a powerful article of support in the *Spectator* he lamented:

> Unfortunately, however, someone associated with the trade gave away the proposals placed before them for consideration with the consequence that opinion is ranging itself on our scheme before any opportunity has been afforded us to state our case.[81]

Strachey replied the next day that he was 'sorry the scheme had been compromised' as it was 'such an easy case to put'.[82] However, two days later the Chancellor received a far less sympathetic letter from the Scottish brewer, and more importantly Scottish Unionist whip, Sir George Younger. Younger's opposition was almost certainly an element in the failure of the drink crusade, as his resistance would be seven years later in the collapse of Lloyd George's Coalition government. 'You cannot nationalize the drink trade without Unionist support,' wrote Younger,

> and while you appear to have made satisfactory arrangements with English leaders you will [need] my support and I insist that if you take over the pubs you must take over the breweries. You need not trouble to discuss the scheme any further in the Cabinet unless you are prepared to take the whole in this case and not merely what may suit you as I can promise you now that no Unionist leader would ever dream of looking at such a scheme for a moment.

It would have to be all or nothing.[83] Younger's self assurance may have seemed overdone but his position in the party was an exceptional one. The Conservative party leader was his fellow Scotsman Andrew Bonar Law who was responsible for his post as whip and for his baronetcy.

Younger's truculent attitude identified a problem within the Unionist party that would be of great importance within the next few weeks and on vastly larger questions than the issue of drink. The difficulty lay in the split in opinion between the lower ranks of the party and the national leadership over the matter of cooperation with the government. The back bench felt that Bonar Law did not press the government with sufficient vigor. This discontent had been simmering at least since the beginning of 1915. In a way, Masterman had been sacrificed as an act of appeasement. Bonar Law was out of step with his party on the drink question.

Twelve days before Younger's letter, on 7 April Bonar Law had written to Lloyd George promising that if drink were shown to be a difficulty in the prosecution of the war 'we shall not, as a party, oppose the proposal' for state purchase.[84] Later, on 17 April, he had written to J.P. Croul, editor of the *Scotsman*, commending purchase and saying that he wanted to free the Tories from the 'incubus of being tied to the Trade'.[85]

On the day he received Younger's letter, 19 April, Lloyd George submitted his plan for national prohibition to the Cabinet. As he no doubt anticipated, his colleagues rejected it immediately. Moreover, as J.A. Pease recorded, the Cabinet proposed that he look into plans for restriction of pub hours, perhaps only in munitions areas, or purchase.[86]

Asquith was more succinct:

> Nothing can be more absurd than to prevent the yokels of Bucks or Kerry from enjoying their modest & accustomed drink because some men engaged in ship-building on the Tyne or Clyde are drinking too much. Altogether the thing is beginning to assume more rational dimensions, and before long they will have nearly reached my own 'reactionary' view, that the main thing to be done is to limit hours of opening, provide really good food & drink in accessible places, and perhaps clap a substantial addition on the taxes on spirits & wine.[87]

Although it was unclear at the time not only national prohibition but wholesale state purchase of the licensed trade had failed. 'The Great Purchase Folly is as dead as Queen Anne,' wrote Asquith to Miss Stanley that evening, even though, he added, McKenna and Haldane were inclined to shed a few tears over it.[88] The Cabinet returned to the subject on 22 April and again on 26 April, but already Lloyd George was backing away. Charles Hobhouse, who personally supported prohibition of spirits, recorded in his diary on 22 April that the Chancellor wanted 'as usual to do something startling,' but 'was very uncertain as to his proposals.' The Cabinet demanded a draft bill.[89] Four days later with a draft bill before them the power of compulsory purchase was finally deleted.[90]

Even if Strachey wrote on 3 May regretting that Lloyd George could not induce his 'colleagues to support you in your scheme of buying out the trade,' it is apparent that Lloyd George's enthusiasm for the grand stroke of state purchase had been declining for some days. He had told Riddell as much at dinner on 18 April.[91] Too many interests opposed him; the political complexities were too diverse and the sums involved were impossible even in wartime.[92] The Cabinet itself was frightened of the consequences Lloyd George reported to C.P. Scott.[93]

He was moving, then, into the third and last phase of the anti-drink crusade, control of drink through taxation and administrative regulation, a kind of guerrilla warfare he had undertaken many times before. On 20 April, the day after the first rebuff in the Cabinet he introduced the third amendment bill to the Defence of the Realm Act (D.O.R.A.).[94] This measure dealt entirely with the control of alcohol. His theme to the House was that the control of drink constituted the third big job in the prosecution of the war. The government had the power to take over manufacturing companies; trade unions had given up restrictive practices; now the state must tackle drink. He referred to the Home Office investigation of the shipyards, to the reports he had received from shipbuilders, and he repeated his warnings in the Bangor speech. Yet he admitted that drink was a most difficult subject for legislation. Every government that had attempted it had been hurt.

D.O.R.A. Amendment No. 3 gave the government the power to proceed by Orders in Council to close down, control or acquire, the private liquor industry in any area, or to open canteens in competition with pubs, in effect superseding at a stroke all the ancient local authority powers in this province of community affairs. Finally, he announced that the measure before the House was in the nature of a budget resolution as it would include taxes on the trade. Accordingly at the end of his speech the House resolved itself into a ways and means (i.e. budget) committee.[95]

In the ways and means committee Lloyd George put down resolutions virtually doubling the taxes on whisky and wines and increasing by nearly ten times on a sliding scale the taxes on heavy beers. What Lloyd George seems to have been doing in this awkward parliamentary maneuver on 20 April was to attempt to incorporate his drink restrictions into already pending government legislation, the D.O.R.A. amendment and the forthcoming budget. Presumably he hoped to limit debate. Instead he prolonged it.

Suddenly the debate came alive. Timothy Healy, one of the few Irish nationalists present, rose in a fury. There had been no notice that this was to be a budget night 'under guise' of a debate on a D.O.R.A. amendment. The new duties were a 'murderous tax' that would kill Irish brewing and distilling. He intended to oppose the government for the first time since the war began.[96]

Healy's anger only reflected that of the Nationalist party at large. Over the following weekend the papers were full of statements by politicians which were enlivened by Lloyd George's release on 30 April of a White Paper on the drinking problem. This rather curious document of twenty pages entitled 'Copy "of a Report and Statistics of Bad Time Kept in Shipbuilding, Munitions and Transport Areas"' was generally a haphazard scrapbook of extracts of reports sent by the Shipbuilders' Federation and of a few Admiralty returns, with an excerpt from *The Times* of Lloyd George's speech to the shipbuilders on 29 March.[97] It excited both comment and derision.[98]

Lloyd George's introduction of a second budget was scheduled for Tuesday, 4 May. The previous day he had met Bonar Law, who clearly now had the sense of his party, and who told him that the Conservatives could not approve taxes on the trade of this size. Lloyd George reported that he had said that then he must drop them and blame the Tories. He affected to believe that the opposition leader was much impressed by this threat.[99]

Whether the awkward imposition of the spirit and beer duties on 20 April was intended, as Lloyd George later claimed, to prevent 'forestalling' — taking whisky out of bond before the new tax was effective — or to suppress discussion of the alcohol duties during the budget debate as the rest of the world assumed, is unclear. In any case the tactic was ineffective. After Austen Chamberlain's angry reply to a budget statement that called for no changes and did not mention the new duties, Bonar Law in a masterly combination of sympathy and menace, professed support for the principle of temperance but admitted that he had been 'inundated' with telegrams calling for resistance by the Conservatives. The sensations of the debate however were Arthur Henderson speaking for Labour, who called the White Paper a 'libel', and John Redmond, speaking for the Irish. The Nationalist leader attacked the White Paper. If drink were a problem in some areas D.O.R.A. was available. The taxes on heavy beer would destroy the market for the most important cash crop in Ireland, barley. More ominously, he reminded Lloyd George, the owners of Irish distilleries, John Jameson for example, were Unionists. He had never expected to find himself in agreement with the voice of Unionism in Ireland, the *Irish Times*, but the paper now absolutely condemned the new taxes. He finished by reading the resolutions passed by the Nationalist party that day which concluded with the words that the party 'will oppose them [the drink taxes] by every means in our power'.[100]

Lloyd George had always commended drink legislation to his colleagues, and indeed to the public, as a political demonstration of wartime unity and of the willingness of the nation to sacrifice. Repeatedly he had pointed to the stirring examples of Russia and France. What he had accomplished by the end of the House sitting on 4 May was the breakup of party unity that had supported the government since the beginning of the war — allowing even Home Rule and disestablishment into the statute book — and the destruction of the illusion that Britain was ready for sacrifice. Any one of several possible combinations of votes between the Unionists, the Irish, and Labour, could defeat the government. There was no course but surrender.

He attempted some further negotiations with the brewers, but on the morning of 6 May he saw Redmond and Dillon and agreed to give up the drink taxes.[101] 'Mr. Lloyd George is in disagreement with at least nine-tenths of public opinion of the country,' said the *Daily Telegraph* the next day,

> upon a piece of liquor legislation and is struggling to get his own way. If he had been able to form a plausible case for his proposals, on the grounds of national need in connection with the war, he would easily have carried the House of Commons and the country behind him.

The general complaint seemed to be that the entire country was being penalized for the failure of a few.[102] Everyone was in favor of sacrifice, but not yet.

As these words appeared, the dropping of the drink tax was announced, the Chancellor's disgrace being covered somewhat by the news of the sinking of the *Lusitania*. That evening Lloyd George spoke to the Newspaper Press Fund. Afterwards George Riddell reflected upon the events of the last few days in his diary.

> LG made a good speech but he has made a sad mess of the drink question, except that as usual he has aroused public attention. His big schemes have all fallen to the ground. He talks too much and flew too high. The Irish Party performed the happy despatch. T.P. O'Connor says, 'LG was very obstinate and took it badly.' The truth is that politics in Ireland are controlled to a large extent by the liquor trade — one of the powerful unseen forces. LG as a constructive statesman is rarely successful. He is a great drummer, a great negotiator and a great force. And he has the power of spotting weak places, particularly in other people's armour. His great schemes however are usually a mistake. His land taxes and insurance for example.[103]

The biographer must address the question: What had happened? The entire episode of the drink crusade had lasted little more than a month. Although the Bangor speech occurred on 28 February and Plender presumably began his investigation soon after, these were the usual trial balloons combined with the accumulation of statistics. Basically the period had lasted from the meeting with the shipbuilders on 29 March to the surrender to the Irish on 7 May, a time, as will be seen, when Lloyd George was busy also with several other important matters. The blaze of publicity began with the shipbuilders and the King's Pledge. When the pledge failed to have any effect he moved quickly from national prohibition to what was probably his own goal from the beginning, state purchase. This was defeated in the Cabinet. However, purchase of the trade was furiously opposed also by Robertson Nicoll of the *British Weekly*, a voice Lloyd George on many previous occasions had taken very seriously indeed, even though he seems to have neglected him during the previous month. Harold Spender records in his autobiography that Lloyd George told him that Nicoll defeated the plan for assumption of the trade which would have been run on the 'Carlisle System'. The state, said Nicoll, should have nothing to do with drink. He used the analogy of opium in India provided by the East India Company. Lloyd George, Spender continued, had insisted that his opposition was not the brewers, with whom he could have dealt.[104] Lloyd George repeated this assertion without providing names, in his

War Memoirs, and it has become the conventional historical explanation of the demise of the anti-drink campaign.[105]

However, this cannot be the whole truth. The so-called Carlisle System was not in existence in 1915. It did not appear until 1916 when the Board of Liquor Control established under the terms of D.O.R.A. amendment number 3 nationalized the brewery and some 170 pubs and licensed hotels in the Carlisle area. (They were sold finally in 1973.)[106] It is clear that Lloyd George's recollections to Spender were made some time after the event he was discussing, possibly when he was seeking an explanation of what had happened. But also, even if Lloyd George had long felt that he must listen to Robertson Nicoll, the rest of the Cabinet had no similar compulsion and such well informed observers as St. Loe Strachey assumed the Cabinet to be responsible for defeat of the plan.[107]

Finally, even if Nicoll opposed state purchase, he was only one, if a powerful, voice and he represented the radical fringe of nonconformity. Sir Thomas Whittaker, MP, a wealthy northern hardware manufacturer, a Privy Councillor, officer of nearly every temperance association in the kingdom and managing director of one of the largest temperance friendly societies, a man who had sponsored Lloyd George on the temperance platform for a quarter century, strongly and publicly supported state purchase.[108]

The proper answer would seem to be that public opinion as a whole was reluctant to involve the entire nation in the solution of what was, on Lloyd George's own evidence, a local problem. To this opinion the Cabinet responded.[109] It could never be stated publicly but intemperance was almost entirely a Scottish, indeed a Clydebank, matter with some echoes among the dockers and the seamen. The Royal Dockyards at Plymouth, for example, were unaffected. Hence, even though the boilermakers insisted publicly that any restriction imposed should be national, the Cabinet decided otherwise and the drink crusade dwindled to powers for local control through Orders in Council remaining under D.O.R.A. amendment number 3.

Lloyd George admitted in his *War Memoirs* that in the national drink crusade he was 'compelled to swallow almost total defeat'.[110] However, he recorded proudly the accomplishments of the Liquor Control Board established in June 1915, after he had gone to the Ministry of Munitions, to administer the powers created under amendment number 3. He showed that the statistics of alcohol consumption fell markedly during the war and that in the budgets of 1917 and 1918, after he was Prime Minister, taxes on beers and spirits were raised to unprecedented levels, all of which is perfectly true. Some of this may have been the result, as he admitted, of millions of men of drinking age being absent from Great Britain, but a more telling point, easily found in any review of tax statistics on alcohol (which for Britain go back well into the eighteenth century), is that since the beginning of the twentieth century, consumption of drink in absolute terms had been falling, steadily if irregularly, despite a growing population with an even more rapidly growing proportion of adults. The reductions in consumption during the war were more than marginal, but not great. In fact Lloyd George remarked to Riddell at the end of January 1917 that he felt the Liquor Control Board had failed to show much enthusiasm for reducing the number of pubs. No doubt, he thought, Asquith had passed word to its chairman not to be too energetic.[111]

The drink problem, in conclusion, was genuine, but small, confined to a few trades in a few industries. Lloyd George probably did himself no harm by turning it into a national issue. He, and everyone else, were properly worried about the slow production and repair of ships. But Riddell also clearly was correct when he wrote that the Chancellor had erred by making too much of it. He forfeited the support of the Conservatives by trying to make it a war measure. The war-time electoral honeymoon was waning despite Asquith's attempts to prolong it. Perhaps the important result was the further stimulation of the shop stewards movement on the Clyde, with which he would have to deal within the year as Minister of Munitions. His reception there at the end of 1915 was distinctly unfriendly.

The growing frustration among the Conservatives, already manifested in their reaction to the drink question and their angry response to Lloyd George's second war budget, symbolized the breakdown of the political accord that had existed between the front benches, almost without interruption since the beginning of hostilities. The tension would burst into the open less than two weeks later bringing down the Liberal government. However, except for the turmoil over the drink duties, the 1915 budget was not only uninteresting, but lifeless. Lloyd George proposed nothing. The standard rate of income tax remained at 2s 6d; super taxes were unchanged although the Chancellor noted happily, without any reference to war profiteers, that there were 15,000 new supertax payers, almost doubling the number in this bracket.[112]

But the war that had cost about £1,000,000 per day in November 1914 was now costing twice that amount and he would have to find £1,132,000,000 in the next twelve months. Of this £862,000,000 would be borrowed, again entirely in the capital market.[113] Perhaps the most interesting parts of the address were in the Chancellor's continual hedging on the duration of the war. In November he had insisted that as the government's financial officer it was his duty to think in the long term, but now he professed to believe that it might be over in six months, but it might not. As there exists plenty of evidence showing that he was perfectly sure the war would not nearly be over in six months this reluctance is curious and suggests pressure from the Cabinet.

In any case the Conservatives were furious, as has been seen, at their inability to discuss the drink taxes which were not in the resolutions before the House on 4 May, while Austen Chamberlain who had warmly applauded Lloyd George in November used his answering speech also to denounce the munitions scandal which existed he said 'despite the soothing syrup administered by the Prime Minister in an unhappy moment at Newcastle.'[114] The clamor over the innocuous, almost invisible, May budget could have told anyone, except the Prime Minister, that his government was in trouble.

II

Asquith had remarked to Venetia Stanley on 18 March, rather idly, that he might create a special munitions post '"Director of War Contracts" or something of that kind' for Lloyd George and relieve him of the Chancellorship. Lloyd George was reluctant to give up his post as Chancellor, but agreed to think about it. As he usually did the Prime Minister appointed instead another committee, composed of himself, Lloyd George, Montagu, and

A.J. Balfour, but not Kitchener, to discuss the appointment of a Munitions Committee. The men met on 22 March.[115]

Kitchener's absence from the planning committee evidently was intentional and was probably Asquith's way of insuring that the deliberations were peaceful for he wrote to Lloyd George later that day suggesting some names for the membership and adding that it was 'essential' that the War Secretary be 'brought in'.[116] What Asquith had first conceived, unclearly, as an executive bureau or sub-department with a full-time ministerial head became, four days later, only another committee. Nonetheless Kitchener was immediately suspicious of an encroachment on War Office control of munitions production. After a fairly temperate meeting with Asquith on 24 March he wrote a letter of protest which the Prime Minister immediately passed to Lloyd George for an answer.[117] Lloyd George replied the same day with a note that could serve as a model of diplomatic persuasion. The committee (whose powers were not yet settled) would not interfere with existing contracts. Kitchener should welcome it, he was busy with other things, time consuming negotiations with labor, etc. No one really wanted to take it on but it might help, although if it could not be effective it should not be appointed.[118] Kitchener answered with a standard reply: the committee no doubt will be a help to the War Office, but production was well in hand and such changes as the Prime Minister proposed needed an Order in Council.[119]

Lloyd George sent copies of Kitchener's reply to Balfour and Churchill, saying to the latter that he would decline to head the committee unless the War Secretary was controlled.[120] Balfour sent a sympathetic reply commenting on Kitchener's innocence in matters of production and saying Lloyd George must see the Secretary of State for War.[121]

The confrontation occurred on 28 March in Asquith's, and apparently Montagu's, presence. It was chiefly a shouting match during which both Lloyd George and Kitchener offered to resign.[122] Finally the War Secretary attempted to forestall Lloyd George's committee by appointing his own, the War Office Armaments Output Committee, announced on 7 April.

Asquith announced the Munitions of War Committee the next day giving it, as he described to Miss Stanley, 'the fullest possible powers'. The new body that would solve all problems was proclaimed in the press on 14 April, and Asquith listed its membership in the House of Commons the following day asserting that the committee could take 'all steps necessary' to 'insure' the production of munitions.[123] *Punch* celebrated its appearance with the famous cartoon of Lloyd George 'delivering the goods', galloping forward astride the near horse of an artillery team inscribed 'Capital' and 'Labour' drawing a caisson loaded with munitions.[124] But in none of the optimistic publicity, all of which was designed to impress the public with the fact that the munitions problem was at an end, was there any indication of what the committee would do or what were its terms of reference.[125]

By the time the munitions committee was announced, it had already met several times. Altogether, between its first meeting on 12 April and dissolution of the committee in the coalition crisis the next month it assembled six times, the last on 13 May. As a factor in the production of munitions the committee was useless as Lloyd George admits.[126] Historically it stands as simply another example of Asquith's lamentable tendency to give the appearance of action by the delegation of a problem. Yet the month of the committee's existence is not unimportant for the story of Lloyd George. He found it almost impossible to extract information from the War Office, and indeed in trying to obtain data he involved himself in the most spectacular row with Kitchener that the Cabinet had seen to that time, but he learned enough to be convinced that weapons and ammunition procurement would have to be separated from Kitchener's department. Thus the munitions committee was, as in fact he put it, 'a stepping stone' to the Ministry of Munitions.[127]

What Lloyd George and the other members of the committee learned was that the War Office had no idea not only of what were the requirements of the army in France, but of how many weapons were being produced. At the first meeting on 12 April with Lloyd George in the chair and Balfour, Montagu and a number of civil servants in attendance, the Chancellor asked the Master General of the Ordnance, Stanley Von Donop, also a member of the committee, to report on the current supply of shells and to what extent industries outside the customary munitions club were being brought into shell making.[128] The request for this simple and rather basic information caused a flurry of anger in the War Office. 'I'll get him the figures,' growled Von Donop to William Beveridge who had been 'provisionally' designated as secretary of the committee, 'but they will delay production of shells for two days. The statistics are absolutely secret, known only to me. I'll have to spend two days with a slide rule on them myself instead of getting on with my job.'[129]

Despite these dismal predictions Von Donop produced a statement the next day with a memorandum by Lord Moulton, an eminent judge and in 1915 chairman of the Committee on Explosives Supply under Von Donop at the War Office. These documents did not indeed tell much about shell supply, but a great deal about conditions in the department of the Master General of the Ordnance. In his statement Von Donop outlined the army ammunition requirement as he saw it. On 1 May there would be 913 eighteen pound guns. At the standard ration of 17 rounds per gun per day the weekly requirement, he calculated would be 108,587 eighteen pound rounds. He expected to receive 51,250 from home manufacturers and 38,750 from abroad for a total of 90,000 per week, leaving a shortage of 8,587. Nearly all the increase in eighteen pound ammunition, he added, apparently not recalling his fights with Lloyd George the previous autumn, was coming from abroad. Production, mostly but not entirely in the United States, would be twice that at home by August.[130]

The minutes do not indicate whether the committee noted that nearly every calculation in Von Donop's document was wrong and that the shortage on his own figures was not 8,587 but 18,547.

The other report, by Lord Moulton, whom Lloyd George would quickly appropriate for the Ministry of Munitions in June, began with a statement by the author of contempt for his superiors. He specifically declined any responsibility for the figures his document contained.

> The fact is that they [the figures] are based upon the contractual obligations of supplies of shells and not upon any estimate of the extent to which these contracts will be punctually performed.

It is of no service to tabulate clerically contractual obligations. No one is keeping his contract even approximately and consequently I am unwilling

to make a return based upon those figures. Nonetheless, Moulton offered samples of the curious War Office accounting for explosives in two columns headed 'Total Estimated Requirement' and 'Actually Used'. These sums show, for example, that in March the 'Requirement' was for 2,347,520 pounds of high explosive and that 588,420 was in fact 'Used', which suggests a huge over supply. In fact a careful reading of the War Office report shows, as Moulton had warned, that 'Requirement' meant simply the amount contracted for and 'Used' the amount delivered.[131]

Among Von Donop's mistakes in his error-filled statement of 13 April was the assertion that by August of 1915, particularly with the increase in supply from abroad, there would be no shortage of ammunition in France.[132] Either at the meeting at which the memorandum was delivered or later, Lloyd George discovered that the Master General was basing his calculations on two armies on the Western Front whereas in fact Britain was building four armies there. Accordingly at the next day's meeting, Wednesday, 14 April, he told the committee that the correct number of troops for which they should plan was 509,000, a figure already given the Cabinet with great reluctance on 12 April by Kitchener himself. The result, in the Cabinet of Thursday, 15 April, was a ringing fight between the Field Marshal and Lloyd George, with most of the members supporting the Chancellor. In the end Kitchener tried to walk out and resign. Lord Beaverbrook assigns much importance to this affair. He suggests the Secretary of State was prevented from leaving the government only because he was physically unable to get through the door of the Cabinet room which opened inward and was being held closed by J.A. Pease. Had he been able to do so he would have brought down the government.[133]

This of course is possible. The government was indeed brought down by the resignation of a less visible martial figure just one month later. The question rather is whether Kitchener intended to carry out his threat. Charles Hobhouse thought not.

Yesterday [15 April] we had a very stormy meeting. K., the moment we met, said he had something very serious to say. Yesterday [14 April] at a meeting of the War Munitions Committee the Chancellor of the Exchequer and Montagu informed the Committee that the number of troops in France was 500,000, and this in spite of the entreaty he had made the figures he supplied the Cabinet should not be divulged; he felt a great responsibility to the Army for having furnished these figures, since the knowledge of them by the enemy might have serious results, and as they had been divulged by his fault he could only resign his position as Secretary of State and immediately withdraw from the Cabinet. Ll.G replied that at the first meeting of the Committee Von Donop, the Master-General of the Ordnance, had produced figures to the Committee which showed that we had two armies in France, and not four, and that by July [August?] supply to these of all munitions would have overtaken demand. He thereon gave the Committee as a basis to work of the number of 509,000 which K had given the Cabinet two days before. It would be a mere farce for them to be working on fiigures which were inaccurate, and neither he nor any other of its members would stay there 5 minutes if they were not to be trusted with the real numbers and requirements. W.S.C. then chimed in to support Ll.G. and said that these figures were probably known approximately to a good many — I interrupted to say they were known to a writer in *The Times* the previous day — and to the Paris correspondent of the *Tribuna* — and that no great responsibility for their being mentioned to a confidential Committee could therefore exist, that everyone had successes and failures, and if things went amiss sometimes no great harm was done. Grey remarked that K. had some cause of complaint as he had particularly asked those figures should be kept secret. Ll.G. answered very hotly that it was childish to withhold such facts from a body which was set up at K.'s request, of which he was Chairman, against his own wish, and only because of K.'s insistence and the P.M. — he was quite ready to resign that or any other position, but he could only continue as long as he was in full possession of all facts and figures. Crewe and Harcourt tried to mediate and then K. broke in saying it was plain that he had lost the confidence of his colleagues and must cease to cooperate with them, picked up his spectacles, pushed back his chair, and took 3 slow, very slow steps to the door. McK., W.R., Lucas, Harcourt, Crewe and some at the far end of the table called out 'No, no' — Grey and the P.M. said nothing. Ll.G., W.S.C. and I also said nothing, they because they were angry, I because I was certain the whole thing was pure farce. Either K. wished to try his strength with the public against the govt. or his case being a bad one, that he wished hereafter to be able to refuse to give information. He tried 'resignation' 3 times with Cromer, and when on the third time it was accepted by telegram and a remark that a cabin on the first homeward ship reserved, it was not again referred to, or proffered. If now accepted it would have made a great fuss, and he would have had to explain that he had resigned because he had withheld from one of his most important military colleagues important information or had authorized that colleague to supply the Chancellor of the Exchequer and a Committee set up in response to a national request with false information, by either of which courses he endangered the state and because his colleagues thought such conduct unwise and corrected it, he retired from Office. That K. has got some underhand game on is almost certain, but that he play it with such bad cards is not likely.[134]

As usual the Prime Minister was in misery and, it would seem, quite shaken by the event. 'Ll.G. & Winston were both (the former having a quite presentable case) aggressive and tactless,' he told Venetia Stanley the next day.

And the situation was for the moment of the worst — particularly as Grey — a good deal to Ll.G.'s chagrin — strongly championed Kitchener, and McKenna was almost openly gloating over the imminent shipwreck of the Committee, wh. as you know he has always hated & sought to frustrate. And all this came literally like a bolt out of the blue, for I had not the faintest premonition of it.

Nonetheless, continued Asquith, he was able to smooth things and bring the Cabinet back to business. 'Still,' he concluded, 'it leaves a disagreeable taste in one's mouth — particularly as Ll.G. (who of course is not quite *au fond* a gentlemen) let slip in the course of the altercation some most injurious & wounding innuendos wh. K. will be more than human to forget.'[135]

No one emerges with much credit from the affair except perhaps Kitchener himself. Asquith displayed his usual complacent weakness, satisfied by being able to continue to number the days he had been Prime Minister, McKenna, his venomous jealousy, the younger men, happiness at seeing a splendid, elderly and inarticulate military figure insulted by two famous artists in vituperation. On the following Wednesday, 21 April, Kitchener sent a note asking Lloyd George, according to Frances Stevenson, who had not seen the Chancellor since the previous Thursday's Cabinet, to call at the War Office. Kitchener, Lloyd George reported, was entirely pleasant and worried about what would be said on munitions in the House of Commons during the coming supply debate, the first since he had come to the War Office. 'I am afraid there will be a great row about it,' Lloyd George reported Kitchener saying.

> 'There is one thing' said C ['Chancellor' i.e. Lloyd George], 'that will satisfy them, and that is the figures you gave me of the men who have gone to the fighting line. If you would only allow me to make public those figures, I think I could make everything all right by showing them how the W.O. has exceeded everything that was expected of them.' K. brightened up. 'Certainly my dear fellow', he exclaimed, 'you may publish them by all means.' 'I will say then', said C, 'that instead of six divisions we have sent more than five times that number.' 'Not five times', said K, 'but six times; & you can add', he continued enthusiastically, 'that every man who has fallen has been replaced.'[136]

This engagement displays Kitchener at his best, a genuinely simple man, eager to do his duty, willing to learn, but bewildered by the nuances of political behavior, and quite willing to forget or to forgive ill treatment. One could add it illuminates again the combativeness of Lloyd George, who would say the most wounding things when aroused, but who carried few grudges.

Lloyd George indeed conducted a powerful defense of the War Office and its accomplishments during the supply debate on 21 April, while providing the Commons and the nation with a detailed lecture, alluded to in the previous chapter, on the new type of war in which Britain was engaged.[137] He used the unexampled demands for a mass army, the onset of siege warfare, the need for artillery and high explosive ammunition, the lessons from General Castelnau as evidence of the overwhelming problems encountered and solved by the War Office under Kitchener. And he pointed out that Britain had now not six divisions in France but six times that many, 'all fully equipped'.[138] As he was at this time at the climax of the drink crusade, he dwelt in some detail on the abuse of alcohol.[139] The next day in the Cabinet he received a hand-written note from the Field Marshal complimenting him.[140]

The Committee on Munitions of War, the 'Shells Committee' as it was usually identified in the press, had not much longer to live and Lloyd George already was clearly disgusted with it. Most of its six meetings occurred in the first two weeks of the committee's existence and its demise merged into the growing newspaper clamor over the 'munitions scandal'. This topic properly belongs within the story of Lloyd George's activities during the fall of the Liberal government. It need only be noted here as it contributed to the committee's extinction.

On the morning of 9 May three corps of the British army mounted a major attack on Aubers Ridge; they were beaten back by nightfall without seizing any ground but with 11,500 casualties. Field Marshal Sir John French, watching the advance from a church tower, ascribed the failure to a lack of artillery ammunition, particularly of high explosive for which, he insisted, he had been asking the War Office for months. Immediately he sent his secretary Col. Brinsley Fitzgerald and an A.D.C., Captain Frederick Guest, Churchill's cousin, to Britain to interview politicians, including Lloyd George. The two officers saw the Chancellor on 12 May, showing him copies of French's correspondence with the War Office and a memorandum explaining the need for high explosive shells in place of shrapnel.[141] Two days later, the first of a series of articles by Lt. Col. Charles Repington, military correspondent of *The Times*, on the scandalous shortages of artillery shells appeared in that newspaper. Repington supplemented this on 17 May with a long report on ammunition to Lloyd George. He pointed out among other things that at Aubers Ridge only seven percent of the shells fired were high explosive.[142] Meanwhile, on the day following Repington's first article, 15 May, a Saturday, the First Sea Lord, John, Lord Fisher, resigned his post as a protest against the Dardanelles expedition and the Liberal government's collapse began.

Lloyd George's part in the complex maneuvers that were the construction of the first war-time coalition were of immense importance, as will be recounted, but his mind continued to dwell upon munitions. On 19 May, when the Unionists were pressing him to replace Kitchener at the War Office — an indication of where many politicians found the burden of the crisis — evidently as a result of Repington's report, he wrote a long letter to the Prime Minister effectively bringing the Shells Committee to an end.

My dear Prime Minister,

Certain facts have been brought to my notice on the question of munitions which I have felt bound to call your attention to. I write to you inasmuch as my appointment as chairman of the Munitions Committee came direct from you.

In order properly to discharge our functions as a Committee it was essential that all information as to the character of the explosive most urgently needed and the present supply available should be afforded to us. I am now informed, on what appears to be reliable information:

(1) That in order to attack highly developed trenches protected by barbed-wire entanglements, shrapnel is useless and high explosive shells indispensible;

(2) That those who are responsible for conducting operations at the front have for months impressed this fact upon the War Office, and asked in the first instance that 25 per cent of the shells sent to France should be high explosive, and that afterwards this percentage was increased to 50 per cent; [this data was contained in Repington's letter]

(3) That notwithstanding these urgent representations the percentage of high explosive shell provided for the 18-pounders has never exceeded 8 per cent; that when the great combined attack to break through the German lines was made by the French and British armies last Sunday week, the French prepared the attack with an overwhelming bombardment of high explosive which utterly demolished the German trenches and barbed-wire entanglements, thus enabling the French to penetrate the German lines for four miles without any excessive loss of life...The Germans rose in their trenches and mocked our advancing troops, then calmly mowed them in thousands. The Germans themselves have barely lost 200 men...

(4) That a full report on ammunition was sent to the War Office weeks ago from Headquarters in France, and that later another report on guns was sent. Neither of these reports has ever been shown to the Munitions Committee, and I gather they have not been seen by you.

If these facts are approximately correct, I hesitate to think what action the public would insist on if they were known. But it is quite clear that the proceedings of a Munitions Committee from which vital information of this character is withheld must be a farce. I cannot, therefore, continue to preside over it under such conditions. *It is now eight months since I ventured to call the attention of the Cabinet to the importance of mobilising all of our engineering resources for the production of munitions and equipments of war.* In October of last year I brought a full report from France showing how the French Ministry for War had coped with the difficulty. The Cabinet at that date decided that the same course should be pursued here, and a Cabinet committee was set up for the purpose. We met at the War Office and it was there agreed, with the Secretary of State in the chair, that steps of that kind should be taken in this country. *I regret to say after some inquiry that action on those lines has not been taken even to this hour except at Leeds.*

A Cabinet Committee cannot have executive power; it can only advise and recommend. It is for the department to act. They have not done so, and all the horrible loss of life which has occurred in consequence of the lack of high explosive shell is the result.

Private firms cannot turn out shrapnel because of the complicated character of the shell; but the testimony is unanimous that the high explosive is a simple shell and that any engineering concern could easily produce it. That has been the experience of France.

Ever sincerely,

D. Lloyd George[143]

So begins the story of the Ministry of Munitions.

5 Conspiracy and Coalition

On 25 May 1915 Prime Minister H.H. Asquith announced the composition of the first war-time coalition government. So ended the ministry of which Lloyd George had been a member since December of 1905, the only single party Liberal administration of the twentieth century.

The story of this political convulsion, which occurred in the ten days following Saturday, 15 May is usually told in terms of Admiral John Fisher's resignation as First Sea Lord in protest against Winston Churchill's Gallipoli campaign and of the growing unrest in the newspapers and the House of Commons over shell shortages caused by Lord Kitchener at the War Office. In effect personalities were the immediate cause of the crisis.

In the narrowest sense these explanations are true. Yet the resignation of a First Sea Lord should not have caused the fall of a government. Two had resigned without fuss since the war began and more would depart quietly in the next three years. The munitions problem of course had been simmering for many weeks.

But historically the fall of the last Liberal government must be viewed first of all as an episode in the decline of Liberalism itself, of the unwillingness of many members of the government to compromise their principles to meet the imperious demands of war, and of their unwillingness to take hard decisions, all combined with an almost fatuous optimism. One cannot help being struck by the number of occasions during these weeks, after the naval attack on the Dardanelles had failed, when the first landings at Cape Hellas were clearly pinned to the beaches and while British troops in France were attacking virtually without artillery support, that men as well placed as the Prime Minister and the Foreign Secretary were predicting the end of the conflict within months. This was not optimism, but blindness. The result was less that bad decisions were taken than that no decisions were made. The fighting of the war was left to the initiative of energetic departmental ministers like Churchill, or indeed to the generals in the field, such as Sir John French. The closest reading of the Cabinet letters and the War Council minutes, for example, will not reveal how it transpired that Churchill was allowed to proceed with the naval bombardment at the Dardanelles without the definite commitment of troops to hold the Gallipoli forts once they had been silenced, which everyone agreed was necessary.[1] And during the critical weeks after the naval attack was cancelled and when the ground assault was being prepared and executed, between 19 March and 14 May, the War Council did not meet at all.

Obviously much of this indictment must be laid upon Asquith himself, the last classical Liberal, the last Augustan. His method of administration in peace and war lay in waiting upon events, exemplified in the phrase 'wait and see'. A problem could be solved by deputizing a committee. He rarely forbade a policy and never originated one. The possibility of running a war from Downing Street as Lloyd George would attempt after December 1916, and as Churchill would succeed in doing a quarter century later, would have been beyond his comprehension. He supported his ministers loyally in the House of Commons and in the Cabinet, as Lloyd George attested many times, got them out of trouble, for example Marconi, and warned them to be cautious. He could say no from time to time as he did to McKenna in 1911, although too infrequently. But he never said: 'This is what we shall do.'

Yet there lay in him an arrogance, a conviction that the office of Prime Minister belonged to him.[2] His undoing proceeded from how little he cared for its demands and how much he valued, not in fact its power, but its status. Only to retain his place would he move quickly and decisively. The instinct for self-preservation is strong among Prime Ministers.[3] He would protect his office at any cost but would do nothing to remove the causes of the discontent.

Asquith's inertia then provided a focus, although one could hardly say a cause, for a third element which turned the relatively minor event of mid-May into a means for unseating the government. Probably the most serious large problem in the spring of 1915 was the waning popular commitment to the war, symbolized on the one hand by the Unionist disenchantment with the party truce which left the opposition isolated, unable to criticize policies of which they did not approve. But it was also a fact that the population at large was beginning to realize that the conflict in Europe was bringing not hardship but high wages and full employment. Enlistments were falling and had virtually ceased in south Ireland. There were no shortages except of housing. Barring those with friends or family members in the services life had changed very little. In a word, the war had become routine.[4]

Lloyd George was of course aware of this sense of relaxation and ease. The sense of engagement, the enthusiasm, the excitement of 1914 was dissipating. This had been the theme of the Bangor speech. Unlike the French, he said, the British did not know what war was. And he understood clearly and had regularly transmitted to the Cabinet the danger of allowing matters of war strategy to drift. The easy presumption that everything that could be done was being done would lead to disaster. Factories that should be turning out war materiel were obstinately declining military contracts to retain their profitable civilian business. The D.O.R.A. amendments had been intended to bring this to an end.

Unionist disenchantment with the handling of the war, already referred to, posed perhaps a greater threat to that party's leadership than it did to the government, but in the end it may have made the coalition inevitable. The Unionist Business Committee formed in January 1915 as a 'ginger group' of 100 back-bench opposition MPs under the chairmanship of Sir Ernest Pollack, but whose hero was Sir Edward Carson, was as impatient with Bonar Law's apparent unwillingness to press the government on military matters as it was of the government itself. Thus at the beginning of May party leadership on both sides of the House were in difficulty with their own followers.[5]

I

At the end of January 1915, through Andrew Bonar Law and Austen Chamberlain, Lloyd George had briefly undertaken some independent soundings on Unionist interest in a coalition along the lines of his proposals of August and September 1910. What Lloyd George had in mind is not entirely clear because for a time he could not find a copy of his 1910 memorandum. Eventually one was resurrected and Chamberlain took a copy with him.[6] As during these weeks Lloyd George was fully occupied with his plan to win the War Council to a Balkan strategy, one may speculate that the inner meaning of his approach was an attempt to gain opposition support for this project.[7] In any case the Unionist back benches and the second rank leadership had no desire for a coalition but disliked the present situation which had all the disadvantages of a coalition and none of the advantages. Their desire was that Bonar Law and Lord Lansdowne should press the government harder.[8]

Asquith evidently was not told of this meeting, but later, at Churchill's urging, he asked Bonar Law and Lansdowne to attend the War Council of 10 March. This was immediately after the Russian ultimatum, already discussed, stipulating that the Greeks must not be allowed to cooperate in taking Constantinople and that Russia claimed the city herself. As the penetration of the Straits was going well at this time, the Conservative leaders were being invited to share responsibility for what was obviously a major change in a British strategic policy nearly a century old for which a decision would be demanded within weeks. The opposition leaders declined to take part in discussions where they had no authority and announced they would accept no further summons.[9]

Lord Beaverbrook states that this encounter was seen by Churchill as a first step toward drawing the Unionists into a coalition and Churchill fully confirms in *The World Crisis* that he believed Unionist cooperation essential and the party's isolation dangerous.[10] Nonetheless, the implicit admission that Asquith's administration was incapable of managing the war alone was bound to stir criticism of the Cabinet and its Prime Minister and to foment among the Liberals suspicions of conspiracy. By the third week of March, even before the meaning of the disastrous battleship sinkings in the Dardanelles Straits or the extent of the munitions crisis were clear, denunciation of the weakness of the Liberal administration was beginning to circulate.

Not surprisingly the first complainant was J.L. Garvin, whose fine-tuned sense of emergency was always quick to detect variations in the public mood. In a leading article in the *Observer* on 21 March entitled 'The Temper of the Nation' Garvin wrote: 'The nation for the first time is uneasy about the Government and itself.'

> It believes in some individual Ministers like Mr. Lloyd George and Mr. Churchill, Lord Kitchener and Sir Edward Grey, but it distrusts a purely party Cabinet framed with no view to the efficient conduct of the war in the greatest of world's crises, and it is beginning to doubt whether we have at the very head the strong directing, yet unifying, force which is a prime requisite for the supreme vigour of our effort, and the triumph of our arms.[11]

Just the week before, Rufus Isaacs, Lord Reading, who had spent the previous week-end at Walmer Castle with the Asquiths, remarked to Riddell upon how 'lightly' the Prime Minister's 'great responsibilities' rested upon him. He had scarcely mentioned the war except during the two hours when he was dealing with the business for which Reading had been summoned. Later that day, asked by Riddell whether Asquith was not 'too easy', Lloyd George for the first time criticized the Prime Minister. 'Things are very unsatisfactory in that respect. . .' he replied.[12]

On the day Garvin's leader appeared the Prime Minister heard from Edward Montagu, who had spent the past week with Lloyd George and A.J. Balfour at the meeting with trade union officials in the Treasury, that in Montagu's opinion both Lloyd George and Churchill showed signs of susceptibility to Balfour's malignant charm and that Churchill believed Balfour should be put in charge of the Foreign Office during the following week when Grey took a fishing holiday.[13]

In the event Asquith took the Foreign Office himself during the week and seemed unconcerned, but four days later he received a more alarming report conveyed through his wife, Margot from H.W. Massingham. Massingham was the highly influential editor of the *Nation*, the bible of radical Liberalism, which had indeed published Churchill's first article on social reform in 1907. Swearing that his story was true and that he could prove it, the editor had said that Churchill was 'intriguing hard' to put Balfour at the Foreign Office not temporarily, but permanently. Writing to Miss Stanley, Asquith agreed that he knew Churchill was under Balfour's influence, invited the former Prime Minister to the Admiralty constantly, and probably told him many things that should be withheld.

'Since I began the last sentence,' Asquith continued:

> Ll. George has been here for his favourite morning indulgence (it
> corresponds in him to the dram drinking of the Clyde workmen) — a
> 10 minute discursive discussion of things in general. I asked him what
> he thought of the Massingham story, & rather to my surprise he said
> he believed it was substantially true. He thinks that Winston has for the
> time being at any rate allowed himself to be 'swallowed whole' by A.J.B.
> on whom he, L.G., after working with him for a week or two, is now
> disposed to be pretty severe. It is a pity, isn't it? that Winston has not
> got a better sense of proportion, and also a larger endowment of the
> instinct of loyalty. As you know. . .I am really fond of him; but I regard
> his future with many misgivings. . .He will never get to the top in
> English politics, with all his wonderful gifts. . .[14]

That Sunday Garvin resumed his attack on the government with one of the first public demands for a step that was already privately called for by many members of the opposition and particularly within the Unionist Business Committee, national registration of men.[15] 'Our own view,' said Garvin, 'is still that all piecemeal, catchpenny, spasmodic methods of raising men are at this stage of the war a public indignity and a great national error.' National registration would show the men in the workshops that they too were soldiers. He concluded by attacking Massingham's *Nation* for saying that the press should not criticize the Prime Minister. Asquith was not doing enough to shorten the war.[16]

The next day the Tory *Morning Post* took up the attack. In a leader entitled 'An appeal to the Prime Minister' it dilated at length upon the Prime Minister's slackness, providing in fact an acute description of Asquith's style of government, excellent for peace, disastrous in war:

> In masterly fashion he has shown how easy it is to combine the
> appearance of personal responsibility with the complete deliverance
> of autonomy to aspiring and unquiet colleagues. During his reign the
> office of Prime Minister has profoundly changed. To spend long hours
> on the Treasury Bench, to take frequent part in debates great or small,
> to keep a firm hold on the domestic, foreign and Colonial policy of the
> country, and to give the touch of a superintending hand to the more
> important Departments of the Government has of late years been
> little more than an interesting tradition in Downing Street...The
> powers which, as Prime Minister, he should have sought [to look into
> manufacturing, supply of arms, conditions of industry] have at length
> been taken over by the Chancellor of the Exchequer: and a Minister
> burdened with the cares of an important Department has stepped into
> the place of his leader, who has none.[17]

All of this proceeded of course from strongly Unionist newspapers with close contacts among Tory radicals and the Unionist Business Committee; they were not calls for a coalition. Rather one can infer the insinuation that a more active and vigorous Unionist leadership would have overthrown so weak a government.

On the morning that this article appeared, the Liberal *Daily Chronicle* published a leader entitled: 'The Intrigue Against the Prime Minister.' Generally it was an attack upon the *Observer* article of 21 March, suggesting that the Unionists wished to replace Asquith because they were impotent so long as he remained in power. There was no suggestion of a Liberal conspiracy and Lloyd George was mentioned only once.[18]

In view of what the *Daily Chronicle's* leader in fact contained, it is difficult to understand why it caused Lloyd George to become so angry.[19] He immediately telephoned George Riddell asking him to get in touch with Robert Donald, editor of the *Chronicle*, and to enquire whether Reginald McKenna, the Home Secretary, had inspired the article. Riddell did so and received a flat negative. Later that day Lloyd George asked for a second enquiry which elicited the same response.[20]

McKenna would figure largely in the events of the next seven weeks but he has remained, perhaps for the lack of a letter collection of any importance, an almost unknown personality in the history of the first two decades of the twentieth century. However his career had paralleled Lloyd George's. As MP for Monmouthshire North, elected in 1895, five years after Lloyd George, a nominal Congregationalist and Londoner, he had been an able and energetic opponent of the 1902 Education Act and rose rapidly. Campbell-Bannerman made him a Junior Whip and in 1907 he followed Birrell at the Board of Education. With Asquith's reconstruction of the government in 1908 he had nearly attained the Exchequer and was consoled with the glittering prize of the Admiralty. He appears to have come to dislike Lloyd George at this time although before the two seem to have been on amiable if not intimate terms.

McKenna's problem was an abiding jealousy and envy which he found difficult to conceal. He had great industry and a keen and orderly mind, much admired by Asquith, who admired also his accomplished wife, Pamela Jekyll, whom McKenna married in 1908. The Prime Minister was a frequent visiter at the handsome, Luytens-designed, home of the 'McKennae' in Smith Square for evenings of bridge, as his letters to Venetia Stanley testify. But Asquith could move abruptly when he felt himself threatened as he had done in the autumn of 1911 when he turned out McKenna from the Admiralty, which he loved, but where he was almost totally under the control of the Board, and replaced him with Churchill. McKenna's rage then turned upon Churchill and did not abate.[21]

At the end of October 1914, at the time of John, Lord Fisher's appointment as First Sea Lord, McKenna denounced Churchill to Riddell in unbelievably fierce terms.

> McK says Winston knows nothing about it [the navy]. He referred to an article in the 'Morning Post' today which uses the phrase 'an untainted mind'. McK says Winston's mind is quite untainted by any knowledge of Naval matters whereas Fisher's mind has been 'tainted' with naval knowledge for 60 years. McK also remarked, 'Winston has plenty of ability but the flatterers by whom he is surrounded deter him from the necessity of learning his job. He is told he knows it and he thinks he does. He is quite incompetent.' McK's animosity to Winston is one of the most virulent and persistent hatreds I have ever known. . .He is very half hearted, I always think, about the war. Too fond of being 'just to the Germans' and paying too small regard to our own poor people. . . He is always talking of 'fighting like a gentleman' of not 'losing our heads' of the 'lack of evidence of German machinations' and of 'the absence of danger' etc. etc.[22]

The fact was that McKenna was a solid Liberal, fair minded where his own interests were not concerned, tolerant and just. Riddell rather liked him despite his spiky personality and worried that those admirable qualities, which Asquith shared, were not the best intellectual equipment for fighting a war. After returning from a dinner with the couple on 20 November 1914, where McKenna had spoken of a committee upon which he sat to investigate German atrocities, Riddell reflected in his diary that such a task for the Home Secretary might be a mistake.

> The truth is that a certain section of the Liberal party still have a sneaking affection for the Germans. They try to persuade themselves that this is not a war of the German people but only of a class and that the time is not distant when the two nations will be embracing one another. McKenna is a curious mixture. LlG told me a few days ago that he had said to Bonar Law that McK was really a nice and able man, but Bonar Law would not have it and replied, 'we all dislike him more than anyone in the Cabinet.' This is all due to his manner. He is very kindhearted and will do more for his friends than most people.

He also has a great sense of justice which often leads him to occupy positions which the public do not understand. His mind always works on mathematical lines.[23]

Bonar Law of course was always saying that the Unionists detested some single member of the government, McKenna, Churchill, Masterman, occasionally Lloyd George, but in fact McKenna's position in the Cabinet was not strong and depended, as one suspects he well understood, upon his personal intimacy with the Prime Minister. All of this made McKenna an inveterate intriguer as he had been since 1908 when he had conveyed to Asquith, newly appointed Prime Minister, the story that Lloyd George had given away to his friend, Robert Donald of the *Chronicle*, the names of the prospective Cabinet.

Still on Monday, 29 March 1915, while Lloyd George was seething about the article on the conspiracy against Asquith and suspecting McKenna, the Home Secretary had indeed gone to Asquith and reported that he had evidence that Lord Northcliffe, publisher of *The Times*, was engineering a plan to supplant Asquith as Prime Minister with Lloyd George. Churchill was part of the plot. Writing to Miss Stanley, Asquith admitted he was worried, but professed to disbelieve the story.[24]

Later in the day Lloyd George came to see Asquith about Kitchener's obstruction of the work of the Munitions Committee and the Prime Minister took the opportunity to say, as he told Miss Stanley in a letter of 7 p.m., that only that day

I had heard sinister and, as I believed, absurd interpretations wh. were being given to the articles in *The Times, Observer, Morning Post* &c. I've never seen him [Lloyd George] more moved. He made a most bitter onslaught upon McKenna whom he believes, thro' his animosity against Winston, to be the villain of the piece & the principle mischief-maker. He vehemently disclaimed having anything to do with the affair: Kitchener, he said, is the real culprit because, in spite of every warning, he has neglected up to the 11th hour a proper provision of munitions: & K. being a Tory, or supposed to be one, the Tory press, afraid to attack him, are making me the target of their criticism. As for himself (Ll.G.) he declared that he owed everything to me; that I had stuck to him & protected him & defended him when every man's hand was against him; and that he wd. rather (1) break stones (2) dig potatoes (3) be hanged & quartered (these were metaphors used at different stages of his broken but impassioned harangue) than do an act, or say a word, or harbour a thought that was disloyal to me. And he said that every one of our colleagues felt the same. His eyes were wet with tears, and I am sure that, with all his Celtic capacity of impulsive & momentary fervour, he was quite sincere...

Of course I assured him that I had never for a moment doubted him — wh. is quite true: & he warmly wrung my hand & abruptly left the room. Darling, does that interest you?[25]

The next morning the *Chronicle*, certainly with Riddell's telephone calls aware that its leader of 29 March had caused dissension in the government, attempted to repair its damage. Blaming the *Morning Post* and citing its article the previous day it unfortunately gave wider currency to the charges.

185

The Prime Minister was accused of displaying none but forensic abilities, of contenting himself with finding formulas of agreement between colleagues without giving the nation any lead, of shirking administration and eschewing initiative.

The *Morning Post*, said the *Chronicle*, compared the Prime Minister's work unfavorably with Kitchener's and Lloyd George's. However both men, who regarded Asquith with 'unswerving loyalty, must certainly deplore this.'[26]

The trouble was that despite the personal loyalty Asquith inspired — and it was widespread and genuine, including Lloyd George — despite his ability to dominate the House of Commons, the charges in the *Morning Post*, repeated by the *Chronicle*, indeed were true. Lloyd George knew it better than anyone. His long memoranda at the beginning of the year, pleading for thought about planning, preparation, logistics, and strategy, were in effect, criticisms of Asquith, although certainly neither he nor the Prime Minister saw it that way. The Prime Minister could help. He could for example lend weight in negotiations to bring Greece into the war without telling the Cabinet, but he would propose nothing.

The next day Asquith brought Lloyd George and McKenna together. '...they came here at 3.30 and we had an hour together,' he wrote to Venetia Stanley that evening.

It was as you may imagine at moments 'rather' exciting. L.G. began on a very stormy note, accusing McK of having inspired Donald to write the article in the *Chronicle* wh. was headed 'Intrigue agst. the P.M.', and in one sentence of which, only one, his name was mentioned. McK as hotly denied that he ever said or suggested to Donald that Ll.G. was in the 'plot', while admitting that he had had a talk with him on the subject of attacks in the Tory press. Ll.G. proceeded to accuse McK of always seeing imaginary plots: e.g. in this very matter. Winston's supposed campaign against Grey, to wh. McK rejoined that the person he really suspected was A.J.B., with whom we all agreed Winston was much too intimate. There was a lot of hitting & counter hitting between them, but I am glad to say that in the end I not only lowered the temperature, but got them into first an accommodating and in the end an almost friendly mood. I told them that I was absolutely certain none of my colleagues was otherwise than perfectly loyal: that the use of the word 'intrigue' instead of 'attack' was calculated to suggest a movement against me from *within* rather than from without; and that while McK never meant that *that* shd. be conveyed to the world, it was not unnatural that Ll.G. should have thought otherwise and even imagined that he was pointed to as the supposed traitor. And so on — you can well imagine the kind of thing. It was at first & for some time a thoroughly disagreeable interview, wh. I do not wish to go through again, but the sky gradually cleared, and the result shows that it is (as I think) always wise to have these things 'out' at once & not to allow the personal virus to curdle, or get inflamed, by suppression, or half hearted approaches at compromise.

In a letter later that night Asquith continued:

My darling — I didn't tell you in any of my numerous letters today about the one really dramatic moment in my interview with Ll.G.

& McK. They were getting very *acharnés* — bandying charges, & apparently quite irreconcilable. I was, I confess, rather disgusted, and inclined to chuck the whole thing (for the moment). So I said, sitting in the chair wh. I always occupied at the Cabinet: 'Very well: in another week I shall have sat in this chair for 7 years. If I have the slightest reason to think that there is anyone among you who has even the faintest doubt or suspicion about me, I will gladly (for what have I to gain or lose?) abandon this chair, & never sit in it again.' I wish you cd. have seen them! Their mutual anger dissolved like a frost under a sudden thaw: and they both with united voices exclaimed: 'The day you leave that chair, the rest of us disappear, never to return!' and I am sure they meant it. Wasn't that a rather fine moment for me?[27]

Asquith was quite satisfied with the results of his mediation and threats. No doubt this was reinforced by a note in the radical *Daily News* commenting for the first time on the conspiracy, and saying that the whole thing was the work of a small group of Tories and that it had been brought to the attention of Lloyd George who was contemptuous of it. The entire Liberal party was behind the Prime Minister.[28] But even if Asquith now felt satisfied about the loyalty of his colleagues, the conditions that prompted the attack on his administration in the first place continued to exist and so the attacks went on.

The argument here is that the events of the last days of March 1915 and those that began on Saturday, 15 May, six weeks later, are part of a single story. Discontent with leadership, if not disloyalty, existed in both parties. The stories of the Prime Minister's easy optimism and indolence in the ultra Tory papers were echoed within the Liberal party, and from time to time by Lloyd George himself. There was indeed chaos in army contracting procedures; there was a shell shortage; the Gallipoli campaign, although it was not yet clear, was in fact heading toward bloody disaster. No formula of words, no simple faith that the war would soon end, would change these facts.

The next Saturday, after lunch and golf at Walton with Lloyd George, Riddell recorded:

He says that the PM has made him a bet that the war would be over in three months. He cannot understand how the PM should be so optimistic. LG made another bet today that the war would not be over by Christmas.[29]

Evidently the second bet was with Grey, who, according to J.A. Pease, offered Lloyd George a box of cigars if the war were not over by the end of the year.[30] Even Churchill was infected. A few days later in conversation with Riddell on attempts to shorten the war the First Lord stated: 'I think the Germans are beat, but every day by which the war is shortened will mean one less day of misery and anguish to millions of people.'[31] Lloyd George's endless lectures on the stalemate in France appear to have had no effect. By the end of the month, with British forces pinned to the beaches at Cape Hellas, Churchill still was reassuring everyone publicly and privately that the military assault on the peninsula was going well. 'I think the Dardanelles Expedition will be successful,' he told Lord Riddell on 29 April.

The whole thing was most carefully arranged...This is one of the great campaigns of history. Think of what Constantinople is to the East...I am not responsible for the Expedition; the whole details were approved by the Cabinet and Admiralty Board. I do not shirk responsibility, but it is untrue to say that I have done this off my own bat. I have followed every detail and I think I am the right man for the job.' Then he laughed. 'In fact I think the country is damned lucky to have me here just now...My critics may snarl and yelp until they are black in the face. They can do nothing. I have a complete answer for them when the time comes.

Two days later Riddell mused in his diary

In thinking over my talk with Winston, I have been impressed with the way in which the McKenna vendetta haunts the scene in all sorts of strange ways. I wonder if Mrs. McK's courtesies and attentions to me during the past two years have not been made partly with the object of detaching me from Winston...[During his conversation with Churchill Fisher had interrupted peremptorily and afterwards Churchill had remarked 'Fisher and I have a perfect understanding.'] I feel sure from Fisher's manner that trouble is brewing.[32]

II

Lloyd George was making headlines with the drink question in the early weeks of April, 1915 and to general applause the Munitions of War Committee under his chairmanship had been appointed in the third week of March under conditions already described, but the attacks on general government weakness and inaction continued, Lloyd George always excepted. On 15 April occurred the famous Cabinet duel between Lloyd George and Kitchener over the figures of munitions production and deliveries. It is difficult therefore to comprehend Asquith's willingness to accept at face value and without further investigation the assurances contained in a note from Kitchener, after a talk with Sir John French, the commander in France, that he 'will have as much [ammunition] as his troops will be able to use in the next forward movement.'[33] This note, promptly passed on to Venetia Stanley, arrived the day before the Cabinet fight which had of course resounded with charges to the contrary. Nonetheless the Prime Minister determined to use the comforting information it provided as the basis for a speech, scheduled for some time, that he was to give in Newcastle in the following week.[34] Asquith was exultant. 'It shows how wicked was the lie invented by *The Times* yesterday that our lack of ammunition at the front was holding back not only our Army but the French,' he wrote to Miss Stanley. 'Of course you won't breathe a word of it.'[35]

Why Asquith, with an acute and trained legal mind, should accept a casual phrase referring only to a specific action already being planned in France and garnered at second hand from a man who also did not wish to admit a shell shortage in the face of so much evidence to the contrary, represents a problem that must bear some discussion even in a biography of Lloyd George. The Prime Minister's unenquiring, indeed innocent, confidence was at the core of his weakness in office and in the end undid him. The effortless superiority that made him a Secretary of State six years after entering the House of Commons, by which time he was already marked as a future Prime Minister, left him arrogant but vulnerable. His biographers continually excuse his inattention to business by remarking upon the speed with which he emptied his despatch boxes. For him the war represented no emergency. He had never failed before. His mastery of debate in the House of Commons, which he never lost, was unchallenged. If legislation could have produced shells the deed would have been done and in fact his defense of his position after the war dwells heavily on D.O.R.A. amendments, nos. 2 and 3.

Newspaper attacks and rumors of conspiracy caused him to be angry and perhaps a little frightened and so he would seek immediately reassurances of loyalty, as from Lloyd George or McKenna, but he would not alter the style of administration or of his life: the bridge games, the afternoons lurking in Mansfield Street for a glimpse of Miss Stanley, or the weekends at Walmer Castle or at the Wharf at Sutton Courtney in Berkshire. He desired serenity; life should be 'fun', a word that appears repeatedly in his letters. He was like the parents, and there are many, who want only reassuring letters from children away at school so that they need not worry about them.

Thus Kitchener's note gave Asquith all he needed. He happily went off to Newcastle on 20 April and that evening, before a large crowd which had expected a statement on drink, he asserted that the army in France was better equipped and maintained than any army in British history, a statement which was perfectly justified, and that there was 'not a word of truth' in arguments in the papers that it was 'being crippled, or at least hampered, by our failure to provide the necessary ammunition'.[36] The Brocks refer to Asquith's Newcastle speech as 'perhaps the most damaging blunder of his wartime premiership.' Stephen Koss, less succinctly, generally concurs.[37]

Although these estimates are correct, the damage was not immediately apparent. The Northcliffe newspapers simply continued their attacks. That the Prime Minister did not know what he was talking about was their general tenor. He never 'removed his blinkers,' said *The Times*.

> That is why we hold that it [the speech] was short of courage. When he came to the specific question of the supply of munitions of war, he made statements that will not bear examination. In particular, he said that the operations of our army had not been hampered by 'our failure to provide the necessary ammunition.' That is an assertion we are reluctantly required to challenge.

Indeed, the paper continued, the army was well equipped and well cared for, far better than any army before, but 'there has been too much jam and too few shells'.[38] Even here there was an ominous approving reference to Lloyd George and the Munitions of War Committee.[39] The *Daily Mail* echoed these sentiments and repeated its call, begun several weeks earlier, for what would provide the true crisis of traditional Liberalism and which, viewed in perspective, would probably contribute more toward the weakening of Asquith and to Lloyd George's succession than any other issue: military conscription.[40]

The intent here is to say that while Northcliffe was an eccentric and unstable man, in this case his newspapers, whatever were the motives of their proprietor, were not wrong but right. Munitions and conscription *were* the questions of the future. Asquith made a mistake in not grasping this and eventually paid the price. He did nothing to solve, only to smooth over, the violent hatreds in his Cabinet. He did not change his manner of living. Yet he was faced by an opposition party whose back bench equally was unhappy with its own leadership, a condition he was unable to exploit.

In all of this there was scarcely any mention of Lloyd George. An answering *Daily Chronicle* leader the next day did not hint at conspiracy. Nevertheless still only three days earlier Charles Hobhouse confided to his diary a highly circumstantial account of a plot conveyed to him by Walter Runciman, including Garvin and Northcliffe, and Balfour and Churchill. These men wished to replace Grey with Balfour, Asquith with someone else, and to dispose of the rest of the Cabinet, except for Kitchener and Lloyd George, 'who was an essential element of success'. Evidently the conspirators had seen Kitchener who professed to be uninterested.[41] Hobhouse, as has been observed on other occasions, was often misinformed, or more frequently misunderstood what he had heard. But apparently Lloyd George had heard some version of the same story for on 29 April he took some trouble to convince George Riddell that he was entirely loyal to Asquith and was not interested in becoming Prime Minister himself. He would not be able to stand the ceremonial.[42] On 21 April, as has been described, he had stoutly defended Kitchener on the army estimates and had gone out of his way not to contradict Asquith's Newcastle speech, which he knew to be based upon faulty information.[43]

Still the pressure did not die away. On 9 May, J.L. Garvin, who for years had been a consistent and honest promoter of inter-party cooperation, and an admirer of Lloyd George, called openly in the *Observer* for a coalition government. His lead article was not an attack upon Asquith in the manner of the Northcliffe papers, but simply a statement that no Cabinet whose members, save Kitchener, had for a decade engaged in partisan warfare could be the proper instrument for fighting a great war. They had not failed in their duty. Any other body of men would have made as many mistakes and the editor placed implicit trust in most of the present incumbents. But could not there be an all party 'Committee of Public Safety'?[44]

This was vintage Garvin, reminiscent of his proposal for the Constitutional Conference and for all party cooperation on national insurance. Two days earlier, on 7 May 1915, the *Lusitania* had been torpedoed causing Balfour to predict Garvin's sentiments, as well as Lloyd George's at Bangor, in a speech at the Westminster Palace Hotel on 10 May. With uncharacteristic emotion he spoke of the barbarity of it all and how it would influence the United States, as indeed it did. But it should also influence Britain. 'I should like to see,' said the former Prime Minister,

> in the conduct of our righteous cause something of that unity of
> purpose and fixity of action which has characterized our German
> enemies in all their wretchedness. And if, as I believe will be the effect,
> this latest outrage is to convince the people of this country that, not
> only our soldiers, but the whole nation is at war, and that every ounce
> of weight in every direction must be directed to bringing that war to an
> end — if that is to the effect of it, then we can thank the Germans for
> this latest instance of their barbarous methods.[45]

The *Lusitania* disaster of course directed attention to the Admiralty and further weakened Churchill. There were charges of 'slackness'. Sir George Riddell, like the good newspaperman he was, immediately visited the First Lord.

Churchill was very sensitive to rumors of inefficiency within his administration and challenged Riddell to name an example. Riddell mentioned a case of six part-time naval surgeons each of whom were paid £5,000 per year. Churchill denied this and then called in Sir James Masterton-Smith, his secretary, who confirmed it. By now Churchill was angry and sent for Sir Arthur May, the Surgeon General who defended the appointments saying they were sanctioned by the Prime Minister. Riddell who obviously knew the background of the posts remarked in his diary that the appointments, approved in 1908, seemed 'to have been a job. Indeed it was hinted that Mrs. A had been instrumental in getting the appointments made.' Churchill, now truly furious, attacked May for keeping him in ignorance saying there were only 500 naval wounded in the country while military surgeons had more work than they could handle. At the end of this unpleasant episode Riddell asked: '"How is Fisher?" Churchill replied: "Alright"' and abruptly changed the subject. 'I wonder whether they have fallen out,' Riddell reflected.[46]

The truth was that despite Churchill's enormous energy, capacity for work, and love of the Royal Navy, he was much less than the ideal First Lord of the Admiralty. His interests lay in technology and naval operations. Internal Admiralty administration bored him and was left in the hands of elderly functionaries such as May and the Permanent Secretary, Sir Graham Greene. McKenna, himself a meticulous administrator, was not entirely wrong in his criticisms. Admiralty 'slackness', despite the heroism of the fleet at sea, would remain a continuing and pressing Cabinet problem during the war at least until the appointment of Eric Geddes as First Lord, and stories about it were an important part of the campaign against Churchill.

Clearly there were rumors of trouble everywhere, of discontent within each party over its leadership, of difficulties within the Admiralty and the War Office. The Unionists had been unhappy with the party truce at least since the beginning of the year, and tales of a conspiracy against Asquith, never proven but never stilled, had circulated since the end of March. Then on 9 May, fewer than three weeks after Asquith's easy assurances about the ammunition supply at Newcastle, British troops were beaten back at Aubers Ridge with very heavy casualties after an attack that was preceded by, for the time, a very heavy barrage of 80,000 rounds, which also exhausted available ammunition.[47] According to his latest, and generally sympathetic, biographer, this failure, for which he needed a scapegoat, caused General French to give Colonel Charles Repington, the military correspondent of *The Times*, the correspondence between himself and Kitchener.[48] Repington's dispatch, and a leader highly critical of the Secretary of State for War appeared on Friday, 14 May.[49] In his published diary Repington insists that French never saw his dispatch, which is not quite the same thing as saying the General did not inspire it, but he further asserts that the data came from R.B. Steven, Commanding Officer of the Second Battalion of his old regiment whom he was visiting.[50]

Everyone but the Prime Minister seemed to realize that politics were in turmoil. Two days earlier, on 12 May, just hours after he had received a note from Venetia Stanley saying that she intended to marry Edwin Montagu, Asquith, in the House, was asked by F. Handel Booth, Liberal for Pontefract and a former member of the industrial insurance lobby, whether the Prime

Minister 'would consider' a coalition government. With the greatest assurance Asquith replied: 'The step suggested by my hon. Friend is not in contemplation, and I am not aware that it would meet with general assent.'[51] Nonetheless within 72 hours the movement toward coalition had begun.

III

The details surrounding the formation, in May 1915, of the first World War I coalition have been analyzed and written about for many years, yet in some ways the story is not as clear as is the sequence of motives and events attending Lloyd George's assumption of the Prime Ministership in 1916. The thesis here has been that pressure had been building for several months. The only person not aware of it, or more precisely who would not allow himself to become aware of it, was the Prime Minister, if one can, as one must, trust the Stanley letters. If there was a conspiracy against Asquith it probably originated with Northcliffe. Lloyd George was not a part of it. However, there is no need to tell here the full story of Asquith's skillful and successful rescue of his position, which at last he realized was slipping from his hands, perhaps to be replaced, as some Unionists seemed to desire at the beginning, by Lloyd George.[52]

The chain of circumstances began with a chance meeting between Lloyd George and Lord Fisher, as Lloyd George told the story to Riddell eight days later, in front of No. 10 Downing Street, evidently late in the morning of Saturday, 15 May. Fisher said he had resigned and was going to Scotland. Lloyd George then went into No. 10 and saw Asquith who characteristically discounted Fisher's action. The First Sea Lord, he said, was always resigning. Lloyd George replied that he believed Fisher meant it this time. Later that day Lloyd George received a telephone call from McKenna, to whom Fisher had gone, apparently at the Prime Minister's suggestion, and with whom Fisher remained friendly.[53] McKenna reported that the Admiral's resignation was final.[54]

So far, no one, presumably, but Lloyd George, the Prime Minister and McKenna knew of Fisher's action. Over the weekend talk was of Repington's revelations.[55] According to Lloyd George's account to Riddell, it was McKenna's telephone call that convinced the Prime Minister that matters were becoming serious. Lloyd George obviously saw the implications even more quickly. The Cabinet would have to be reconstituted. That evening Frances Stevenson wrote in her diary:

> He says if Fisher's resignation is accepted, Churchill will have to go. He will be a ruined man. 'It is the Nemesis', said C. [Chancellor] to me, 'of the man who has fought for this war for years. When the war came he saw in it a chance of glory for himself, & has accordingly entered on a risky campaign without caring a straw for the misery and hardship it would bring to thousands, in the hope that he would prove to be an outstanding man in this war.'
>
> C. tells me that when the Cabinet gave their consent to a bombardment of the Dardanelles forts (very unwillingly) it was on the strict understanding that the operation should not be announced in the first place, so as not to commit the Government & to enable them, if the thing should turn out to be impossible or a more lengthy

proceeding than was anticipated, to withdraw from the campaign without any discredit to themselves. This did not suit Churchill, however. On the first day that the bombardment commenced, he broke faith with his colleagues & caused the announcement to be made in the Press with great eclat that we had begun the bombardment of the Dardanelles forts, & intended to force the Straits. Therefore it was of course impossible for the Government to withdraw.[56]

Obviously Lloyd George had little sympathy left for Churchill, a fact Churchill would come to appreciate as the crisis developed, although one may speculate the earliest voice to suggest to the Prime Minister that the First Lord would have to go was McKenna's. However, the Chancellor's comments to Miss Stevenson on Churchill's failure to obey Cabinet instructions on the announcement of the bombardment were, to say the least, unfair. As has been discussed in a previous chapter, the Dardanelles operation emerged in the first place only as a cheap and easy way to do something quickly on behalf of Russia. In Lloyd George's mind, and Asquith's, it was principally an avenue to the larger concept of an alternative front in the Balkans, symbolized by the Salonika proposal. There was little doubt or consideration on whether the battleships could get through. Thoughts turned rather on what they would do when they reached the Sea of Marmora. Would the pre-dreadnought vessels employed be able to handle the powerful *Goeben*? How could Constantinople be held without troops? The unspoken conclusion was that troops might not be needed in the initial stages of the operation. No doubt they could be found when the time came. That the passage of the narrows could be defeated by field guns operating against trawlers being used as mine sweepers was never considered.

Moreover, these assumptions — it is hardly accurate to call them decisions — proceeded from rambling conversations over a number of days. Crisp decision making was simply not Asquith's Cabinet style. And after the first few days, when the outer forts had fallen, the Prime Minister as well as everyone else was pleased. There was no thought of calling off the operation. More than any military operation in modern times the Dardanelles expedition was conceived and authorized in a fit of absence of mind. The fault, if it must be found, lay with the Prime Minister although the First Lord of the Admiralty would have to bear the punishment.

Churchill's agony began immediately even though initially he does not appear to have recognized his danger. On Sunday, 16 May, the political world seemed quiet. Asquith, as usual, departed serenely for The Wharf where Churchill visited him in the afternoon and made clear that he had replaced Fisher with A.K. Wilson, whom he had peremptorily discharged after becoming First Lord. He made the routine offer of resignation which Asquith declined, while inviting Churchill to remain for dinner.[57] He prepared a statement for the House of Commons telling of Fisher's resignation and announcing the new Board of Admiralty. Early Monday morning he saw A.J. Balfour. Briefly the crisis appeared to be over.[58]

But there were other movements. On Sunday, 16 May Fisher wrote to McKenna, 'my beloved Friend', reaffirming his resignation and saying that he would see no one, neither Churchill nor the Prime Minister. McKenna considered this letter important enough to take to Asquith immediately.[59]

Also on Sunday, Northcliffe telephoned Riddell asking the latter to arrange an appointment with Lloyd George for the following day.[60] The two men met evidently early in the morning and probably discussed munitions for later on Monday Northcliffe telephoned again to say that Lloyd George had asked to meet Repington at Riddell's house. By the time the military correspondent arrived, at 7 p.m., Lloyd George was at the House of Commons and had asked that Repington be taken there. Riddell, present at neither meeting, mused in his diary afterwards: 'LG did not tell me what had transpired, but I rather suspect that some sort of an understanding was arrived at between him and N.' So far Riddell knew nothing of the political crisis.[61]

Whether this surmise was true cannot of course be established. Lloyd George had little to gain among the Liberals, and much to lose if an association with Northcliffe were known. Although he would be accused by many in the next few days of wanting to become Prime Minister (and by some historians), there is no evidence beyond the statements by peripheral Liberals such as Pease and Hobhouse, who did not like him in any case.[62]

What is clear, however, is that from the meeting with Repington and from the documents he subsequently received, Lloyd George realized that the munitions problem was not simply serious, but an emergency.[63] His letter to Asquith quoted in the previous chapter, proclaiming a shell crisis, resigning the Munitions of War Committee, and urging a ministry for munitions went off two days later. And the next morning, Tuesday, 18 May, *The Times*, in a stinging leader demanded Churchill's removal from the Admiralty.

On Monday morning the Admiralty problem became a political emergency. Bonar Law appeared at the Treasury to see Lloyd George having received newspaper clippings which seemed to indicate that Admiral Fisher had resigned. Lloyd George confirmed that the First Lord indeed had resigned. The story of the conversation between the two men has been told by Lord Beaverbrook, presumably with Bonar Law as a source, and by Lloyd George in his *War Memoirs*.[64] The two accounts do not differ substantially except on the matter of which man first suggested a coalition and both stories agree that the burden of the Unionist leaders' argument concerned the discontent with the present state of things in the House of Commons and its dislike of Churchill. If the First Sea Lord were to go, Churchill could not be allowed to stay at the Admiralty. Bonar Law could not, nor did he wish to, prevent a row in the House of Commons. A point to note here is that the center of the controversy really was Churchill far more than Fisher. Destruction of the former was far more important than the rehabilitation of the latter. The Unionists were prepared to end the war-time truce to attack the First Lord. Lloyd George in his account adds that Bonar Law also was concerned at the government's evident complacency about ammunition supplies. His party's alternatives were full cooperation or all out opposition.

According to Beaverbrook Lloyd George grasped the situation immediately and replied: 'of course we must have a Coalition for the alternative is impossible.' Lloyd George relates that he left the Treasury and went to No. 10. Asquith understood the position at once and Lloyd George then returned and brought Bonar Law through the passage that leads from the back of the Treasury to No. 10 and No. 11. The three men concluded that Bonar Law would write a letter to the Prime Minister demanding a debate on government policy but implying, as an alternative, the offer of a coalition.[65] The Liberal government was dead by noon on Monday, 17 May.[66]

One must question at this point why Asquith who had so airily passed off the suggestion of a coalition less than a week before now accepted one in a few minutes' conversation. This puzzle has some importance for Lloyd George's career in the next year. Bonar Law in his letter, the form of which the three men had agreed upon, dwelt at length on Fisher's resignation saying that if it could be 'postponed we shall be ready to keep silence now.' In other words there would be no debate. Everyone knew that Fisher would not serve under Churchill, but there was a good deal of evidence that Fisher heartily wished to remain at the Admiralty and serve as a uniformed war minister in the style of Kitchener at the War Office. Subsequently in a note to Asquith on 20 May, Fisher made this quite clear himself. The point is that Churchill easily could have been sacrificed. Not a dog would have barked in either the Unionist or the Liberal camp. The evidence presented in the previous chapter appears to show that the Prime Minister would have found the First Lord's departure a trifle saddening but a great relief. For Asquith, Churchill's departure was a symbolic matter. But the endless charges of weakness and indecisiveness, centering on the failure of munitions supply, were a real issue. The contradictions of his Newcastle speech were an embarrassment. In his memorandum of 17 May to the Cabinet thanking them for their services the Prime Minister gave equal weight as a cause of the crisis to the 'alleged' shortage of munitions and in his conversation with the King's private secretary Lord Stamfordham two days later, explaining his actions for the King, he evidently dwelt at length on Kitchener's assurances, the Newcastle speech, and Repington's dispatch.[67] The munitions crisis then was real. As it was Kitchener's responsibility he too would have to be replaced. This by itself meant a coalition. He could remove Kitchener only with Conservative support and not without it.

Monday, 17 May 1915, then became the day of decision in the death of Britain's last Liberal government. Bonar Law retired to Lansdowne House to write the agreed letter intimating that the Unionists considered Fisher's resignation a matter serious enough to warrant a full debate in the House of Commons, but suggesting 'some change in the constitution of the government' as an alternative and Asquith responded by sending the note already cited to each Cabinet member thanking him for his services, in effect telling him he had resigned. He referred to it as the discharge 'of a most repugnant but most important duty'.[68] To most members of the Cabinet, particularly the junior members, it was a complete surprise. Charles Hobhouse records that he was talking with McKenna, late in the evening, when Maurice Bonham-Carter entered with letters for the two. Both men were astounded and decided that Balfour and Lloyd George were at the bottom of it. Balfour wanted revenge against the Tories and Lloyd George wanted to be Prime Minister.[69]

Churchill was devastated. He wrote later that he had seen Balfour early in the day and had intimated that a reconstruction of the Board of Admiralty was required. This was simple enough. Only later at the House of Commons with a speech in hand to explain the changes both Lloyd George and Asquith had made clear that there would be no speech and that he must go.

Two days later Lloyd George recalled the scene for George Riddell. Churchill, he said,

> came in with a face like the face we used to see on old mugs. Winston said he intended to make a statement to the House of Commons and that he had prepared it. LG told him he could not carry out his intention, as the effect upon foreign politics would be disastrous, particularly with Italy hanging in the balance. Winston said, 'You forget my reputation is at stake. I am wounded.' LG said, 'I read his statement. When I came to the parts in which he referred to his own services, I could see his eyes filling with sympathy for himself. However, I persuaded him that the statement could not be made, and off he went.' (A ruthless game this politics. No quarter and no sympathy.)[70]

In the evening of Wednesday, 19 May, Lloyd George and Riddell were walking home from the Savoy. Lloyd George told Riddell that Churchill would have to leave the Admiralty.

> He is a dangerous fellow. He also said that Samuel and Runciman had not done well. Samuel will probably have to go. A place would have to be found for Winston. McKenna who is supposed to have done badly will stay. (Strange metamorphosis. LG is now evidently working with McKenna of whom he formerly held the poorest opinion. Think of the day when LG and Winston were bosom friends and spoke of McK in contemptuous terms.)[71]

Nevertheless on Monday despite this rebuff Churchill, whose political obtuseness never left him, did not yet understand that in a real sense the crisis at the moment raged over himself. At midnight after receiving Asquith's memorandum dismissing the Cabinet he replied with a remarkably tranquil letter, of which he prints only a part in the *World Crisis*, saying that he would be sorry to leave the Admiralty but would accept only a service department (the War Office?), while giving avuncular advice on other appointments. Lloyd George ought not to replace Kitchener although Balfour, whom he had already recommended for the Admiralty would be good. Lloyd George could take on munitions.[72]

However, after seeing the morning papers the next day in which the crisis was first announced by the Conservative papers and which included the vicious attack upon himself in *The Times*, Churchill's self assurance evaporated.[73] He now sent the Prime Minister a second, far more modest, letter, not mentioned in the *World Crisis*, saying that he would accept the Colonies, which Lloyd George had rather casually suggested for him the previous day. 'I could not measure the situation yesterday as it concerned me,' he explained. But 'above all things I should like to stay here and finish my work.'[74] That afternoon, over the initials of its editor J.L. Garvin, the *Pall Mall Gazette* announced to the world that Fisher's resignation had not only destroyed Churchill but had put out the Liberal government as well. 'You can no more put it back than restore Humpty Dumpty.'[75] In effect the Churchill phase of the crisis was over, even though he could not believe it. On the next day, Wednesday, 19 May, he sent George Lambert, the junior Civil Lord of the Admiralty, on an embarrassing mission to see Fisher and to offer him anything he wanted, including a seat in the Cabinet, to remain. Maurice Hankey was with Fisher when Lambert arrived.[76] The First Lord would later make a number of other ill advised attempts to hold on to his post, including a letter to Bonar Law and a letter by his wife to Asquith.

Throughout the week Churchill, like a man about to be executed, denied his fate. On 20 May Riddell saw him at the Admiralty. He was hysterically irrational, as his biographer put it, about to die of grief.

'I am stung by a viper. I am the victim of political intrigue. I am finished.' I said 'Not finished at forty, with your remarkable powers!' 'Yes,' he said. 'Finished in all I care for — the waging of war; the defeat of the Germans. I have had a high place offered to me — a position that has been occupied by many distinguished men, and which carries with it a high salary. But that all goes for nothing. This is what I live for. LG has been partly responsible. Fisher went to him and he told him to resign, or at any rate did not dissuade him. I have prepared a statement of my case, but cannot use it. The foreign situation prevents me from doing so. I will show you this statement. [Churchill showed Riddell his statement.] This is a political intrigue. It centers around LG. He thinks he sees his way to go to the War Office. Is he going to be Minister of War? What has been decided?' I said: 'He does not want to go to the War Office.' Winston replied, 'You are wrong. He does!' He then went on to speak of Balfour and Bonar Law. He said, 'They insist on high offices. Bonar Law also wants the War Office.' I said, 'I think you are wrong.' Winston, however, insisted on his point. 'The poor devil [French] is fighting for his life. Had I spent some of my time in lobbying newspapers instead of working twelve hours a day, I should not be in this plight. This is a Northcliffe Cabinet. He has forced this.' R.: 'Do you think the PM has been weak in the conduct of the war?' Winston: 'Terribly weak — supinely weak. His weakness will be the death of him.' Thus closed. . .a most painful and eventful interview and I left this broken man pacing up and down in his room. Early in the conversation he said that his fate was not yet sealed. It think it is. How soon men forget, or appear to forget. I wonder whether Winston remembers McKenna's downfall.[77]

Nonetheless the old Cabinet was dead. The question now was what would go in its place.

IV

The argument has been made, repeatedly, that the underlying cause of the May crisis was Asquith's weakness: 'supine, sodden, supreme' lamented Churchill in his misery.[78] Both Conservative and Liberal newspapers agreed upon this, albeit in different ways. The opposition dwelt upon the 'drink muddle', and the 'shell scandal'. Among these the failure to control Churchill was only another notorious example.[79] The Liberal papers acknowledged that the Prime Minister was under attack, albeit unfairly, by the Northcliffe papers and hinted at a press conspiracy reaching back to the end of March.[80]

That Asquith understood all this cannot be doubted. The immediate disposal of Churchill and the agreement upon a coalition were the easy decisions taken on 17 May. The more difficult phase, now at hand, was the balancing of interests in the new government. All of this was made the more complex because Bonar Law was under similar pressure to take action, either to fight or to join. Here the leader of the insurgents was easily visible in the person of Edward Carson.

As has been seen, despite many protestations to the contrary, Carson despised Asquith as a lazy weakling, but it is hard to be certain that he had much more admiration for his own party leader, and it is quite clear that Bonar Law himself feared Carson's prestige and influence among the Unionist rank and file. He had to be sure of Carson's position before committing himself. Bonar Law evidently got in touch with Carson immediately after leaving Asquith and Lloyd George on Monday, 17 May, for Ruby Carson recorded in her diary that her husband told her at 1 p.m. on Monday that there would be a coalition. The next day, before any appointments had been discussed, Carson reported to her that he would be in the Cabinet and on Thursday, 20 May, Bonar Law, at dinner at Carson's house in Eaton Place, confessed that he felt he could enter a coalition government only because Carson had agreed to do so.[81]

Carson's inclusion in the coalition therefore was as politically necessary as Churchill's departure. Thus there were three Unionists, Bonar Law himself, and Carson, and Balfour for whom places had to be found. Balfour, Churchill had already suggested for the Admiralty on 17 May, admitting the collaboration between himself and the former Unionist leader that had given rise to so much speculation in previous months: 'I made him a party to all our secrets.'[82] However Asquith seemed well satisfied and the appointment quickly was made. At the same time Carson became Attorney General with a seat in the Cabinet.[83] The problem lay with Bonar Law and intimately involved Lloyd George.

Generally the assumption had been, among leaders of both parties, that Lloyd George would replace Kitchener at the War Office with Kitchener perhaps taking command in France, or as was later suggested assuming the revived post of Commander-in-Chief. Asquith had mentioned this to Churchill on 17 May. Churchill later accused Lloyd George of fomenting the crisis in order to gain the War Office. Here, however, the logic was that as the War Office controlled munitions production and as Lloyd George had made munitions his province, the War Office was where he belonged. However, the need to eject Kitchener was clear, although only the Northcliffe newspapers, first on 21 May, referred to it. But it could be accomplished only when the Opposition was entering the government and Kitchener could not be replaced with a nonentity.

Lloyd George seems briefly to have agreed to replace Kitchener. He was being bombarded with documents on War Office slackness by Colonel Repington, who assured Lloyd George that he would be 'welcomed' there.[84] Lloyd George told Frances Stevenson on 17 May that she would be coming with him. But his interest in the work there centered chiefly on munitions and his motives for taking the post derived from anger that the War Office had misled him.[85] By the next day he was beginning to change his mind. Riddell warned him against the War Office and evidently Maggie opposed his going there.[86] On the 20th Repington wrote to him warning 'for heavens sake don't give Lord K the Command-in-Chief in France! That would be too high a price to pay for your arrival at the War Office!'[87]

Stimulated by Repington's revelations but perhaps also to forestall pressure toward the War Office, Lloyd George had written his long letter to Asquith of 19 May, already discussed, resigning the Chairmanship of the Munitions Committee and stating that a department for munitions alone could take action. In effect munitions supply should be separated from munitions use.[88]

There is a coincidence in this recitation suggesting at least some collusion between Lloyd George and Lord Northcliffe, as George Riddell had long suspected. As has been seen, Northcliffe saw Lloyd George for an hour on 17 May, a meeting at which Riddell was not present but which Northcliffe later described as 'very useful'.[89] Northcliffe saw Lloyd George again on Sunday morning, 23 May.[90] The point is that the morning after the first meeting *The Times*, after announcing that Churchill's departure was 'a *sine qua non* of [Cabinet] reconstruction,' stated equally flatly that 'the great driving power of Mr. Lloyd George will of course be retained'.[91] More important, on Friday, 21 May, the burden of Lloyd George's letter to Asquith appeared in its leader columns. On the same day the *Daily Mail*'s more violent attack on Kitchener, subsequently burned on the floor of the stock exchange, appeared.[92]

The Friday leader in *The Times* announced that Kitchener 'must be relieved of the business of supplying our troops at the front and at home with munitions and other necessaries of war. . .Mr. Lloyd George. . .is the obvious man for the undertaking.' Accompanying the leader was a special article calling among other things for the creation of a new 'Minister of War Supplies'. Mr. Lloyd George, as the man 'of push and go', has been 'frequently mentioned' for this post.[93]

Taking all the testimony together, one must conclude that Asquith's interest in Lloyd George's going to the War Office was in the replacement of Kitchener. But Lloyd George's interest was the enhancement of munitions supply. When it occurred, first apparently to Lloyd George, that munitions supply might be separated from the War Office, the Chancellor changed his mind and Kitchener's place was saved. The two events, in any case, occurred almost simultaneously. The letter to Asquith proposing a separate munitions department was written on 19 May and the next day he informed Maggie that he was absolutely refusing the War Office.[94] The evidence would seem to show that Lloyd George was using Kitchener's ill behavior as a vehicle for the mobilization of political opinion for an independent munitions ministry. In any case once the munitions ministry became a possibility the attacks upon Kitchener began to subside.

But one has to wonder whether the decision not to make a change at the War Office was prompted not only by Lloyd George's reluctance to take the post but also by Bonar Law's clear desire for it. On Thursday, 20 May, Riddell saw Sir Reginald Brade, Permanent Secretary at the War Office throughout the war, who told him of a meeting the previous evening with Max Aitken (who became Lord Beaverbrook in 1917) and with Bonar Law, Lloyd George and McKenna the following morning. The upshot of the two meetings was that Lloyd George would not go to the War Office, even though Bonar Law was adamant that Kitchener should not remain in his place. The implication seems to be that if Bonar Law were able to force the departure of Kitchener, the War Office would be his. Hence Kitchener, with all his faults, stayed.[95]

Asquith who had been wondering what to do with the glittering pro-consul should he leave the War Office — he was too old for India or a field command — was surely much relieved.

But if Lloyd George was not to go to the War Office could he not stay at the Treasury? There were many letters from the City urging that he remain and Frances Stevenson records that on the morning of 20 May, Walter, Baron Cunliffe, Governor of the Bank of England, came in tears to see him to plead that he remain at his post.[96]

On the other hand Lloyd George's person had been associated with munitions in the public mind since at least the Bangor speech at the end of February and certainly his own interest in the question was older. For six months he had thought of nothing but the organization of industry and industrial workers, and of temperance and munitions supply. All of these could be comprehended under the production of munitions of war. One cannot escape the belief that he understood this. The letter of 19 May meant therefore not only a separate executive department of munitions but himself at the head of it.

However, one needs always to be a little cautious with Frances Stevenson's descriptions of the tides of the political world. Her only source was Lloyd George. When she wrote therefore on 24 May that 'everyone is keen on his [Lloyd George's] taking up munitions of war,' it may have meant only that Lloyd George intended this would soon occur.[97] He never said such things to George Riddell. In this case however, the diary entry, which covers events of the previous five days, was likely an accurate description. As has been seen *The Times* was clearly demanding precisely this translation.

But there remained the problem of Andrew Bonar Law. As Leader of the Opposition Bonar Law could expect, and did demand, a major office. He, with Austen Chamberlain, was one of the few important Unionists with experience in business. If Lloyd George were to remain at the Exchequer and Kitchener at the War Office Bonar Law could reasonably claim the department of munitions.[98] But equally, and this may have been more compelling, if Lloyd George took munitions, the Unionist leader as the second ranking man in the government had every right to the Exchequer. This, the Prime Minister was determined to avoid, for the public reason that the Liberals would never stand for a tariff reformer in charge of tax policy and budget making, but privately, and possibly at least as important, he had another man in mind, Reginald McKenna. (Asquith thought briefly, evidently at Riddell's suggestion, of holding the Exchequer himself. No doubt McKenna would have been Financial Secretary.)[99]

There is however another factor commending Lloyd George to munitions, of which the Chancellor may not have been aware. On the critical day of 20 May, Asquith received a note from John Bradbury, Permanent Secretary to the Treasury since 1913, asking to be relieved of his duties and transferred to any other post however humble. Were he not a married man, he said, he would resign altogether. As it was he had only about £100 a year. But he could no longer work with Lloyd George, and would not stay if the present Chancellor remained. He had seen Lloyd George only rarely in the past few months and had been consulted only on brewery purchase. His office had sunk to the level of a minor clerkship. Finally, he said, work was much more complicated now than it had been during the financial crisis which the Chancellor 'handled with so much apparent success at the beginning of the war'.[100] This was a damning indictment by itself, but coming, as it did, only two years after the resignation of Sir Robert Chalmers, which indeed had followed the resignation of Sir George Murray in 1908 from the same post for almost exactly the same reasons, Asquith took it seriously. He saw Bradbury immediately and asked for details. Bradbury replied he would give them if required, but that his motives for leaving were the same as his predecessors. 'Accordingly,' wrote Charles Hobhouse, 'McK goes to the Exchequer where he will do admirably, and they are to invent a new post for Ll.G.'[101]

Hobhouse, as usual, knew only part of the story, but he was close to Asquith, and he had worked with Lloyd George long enough to know, and to despise, his administrative methods. His diaries are full of complaints. Yet in the narrow sense Bradbury's charges against the Chancellor were quite true. Lloyd George had spent almost no time on purely Treasury business since the August crisis of 1914, as the preceding chapters show, except for two remarkably unimaginative, and indeed inadequate, budgets. As a result Britain was fighting the war almost entirely on City credit and worst of all, on a ballooning overdraft at Morgan's in the United States as a result of the contract of January 1915. Already there had been questions in the House of Commons, the pound had begun to fall and his inattention to business was worrying bankers both in Britain and the U.S. On 19 February the Grenfell bank in London had written to Morgan's in New York complaining that it could not induce the Chancellor of the Exchequer to put his mind to the strengthening of Britain's currency. 'H.P. Davison,' the cable concluded, 'knowing the mentality of the Chancellor of the Exchequer will appreciate our difficulty.'[102] The man who had so cogently and properly urged upon Asquith that the Cabinet take a larger, more comprehensive, view of the war, that it plan for years, that it explore contingencies and search for new ideas, had never applied these splendid precepts to his own department.[103] The Treasury was living hand to mouth. Lloyd George disliked civil servants as they disliked him. His genius was of imagination, the pulling open of unknown doors of possibility, not in marching along well-known corridors of regulation. As has been noted no one but he could have imagined the Bank of England as a wholesale bill broker. But the Bank had entered the field and moreover was making money at it. No wonder the Governor, Lord Cunliffe, wept. But still Bradbury was correct. The entire basis of British war finance would have to change. More long term funding had to be found, and soon. Fortunately Lloyd George, who had never seen a bond, escaped these problems. They became McKenna's.

It is not too much to say that when Lloyd Geroge went to the Ministry of Munitions, the pound-dollar currency market, which generally he had left to Lord Cunliffe, was in a shambles. Dollar liquidity in London had practically disappeared and in July the pound, which had remained remarkably stable since the beginning of the war, had begun to fall. In mid-August Morgan Grenfell had written to him saying that in two days $17,000,000 was due on orders delivered and that the British account in New York held only $4,000,000. Moreover since the decline of the pound it was becoming difficult to sell 'any considerable amounts' of pounds even below $4.70. The letter concluded rather desperately: 'We presume that the authorities have the matter in view and contemplate steps to meet the situation. . .'[104]

A fascinating chart derived from Morgan and Co. figures in the United States Senate Documents illustrates starkly the change in British financial strategy that occurred under McKenna. Under Lloyd George Britain had paid for arms entirely by the sale of sterling and the shipment of gold, the conventional method of paying for imports. McKenna's first act was to sell about $35,000,000 in securities, and negotiate a $50,000,000 loan from Morgan's. By October he had stopped almost entirely the sale of sterling.[105]

Asquith's attempts to make McKenna Chancellor in 1908 have been recounted. Since that time he had proved to be a loyal and efficient supporter, enduring without public complaint some remarkably hard treatment from the Prime Minister in 1911. He was a reliable hater of Churchill and with a few interludes, maintained a seasoned dislike of Lloyd George. He had no friends but Asquith. There would be no intrigues against the Prime Minister with him at No. 11 (although he would not for a time occupy that house). And he had a handsome and talented wife in Pamela Jekyll whom Asquith always delighted in capturing as a bridge partner, perhaps the more so after the departure of Venetia Stanley.

The problem in McKenna was his unpopularity in both parties. He was distinctly a second-rank figure. Generally it was assumed that his career was in decline. Therefore it would be hard to justify his translation to the Exchequer against the demands of Bonar Law, who quickly learned of the plan and was clearly furious.

However modest and unassuming in demeanor the Unionist leader was, as Lord Beaverbrook remarked, 'meekly ambitious', he had never sat in Cabinet and, as Lloyd George reported to Miss Stevenson, he possessed firm notions about the status of the party leader.[106] Could he be pushed aside? The difficulty was removed by a subterfuge evidently worked out, probably on 24 May, by Asquith and Lloyd George although one must comment that the scheme bears all the marks of a typical Lloyd George solution. Lloyd George, it was decided, would see Bonar Law who now wanted the Exchequer and who had been urged by his colleagues to accept nothing less and to explain that he would have neither munitions nor the Exchequer nor the War Office, but for any number of high minded patriotic reasons he ought to be content as Secretary of State for the Colonies.[107] Asquith composed a memorandum to himself on 26 May setting out this strategy. It is partly printed in J.A. Spender's biography, which leaves out a sentence saying that it was designed to keep Bonar Law from any major office.[108] The reason Bonar Law would have to take the Colonies, it was to be explained, was that Lloyd George was not, in fact, leaving the Exchequer at all. He was going to munitions only temporarily. He would remain Chancellor and live at No. 11. When shells were on a 'sound footing', as he told Maggie, he would return. McKenna would be only a locum tenens. Hence the Exchequer was not available for the Unionist leader. Bonar Law accepted this fabrication and agreed, to his colleagues' surprise, to take the Colonies.[109]

However, the news that McKenna would be at the Prime Minister's elbow at the Exchequer turned out to be nearly as controversial and incomprehensible as the resignation of Fisher had been in the first place and quite eclipsed the expected departure of the unhappy Churchill. Even one so well informed as Riddell could hardly believe it.

> The political situation has taken an amazing turn this week. McKenna, who has been the most unpopular member of the Cabinet and who has never been in the inner circle, has suddenly wriggled his way to a front place. In September 1913, when I was staying with him at Dornoch, he did not even know that Asquith and other prominent members of the Cabinet were meeting at Percy Illingworth's. Even I knew more than he did. I can remember L.G.'s sneering account of how McKenna who 'was with child' (Mrs. McK was in a family way) had wept at the proposal to eject him from the Admiralty and how he had ignominiously gone to the Home Office like a chastened dog. The inner conclave were the P.M., L.G., Grey and Winston. No one else really mattered. Now McKenna seems to have replaced Winston. His friendship with Fisher has enabled him to score. An interesting metamorphosis which shows that if a man is courageous and prepared to eat enough dirt and submit to enough insults he may triumph in the end. He is very shrewd and cunning, but, as with most of us, the turn of events has done the business for him. It would however be interesting to know whether he conspired with Fisher to bring about Winston's downfall. . .He would have stopped at nothing — not even at stabbing him in the back in a dark lane. His feelings may [not?] have been justified, but I have correctly described them. Now in 48 hours, he has become one of the four chief actors in the Cabinet's drama. But he is a small man with bad judgement, vain, but kind-hearted and with the courage of a lion.[110]

The Unionists were equally incredulous. Even though the arrangement could not possibly have been settled by that time Cynthia Asquith, Lady Elcho's daughter and wife of Asquith's son Herbert, learned at lunch at Downing Street, apparently from the Prime Minister himself, on Friday, 21 May, that McKenna, 'whom every man in the street would like to expel before anyone, with the possible exception of Haldane, is the one fixture about whom there has been no doubt.'[111] Next day at lunch with her mother and Arthur Balfour, the prospective First Lord of the Admiralty compared the positions of the presumably incoming and outgoing Chancellors of the Exchequer.

> He said it was curious how very much more popular Lloyd George — whom everyone would expect to be such a rock of offence — was with both sides of the House than McKenna. Lloyd George appears to have a kind of licensed irresponsibility and people forgive what they, at the time, considered the most heinous crimes. Of course, he had personal charm, whereas poor McKenna is calculated to jar nearly every nerve in everybody. Lloyd George appears to have gained the appreciative confidence of the City by asking, and taking, the best expert advice in the financial crises of the war.[112]

By the next Sunday after Fisher's resignation, 23 May, the crisis was nearly over. Northcliffe had seen Lloyd George that morning, still urging the Chancellor to go to the War Office as he subsequently told Riddell, but the important posts had been fixed except for the persuasion, or coercion, of

Bonar Law.[113] Balfour at the Admiralty and Carson as Attorney General were in place. Haldane was gone as a symbolic sacrifice. Churchill would leave the Admiralty amid general applause. Asquith, who hated this sort of pressure, had seen the First Lord on Saturday and reiterated the burden of a letter of the previous day. There was no alternative. The Prime Minister, who could hardly make a decision in any other matter, had moved swiftly and decisively in this personal one, even at some cost in composure. Cynthia Asquith recorded that the Prime Minister, to her always the most serene of men, 'looked really rather shattered with a sort of bruised look in his eyes'. She heard that even his bridge, 'always bad' had grown worse during the crisis.[114]

On Sunday, 23 May at dinner with Lloyd George at his house at Walton, Riddell heard the story of the previous week. After telling of Fisher's appearance in Downing Street Lloyd George unburdened himself about Churchill.

> L.G. said that Winston had acted badly inasmuch as he had not told the Cabinet that all the Naval Board were of the opinion that the Dardanelles operation should be a combined sea and land attack.

> L.G. said that he had fought to get Winston high office — the Colonies, the India Office, the Viceroyalty of India — his colleagues would not, however, agree to Winston's having anything but a minor position. They would not listen to India where things were in an unsettled state. L.G. said that McKenna had never said a word against Winston's appointment to any of the offices although he said nothing in his favour which could not be expected. He said that Winston had acted unwisely. He had written some foolish letters to the P.M., who had been angry and who had written Winston a sharp letter in reply. Amongst other things Winston had said 'no one but I can carry the Dardanelles operation to a successful conclusion.' R: 'When any man talks like that he is on the way to a lunatic asylum.'[115]

Lloyd George was clearly aware that he could not work with Kitchener at the War Office if Kitchener were Commander in Chief, a proposal made by St. Loe Strachey that day.[116]

> Kitchener will never act as a subordinate. He wants a tame colleague who will be useful but who will sign what he tells him. If he wants to reprimand French, the new Secretary for War will have to sign the dispatch without comment. That would not suit me. K. is either incompetent or he is tricky. You cannot get away from it.

Riddell mentioned at this point that Sir John French was using Alec Murray. People had been telling French to put himself right with the public. Lloyd George made no comment, but Riddell reflected that Lloyd George was also working with Northcliffe.

After commenting on new appointments rumored, Simon declining the Lord Chancellorship, Riddell ventured:

> McKenna has had a remarkable stroke of luck — the most despised amongst Cabinet ministers has become one of the inner circle. L.G.: Yes, the Tories wanted to get rid of him but the P.M. would not agree. R.: The inner circle consisted of the P.M., yourself, Grey, Winston and Crewe. L.G.: Yes, but since the war Winston has been intolerable, or

rather he was during the first few months. If the P.M. was late [to Cabinet] he would not talk to anyone but Kitchener. The little dogs were not worth his notice. I am afraid he is angry with me just now. He came up to me in quite a menacing way and said 'I can see you don't mind what is going to happen to me' or something to that effect. I replied, 'you are quite mistaken. We all have our ups and downs and must make the best of it.'

Lloyd George concluded by telling Riddell that he had no intention of going to the War Office and repeated the fiction that he was staying at the Treasury, recounting the story of Lord Cunliffe's appearance in tears to attempt to keep him there.[117]

This conversation took place on Sunday evening, 23 May 1915. Except for the suborning of Bonar Law, which occurred on Tuesday, 25 May, all the pieces were in place, and on the evening of that day the names of the new Cabinet were given to the newspapers. The Prime Minister with evident relief composed a note of thanks to Lloyd George.

I cannot let this troubled & tumultuous chapter in our history close without trying to let you know what an incalculable help & support I have found in you all through. I shall never forget your devotion, your unselfishness, your powers of resource, what is (after all) the best of all things your self forgetfulness.

These are the rare things that make the drudgery and squalor of politics, with its constant revelation of the large part played by petty & personal motives, endurable, and give to its drabness a lightning streak of nobility.

I thank you with all my heart.
  Always yours affectionately
    H.H. Asquith[118]

Lloyd George deserved this accolade. Asquith, one has to believe, meant what he said. He seems for a time to have been in a panic. He sensed he was the cause of trouble, McKenna told Hobhouse later, and Hobhouse recorded that he had himself been informed by Margot that the Prime Minister was in tears for three days after asking for the resignations of his colleagues.[119] Lloyd George's function may have been first to stiffen the Prime Minister's determination by reminding him that given the present circumstances he could remain at his post, and second by pointing out that Bonar Law could be easily coerced. The prospect of all out Unionist opposition had frightened Asquith, but it was not real. If the Unionists denounced the party truce, Lloyd George was sure, the leader of the attack would not have been Bonar Law but Carson. Lloyd George could see this and was sure that Bonar Law, no fool, saw it also. Alternatively with Carson in the Cabinet Bonar Law, in the last analysis, had to take whatever post he was offered, as finally he did. This essential weakness of the Unionist leader's position and the strength of Carson's, combined with the latter's contempt for Asquith, would become a central factor in the political events that made Lloyd George Prime Minister nineteen months later.

For Lloyd George there were no regrets about the formation of the coalition.

His frustrations since the beginning of 1915 were reason enough to welcome a change. The mobilization of Britain's industrial power, which he had so long demanded, could now begin. Riddell saw him at Walton on Wednesday, 26 May after the names of the new Cabinet had appeared in the papers. Lloyd George still insisted that the translation to munitions was only temporary, and that No. 11 would probably be the offices of the new ministry. All in all the shell scandal was a step forward, he said, even though Field Marshal French was wrong in giving information to Repington.

> 'Northcliffe was right in his facts and I am not sure he was wrong in directing public attention to them as he did.' LG did not mention that he had seen Northcliffe again on Sunday 24th [i.e. 23rd]. I have a shrewd suspicion that LG has been a party to the attack on Kitchener in the 'Times' and the 'Daily Mail' and the 'Manchester Guardian'. He did not appreciate how powerful Kitchener is in the country or how much Northcliffe is hated by the Press generally and distrusted by the public. LG is very deep and subtle in all his proceedings. He rarely tells *all* the story.[120]

Riddell may well have been correct. By mid-May Lloyd George was furious at Kitchener, as his letters attest, and could easily have encouraged the attack upon him in the Northcliffe newspapers. On the other hand there was little Lloyd George could tell Northcliffe that the newspaper proprietor did not already know. The information for both men came from Repington. In any case once it became likely that if Kitchener left the War Office Bonar Law would go there, unless Lloyd George himself claimed it, which he did not want to do, Kitchener remained in place. This failure to take action when it was possible, of course, would soon be regretted by everyone, Lloyd George included. Nonetheless even after Kitchener's departure a year later Lloyd George again moved to forestall Bonar Law's appointment to a War Office by now stripped of most of its powers.

The other figure in the drama almost unnoticed by the time the Cabinet was announced, was Churchill, who would be Chancellor of the Duchy of Lancaster. Riddell saw him at the Admiralty, also on Wednesday 26 May, and accompanied him to the Bath Club. His rage against Lloyd George was unbounded.

> I leave the nation a navy in a state of perfect efficiency. I cannot say more. Lloyd George is responsible for the coalition government. He has treated me disgracefully. He has no sense of honour. Notwithstanding our former relations, notwithstanding how I stood by him in the Marconi days, he did nothing to help me. He never put out a hand. He acted just as if they had been killing a rat. I shall never work with him again. He never hesitates to sacrifice a friend if he stands in the way of his game. He might act differently to some of his old Welsh friends, but we English are a different race. You remember what I say. He will treat you in the very same way if it serves his purpose. I have no complaint to make of McKenna. I am glad he has gone up. All this is due to Lloyd George's intrigues. But it is all over now. I shall stay on until the Dardanelles expedition has become an assured success. I shall give the Government my support. I shall make a few speeches and then

I shall go to the Front. I could not continue to hold a sinecure office at such a time. Fisher has acted like a treacherous devil. His Malay blood has come out. At the last he was attacked by nerves. He is suffering from a nervous breakdown. He is an old man. There is that to be said for him. This is all for your private ear, but remember what I say regarding LG. Whatever your friendship or relations with him may have been he will never scruple to sacrifice you if you stand in the way of his plans.[121]

Charles Masterman, once, save Churchill, Lloyd George's closest friend, had said nearly the same thing six months earlier.

6 Machines or Men for War

As Lloyd George himself recounted many times afterwards, when he became the Minister of Munitions he had nothing, no premises, no staff, no table of organization. He was, in his person alone, the Ministry of Munitions. Legally it did not yet exist and would not until 9 June 1915. His first act, taken in the afternoon of 26 May, the day the new Cabinet appeared in the papers, was to appoint Christopher Addison Parliamentary Under-Secretary and Sir Hubert Llewellyn Smith as General Secretary. Both men of course had been associated with Lloyd George before.

Smith was, and remained, Permanent Secretary at the Board of Trade (hence his title of General Secretary of Munitions), where he had been since 1907, being appointed within Lloyd George's tenure as President. He returned to the Board in January, 1916. He had been most effective during the threatened railway strike in the autumn of 1907 and appears to have been one of the few established civil servants with whom Lloyd George could get along. His presence may account for the fact that the first office of the new ministry was in the house of William Lockett Agnew, the art book publisher, at No. 6 Whitehall Gardens where Gladstone had once lived, next to the Board of Trade. Here President Woodrow Wilson's representative, Edward M. House, saw Lloyd George on 2 June. He recalled that the Minister of Munitions' office contained one chair and one table. Lloyd George occupied the chair and House the table.[1] Eventually, in March 1916 Lloyd George moved his office to the Hotel Metropole on Northumberland Avenue facing Trafalgar Square, which the ministry had occupied. It had in the meantime taken also the new Ministry of Agriculture building in Whitehall, renamed Armament Building.

Lloyd George, it could be noted, had first talked to Llewellyn Smith about the Ministry of Munitions on 21 May when he was still insisting to everyone that he intended to stay at the Exchequer.[2] Indeed only two days before, in his letter to Asquith resigning the chairmanship of the Committee of Munitions of War, he had first proposed a separate Ministry of Munitions.

Addison, a physician and former teacher of anatomy at Sheffield and London, was a more recent acquaintance. He had entered the House of Commons in January 1910 for Shoreditch and Lloyd George had consulted him occasionally on national health insurance although his influence was not so great as he suggests in his memoirs. Among the Liberals he was counted as a solid radical of the younger 1906 generation; his introduction to Lloyd George came through Masterman whose duty it was to keep the Chancellor in contact with those people. After Masterman's disappearance from the House in February 1914 Addison had begun to replace Masterman as the shepherd of this frequently troublesome flock of Members. Addison had signed the petition against British intervention in the war circulated among them at the end of July 1914. Nonetheless Addison was not a doctrinal pacifist. He had been an officer in the Hallamshire Rifles for twelve years and when the government was reshuffled in August 1914 he had taken office as Parliamentary Secretary at the Board of Education under J.A. Pease. This post he was unhappy to leave, but his close association with Lloyd George during the next six years would be of great importance for both men.

A third important early appointment who, like Addison, would remain a part of Lloyd George's official life for years was that of Eric Campbell Geddes. Lloyd George apparently first heard of him from Sir Edward Grey who had been Chairman of the Northeastern Railway until he became Foreign Secretary, but had remained in touch with its affairs since 1905.[3] Geddes, after a career in lumbering and railroading throughout the world, had gone to work for the railway in 1904 and was a great success. In 1914 he became Deputy General Manager of the railway with the prospect of succeeding to General Manager.[4] On this basis Grey drew Lloyd George's attention to him on 27 May and Lloyd George and Addison interviewed him the next day.

Geddes, according to Addison, was an immensely self-assured and ambitious man, in 1915 just 39 years old, who was eager for an important job at the Ministry of Munitions.[5] Lloyd George appointed him Deputy Director General of what within a year became two departments: Guns and Equipment, and Small Arms Ammunition, under the Director General of Munitions Supply, Major General Sir Percy Girouard.

Girouard came to the ministry from the Armament Output Committee of the War Office, a group that had been put together by the Master General of the Ordnance to show, in the face of many charges to the contrary, that he was doing something to produce weapons of war. He was in fact a man of great talent, a Canadian engineer officer who had retired in 1912 to run Armstrong's enormous shop at Elswick, Newcastle. He did not, however, remain long at the Ministry of Munitions.

Girouard turned out to be a difficult colleague, an expert among amateurs, and worst of all, among politicians. He was deeply concerned about questions of precedence and power and Lloyd George had been in some doubt about appointing him at all.[6] As Director General of by far the largest division of the ministry, he saw himself as the sole channel of communication to the Minister. This was intolerable for a man like Lloyd George who, however disorderly his work habits, chose always to give orders directly and in person to the man who would carry them out. Girouard thus became, within weeks, the ministry's greatest problem.

The end came quickly. Early in July Girouard arranged for the King to visit factories in Coventry and selected himself, without telling Lloyd George, to attend His Majesty as 'representative of the Minister'. The visits took place during the middle of July when Lloyd George was in Wales settling a coal strike. When Lloyd George returned he was furious. 'I hear even the P.M. is up in arms about this performance,' wrote Addison, who disliked Girouard more than most. 'L.G. has at last got to the end of his tether and decided that he must part with Girouard.' That afternoon, 22 July 1915, Girouard received a letter asking for his resignation.[7]

This otherwise minor affair is illuminating in regard to the character of Lloyd George. No man was less concerned with ceremonial opportunities. He had not at the time gone to Buckingham Palace to procure his seals of office as Minister of Munitions and had enquired whether they could not be sent. He was, he explained, very busy. Yet neither did he like to see the grasping after status in others. He understood instinctively that in a huge new administration, without precedents or established channels of communication, personal relationships were of vital importance. He began immediately the practice of weekly meetings of department heads in his office, which he believed were extremely useful although evidently some of his subordinates found them a waste of time.

But more than that, probably the basis of his charge against Girouard, he made a clear distinction in his mind between the expert and the administrator. Good administrators, he told the House of Commons on 23 July, the day after Girouard had been told to resign and indeed before he had done so, may lack technical expertise, but experts were rarely good administrators.[8] In effect, without any expertise whatever, he intended to run the Ministry of Munitions his own way and in his own name. He would not, and never would be, dominated by his officials. He always solicited advice, but the decisions were his and his cruelty to advisors became notorious. It could be noted that he quickly received two nominations from Asquith for a replacement for Girouard. Both were rejected.[9] Girouard was succeeded on 4 August by Sir Frederick Black from the Admiralty.

A second recruit from the Armament Output Committee, interviewed on 28 May, was George Macaulay Booth, a director of Booth's Steamships and the Bank of England and the second son of Charles Booth, the investigator of poverty and pension reformer. Although always identified as the genuine 'man of push and go', he was neither according to Lloyd George, but rather a man of tact and geniality, not a driver but a conciliator.[10] He was made Deputy Director in charge particularly of area organizations, perhaps Lloyd George's greatest personal contribution to the structure of the ministry, and, as one depending largely on voluntary effort, requiring reservoirs of good will. Booth indeed seems to have suggested the area organization on 28 May.[11]

The plan of the Ministry of Munitions' departmental organization was evidently worked out largely by Booth with help from Girouard. The two presented a draft on 1 June.[12] At the time of its foundation the ministry was organized into four main operating divisions: by far the largest, Munitions Supply, was under Girouard. There were in addition an Explosives Supply Department under Lord Moulton, an Engineering Department under Brigadier General L.C. Jackson and a Secretariat and Labour Department under William Henry Beveridge.

A final appointment made in the very early days of the life of the Ministry was of David Alfred Thomas who was to go to America to look into the existing and potential sources of munitions supply. For months Lloyd George had been receiving letters about the inefficiency of the War Office purchasing system in the United States. Most traditional arms producers were already operating at full capacity and the purchasing agent, J.P. Morgan was reluctant, on its own, to place orders with second rate companies. A reduction of new orders would be a good idea.[13] For Lloyd George, Thomas represented an unusual choice. As the member for Merthyr from 1888 to 1910 he had been Lloyd George's most determined and successful opponent during the latter's campaign to create a Welsh political party and had taught the young Member for Caernarvon District a lesson in political tactics in January 1896 when he lured Lloyd George into a packed meeting in Newport and allowed him to be shouted down.

Thomas, an immensely wealthy man, a coal broker and mine owner, had remained a force in South Wales politics until his retirement from the House of Commons in December 1910. But he had not, so far as can be seen, come to terms with Lloyd George. Moreover he had returned from the United States with his daughter only the previous month on board the *Lusitania* and had survived its torpedoing off the coast of Ireland on 7 May. Another ocean trip only little more than a month later required some resolution. Finally his health was far from good. He would die in 1918.

Thomas was above all a man of resolution, courage and patriotism. He replied to Lloyd George's letter of 8 July quickly, agreeing to return to America although reminding the minister of the *Lusitania*.[14]

The question was: what was Thomas to do in America? Although deliveries from the United States, principally at this time rifles and shell cases, were much in arrears, Lloyd George seems not to have fully considered precisely what Thomas was to do to increase them. Morgan & Company was the official British purchasing agent. But there existed no British mission beyond a number of War Office inspectors.[15] Hence in the days before Thomas left there occurred a spirited debate between Addison and Lloyd George over Thomas's charge. Addison was adamant that Thomas not be allowed to place orders and so undercut Morgan's so-called 'Export Department'.[16] This turned out, in the event, to be good advice. As a supply executive Morgan's no doubt could have been replaced, but, as Cecil Spring-Rice, the British Ambassador, made clear to Thomas once he had arrived, as a financial representative, rounding up dollars from United States banks to pay Britain's mounting bills, Morgan's was invaluable.[17]

Lloyd George announced Thomas's appointment to the House of Commons on 23 June with very little explanation, and Thomas sailed from Liverpool two days later.[18] He arrived in New York on 5 July and remained in the United States until the end of November 1915. His achievements there were of considerable importance and are hardly mentioned in his daughter's biography. At the time that Lloyd George's contract with Morgan's had been signed in the middle of January 1915 the War Office had insisted that orders in America would not exceed £10,000,000. Hence the stipulation in the contract, Clause 11, that Morgan & Company would receive two percent on the first £10,000,000 of orders and one percent thereafter.[19] Within four months £60,000,000 had been spent. Hence it had been suggested to Thomas that the contract might be renegotiated. He was in addition to see, in view of the huge sums involved, whether Morgan's 'Export Department' was sufficiently protecting British interests. After he arrived, he found the department, under Edward R. Stettinius, President of the Diamond Match, to be entirely efficient to the point that it was growing unpopular around the country. Moreover, he reported Morgan's seemed to be embarrassed about the huge sums they were receiving. J.P. Morgan had told Thomas early in his stay that henceforth Morgan would base its commission not on the value of goods delivered but only upon the cost to the House of Morgan of running the 'Export Department' and would refund to the Treasury amounts already paid above this formula.[20]

Thomas's great achievement in the United States was in the establishment of the British Munitions Board. While he reported that he was entirely satisfied with the care for British interests exercised by Stettinius he saw the need for more experts on the spot to examine the facilities of bidding contractors and to see to transportation of the finished product, which should not be left to the contractor.[21] He noted that Stettinius entirely agreed.

The resulting agency, which came to be called the 'Moir Organization' when it was taken over by E.W. Moir of the Ministry of Munitions Invention Board on 13 December 1915, was a great success and continued, including an expanding intelligence division, until the end of the war. Anonymity was thought to be desirable, even though officially the organization was only an agent of Lloyd George's Ministry of Munitions, and so its offices in the Equitable Building on Broadway were registered in Moir's name alone. On the other hand Thomas advised that Lloyd George should not under any circumstances deal with representatives of American armament firms in Great Britain, even though it might seem easy and attractive to do so.[22]

Thomas's second important achievement lay in bringing Canadian firms into British contracting on a regular basis. He states in his report that he had been instructed to do this before he left Britain, but this may have been reinforced by a letter passed on to Lloyd George in September by Walter Long and apparently forwarded to Thomas from a 'leading man' in Canada [Max Aitken?].[23] Thomas, the anonymous letter stated, was entirely in the hands of Morgan's. They 'met him at Ambrose Light with a steam yacht. They are with him day and night.' He saw only what they chose him to see. 'They have a fine business organization and he of course is attracted by it' but the result was preference for American firms. Much of this of course was not true. Lloyd George quickly replied that Britain was doing everything it could to direct business to Canada even though Canadian prices were higher, but that Thomas would be notified.[24]

In the end Thomas spent a good deal of the latter part of his stay in Canada and established the Canadian Pacific Railroad as purchasing agent. He was able to negotiate a contract that Canada would be favored over the United States where possible even at higher prices and longer contracts, and that the Canadian Pacific would be paid only half Morgan's commission, in effect one percent on the first £10,000,000 and a half percent thereafter.[25] Thomas left New York on 29 November 1915.

All of this including Thomas's appointment had taken place while there was still, legally, no Ministry of Munitions in existence. The Ministry of Munitions Bill was introduced only on 3 June by the new Home Secretary, John Simon and received the Royal Assent on 9 June. Its terms were the simplest, one may infer by Lloyd George's design. The operative sentence appeared in the second of seven short clauses stating that the Minister of Munitions 'shall have such powers and duties in relation to the supply of munitions for the present War as may be conferred on him by His Majesty in Council and His Majesty may also if he considers it expedient' extend such powers and duties.[26] That was all. The minister would receive £5,000 per year and would not have to stand for re-election. Everything else would be decided in the Cabinet. It follows then that Lloyd George himself determined his own powers in the Order in Council, published on 16 June, which stated:

> It shall be the duty of the Minister of Munitions to examine into and organize the sources of supply and labour available for the supply of any kind of munitions of war, the supply of which is in whole or in part undertaken by him and by that means, as far as possible, to ensure the supply of munitions for the present war as may be required by the Army Council or the Admiralty or may be otherwise found necessary.[27]

In his memoirs Lloyd George proudly italicizes the last line of this quotation and explains he made ample use of these powers.[28] He was, in effect, thus empowered to produce anything he chose that could be called munitions of war, whether requested by the military or not, and in any amount.

Still, there exists in the Lloyd George papers a curious letter from Llewellyn Smith to the War Office, evidently to the Permanent Secretary, Reginald Brade, written on 5 June at a time when the Ministry of Munitions Bill was before the House of Commons and the Order in Council defining the Minister's power was unwritten, or at least unpublished. It defined the ministry's powers in a much narrower way.

> It is understood that the duties of the new Department. . .will begin when the requirements of the War Office have been made known to it . . .and they will end when the delivery of such munitions. . .has been made to the War Office. . .[29]

Lloyd George comments upon this letter at length in his *War Memoirs*, except that he states that the letter originated in the War Office, was sent by that department to the Ministry of Munitions, and illustrated the 'rigid and hardened mentality' of that department.[30] The historian must conclude either that Lloyd George made a mistake in the composition of his memoirs or that the letter was a deliberate attempt to mislead Kitchener.

Nevertheless, on the basis of the total freedom he was able to accord himself was founded the big gun program, the order for the construction of artillery of 4.5 inch caliber and larger, far in excess of the War Office's stated requirement. This began in the summer of 1915 and continued throughout Lloyd George's tenure at the ministry. By the time the program was complete all the guns were needed, and more. Nonetheless the big gun program provoked bitter disputes in the Cabinet with McKenna and with the War Office. But beyond the creation of the ministry itself it may have been Lloyd George's most important contribution. The war on the battlefield was won with big guns. Lloyd George provided them.[31]

I

Lloyd George probably did his most valuable work at the Ministry of Munitions in the first six months, perhaps the first three months, of his time there. By 27 November 1915, when he snatched the Ordnance Board from the War Office and from its departmental chief, the Master General, Stanley Von Donop, the ministry's structure was essentially complete. Manufacture had been entirely in his hands since the acquisition by the ministry in August and September of the Royal Ordnance factories. The Ordnance Board provided control of the critical component of design and specification. The board was reproduced in Munitions as a staff organization of the minister under Major General John P. DuCane who had been chief of artillery in the General Headquarters in France and whom Lloyd George first met at Boulogne on 19 June 1915.[32]

As was remarked in connection with national health insurance, it is frequently difficult to determine the precise origin of the various components of Lloyd George's projects: the Medical Research Committee in health insurance for example. Who suggested the Development Commission in the land program? The answers can only be guessed at, perhaps a chance remark by some expert or a recollection from his Welsh childhood. No doubt many ideas were worked out in conversations with colleagues. After all that is what men like Masterman and Addison, and in earlier days Churchill, were for. He could trust his instinct — perhaps it could be identified as genius — to tell him whether the proposed structure would work, always secure in the knowledge that if it did not it could be discarded, or starved to death. One suspects that frequently he did not know himself where his projects came from and so he would make up fanciful, usually simple, explanations for extremely complicated initiatives: for example his assignment of the motive for the Balfour Declaration, to Chaim Weizmann's invention of a new process for the manufacture of acetone.

Hence, Lloyd George's own contribution to the great success of the Ministry of Munitions, beyond his boundless energy, his talent and courage in choosing executives, and the political power which enabled him to wrestle every phase of the weapons supply process from the War Office, is very hard to delineate. But the historian must answer the question: why did the ministry work? In what way was it an improvement over War Office arms procurement? One can proceed only by inference with some help from chronology. Two innovations that clearly belong to Lloyd George, simply because he had been talking about them for months before the ministry was established, were the need for national industrial mobilization and for the large scale ordering of weapons. On both of these topics he had been bombarding the Cabinet since his first trip to France. He took care in the Orders in Council to ensure that weapons and ammunition procurement would be governed by his own initiative and not bound by the pinchpenny customs of the War Office all based upon the fatuous assumption, which hovered over British official thinking at least for the first 12 months of the conflict, probably until the battle of Loos at the end of September 1915, that the war would end soon.

The big gun program, the highly controversial symbol of all-out weapons production, will be discussed. In it lies the essential difference between Lloyd George and his colleagues. He seems to have understood certainly since the beginning of 1915 that any limits on Britain's effort in any area, not only weapons, were not only obsolete but meaningless. Even discussion of whether the army would be 2,000,000 or 3,000,000 men, which had occurred, was meaningless. What was needed was not two, or three, million men, but every available man and, by implication, every available gun. Britain must not make a measured effort, however large, but a maximum effort, which would include conscription. Genius, it has been remarked many times, is not knowledge but understanding, the light that enables a man to see things before others do; it is charisma, a gift not of universities, but of God. Lloyd George comprehended total war.

Mobilization of industry through local Boards of Management, on the other hand, came immediately and successfully with the Ministry of Munitions. Surprisingly Lloyd George says little about it in his *War Memoirs* — no doubt to him it seemed obvious — but the idea remained with him, probably becoming the germ of his Councils of Action program in 1935 as a part of the New Deal for Britain campaign, his last major political initiative. The theme that Britain's enormous industrial resources were not being fully exploited for the war effort had appeared in nearly every public speech Lloyd George made in the spring of 1915, most notably at Bangor and in his introduction of D.O.R.A. Amendment No. 2. But while he continually attacked Kitchener's secrecy and mendacity about military supplies, he did not refer to the War Office practice of dealing only with a limited number of prime contractors, the War Office List, which was at the root of the problem. (Apparently the official list of prime contractors at the beginning of the war included just 29 firms. By the time the Ministry of Munitions was established this had grown to 279 with about 3,000 subcontractors.)[33] Manufacturers outside this ring were unused for arms and ammunition, except as subcontractors.

By the beginning of June, that is before the Ministry of Munitions officially existed, Lloyd George clearly had the idea of direct contracting by the government with small firms who would convert their shops to component manufacture of guns or ammunition. In the first two weeks of that month, while the bill creating his ministry was before the House of Commons, he made a tour of Wales and the west of England explaining to the nation what he intended to do. In ten days he gave four major addresses, generally to union leaders and businessmen: at Manchester on 3 June, Liverpool on 4 June, Cardiff on 11 June, and concluding at Bristol on 13 June.[34] All of the speeches contained the same message. Britain was about to mobilize for war. Machines, wealth, and men were all to be in the service of the country. In each with varying emphasis he pointed to the example of the French munitions effort. That country had undertaken the wholesale conversion of small non-military manufacturing shops to war work. Automobile factories could produce artillery. Manufacturing jewelers could make shell fuses. All of this was presented as an appeal to patriotism. 'When the war is over,' he said at Cardiff on 11 June, echoing Shakespeare's *Henry V*,

> it will be something that will be talked about in every family and on every hearthstone till this generation passes away. Every man and every woman will have their toll of sacrifice. There will be many with their toll of heroism. It will be a topic of conversation and think how it will fare then with those who have worked today. They could say: 'when the summons came to us to do what we could to support our troops at the front, we never waited. We turned our works at once to the purpose of producing every shell that our machinery could possibly yield.' It will be a matter of pride and of boast, and of legitimate pride and boast, as long as they live, that they so behaved. Yes but think

of the others when the talk goes round, of what happened, when somebody will say to them 'when the government asked you to do your best to support our soldiers what did you do?' I should like to know whether he could say: 'I refused. I was not going to upset my works. I was not going to lose my business. I was not going to damage my trades.' I defy any man to say that in the years to come without a blush on his face.[35]

Obviously French experience provided a model for Lloyd George in building his ministry, although one must not forget that he routinely admired most things French, got on well with Briand and with Albert Thomas whom he would soon meet, even though he could not speak their language nor they his. He constantly referred to French national spirit and military ardor as well as their organization for munitions production. One must remark that in France organization had been immediately necessary. She was the least industrialized of the Western military powers with many small, by British standards, highly specialized family-run workshops. He had been told when in France in October 1914 by General St. Clair Deville, the inventor of the revolutionary 75mm field gun, of the French system of organizing small establishments on a voluntary regional basis.[36] The nation's fierce conscription law had called every able bodied man into the army at the outbreak of war on the assumption, universal at that time, that the war would be short and fought with existing equipment and ammunition. But the need for industrial mobilization was clear almost from the beginning and included, Lloyd George noted, both the release of skilled workmen from the army and the employment of women. He reports that General Deville offered to explain the French system to the British War Office, but there was no response.[37]

Lloyd George obviously had intended, well before the Ministry of Munitions, the wholesale conversion of British industry to war work. The government had the power to enforce this change under D.O.R.A. Amendment No. 2. What was needed was the administrative structure to handle this mass participation of small shops. They should not be subcontractors of established munitions firms, who had already shown that they were unable to enforce delivery commitments on their existing subcontractors, but in a direct legal relation with the government. The response was the regional organization which would at once provide a channel for the local patriotism to which he appealed in his June speeches, but which would also prevent subcontractors from accepting competing orders from several large firms for the same work, bidding up prices.

Lloyd George explained his plan to the House of Commons on 23 June during the debate on the Munitions of War Bill. (A different measure from the Ministry of Munitions Bill. Generally it defined the powers of the Minister in the control of capital and labor. In effect it put into law the terms of the Treasury agreement.) Subcontracting, said Lloyd George flatly, has been a failure. He proposed instead to bring local businessmen into direct relationship with the Ministry, to 'invite the businessmen...to organize themselves, and to assist us to develop the resources of their district. They have the local knowledge, they have the skill, and they are on the spot. . .'[38]

He showed the House a fuse for a high explosive projectile, apologizing to the Speaker if he was not in order. It was very complicated, required fine machinery, but many small workshops, even in London, could make it. However, no one but the managers themselves knew the capabilities of their own firms. He appealed, as he had done earlier on his speaking tour, for businessmen to come forward.[39]

By the time he spoke the area organization was laid out, if not in place. One of the businessmen who had come forward offering his services was James Stevenson, managing director of John Walker and Sons distillery, who earned, it was said, £14,000 per year and who in twenty years had changed Walkers from a minor Kilmarnock blender into Britain's largest whisky distiller.[40] Stevenson knew nothing of munitions, but he knew marketing and the invisible network of commerce in the United Kingdom. In an hour, on a W.H. Smith map, for which, he claimed, he was never reimbursed, he had divided the United Kingdom into ten munitions regions, seven in England and Wales, two in Scotland and one in Ireland. (Later this was increased to twelve, providing eight in England while Dublin and Belfast in Ireland were separated.) Within each region, in the principal town, was an Area Office representing the Ministry of Munitions to provide specifications, information, labor liaison, and applications for rationed raw materials. However, the actual contracting authority were some forty Boards of Management, made up of local businessmen serving without remuneration although legally the Boards were agents of the ministry. To the Boards went orders for arms or munitions, and it was at this level, through the local knowledge and experience of Board members, that the great unused potential of British manufacturing became engaged in the work of war. The Boards were empowered to bind the ministry in contracts which were then reviewed by the Contracts Department in London.[41] There is some suggestion in the official history of the ministry that the Boards of Management did not work well, although Lloyd George does not mention this in his *War Memoirs*.[42] As time went on more and more contracting was done from London. However, the Boards' vital function in the process of the mobilization of British civilian industry, that of providing the intimate local knowledge of what hundreds of workshops in each area were capable of doing and of bringing them initially into government service, had already been accomplished. Renewals were uncomplicated.

The Boards' local information was being supplemented, even as Lloyd George introduced the Munitions of War Bill, by a massive national survey of the industrial resources of the United Kingdom. Between 19 and 26 June 65,000 questionnaires were sent by post to every industrial establishment of which there was any record asking for details on the machinery it contained and the work currently being done. Unusually for such bureaucratic intrusions, the response was immediate. Within three weeks there had been 45,000 replies. One may comment that for Lloyd George, even though to him numbers were little more than toy balloons used in speeches to entertain or to attract attention, this survey was a customary part of his pattern of management. His great strength as an administrator lay in the comprehension of the magnitude of his task and in imagining a solution. The path toward the solution could be worked out by trial and error. This others could do. The industrial census inaugurated during his tenure at the Board of Trade, and indeed the Land Surveys, were predecessors.

But in this connection, particularly after his battles with Kitchener during the spring over munitions figures, he was adamant that he should know how well his ministry was doing. As a result there existed from the beginning a statistical department, within the general division of Munitions Supply, under Walter Layton, at that time a university lecturer in economics and later editor of the *Economist*, who remained with the ministry throughout the war.

Layton had designed the industrial survey as his first work at the ministry and came to have a good deal of respect for Lloyd George as an administrator while Lloyd George seems to have used him as a channel for working off complaints about inefficiencies in other parts of the organization. Layton noted in his diary that the thick weekly statistical return on production that was his principal task always came back filled with underlining, exclamation points and queries.[43]

As Lloyd George emphasized in his *War Memoirs* the Ministry of Munitions had been founded because of a shortage of artillery ammunition particularly.[44] The military lesson of the early months of the war seemed to be that Germany's rapid advances had been achieved by a huge superiority in heavy artillery with unlimited supplies of ammunition, not because of any special excellence of her infantry. Conversely the professional B.E.F., without anything approaching adequate artillery, had sustained bloody losses without advancing.

But the ammunition problem had been complicated by external factors not under the government's control and which could not have been foreseen. One, of course, was the burden of the experience in the South African war in which the lesson was the need for mobility. Battles were won with quick maneuver and surprise. For artillery this meant light easily movable guns and shrapnel ammunition. But in the static siege operations in France the need, as the German success showed, was for heavy weapons and high explosive ammunition to bury trenches and break down barbed wire. When the war began not twenty percent of Britain's artillery ammunition reserves were high explosive and one part of Lloyd George's continual battle with the War Office had turned upon his attempt to increase production of this shell at all calibers. Fortunately it was much simpler to produce.

But there was another difficulty. Just two or three months before the war broke out the British army had adopted trinitrotoluene (T.N.T.) as its explosive, abandoning Lyddite, which it had used since the nineteenth century. The result, Lord Moulton, the Director of Explosives Supply, explained to Lloyd George, was that production of Lyddite had stopped altogether for lack of a market and Moulton doubted whether 20 tons of T.N.T. a week was being produced in the country. To make a comparison, he added gloomily, he estimated that the Germans fired off 800 tons of T.N.T. in two days.[45] There were ways of extending Lyddite supplies and T.N.T. could be used as a catalyst for other explosives, diluting it by as much as one in ten, but the situation was serious.

Finally there was the complication of Woolwich. Traditionally all shell filling, that is filling the shell body with explosive, capping, and fitting the fuse and gaine, the tube which led from the fuse to the interior of the projectile to ensure an explosion, had been done at this great arsenal. It was controlled entirely by the Master General and the Board of Ordnance which was supposed to meet at the Tower of London, theoretically in the presence of the monarch, hence the style 'Royal Artillery'. These ceremonies had faded, but Woolwich and the other three Royal Ordnance factories, at Enfield Lock, Waltham Abbey and Farnborough continued to be governed by a mysterious document, the 'Extract', an extract from the proceedings of the Board of Ordnance which went to each factory individually. The Extract, in effect a work order, meant that each factory worked entirely and solely for the Board and prevented any cooperation or consolidation of functions among them. Woolwich possessed accordingly, and intended to keep, its monopoly of shell filling. Woolwich, when Lloyd George inspected it, was full of empty shells but was producing far too few completed projectiles.[46]

Shell filling and finishing had therefore the highest priority. Two national filling factories were established in July 1915 and in August and September ten more. Eventually there were eighteen. The work was simple, although heavy, and hideously dangerous. All that was needed was a series of sheds, each separated from the other by a revetment, with a solid roof that would not fall and thin walls so that any blast would go outward. These factories were run by each of the three divisions of management into which the Ministry came to divide itself: the Boards of Management firms, already described, by the Ministry itself, or by the War Office List firms working on a cost plus percentage basis. The last was a compromise worked out by Lloyd George as the great armament firms saw government operated shops invading their markets.

For the historian the important interest of shell filling lies in the fact that it was here that the great social revolution brought by the Ministry of Munitions first appeared, the massive employment of women. Lloyd George had obviously foreseen this for the June speeches are full of references to it. But at this time he was speaking usually of the introduction of women, or unskilled, unapprenticed, men, into simplified operations within the engineering trades. However, the shell-filling plants became the first large scale employers of females. Because they were new and government owned, and the work at best only semi-skilled, the problems with unions over dilution did not occur. The women's suffrage organizations were, of course, enthusiastic over all of this and attempted to inject themselves into the management of the factories. The Lloyd George papers contain a thick file of correspondence covering the first six months of 1915 from suffrage leaders dealing with women at work and with the far more difficult problem of introducing women into the engineering trades where hitherto only men had been employed.[47] Although Emmeline Pankhurst led a noisy demonstration in London on 19 July demanding women's 'Right to Serve', which Lloyd George addressed, he had always assumed that women would participate in war work. In effect there was no controversy between the women's movement and the Minister of Munitions. The opposition to women appeared among union leaders in the established trades and caused a problem Lloyd George never was fully able to solve.

However, for Lloyd George a particular fascination in the large scale employment of women in government-owned factories was in the opportunity it offered for complete supervision of living and working conditions. Here was a species of social welfare he could understand. As has been seen many times he was in no sense a socialist and had no quarrel with private capitalism but the neglect, coupled with the exploitation, of the worker, the miner, or closer to home, the Nantlle quarrymen, drove him into a rage. Now the Ministry of Munitions could be a model employer.

Because of the nature of their work shell-filling plants had to be isolated. This meant usually the provision for the accommodation for women workers and all that followed: canteens, facilities for recreation, medical care, religious service. These things done well, he was convinced, would result not in greater expense but higher productivity.[48] He could spend a happy afternoon choosing window curtain fabric for dining halls. Here, one suspects, he saw the answer to socialism.

The shell-filling bottleneck was relatively easy to break.[49] The War Office had always insisted that projectiles should be made only in its designated factories and had resisted strenuously earlier in the spring an offer by a group of businessmen in Leicester to found one in their community.[50] But finally on 28 April 1915 only about six weeks before the Cabinet crisis, with the Munitions of War Committee already in operation, Kitchener had given permission to Girouard and Booth to proceed with a plan for the establishment of national shell factories 'without further reference to the Secretary of State'. Girouard, two days before, had proposed this to Lloyd George's committee and had received an enthusiastic endorsement. Although nothing under these new powers was accomplished in the short time left before the advent of the Ministry of Munitions, Kitchener to his credit, had allowed at last a breach in the tight wall of the War Office List.[51]

By the end of December 1915, 'national factories' as these enterprises were designated numbered 73, of which 49 were engaged principally in the manufacture of artillery ammunition. Very quickly the munitions factories were divided between 'national shell factories' producing 4.5 inch and smaller, principally 18 pound shells, and 13 'national projectile factories' producing 60 pound shells and larger, up to 15 inch. These latter were government owned but operated on commission by the traditional munitions manufacturers. By the end of the war the Ministry of Munitions owned and operated either directly or under contract 218 national factories producing not only ammunition but nearly every sort of weapon of war, some not even developed at the time Lloyd George left the office. This figure included the four Royal Arsenals but does not include the traditional munitions firms and thousands of others producing under contract for every sort of military need from machine guns to steel helmets.[52]

II

In his memoirs, Christopher Addison insists, and Lloyd George on the whole concurs that so far as Lord Kitchener was concerned the transfer of functions from the War Office to the new Ministry of Munitions generally was conducted with good will.[53] Lloyd George received a courteous note from Kitchener on the day his appointment was announced: 'Delighted you are coming to help me.'[54] Kitchener was undoubtedly an autocrat, but he was also a patriot and too sure of himself to be jealous of any man. As a result there was no obstruction from the Secretary of State for War, but as Addison notes rather obliquely the Master General of the Ordnance was reluctant to part with more of his functions than was required.[55] Lloyd George's mistake, of which he immediately became aware, was to have defined the powers of his ministry too loosely. The Ministry of Munitions Act and the subsequent Order in Council had stipulated in very large terms that the Ministry would provide ammunition and weapons for the War Office and Admiralty but the legislation had not said the ministry could design weapons, nor inspect them, nor that no one else could manufacture weapons. Thus there began immediately a struggle with General Stanley Von Donop first of all for control over the Royal Arsenals which was soon extended to the Ordnance Board and design. The ministry eventually won these battles as has been seen, in fact rather easily. Kitchener was no match for Lloyd George in Cabinet maneuver and the Prime Minister may have been so embarrassed about earlier mistakes on munitions that he was prepared to accede to any request of Lloyd George. But the question is important because the drive to extend the functions of the Ministry of Munitions soon became entangled with Lloyd George's rapid expansion of the weapons program first of all in big guns and machine guns, and in the demand for the return of munitions workers from the army. All of this projected the Ministry into Cabinet politics.

'Von Donop should be shot' declared Lloyd George to Riddell and Robert Donald of the *Chronicle* in the presence of a number of politicians, while the group was at golf on Walton Heath on 26 June. Removal would be easier, he continued, if Donald would begin to attack him in his newspaper. Might this not be dangerous, asked Donald. Riddell agreed that it would and later mused in his diary: 'Surely if Von Donop has acted badly the Cabinet should deal with him, not the newspapers. Our Government seems lamentably weak.'[56]

This was only the beginning of Lloyd George's troubles. In the first days of July the attempts to get the Royal Arsenals for the Ministry of Munitions became confounded with the ancient myth that no munitions shortage existed at all, and with Lloyd George's attempts to bring back to munitions work skilled engineers from the army. All of this was associated in his mind with conscription or indeed with its larger expression, national service.

'Last night,' wrote Riddell, 'there was a devil of a row in the House of Commons regarding Woolwich. I called to see [Reginald] Brade, who seemed worried. *He says Kitchener asked the P.M. what he should do regarding Von Donop. Asquith replied, "Leave him where he is."*' 'The whole affair is a scandal,' growled Lloyd George. The next day Lloyd George reported to Riddell:

> McKenna denies shortage of high explosives, etc., and will probably lead him (L.G.) to state facts, as he will do if any of his colleagues, whoever it may be, makes this statement in public. L.G. says P.M. likes McK because he does not like inconvenient facts.
>
> L.G. says that we are exporting to France only 150,000 high-explosive shells per month, whereas the Army ask for 200,000 per day![57]

Lloyd George of course succeeded, with the Prime Minister's help, in bringing the Royal Arsenals under ministerial control in the next month, but by this time he had announced his big gun program and the battle with McKenna began in earnest, to be exacerbated by the question of conscription.

A long conversation with Riddell on the way to Folkestone on 20 August may serve as an introduction to the problems of the Ministry of Munitions in the next six months.

He told me that McKenna was opposed to his proposal to order more big guns, on the grounds of expense and because he alleged naval requirements would be prejudiced. [Throughout the war the Admiralty rarely used the Ministry of Munitions and depended entirely upon its own sources, the War Office List, for ordnance.] L.G. inquired of the P.M. whether he was to proceed with his orders [for guns] or not. The P.M. said he had better go on. [Asquith had agreed, just the day before, to the transfer of the Royal Arsenals.] McKenna is strongly opposed to conscription in any form. L.G. who strongly favours it, said that before it was raised in the Cabinet the facts should be ascertained, and that it was very important to secure Kitchener's support. If he declares in favour of conscription opposition would be almost impossible; whereas if he declares against it, the supporters of the policy would have a hard task before them.

Lloyd George showed Riddell letters from Colt Arms in the United States offering to supply machine guns in October 1914 and again in February 1915, but the War Office had declined. Unbelievably the War Office and indeed the army were deeply divided on the large scale adoption of machine guns.

'The P.M.' said Lloyd George, 'is treating the war as if it were Home Rule or Welsh Disestablishment.'

Since L.G. has been at the Munitions, the P.M. has never asked how things are proceeding or how is he getting on. When a subject is forced on his attention his judgement is admirable, but he never searches out weak places. Every Minister is left alone until some huge rock looms and action is inevitable. I said, 'Has the war aged the P.M. much?' He said, 'No.' We talked of political friendships and antagonisms. L.G. said that Lord Rendel had told him, almost at the outset of his (L.G.'s) political career, that when he got into office he would find there were no real friendships at the top. L.G. found that this cynical remark was quite true. Look, for example, at Haldane's downfall. His close friendship with the P.M. had not saved him. . .He said that in the Cabinet no important questions were decided by vote. The P.M. usually declared that the general opinion seemed to be so and so.

And of considerable significance for the Cabinet battles to be recorded here, Riddell continued:

L.G. gave me a highly amusing account of the P.M.'s love affairs. Mrs. McKenna, before her marriage, was his old love. Then he became enamoured with Venetia Stanley, who has recently married Montagu, much to Mr. A's annoyance. Now he has returned to Pamela McK.[58]

The complex and mingled difficulties of the return of skilled workmen from the army, of the control and dilution of labor and the relaxation of union rules, and of conscription will be discussed separately. Lloyd George was never able, during his year at munitions, to solve any of them entirely satisfactorily. But his initial arms production program, the manufacture of heavy artillery far beyond the War Office requirements of the moment, in the face of opposition from the War Office and within the Cabinet, stretched his powers to the limit, and was a fully justified success. His victory confirmed not only his well known political skills but the truth of his conception of the nature of the war. As such it requires some discussion.

Virtually Lloyd George's first act once the Ministry of Munitions Bill had been passed and his June speaking tour completed was a quick trip to Boulogne to visit French artillerymen. In the company of Llewellyn Smith, J.T. Davies his personal secretary, and General Ivor Philipps his Parliamentary Military Secretary, he arrived early on Saturday 19 June 1915 and returned late the next day. The Boulogne Conference proved to be a critical learning experience for Lloyd George in a number of ways. To begin with, here he met for the first time the new French Under-Secretary of State in the Ministry of War in charge of artillery, Albert Thomas, who had been appointed on 18 May. Thomas had written a cordial letter to Lloyd George three weeks before congratulating him upon his appointment and suggesting that an exchange of views was always desirable.[59] Thomas was a short, bearded, bespectacled, stocky man, a Jew and a socialist, who looked much like a rabbi, and a scholar, the biographer of Napoleon III for the *Encyclopaedia Britannica*. He had come into the government only in October 1914 to organize the railroads, and was not, in the summer of 1915, a minister.[60] Lloyd George had heard of him through Paul Mantoux whom Thomas sent to London immediately after entering the Ministry of War.[61] In the months that followed Lloyd George and Thomas became fond of each other and worked closely together not only on munitions but on the political and strategic relations between the two governments.

According to his *War Memoirs*, Lloyd George had asked Thomas to come to Boulogne and to bring with him some officers who had experience with artillery in the lines. He was searching for information the War Office would not provide. He had also requested that Field Marshal French provide an artillery expert, who appeared in the person of General John DuCane, shortly to come to the Ministry of Munitions himself. At the first meeting of 19 June, with only the British present, Lloyd George asked DuCane for an estimate of the requirements in guns of all calibers for an army of 1,000,000 men and of the number of shells necessary for a bombardment undertaken to support a major attack.[62] Lloyd George does not provide DuCane's response in his account but DuCane's own notes show that he believed, and the French later agreed, that there should be available as many heavy guns, over 6 inches, as field guns, and that nothing between 3 and 6 inches was of much use.[63] In order to comprehend the magnitude of what Lloyd George was proposing it should be noted that there were in France at that time 1,263 field guns, most 18 pounders, in effect 3 inches, but some as small as 13 pounds, and just 61 guns of 6 inches and up.[64] Before a major attack the artillery should have available 1,000 rounds per heavy gun, all high explosive with delayed action fuses, and 2,000 rounds per light gun, three quarters high explosive.[65] Britain the previous week had delivered to France 125,000 rounds of all sizes, largely shrapnel, in effect about one tenth the amount needed for an offensive. In quiet periods 200 rounds for the heavy and 500 for the light guns would suffice. At that time the British were trying to achieve 17 rounds assured supply per day for the 18 pounders and the Germans had received in the previous week 1,750,000 rounds, all high explosive.[66] The French reported they were producing 'rather under' 700,000 rounds per week.[67]

Lloyd George records that the French general present, a 'General Gossot', was as obstinate and antiquated as British generals. 'He had the same superstitious belief in the efficiency of the "*soixante-quinze*" [the famous 75mm field gun, the equivalent of the 18 pounder] for all purposes as our own generals had in the all-round potency of shrapnel. I had to contend with a priesthood not a profession.'[68] But DuCane's account indicates that except for the French insistence that field howitzers were useless — the British 18 pounder which could elevate to 16 degrees was close to being such a gun; the French 75mm was not — the conference was entirely amicable.[69] At Boulogne Lloyd George found what the historian must conclude he was looking for. His instinct had told him, as these pages show, that Britain was engaged in a war of machines. Of all war machines the big gun was the monarch. He had what he needed to begin, on his own authority and against strong resistance, the 'Boulogne Program'. He would make the B.E.F. a big-gun army.

The second meeting of two the next day, Sunday, 20 June, was occupied principally with conversations between Lloyd George and Thomas concerning manufacturing. Both the French underminister and Lloyd George were eager to establish systematic cooperation between the two nations. Competition in the United States hurt both. France, with much of her capacity in German hands, needed steel. Thomas was preparing to organize the entire Swiss clock-making industry for the production of shell fuses and would give Britain a share.[70]

After the meeting Lloyd George, who had begun to admire DuCane immensely, rode with him to the boat. He reports that DuCane admitted he had learned that the British artillery standard of requirements was inadequate and that he would consult with the Commander in Chief, Sir John French, about it.[71] Very likely Lloyd George himself asked DuCane to be sure that French understood the new importance of big guns. In any case five days later the Commander in Chief of the B.E.F. composed the first of several letters fully supporting Lloyd George's position. Lloyd George now had military support for his program.

French's emphasis centered upon German capabilities. Germany, he wrote, began the war with an obsolescent field gun, but instead of remedying this she had put all of her efforts into building big guns, above 5.9 inches. (However, the Germans were already designing, and would in 1916 build, the first model of the fearsome 88mm gun that became famous in World War II.) One third of all her artillery was now of this size or larger. The B.E.F. at the moment, continued the Field Marshal, had 1,080 field guns, 336 of 4.5 and 5 inches and 71 guns of 6 inches or larger. Just to bring his force up to present parity with Germany he would need 400 sixty pounders, 400 6-inch guns and 290 8-inch or larger.[72]

The War Office accepted French's ordnance requests. Part of this unusual accommodation proceeded from Kitchener's determination, announced on 7 July at a conference of Allied leaders in Calais at which Lloyd George was not present, to put 70 divisions into the field by 1916.[73] This figure is important for it turned out to be, whether Kitchener realized it at the time or not, precisely the maximum that the population of Great Britain and North Ireland could support even with military conscription, given the manpower demands of industry and the navy. (Enlistment in southern Ireland by this time had virtually stopped.)

This decision by itself entailed a huge new program. Hitherto all calculations, both the War Office's and Lloyd George's, had been based upon an army of 50 divisions. Originally the Boulogne program had simply envisioned an increased proportion of heavier guns. As Lloyd George explained to the Cabinet War Policy Committee (essentially the old Committee of Imperial Defence), on 16 August, Britain simply did not have the manufacturing capacity to match heavy artillery and light equally. But nevertheless his numbers were astounding. For example, on 31 May 1915, when the Ministry of Munitions was established the army possessed 79 60-pound guns with 148 on order. By December 1916 he intended to have 800. Of the biggest, the 12 inch, there were now five, by next March the army would have 48.[74]

Lloyd George referred constantly during this long recitation to the lessons he had learned at Boulogne. This was a new war, a 'war of mechanics' and of machines, as he had put it in his June speeches, in the Treasury Conferences in March 1915, and at Bangor in February. But then he was simply trying to inspire labor, to tell the working man how important he was. Now he was beginning to formulate a new military doctrine of machines which, whether he understood it or not, contradicted precisely the British, and indeed the French, military view of how the clash of arms on the battlefield was resolved. This struggle between the machine and what the generals chose to call the 'human' battlefield only began with the big gun program. It would continue in the debate over the provision of machine guns, the proper use of tanks, and would inform Douglas Haig's defense of his tactics in France in the debates with Lloyd George during the last two years of the war. Essentially the question for Lloyd George was whether machines served men or were the men to serve machines. He gave a succinct answer in December in the House of Commons during an account of his first six months stewardship at Munitions, when the argument over machine guns was at its height.

> The machine spares the man. The machine is essential to defend positions of peril and it saves life because the more machinery you have for defence, the more thinly you can hold the line, therefore few men are in position to jeopardy of life and limb...What we stint in material we squander in lives.[75]

Machines therefore were paramount.

This speech was made at a critical period in the life of the Ministry of Munitions when Lloyd George was under heavy fire within the government for wasting money on weapons the War Office did not want, while, outside the government, he was about to collide with organized labor. And he was at the moment thinking principally in terms of machine guns, as will be discussed. But the germ of the new doctrine is clear. The days of masses of men on the battlefield already were coming to an end. The truth of his conception had to wait another twenty-five years for realization.

Lloyd George's program presented to the War Policy Committee on 16 August was known within the ministry as Program B.[76] It was based upon the

Boulogne lessons and Kitchener's decision to raise the army establishment to 70 divisions. But even as he presented it, Program B was growing obsolete. In the middle weeks of August the Allied cause suffered a number of military disasters which caused Lloyd George to wonder seriously whether Britain's effort at its present scale could win the war. On 4 August the Russians evacuated Warsaw. Three days later it was clear that the surprise landing on Gallipoli at Suvla Bay, the last chance to take the peninsula, had failed. Within ten days, with the Russians now in full retreat, the Germans invested Brest Litovsk which fell on 25 August. Meanwhile Bulgaria, certain after the Suvla Bay disaster, that Turkey would not be driven from the war, prepared to attack Serbia. With the Serbs defeated large Austrian forces would be released to attack Russia. The Russians already were virtually gone from Poland. For Lloyd George the question was whether the Czar's empire could remain in the war.

On 18 August before the War Resources Committee, he brought up the possibility of a total Russian defeat. This committee had been appointed in the aftermath of the Calais Conference to consider what size army Britain could support in 1916, thus involving conscription. It was chaired by Lord Crewe and included Lord Curzon, Lord Selborne, Austen Chamberlain and Churchill. After making what were now becoming routine complaints about the slackness of organized labor, Lloyd George warned Russia could break up. She was losing rifles at the rate of 120,000 per month. The first big order from America would not commence delivery until January 1916. By that time she would have left, he estimated, only 1,200,000 rifles.

He recalled that he had pointed this out as early as the previous February, 1915 and was always told that the Russians invariably lied and so they probably had millions of rifles stored somewhere. 'Upon that flimsy basis we assumed everything was alright. Now it has turned out things are not alright.' He concluded:

> If the figures which I give now represent approximately the facts, where are we if the Germans get through to Petrograd and break up the Russian Armies? The whole burden of the fight falls on us practically. The French are doing as much as any nation can do. The Italians are not really worth much.

They were an admirable people, but not military.

What then could be done? Lloyd George proposed national service. Lord Crewe interjected to say that beside trenches and munitions there was ordinary domestic service. Would Lloyd George use compulsion here?

> I certainly would [this is altered in pencil corrections in the typescript to read: 'It would help']. I would say that every man and woman was bound to render services that the state required and which in the opinion of the state they could best render. I do not believe you will go through this war without doing it; in fact, I am perfectly certain you will have to come to it.

He proposed starting with military conscription.

> You will not get through without some measure of military compulsion or compulsion for military service. The longer you delay the nearer you

will be to disaster. I am certain you cannot get through without it. I do not believe, for instance, that you can keep your armies at the front without it, unless you are going deliberately to cut their numbers down to a figure which will be inadequate, and which is known to be inadequate in advance. The number of men you should put at the front does not depend on us in the least. It is going to depend on the Germans and what the Germans are going to do during the next three months in Russia. If they succeed in putting the Russians out of action during 1916 as a great offensive force, for us simply to keep 70 divisions at the front is suicide. Not only that, it is murder, because to send a number of men who are obviously inadequate is just murdering our own countrymen without attaining any purpose at all. . .[77]

The peril of a Russian collapse, couched in surprisingly forthright terms, became a theme of Lloyd George's speeches in the autumn of 1915.[78] But his immediate reaction was to prepare for a huge increase in the British military effort, including conscription. By the end of August, Lloyd George and General Ivor Philipps prepared a revised schedule for artillery manufacturing, known in the ministry as Program C, appropriate for an army of 100 divisions equipped at the Boulogne scale.[79] It was this step that brought Lloyd George into collision with the War Office and with a faction of the Cabinet. His increase was of course justified; by the time the guns were produced the army needed them, and more. But Britain did not have the manpower for a 100 division army even though the War Resources Committee reported favorably on such a step on 2 September arguing that such a force represented a 'proportionate' British contribution to the Allied line of battle.[80] Indeed her military forces never reached Kitchener's establishment of 70 divisions within the then existing 12 battalion table of organization.[81] Lloyd George may not have appreciated this. No one at that time knew what were Britain's resources in physically fit men.

Lloyd George's part in the fight for conscription will be discussed. Here, within the story of the Ministry of Munitions, it is necessary only to say that his appearance as a whole-hearted supporter of compulsory military service was a product of his appointment to the ministry. He was appalled at the slovenliness of labor, at Holy Monday, at trade union restrictions, matters which in fact, despite his experience in the settlement of strikes and his sympathies for the Penrhyn quarrymen, he now encountered for the first time. So he moved from the position he had held during the spring of 1915, that the British worker must learn what war was, and this meant hard work and abstinence, even at the cost of government control of drink and the relaxation of union limits on production, to a conviction that labor had to be controlled as was capital already, by national service. The French showed how easy it was with iron-clad national conscription to move men to the army and back again. It was a matter of survival.

In September 1915, Lloyd George put these thoughts together in a widely publicized foreword, which *The Times* printed and followed by an admiring lead article, to a collection of his wartime speeches, entitled *Through Terror to Triumph*, a phrase taken from his Queen's Hall address. Quite explicitly he told of Russia's peril, which was Britain's problem and which might mean conscription. The nation must not hesitate 'when the need is clear, to take the necessary steps to call forth its manhood to defend its honour and existence.'[82] British military efforts in the next three months, he warned, might determine the course of the war. This statement was widely praised, but also denounced, among others by Robertson Nicoll.[83] To mollify his powerful critic, Lloyd George, as he told Riddell, wrote 'the usual letter' to *The Times*.[84] This letter, to an unnamed, and probably non-existent, correspondent, featured on the leader page, denied that the government was divided over conscription. It could not be divided because it had not discussed the matter. Let figures be developed, said Lloyd George. If they show conscription necessary Britain must have it. If otherwise, there would be no conscription.[85]

In his *War Memoirs* Lloyd George tells in some detail the story of his struggle with the War Office to secure approval of the 100 division big gun program at the Boulogne standard and how he was vindicated by events.[86] Curiously however, he assigned the reasoning behind his decision not to his growing fears of a Russian military collapse and the consequent need for Britain to raise 100 divisions through conscription, which was clearly the case, but to the more prosaic impulse of manufacturing convenience: firms assured of larger orders would expand plant and install extra machinery thus speeding delivery. He quotes a letter from H. Llewellyn Smith to the War Office, sent evidently about mid-September explaining the new program as one in which

> The Minister has been influenced in providing such a margin [of extra guns] by the important considerations that the ordering of those large quantities will make it worth while to have new machinery on a larger scale installed. . .which will hasten the dates at which considerable deliveries can take place in 1916. A larger number of heavy guns will by this plan be delivered during the critical first months of 1916 than would have otherwise been possible. . .[87]

In the meantime Kitchener had replied to Sir John French's request for a larger establishment of heavy ordnance in the B.E.F. French said the War Secretary had reiterated that the already approved requirements fulfilled his needs and that the extra guns should be given to Russia. To this Lloyd George retorted that he was not prepared to cancel his program except at the direction of the Cabinet. So the battle moved elsewhere.

For the Cabinet Kitchener provided the substantial memorandum already cited in connection with General DuCane's notes on the Boulogne meeting.[88] Basically he argued that Lloyd George's proposal for 639 extra guns of 60 pounds and larger were in the heavier calibers, sufficient not for thirty but nearly fifty divisions and there were not enough artillery personnel, let alone officers to man them.

The discussion in the Cabinet does not appear in Asquith's letter to the King, but one may imagine it occurred in the Cabinet of 12 October already overwhelmed by the failure at Loos at the end of September despite the first large scale use of poison gas by the Allies, and by the news on 9 and 11 October that Serbia had been invaded on the north by Germans and Austrians and on the east by Bulgarians. The disasters Lloyd George had predicted were beginning to occur. Meanwhile the Cabinet was literally being torn apart by the battle over conscription.[89]

Asquith's response was predictable. He appointed a committee under Lord Crewe to resolve the big gun dispute as if it were a question, as Lloyd George had already noted, concerning Welsh Disestablishment or county council powers rather than a critical issue of Britain's survival. The committee, according to Lloyd George's account, met once, at the Ministry of Munitions. Kitchener made his case. Lloyd George sat almost completely silent. The committee adjourned to reflect. After it was over William Sutherland, who acted chiefly as Lloyd George's patronage secretary but who was present taking notes, recorded that J.T. Davies asked: 'I suppose, Sir that means the end of your programme.' 'No,' replied Lloyd George, 'it means the end of the Committee.'[90]

So it proved to be, but Lloyd George is not quite correct in saying that the matter had now ended. Rather the big gun program's cost became an item in Reginald McKenna's litany of charges against Lloyd George with which he sought to influence the mind of the Prime Minister, so inflaming further the poisonous struggles over conscription and the rescue of Serbia. On 18 October Edward Carson, to the dismay of senior Unionists, above all his party's leader, resigned over the failure to aid Serbia. Lloyd George, utterly discouraged, was already thinking of doing the same.[91] But the big gun program was safe. Twenty years later, when he had no reason whatever to be fond of Lloyd George, Christopher Addison published his diary including an extract he had written late in November 1916 as Romania was being invaded and Russia, by now near collapse, found itself unable to help her. Lloyd George's greatest fear was about to be realized. Lloyd George, Addison wrote in honest admiration,

> insisted on the big gun programme against the advice of Kitchener and the staff and even against the open opposition of many Members of the Cabinet. As I think I said at the time, he refused to withdraw his proposal except at the written instructions of the Cabinet, which, of course, they dare[d] not give. There is not now a soldier or a Minister in the whole ranks of the Allies who, if they knew, would not thank God that he went far beyond the gun programme of the artillerists. As we know, they require even more at the present moment than the great programme of that time forecasted and, if it had not been for that programme and for turning the country upside down to meet it, we should have been in a hopeless position today.[92]

III

The fight with the War Office over big guns and the control of design was parallelled by a similar conflict over the supply of machine guns. And here again Kitchener had at his side the economizers in the Cabinet. Yet in some ways the issue in this debate was less the matters of expense and waste of manpower, which the Secretary of State for War had emphasized in his memorandum to the Cabinet of 6 October 1915, than the organic nature of battle itself: how in fact was battle won?

Lloyd George realized, as he made amply clear in his *War Memoirs*, that there was a prejudice among professional officers against the machine gun, although he could not understand it. For the soldiers it was considered a weapon of opportunity, suitable only for very specialized combat situations.[93] The B.E.F.

was supplied with only two per battalion, yet the Germans had fourteen and were working toward sixteen. He had been horrified at photographs of High-landers in perfect rank and interval lying dead in front of the German trenches at Loos. (The approaches to the Hohenzollern Redoubt achieved some fame in the German army as *Das Leichenfeld*, the corpse field.)[94]

There had been endless debates in the Army Council and in military journals in the years before the war about whether the machine gun or the bayonet and superior Japanese courage and discipline had won the war in 1904-5 for the Japanese in Manchuria. The fact was that the machine gun did not fit within the doctrine of battle set out in the Field Manuals and taught to a generation of British officers. The battlefield was a place occupied by men: there would be the 'wearing out battle', which phrase appears any number of times in Douglas Haig's diary, followed by the 'decisive assault'. Assault was the key. Glory would belong to the army with the most determined soldiers and the most skilled commanders. The stout heart of the British infantryman with his Lee Enfield .303 short service rifle and long bayonet would win the war, not machines. Victory was above all the triumph of the human spirit. This was not opinion, but doctrine.[95]

One must quickly add that all of this, the 'human battlefield', did not preclude the use of greater and greater amounts of artillery, which Douglas Haig, who replaced French as Commander in Chief of the B.E.F. soon after the Battle of Loos, readily understood. Big guns were part of the wearing out process. (Haig's concession to the new technology, demonstrated in his plans for the Battle of the Somme, was embodied in his phrase of 'Artillery con-quers, infantry occupies'.) Haig, throughout the war, was determined not to be found lacking in will. The final decisive assault would be his vindication.

But the Vickers machine gun adopted by the British Army in 1912 weighed about 34 pounds with its water jacket filled and the tripod another 49 pounds. At least two men were required to carry it, with any number more for am-munition. It was anything but an assault weapon. There was no enthusiasm for it in either the War Office or in the British command in France, although by the autumn of 1915 the men in the trenches knew better. From Lloyd George's point of view if the new weapons did not coincide with doctrine, the doctrine should adapt. The war on the Western Front was a siege, not Omdurman. It should be remarked that Haig's implacable devotion to infantry assault interfered equally with the deployment of tanks which he regarded as auxiliaries to the foot soldier, although it must be said he was glad to get them.

Evidently Lloyd George had determined on a great increase in machine gun production at the time the Ministry of Munitions was established for D.A. Thomas had been instructed to look into this, among many other things, when he went to the United States. He reported that only Colt Arms could build the Vickers model.[96] But perhaps most important for the political sup-port Lloyd George needed was Asquith's first trip to France, in June 1915, when he visited the front and came back impressed with machine guns.[97]

The next step, desirable but not vital, lay in procuring interest from the War Office. Lloyd George gave Geddes, in charge of small arms for only a month, the task of confronting Kitchener and asking support for an increase above two per battalion. What numbers in machine guns, he asked Kitchener, would the army need in nine months? 'Do you think I am God Almighty?' retorted the great man. Eventually Kitchener agreed that two per battalion were essential, four were desirable, and anything above four was a 'luxury'. Geddes induced Kitchener to initial a note to this effect.

When Lloyd George saw the War Secretary's requirement he was indignant. 'Geddes records that I said to him,' he wrote '"Take Kitchener's maximum; (four per battalion); square it, multiply that result by two; and when you are in sight of that, double it again for good luck."'

Lloyd George adds that in November 1915 the War Office raised its establishment to sixteen per battalion, meeting the new German equipment, and this figure later was nearly doubled again. With the life of a machine gun in action not much more than six months the demand for reserves was heavy, and after the development of the interrupter gear the ministry was called upon to furnish large numbers of air cooled Vickers guns for the Royal Flying Corps. Thus by the end of the war, he records proudly, there were, for one use or another, over 80 machine guns per battalion in France with further huge numbers stored in Britain.[98]

One may speculate that Lloyd George prized the sturdy, utterly dependable Vickers heavy machine gun even more than the heavy artillery he forced upon the army in the Boulogne program. Certainly in the early days of the ministry he jealously guarded their numbers. George Booth's diary records an entertaining, and highly characteristic, encounter between Lloyd George and General Pasolino Pasolini of the Italian army over the Vickers gun. This highly decorated officer had arrived in London to claim the 500 heavy machine guns that Italy had been promised before entering the war. In the midst of debate over the production and use of the weapon Lloyd George was unwilling to part with so many.

On the other hand Lewis machine guns, a much lighter weapon, almost an assault gun, were cheaper and easier to supply. Therefore in a brilliant display of bait-and-switch salesmanship he convinced the Italians that the Lewis guns were what they really needed.

'When Lord Kitchener suggested we should supply you with 500 Vickers guns,' he explained to General Pasolini, 'the position of the war front was very static.'

> The Vickers gun is appropriate for an emplacement, a gun for defence; but now things are becoming more fluid and with you Italians coming into the war it will soon be a matter of advance. The lighter Lewis gun is therefore what we recommend. You brave Italians will be rushing forward and will not be hampered with the heavy emplacement Vickers gun.

Without demur the Italians took the Lewis gun and went away apparently happy. However, throughout the interview, despite frantic notes pushed under his nose by Booth, Lloyd George had always referred to Pasolini as 'General Gasolini'. After Booth had congratulated him on his abilities as a salesman, he told the minister of his mistake. Lloyd George roared with laughter and suggested Booth invite General Gasolini to dinner with his daughter Donna Kerosina.[99]

The battle over machine guns did not end with Lloyd George's orders for increased production. Operating on the assumption, customary for him at this time, that in decisions on military matters German practice was probably correct and the British War Office usually wrong, he began to press for the formation of a machine gun corps to be made up of machine gun companies, unattached to any battalion, which could be thrust into the line as needed. He succeeded in obtaining a Royal Warrant authorizing the corps on 22 October but the War Office remained unwilling to move forward in the formation of units. Even though it was far outside both his area of authority, or indeed of his special competence, his belief in the rightness of his own judgment prompted him to take the matter to the Cabinet War Committee (which had recently succeeded the Dardanelles Committee which itself had succeeded the earlier War Council in June). As Lloyd George's memorandum, laid before the committee on 13 November, expresses so well his conception of the mechanized battlefield and indeed the notion he would develop much further as the war progressed: that machines could be used to release men for duties on other fronts so restoring movement to the conflict, it deserves to be quoted at length.

The machine gun takes the place of rifles and riflemen he stated. As this is true, did Britain really need a rifle with a range of 2,000 yards?

> I believe that one machine gun, with its detachment of ten men is,
> at a very low estimate equivalent in destructive power to fifty riflemen,
> especially on defensive. If that is a correct basis of comparison we could
> make up for our shortage in men and obtain equivalent fighting value
> by training 200 machine gunners instead of 1,000 riflemen. In other
> words, with 50,000 machine gunners we could do the work of 250,000
> infantry. We could also save in rifles, in which, so far as I can see, the
> Allies are never going to obtain the numerical superiority over the
> Germans necessary for a decisive victory.

> It seems also, that if our machine guns are employed on a large scale,
> on a comprehensive plan, they will, in conjunction with barbed wire
> and fortification, give us the strategic power *so far enjoyed by the Germans
> alone* of taking large numbers of troops away from one front, where no
> offensive is in contemplation, and transferring them to a quarter where
> active operations are intended.

> This is what the Germans have done on the Western Front, to release
> men for the thrust against Russia, and what they are doing on their
> Eastern Front, to set free men for attacking Serbia, and for action on
> the Western Front. This power to replace men, which amounts to
> strategic elasticity, applied especially, I think, to our present intentions
> on the Western Front.[100]

Strategic elasticity, in Lloyd George's view, was a concept the War Office and the command in France did not understand. As he wrote his paper he could reflect that the disasters he had predicted earlier in the autumn were occuring. The decline of Russian power shown by the loss of Poland was compounded with the Czar's assumption of direct command of the army on 5 September. Bulgaria had declared war on the Allies and Serbia was gone. The Cabinet was mired in the three linked decisions of military conscription, the evacuation of Gallipoli and again, as at the beginning of the year, of the dispatch of a British force to Salonika, with no sign that any resolution would come soon. Strategic elasticity was more than an appealing theory. It was a necessity.

It should be remarked that in his many fights with the War Office, which of course began well before he came to the Ministry of Munitions and continued after his appointment as Prime Minister, Lloyd George was always buttressed by a large fund of private information about conditions at the front. He encouraged serving soldiers to write to him and maintained a regular correspondence with General DuCane until he came to the ministry.

A second important source, as Lloyd George acknowledges in his *War Memoirs* was Colonel Arthur Lee, a Unionist Member of Parliament who had been active in the budget battles of 1909, and who came to munitions early in November as Lloyd George's military secretary when General Ivor Philipps was appointed to command the Welsh Division.[101] Lee would remain an important political associate of Lloyd George until well after the war.

Contacts such as these, supplemented by a continual stream of roving enquirers in France, who visited commands at all levels, gave Lloyd George the private information with which he frequently astounded his colleagues and which he would use with effect in the years to come in arguments with generals, above all William Robertson. Arguably it was here, in the systematic collection of data from what might be called the 'consumer' sources of the Ministry of Munitions that he departed most completely from the earlier procedure of the War Office. Field Marshal French's clumsy attempt to appeal for help through the newspapers, in reality a cry of desperation which had played so large a part in the fall of the Liberal government in May, would not have been necessary two months later.

However, one must question, parenthetically, how well some of the early attempts at direct communication worked, or at least how knowledgeable were some of the collectors of information. Douglas Haig recorded in his diary on 1 August 1915 that he was visited by two Members of Parliament from Lloyd George's 'Armament Committee' who came to enquire about the First Army's needs. Haig patiently confirmed to them that artillery ammunition was indeed important and explained the difference between high explosive and shrapnel. When he was finished he was asked whether there was any requirement for 'round cannon ball'.[102]

IV

During the June speeches Lloyd George had referred often to a projected 'Labour Volunteer Army', the 'King's Squad' which would be recruited and organized by the trade unions to provide a large body of mobile, skilled men who could be moved about the country as required. All of this was associated in his speeches with the need for relaxation of trade union rules, organization, sacrifice and, by implication, of the need for national service. The latter was a 'serious question' for the 'near future'.[103] However, if the workers responded satisfactorily industrial conscription obviously would not be needed.

This was the first time Lloyd George had mentioned conscription publicly, although Tory newspapers had been calling for it for months.[104] There was indeed already in preparation a bill to require national registration of all men and women between the ages of 15 and 65 with the declaration of industrial skills. While the Cabinet saw this measure as a way to prevent the enlistment of skilled workers, and indeed the system of 'starring' skilled men (the provision of a lapel badge to shield men in essential trades from the importunities of super patriots and recruiting sergeants) was a product of it, many radicals saw it as a step toward compulsion, as it proved to be.[105] However, in early June Lloyd George was thinking of national service in terms of industrial mobilization for which he had been calling for months. 'It is the elementary duty of every citizen to place the whole of his strength and resources at the disposal of his native land in its hour of need,' he had reminded the assembled trade union leaders and manufacturers at the Manchester Town Hall on 3 June 1915.

> No state can exist except on the basis of a full recognition of that duty on the part of every man and every woman in the land. To what extent and in what direction the moral duty of each citizen to give his best to the State should be converted into a legal duty, a question not of principle but of necessity, is to be decided from time to time as the emergency arises during a period of war.[106]

It is clear that at this time Lloyd George was using the threat of compulsion as a way of securing recruits for the Labour Volunteer Army. A few minutes later he told the audience, rather unclearly, that while conscription for the military forces might be unnecessary for the time being they 'ought not thereby assume that it is unnecessary to enable us to mobilize the industrial strength of this country.'[107] How seriously he took all of this is hard to say. As always when faced with a massive problem, the proportions of which were unfamiliar to him, he was feeling his way forward trusting his instinct to guide him, although his anger after the plan's failure was real enough.

After the second of his June speeches, at Liverpool on 4 June, he had returned to London. There on 10 June and again the following week on 16 June, after the series of addresses was complete, he met privately with Britain's trade union leaders, essentially the same group that had attended the Treasury conference in March. Here he urged the union leadership to take charge of the Labour Volunteers. They would be backed by legislation, and he produced a draft of the Munitions of War Bill which was intended to put into law the conclusions of the Treasury Conference including the limitations on the profit of munitions industries. He did not want military conscription. The army still had more men than it had rifles to distribute.[108] This was quite true. Addison had written only a week before that on 1 March 1916 there would not be more than 1,000,000 rifles available. Was it really useful, he asked, to draw men from civilian employment so rapidly?[109]

As events would quickly demonstrate, the apparent agreements arrived at in the meetings with labor leaders were far from conclusive. Lloyd George's troubles with labor were only beginning although he did not yet realize it. At lunch with C.P. Scott after the second meeting, on 16 June, he spoke with the assurance of a man whose problems have been solved. '1. All Trade Union rules to be suspended in Munitions workshops,' Scott recorded Lloyd George had announced (presumably this referred only to government owned establishments).

> 2. All workers in them to be placed under military discipline and made punishable for breaches of regulations.

3. Acceptance of service to be voluntary provided Trade Unions can within a week enlist a sufficient number of workers.
4. All private firms engaging munitions workers to be compelled to require a certificate from previous employers so as to prevent desertion from munitions works.
5. On the other hand war-profits to be annexed by the state.

Failing the enlistment voluntarily of a sufficient number of workers I gathered that Lloyd George's original scheme of universal compulsory service for home defence would take effect, such service to be either in a home defence army or in industrial service sanctioned by the State.

As to Russia she was 'done for'. The Dardanelles was 'a mad enterprise'.[110]

The 'trade union army' scheme was officially announced in the House of Commons on 23 June during the debate on the Munitions of War Bill. Recruitment, said Lloyd George, would begin the next week and last for seven days. Trade union leaders would sit in 180 town halls throughout the country to take enlistments from skilled men who would go where they were needed. He emphasized that union leaders were sure the scheme would work but also admitted that compulsion was inevitable if it did not.[111]

As finally settled, evidently in some haste for Lloyd George did not provide these details, the workers would enroll for six months. They could be transferred anywhere but would receive railway fare if they were required to spend more than one half hour in travel one way to their shop or mill. They would be granted 2s 6d per day if living away from home and were to be paid either their regular wage or the local rate, whichever was higher.[112]

For a moment it seemed that the plan would work. The Volunteer Labour Army was a 'great success' wrote Addison in his diary on 6 July. Eighty thousand men had signed up. There was no need for industrial conscription.[113] But the figures were deceiving. At the end of the month Lloyd George asked for a return of the numbers of volunteers actually placed in employment. Of the nearly 100,000 men enrolled by that time, J.T. Davies replied, only 2,176 in fact had moved to munitions work.[114] The problems were that many workmen inspired by the appeal to patriotism had enrolled in the Volunteers while being already in essential industries. A great many more had overstated their skills. (One suspects that union leadership, wishing to show labor's enthusiasm and anxious to intercept any move toward compulsion, had not enquired rigorously about work qualifications.) Others were not genuinely available for a variety of reasons of domestic hardship. In effect, the Volunteer scheme, a huge pool of skilled mechanics to be sent anywhere as they were needed, was not going to succeed. Britain's vast labor resources would not be brought into national service in this way. Addison records that eventually, evidently well after Lloyd George left munitions, the 'Labor Army' amounted to about 38,000 men who were of moderate usefulness, particularly in starting up new factories.[115]

There was, however, another large body of trained workmen whose unavailability had disturbed Lloyd George for months, well before the advent of the Ministry of Munitions: those who were in the army. Early in May, as Chairman of the Munitions of War Committee, he had asked Llewellyn Smith for an estimate of figures in this category and received the reply that among the 600 largest engineering firms in the country employing 281,000 men pre-war, 45,754 had enlisted by February 1915 according to trade union returns. Worse, in the next two months nearly 4,000 more had gone even as the government began spasmodic attempts to get such men back. Extrapolating from these figures Smith estimated that from all engineering firms, large and small employing altogether 665,000 men about 8,000 men had enlisted in March and April at a time when engineering labor was critically in demand.[116] Here again, Lloyd George pointed out any number of times, military conscription could help him. If he could get 120,000 skilled men from the army the manpower stringency would be ended. He could get them if he could promise Kitchener 120,000 unskilled men as replacement.[117]

The Munitions of War Committee elicited a promise from Kitchener on 12 May to take steps to prevent the practice of enlisting skilled men. Nevertheless enlistment continued even after 'badging' began reinforcing Lloyd George's conviction that skilled men must be returned from the army. The release of men was pushed vigorously during Lloyd George's tenure at the Ministry of Munitions. Ultimately it was more successful than the Labour Volunteers although as Lloyd George remarked it was like 'a process of extracting teeth'.[118] Not only was there War Office obstruction and resistance from unit commanders, but from the men themselves. Battalion solidarity, the sense of comradeship and shared sacrifice that distinguishes an army from a mob, often made the individuals reluctant to leave. The earliest efforts to recall men, begun even before the Ministry of Munitions, involved identifying valuable men through their previous employers as individuals and tracing them through army records. This was time-consuming and often fruitless. More successful was the so-called 'bulk scheme', begun in July 1915. Ministry of Munitions inspectors visited army units, at first in Britain only but later in France, paraded the men and invited skilled mechanics to step forward. After suitable testing those accepted returned to factories. They remained, it should be noted, under military discipline and received either army pay and allowances or the prevailing wage, whichever was higher. Altogether during Lloyd George's tenure at the ministry, he succeeded in retrieving 43,231 men from the armed forces, two thirds under the bulk scheme, who constituted a skilled and mobile labor force similar to the body he had envisioned in the Labour Volunteers.[119]

During the incredibly busy weeks of June, after four major speeches, while appointing the personnel of the Ministry of Munitions and negotiating with trade unions, Lloyd George was also planning the Munitions of War Bill, which he introduced on 23 June three days after his return from the fruitful conference at Boulogne.[120] Basically the bill gave legislative effect to the rather tentative agreement arrived at between Lloyd George and the trade union leaders at the Treasury in March. It stipulated, first, the limitation of profits in munitions industries to 20 percent in excess of the average of the last two fiscal years before the war. Wages and salary scales were to be fixed. Any firm could become a so-called 'controlled industry' by proclamation and some 4,000 were brought into this category during Lloyd George's time at the ministry. But as a balance for state supervision of employers, labor would be brought under control.

Clauses on industrial relations hence constituted by far the largest portion of the act's provisions. In fact as Lord Curzon made amply clear to the upper house the 'sole object' of the act was the mobilization of labor.[121] All disabilities and controls on employers were to be understood as a means to that end.

The central provision of the bill was that in controlled establishments all trade union rules were to be suspended and disputes were to be handled by arbitration. Strikes were illegal except in coal mines and cotton trades where labor representatives had refused agreement. However, large powers existed under other clauses to end strikes by decree. An amendment accepted by Lloyd George during passage insured that these concessions would disappear with the end of the war.

Finally, a worker might not leave any firm doing government work, whether a controlled establishment or not, without the written permission of his employers, the so-called 'leaving certificate'. Should he do so no other employer was permitted to hire him for six weeks. This was the infamous Clause 7 of the bill, which according to William Henry Beveridge, director of the Labour Department, employers sometimes misused by withholding the certificate from a workman they desired to punish.[122]

For the British working man, in conclusion, Lloyd George's central intent in the bill, as Clause 7 indeed made amply clear, was the enlistment of the worker in the war effort not quite as a soldier under military discipline, but at least as a directed civilian. By taking employment at a controlled establishment a worker gave an undertaking that could result in civil penalties if not carried out. Only the enlistment, as in the peacetime army, was voluntary.

An important fact to note in the parliamentary story of the Munitions of War Bill's subsequent stormy history is that it had been presented to the Commons as an agreed measure, always Lloyd George's favorite tactic. And it was, to be sure, supported by the leaders of the Labour party. Only Philip Snowdon, eventually Ramsay MacDonald's Chancellor of the Exchequer, rose to point out that Lloyd George had dealt only with union leaders. The unions themselves had been given no opportunity to approve or disapprove.[123] Here lay a warning. The trade union leadership, of whom Lloyd George thought very little in any case, might not represent correctly the mood of their membership. Surprisingly this was something Lloyd George, usually able to sense nuances of this sort, for example animosity between the poorer doctors and the British Medical Association, failed to understand.

The Munitions of War Act received the Royal Assent on 2 July 1915. Its strength as a weapon in the control of industrial disputes was tested immediately. While the measure was before parliament a wage dispute in the South Wales coalfield was moving toward a crisis. Its central feature was simple enough. Since the beginning of the war coal prices had increased about 25 percent while the miners wage, set by arbitration panels under the Coal Mines (Minimum Wage) Act of 1912 remained at levels set in March 1913.[124] However, there were complications the most important of which was the miners' demand for a new minimum wage standard in order to prevent the miners remuneration, theoretically linked to the price of coal, from falling after the war when presumably coal prices would come down.[125]

A coal strike in South Wales would be more serious than almost any other labor dispute. All of the larger vessels of the navy except the newest dreadnoughts got up steam with Welsh bunker coal and the admirals would use no other. Moreover France, with almost all of her mines in enemy hands, was completely dependent upon exports from Britain. Technically the coal industry was not covered by the Munitions of War Act. The miners' union representatives had withdrawn on the third day of the Treasury Conference on the argument that with their wage tribunals and arbitration provisions they did not need the new machinery. Yet about 200,000 men were involved.

Through the spring of 1915 the government had taken little notice of the growing discontent in the coalfields and only at the end of June, with the miners' agreement due to expire on 30 June, was Walter Runciman, the new President of the Board of Trade, sent to Wales, where on 1 July he was able to obtain an agreement with both the owners and the Miners' Council granting generous wage concessions but, on Sir George Askwith's suggestion, deferring discussion of a new minimum wage until after the war.[126]

The miners' executive had accepted Runciman's proposal reluctantly, as indeed had the owners, and had recommended it to the membership by a vote of only 123 to 112. Such division in the leadership was of course an invitation to seek new concessions which promptly began with the demand for 'interpretations' of the extremely complicated agreement. Runciman wrote to Lloyd George on 7 July saying that he had obtained compromise only with difficulty and asking whether he could proclaim the mines controlled establishments under the Munitions of War Act, now five days old. Lloyd George replied the next day saying he should not hesitate to invoke the act.[127] As a result, on 12 July a mass meeting of miners rejected the agreement 1,800 to 1,000 and threatened to strike. The next day the South Wales coal industry was proclaimed essential war work and strikes were officially prohibited. On 15 July 200,000 miners went on strike.

The government suddenly recognized the crisis. On 19 July a long Cabinet meeting devoted entirely to the strike resolved to send Lloyd George to Wales. Despite the apparent unanimity of the men in going on strike there was reason to believe that many were nervous about what they were doing. The same meeting that had rejected the agreement on 12 July had refused also to hold a ballot of miners, but nevertheless all of them were breaking the law. Therefore, as Asquith wrote to the King:

> In the end the Cabinet agreed that before any steps of a preventative or punitive kind were resorted to Mr. Lloyd-George shd. be authorized to go to South Wales to-night or early to-morrow to make a final appeal to the great body of the miners to resume work on patriotic grounds, and if necessary to hold a ballot on the subject. It should (if it seemed expedient) be intimated that the Govt. wd. be willing that they shd. go on from day to day on Runciman's terms on the understanding that the margin between those terms and their demands wd. be submitted to an Arbitral tribunal.
>
> He wd., at the same time, make it clear to them that if they did not respond to his appeal the Government wd. at once proceed to take all necessary measures to paralyze the strikes, by preventing meetings, speeches and the receipt of strike pay, by taking over as 'controlled businesses' such pits as are needed in the public interest, working them

for the profit of the State alone, by securing that they were adequately supplied with Labour and by providing for the proper protection of these who were engaged in working them.

Incitement to strike, the Prime Minister concluded, might be made a treasonable offense.[128]

These were strong words. Whether the Cabinet was as determined to use coercion as Asquith's letter indicated cannot be known. Lloyd George certainly was not prepared to use force. He consulted Riddell who was apparently in touch with an informer within the miners' leadership, referred to as 'our friend'. Riddell urged Lloyd George to make no threats. Government control of the mines was what the extremists desired and they would gladly foment a strike to cause it. Moreover the owners were making huge amounts of money.[129] Lloyd George made up his mind that further compromise was necessary, even before he appeared in Cardiff aboard a special train on 20 July.[130] He immediately conceded, much to Runciman's and the Board of Trade's labor advisor Sir George Askwith's disgust, all the miners' demands including an increase in the minimum wage. He did not speak publicly to the miners until 21 July when the settlement was complete. Nonetheless the miners were back at work and his additional concessions, he reported to the Cabinet on 22 July, 'were relatively unimportant, of small pecuniary value.'[131] In a sense this was true but the grant of an increased minimum wage would cause Lloyd George endless trouble after the war when coal prices indeed fell. Worse still the precedent of government capitulation to big unions, according to Askwith, 'did more to cause unrest during succeeding years than almost any other factor in the war. . .'[132] Certainly Lloyd George sensed this. He would handle differently his next confrontation, on Clydebank, with militant labor.

V

Probably no aspect of Lloyd George's work at the Ministry of Munitions was more time-consuming nor troublesome and, in the long run, less successful than his efforts to enforce the relaxation of trade union rules and traditional craft exclusiveness, an exercise termed 'dilution', a name coined by Christopher Addison. Yet dilution was now the center of all his plans for industrial mobilization. The Treasury Conference, although the word did not yet exist in this context, had been about dilution.

At its simplest dilution meant the division of skilled machining tasks into simpler components which could be undertaken, with supervision, by unskilled or semi-skilled workers, men or women. But it involved also not only the introduction of unapprenticed non-union labor onto the shop floor but the reorganization of the manufacturing process itself, the breaking down of craft demarcation lines and the erosion of craft wage premiums. And as the war progressed it entailed the introduction of automatic or semi-automatic machines and the disappearance of jobs. Dilution thus was the lash driving British industry into the post-Ford industrial revolution of mass production and assembly line manufacturing in which a highly complex mechanism, a tank or a machine gun, could be built entirely by only moderately skilled workers.

One has to doubt whether Lloyd George, the most unmechanical of men who never seems to have learned to drive a car, understood this, but others like Addison did understand.[133] And the skilled workers saw it instinctively. Their world was evolving. Wages were high, work was plentiful, but who would be needed after the war. If women and boys could produce a machine gun they could make an automobile. To be sure the introduction of women was a shock, but dilution was more than this, it portended revolution.[134] The resistance to dilution thus was not entirely a result of trade union opportunism or radical shop-steward conspiracy. There was an element of Luddism.

Britain's late nineteenth-century industrial power was based not only upon a permissive political climate and vast capital resources; other nations, the United States and Germany, had these advantages also, as well as far larger populations and perhaps greater marketing skills. But Britain had in addition, certainly not uniquely, but in great depth and quantity, in its engineers, boilermakers, ironfounders, or tool makers, a national genius, a huge body of skilled workmen, who, given specifications, could build literally almost anything. The tank, for example, has been written about in many contexts, but one, hardly mentioned, is that, going from conception to production in little more than nine months, it was a manufacturing miracle. Experimental models were put together within weeks.[135] The men who constituted this industrial army were conscious of their skill and importance, and were well organized, conservative, and pugnacious.

Nonetheless, for Lloyd George, dilution in its largest sense encompassed everything he had fought for since the beginning of the year. Everyone in the nation must in some way contribute to the war effort. Peacetime work rules should no more be allowed to hinder weapons production than peacetime political usages should prevent wartime decision making. National service, a word he frequently used and that he eventually assigned as the name of a ministry, meant a nation mobilized. Each citizen must work or fight. He had described this ideal, unclearly, in the Manchester speech on 3 June horrifying a number of Liberals who assumed he was speaking of military conscription. As he made clear to the Committee on War Resources in the middle of August he supported military conscription but chiefly as an avenue to the achievement of the goal of national mobilization. Conscription made real, as the French had shown, the challenge to work or fight.

August however brought the Russian disasters and Lloyd George's determination to prepare for a 100 division army equipped at the Boulogne scale. At the same time, by early August, it had become evident that the War Munitions Volunteers scheme would not yield the hundreds of thousands of men expected.

In the June speeches, in his speech on the Munitions of War Bill, and in the innumerable other public utterances since, he had always implied, already noted, that if the munitions volunteer plan did not work the unions were obligated to accept national service. Whether he seriously believed this may be questioned, but one cannot doubt that he hoped to institute some form of national service for labor, of which the Labour Volunteers would have formed a nucleus, and certainly he used the threat of legislative compulsion during the fights over dilution in the months to come. But in any case when Llewellyn Smith informed him on 27 August, that the volunteer scheme clearly had failed he turned his attention not to compulsory service but to dilution.

Of course he had been pressing the case for unskilled labor for months. For example the women's march in London on 17 July, the 'Munitionettes', had been paid for by the ministry, although publicly it was sponsored by the suffragette movement.[136] But now at the end of August, with the dozens of new factories to be completed within the next few months, labor had to be found. The National Labour Advisory Committee, a small group of labor leaders chaired by Arthur Henderson, Labour's representative in the Cabinet and President of the Board of Education since May, who had in fact proposed the committee six months earlier, suggested that he begin his campaign with a speech to the Trades Union Congress which was meeting in Bristol between 6 and 11 September. He appeared there on 9 September.

Lloyd George faced a difficult task. (*The Times*, in this period applauding his every act, featured his 'exemplary courage' in a leader.) The response to his opening sentence: 'I come before you as the largest employer in the land' set the tone. There was some laughter, but also jeers and hisses. As the speech progressed, he was frequently interrupted.[137]

The speech was a call for union agreement to dilution. The war was a conflict between German workers and British workers. Britain could not win without the workers' help and would surely lose if they withheld it. Russia was already in peril. He showed the assembled men a 4.5-inch shell. Women could make it, he said, and were doing so in France and Germany. Sixteen new national factories were already completed with more on the way and many existing factories were understaffed. Eighty-thousand skilled men and 200,000 unskilled men and women were needed immediately. He reminded the T.U.C. of the resolutions of the Treasury Conference and of the fact that the state was already limiting the profits of 715 controlled establishments.

While there was clearly much solid masculine antipathy to the entrance of women into workshops under any circumstances — Lloyd George cited such a resolution from the men at Woolwich — the more reasoned fear apparent in interruptions was that piecework rates for unskilled work at simple tasks would be lowered, so undercutting time-wages. Lloyd George invited the men to send him any evidence of such reductions. In fact as it turned out the effect of piecework was the opposite, but caused equal discontent. As had been apparent even to Adam Smith over a century before in his discussion on the manufacture of pins, the division of a task into simple discrete processes each performed by a single individual speeded production greatly. Hence if paid for at piece rates it might result in larger not smaller earnings. So it proved at the Ministry of Munitions. Some well paid skilled workers eventually discovered to their fury that they were earning less than the unskilled men and women they supervised.

At bottom the question was who would profit if a skilled task were divided into several easier, more elementary jobs. A skilled workman's daily round could be separated into, say, five components, each capable of being accomplished by women. The result would be five, or more, times the production but at considerably smaller cost. Who ought to benefit? If the benefit were to go to the owners there would be no dilution, but the owners, understandably, were unwilling to pay full craftsman's wages for, say, scraping lathe beds at John Lang's, which was only a part, and a rather simple part, of the work of an expert lathe builder. In the end the workers' response was, so far as possible, to keep women out altogether.

The Bristol speech stirred up a noticeable controversy within trade union branches. There was a flurry of resolutions contradicting points made by Lloyd George about work stoppages and resistance to dilution.[138] The speech greatly embittered relations between Lloyd George and the trade union rank and file, an animosity which lasted for months and was certainly a factor in the unpleasant episode in Scotland at the end of the year.[139] Back in London Lloyd George maintained the pressure in a meeting with Henderson's National Advisory Committee with a reminder that with the volunteer scheme unsuccessful dilution was the only alternative to compulsion. Workers had to be found. The unions should take charge of it.

The critical union for beginning the dilution process was the Amalgamated Society of Engineers, the oldest, best organized, probably the wealthiest of the craft unions, whose membership was precisely at the center of munitions making. On 13 September Christopher Addison, and four days later Lloyd George, met the A.S.E. leadership. Both men conveyed the same message: if the union did not want industrial compulsion it would have to make dilution work.[140] Lloyd George stated the alternatives clearly:

When Mr. Brownlie [J.T. Brownlie, Secretary of the A.S.E.] stated his views on industrial conscription all I can say is this, the stronger your views about the undesirability of conscription, the more bound are you, if I may say so to enable the volunteer system to work. You cannot have it both ways. You cannot say, 'We will not have compulsion, and at the same time we will take the fullest advantage of the voluntary system to make it difficult for you to get the best out of the men.' You must choose one or the other.

There was, he admitted, a third alternative: 'that the State should perish.'

To the extent that he was able to secure agreement from the union leaders present, Lloyd George was successful. The labor leaders and the National Advisory Committee quickly agreed to participate in a joint committee to manage dilution, made up of representatives of the N.A.C. and the Ministry of Munitions. This became the 'Central Munitions Labour Supply Committee' announced on 18 September.[141] Henderson again was chairman but the committee of fourteen included also W.H. Beveridge and C.F. Rey from the Ministry of Munitions and J.T. Brownlie of the A.S.E. as well as Mary Macarthur, the pioneer women's trade unionist.

Addison refers to the labor leaders' participation as an 'invaluable agreement' and so it may have been, but the struggle for dilution was only begun. Addison did not yet understand, nor did Lloyd George, that the war was dissolving the lines of authority within the British labor movement. Union leaders in the Cabinet like Henderson, as stable and earnest a trade unionist as ever lived, or leaders conferring with ministers as equal representatives as if they were foreign powers obviously enjoyed great status. But what they won in status they lost in the power to command. The South Wales coal strike, indeed the Clyde disturbances of February 1915, had given warning. On far too many shop floors union leaders in government were leaders no longer and power had devolved to the workers themselves. To a considerable extent it remained so for well over half a century. Such were the origins of the Clyde Workers Committee, which was the core of the famous 'shop stewards movement'.

Attempts at dilution had begun before the formation of the Labour Supply Committee and as has been seen large numbers of women were already being hired by the national shell factories. However, the first labor trouble appeared in August, significantly on the Clyde at John Lang and Sons machine tool makers in Johnstone. The Ministry of Munitions' Machine Tool Committee had issued instructions on 7 August to bring women into the shop. The local branch of the A.S.E. promptly resolved that 'no woman should be put to work on a lathe'. Lloyd George and the engineers' leaders discussed this matter, among many others, at the meeting on 17 September.[142] Lloyd George agreed that the instructions should not have been sent without his knowledge but urged the A.S.E. to press its branches to allow dilution and on 30 September, with the Labour Supply Committee now in place, the ministry announced that Lang was going to hire twelve women, at 15 shillings per week on gear cutting, light drilling, and milling machines.

Reports of discontent in Scotland quickly reached London and on 13 October the Council of the A.S.E. asked for a conference with Lloyd George, which was held the next day. At this meeting the A.S.E. leaders asked sensibly that branch discontents be settled before dilution was proceeded with and unrealistically that workers be represented on boards of management, to which Lloyd George retorted that this had nothing to do with dilution. Nonetheless on 27 October the A.S.E. leaders agreed again to support dilution and on 29 October Messrs Brownlie, the Secretary, and Gorman of the Council travelled to Scotland to meet the Paisley District Committee. They reported on 1 November that they had made a strong appeal and believed they had succeeded. In the next six weeks Lang put 19 girls on milling, drilling and gear cutting and found the results satisfactory. But then on 15 December shop stewards informed the company that local trade union members had met and determined to strike if another girl were employed.[143]

The story of Lang's trials with dilution has been set out at some length, because it shows the problems of an early experiment with dilution. It also illustrates perfectly the appearance, already alluded to, of the sudden and massive division that appeared in most large British unions during the war between the nominal leadership with whom the government had to deal and the shop floor activists, the stewards, whose consciences, pacifist inclinations, or socialist convictions made final decision-making almost impossible.

The fact was that most Clydebank employers were watching Lang's experiment closely. There had been other threatened strikes — one at Fairfield's shipyard in Govan at the end of October — but against the abuse of leaving certificates not over dilution. (The arbitrary powers given to employers by the leaving certificate were reduced by the Munitions of War (Amendment) Act which became law in January 1916.) At Fairfield's the government intervened at the last moment, but eventually surrendered and released three workers who had been jailed.[144] After the Labour Supply Committee issued its first circulars in the early autumn accompanied by a letter from Lloyd George dated 4 October, employers had felt themselves to be under pressure to begin dilution. But they could not obey the minister's orders, the employers association wrote on 12 October, so long as the unions 'are permitted to flout government instructions'.[145] The employers felt themselves to be trapped in the middle of a struggle between the unions and the government in which they had no real interest. They were making money in any case. To obey orders from London which resulted simply in the disruption of their shops and an embittered work force to whom the government finally would surrender, made no sense.

If dilution were to succeed the Ministry of Munitions, which seemed to mean the minister himself, would have to try conclusions with the workers. The men on the shop floor would have to be convinced, or forced, to allow unskilled workers to undertake industrial tasks they had always regarded as their own. Neither the employers in Scotland nor the union leaders in London could control the men.

All of this was obvious enough to Lloyd George although typically he blamed it on Beveridge and the Labour department. That department was, he wrote, the worst of all the ministry's departments. It had bungled the munitions volunteer scheme. Its reports told him nothing.[146] On 22 December he left London and after stopping briefly at Newcastle arrived in Glasgow on 23 December accompanied by his old friend Alec Murray, now Lord Murray of Elibank, who would work briefly in the Ministry of Munitions, and with Arthur Henderson and J.T. Davies.[147] Lloyd George rarely underemphasized the difficulties or danger of the problems he faced when describing them to Miss Stevenson but her diary suggests a real concern about the Clyde. 'Mr. [J.T.] Davies [Lloyd George's secretary] says that he was very doubtful as to whether they would return alive,' she wrote afterwards.

> D[avid] says that the men up there are ripe for revolution, that they are completely out of hand. They have been told that the war is Labour's chance. But D. is convinced that there is German money up there. The men are certainly misled, for they say that the war has been engineered by the capitalists in order to enthrall the working classes, and that the war for them is not against Germany, but against the capitalist.[148]

When Lloyd George arrived in Glasgow (on Thursday, 23 December although he put it on 24 December in his memoirs) he asked that the large meeting to be held in St. Andrew's Hall which he was to address that evening be postponed. He wanted to talk to shop steward representatives first. Evidently it was then that he was told that the shop stewards committee he had asked to see refused to meet him. This was a bad beginning. Nevertheless he was determined to talk to the men who were reported to be at the core of the trouble and so drove to Beardmore's Parkhead Forge, the largest employer of engineers and the largest producer of heavy artillery in the area. Here he met David Kirkwood, at that time a convenor (chairman) of the Parkhead shop stewards and later a Labour Member of Parliament and a baron, whom he asked to let him address the stewards. At Murray's suggestion Kirkwood introduced the Minister of Munitions:

> This is Mr. Lloyd George. He has come specially to speak to you and no doubt you will give him a patient hearing. I can assure him that

every word he says will be carefully weighed. We regard him with suspicion because every act with which his name is associated has the taint of slavery about it.[149]

Lloyd George's speech was wholly a plea for dilution as a means of winning the war of the sort he had given many times before. Workers were soldiers and so on. After he had finished Kirkwood made a statement giving perhaps a clue to the real objection to dilution, already alluded to. The problem was not the introduction of unskilled hands but the simplification of the manufacturing process. He asked whether the government was prepared to give workers a share in the management of the works.

As socialists, they welcomed the dilution of labour, which they regarded as a natural development in industrial conditions. They were not like the Luddites of another generation, who smashed new machinery. But this scheme of dilution must be carried out under the control of the workers. Otherwise cheap labour would be introduced. Unless their demand was granted they would fight the scheme to the death.

This sober prose from the 'History of the Ministry of Munitions', a volume probably written by William Beveridge, may have contained an important statement.[150]

Kirkwood went on to deny in harsh terms that the union leaders in London, Henderson, who was present (and who was in any case not an engineer but an ironfounder), and Brownlie had any right to speak for the Clyde workers.

We repudiate this man. He is no leader of ours. Brownlie has been told the same to his face. And if you, Mr. Lloyd George, want to know the mind of the workers don't go to these men. If you wish to do away with the discontent in the workshops, do away with the cause.[151]

Lloyd George had provoked this outburst by saying, as he did much too frequently in situations like this, that he was not responsible for the Munitions of War Act. It had been written by the union leaders. But it should have provided a lesson. He was dealing not only with a problem he did not understand, but with the wrong people. Despite his insistence two days later at St. Andrew's Hall, on 25 December, that he had been brought up in a worker's home and knew as much about a worker's life as any of his audience, the world of factories, wage labor, unionism and socialist ideology was foreign to him. He understood the hatred of the landlord but he was not, and never became, anti-capitalist.

The next day, 24 December, he at last received a delegation from the Clyde Workers Committee, headed by J.W. Muir, in fact a radical labor journalist. Again he was treated to a lecture on the necessity for workers' control of any dilution process. 'Industrial evolution must be accompanied by social evolution.'[152] Muir was far more pugnacious than Kirkwood and would contribute as much as any individual to the tumult of the meeting at St. Andrew's Hall.

Lloyd George's address to the assembly on the following day, 25 December, of some 3,000 workmen and C.W.C. members who had received four shillings from their employers for attending on Christmas morning, has been variously reported, but usually as a generally placid meeting, disrupted only by a minority of trouble makers who were quieted by Kirkwood. (Evidently elected union leaders had been urged to boycott the meeting which was then packed by C.W.C. activists.) This is Lloyd George's own story and that of *The Times* which printed the official account provided by the Ministry of Munitions on 27 December.[153] Perhaps not surprisingly the violence of the meeting, and indeed the meeting itself, is equally de-emphasized by historians of the Labour party who perhaps wish to leave Lloyd George with no excuse except malice for suppressing the *Forward* which on 31 December 1915 printed a full and entirely temperate account of it (which no historian appears to have seen, although it is printed as Appendix XIX in Volume IV, Part 4 of the 'History of the Ministry of Munitions').[154] In fact Lloyd George wished to suppress his humiliation at Glasgow, was angry over publicity about it as William Beveridge well understood, and made without much consideration one of his all too frequent small-minded decisions which he found difficult to explain later and which caused him endless problems.

The *Forward*'s account of the 25 December meeting began by noting that the official account which it had already published, although it gave a fair summary of Lloyd George's speech, had been misleading in suggesting that interruptions were confined to a small section of the audience. 'We are all for free speech,' continued the paper, 'and free speech not only for ourselves but for our opponents.'

> We therefore associated ourselves wholeheartedly with the Socialist effort to secure Mr. Lloyd George a hearing, and regret that a mean spirited Press Report should seek to convey the impression that it was the Socialists (called 'Syndicalists') who sought to break up the meeting.
> The meeting began with a storm of hissing and booing, and the Chairman (Mr. Henderson) suffered a running fire of interruption. In our opinion he would have done better to have explained the admirable part he played in getting Jas. Marshall, of Parkhead, released from jail rather than to attempt as he did a rather general patriotic appeal. Here is the sort of thing he suffered: —
> 'I am delighted to have the opportunity of appearing in this hall with the Minister of Munitions — ("What about the hall for the workers.") [Socialist societies were regularly refused permission to rent public halls.] — to lay before you the great issue of the present moment so far as the war is concerned. ("Ay! and profits.") You are all aware of the fact that we are engaged in probably the greatest war — ("At hame") — that ever the old country has been concerned with.

Henderson endured this sort of thing for another ten minutes with the stoic calm for which he was famous and then appealed to the crowd to hear Lloyd George. The *Forward*'s account continued:

> On rising to speak Mr. Lloyd George was received with loud and continued booing and hissing. There was some cheering, certainly, and about a score of hats were waved in the area, but the meeting was violently hostile. Two verses of 'The Red Flag' were sung before the Minister could utter a word. Owing to the incessant interruption, and the numerous altercations going on throughout the hall, it was quite impossible to catch every work of Mr. Lloyd George's speech.
> 'My first duty,' he said, 'is to express regret to you because I could

not address the meeting on Thursday.' ("Leave that alone") At this stage a delegate in the area stood upon a seat and endeavoured to speak. He got only to the length of saying 'Mr. Lloyd George' when apparently he was pulled down. There were loud cries of 'Free Speech.'. . .

Lloyd George invoked the name of Ramsay MacDonald, which brought a cheer, and Albert Thomas, which brought bewilderment, and said that both these certified socialists were friends of his. He dwelt upon the success of the French munitions effort calling forth cries 'What about the Munitions Act'. Eventually he called upon Kirkwood to quiet the crowd so that for a time he was allowed to speak. He spoke of the gravity of the war and the workers' part in it, but unhappily digressed to say that the 'responsibility of a Minister of the Crown in a great war is not an enviable one,' which of course provoked shouts of 'the money's good' and much laughter.

Eventually he was able to get through his peroration and closed with a promise of a great future for workers after the war. He promised to answer written questions until twelve o'clock but now John Muir, who had denounced him the previous day, stood upon a chair and said that he had been promised an opportunity to state the case for the workers. Muir refused to be silenced and as it was impossible to hear either Lloyd George or Muir, Henderson closed the proceedings and the meeting broke up in disorder.[155]

Miss Stevenson records that Lloyd George gave a Christmas dinner for everyone in his party during the railway journey from Glasgow to London and afterwards, evidently in high spirits, organized an impromptu concert. Lloyd George, further, states flatly in his memoirs that after December, with the passage of the Munitions of War (Amendment) Act somewhat limiting employers powers over leaving certificates, 'dilution made rapid headway'.[156]

In fact the dilution struggle was approaching a crisis. On December 27 the major London newspapers published a heavily sanitized version of Lloyd George's meeting in St. Andrew's Hall which generally gave only the prepared speech. But then, almost certainly to his surprise, Lloyd George learned that on 31 December a small socialist paper, the *Forward* had published the stenographic account printed above. It was later remarked in the House of Commons that the Press Censor had asked all newspapers to refrain from printing any story of the tumultuous Christmas Day meeting other than the one provided by the Ministry of Munitions but for some reason this request was never sent to the *Forward*. Later in the day of 31 December, Lloyd George received a telephoned transcript of the *Forward*'s story and a meeting that evening of Lloyd George, Addison, H. Llewellyn Smith, W.H. Beveridge and C.F. Rey decided to suppress the paper. On 2 January the police were instructed under regulation 51 of D.O.R.A. providing that no person should 'spread false statements likely to cause disaffection,' to close the Civic Press, which printed the *Forward*, and pick up all copies of the 1 January issue.[157]

The chronology of these events is of some importance because Lloyd George, as he often did when his decisions turned out badly, sought to dissociate himself from the suppression of the *Forward*, claiming it was solely a police matter, and to blame someone else, in this case the Labour Department of the Ministry of Munitions. He was of course conscious that amid the many achievements of his ministry, good relations with labor were conspicuously missing and in consequence was continually furious with the Labour Department. Just two days before the suppression of the *Forward*, when he was publicly affecting to believe all labor problems were solved, he had written angrily to Walter Layton about the Labour Department:

> We created a separate Department, brought together a considerable staff, borrowed experienced men from the Board of Trade to advise and direct it. . .and. . .after six months all we had to show for it was a colossal failure called the 'Munitions Volunteers.'. . .[158]

Similarly, when it became clear in the first days of the new year that the suppression of the *Forward* was a political error and, more important, a personal reflection upon himself, he denied all connection with it. Even Frances Stevenson was told:

> The suppression of the Forward caused trouble. It was done in a hurry, because the excitable Labour branch of our Department were scared at the vivid accounts given of the Glasgow meeting. D. had to work up a case afterwards to justify himself. It would have been far better not to have suppressed the paper, but D. has not time to attend to everything himself, and the Labour Dept. are continually letting him down. . .[159]

The universal, and probably correct, assumption within the ministry and the political world of Westminster was that Lloyd George had ordered the *Forward* closed out of embarrassment at its reporting of his treatment in Glasgow, a matter which he had believed was hushed up. Beveridge takes this for granted in his memoir and notes that when he was ordered without warning to build a case for the action he could find nothing in the *Forward*'s story of the St. Andrew's Hall meeting that was remotely treasonable and was forced to lift quotations from previous issues, which the government had never before noticed, that might be so construed.[160]

There were, of course, immediate questions in the House of Commons, particularly from the Scots, both Liberal and Labour and from members of the Independent Labour party to which Kirkwood himself belonged.[161] The first official response was that the suppression was the work of the military authorities. But on 10 January 1916, on a motion for adjournment, Lloyd George was forced to defend himself. Fortunately for him, when the police authorities went to the Civic Press they found not only the *Forward* which they had come to seize but also the uncirculated print run of a far more radical paper, the *Vanguard*. In the House, therefore, Lloyd George sought to link both papers in a single conspiracy, painting the *Forward* with the treason of its sister publication. He read what he claimed were excerpts from both papers, concerning for example the Royal Family, and usually ignored shouts demanding identification of the source of his quotation from Members, who were clearly well aware of what he was doing. So far as can be detected he read nothing from the 1 January issue of the *Forward* which had caused the paper's suppression in the first place. Again and again he angrily denied that wounded ministerial vanity had anything to do with his action against the paper.[162] It was not a creditable nor an honest performance. William Beveridge, who had listened from the official gallery, found that the Minister of Munitions used nothing from the brief he had prepared, but felt that he had witnessed a parliamentary triumph and that Lloyd George had carried the House of Commons with him.[163] This is not evident from the debates. Lloyd George survived, but left a thin House angry and dissatisfied.

The lesson of the *Forward* incident for Lloyd George seems to have lain in convincing him that although dilution would have to be carried forward at all costs, henceforth he would, himself, remain in the background. As a result when the decisions to enforce dilution on the Tyne and Clyde were made after a series of conferences in the middle of January 1916 the ministry was represented by local dilution commissioners with full power to enforce the law. There were no public interventions by the Minister of Munitions of the sort that had occurred in South Wales and at St. Andrew's Hall. As it turned out the Clyde continued to be the center of trouble. There was another newspaper suppression, the *Worker*, a number of strikes and eventually the arrest and deportation of several members of the Clyde Workers' Committee. Lloyd George remained in touch but did not appear.[164] But dilution went forward, although the results were not large. Shortly before Lloyd George left the ministry the official figures showed that slightly more than 10,000 women had replaced 7,436 skilled men in 150 controlled establishments (this figure is of course in addition to the hundreds of thousands of women in the national shell factories).[165] Nor, contrary to what Lloyd George would observe in July 1916, was the labor problem 'solved'.[166] In his first year as Prime Minister he would see even greater difficulties.

However, in the new year, 1916, Lloyd George's attention turned again, as it had in the spring of 1915, to the weakness of the government of which he was a member. The intractable divisions already existing in the Cabinet were inflamed by the conscription issue and made more dangerous by the emergence in January 1916 of Sir Edward Carson at the head of a group of about 100 Unionists, the Unionist War Committee, which was apparently determined to destroy Asquith. Lloyd George was uncertain where his own loyalties belonged.

7 The Cracking of Liberalism: Carson, McKenna and Conscription

During the year between the summer of 1915 and the summer of 1916, while he was at the Ministry of Munitions, Lloyd George moved from a position as Herbert Asquith's aide and collaborator, the warmly thanked advisor in the May Cabinet crisis, to the place of a potential rival as Prime Minister. This is not to say that at this time he sought the post, nor, it must be quickly added, is there much evidence that Asquith suspected him of conspiracy even though with McKenna at his side the Prime Minister surely received plenty of whispered allegations. Rather the story is the unhappy one of the continual decline in the effectiveness of the Prime Minister to a large extent as a result of hesitation and delay over the enactment of military conscription. This came, it would seem, partly a result of his own decision as a matter of political tactics to allow it to appear that conscription had been thrust upon him. Thus he was able to hold, after the passage of conscription, the loyalty of the principal Liberals within the Cabinet and of the leading radical Liberal newspapers. But he lost the respect of many other Liberals, more numerous than he realized. Probably as important he stimulated an active movement against himself within the Unionist party which looked forward to destroying not only Asquith himself but, with almost as little compunction, their own Unionist leadership as well. At its head was his old nemesis, Edward Carson. In effect the Prime Minister lost within six months the padding or protection for his administration that the May coalition had been intended to provide. 'More than any single person' the biographer of Bonar Law declared, '[Carson] was responsible for Asquith's fall.'[1]

The May 1915 reconstruction, it should be recalled, had been easy for Asquith because the opposition leader, Andrew Bonar Law, was also under attack for weakness by his own back bench although there was no widespread desire within the party for a coalition. Bonar Law was able to agree to enter the government only because his chief opponent, Edward Carson, agreed at the same time to do so. However behind these personal political considerations lay a genuine and widespread feeling in the country, promoted by newspapers of both parties, that the Liberal government was inadequate. Publicly this sentiment was symbolized by the shell scandal, which indeed was real enough, and in the narrower world of Westminster by the universal detestation of Churchill, whom the Prime Minister seemed unable to control. All of these convictions Lloyd George of course shared, without any disloyalty to Asquith.

But coupled with the generalized sentiment that old fashioned single party government was unsuited for the urgencies of a great war, lay the belief that coalition would bring efficiency, direction and decisiveness. The Ministry of Munitions with Lloyd George at its head seemed to promise this. For a time newspaper, and indeed parliamentary, support for the ministry, all assiduously promoted by Lloyd George himself, was almost universal.[2] To be sure, in the struggles with the War Office Asquith provided unwavering strength. The private complaints of Kitchener and Von Donop about excessive production of artillery or of McKenna about a waste of money were firmly brushed aside. For a few weeks all was well.

Then in August and September, 1915, under the pressure of military disaster, good will began to dissolve. Lloyd George's endless calls for national mobilization and warnings of disasters to come coupled with the march of events — Russia's collapse in Poland and the British failure at Suvla Bay in August, Bulgarian mobilization and Loos in September, the fall of Serbia in October — could mean only rising contempt for one, who, when a Prime Minister, appeared to believe that the war was about to be won.

Lloyd George's concerns during the summer and early autumn months of 1915 were almost entirely within the Ministry of Munitions. He missed many Cabinet meetings, telling Frances Stevenson that they were a 'waste of time'. A.J. Balfour was reported to have enquired what had 'become of the little man'.[3] Yet before the new coalition was two weeks old, on 6 June 1915, such an ernest scavenger of gossip as Lord Esher could write to his son 'People say that Lloyd George will oust Asquith. It is possible. He has the ear of the groundlings, and the Tories have taken him to their bosom as I always knew they would.'[4] Within the week Esher was telling the same to the King.[5]

There is no evidence that Lloyd George at this time was thinking of anything but the mobilization of British manufacturing and industrial manpower — he was in the midst of the June speeches — but he was becoming closely and dangerously involved, to George Riddell's distress, with a man who believed he had narrowly missed overturning Asquith in May and was determined to try again, Alfred Harmsworth, Baron Northcliffe.

On 5 June at a Printer's Charity dinner Riddell sat next to Northcliffe.

> He spoke to me at length regarding the war. He said he intended to attack Kitchener again, and also to attack Asquith, of whom he spoke in slighting terms. He also spoke in the same sense of all the Ministers but L.G., who, he said, would have to become Premier...N. prophesies the war will last for years...I said, 'You must give the new Government a chance. You have no better to suggest.' To this he replied, 'Someone will turn up. The war will disclose a genius. Kitchener knew that I saw L.G. last Sunday [30 May]. He has his spies watching me. My letters are opened and my telephone is tapped. But I have my spies in the War Office.' [Riddell believed that one of Northcliffe's spies was Alec Murray, still deeply in debt, wandering Whitehall in search of employment. Within a few months Lloyd George appointed Murray to the Labour Division of the Ministry of Munitions.[6]] He also says that Moore [G.G. Moore, an American friend of Field Marshal French in whose house French usually lived while in London, and evidently a contact with the press] is being watched by detectives but that his brother Rothermere says that Moore is a reliable man.[7]

Northcliffe earlier in the day had repeatedly telegraphed Riddell asking for an interview with Lloyd George for the following day, Sunday, 6 June. Perhaps he could play golf with Riddell and the two afterwards could walk over to Lloyd George's house on Walton Heath. Lloyd George, back in London between the speeches at Liverpool and Cardiff, proposed instead that Northcliffe drive straight to his residence.

> N. is a crafty cunning fellow and I gather he wants the public to know that he is in touch with L.G. and thus secure support for his recent action against Kitchener. I did not feel disposed to be seen playing golf with N. . . .[8]

Riddell was and would remain most unhappy about all of this. At 10 a.m. the next morning he hastened to see Lloyd George and declared:

> It would be a great mistake to allow N. to identify himself with you and treat you as an ally. You saw what Winston said in his speech yesterday regarding the inadvisability of suppressing press criticism.

On 5 June 1915 in his constituency in Dundee Churchill had made a remarkably incautious speech, which can only be compared with his unbelievable proposal in the House of Commons early in 1916 to bring back Lord Fisher to the Admiralty. Ostensibly he was simply accounting to his constituents for his stewardship as First Lord but, perhaps inevitably, the address became an attack upon those he believed had caused his fall. He announced that he 'did not believe newspapers ought to be allowed to attack responsible leaders of the nation' particularly those in charge of the fighting services. And gratuitously, in reference to nothing, he declared himself to be opposed to conscription. Lloyd George had made his first tentative proposals for national mobilization of labor two days before at Manchester.

> LG: I don't agree with that.
> R: That is not my point. Northcliffe says you have enemies in the Cabinet and that Winston is very bitter against you. Just think what a rod you would furnish him with if you enabled him to say you were working with Northcliffe.
> LG: Yes that is true. Winston has been saying some very foolish things about me.[9]

Later in the day, Sunday, Riddell saw Lloyd George again after Northcliffe's visit. Lloyd George insisted he had no idea why the newspaper proprietor had come. 'N said nothing of moment and asked no questions.' Riddell suggested, as he had earlier, that the motive had been to publicize his association with Lloyd George. He had however told Lloyd George a good story making the rounds among Unionists. The party, it was said, was run by two old men: one aged 70 (Lansdowne) with no bladder and one aged 55 (Bonar Law) with no brain.

The two discussed again the Asquith, McKenna, Kitchener axis in the Cabinet, the latter two cooperating to manipulate the Prime Minister's well-known aversion to inconvenient facts to convince him that no shell shortage existed. Such manipulation had occurred in a recent War Council, Lloyd George said. Kitchener simply lied and McKenna supported him. Asquith's

Newcastle speech was a recent example of how easily and dangerously he was led astray.[10]

Lloyd George's dangerous flirtation with Northcliffe, which Riddell had suspected and deplored at least since the beginning of the war, probably did him no real harm until after he became Prime Minister, and indeed may have helped him achieve that office, but at this time it was innocent enough even if others suspected political ambition.[11] Surely, Lloyd George saw in Northcliffe only a powerful, if dangerous, ally in the struggle to awaken a Cabinet dominated by men who for various reasons, jealousy, innocence or indolence, wished to believe at the nation's peril that no munitions shortage existed. He was descending to the level of political warfare that was natural for him: Cabinet differences fought out within the forum of public opinion, the assault through the press. If he could find a paper that would publish the truth as he saw it he would cooperate; he had done the same in the *Daily Chronicle* interview at the beginning of the previous year.

Hence despite Riddell's warnings he and W. Robertson Nicoll, the influential editor of the *British Weekly*, whose support Lloyd George always considered vital, composed a letter to Northcliffe saying that Lloyd George would confirm *The Times* proprietor's charges against Kitchener and saying that he would resign if he were not given freedom at the Ministry of Munitions.[12] From this letter and evidently from other conversations at the same time, Nicoll published in the *British Weekly* on Thursday, 10 June a sensational account of the new Minister of Munitions' problems.

> He [Lloyd George] accepted the new post of Minister of Munitions, and he has been called to it by a nation universally of the opinion that if he cannot accomplish the titanic task no one else can do it. Lloyd George should not be hampered in this work by the government or the House of Commons. If he is he will and he should refuse to go on. He is the last man to be influenced by pique. . .it is not and cannot be his duty to undertake a task which he knows is hopeless from the beginning. He must be trusted. Humanly speaking, everything depends upon him.[13]

One may suspect that such public threats to resign were only Lloyd George's way of ensuring that the Orders in Council defining his powers as Minister of Munitions, which were probably before the Cabinet at this time, would give him the wide latitude that made such a success of his career at munitions. Indeed Llewellyn Smith's letter to Reginald Brade of 5 June defining the minister's powers far more narrowly, already cited in Chapter 6, may have been a diversion in the same campaign designed to forestall resistance from the War Office. Nonetheless these, from Lloyd George's point of view innocent, activities designed only to enable him to produce weapons of war evoked much angry comment. *The Times*'s Political Note the next day remarked that the *British Weekly* interview was being widely read and interpreted as the threat of a general election while noting that Lloyd George had not been seen in the House of Commons since the formation of the new ministry.[14] Riddell spoke to Lloyd George with unusual violence.

> The public will believe you suggested the article in order that Northcliffe might quote it in support of his policy. You will have to be careful. The

Liberal journalists are very suspicious of you. They hate Northcliffe so much that they will not scruple to attack you and your policy if you identify with him. He is trying to shield himself behind you.

He admitted he did not know what Lloyd George was doing or had in his mind but the radical Liberals were growing angry.[15] He later recorded that Reading and also McKenna, not surprisingly, agreed.[16]

The skirmishes attending the birth of the Ministry of Munitions have been traced in some detail because they help to account for Lloyd George's singular isolation in the battles over the big gun and machine gun programs that came in the autumn and, more seriously and longer lasting, over the revived question of an alternative front in Salonika and finally over conscription. One sees here the breakup of the nonconformist, radical, pacifist coalition which Lloyd George had put together after 1906 and which had brought him the years of political success he had enjoyed down to 1914. Soon in fact, he was without political friends. Churchill was hostile and weakened, Masterman was gone. His huge ministry provided none of the usual patronage. It was filled with businessmen who were not concerned with politics. Asquith supported him loyally on munitions affairs but in everything else appears increasingly to have depended upon the McKennas, Reginald and Pamela. Lloyd George's isolation, his anger, and his difficulty in forcing decisions, drove him inevitably toward the Unionists. The entente with Edward Carson with all its consequences for Liberalism and for Britain began as this alliance of convenience.

I

As has been discussed at length, Lloyd George first approached military conscription as a concomitant of the larger question of national industrial mobilization. He sensed that the former would make the latter easier. His famous speech at Manchester on 3 June, which many people believed to be a call for compulsory army service, in fact differed only in rhetorical detail from that given at Bangor at the end of February: Britain must wake up and learn what war is; everyone must fight or work; all are called to sacrifice, etc. He realized that an assured supply of new drafts for the army would make simpler the recapture of skilled men from the service. But in the summer of 1915, while he was calling for national service, he was well aware that the munitions crisis remained acute, that even service rifles were scarce. In effect it is a mistake to identify him in the first few months at the Ministry of Munitions as an all out military conscriptionist as one would Churchill, Curzon, Walter Long, Alfred, Lord Milner or Lord Derby. His concern was the control of industrial labor. He cannot have missed Briand's ending of a railway strike in France at a stroke of a pen, converting civilian workers into soldiers under military discipline.

Even after the question of undiluted military conscription had fractured the Cabinet, Lloyd George's approach to it, as always, was larger. He was afraid, of course, that the Allies would lose the war unless Britain did more. The symbol of this concern became the unattainable 100 division British army. But more compelling, one is forced to conclude he was convinced that the inability of the government to make a decision on the vital question of military manpower displayed to the world the shuffling doubt and irresolution that had characterized Britain's executive administration since August 1914. Every decision had to be forced upon the Cabinet. Indeed exterior circumstances were frequently arranged, as with conscription, so that personal determination was not required. At the center of it all was the Prime Minister. At his elbow was Reginald McKenna.

Lloyd George's severance from the Cabinet Liberals, whose leader was McKenna, begins then in the autumn of 1915. Of course for years, since 1908, McKenna could hardly be identified precisely as a friend. However, the relations between the two men waxed and waned, to some extent in indirect relation to Lloyd George's comradeship with Churchill whom McKenna hated even more. Because McKenna would become a central figure in Cabinet politics in the eighteen months between the summer of 1915 and the end of 1916 and would use his position at the Exchequer, as well as his intimacy with the Prime Minister, to influence policy in many directions, Britain's financial situation in the middle of 1915 for which he was responsible needs some brief attention.

McKenna continually insisted that the nation could not afford the scale of military effort that Lloyd George demanded. It could not afford the big gun program; it could not afford the complete mobilization of industry for war and its twin, military conscription. He questioned, for a time, the reality of the shell shortage. Lloyd George of course assumed that these assertions proceeded only from jealousy and spite and that McKenna was secretly pacifist, or worse, pro-German. Of McKenna's uncomfortable personal manner there can be no doubt, nor of his real distrust of Lloyd George which was far older than the war. But when he assumed the Exchequer he was confronted with precarious financial difficulties, which were not fictitious and which to a great extent were the result of Lloyd George's casual management of that department since August of 1914.

The immediate trouble proceeded from the decline of the value of the pound against the dollar and was a consequence of Lloyd George's initiative for large scale purchases of munitions in the United States. Until the beginning of 1915 the pound-dollar exchange had remained remarkably stable at 1:4.86 principally because in 1914 Britain bought little abroad, civilian exports continued, and the City held large dollar balances. The United States, it must be recalled, was a net debtor in 1914. But in the spring of the next year, after the Morgan contract of January, British purchase began in earnest and by April the value of the pound was down to $4.80. To all of this Lloyd George was oblivious, as Morgan's, which was worried, understood. Lloyd George's eyes were fixed entirely upon the mobilization of British industry for war which, one could add, would reduce civilian exports and drive the pound down further.

The crisis arrived in July. On the twentieth of that month McKenna, barely six weeks in office, was informed by Morgan Grenfell that Morgan's could not buy dollars with pounds at $4.77 and was afraid to test the market for fear of reducing it further. This immediate danger was quickly surmounted by a loan, arranged by Morgan's, of $50,000,000 secured by $40,000,000 in American securities put at the government's disposal by the Prudential Insurance Company and by a shipment of gold.[17] Such Victorian expedients were still possible in Britain in the summer of 1915. They soon disappeared.

But this was only the beginning. On 14 August Lloyd George, at the Ministry of Munitions, learned that for contractors payments due the following week amounting to $17,000,000, Morgan's held only $4,000,000.[18] The July crisis had moved Asquith to inform McKenna in stringent terms only two days after the Morgan Grenfell letter of 20 July, that Britain was immediately to take every possible step to support the American exchange by withdrawing gold from circulation and, far more difficult, by requiring owners of American securities to sell them to the government.[19]

McKenna was crushed. He had discovered that one of the few things that seemed truly to exercise the Prime Minister was the American exchange. Here could lie his undoing. And Lloyd George's Ministry of Munitions was by far the most profligate and wasteful American spender.

The long range solution to the problem of the weakening pound was the raising of a large dollar loan in the United States private market. Lloyd George had looked into this possibility very casually in the spring but had done nothing. Now in August, in conjunction with the French, McKenna appointed a strong group of British and French bankers, headed by Rufus Isaacs, Lord Reading, to negotiate an American loan. The mission sailed for the United States on 1 September 1915.

The story of the difficult bargaining between the Reading mission and a consortium of American banks headed by Morgan's is not part of the life of Lloyd George but it is important to note that the mission remained in the United States for six weeks, was several times close to failure, and in the end achieved somewhat less than the British government had hoped.[20] All of this must be remembered when considering McKenna's bitter and frequently unjustified attacks upon Lloyd George's attempts to expand Britain's military potential. The two men literally were fighting different enemies: one the Central Powers, the other the dollar.

McKenna outlined his ideas on the war, rather plaintively, to L.T. Hobhouse, an eminent sociologist and friend of C.P. Scott's on 24 September. He trusted Hobhouse, as staunch a champion of the True Principles of English Liberalism as he was himself. His argument, that Britain should participate in the conflict as she had done in the French wars of the eighteenth century, as guardian of the seas, banker and manufacturer, illustrates the unexampled importance of Kitchener's thoughtless decision in August 1914 to build a mass army.

Hobhouse had asked McKenna why he was so opposed to conscription. Wrote Hobhouse to Scott:

> McKenna's objection is not so much that it would divide the country, as that we are unable to stand it industrially. He argues 'we have to provide 1,590 millions viz about 2/3 of the national income for the war. All the Allies call upon us. . .The Allies have plenty of men, but not equipment. There is a limit to what you can get from the U.S.A. You must in any case pay for what you get. . .Therefore you must keep our own industry going. Now every time you withdraw men on a large scale you give it a shock. It recovers slowly as new workers, women and older men and boys, are gradually drawn in and slowly made efficient. But then you come and draw more men and industry runs down again.'

McKenna agreed he would not stop recruiting but would slow it down to 5,000 or 10,000 a week, 'if it goes much faster exports will fall and the exchange goes against us.'

> He wholly scouts defeat. Where are we touched? We can go on ten years if they will only leave industry alone. . . .There are 100 ways of winning the war and only one of losing — conscription.[21]

One has to conclude that McKenna truly believed all of this, that he was convinced the war could be won with the Pitt System. In any case with the Reading mission still struggling to conclude a loan in the United States, and by no means sure of success as he read every day in cable messages, there was no other way. However, the significance of this philosophical dichotomy in the Cabinet was vast. Within months it had destroyed whatever ideological unity existed in the party coalition. On one side were the old Liberal purists, among whom Lloyd George once would probably have counted himself, McKenna, Runciman, Simon, Samuel Harcourt and probably Montagu, supported usually by Crewe and Grey whose loyalty was chiefly to Asquith, and buttressed by a large body of the 1906 generation of radical Members of Parliament and by a substantial portion of the old advanced Liberal press. Many, although of course not all, of these men had opposed the war at its outbreak and from them chiefly came the constant murmurings that the war would be over soon. Even in the autumn of 1915 they declined to see any military emergency, as McKenna's interview with Scott, which occurred precisely at the moment Highlanders were being mown like wheat by machine gun fire before the Hohenzollern Redoubt on the battlefield at Loos, had shown. In the final break in December 1916 these men, virtually without exception, would support Asquith. Indeed the assurance that the solid heart of old Liberalism supported him no doubt impelled the Prime Minister to let fall the compromise with Lloyd George arrived at on Sunday, 3 December and to push the disagreement to resignation.

To an extent the Prime Minister suffered also from his own enormous prestige within his party. Those around him and the newspapers which supported him increasingly lost touch with reality. For Lloyd George, they argued, to assert that the war was going badly or even that a shell shortage existed was to denounce the government. To denounce the government was to denigrate Asquith, no one else really counted. It followed therefore that for Asquith loyalists there could be no shell shortage and the war was going well.

These conclusions were for the future. Here it must be stressed that the fatal divisions of the fall of 1915 over conscription were exacerbated on McKenna's part by Lloyd George's exorbitant spending on munitions and by the Chancellor's venomous dislike of the only two Liberal conscriptionists in the Cabinet, Lloyd George and Churchill. Thus the split between the hard liners and the ideologues that had so weakened Asquith in the spring of 1915 reappeared in the autumn, with the difference that the Unionists, instead of sulking on the outside over the government's feebleness, were now sulking within the Cabinet and the leader of the malcontents was not Bonar Law but Sir Edward Carson.

For Lloyd George, as has been seen, these were trying times. He was distrusted if not disliked by most, not all, Unionists and was becoming aware as the autumn progressed of the real bitterness against him among most Liberals in the Cabinet, even more in the House of Commons, and in the radical press, which once cheered his every word. Such friends as he had were among the Tories, and Northcliffe. Lloyd George of course suffered at all this, but the historian should remember that it did not last. Nonetheless one should record J.L. Garvin's comments to Scott in the second week of November:

> He spoke rather sadly of Lloyd George of whom he had seen a good deal lately, blamed him for quarrelling with his own party. The Labour men, the Irish and the Radicals all now against him. A man should always stick to his own party because there lies his influence. What was the use of Lloyd George breaking with the 'Daily Chronicle' and the 'Daily News' and cultivating the 'Daily Mail' and 'The Times.' He seemed to have lost his nerve as well as influence and, whereas Churchill had gained in force and character, he had lost. On the new War Council he was in a minority of one. Asquith and Balfour both belonged to the other camp in the Cabinet, McKenna was his sworn enemy, Bonar Law had a serious grudge against him for preventing him being Chancellor of the Exchequer in the Coalition Government when Lloyd George took the Munitions Office. In putting McKenna in and keeping Bonar Law out Lloyd George made the mistake of his life. McKenna was overjoyed 'trod upon air' and ever since had been counter-working George. He had acquired an extraordinary influence over Asquith largely by saving him the trouble of thinking. It was the influence of a narrow, second-rate, efficient business mind with ready-made solutions over a much more powerful but cold, indolent, and self-indulgent nature. In fact we were now living under a McKenna regime. It was a wretched position for Lloyd George and he ought not to have accepted it. But he seemed to have lost his old self-confidence and courage and could no longer take risks.[22]

This isolation of Lloyd George was not only Scott and Garvin's conclusion. Less than a week earlier Riddell had mused in his diary:

> It is evident that Lloyd George is working closely in touch with Northcliffe, and gradually shedding the sentimental section of the Radical Party — men like Whitehouse [Liberal for West Lanark since 1910, a Ruskinite and boy's club enthusiast, briefly a secretary to Lloyd George at the Exchequer, and in 1915 a strong anti-conscriptionist] for whom he now has the heartiest contempt. None of the Radicals in the Cabinet are [sic] working with him. McKenna, Simon, Runciman, McKinnon Wood, Buckmaster, Harcourt, etc. are opposed to him. He finds his supporters among the Conservatives. It looks as if he is going the same road as Chamberlain. L.G.'s attitude to the war makes his severance from the Radicals inevitable. . .Bereft of his associates on the great question of the day, he is obliged to seek support elsewhere. L.G.'s future is interesting.[23]

One has to doubt whether Lloyd George's relationship with the Northcliffe press was ever so influential as both he and they from time to time seemed to think.[24] But still the matter is important not simply because the appearances of comradeship with Northcliffe continually vexed George Riddell. Rather as the fall and winter of 1915–16 passed, *The Times* proprietor's unseemly presence lay at the center of all the charges levied against Lloyd George by his old friends in the radical press. Lloyd George's first indiscretion, already alluded to, was the widely printed preface to a new edition of his war-time speeches, which appeared on 13 September 1915 and which appeared to call for military conscription although, as has been discussed, Lloyd George, at the time, was obviously thinking more along the lines of some sort of national industrial service:

> If we are not allowed to equip our factories with adequate labour
> to supply our armies, because we must not transgress regulations
> applicable to normal conditions; if practices are maintained which
> restrict the output of essential war material; if the nation hesitates,
> when the need is clear, to take the necessary steps to call forth its
> manhood to defend honour and existence; if vital discussions are
> postponed until too late; if we neglect to make ready for all probable
> eventualities; in fact we give ground for the accusation that we are
> slouching into disaster as if we were walking along the ordinary paths
> of peace without an enemy in sight; then I can see no hope. . .[25]

These words evoked the first of several attacks from A.G. Gardiner, the great editor of the *Daily News* who, with J.A. Spender and C.P. Scott, represented the heartbeat of old nineteenth-century Liberalism.[26] Beginning more in sorrow than in anger, as the months passed Gardiner's indictments came to include nearly all that post-war Liberalism held against Lloyd George for the rest of his political life: consorting with Tories and with Northcliffe, of slandering Britain as a 'nation of slackers' and of using conscription to undermine Asquith, and finally, by the spring of 1916, 'caught by the flair of a great occasion, impatient with democracy, [you have been] seized with a sort of apocalyptic vision of yourself as a saviour of Europe.'[27]

This rising invective is important and would become more so as the campaign for conscription progressed because the charges came to be repeated in more personal terms by other Liberals whom Lloyd George for decades had counted as friends, Llewelyn Williams for example. But more to the point the reciprocal of these denunciations, the equivalent praise, growing proportionately in volume through the winter, fell upon Reginald McKenna. As Lloyd George declined McKenna was the coming man, the rising hope of Liberalism. His attempts to stabilize the pound even at the cost of import duties were applauded as pure Cobdenism,[28] while his approach to the war, already referred to, that Britain could not at once control the seas, finance her allies, build a mass army in France, and maintain her industrial base, was endlessly reiterated.[29]

At the end of November, 1915 over golf and lunch, Riddell noted Lloyd George's discouragement.

> He says things are very unpleasant in the War Council. Chiefly for
> reasons of personal antagonism, McKenna opposes almost every
> project which LG suggests or supports. As a result the atmosphere is
> unpleasant and unfavourable to the transaction of business. He thinks
> McK narrow, vindictive and lacking in imagination. He says that
> McKenna, Simon, Runciman, Buckmaster and Samuel are dominated by
> old party prejudices and catchwords. They fear to see the old Radical

THE NEW CONDUCTOR.
OPENING OF THE 1917 OVERTURE.

Punch cartoon, 20 December 1916. The new government was announced on 10 December 1916.

Punch cartoon showing Lloyd George as Asquith's solver of problems. It refers to the government's decision to reform the government of Ireland after the Easter Rebellion in April 1916. Note the map of Ireland on the Prime Minister's desk and the pictures of Carson and Redmond on the wall.

PRESS THE BUTTON, AND UP COMES THE GENIE.

An illustration from Riddell's published diary: Lloyd George on the Walton Heath golf course. The third man from the left (excluding the caddies) holding a golf club is Sir George Riddell.

THE LIBERAL CAVE-MEN;

OR, A HOLT FROM THE BLUE.

Harassed Chancellor. "It's not so much for my feet that I mind—they're hardened against this kind of thing; but I do hate rocks on my head."

(Above) Punch cartoon, 15 July 1914. The 1914 land budget fiasco: 'Holt' refers to Richard Durning Holt, Liberal MP for Hexham, Northumberland, since 1907, a Liverpool shipping magnate, who organized resistance to the local authority grants.

(Left) Lloyd George 1915-16. His hair and mustache had become white by the end of the war.

A contemporary postcard–a perceptive caricature. Lloyd George smiled frequently and his eyes were bright, they 'twinkled' it was said. In fact his eyes were piercing and hard.

the Chancellor of the Exchequer

A sketch from *The Illustrated London News* showing Lloyd George as Minister for Munitions speaking in the House of Commons in 1915. He is holding a fuse for a high-explosive projectile, and apologized to the Speaker if he was not in order.

MR. R. McKENNA,
Minister of Education, Engaged to Miss Jekyll.

MISS MARGARET JEKYLL,
Engaged to Mr. McKenna, M.P.

The announcement in *The Illustrated London News* of the engagement of Reginald McKenna to his wife, Pamela (inexplicably called Margaret here).

Lloyd George with Sir Rufus Isaacs and C.F.G. Masterman in 1911, probably in Criccieth.
(Gwynedd Archives)

Sir Douglas Haig and General Joffre talking to Lloyd George in September 1916 with Albert Thomas looking on. The man in the background with hand on hip is probably General Henry Wilson.
(Imperial War Museum)

Party weakened or destroyed because they believe that they would thus lose their own power and influence. They do not appreciate the necessities of war.

Lloyd George reported that he never saw Masterman anymore but that Masterman and McKenna 'are as thick as thieves'.[30]

The McKenna-Lloyd George division is of considerably greater importance than simply the pain it gave to both men. In fact what one sees here, a year before the fall of Asquith, is the beginning of the breakup of the Liberal party, not really over personalities, although Lloyd George's ambition was for A.G. Gardiner the symbolic issue, but over principles. If Liberalism did not stand for the rights of the individual it stood for nothing. Yet since the formation of the Ministry of Munitions in June 1915 Lloyd George had been busily at work attempting to organize — his opponents styled it 'Prussianize' — the nation, control capital, control factories, control labor. McKenna saw, quite correctly, that military conscription was only the most dramatic part of a much larger whole. Britain he argued neither needed it nor could afford it and within such a system the Liberal party would not survive.

But of much more immediate importance, providing the link between the controversies of the winter of 1915 and the fall of Asquith a year later, was the misperception apparent in Gardiner's articles, McKenna's whispered asides to journalists, and quite clearly in his mistaken advice to Asquith when the final crisis began: that Lloyd George was almost entirely alone and was motivated by nothing more than personal ambition. He had no Liberal support except for Churchill — and after all 'Mr. Churchill is Mr. Churchill' sneered Gardiner, not to be taken seriously.[31] Among the opposition he was only tolerated as potentially useful by a few Tory grandees, led by Northcliffe, and by hotheads led by Carson, who chiefly were disgusted with the official leadership of their own party.

Churchill, as the other Liberal outsider, suffered even more than Lloyd George in this period, burdened as he was by loss of office and the clearly deteriorating situation in Gallipoli. His end, apparently also McKenna's work, came on 11 November when the new War Committee, appointed to replace the so-called 'Dardanelles Committee', which since summer had been the term for the War Council, was announced. To Churchill's rage and the political world's surprise, he was not named a member of the new committee, but McKenna was appointed.

C.P. Scott saw Clementine Churchill the next day when he called to say good-bye to her husband who in fury was going to join his regiment in France. He had expected to become a Lieutenant-General. He was instead a Major and his political life seemed to be over. Mrs. Churchill, thought Scott, 'looked as if she had nearly cried her eyes out' and she nearly broke down again as they talked. Churchill did not know it but he was a significant victim of McKenna's influence over the Prime Minister. Lloyd George, however, was furious.

McKenna had just induced Asquith to appoint him to the new War Committee, Lloyd George growled to Riddell over dinner on 14 November. He was not playing the game. It had been agreed that no one would press claims on the Prime Minister so that he would be free to choose his own committee. 'The P.M. has been spending the weekend [obviously 5, 6, 7 November] with the Jekylls,' Riddell later reflected,

> and has no doubt been subjected to much feminine influence. Mrs. McKenna, L.G. thinks, has been working hard in the interests of her husband. P.M. has, or is supposed to have, a great liking for her, as well he may, she is a very clever little person.[32]

Lloyd George told generally the same story to Frances Stevenson the next day with the additional information that McKenna, 'conceited, self-confident, persistent' as Miss Stevenson put it, had in the beginning asked the Prime Minister outright at Cabinet for a place on the committee and had been refused.[33] This could be another of Lloyd George's self-serving and simplistic explanations of a complicated or awkward event. But Asquith's Cabinet letter of 4 October, when the new committee was first projected, shows Churchill as a member with McKenna excluded and while Churchill was not present at the committee's first, unofficial, meeting on 5 November, neither was McKenna.[34] In France, Churchill several times was nearly killed. At the time he might have welcomed such a consummation.

II

The military need for conscription, as opposed to the demand for it as a symbol of commitment or sacrifice, appeared in the summer of 1915. Edward, Lord Derby, who had become the highly successful chief recruiting agent for West Lancashire, noted in his letters in July that enlistments were falling off rapidly and, significantly, men were responding that they would go into the army when they were 'fetched'.[35] By June 1915 the advertised minimum physical requirement for the height of volunteers was 5 feet 2 inches with a chest measurement of $33\frac{1}{2}$ inches.

Derby became an important part of the campaign for compulsory enlistment in the months that followed, but the key figure, as Lloyd George and everyone else believed, was Lord Kitchener. His menacing face and pointing finger on thousands of posters calling Britons to their duty had brought the New Army into being. His popularity and prestige in conscription's support would make passage easy. Whether or not he could control the War Office, he could control opinion in the nation. 'K. plants himself simply upon the Registration Act,' wrote the Solicitor General, F.E. Smith, a close friend of Churchill's and a Unionist, to Lloyd George on, probably, 9 August,

> and says if the result shows a real reservoir of strength he will not hesitate to tell the Cabinet we must have compulsory service — not a bad argumentative position especially as he claims French as an ally.[36]

This letter, mentioning also a meeting on conscription which Bonar Law would be unable to attend, symbolized an opening phase of the Cabinet battle between Lloyd George and McKenna. Unfortunately Smith had addressed it simply to 'The Chancellor of the Exchequer' forgetting that for six weeks McKenna had held that office. McKenna had opened it, as he was entitled to do, and had realized it was meant for Lloyd George. However, instead of immediately sending it on he held it for some days and apparently showed it to others, evidently at least to Walter Runciman who wrote to

Kitchener on 12 August warning him that he had seen evidence that the conscriptionists were proposing to use him to hurt Asquith. He may well have also showed it to the Prime Minister, or his wife, for Margot Asquith also wrote to Kitchener on 18 August saying much the same, more forcefully, and naming Lloyd George.[37] Finally McKenna sent the letter to Lloyd George on 11 August with a terse explanation. Lloyd George wrote a furious and characteristic reply saying, as he told Frances Stevenson, that the next time McKenna received a message for someone else 'he should put it back in the same box & send it on to the right person at once — after he had read it of course. D[avid] also intimated [to McKenna] that had any other of his colleagues done a similar thing, he would have experienced some surprise.'[38]

One cannot say that the missent letter began the conscription struggle, but clearly it provided evidence for the argument that the anti-conscriptionists took within the Cabinet: that conscription was unnecessary or too expensive, or impossible because the numbers of men did not exist, or that it was abhorrent to Liberal principles — any argument would suffice. It was being pursued only because its Unionist supporters hoped to use it to discredit the Prime Minister and put Lloyd George in Asquith's place. This was not only Lloyd George's own estimate of the tactics of his opponents, manifest in any number of places in Miss Stevenson's diary. Maurice Hankey, the secretary of the Dardanelles/War Committee, who, although unfailingly loyal to Asquith, must count as a disinterested observer, believed the same. 'It appears that Ll.G. is out to break the Govt. over conscription if he can. . .' he wrote on 16 October after lunch with the Prime Minister. Later that day he received the usual hysterical note from Margot urging him to see people and do something about it.[39]

What Asquith honestly thought one cannot tell, but there is no question that he felt an emotional dependence upon Lloyd George for his fertility of mind. His friends brought him problems and worries, rumors of conspiracy. Lloyd George never withheld unpleasant information, but always provided also ideas, hope and plans for action. The two men had lunch toward the end of September at the troubling time of the commencement of the Battle of Loos, the first large operation of the new armies. Miss Stevenson recorded what she had been told of their conversation.

'It would be a pity for us to quarrel,' said the P.M. to D. in a frank talk. 'I have never believed the stories that have been going round about your intriguing against me. I have always replied to any suggestion of this kind that during all the years we have worked together you have been the most loyal of colleagues. I will be quite frank with you,' he continued. 'There are only two men in this Cabinet who count at all, and we are those two. If we quarrel it will mean disaster.' They parted good friends, D. having persuaded the P.M. to insist on a small Cabinet of 6 or 8 members. [This eventually became the War Committee from which Churchill was excluded.][40]

As is inevitably the case in political affairs, the fight over conscription was entangled with exterior matters over which the Cabinet had no control. The key event, already mentioned, was the failure of attempted landings at Suvla Bay on the north coast of the Gallipoli peninsula on 7–8 August. This disaster was doubly lamentable, first because it constituted a real chance to end five months of heartbreaking stalemate and to win the campaign by the use of surprise and the mobility provided by seapower and imaginative tactics, indeed involving specially built landing craft, qualities not usually associated with British generalship at this time. But second, it was also disappointing because the failure was more clearly than usually the case the fault of the commander on the spot, Lieutenant General Sir Frederick Stopford, who seems to have been forced upon the theater commander, General Ian Hamilton, by Kitchener.

Lloyd George was furious. Kitchener 'is a liar', he announced to Riddell some time after the Secretary of State had given his explanation of the tragedy.

> He has the Oriental notion of the truth. . .he told the Cabinet that Ian Hamilton had asked for Stopford. He had asked for other generals whom K declined to send because they were junior to Mahon. [Lieutenant General Bryan Mahon, the General Officer Commanding the Tenth (Irish) Division.] K gave Hamilton a selection from four worn out men. He took Stopford [who had a fine field record in the nineteenth century] because he thought he was as good, or rather no worse than, the other three. You know the tragic results.[41]

After Suvla the prospect for success in Gallipoli was at an end. Eventually Britain would have to get out. The question, as torturing as conscription, was how to do it. Immediate pressure came from a highly secret report to the Prime Minister of Australia, Andrew Fisher, by a young newspaperman, Keith A. Murdoch, leaked to Lloyd George and Carson, condemning the entire operation. Murdoch evidently had been commissioned to look into the treatment of Australian troops by the British.[42] He denounced in the strongest terms the lack of training, staffwork and generalship. Certain officers, all British, should be recalled. He concluded, along with comments on the poor physique of English soldiers in comparison with the Australians, with a bold hint that in the absence of reform Australia should consider withdrawing its forces.

Two days before he received Murdoch's report Lloyd George proposed in the Dardanelles Committee that all troops be evacuated from Suvla Bay and moved to Salonika.[43] He had been suggesting this of course for months. In July Lloyd George had proposed that only 50,000 men be left at Gallipoli to hold Cape Hellas and the rest be sent to Salonika to help Greece coerce Bulgaria.[44] But Bulgaria was now past coercion. Her King Ferdinand (always identified as 'the Fox') had determined after Suvla that as Turkey would continue to occupy the Allies, the time had arrived to accomplish what had eluded him in 1912 and 1913, the seizure of Macedonia from Serbia. For Bulgaria this would be the third Balkan War, in which she would have now the support of Germany and Austria. Finally, like a good many other rulers he believed in the autumn of 1915, as Russian strength declined, that the Central Powers would win in Europe. The day for the big Bulgaria of San Stephano had arrived.

In all this Allied diplomacy was helpless. Bulgaria could neither be frightened nor bought. The territory she most coveted was Serbian and although for months Grey sought to induce Serbia to offer her neighbor some concessions, the Serbs, unaware of their own peril, stubbornly refused. Lloyd George and Churchill, the Prime Minister wrote to the King in June, 'were of the opinion that a high price (at the expense mainly of Greece) was worth paying for the prompt adhesion of Bulgaria.'[45] In any case, in the auction of Serbian territory the Central Powers could afford to be more generous than the Allies, bound as they were by commitments to Italy which had its own plans for the acquisition of South Slav territory.

By the end of September a large Bulgarian army was massed on the eastern Serbian frontier while a substantial German-Austrian force was preparing to cross the Danube from the north. Serbia, for whose independence indeed the war had begun, was about to fall. In London the Cabinet was paralyzed and miserable but hardly contrite. 'Thus ends one of the most important chapters in the history of Diplomacy,' wrote Asquith to the King on 2 October.

> The discredit for the result must be divided between Russia, but for whom Bulgaria wd. probably have been brought in months ago, and Serbia whose obstinacy and cupidity have brought her to the verge of destruction.

The whole world knew, the Prime Minister asserted, that Macedonia belonged to Bulgaria.[46]

The entrance of Bulgaria into the war — which duly occurred on 11 October — and the overrunning of Serbia meant far more for Britain than the imputation of feebleness. Germany now had, or soon would have, a direct land route to Constantinople. Turkey would be rearmed. The armies on the Gallipoli peninsula now were liable not to frustration but destruction. Thus the issue of evacuation, hitherto always evaded in Cabinet, now had to be faced. But the murder of British troops in Gallipoli would be not only a military disaster. It meant, as Lloyd George and many others believed, the admission of the collapse of British power in the East. The Suez Canal, indeed India, were involved.

One senses that the weeks surrounding the end of September and the beginning of October of 1915 mark a new phase of the war, and a species of revelation for Britain's political leadership. The failures of Loos and in the eastern Mediterranean made clear to all but the blind that the conflict would not end soon. The munitions crisis, invisibly, was coming to an end, to be replaced by the dilemma of manpower. It was as if the conflict were starting over again. The decisions not made at the beginning of the war now had to be taken.

For Lloyd George the Allied collapse in the eastern Mediterranean was utterly discouraging. 'The Eastern situation very grave,' wrote Frances Stevenson on 5 October. Lloyd George had told her that he had heard on 2 October from Noel Buxton, who continued to be his chief source of intelligence, that the Germans would be in Constantinople by Christmas.

> 'But,' said I, 'if they once get to Constantinople, our Dardanelles campaign is at an end.' 'My dear Pussy,' he replied, 'I am very much afraid that the whole of the Eastern empire is at an end.'

And now that it was too late Miss Stevenson learned that troops were being sent to Salonika.[47]

The revival of the presumably discarded Salonika expedition while Serbia was in the process of being overrun has mystified historians since 1915, as it did contemporary observers. However, the initiative this time came from the French, a product of the usual Byzantine French military politics. General Joseph Joffre, who in March 1915 had declined to consider an army in Salonika, discovered in August 1915 that he needed a foreign command for the excessively popular General Maurice Sarrail. Sarrail had been a hero of the Battle of the Marne, was a Freemason and had been a violent Dreyfusard while only a battalion commander. Sarrail was known as the 'Jacobin General'. Lloyd George's friend, Aristide Briand, still Minister of Justice and a confirmed easterner, suggested Sarrail be sent to Greece and on 3 August he was named Commander of the newly founded 'Army of the Orient' without however any troops or clear indication of where he would be assigned. Then events in the Balkans provided the determination. On 22 August, after a victory for his party in the June elections, Eleutherios Venizelos, the friend of the Allies, became again Greek Prime Minister. He was reappointed most reluctantly by King Constantine, who had received his education in Germany, was a field marshal in the Prussian army, and whose wife, Sophia, was the German Emperor's sister. Within days after Venizelos's reappearance the threat to Serbia by Bulgaria was clear. Greece was bound by a treaty of 1913 to defend Serbia against Bulgaria. Accordingly Venizelos ordered Greek mobilization and called for Allied support, supposedly with the King's consent. Thus it was to Salonika that Sarrail would be sent with a French division from the Dardanelles.[48]

Sarrail left France on 7 October 1915. On the same day German and Austrian troops crossed the Danube. By this time, on 5 October, the first British troops had landed at Salonika, and Venizelos had been dismissed a second time by Constantine.[49] Nonetheless, on 11 October Bulgaria not intimidated by the Allied presence in Greece invaded Serbia. How great was Lloyd George's belief that an Allied force at Salonika, a city with only a rickety narrow-gauge railway running to the north, could save Serbia is in doubt. His lonely arguments in the Dardanelles Committee and the Cabinet for a force in Greece turned generally on the matter of prestige although he usually added that Salonika provided an alternative to Gallipoli, which now he regarded as an irretrievable failure. Britain was always late but she must send troops to Salonika to show she was not beaten. The army could hold on at Cape Hellas with 50,000 men. The 45,000 at Suvla could be used to show the flag in the Balkans, he urged on 23 September as Bulgaria mobilized.[50] After external events intervened his argument was the same. On 11 October, as the Bulgarian invasion began, he reminded the Dardanelles Committee that it appeared that Britain could not protect her friends. First Belgium had been lost, now Serbia.[51]

The Dardanelles Committee meeting of 11 October and the Cabinet of the following day, were of critical importance for the future, not only for policy in the eastern Mediterranean, but for the course of British politics at Westminster. Lloyd George gives an extended account of their deliberations and conclusions in his *War Memoirs*.[52] Basically the military held that any substantial diversion of troops from France to the aid of Serbia would have to wait upon the outcome of further operations around Loos. Eventually the

Committee acquiesced and determined that a force could be sent to Egypt as a staging point for unspecified engagement elsewhere. In effect Serbia, as Lloyd George put it, 'would be left to her doom'.[53]

That evening Lloyd George dictated to Miss Stevenson a memorandum for circulation to the next day's Cabinet.[54] Although most of this document is printed in his *War Memoirs* its importance in marshalling his objections to the present conduct of the war, and indeed to the western orientation of British military planning in the next three years, compels that it be quoted at length.[55] Taken together with the memoranda submitted in January and February it counts as a comprehensive statement of his conception of Allied strategy. 'The helplessness of the great Powers' Lloyd George began

to save from destruction one little country after another that relied on their protection is one of the most pitiable spectacles of this War.

The appreciation of the existing situation in the Balkans circulated by the General Staff is a distressing document. It might all be compressed into two words: Too late! It might easily have been foreseen that a march through Serbia into Bulgaria would be one of the most obvious and profitable moves for the German General Staff to contemplate, by connecting up their railway system with Turkey:

1. They could aim a most direct and effective blow — in fact the only direct and effective blow they could possibly aim — at the British Empire.

* * * *

3. They could have a fair chance of destroying the great British force which is now holding on by tooth and claw to a rim of the Gallipoli Peninsula.

4. They could strike a ringing blow at our prestige in the east.

5. They could render perfectly nugatory our sea-power in so far as South-Eastern Europe and a large part of Asia are concerned.

By equipping the Turks, perhaps the Afghans, they could extend the war to Egypt, even to India, and force large diversions of troops from France in 1916. The same activity would bring pressure on the Russians.

8. All this they could achieve by overcoming the resistance of an ill-equipped army of 300,000 Serbians, a considerable portion of these having their attention engaged by the prospect of a hostile Bulgarian army attacking them from behind. Not a very formidable proposition for the military power that has rolled up the great armies of Russia, whilst at the same time holding in check the combined forces of France and Britain! It was therefore obvious even to the civilian mind that it was too tempting a project for the Germans not to seize upon.

(In fact the Germans, Austrians and Bulgarians needed only a month to subdue Serbia. General Sarrail's British detachments were under strict instructions not to move into Serbia and consequently the small Salonika force made a few gestures but nothing more.)[56]

Lloyd George continued by noting that in December, in effect 1 January

1915, and again in February he had called attention to the possibilities in the Near East and often offended his colleagues by referring to it.

> It perplexes a mere civilian to find any explanation for the neglect of the military authorities to provide against so disastrous a blow to our Empire, when it was so clear to any careful observer that it was impending. It is incredible that the fifth day after the blow had actually fallen finds us without a plan — unless the sending of some general — not yet fixed upon — to the eastern Mediterranean to scout for a scheme of operations can be called a plan. The Cabinet may depend upon it that when it became clear to the British public that we have been taken by surprise and that we have not made the slightest preparation to counter the German thrust, confidence will vanish in our capacity to conduct the War, and rightly so.

But there remained much that could be done. A large and firm British and French commitment of troops to the Balkans would bring in Greece and Romania for one more effort to save Serbia.

> There are two reasons for doing so. The first is that the abandonment of Serbia to her fate would be fatal to the prestige of Great Britain among the Allies and throughout the world. The hostility of Bulgaria and the neutrality of Greece and Rumania are attributable to the conviction which has permeated all neutral countries that Germany is irresistible and that we are impotent to protect nations which have incurred her wrath. . .

The second reason was, again, the menace to Egypt, to the Muslim world of northern Africa and India, and of a revived and rearmed Turkey. Only the expulsion of the Germans from Serbia could prevent the crumbling of British power in the Mediterranean and beyond Suez. 'Surely the averting of such a catastrophe is worth one grand final effort. Is such an effort beyond our compass?'

* * * *

> The Situation is desperate, and nothing but prompt, courageous, and even daring action can retrieve it. What risks do we run by making this promise?

> 1. We should have definitely to postpone the offensive in the west. When it [Loos] has failed now, after the most prolonged and careful preparation, why should it be assumed that it will succeed three months hence? The French and ourselves will not be appreciably better off in the matter of big guns — not until the late spring of next year. We have already lost — French and British — between 500,000 and 600,000 men in the two great attempts made since last May to pierce the German line. To ignore the costly lesson thus given us and to make another effort of the same kind without adequate equipment of heavy guns and ammunition would be wantonly to throw away the lives of the very fine body of men who have volunteered for the new armies.

Lloyd George concluded with a plea for a reduction of the Gallipoli effort, although he stopped short of proposing outright evacuation. But any attempt at another massive attack was 'insane'.

We have failed repeatedly when the Turks were short of ammunition.
Are we now to succeed when they are reinforced with German
heavy guns and [an] abundance of ammunition. It is by no means
improbable that the Turks might drive us into the sea before
reinforcements reached our army on that Peninsula.

Lloyd George's memorandum produced a generally approving letter from
Grey and an almost unbelievable one from Kitchener who proposed that the
way to save Serbia was to induce Bulgaria, whose armies were at that moment
pouring into Macedonia, to join the Allies.[57]

Viewed in perspective then, the fall of Serbia slammed shut the window
of opportunity that had been opened by Turkey's declaration of war. The
Ottoman Empire, the sick man, proved to be, despite its legendary corruption,
Britain's most formidable and successful antagonist after Germany. The
Germans, not the British, captured Constantinople. A warm water route to
Russia was not opened nor was a secondary front against Austria established.
The leverage provided by the unanimous hatred of the Turks in the Balkans
was thrown away.

III

In political, as opposed to military, terms the devastating result of Bulgaria's
invasion of Serbia appeared also on 12 October with the resignation from
the Cabinet of Sir Edward Carson, thus beginning the unravelling of the
highly artificial unity that had been stitched together in May with the formation
of the coalition. After some weeks of intermittent illness Carson would begin,
in January 1916, to organize a Unionist opposition that eventually drove
Asquith from office. Moreover his departure was scarcely more dangerous to
the Prime Minister than to the leader of the Unionist party, Andrew Bonar
Law.

Carson, it must be quickly said, had been unhappy in the Cabinet long
before the Serbian crisis. He detested the handling of the Gallipoli operation
and had in Lieutenant General Bryan Mahon, a schoolmate at Portarlington
years before and now G.O.C. of the Tenth Division, a copious and dependable
source of information. In a flood of letters Mahon cried out against the
expedition. Everything, the smallest thing, was immensely difficult. If only, if
only troops had been landed at the time of the first bombardment. And so
on.[58]

His biographer makes clear that Carson's grievances were the general ones
that also afflicted Lloyd George: indecision, lack of precision, planning and
initiative, the 'policy of drift', not specifically the failure to protect Serbia;
there is no indication that Carson saw the fatal strategic implications of the
fall of that country. However, he was much affected by Keith Murdoch's
report which he saw on 23 September after Murdoch came to London. He
immediately sent the Australian to see Lloyd George, who reported to him
the next day:

My Dear Carson

I saw Murdoch the Australian yesterday. He struck me as being
exceptionally intelligent and sane. That makes the account he left me
of his visit to the Dardanelles much more disquieting. He left on my

mind an impression of impending disaster, and he is angry at the ignorance and apparent indifference of the men here who are directing operations.

After saying that he urged Murdoch to show his report to the Prime Minister and describing other points of his conversation — the inhospitable environment, surprising efficiency of the Turks, the sickness among the troops and the low morale, even among the Australians — Lloyd George concluded his letter with a statement of alliance.

As you know, I have always opposed this Gallipoli enterprise, and so have you. I opposed it at the start, and you have opposed it since you joined the Ministry. But we have also agreed that if it was to be proceeded with, it ought to be pressed on with forces which are in some measure adequate to the tremendous character of the operation. I have never thought that success was possible unless the Turkish forces were engaged elsewhere, so as to deprive the Turks of the necessary reinforcements of men and ammunition for the Peninsula.[59]

Lloyd George sent a copy of this letter to Bonar Law adding the telling point that Murdoch believed the Turks could drive the Allies from the peninsula if they chose but forbore in the belief that in allowing the Allies to stay more men would die, particularly of sickness.[60]

For a moment it appeared that failure at Gallipoli would be balanced at last by vigorous intervention in the Balkans. On 28 September, just three days after Lloyd George's despairing letter to Carson, Grey, who finally had allowed himself to be convinced that Bulgaria was preparing for war pronounced, in reply to a question, a firm warning in the House of Commons.

If. . .the Bulgarian mobilization were to result in Bulgaria assuming an aggressive attitude on the side of the enemies we are prepared to give our friends in the Balkans all the support in our power, in the manner that would be most welcome to them, in concert with our Allies, without reserve and without qualification. . .[61]

Grey does not mention this declaration in his memoir. Nor does his biographer G.M. Trevelyan, a Balkan expert as well as a distinguished historian, refer to it, although Trevelyan admits that Grey's failure in the Balkans represents 'the greatest defeat of his diplomacy in the war'.[62] How or when it was authorized is unclear. The Cabinet had by no means settled upon a Salonika expedition. Its importance here lies in the fact that Lloyd George and Carson believed it meant that Britain had promised to defend Serbia 'without reserve or qualification' and that within weeks that promise had been broken. Their disgust was clear in their writing and subsequent actions.[63]

How Grey, honorable and intelligent, could have made such a diplomatic, not to mention political, error deserves a word of explanation. Even as the Germans and Austrians were massing north of the Danube he was apparently convinced that the Central Powers were at the end of their strength. In effect he was still afflicted with the fatal optimism that for nearly a year and a half had stifled and warped strategic planning and weapons procurement in the British war effort. He believed that the threat of Allied intervention would prevent an attack on Serbia from the north. It would not take much, he evidently believed, to overawe the Germans. The previous week he had written to Sir George Barclay, British Minister to Romania, urging that he stimulate action in Bucharest.

> ...Germany is getting weaker in men and money, all our information shows this to be so in spite of her temporary successes against Russia, which are themselves exhausting her. An understanding between the Balkan states would make invasion of the Balkans too formidable a task for Austria and Germany to attempt.[64]

Carson was present at the Dardanelles Committee meeting of 11 October, already discussed, at which the military members were able to force the decision, over the objection chiefly of Lloyd George, to press ahead again on the Western Front and later send a force to Egypt. Even though General Mahon's 10th Division was already ashore at Salonika they were to receive no reinforcements.[65] Lloyd George's angry memorandum was dictated that evening. On the same day, Monday, 11 October, *The Times* reported that Carson had resigned.

Surprisingly the next day's Cabinet was devoted entirely to conscription. On 22 September Asquith had asked the Earl of Derby to take the new post of Director General of Recruiting. This appointment had been announced on 5 October.[66] A Cabinet on manpower supply may therefore have been appropriate, but in the midst of the Balkan danger, Lloyd George was furious. 'With the Balkan crisis as it is, and an army sitting and doing nothing at Salonika, and Serbia sending telegrams every few hours for help, the Cabinet *did not even mention* the situation in the East. It is incredible: it would be laughable if it were not so dreadful,' wrote Miss Stevenson.[67]

It is not clear whether Carson attended the unhappy Cabinet meeting of 12 October. He had in any case warned his secretary that morning that he would not be a member of the government by evening and had written a short letter of resignation which he delivered to the Prime Minister at noon, promising a longer explanation by evening. Evidently he saw Lloyd George at about the same time and told him of the action. Lloyd George entirely approved, admitting that he ought to be doing the same thing.[68]

Asquith's fine political mind comprehended the danger immediately. Suddenly a potential Leader of the Opposition had been born who had at his back a disciplined force of Tory die-hards mobilized in the battles over Home Rule who would now contest not the future of Ireland, but far more important, the quality of prime ministerial leadership. It was a challenge not unlike the one he had faced in the middle of May. Within minutes, Carson had a letter in his hand urging him to desist.

Asquith delayed announcing the resignation even though Carson ceased attending Cabinet and wrote to the Prime Minister two days later asking him to send his letter to the press. Meanwhile the Prime Minister brought all possible pressure to bear upon the Attorney General. The other Unionist leaders needed no urging. Both Bonar Law and Walter Long spoke and wrote to him repeatedly. Their own danger was as great as the Prime Minister's.[69] At the same time Carson's followers among the Tory radicals advised him to find other malcontents to take with him. 'Don't go out alone if you can possibly help it,' wrote Leo Amery on 14 October. 'If you and

Lloyd George go that is another matter. Then you have the nucleus of something to go upon afterwards.'[70]

The week following Tuesday, 12 October, trying to undo damage already done, was clearly a difficult time for the Prime Minister. Indeed on the following Monday he announced in Cabinet that he felt ill, turned over the meeting to Lord Crewe and took to his bed for several days. Generally he searched for expedients. On the evening of 12 October Churchill and Lloyd George were permitted to send a telegram from the Foreign Office to Romania and Greece offering the support of 150,000 men if the two powers would defend Serbia against Bulgaria.[71] This was promptly refused but on 16 October Grey offered Cyprus to Greece for a declaration of war. Meanwhile, faced by a Cabinet revolt of Lloyd George, Churchill, and as Lloyd George calculated, six Tories, Curzon, Carson, Bonar Law, Long, Lansdowne and Kitchener over conscription, Asquith produced on 15 October what became known as the 'Derby Scheme' for recruitment. How much coercion actually was applied to the Prime Minister is unclear. Obviously he was unwell, floundering and desperate.[72] Lloyd George, himself ill with toothaches, seems to have told Frances Stevenson, and even allowed C.P. Scott to infer, that the eight men threatened resignation.[73] Yet among the rebels he counted Carson whom he knew already had resigned and Kitchener who as even Miss Stevenson understood hardly would have participated in such a cabal. In any case the Derby scheme, the last step on the road to conscription, as probably Asquith intended it should be, was born. It was to be tried for six weeks. He had bought some time. (The Derby scheme involved the individual solicitation of all physically fit men on the national register who were not engaged in essential work to attest their willingness to serve when called upon. Hence it would at the very least provide a measure of the size of the pool of men available in case of compulsion.)

The announcement of Carson's resignation could not be longer delayed. The press was full of rumors and mutterings. On Monday, 18 October Carson wrote to Asquith asking him to announce it. Otherwise he would reveal it himself. The Prime Minister replied immediately saying that he ought to see the King first to explain his reasons. Carson apparently replied for that evening Maurice Bonham Carter wrote again that the Prime Minister was ill and asleep, but that Carson still should see the King.[74]

This was enough. Still later that evening Carson gave the story of his resignation to the press.[75] It has 'for the moment overshadowed every other topic of discussion in the world of politics' said *The Times* the following day. It was 'a political event of the first magnitude,' it noted with a glance at Lloyd George, 'none the less because for the moment it seems likely to stand alone.'[76]

The linking in the mind of the press of Carson and Lloyd George would continue and grow after the resignation. Lloyd George was aware of the importance of this new perception and pondered it. Again and again in the next months, he considered resignation, consulted people about it, asserting continually that he should have departed with Carson.[77] (However during the second week of October he was almost totally occupied by the struggle with Kitchener over the Boulogne big gun program.) Certainly he foresaw the trouble Carson would make for a supine government of which he was a part, criticizing it for the weaknesses he himself deplored. *The Times* warned obliquely that the sickness of the government was likely to be fatal.

> Sir Edward Carson is no office seeker, but is still less likely to seek the 'lonely furrow' of a dramatic resignation. If at last he has been driven to the conclusion that he can take no further part in the present conduct of the war then we may be perfectly certain that he has weighed, and found wanting, the whole case for remaining with his colleagues and preserving the semblance of Cabinet cohesion at such a time.[78]

Carson made a temperate statement in the House of Commons on the day *The Times* leader appeared acknowledging that he had been treated with nothing but courtesy by Asquith and denying any political motive for his departure. As a cause he specified only Grey's exhaustion of Germany statement of 28 September.[79]

However, on 2 November, even as Asquith returned to the House to make a long statement on the war effort, including the declaration that the failure of the Derby scheme would surely bring a public demand for conscription that he, the Prime Minister, would be bound to heed, Carson began the offensive that eventually would overturn Asquith's government. A Cabinet of 22 men, he announced on that day, perhaps suitable for peacetime, made too many mistakes. Suvla Bay was the most recent example, but a war committee subsidiary to the Cabinet, however small, meant only that every issue had to be debated twice. He recommended instead that the Cabinet itself be reduced to six or eight members. He pointed again to Grey's statement of 28 September. He thought it had been made with authority. It had not. Serbia would now be crushed and with the Germans in Constantinople the Gallipoli expedition faced murder. 'I am bound to say,' he concluded, 'that nothing has ever astonished me more than the gyrations which we have gone through in relation to our policy in the Balkans.' He demanded a concentration of troops at Salonika.

Finally he read, after shouts demanding that he do so, the second, longer, letter of explanation he had written to the Prime Minister on 12 October. Again he mentioned Grey's statement.[80]

IV

In the days following Carson's resignation, Lloyd George had several teeth extracted, for him a very weighty matter entailing much anxiety, postponement and consultation. Meanwhile he considered his own resignation, causing almost equal ceremony. Inevitably he talked to Robertson Nicoll, as well as Reading, now returned from the United States, and C.P. Scott, as well as George Riddell. 'He is perplexed as to the course he should take,' wrote Riddell on 23 October.

> He is convinced that unless our methods are changed we shall have a great disaster in the East, and that we shall ultimately be beaten in the war. He thinks the nation should be told the truth. . .He is evidently pondering alternative courses of action; he does not know how to act. . .

L.G.: The reorganisation of the Cabinet is what is wanted; we are sure to be beaten under our present regime. One course I have thought of would be to resign my seat in the Cabinet and continue my work at the Munitions Department. I should then escape this horrible responsibility for things I cannot alter.

* * * *

I [Riddell] have omitted an important observation he made. He said, 'The public will have to come into this. I see no other way of improving matters. I do not want to be in the Cabinet just now. There is going to be a disaster; I have done my best to prevent it. My advice has not been taken. I don't wish to feel that I am responsible for what I cannot avoid.'[81]

Six days later, again at Riddell's house, with Reading and Nicoll, he sought further advice. This time his complaints centered upon Kitchener, whom, he said, 'the whole Cabinet considered incompetent but the P.M. cannot make up his mind to act. Last night L.G., Grey and Crewe had dinner with the P.M. and all told him their views of K. . .'

Lord R[eading] said he hoped L.G. would not resign, as this would be a national calamity. In any event he must base his resignation case on some specific issue. Nicoll thought he should resign. L.G. said he agreed. I said the specific issue was the military conduct of the war, but that the P.M. would no doubt institute reforms rather than that L.G. should resign. L.G. said he had not yet threatened resignation. If he resigns he would rather do so alone. Resignation in company with a group of Tory Ministers would lay his action open to misconstruction. He will have to determine how to act before Tuesday [2 November] when the P.M. makes his statement [the speech already cited that preceded Carson's first attack on the government]. . .He repeated his diagnosis of the situation which I have related in my notes of earlier conversations, and said he thought the nation should be told the truth. The existing Parliamentary Opposition was negligible, but if he were to resign, he and Carson would form the nucleus of a strong critical party.

He complained also of the attacks to which he was being subjected in Liberal radical newspapers and blamed McKenna.[82]

Two matters should be noted, which may justify these extended quotations. First there are the repeated references to the involvement of the public. Instinctively Lloyd George was thinking, as he always did when faced with an intractable political problem, of a public campaign. Mobilization of the voters against his political enemies, over the head of parliament, had been his normal operating procedure since the days of Welsh disestablishment. He had used it against Chamberlain and tariff reformers, the dukes, and indeed Winston Churchill. But he probably realized quickly that public denunciation of the scope or direction of Britain's war effort was out of the question. He was, in effect, deprived of his most potent weapon.

On the other hand there was Carson, tall, cruel, fierce, with a face like a skull, who combined a talent for passionate oratory the equal of Lloyd George's with almost unrivalled legal knowledge and yet, when he chose to display it, a winning Irish charm that captured followers. The two of them together, the most dangerous pair in the House of Commons, could accomplish, at least in normal times, almost anything.

Thus he had conflicting arguments for and against resignation, to which must be added a reluctance to leave the Ministry of Munitions which work, one senses, he genuinely enjoyed. In any case, two days after the discussion with Reading, Riddell and Robertson Nicoll, who came to be identified as Lloyd George's 'three Rs', he dictated what must be styled a conditional letter of resignation coupled with a firm warning. The occasion officially was the reconstitution of the Dardanelles Committee into the new 'War Committee', which Lloyd George had first bruited at his amiable lunch with Asquith in the third week of September. His letter was officially a reply to one Asquith had written him on 28 October outlining the constitution of the new committee.[83]

> My Dear Prime Minister
> I am sorry to trouble you when you must be worried with the anxieties of the situation, but I feel I must put to you my view of the position before you come to a final decision. The appointment of a small Committee with fairly full powers will undoubtedly be a great improvement on the sort of Duma which has been sitting on war problems up to the present. But unless there is a complete change in the War Office the new Council will be just as impotent as the Cabinet and the old Council proved themselves to be. Our War Administration have committed every blunder the enemy could wish them to be guilty of. It was quite clear, even to the civilian mind, soon after the war began that this war would ultimately be decided by superiority in quality and quantity of material, and by the wearing down of the enemy in numbers. The Allies had the advantage in both respects, and the War Office have by an incredible lack of foresight and energy thrown away both the advantages.

He provided a long list of the misfeasances and nonfeasances of the War Office: the failure to order in adequate quantities, the failure to coordinate orders for component parts, Woolwich again cited, the failure to provide information.

Lloyd George continued with a personal attack upon Kitchener, generally upon the failure to anticipate events in the Balkans, while reminding the Prime Minister that he himself and the War Council had been calling for preparations in this theater since the beginning of the year. Kitchener had not listened, 'not even a mule had been bought.' '*Kitchener never knew,*' he wrote with angry underlines, '*that they* [the Germans and Austrians] *had crossed the Danube 20 hours after the news reached the War Office that they had effected a crossing at five points.*' The public's 'delusions' about Kitchener would vanish if the House of Commons were told the facts, and he warned Asquith that the government's position, as well as the Prime Minister's own, was not strong.

> If I thought the appointment of a small Committee would put an end to all these amazing series of blunders, I should be satisfied. But I have gone on for months always thinking that every mistake must surely be the last, and finding myself constantly surprised by the capacity of our

great War Lords for blundering. I wrote to you in December last calling your attention to the stupidity of the War Office, and telling you that, in my judgement, unless we showed greater grip as a Government in management of the war, it must end in inevitable disaster. I have protested at each stage, sometimes in writing, sometimes by intervention in the Cabinet and at the War Council. I did so long before the Northcliffe Press began its campaign. At best the chances are against the next few weeks bringing much cheer — they might bring ruin to Serbia and for us retreat in the Balkans and disaster in Gallipoli.The nation would endure this and a good deal more if they knew everything was being done that human effort and foresight could compass to ensure final victory; but their confidence has been rudely shaken by what they can see of our unpreparedness in the Balkans. The friendly press are showing marked symptoms of mutiny. The steadfast loyalty of our party to your leadership has so far saved the Government, but you will forgive me for saying that I doubt whether that would save us if a catastrophe befell Serbia or our forces in the Dardanelles and all the facts on the conduct of the war were dragged out as they would be. Every mistake and omission would then be brought out with accumulative force. The row in Commons will come last. Press and public will be moved before the party politician, but in the end he will follow public opinion, and we must have a good answer when the time comes. There is only one answer that can satisfy the public, and that is that you have already made an end of the futile régime that stumble along from one fatuity to another. I am quite willing to face the inevitable tumult when it comes if this answer can be given, but I have reluctantly come to the conclusion that I can no longer be responsible for the present war direction, and at the Cabinet to-morrow I propose with your permission to raise the real issue.
Ever sincerely,
D. Lloyd George[84]

The menace evoked here was a double one: Lloyd George might resign of course, but the danger from Carson, although not mentioned, was clear and present. The aimlessness of the government therefore would come out. Lloyd George was saying he might help to defend it, or he might not. Asquith's reply was dated 3 November 1915, the day after he returned to the House of Commons, although marked 'Secret and Immediate,' which suggests that Lloyd George may not have sent his letter on the date he assigns in his War Memoirs, 31 October. There is the reference at the end to 'tomorrow's Cabinet'.[85] On 31 October the Prime Minister remained ill in bed.[86]

Asquith was clearly alert and in action by 3 November and no doubt suffering from the preliminary barrage laid down by Carson the day before in the House of Commons. He agreed to everything. He had 'arranged', he wrote that day to Lloyd George, that Kitchener would be shipped away. He would proceed immediately, the following day, to the eastern Mediterranean to confer with 'all our military and diplomatic experts in that quarter of the world. . .' Obviously this would take some time and meanwhile Asquith would manage the War Office. While there he promised to put things 'on a better footing and in particular come to a complete understanding with you' on relations with the Ministry of Munitions. He concluded:

We avoid by this method of procedure the immediate supersession of K. as War Minister, while attaining the same result. And I suppose even B.L. [Bonar Law] would hardly object to such a plan.
Yours very sincerely,
H.H.A.[87]

On 1 November Bonar Law had written to Lloyd George asking whether Lloyd George would object if he spoke to the Prime Minister saying that only 'disaster' lay ahead if Kitchener remained at the War Office and that he agreed that Lloyd George could not continue to take responsibility for events.[88]

Kitchener's odyssey, which caused immense bitterness later in the army and was at the root of much of Lloyd George's trouble the following autumn with General William Robertson, nevertheless made things immediately simpler at the Ministry of Munitions. In the vital matter of the concentration of ordnance design and inspection under the Ministry of Munitions Asquith, of course, was as good as his word. After a reminder from Lloyd George, which pointed out that in France Albert Thomas had complete control of everything, the Prime Minister summarily abstracted General Von Donop's remaining functions, leaving the Master General with nothing to do, and lodged them in munitions. Von Donop retained his title until Lloyd George became Secretary of State for War.[89]

It would seem, thus, that Kitchener's almost useless mission to the eastern Mediterranean was to a large extent prompted by the Prime Minister's perception that he must choose between Lloyd George and the War Secretary. Lloyd George's letter, containing more than a hint of resignation, blaming the War Office for all the disasters of the past months, clearly reinforces this conclusion. The decision may not have been easy for the Prime Minister. Only two weeks before Asquith had described Kitchener's place in the government in nearly the same warm terms he had used with Lloyd George in September. 'So long as you and I stand together,' he had written on 17 October, 'we carry the whole country with us. Otherwise the Deluge.'[90] In dealing with conscription, which was the pressing political problem of the moment, this was undoubtedly true as even Lloyd George acknowledged, and the Prime Minister sincerely valued both men. Yet in the autumn of 1915 Kitchener's days were over. The journey to the Orient was the beginning of his sad decline and a victory of sorts for Lloyd George.

V

The decisions put off in the summer and autumn of 1915 had to be faced before the end of the year. On 9 November, Nish (Nis) in Serbia on the Bulgarian border fell to the Germans. The direct railway link to Constantinople was now open. The Germans could rebuild and rearm the Turkish army. The British position on Gallipoli, hopeless for offensive purposes since the failure of the Suvla operation, would within months become untenable. The decision to evacuate, over which the government had been dawdling for months, was imperative. (His control of the agenda constituted one of Asquith's favorite tools of Cabinet management. Questions that were likely to be divisive or unpleasant, conscription, Salonika, or the evacuation of Gallipoli, simply were not allowed to come up. He would adjourn the Cabinet for tea.)

But this involved a second decision. What of the recently arrived force at Salonika, badly supplied, with little artillery, occupying potentially hostile Greek territory and faced by a large and newly triumphant Bulgarian army? Should it, could it, be allowed to remain in Greece, particularly if the much more powerful force on the Gallipoli peninsula, a potential reinforcement in an extremity, were pulled out? However, to make matters more complicated, there was still a large, demonstrably brave, Serbian army retreating to the southwest down the Vardar valley. The war had begun for the defense of Serbia. Were the Serbs to be abandoned?

This led then to the third dilemma. If the iron logic of bayonet strength and weaponry dictated that both expeditions should be withdrawn at once, what became of Britain's military position on the southern shore of the Mediterranean and in the Orient east of Suez, not to mention its prestige in the Islamic world? Hundreds of thousands of Turks concentrated for a year to defend their capital city, all newly rearmed, would be released to destroy a tiny force under Major General Charles Townshend already endangered in Kut in Mesopotamia. With Mesopotamia cleared where would the Turks go next, possibly into Persia or, infinitely worse, to the Suez Canal.

The fact was that Asquith's machinery for the direction of the war and indeed the temperament of the Prime Minister himself were ill-equipped to make these decisions. The story of the Salonika force became a comedy of uncertainty. Three days after the fall of Nish the new War Council at its first official meeting, on 12 November, decided to warn the French that the British were determined to inform the Greeks that unless they joined the Allies, Salonika would be neutralized.[91] To this the French agreed, although stipulating that coercion should not be announced until Salonika was secure.[92] Three days later, with the Serbians still withdrawing to the south toward the Adriatic and the railway to Monastir in danger from the Greeks, the War Committee declared that even though it was too late to open communication with the Serbs, Salonika should be held to prevent it 'becoming an enemy submarine base'.[93]

These were robust decisions. However on 1 December Kitchener returned. Two days later, in the Cabinet, after going over the disasters in the Eastern Theater — Mesopotamia (Kut was finally surrounded on that day), Gallipoli and Salonika were impending catastrophes, not to mention Egypt — he announced, according to Asquith's letter to the King, that 'he could take no further responsibility for the conduct of the war unless our troops were at once withdrawn from Salonika and the earliest and the most certain of these catastrophes thereby averted.'[94] The Cabinet promptly reversed itself and agreed. (In defense of this remarkable change of opinion it should be noted that the Cabinet had before it a recent letter on Greek opinion by a Mr. J.J. Stavridi which warned that there was absolutely no war sentiment in Greece. She would not honor her alliance with Serbia no matter how many Allied troops were in the country. Moreover, King Constantine probably represented the public consensus that the Germans would win the war better than did Venizelos who had invited the Allies in.)[95]

At the meeting of 3 December the Cabinet after dithering for some time about how to tell the French that Britain now intended to leave Salonika finally approved a telegram to Paris announcing its decision. That evening came a stinging reply from the French accusing the British of disloyalty. The result was an emergency meeting at Calais the next day, 4 December, between Briand, since 29 October French Premier, and Generals Joffre and Galliéni, and Asquith, Balfour and Kitchener. Lloyd George, pointedly, was not invited.[96]

The meeting clearly was an unhappy one. Just two days before, on 2 December, Briand had appointed Joffre supreme commander of the French armies, thus giving him responsibility for the Eastern Mediterranean Theater over Sarrail. Joffre now wished to stay in Salonika but Kitchener announced that he intended to stay instead in Gallipoli and would resign unless the Allied force were evacuated from Salonika. Townshend earlier had been repulsed at Baghdad — the Turks must not be able to claim victory everywhere.[97] After an hour's private conversation with, as Albert Thomas later recounted to Lloyd George, 'a pistol to their heads,' the French delegation agreed.[98] The British could withdraw. But by the time the French had returned to Paris everything had changed. Sarrail had been defeated by the Bulgarians, and the Socialists, upon whom the *Union Sacré* depended, insisted that Salonika should be not evacuated but reinforced.

Such was the background of Albert Thomas's famous mission to London on 6 December where he and Lloyd George induced the British government to change its mind yet again about Salonika. Thomas had sent, prior to his arrival, a telegram, with a warning that the Briand ministry would fall if Salonika were evacuated. Clemenceau would come in and President Poincaré might resign. This was discussed at the War Committee meeting earlier in the day where Kitchener repeated his threat to leave office and, according to Frances Stevenson, Lloyd George said that the Germans had told the Greeks that they would allow an Allied withdrawal which the Greeks could supervise. 'It is a good thing that the British and the Germans have found something to agree upon at last,' growled Lloyd George to the War Committee as he told Frances Stevenson.

> Here are the Germans asking for our withdrawal and here are we replying that it is the thing we wish most to do at present! It is a long time since the British and the Germans have been so unanimous upon any point! Surely this must be the beginning of concord between us and the enemy![99]

Apparently Albert Thomas arrived in London immediately after this acrimonious morning War Committee meeting. In any event he appeared in time to have lunch with Asquith at No. 10, which Lloyd George claimed to have arranged, and changed the Prime Minister's mind again. The British would stay. Lloyd George recounted three years later to Robertson Nicoll on 30 September 1918, having received that day Bulgaria's surrender, how Thomas's wit and cogency, translated by Paul Mantoux who also became a source for this encounter, charmed Asquith. Thomas did not apparently discuss the political repercussions in France were the Salonika army to be evacuated.[100]

Lloyd George insisted in this later account of the affair that Asquith's conversion was chiefly Thomas's work. On the same day, 30 September 1918, Lloyd George wrote to Thomas congratulating him: 'Without your opportune intervention the Austrians would have occupied Salonika. Greece would have become in reality a German colony and the great victory on the flank of the Central Powers, occurring at this moment, would never have been produced.'[101]

Thus British eastern strategy changed again, although typically Asquith allowed the decision to be blurred. Apparently at Lloyd George's suggestion, Grey, and Kitchener, whose mind already was changing on Salonika as it had so frequently over troops for the Dardanelles, were sent to Paris to settle matters as they thought best.[102] Grey, who comes as close in his memoirs as he could to admitting a mistake on Bulgaria, came back from Paris believing that at least he had saved the Briand government.[103]

A year later, in November 1916, Lloyd George, clearly still furious, put together his thoughts on the failure of Britain's eastern strategy in a memorandum to be presented to the French at the annual military planning conference at the French headquarters at Chantilly. Although this document appears in full in his memoirs, the paragraph on Salonika, excised by Asquith lest it offend the French command, summarizes perfectly the argument of this study on the critical mistakes of November and December 1915.

> I hold in the history of 1915 the case of Serbia to be the most unpardonable and, I fear, the most irreparable of all the Allied failures. We realize now how important it was for us to block the German road to the east. We could have cut off their supplies. We should have given the German people the sense of being hemmed in, and what would have been more destructive to their morale than the consciousness of that fact? We could have won Bulgaria and organized a great Balkanic Federation with a reserve of 2,000,000 fighting men, which we could have gradually equipped and made formidable armies out of for attacking the Germanic Powers in a ring of flame. Turkey, with very little ammunition and hardly any power to manufacture it, would soon have collapsed from sheer exhaustion. This could have been accomplished by the timely occupation of the Vardar Valley with half the forces which are now in Salonika, and a third of the men who fell in fruitless and fatuous attacks on German barbed-wire entanglements in the Western campaigns of 1915. Instead of this, what has happened? The German road to the east is open from Belgrade to Baghdad; she is supplied with corn, cotton, coffee, tea, copper and, what is still more important, with first-class fighting men. These facts have given her people new hope. Bulgaria is equipped, Turkey is reorganized; Greece is overawed with a third of her people hostile to the Allies; Serbia is destroyed;...An attempt was made to occupy the Vardar Valley in November, 1915. We realised at last how vital it was to seize the bridge to the east. But it was then too late. The Balkans, which might have been an asset, are now a heavy burden.[104]

The effective end of the Derby recruitment scheme came on 11 December just days after the resolution of the Salonika crisis. On 22 December 1915 the Cabinet met to consider his report.[105] In the interval the withdrawal from Gallipoli had begun with the evacuation of men from Suvla Bay and Anzac Cove in which, against all predictions, there was not a single loss of life. Derby's statistical conclusions were stark. The Prime Minister had promised that married men who signified their willingness to serve (i.e. to 'attest') would not be called until the available unmarried men were called up. Accordingly two thirds more married than single men had attested. But the cold figure remained that there were well over two million men of military age in the nation, not in munitions work, who were presumably available for military service and Asquith had warned on 2 November, albeit obliquely, that if the Derby Scheme were unsuccessful in producing enlistments, compulsion would have to follow. Everyone knew what the numbers meant. 'The moment that one emerges from any crisis,' wrote Asquith to Mrs. Henley that day,

> one is engulfed in another. The Cabinet met for the first time to consider the Derby Report. The impression left upon me is profoundly disquieting.
>
> The discussion unhappily followed party lines (Lloyd George and Henderson were away), and to judge from today's experience we seem to be on the brink of a precipice. The practical question is — Shall I be able during the next ten days to devise and build a bridge?[106]

The Prime Minister probably was relieved that Lloyd George on 22 December was absent from the Cabinet on his way to the unpleasant meetings in Glasgow. Two days before, on 20 December, Lloyd George had delivered what certainly must rank as one of the most powerful of his war-time parliamentary addresses, the famous 'Too Late' speech, already discussed in connection with the Ministry of Munitions. Indeed nearly all of it was devoted to a recitation of what he had accomplished there. But in his peroration, apropos of nothing that had gone before, he launched a powerful denunciation of 'British sloth and indecision'. He almost certainly was aiming at engineering employers and workmen in Scotland, but he was widely interpreted to be attacking the War Office or the Cabinet, or the Prime Minister.

The nation, he declared, had a contract with labor.

> We are carrying it out. It can be done. I wonder whether it will not be too late? Ah! Two fatal words of this War! Too late in moving here. Too late in arriving there. Too late in coming to this decision. Too late in starting with enterprises. Too late in preparing. In this War the footsteps of Allied forces have been dogged by the mocking spectre of 'Too late'; and unless we quicken our movements damnation will fall on the sacred cause for which so much gallant blood has flowed. I beg employers and workmen not to have 'Too Late' inscribed upon the portals of their workshops: that is my appeal.[107]

Part of Lloyd George's genius in oratory lay in the calculated inspecificity of his warnings or denunciations. Every Briton had been made to understand that he was defrauded by the dukes, oppressed by the Church, or called upon for national service in war. Such was the effect of the 'Too Late' address, even though nineteen twentieths of it was devoted to the accomplishments of the Ministry of Munitions. Some cartoonists saw it as an attack upon the government or Asquith for dawdling over conscription. Many others believed it directed at the War Office. Lord Derby asked Riddell afterwards how Lloyd George and Kitchener could remain in the same Cabinet. Frances Stevenson recorded that Von Donop was going over it line by line.[108]

Lloyd George returned to London from Glasgow on 26 December. The next day the Cabinet was to meet to deal with conscription in the light of the Derby figures. At noon Lloyd George sent Asquith a note, via Lord Reading, saying, according to Frances Stevenson,

> that if the P.M. kept his promise to the compulsionists, he (D)[avid] would stand by him through thick and thin; that if there were a general election, he (D) would do all the dirty work up & down the country — speaking & the like and would work for him like a nigger. If however the P.M. did not see his way to keep his promise, he (D) would be obliged to send in his resignation, but whatever happened, D. made it quite clear to the P.M. that under no circumstances would he take office in a Tory government.[109]

This last statement according to Reading greatly pleased Asquith. The consensus among anti-conscriptionists was that Lloyd George was using conscription to force an election, which the Conservatives would win overwhelmingly. Bonar Law would become Prime Minister to be controlled by the 'sinister alliance' of Carson and Lloyd George.[110]

Lloyd George of course was always threatening to resign and had done so in the past autumn, or at least had implied it. But this threat evidently was genuine although the letter seems to have disappeared. That morning he had written to Maggie:

> [In Welsh] A very important Cabinet this afternoon. P.M. & his gang trying to sneak out of their pledges. If they do I wash my hands & come out. I have made up my mind. My path is clear in front of me & as you know under these conditions I am always happy, whatever happens. By 5 p.m. I may be plain Lloyd George.[111]

As it turned out Asquith adjourned the Cabinet at 5 p.m. without a minute's discussion of conscription. The entire meeting was devoted to the admittedly critical matter of the evacuation of Cape Hellas. Now that the troops at Anzac Cove and Suvla Bay had been withdrawn, the Turks would be expecting it.

In the Cabinet, according to Miss Stevenson, Lord Curzon shouted that the Prime Minister had been deliberately wasting time to avoid the discussion of conscription. Asquith agreed to another meeting the next day. As a result on 28 December Britain adopted conscription. 'Cabinet satisfactory', Lloyd George wrote to his wife. 'P.M. dropped on the right side. Compulsion for unmarried men. There may be resignations. Not certain. Simon, Runciman & McKenna threaten — but doubt it.'[112]

Considering the monumental importance of the decision — the inevitable corollary of the unconsidered decision in August 1914 to send a mass army to France — Asquith's note to the King was terse. The Cabinet, he reported, considered the Derby scheme.

> Much difference of opinion was manifest.

> In the end a proposal by the Prime Minister to the effect that unmarried men of military age, who did not within a prescribed time — perhaps three weeks — satisfy the local tribunals that they had good ground for exemption, should be deemed to have attested and liable as such, was agreed to.

The Prime Minister noted 'reservations' by McKenna and Runciman.[113]

So appeared the first British military conscription bill, the so-called 'Bachelor's Bill', which was based upon Asquith's logic applied to the Derby scheme: that if British men were to be pressed for military service unmarried men should come first. The politics were peculiar, a typical Asquithian fork. Those most opposed to conscription were the principled, earnest, generally younger Liberal radicals, who in earlier days had supported and revered Lloyd George and cheered land reform but who now revered Asquith. Many had signed the petition against British intervention in France a year and a half earlier at the end of July in 1914. For them military conscription would lead inevitably to industrial conscription which was not necessary; the Derby figures were wrong. In any case conscription would turn Britain into the Prussianized state that the war was supposed to prevent.[114] Yet to vote against detested conscription meant not only to vote against the wishes of their beloved Prime Minister but to vote for a general election which everyone was convinced would result in a figurehead Bonar Law government controlled by Lloyd George and Carson, and for the end of the 'great career', as Dillon put it, of H.H. Asquith.[115] To vote for one's conscience was to play into the hands of the enemy. Lloyd George himself of course was a puppet of Northcliffe. Hankey described their dilemma succinctly a few months later during the debate over the second Military Service Bill: 'Those who want compulsory service don't want Asquith, while those who want Asquith don't want compulsory service.'[116]

Asquith, one cannot doubt, understood all this perfectly well. As he had done on several occasions before, notably in the Marconi vote, he allowed the whips to circulate the warning that if the vote against the Bachelor's Bill exceeded 150 he would dissolve and the Tories would be in office for 20 years.[117] He was pronouncing the extinction of the old Liberalism.

However, there remained another immediate, non-ideological imperative pressing the Radicals to disregard their consciences, hardly mentioned by newspapers, yet evidently discussed in Cabinet and clearly present in the minds of the desperate and angry Liberal and Labour purists seeking to retain some vestige of the creed to which they had devoted their political lives. As the Bachelor's Bill, technically the Military Service Bill, lay on the Table of the House of Commons at the beginning of January 1916, the Parliament Act (Amendment) Bill extending for a year the life of the December 1910 parliament was before the almost totally pro-conscription House of Lords. The failure to approve it by the upper house would bring an automatic general election in which the country surely would commend their Lordships' action by bringing the Unionists to power. Prolongation of parliament hung, as Llewelyn Williams put it during the first reading of the Bachelors' Bill, like a Sword of Damocles over the government and the debates on conscription.[118] The alternatives were the destruction of old Liberalism or the murder of the Liberal party.

In the event, the Military Service Bill — introduced by Asquith on 5 January 1916; it became law on 27 January — passed quickly if not quietly. On the First Reading the vote was 403 to 105. Of those opposed 34 were Liberal, including Simon and Runciman from the Cabinet, and 11 Labour. The rest were Irish.[119] On the Second Reading only 27 Liberals opposed the bill. John

Simon spoke against it alone. Lloyd George, present and voting, did not speak, but his influence was evident.

Remarkably, among the anti-conscription Liberals recorded against the bill there were few Welsh MPs, who usually counted as Radicals. Most of the leaders of the party, including some with whom Lloyd George had been associated for years, notably Ellis Griffith and Herbert Lewis, supported the measure. Among the small number against it, however, was Llewelyn Williams, who with Herbert Lewis perhaps Lloyd George's oldest living political friend. Williams spoke angrily against the conscription bill, the government that had produced it, and suggested that there had been pressure from Lloyd George. He would rather see such a measure from a Tory government which at least believed in it, Williams declared, than from a Liberal one which professed volunteerism 'while cutting its throat'. He noted that the House of Lords could put the government out in a moment. If so, he admitted, the House may have heard his voice for the last time. The Minister of Munitions had great influence in Williams's constituency.[120]

The Bachelor's Bill was only the beginning of the conscription debates. They would break out again with even more fury in May with the second Military Service Bill. As Williams had explained the January measure was the least that could be put before the House, designed only to establish the principle; the real measure would come later.[121] But the January divisions were of some importance for Lloyd George. Asquith was forgiven the odium of military conscription, even the comprehensive second bill. The story already current in the Liberal newspapers, that it was forced upon him by Lloyd George in conspiracy with the Tories, became conventional Radical wisdom. In a sense, of course, this was true although the second part of the story: that Lloyd George hoped to eject Asquith from office was not. No one seems to have doubted that in a general election the Liberals would have been heavily defeated.

Yet it must be said again, the winter of 1915–16 saw the beginning of the rot of the new Liberalism of which Lloyd George had been the steward and architect if not designer. Economic, as opposed to political, enfranchisement, care for the sick and elderly, the pillorying of the dukes, symbols of the establishment, the destruction of the land monopoly, the attacks on dreadnoughts, had dazzled an entire generation of young MPs who had flocked to his side. Masterman, then Addison, were their shepherds. To be sure, some had disappeared in the elections of 1910. But many remained. Any scrutiny of the list of dividers against the Bachelor's Bill will show that of the 45 Liberals and Labour, leaving aside the Irish who opposed the bill, 34 would enter the lobby against Lloyd George on 9 May 1918 in the division over a Select Committee to investigate General Maurice's charges about British troop strength in France. And not one anti-conscriptionist supported him.

One must conclude then that even though many were disappointed with Asquith over conscription, the same men came to hate Lloyd George. But finally it may be too much to say that military conscription alone separated Lloyd George and the Liberal radical reformers who had supported him for so long. A.G. Gardiner's newspaper attack on 18 September it will be remembered had been provoked by Lloyd George's forward to the collection of his speeches which had appeared in *The Times* on 13 September and, as a call for national service coupled with a warning of the weakness of Russia, was in reality simply a demand for greater organized effort in Britain. Indeed at that time some Liberal idealogues, J.A. Pease for example, believed conscription was dead.[122] Lloyd George's anger had proceeded from his dismay at the slackness of labor. The unpopular speech to the T.U.C. at Bristol a few days later was another manifestation of the same anger. Basically the divisions of 'Prussianism' in organization, as opposed to what Llewelyn Williams had styled 'voluntarism', the essential Liberal belief in individual rights, was a far larger matter than simply military conscription. A war for the defense of freedom could result in the destruction of freedom. How seriously the rump of Asquithians took all of this may be seen in their long and anguished debate over the matter after the war, which continued well into the Hitler period.[123]

Over all of this debate hung the shade of Lloyd George's connection with Northcliffe, unclear but always denounced as pernicious. What benefit Lloyd George derived from this association beyond a certain amount of support from powerful newspapers is hard to say. He was always singled out for praise in the general denunciations of sloth and uncertainty in the Asquith government. And despite Riddell's repeated warnings of danger to come from the connection, it was Northcliffe who sought out Lloyd George, not the other way around. Of course Northcliffe appeared as a political monster to A.G. Gardiner and the rest of the Liberal press but it is hard to believe that had the relationship with Lloyd George never existed, the Minister of Munitions would have fared better. The gulf was too wide. 'Humdrum Liberalism,' Lloyd George had observed in 1885 as he excitedly watched Joseph Chamberlain try to inject some new ideas into the party to which he belonged, 'won't win elections.' Thirty years later he could have remarked that it would not win wars either.

In the last reckoning, the disease spread in politics by the military disasters of 1915, to which conscription was little more than the chief response — the Balkans, the Dardanelles, the Battle of Loos, the Russian loss of Poland — weakened Asquith most of all. In the first week of January 1916 precisely as the first reading of the Bachelor's Bill took place, Sir Edward Carson, recovered from illness, returned to the House of Commons and announced the formation of a Unionist War Committee. By the following week 80 Conservatives had joined the group and soon it contained nearly all the Unionist back-bench Members not in active service.[124] Its stated goal was more vigorous prosecution of the conflict, but its real goal was the destruction of the Prime Minister.

For Lloyd George, no less than for Asquith, the events since May were critical. By the end of 1915 he had lost most of his personal political following, the new Liberals. He never was able to establish one again. Most of these men, not all, Llewelyn Williams for example, simply became Asquithians who revered Asquith whether he was successful or unsuccessful. They voted with him in the Maurice debate and saw their political careers die in 1918. With their colleagues in the press they deified him after his death as the last of the Augustans. Lloyd George had no one.

So long as the war lasted this counted for little. There were plenty of men in both parties, including many who actively disliked Lloyd George, who felt that Asquith would lose the war and that Lloyd George, perhaps only Lloyd George, could win it. He was not trusted but he was indispensable. Eventually this sense of necessity would make him Prime Minister, but he remained Britain's political Ishmael for the rest of his life.

8 Conscription, Ireland and the Crumbling of Liberalism

Among the political-military events of the tortured month of December, 1915, beside the replacement of Sir John French as Commander in Chief in France by Sir Douglas Haig, hitherto General Officer Commanding the First Army, was the curious partial supersession of Lord Kitchener as Secretary of State for War by General Sir William Robertson. The complaints about Kitchener have been recounted. Kitchener himself, while in the East, had determined to resign and take either command in Egypt or a post, as Hankey understood it, of roving Commander-in-Chief.[1] However, Kitchener had written also, perhaps while still away, to General Robertson, Chief of Staff of the British Expeditionary Force in France, asking him to come to London to replace General Sir Archibald Murray as Chief of the Imperial General Staff.

These changes brought two new figures, neither of whom Lloyd George knew well at the time, into the political world. Indeed even after he became well acquainted with both, he was never able to understand them. In the end it was against this pair of officers that Lloyd George waged one of his longest and perhaps most futile political campaigns, at its center over strategic alternatives, but in a larger sense over political control of the army. Although he succeeded in destroying, for practical purposes, Robertson's career, Haig emerged from the war, a hero and an earl, with a £100,000 grant from parliament. More important in his war with the army Lloyd George spent a large piece of his political capital, but in the end he failed, nonetheless, to replace the Western Front as the chief theater of conflict.

Haig, born in 1861, was a Scot, a devout Presbyterian, and a wealthy man with connections to John Haig distillers. He was on good terms with the King. He was considered something of an intellectual and had done a certain amount of writing on military topics but his interest in innovation in the soldier's art did not provide him with a willingness to accept suggestions about his business either from subordinates or from politicians. His convictions on tactical doctrine, the nature of battle, the supremacy of the bayonet — the wearing out battle and the final, victorious assault with bayonet — were implacably traditional. Moreover, he was a little shy with the politicians he detested and although forthright and articulate in writing he was unable to present oral arguments forcefully. When questioned by his political superiors he tended to retreat into stubborn silence.

Unlike Sir John French, whom he replaced, Haig, and the military command establishment he symbolized, was unpopular with soldiers in the trenches, both officers and enlisted men. He seemed to be aloof, absentee, uncaring.

He could never bring himself, the tradition went, to understand that his two great offensives, the Somme and Passchendaele were demonstrable failures days after they had begun. Accordingly after the war there grew a volume of legend about British command incapacity to which Lloyd George himself contributed in his memoirs.

Yet Haig was, in fact, a meticulous organizer as he proved militarily at the Battle of Amiens on 8 August 1918, and much earlier in the admirably efficient housekeeping arrangements of the B.E.F., at which the French could only marvel. Such necessaries as regular food, the division canteens for hot meals to and from the front, mail, footgear, care of animals, heavy clothes and the invaluable ground sheet, medical evacuation, railway transportation, particularly light railways parallel to the lines about which there were continual disputes with the French, were all matters in which Haig took a personal interest and demanded peremptory supervision. Many social historians have noted the beneficial physical effects upon men of military service in the First World War. Recruits, particularly from city slums, grew sturdier, put on weight, seemed indeed to be taller, and had had their teeth attended to for the first time in their lives. Haig was unimaginative and depressingly single minded, but was not, as Lloyd George believed him to be, stupid. Significantly when Lloyd George sent Jan Smuts and Maurice Hankey to France early in 1918 to find a better replacement for Haig within the platoon of battle-hardened generals who were by that time available, the two men had to report that there was no one.

In this connection one must take note of Lloyd George's comment in his memoirs that the best general of the war was a colonial officer whom he did not name. This is certainly Sir John Monash who is justly famous in Australia but unknown in Britain. He would have been considered totally unsuitable as a commander. Besides being a colonial, he was a part-time soldier, an engineer by profession, and a Jew.

Sir William Robertson, always known as 'Wully', was a less complex and in many ways a more attractive character than Haig. Born in 1860 in Welbourn, in the most English of counties, Lincolnshire, where his father was the tailor and village postmaster, he was, despite the name, the quintessential English soldier, bluff, hard working, commonsensical. He had joined the Army in the ranks in 1877, received a commission through sheer hard work in 1888 and had risen rapidly. Twenty years later he succeeded as Commandant of the Staff School at Camberley Henry Hughes Wilson, who left Robertson, without resources except his salary, a large debt for furniture. In his last year at Camberley Robertson received the K.C.V.O. He records in his memoirs that he was unsure of what to do and so after being dubbed, when the King extended his hand for the kiss of homage, Robertson, like an honest Englishman, rose to his feet and shook it. There was some consternation but His Majesty was amused. In 1915 Robertson was a Major General.

Well before his appointment as Commander of the Imperial General Staff Robertson was something of a celebrity. Riddell records being told by John Seely, then Secretary of State for War, whom he had asked about Robertson, that the General was 'a wonderful man' who would probably become Commander in Chief one day. Everyone, Riddell noted, spoke this way of Robertson.[2] Riddell further notes that Lloyd George, who had not then met

Robertson, remarked in October 1914 that the general should be appointed to C.I.G.S. to do something about the War Office's slackness.[3] Lloyd George seems to have encountered the general for the first time during his trip to France in the first week of February 1915, when he went to see the Russian and French Ministers of Finance while trying to build support for the Salonika alternative. He came away much impressed and again declared he would press for some high command for Robertson.[4] Riddell noted that Churchill had told him that he would rather meet Robertson than anyone he did not know already. At the same time Lloyd George told Frances Stevenson that Robertson was by far the ablest general he had met since the war began, except for Kitchener.[5] These judgments would change.

Haig shared these opinions of Robertson and proposed in November 1915 through Lord Esher that Robertson take over and make something of the post of C.I.G.S., which under Archibald Murray amounted to nothing.[6] Haig was still only General Officer Commanding the First Army but he understood, as did the entire political-military world including Sir John French himself, that the failure at Loos would mean a change in the command of the British Expeditionary Force.

Robertson's appointment followed immediately upon Kitchener's return from the Mediterranean on 1 December 1915. Robertson had replied to Kitchener's invitation on 5 December by stipulating that only the C.I.G.S. would give advice on military operations to the Cabinet. This change would mean also that the normal channel of communication between the army in France and London would be the C.I.G.S. leaving the Secretary of State with control only of recruitment, supply, and discipline at home. To all of this Kitchener agreed telling Asquith that he wished to resign.[7] As it turned out Asquith was able to persuade Kitchener to stay even with his much reduced powers. The appointments of Haig and Robertson were announced in the second week of December, and Robertson's arrangements were formalized by an Order in Council.

The humbling of Kitchener had an immediate and curious sequel, which in view of what happened after the Secretary of State's final departure is of some importance. In the middle of January 1916 Lloyd George was invited to dine with Lord Reading, Reginald McKenna and Edwin Montagu. As these men except for Reading were hardly his friends, the point of the occasion was not clear. It transpired that the Prime Minister believed Kitchener would soon resign and Asquith wanted Lloyd George's opinion on a successor. Lloyd George responded that anyone would be better than Kitchener, even J.A. Pease. Eventually Montagu asked the critical question: would Lloyd George take the War Office with the promise of support from all? Lloyd George admitted that his work at the Ministry of Munitions was practically done but that the War Office would be 'frightfully difficult' and there were 'disasters still to come'.

As part of the celebration of good will McKenna proposed to Lloyd George that the two of them stop feuding. Together, he declared, they made a strong team and the endless quarreling upset the Prime Minister. They separated, according to Miss Stevenson, good friends, although she wondered how long it would last.[8]

One way to discern the goals that Lloyd George had in his mind at a given time is to note carefully the posts or ministries which he said he did not want. In May of 1915 he had told anyone who would listen that he was happy at the Exchequer and had no idea of moving to a new ministry. In January, with Kitchener effectively removed from control of military operations but consenting to remain at his post as a symbol, perhaps only temporarily, Lloyd George was denying any interest in the War Office, to which nevertheless he finally went in July on the same degrading terms that Kitchener held it.

The events that led to Kitchener's voyage to Russia in June 1916 may be therefore recorded briefly here, because they also involved a continual problem that had troubled the Ministry of Munitions since the beginning of Lloyd George's tenure there: the needs of the Czar's empire. Lloyd George had never doubted that without Russia the Allies were lost. This had been the argument for the 100 division British army and everything that went with it such as national service.[9] Russia constantly clamored for supplies of all kinds, but frequently it was not clear what the nation needed, or could use.[10] Although it had been granted huge loans since Lloyd George had admitted it to British financial markets in the autumn of 1914, Russian ordering procedures, both in Britain and in the United States, were wildly disorganized. By the beginning of 1916 with the Ministry of Munitions getting into stride, shipments to Russia were substantial. For example, three hundred heavy guns, Boulogne program production, were scheduled to be delivered in the three months of February, March and April 1916.[11]

The problem of Russian munitions became more complicated with the opening of the huge German attack on the French fortress of Verdun on 21 February, which greatly increased French claims both for larger deliveries of raw materials from Britain and for a major British military effort. Meanwhile strikes in Russia were slowing production there. On 25 April Albert Thomas wrote that he and René Viviani, a former Premier, were going to Russia simply to discover what Russia had in the way of munitions. On his return he hoped to pass through London to see Lloyd George so that the two could discuss the problem.[12]

The supply of Russia finally came to a head in a memorandum by McKenna dated 2 May 1916, put before the War Committee on 4 May. Russian credits granted on 30 September 1915, he announced, were now exhausted. Russia ordered everything with abandon and about two-thirds of the money borrowed in Britain was spent in the United States. No one could tell whether what was ordered was important. Were shoes, for example, more important than railway track? The Treasury was not in a position to make these determinations. A settlement with the Russian government was imperative. The War Committee agreed. A special emissary would be sent to explain to the Russian government and military leaders 'the essential connection between British finance and the cause of the Allies as a whole.'[13]

Such was the origin of the Kitchener mission to Russia. Maurice Hankey understood that Kitchener had already proposed that he go to Russia and that Hankey accompany him, while suggesting that the journey was simply another attempt to remove Kitchener from the War Office for a time. However, McKenna's memorandum described a situation that he considered genuinely serious and was consistent with everything else he believed about war finance.

In his memoirs Lloyd George states that Asquith 'had approached' him to go to Russia with Kitchener, an invitation he 'could not refuse', and that he was prevented from going only by the request from Asquith on 22 May to 'take up' Ireland as a consequence of the Easter rebellion.[14] To an extent — that Lloyd George perhaps should go to Russia with, or instead of, Albert Thomas — Maurice Hankey corroborates this.[15] But the British ambassador in Petrograd had replied immediately after the Russians had been informed of Kitchener's projected trip that the Czar's government wanted also to discuss the negotiation of more credits. Could not the Chancellor of the Exchequer come too?[16] This would have been McKenna, not Lloyd George. Nevertheless, the failure to leave with Kitchener became part of Lloyd George's personal mythology; it provided drama to his life. But like many other Lloyd George stories there are no independent sources. Frances Stevenson certainly would have commented upon the dangerous projected trip and Hankey's remarks deal with events in April. Finally, Asquith's request to Lloyd George to settle the Irish question came only two weeks before Kitchener's departure. On 5 June 1916, Kitchener was gone forever, and a month later Lloyd George's battle with the generals entered a new phase.

I

McKenna's distress over the strains imposed by the war upon British finances, always in the background of the Chancellor's opposition to Lloyd George, to his dislike of conscription, to aid to Russia, and much else, provided an undertone of despair in Cabinet debate in the winter of 1915–16. Just as British armies at last were becoming trained and equipped to an extent that would enable them to operate independently in the West, the nation was faced with bankruptcy.[17] According to a paper written by John Maynard Keynes, reported Lloyd George scornfully, the critical date was the end of the then fiscal year, 31 March 1916, after that the deluge. This paper, one of several submitted by McKenna, led to the appointment at the beginning of 1916, of the so-called War Resources Committee, chaired by Asquith, of which Lloyd George pointedly was not a member. The committee was officially the Committee for the Coordination of Military and Financial Effort. The members were Asquith, McKenna and Austen Chamberlain. The War Resources Committee, a typical Asquithian shuffle designed certainly to overcome McKenna's objections to conscription, has some importance as a learning and planning experiment of the sort that would be routine in World War II. For the first time manpower as opposed to money was examined as a finite resource. Thus for the historian the committee seems to mark the beginning of the movement from the crisis in munitions to the crisis in men. British strength was not infinite, wrote Austen Chamberlain to Lloyd George shortly before he gave evidence to the Committee. There could be such a thing as full mobilization. Seventy divisions, he thought, were a maximum and those not possible without conscription.[18]

All of this is a matter of some importance for Lloyd George's career, first because McKenna's hesitations caused Lloyd George's original encounter, evidently at some time in February 1916, with John Maynard Keynes whose subsequent influence over Lloyd George's financial thinking has become a matter of some discussion. But second, because Lloyd George's descriptions of Keynes written for his *War Memoirs* in 1933 are pungent and unflattering, they need to be quoted, with the reminder that Lloyd George is writing nearly eighteen years later. (It must be remembered that in the same year, 1933, Keynes had published his *Essays in Biography* with the always quoted sketch of Lloyd George: the 'goat footed bard, this half human visitor to our age''rooted in nothing'. (This, although written more than a decade before, Lloyd George may have seen.) McKenna had mobilized Treasury experts to convince the Cabinet that Britain could afford neither the money nor the men who would be lost in universal military conscription.

> The Chancellor [McKenna] and the President of the Board of Trade [Walter Runciman] more than hinted at the possibility of starvation for our sea-fed island. Mr. M'Kenna's nerve was shaken by the vaticinations of his chief advisor, Mr. J.M. Keynes. The latter was much too mercurial and impulsive a counsellor for a great emergency. He dashed at conclusions with acrobatic ease. It made things no better that he rushed into the opposite conclusion with the same agility. He is an entertaining economist whose bright but shallow dissertations on finance and political economy, when not taken seriously, always provide a source of innocent merriment to his readers. But the Chancellor of the Exchequer, not being specially gifted with a sense of humour, sought not amusement but guidance in this rather whimsical edition of Walter Bagehot, and thus he was led astray at a critical moment. Mr. Keynes was for the first time lifted by the Chancellor of the Exchequer into the rocking-chair of a pundit, and it was thought that his signature appended to a financial document would carry weight. It seems rather absurd when now not even his friends — least of all his friends — have any longer the slightest faith in his judgments on finance.[19]

At the time these paragraphs were written Keynes was working on *The General Theory of Unemployment.*

These of course are Lloyd George's sentiments of the early 1930s. Historical impartiality was not a conspicuous feature of his mental processes. There is no record of his reaction at the time to Keynes's paper or to a similarly gloomy one by John Bradbury. However, later in the spring of 1916, in one of his endless debates with McKenna over finance, in this case over aid to a France locked in the terrible battle at Verdun, Lloyd George provided a hint of his view of national mobilization at once simple and revolutionary, yet precisely the view taken by Keynes himself in the Second World War. France, McKenna had said, could not go on without money, but Britain could not afford to help her any longer. Money, Lloyd George retorted, 'was not relevant. It [war] was not a question of cash supply. If it meant the supply of coal or steel he agreed.'[20] The limits of a nation's fighting capacity, in effect, were not measured in debt or currency but in the hard numbers of steel and men. During the Second World War Keynes, with the resource budget he imposed upon the Treasury, would show that he also understood this.

Although Lloyd George emphasized in his *War Memoirs* that financial deadlines came and went without the heavens over Britain rolling together like a scroll, he was as aware as anyone that British resources were not un-limited. A shortage of shipping, as the President of the Board of Trade, Walter Runciman, was constantly predicting could quickly stifle Britain's war effort and the Germans it was known had begun construction of a fleet of large, long range, deep sea submarines. As has been mentioned, he knew that the Allied preponderance in manpower, constantly alluded to in the newspapers as insuring victory, depended entirely upon Russia. Lloyd George was one of the few who had never questioned Germany's strength. Accordingly he took an unusual interest in the two visits of Edward Mandell House, confidential advisor to the American President, Woodrow Wilson, to Britain in January and February 1916. For the biographer of Lloyd George these visits, although little came of them diplomatically, have a good deal of importance as indications of the progress of his consideration about the post-war settlement and of his anxiety, apparently alone in the government at this time, to bring the United States actively into the war on the side of the Allies. Finally, because he seemed to welcome the American proposals for a negotiated peace, his departure from this position and his public announcement in an interview with Roy Howard six months later that Britain would win the war at all costs and would countenance no negotiations caused a good deal of anger in the United States.

House arrived in Britain on 6 January 1916. On 11 January at a dinner at the American embassy with Ambassador Walter Hines Page, McKenna, Lord Reading, Austen Chamberlain and Lloyd George, House described his commission. 'The United States,' he said, 'would like Great Britain to do those things which will enable the United States to help Great Britain win the war.'[21] Quickly this became a plan for the Allies and Germany to consider war aims which would be preliminary to a conference to negotiate a peace. Should Germany decline to attend or to leave such a conference, as House clearly expected, the United States would throw its weight with the Allies.

This was a clumsy plan. Wilson's constitutional inability to commit the United States to war was its most obvious defect. Moreover it would appear that House, far more than Wilson, desired to intervene in Europe.[22] Finally, apparently coming to light for the first time in 1970 in the biography of Maurice Hankey, the Directorate of Naval Intelligence, the famous 'Room 40', had quickly broken the American diplomatic code and House's dispatches to Washington were in the hands of the British government. Hankey, who often reflected the Prime Minister's thinking, was scornful of the American initiatives; 'humbug and a mere manoeuvre of American electoral politics.'[23]

Alone among his colleagues except for Foreign Secretary Sir Edward Grey, Lloyd George took, or seemed to take, the American proposals seriously. House had felt the meeting at the American embassy was 'hopeless'. But at some time during the evening Reading confided that Lloyd George would like to see him alone.[24]

Three days later Lloyd George, House and Reading dined in a private room at the Savoy Hotel. Lloyd George had recently seen the film 'Birth of a Nation' and was interested in Reconstruction. However, House confided to his diary, 'I found him as ignorant as ever about our public men and affairs . . .' Lloyd George believed Britain would come out of the war healthier and more productive and wealthier. On the other hand he believed the war could go on indefinitely. At its end the Turkish empire must go. 'I tried to scare him as I have others,' wrote House, clearly not realizing Lloyd George had been talking for months of the same disaster, 'regarding Russia making a separate peace. . .'[25]

House amplified these private notes in his dispatches to President Wilson on 15 January. They were agreed that only Wilson's intervention could end the war. This should come, thought Lloyd George, at about the beginning of September 1916. It was clear there would be no victory by that time, but by then both sides would be equally exhausted and Wilson could dictate the terms of peace: an independent Poland, Alsace and Lorraine returned to France, Germany compensated in Asia Minor and Turkey 'eliminated'. Lloyd George insisted, House wrote, that he wanted a peace that would leave Britain and Germany friends.

Lloyd George believed it was vital that American diplomatic intervention should begin with a 'large' military and naval program. It might not have to be carried out, but it would enormously strengthen the American hand. Indeed such an initiative might fail if Wilson did not address this. Significantly two weeks later Hankey was recording in his diary the conviction that 'we must also educate Col. House that America's rôle, if she becomes involved in the war, will be one of finance and supplier to the Allies, not military. . .'[26] The only disagreement at the Savoy meeting, one indeed that would continue and appear at the end of the war, involved Lloyd George's unwillingness to admit the principle of freedom of the seas.

Lloyd George had obviously prepared a speech, which included, as always, a peroration and which showed he had divined correctly that there was in President Wilson more than a spark of vanity. House concluded:

> During the conversation he said that no man had ever lived with such an opportunity [to end a great war], and that if the world went on for untold centuries history would record this as the greatest individual act of which it had record.[27]

The next day House saw Grey and A.J. Balfour at No. 4 Carlton Gardens where Balfour stayed. He told them of the conversation with Lloyd George and of the important words for Woodrow Wilson. Had he discussed his ideas with them? 'They replied, "Not at all; he probably thought the thing out and seized upon your being in London to discuss it with you. . ."[28]

'I wish Lloyd George was Prime Minister,' wrote House in his diary four days later as he prepared to leave London for Berlin, 'with Sir Edward Grey as Foreign Minister, for I believe then we could do something. The Cabinet are all too conservative and boldness is needed at this time. George had this quality I believe. . .'[29]

Back in London on 10 February 1916 after visits to Berlin and Paris, Reading came to see House saying that Lloyd George wanted to continue their talks. The two men met the following evening, 11 February, with Reading. House was pleased by Lloyd George's interest but was disappointed that he was reluctant to endorse a peace conference, which Woodrow Wilson wanted before United States intervention in the war. A proposal for a conference would not be popular in Britain.[30] Lloyd George had no doubts about Britain's determination to win, but he questioned, as he had many times before, his nation's initiative and organization.[31]

Evidently at the same time that Reading had proposed the private meeting with Lloyd George, he had invited House to a larger gathering on 14 February. The dinner at Reading's house in Curzon Street three days later included, besides Reading, Lloyd George and House, Asquith, Grey, Balfour, and the American ambassador. Lloyd George himself in his *War Memoirs* conveys the impression that this was his only meeting with House while saying also that House's account was incomplete.[32] In any case at Reading's house, Lloyd George outlined before his colleagues essentially the same terms he had given House at the Savoy dinner the month before, the restoration of Alsace-Lorraine, Belgium and Serbia, the opening of the Straits, the cession of Italian areas held by Austria.[33] Lloyd George did not record that he suggested any plans for the compensation of Germany in the east, but in fact his conviction that Germany should not be left reduced, angry and bleeding after an Allied victory — that she should remain, on the contrary, a friend of Britain — would remain in his mind. Generally he thought in terms of compensation in the east, in Turkey of course, and, after the November 1917 revolution, in Russia as well.

Two days later, 15 February 1916, House had lunch and drove to the House of Commons with 'X', surely Lloyd George. Given the attendance at Reading's house it could have been no one else. The two discussed Asquith's silence the previous evening. He had take no part in the conversation. X had said this was the Prime Minister's weakness and he did not realize it, he appeared willing to sit 'as a passenger'. House found it odd that it was necessary to get opinions that should come from the Prime Minister from other ministers. X had insisted he had no wish to be Prime Minister under the present circumstances. (Had House suggested that he wished X were Prime Minister?)[34] House returned to the United States on 25 February.

The biographer must account for Lloyd George's activity in this short period, little more than a month, during which he attempted to inject himself into a large issue of foreign policy, British-American relations. After all, the initiative during the House visit was clearly his and came at a time when he was busy with the still simmering strike over dilution at John Laing's, the suppression of the *Vanguard,* and the general labor problem on Clydebank. Obviously he was inviting some form of American intervention in Europe by conveying to President Wilson Allied war aims that were eminently fair and reasonable and which the United States could support. Those proposals, including equitable treatment of Germany, would, he hoped, become the basis of a conference. Although he feared the popular reaction to the announcement of a conference, as did Grey, he would risk it for the assurance of American support particularly if American intervention was preceded by a substantial rearmament program. (Wilson was, in fact, touring the eastern United States during January and February, 1916 making speeches on precisely this point, referring to it as 'preparedness'.)

Yet, in all this, even with much sympathy from Col. House himself and evidently, according to House's diary, a good deal of support from Sir Edward Grey, he was bound to fail. First because Wilson constitutionally could not promise American participation in a European war should Germany break up a peace conference or decline to attend one. But second, more immediately difficult, the Allies and the United States were divided about the goals of the exercise upon which they were engaged. Wilson's biographer makes clear that the President sincerely wished for peace in Europe, hoped he would be able to bring it about, and personally was willing to do nearly anything toward this end.[35] But there was a clear difference in orientation. Wilson aimed toward peace, the European Allies wanted American participation to insure victory, not a negotiated settlement. There were exceptions among individuals, Grey being one. He became truly horrified at the international catastrophe for which he felt responsible as becomes clear in House's diary.[36] (Grey insists in his memoirs that he kept no written records of his conversations.)[37] But the French, Wilson soon learned, were adamant on this. They had no interest in a compromise settlement but they would have been glad for American participation in the war.[38] Clearly Wilson realized this, that he was being led, not toward the sponsorship of a European settlement, but toward American belligerency. Thus in the final memorandum written by Grey on 22 February to be taken by House to the United States for approval, the President inserted the caveat 'probably' in the critical sentence: 'Should the Allies accept the proposal [for a peace conference], and should Germany refuse it, the United States would *probably* enter the war against Germany.'[39] After this change, the House proposals, like many other decisions before the Asquith government, simply were allowed to drop.

For Lloyd George the House mission may be taken as a step in the solidifying of his position as a leading proponent of the hard line, victory at all costs. One has to doubt that he, who asserted more frequently than anyone the growing strength of Germany and the weakening of Russia, really believed that the enemy would agree to a conference. Yet he was conscious also of the military stalemate and soon came to fear a loss of determination, if not in the public at large, among his colleagues. The dithering over the cost of the war and conscription indicated a weariness that would grow more pronounced as 1916 progressed and would indeed become a large factor in the fall of the Asquith government. Hence Lloyd George took perhaps more seriously than any member of the government except Grey relations with the United States. He had seen America as a vital source of supply within weeks after the war began and had literally forced an unwilling military establishment to place orders there. 'D says that unless the U.S.A. come in to help us, we cannot hope for victory' wrote Miss Stevenson on the day following House's departure to America.[40] And so he welcomed, in the face of Asquith's manifest lack of interest, the tentative and probably unworkable offer of American intervention in Europe. Later in the year, in September, after the military disasters of the summer became coupled with growing impatience in America over rigorous blockade restrictions and the Irish crisis, he lectured the journalist Roy Howard in an interview controversial in both Britain and the United States on Britain's determination to see the war through to victory at any cost. But in January and February he sought for an American commitment. At this stage at least, most of the Cabinet thought it irrelevant.

II

Between House's first and second visit to London, from 28 to 31 January 1916, Lloyd George spent a week-end in France with Bonar Law chiefly at Haig's headquarters at St. Omer. Haig thoughtfully had recalled Lloyd George's sons Richard and William from the lines making the trip something of a reunion.[41] This was entirely pleasant, but the trip had some larger importance. Lloyd George came back much impressed with the new

Commander-in-Chief. The headquarters was 'business-like'. There was 'energy and more grip on affairs,' he related to both Riddell and Frances Stevenson. Under French there had been an atmosphere of a 'picnic'.[42]

There is no doubt Haig was efficient. The British army in World War I was well-administered if not imaginatively commanded. Lloyd George never admitted an earlier opinion with which he later disagreed, but Lloyd George's good opinion of Haig seems to have survived for at least six months, that is until the battle of the Somme.

Lloyd George visited also, on 31 January, Max Aitken's headquarters at St. Omer. Aitken, a Canadian, who became Lord Beaverbrook in December 1916, was a political associate of Bonar Law, and was the official Canadian observer in France, a congenial appointment that enabled him to move at will between France and London. As Aitken soon would become an important figure in Lloyd George's, and Churchill's, career, becoming as well a political force in his own right, one must note that at this time he was regarded in London as a somewhat mysterious, and slightly disreputable, figure. The patronage of Bonar Law had secured him a seat in parliament in 1910 and a knighthood in 1911, but he was widely distrusted. George Riddell did not like him even though, surprisingly for such a well-informed man, he did not know much about him. In August 1916 he wrote:

> Griffith, the Assistant Canadian High Commissioner, tells me that Max Aitken is endeavouring to get appointed High Commissioner. The outcome will be interesting. Aitken is said to have kept a skittles-alley in Calgary only a few years ago. His reputation is shady but he is an energetic, clever man. The position he has secured here is amazing, no doubt due in the first place to his friendship with Bonar Law who gave him the introduction to 'high circles'. Notwithstanding all criticism Bonar Law sticks to Aitken like a leech. The rumour of Aitken's financial misdeeds are persistent, but no specific evidence is forthcoming. Meanwhile judgment is suspended. He is good-natured but handicapped by his face, which does not inspire confidence.[43]

At Aitken's headquarters with Bonar Law and also Churchill, who had hurried up from his unit at Ploegsteert bringing in addition F.E. Smith, the five men had a serious political discussion. No notes were taken except by Churchill's aide, Lt. Hakewill Smith, which were to the effect that 'there was full and complete agreement that Asquith had to be got rid of at all costs.' There was also a hint, contrary to what Lloyd George had told McKenna and Montagu only two weeks earlier, that Lloyd George would like to be Secretary of State for War. Churchill's biographer suggests that this conversation may have reawakened in his subject his fascination for politics and inspired him to think of leaving France to return to Westminster.[44] Apparently Lloyd George told none of this to Miss Stevenson.

Finally on this visit, happy after seeing his sons and on his way home, Lloyd George had his initial encounter, in a military hospital, with the ghastly destructiveness of modern weapons upon soldiers. Miss Stevenson records that he was terribly depressed when he arrived in London very late on 31 January and spent most of the next day with her at a flat she had rented at 41A Chester Square. The sight of the unbelievable disfigurement caused particularly by the new bursting devices, shrapnel, shell splinters and grenades (to which land mines soon would be added), so unlike the clean wound of a rifle, seems entirely to have destroyed his composure. 'I feel I shall break down if I do not get right away from it all' he declared to Miss Stevenson as his first words.[45] Among others he had seen was the only son of John Hinds, Liberal MP for West Carmarthen. Part of young Hinds' head was blown away. Lloyd George reported that he had attempted to find specialists to help. However, the young man died soon afterward. 'I was not made to deal with things of war,' he confessed, '. . .this visit has almost broken me down.'[46]

Lloyd George was not a man to understate the depth of his feelings on any occasion, and the horror of modern war would afflict hundreds of thousands in Britain only months later after the beginning of the battle of the Somme causing a singular species of national trauma. But there may have been more here than theatrics. The cordiality of Haig's headquarters faded soon. What remained in him was undiluted bitterness at the carnage of stalemated trench warfare. He had of course known this since the autumn of 1914, but the concept of immovable lines, or even Highlanders felled by machine guns at Loos, were numeric statements. Lloyd George's mind always fixed on the individual. In the years of the new Liberals before the war the objects of his compassion had been the unemployed fathers of families, tramping from one factory gate to another, 'begging for work as they would for alms' or the weeping widows and hollow-eyed children of men killed in quarry disasters. The visions of individuals, not statistics, had inspired the national insurance program. On one hand there were statistics, on the other, people. And so Haig's cordial reception at St. Omer quickly disappeared from his mind. The Somme he regarded as a futile abomination, and Passchendaele a fiendish conspiracy against reason, the more repulsive because he, himself, was by then Prime Minister and might have forbidden it. He fills many pages of his *War Memoirs* with an explanation of why he did not do so.

He moved quickly from hating the huge setpiece battles to hating the commanders who doggedly ordered them while refusing to countenance any alternatives. Thus within six months began the struggle with Haig and Robertson, men so much admired at the beginning of 1916. Perhaps more than any other, this issue would set the tone of politics until the end of the war.

On 10 February 1916, the day, as it happened, that E.M. House returned to Britain from the continent, Ruby Carson, wife of Sir Edward Carson, noted in her diary:

> Mr. [H.A.] Gwynne [editor of the Morning Post] came to see me in the evening, said Lloyd George would soon resign, but saying on grounds of health, he said Asquith was quite useless & he could work with him no longer. LlG said Edward was the only man to save the Empire & he would do all he could to help.[47]

Carson and Lloyd George were by no means intimate at this time although each was going about London saying flattering things about the other in the peculiar minuet that often preceeded a political alliance. Just after his own resignation Carson, in the presence of one of the central retailers of parliamentary gossip, Almeric Fitzroy, had praised Lloyd George and Churchill as the only useful men in an otherwise worthless Cabinet which included his own nominal party leader, Andrew Bonar Law.[48] Lloyd George had lunched with Gwynne on 8 February, two days before the editor saw the Carsons, saying that as the Liberal papers were attacking him he needed a friend. The editor, according to Frances Stevenson, had told him that he and Carson were the only two men in the country who counted.[49]

Lloyd George's threats to resign had been, of course, so numerous that the writer of an account of his life feels constrained soon to ask forgiveness for reporting them, yet the Prime Minister seemed to take them seriously. Most recently, after all, such a threat had produced Kitchener's odyssey to the Levant and helped to bring about the Bachelor's Bill. But that measure, as Llewelyn Williams had quickly divined, was the weakest possible token to the principle of compulsion, intended chiefly to intimidate or reassure doctrinaire Liberals while causing the smallest possible reduction in the labor force. McKenna and Runciman, the senior Liberal purists in the Cabinet had voted for it.

Asquith evidently was much pleased with himself at having weathered the conscription hurricane with only one minor, and unimportant, resignation, that of John Simon. Margot Asquith, inevitably, advertised his complacency by putting it about, apparently widely; 'Nothing but God Almighty himself will drive Herbert out of Downing Street.' Lloyd George heard this from John Dillon.[50] Four days later C.P. Scott recorded being told almost precisely the same thing by Admiral Fisher.[51] Yet it hardly could have been expected that the first military service bill would work well and soon after the measure became law the Army Council was complaining that the actual intake of men under compulsion was lower than under the voluntary system.[52] In all this Lloyd George was hardly involved. He had not been included on the War Resources Committee. He was depressed. He felt tired and ill. He gave up his short morning conversations with Asquith on politics in general which the Prime Minister joked about but nonetheless depended upon. In the weeks after his return from France he referred constantly to the Hinds boy, who had died on 3 February. He deliberately stayed away from several Cabinet and War Committee meetings pleading illness, rarely attended the House and usually spoke only to answer questions on the Ministry of Munitions. He talked incessantly about leaving the government. His complaint, as conversations with Riddell, Scott, and Miss Stevenson all make clear, was not conscription but the general conduct of the war by the Prime Minister.[53] Meanwhile he waited for Carson to recover his health and return to London. Ronald McNeill, Carson's lieutenant wrote on 22 March:

> Lloyd George sent to me to-day to ask anxiously when you would be
> back. It may be significant of the way his mind is turning that he told
> me to tell you he thinks it very urgent that the question of settling
> the electoral register should be considered and some common line of
> action concerted. He will want to see you as soon as you come back.[54]

Carson had publicly cancelled all engagements on 8 February and in early March had retired to a house in Birchington, Kent, near Westgate. On 6 March, just before the couple left London, Lady Carson recorded, 'Bonar

Law came to see Edward & had tea, he thinks Asquith is the best man for Prime Minister. I am amazed, the first time he said it I thought it was a joke.'[55] Bonar Law was by no means the only man to feel the weight of the Prime Minister's powerful personality. Lloyd George also acknowledged it. But Carson, a fighter who saw only Asquith's distaste for controversy, his laziness and indecisiveness, was the wrong man to whom to make this admission. It only increased further his contempt for his party's leader.

In Birchington Carson received a stream of visitors generally wanting to discuss Asquith. On 25 March Lord Milner, Governor General in South Africa during the Boer war, a particular object of hate among all Liberal radicals and the focus of diehard anti-Home Rule and pro-conscriptionist sentiment in the House of Lords, and Geoffrey Robinson, editor of *The Times*, came for tea.

> ...they all made plans that Asquith must be *forced* [underlining in original] to go & say if not we shall lose the war. He has gone to bed because there is another crisis on & they say he is not the least ill. Lord Milner is splendid.[56]

The crisis referred to was General William Robertson's rising anger over the declining intake to the army. He was pressing the government all he could, he wrote to Haig on 22 March and was

> endeavoring to keep on a straight and simple road, and I shall not abate one jot of my purpose to get you men. I daresay this question may break up the Government before we have finished, and perhaps that is not altogether to be regretted...There is great agitation in London the last few days in regard to men...The present Military Service Act is a farce and failure. It was a regular political dodge, and of course political dodges will not stand the stress of war with Germany. We want men.[57]

One must say again that it seems impossible so astute a political manager as the Prime Minister should have expected the time bought by the Bachelor's Bill to be long. With a powerful and active C.I.G.S. as the effective spokesman for the army it could have been expected that the forces that had brought the first, weak, compulsion measure would press even more strongly for its extension. However Lloyd George, at this point feeling his isolation in the Cabinet and, as he told C.P. Scott a month later not wishing 'to alienate his radical supporters more than he could help' was not part of the conscription drive publicly and wished only to resign.[58]

Yet Asquith sensed a conspiracy. This could have come, of course, from McKenna but there may have been confirmation from his friend, the journalist J.A. Spender, who somehow came to possess notes of a conversation between Bonar Law and John Redmond on 15 March. The Unionist leader was even more gloomy than usual. He was convinced the present political situation could not continue. The government could be easily beaten if the opposition had a leader. Carson (still at Birchington) could do it if he had better health. Bonar Law did not think he was himself an alternative. What about Lloyd George, asked Redmond. Bonar Law replied 'You know George as well as I do.' Throughout the conversation Bonar Law, nonetheless, professed the greatest admiration for the Prime Minister.[59] In any case a long projected inter-Allied conference was to meet in Paris at the end of the month, made more important because it was the first Italy would attend as a belligerent. Lloyd George had not been asked to go to France but suddenly, as Hankey records 'There is a rumour of a political plot to be got up in his [Asquith's] absence by Lloyd George, Carson, and Churchill.'[60] It would appear that for once Asquith took the warning seriously. Lloyd George, who had no interest in the meeting was told that he must come because the French wanted him and Albert Thomas appeared fortuitously in London urging him to attend.[61] As it turned out he stayed in France only two days, recalled by labor trouble on the Clyde.

The inclusion of Churchill among the conspirators makes it likely that Asquith indeed had heard something of substance. Perhaps again he had heard (from Hankey?) of the meeting at Max Aitken's headquarters at St. Omer. Churchill himself by this time hated the Prime Minister more than any man alive. He was beginning to fear the bouts of depression, 'my disturbing moods', which afflicted him in France.[62] He longed to return to Westminster and help to lead an attack on the Prime Minister. This meant, as he realized, making peace with Carson. Carson, for his part, disliked Churchill intensely. Ruby Carson records in her diary an occasion in May 1915, when Sir Ernest Cassel, Churchill's friend and benefactor, had asked them to a gathering to meet Winston and Clementine Churchill, her husband had declined saying that he would not speak to the Churchills.[63]

The story of Churchill's return to politics is an unhappy one. Within days after the St. Omer meeting, on 2 March 1916, he came to London on a regular week's leave and upon hearing that naval estimates were to be debated determined to intervene to make the announcement that his participation in the war henceforth would be at Westminster Palace. Urged on by C.P. Scott and J.L. Garvin, editor of the *Observer*, he prepared an address that he hoped would combine a ringing denunciation of the Asquith government's management of the war with the settlement and reconciliation of feuds of the past, a combination of pugnacity and large mindedness, which would be, no doubt, Churchill's description of himself. Churchill, Lloyd George and Carson, Scott said to Churchill on the day before the speech, 'were the only three men in the front rank with the instinct for action and capacity for carrying on a great war. Carson was ill. George was for the time being under a cloud and Churchill alone remained.'[64]

These words from a Liberal sage who, as editor of a great newspaper, had been a power in party affairs when Churchill still was struggling with Greek at Harrow, may have occasioned the disaster that followed.[65] Churchill's speech, on 7 May, began as an admirable and informed dissertation on indecision and inaction at the Admiralty, particularly in warship construction, emphasizing the failure to complete programs begun by himself and Admiral Fisher more than a year earlier.

So far the speech had been excellent, commanding close attention from the House. However, at its conclusion Churchill offered, as he had promised, a practical proposal for improvement: Lord Fisher should return to the Admiralty. [66]

The House was stunned. Lloyd George, who was present, could not believe it. Churchill had insured, he told George Riddell, that Fisher would not return to the Admiralty. 'On the other hand, if he meant to improve his own position, he made a great mistake.'[67] Violet Bonham Carter who had been in the gallery records that she rushed to the Prime Minister's room where she found her father speechless with rage and Churchill's secretary, Edward Marsh, with tears in his eyes.[68] On 8 March Asquith talked to C.P. Scott who found him still furious. The speech variously was a piece 'of the grossest effrontery' and 'of impudent humbug'. Fisher and Churchill had done nothing but quarrel. Had it not been for that there would have been no coalition.[69]

The next day Churchill saw Asquith who gave an account of the meeting to his daughter, Violet. Evidently it was unpleasant. When they parted Churchill had tears in his eyes although Asquith professed to have insisted he had nothing but affection for the former First Lord. She recalled that her father had said

> that it was strange how little Winston knew of the attitude of others toward himself. He had spoken to my father, as he did to me, of the many ardent supporters who looked to him for leadership and my father had said to him, 'At the moment you have none who count at all.'[70]

These were weeks of misery for Churchill and for his wife, Clementine, who, with political instincts far more keen than his, had urged him to stay in France. There at least, one may say, he could die only once. Asquith's perception of course was correct. Churchill could not look beyond himself. He had immense courage, industry and intelligence, but he was and would remain totally self centered. He could see no point of view but his own. He could not compromise.[71] This characteristic made him impossible in Cabinet and had nearly cost him his portfolio early in 1914 during the debate with Lloyd George, who allowed him to prevail over the naval estimates. But it had brought almost universal anger among a far wider group of Liberals in the autumn, after the war began, over his outrageous behavior at Antwerp and over the general sense he conveyed that the war was his personal possession. No one mourned his departure. But despite Asquith's cruel assertion, he had still one friend 'who counted', David Lloyd George.

Churchill departed for France on 13 March 1916 sick at heart. On her return from Dover Clementine stopped to visit the Carsons at Birchington. Although Carson's biographer mentions the visit, it seems clear from Ruby Carson's diary that her husband had not expected the call, nor did he welcome it.[72]

> Mrs. Churchill came on her way back from Dover. She brought some letters for Edward to see. Apparently he [Churchill] has quite decided to come back and lead the Rad.[ical] War Committee & Asquith has tried to dissuade him. How funny it seems to think of her coming to us after all that has happened. She seems very upset & really cried to me as she explained Winston had tried to do as he thought right. Edward told her W. had made everything very difficult the way he dashes off first on one thing then on the other. I really liked her she is so pretty.[73]

C.P. Scott shows that among the letters brought for Carson to see was one to the Prime Minister asking that Churchill be relieved of his command, much to Clementine's distress.[74]

The meeting was not a success and Carson wrote Churchill a terse note on 23 March urging him to stay in France. A return without some particular necessity for his presence would make it difficult for his causes and might convey the 'impression [that] you acted spasmodically and without sound and deliberate judgement. . .'[75] The Carsons dined with the Churchills when Winston returned in April to attend the secret session of the House of Commons on conscription, but the suspicion of Churchill's judgment and stability continued. 'E. and I dined with the Winston Churchills,' wrote Ruby Carson. 'Who would have thought that ever could have happened? He talks an awful lot and gave me the impression his tongue works faster than his brain, though it goes pretty fast. I wonder how honest he is. . .He now loathes Asquith, soon he won't have a friend in the world except the Germans.'[76]

Churchill had become, or had made himself, one of the peculiar tragi-comic figures in politics, of whom there are a number of examples, the pariah, whose support would immediately disrupt any cause he chose to touch. One man no longer urging him to remain in France was the Prime Minister, who saw, quite correctly, that Churchill's return would bring nothing but confusion to the government's enemies. He promised to relieve Churchill at any time.

Through March the political-social world occupied itself with ridiculing Churchill, while the Cabinet, with Lloyd George frequently absent, searched for a way to defend London against intensified Zeppelin raids, to deal with increasingly active submarines and with a projected shortage of shipping.[77] Lloyd George meanwhile impatiently waited for the return of Sir Edward Carson to London. On 22 March, as has been seen, he had asked Ronald McNeill to arrange a meeting when the Unionist leader came back to town.[78] Carson finally returned on 26 March, evidently to attend to the affairs of the Unionist War Committee, which without him was unable to act.

One has the sense that Lloyd George's resignation, so long projected and endlessly reflected upon in conversations with Riddell and Frances Stevenson, depended upon an agreement with Carson. Both men understood that the two together would be formidable. Churchill, of course, saw himself a future partner in this team.

The day after Carson returned Lloyd George had been conscripted into the mission to France from which labor troubles forced him to return on 29 March. Two days later he had a long political conversation with his Military Secretary at the Ministry of Munitions, Col. Arthur Lee.

Lee had been Unionist MP for Fareham since 1900 and was in 1916 a member of the Unionist War Committee. Although he had been Civil Lord of the Admiralty between 1903 and 1905 and credited himself with the invention of the cry 'we want eight and we won't wait' in the Dreadnought debate of 1909, he was in no sense a party leader. Usually he is remembered as the minor, pushing, politician who gave Chequers to the nation presumably in return for a peerage. However, his considerable wealth, derived from his wife, and his long standing connections among the radical Tories made him valuable to Lloyd George who kept Lee at his side until 1922. Lee served as an avenue for Lloyd George to the younger Tories as Masterman and then Addison provided among the advanced Liberals. Some within the inner political world distrusted Lee, among them Max Aitken and Riddell. Riddell, obsessed with the subject, believed the proprietor of *The Times* was behind him, and perhaps saw him as a competitor, as wealthy or powerful men often regard each other. 'LG has gone to spend the week-end with Col. Lee,' he wrote on 21 May, 'who acts as Northcliffe's envoy. He looks like a Jew [although Lee's father was a vicar]. He is a professional husband having married a wealthy American [Ruth Moore of New York].'[79] In fact Lee emerges from his own memoirs as a rather attractive, painfully honest, highly patriotic man, a close friend of Theodore Roosevelt, whom he had met when a military observer in Cuba, and a compulsive volunteer to worthy causes, who remained faithful to Lloyd George long after his departure from the Prime Ministership.

In a letter to his wife on 31 March Lee recorded telling Lloyd George that soon he would have to vote against the government and that Lloyd George therefore had better look for a new Military Secretary. He had offered his personal advice that Lloyd George ought not to be running the Ministry of Munitions but rousing the country. Lloyd George agreed. The letter ended with the significant news: Lloyd George 'will see Carson tonight'.[80] That day Ruby Carson wrote 'Edward and I dined with the McNeills to meet Lloyd George as he wanted to see Edward quietly.'[81]

Unfortunately Lady Carson did not record the conversation between her husband and Lloyd George but clearly it concerned the latter's resignation. Lloyd George told Riddell the next day that he had dined with the Unionist leader the previous evening and continued:

> L.G. told me that he is much dissatisfied and thinks he must leave the Cabinet. He feels he is taking part in a fraud which is sacrificing and will sacrifice hundreds of thousands of lives. Mr. A. has no plan, no initiative, no grip, no driving force. He made a poor showing at the conference [in Paris from which Lloyd George had returned on 29 March]. L.G. thinks he will have to resign soon. The condition of affairs is serious.[82]

In this conversation Lloyd George had remarked upon Christopher Addison's successful handling of the ever-troublesome Clyde labor leaders. '. . .he is,' said Lloyd George, 'a clever, courageous little man.'[83] During the next year, at least into the summer of 1917, Lloyd George would lean heavily upon Addison, both as an industrious administrator and perhaps more important, as an authentic voice of the old radical Liberalism that had meant so much to him for so many years. Five days after the dinner with Carson, evidently without telling Addison, who would have seen it as supping with the Devil, Lloyd George discussed resignation with Addison at lunch. Addison was sympathetic, but typically practical. Lloyd George needed a reason larger than general dissatisfaction and he needed to keep his old friends together.

> I told him that it was to court failure if he went out solely with the backing of the Harmsworth Press [which still applauded Lloyd George daily], the wild men among the Tories only a small following among the Liberals. The urgency of securing detailed consideration and decisions in advance was obvious, as well as the necessity for getting rid

of incompetence whether at No. 10 or the War Office: but I could not envisage his carrying a campaign in the country, powerful as he might be with his speeches, and influential as was a section of the Press which might support him in certain directions, unless it rested on a more solid basis. He would alienate the rank and file of Liberalism simply because he was supported by Northcliffe & Co. and his efforts would take on the appearance of an intrigue against the P.M. He eventually agreed, provided it was possible to choose the time.[84]

Lloyd George, as was his custom, solidified his thinking in dialogue. He discussed with Lee the question of how to support himself on 5 April. His salary would drop from £5,000 per year to £400. Lee mused that Theodore Roosevelt's Metropolitan Magazine would pay £5,000 per year for a weekly column.[85] On 6 April he spoke of resignation a second time with Addison, who warned him again about Northcliffe, and the next day he lunched with Carson at Lee's home, Abbey Garden.[86]

In the next eight months Carson and Lloyd George would meet many more times at Abbey Garden. Lloyd George trusted Lee, as he did not Max Aitken, the generally recognized chronicler of the story of the decline and fall of the first coalition, a fact Aitken backhandedly acknowledges.[87] One could add that almost exactly five years later in 1921 when Carson and Lee were dining together Carson, perhaps remembering the first meeting, leaned across the table to Lee. 'Do you remember those days at Abbey Garden when you and I made LG Prime Minister. For we *did* do it there!'[88]

In all these discussions further measures of conscription had played little part although on 28 March 1916 the Unionist War Committee, with Carson again in the chair, had passed a resolution demanding universal compulsory service.[89] Despite Robertson's continued pounding, the Prime Minister, fortified by McKenna and Runciman, sought to put off the evil day as long as possible. However, the need for a decision became inescapable on 7 April, the day Lloyd George and Carson met at Abbey Garden. That afternoon the War Committee, by now essentially the entire Cabinet, met to consider a request from Haig, dated 4 April for approval of a 'general offensive on all Fronts'. This would be the great 'wearing out battle' first discussed at Chantilly the previous November. The Army would need a large and dependable supply of drafts. On this point Addison noted in his diary, probably on a report from Lloyd George, that Robertson had told the Committee that one third of the unmarried men called up in January had not reported.[90] The debate in the War Committee turned less upon the feasibility of the operation than upon whether the French, heavily engaged as they were at Verdun, would participate. Haig's letter suggested the belief that Germany had been hurt more than the French in that battle and hence an attack was appropriate. (The historian must comment that by autumn he was saying the opposite, that British attacks were necessary, instead, in order to save the French.)[91]

The conscription problem had returned. On Friday, 14 April the Cabinet met to consider manpower needs and had come to no decision. Discussion was adjourned until Monday, 17 April. The day before Carson had written to the Prime Minister asking when he proposed to make a statement on the 'recruiting' question and telling him he intended to put down a resolution 'some of us wish to discuss'. He hoped that after Asquith's statement it would become unnecessary.[92]

Scott's diary suggests that Carson's threatened resolution told Lloyd George that the moment had arrived. The *Guardian* proprietor had gone to look for him at the Ministry of Munitions on the morning of 13 April and had met him, apparently by accident.

> He told me of his strong and increasing dissatisfaction with the conduct of the war and his intention to bring matters to a head by resigning if a measure of general compulsory service were not adopted on the lines of the motion of which Carson had given notice for the following Wednesday[,] after the Prime Minister had made his promised statement on Tuesday as to the intentions of the Government based upon the report of the Cabinet Committee.[93]

Asquith of course understood perfectly what the revived conscription issue meant for the safety of his government. If Lloyd George resigned and joined Carson the rest of the Unionists in the Cabinet, save perhaps Balfour, would go also. Even Bonar Law, despite his loyalty to the Prime Minister, could hardly remain.[94] The coalition would break up. Could he fight an election in which his hesitation on conscription would be used, perfectly patriotically, as a symbol of insufficient vigor in prosecuting the war? Accordingly on 13 April he took the unusual step of asking Christopher Addison whether he believed his departmental chief would resign over the matter of compulsory service for married men. Addison replied that he thought Lloyd George would indeed resign unless some other means of finding men were devised.[95]

Lloyd George was already busy collecting opinions on his resignation. Although the dates in Riddell's diary do not correspond with those in Scott's, it appears that he had asked Riddell to invite Robertson Nicoll to lunch at Riddell's house in Queen Anne's Gate before the Cabinet meeting and then, after encountering Scott at the Ministry of Munitions, had decided to include him also. (Scott records that he was not particularly anxious to meet Nicoll and found him a pompous, affected, professional Scotsman.)[96] The conversation between these four men summarized Lloyd George's position in the spring of 1916. His concern was not the adoption of compulsory service, or any other measure, but victory in the war. 'We have had a Cabinet today [Riddell dates this passage 13 April but the Cabinet was Friday, 14 April] to consider the recruiting question,' said Lloyd George.

> The Army Council made a strong report.[97] We came to no decision. The discussion is adjourned until Monday...Now Sir William [R. Nicoll] what is your opinion? Do you think I should go out? You will remember the interview we had in this house some time ago when you advised me to leave. I did not take your advice and I regret not having done so. But there is this to be said on the other side: Since then I have put munitions on a more satisfactory footing; the stuff is beginning to roll in. The Army are well supplied; General Haig, who is over here, says he has enough. That is something to have accomplished. Perhaps I did the right thing.
>
> Nicoll: May I ask you a question? On what are you thinking of going out? On the enlistment question?

L.G.: One must have an immediate reason. Enlistment would furnish this, but I should really resign as a protest against the general conduct of the war. We never do anything until we are prodded into it, and then we are always too late.

R: You seem to have no plan. The war appears to be conducted haphazard.

L.G.: Yes; that is the trouble. There is no grip. Asquith and Balfour do not seem to realize the serious nature of the situation. They believe the Germans are becoming exhausted, but there is no evidence of that.

Scott: Recruiting would be the occasion but not the cause.

L.G.: Quite true.

Nicoll (after profound meditation): I think you should go out. You will be of more service out than in.

L.G.: I am glad to hear you say that. That is my opinion and Scott agrees. What is your view Riddell?

Riddell was less certain than the others citing the shock Lloyd George's departure would have upon public confidence. How could he explain his going without betraying secret recruiting statistics?

Scott: But you must not confine yourself to a destructive policy; you must put forward a constructive policy.

L.G.: I agree. Carson is improving daily. He is managing his little group with great skill. He is a fine fellow.

Nicoll: He has no following in the country.

LG: Perhaps you are right about that. However I have quite made up my mind. Unless they accept the Army Council recommendations, I shall go out on Monday.

* * * *

LG: Much depends on General Robertson. The question is whether he will stand to his guns. Asquith has treated him most unfairly. Robertson was a member of the first Cabinet Committee on Recruiting, but Asquith has excluded him from that which has just reported, although his subordinates are members of it.

R: Why?

LG: I suppose he thinks Robertson will be awkward.

The interview lasted for nearly two hours. L.G. seemed in good spirits. He went away with Scott.[98]

In their conversation after leaving, Lloyd George asked Scott to come to Walton Heath on Sunday and review his letter of resignation.[99]

The next day, Saturday, 15 April, Asquith, having spoken to Addison on 13 April, played a second card: 'As I anticipated,' wrote Riddell, 'the LCJ' [the Lord Chief Justice, i.e. Rufus Isaacs, Lord Reading],

appeared on the scene this morning. He drove down to Walton with L.G., lunched and played golf in the afternoon. He told me that last

Sunday he stayed with the P.M. at his house on the Thames [The Wharf, in Oxfordshire]. What happened he did not relate, but I have no doubt that wily Henry arranged for tactful Rufus to bring his power to bear on L.G. The same procedure always happens when L.G. kicks up his heels. Sometimes it is the L.C.J.; at others it is oily Alec Murray and in cases of dire distress a combined attack. Just now Murray is *hors de combat.*

* * * *

L.G. says he doubts if Asquith will give way. Asquith feels he is committed against further conscription.

Lloyd George concluded: 'I think I shall be out on Monday — that is if Robertson remains firm.'[100]

Lloyd George had asked Scott to come to Walton Heath on Sunday to help in the composition of his letter of resignation. Upon arriving Scott found Col. Lee already there and the two men combined forces in urging Lloyd George to leave the Cabinet. He would do more good for the war effort on the outside. They appeared to be having an effect, thought Scott. Lloyd George retired to write his letter but went to sleep in the middle of its dictation. Meanwhile the King's private secretary, Lord Stamfordham, called asking Lloyd George to see him in London and so with Scott and evidently Lee, Lloyd George drove back to No. 11 Downing Street, which to the annoyance of McKenna remained his London address.[101]

Obviously Asquith was using all of the considerable resources of influence available to a Prime Minister. Possibly because Lloyd George so frequently protested that ceremonies of royalty meant nothing, Asquith suspected that the intervention of the Monarch would have an effect. In any case Stamfordham was undone within minutes with an appropriately patriotic platitude. The King wished he would not resign but he must, Lloyd George said, no doubt solemnly. '"I have sworn an oath of allegiance to His Majesty, and for that reason I cannot give in. If I had not taken that oath, I might."' Stamfordham went away nonplussed.[102] Lloyd George was so proud of this riposte that he repeated it both to Miss Stevenson and to Scott.[103]

On the evening of Sunday, 16 April, there seemed no possibility of compromise. Lloyd George had proclaimed as publicly as he could that he would resign on Monday unless Asquith promised general compulsion. Most of the Unionists would join him. The Prime Minister either would surrender or the government would collapse amid thunderous applause from the Northcliffe press and also, incidentally, from Churchill who relished the thought of returning to the House to fight in the company of Lloyd George and Carson. Asquith's anxiety was manifest, yet the biographer must remark that he, apparently, had not yet seen Lloyd George himself as would have happened routinely six or eight months earlier. Lloyd George dined alone with Bonar Law on Sunday evening.

By evening the next day all had changed. Lloyd George would not resign. There would be compromise, another conscription committee including Lloyd George; the nation now needed Asquith. Here one has to be annoyed with Lloyd George's own evidence on his motives. Letters to Criccieth are suddenly abundant, self justifications to Miss Stevenson and carefully balanced explanations to fully knowledgeable observers such as Scott and Riddell become repetitive. In his papers there is no private information.[104]

What happened is clear enough. At two Cabinet meetings on Monday afternoon, Lloyd George discovered that Arthur Henderson and the Labour party opposed immediate general compulsion although there was room for compromise and that the solid Unionist rock of compulsionists in the Cabinet was crumbling. Also he did not wish to leave the Ministry of Munitions just yet. He told this story in nearly identical terms to both Scott and Miss Stevenson.[105] Moreover he conveyed to Miss Stevenson that the plan the Cabinet accepted was his. By 20 April Miss Stevenson understood, as did George Riddell and William George in Criccieth, that the crisis was over and that Lloyd George and General Robertson, 'a splendid fellow', had won some sort of a victory.[106]

In fact Lloyd George had won no victory and the crisis was not over. What Lloyd George had done at most, with Arthur Henderson, was to induce Asquith to accept the report of the Military Finance Committee, with the proviso imposed by Henderson, that the existing Derby scheme be worked harder for a trial period. This was the same report, somewhat amended by Hankey, that Lloyd George had attacked in Cabinet only a week before. The Military Finance Committee proposed three measures which did not together, as it admitted, amount to anything like general compulsion, but which cumulatively would increase the intake of men.[107] First the discharge of time-expired regulars, whose enlistments at the beginning of the war all had been extended by one year, should be stopped. This alone was costing the army in April 1916, 5,000 invaluable, fully trained, men per month. Second, Territorials would be ordered to serve in any unit needed. Third, all young men turning age 18 would come under the terms of the Military Service Act. In time this component, mostly unskilled, presumably fit and unmarried, would produce a substantial number of new soldiers. If these provisions and a new attempt to obtain attested unmarried men under the Derby Scheme did not satisfy the Army Council within six weeks, it was agreed, there would be general compulsion. The contest between Lloyd George and the rest lay only in Lloyd George's proposal that a bill for general compulsion be passed immediately with a six week's delay in application. The others, and the Prime Minister, insisted that there be nothing but a Cabinet resolution. In any case the final decision lay in the predictable determination of General Robertson and the Army Council.[108]

Except for the fact that, after further debate, general conscription would presumably come, this was a paltry, miserable response to the commitment that the government had allowed Kitchener to make at the beginning of August in 1914. It was another example, as *The Times* put it, of Wait and See.[109] Munitions, money and men were the legs of the tripod supporting modern war. Lloyd George had quickly understood the first and had overseen, literally, an industrial miracle. He had indeed shirked the second. The despised McKenna, far more expert if unimaginative, understood the alternatives of taxation and foreign borrowing, as opposed simply to drying up the financial liquidity of the City, and had seen to it that the immense credit resources of the United States would help to pay for the huge British, and Allied, purchases in that country. The Allied war effort partly would be paid for in American owned, not British owned, dollars. Finally, in June of 1915, to the dismay of advanced Liberals everywhere, Lloyd George had begun to call for national control of manpower. What this would lead to was unclear, above all to him one may say confidently. But national mobilization meant control: of factories and profits, of civilian consumption, among other things of drink, and of men. All of this developed during the months of fall to spring 1915 and 1916, an intuitive continuum aimed toward winning the war. Why then had he drawn back?

The easiest answer, not always the wrong one, is that he was simply throwing a bone to Carson, and perhaps to the Prime Minister. The only evidence lies in what finally transpired. If he could induce the government, he may have reasoned, to accept and to present to the House of Commons the threadbare collection of half-measures that the Military Finance Committee had proposed, he could depend upon Carson and the blood-thirsty Unionist War Committee to tear it to shreds.[110] Asquith could then honorably surrender and allow himself to be forced into introducing general compulsion. Lloyd George would get what he, and probably Asquith, wanted and nobody would have to resign. As he had told Frances Stevenson, no one but Asquith could get compulsion through the House of Commons. The Liberal radicals again would swallow conscription to save their revered leader.

One must wonder whether Asquith did not understand this also. He too spoke constantly of resignation and on 19 April announced the Easter Recess of the House until 25 April with the warning that the government was in danger of breaking up. If this tactic was designed to frighten the anti-conscriptionists it worked perfectly. The next day there was a meeting, of which Simon was the spokesman, of about 100 Liberal MPs marked by loud protestations of loyalty to the Prime Minister and equally loud denunciations of Lloyd George. On the same day, 20 April, the *Manchester Guardian*'s parliamentary correspondent produced a paragraph declaring that Lloyd George had no following in the House and was disliked by most members of both parties.[111] Two days later on Saturday, 22 April, appeared A.G. Gardiner's vitriolic attack on Lloyd George in the *Daily News*.

As this open letter, although noted before, represents historically the beginning of the last phase of Lloyd George's break with radical Liberalism, and because it was taken seriously at the time by many politicians, including Lloyd George, it must be quoted briefly. After an opening paragraph asserting that those around Lloyd George had remained silent about his misbehavior for too long, surely a statement open to question, the editor continued:

> They have refused to see your figure flitting about behind the scenes, touching the strings, prompting the actors, directing the game, and have agreed to talk of Lord Northcliffe, Sir Henry Dalziel, and the Reverend Dr. Sir William Robertson Nicoll when the name that has been in their minds has been the name of Mr. David Lloyd George.

The nation would have to choose between Asquith and Lloyd George. The Prime Minister, Gardiner stated

> has sought to carry the country step by step, to deserve its confidence and hold its confidence, to weld it [Labour] into the solid mass of the nation, to free it from its fears and direct its energies against the

310

enemy. You, caught by the flair at a great occasion, impatient at democracy, seized with a sort of apocalyptic vision of yourself as the saviour of Europe, have turned to compulsion, not with the cold philosophy of Lord Milner, who is not only German in origin but German in thought, but with a fine Celtic frenzy of one who has no philosophy, only a revelation.[112]

Lloyd George received of course the customary reassurances that Gardiner's open letter had done him more good than harm: it had angered the Unionists and rallied them behind him and, as he told Riddell, it had finally cut him off from the Radicals.[113] It will be recalled that Lloyd George only a few days before on 17 April had given Scott as one of his reasons for compromise on conscription the desire not to antagonize his Liberal friends any more than necessary. Now such caution was useless.

The *Daily News* attack had another result which turned out to be of critical, if momentary, importance eight months later. The faithful Addison, still a good Radical, determined after the article appeared to investigate the depth of Lloyd George's support among the Liberals. Quickly he developed a list containing as he recorded in his diary 'a good body of Members' who supported Lloyd George. Evidently he did not show this list to his chief at the time but the list was invaluable in December 1916.[114]

On 19 April 1916 in his warning to the Liberal world that his government was in danger of breaking up, the Prime Minister had postponed yet a third time the statement on the needs of the army that Carson had demanded. He would speak the next Tuesday, 25 April. The next day Arthur Henderson announced in the Cabinet that the Labour party could not support general compulsion unless it had all the facts. The party wanted a secret session. This the Prime Minister reluctantly granted, a step toward the consensus building that was his style of government.[115] Until a general agreement, to which he could bow, was established, he would not move.

The secret session, which lasted in fact into Wednesday, 26 April, was not a success. Addison found it dull. He heard nothing new and left. Asquith spoke badly and was aware of it.[116] Generally he outlined the details of the compromise worked out by the Military Finance Committee with the provisions insisted upon by Labour that the Derby scheme be given until 27 May to produce 50,000 men and 15,000 per week after that. Otherwise there would be general compulsion. A bill would be introduced on Thursday.[117]

Thursday then became the day when the balance of British politics began to tip against Asquith's government. When the sitting was over, the weight of its authority was sensibly diminished. Asquith himself was not present, detained it was said by events in Ireland. One has to believe he had anticipated what would happen, but not the violence with which it took place.

The new Military Service Bill was introduced by Walter Long, the President of the Local Government Board, not, it may be suspected, because he had anything to do with its framing, but because he was a popular, and senior, Unionist. The new champion, the figure absolutely dominating the proceedings, was Edward Carson. In five minutes dealing only with the proposal to extend the term of regulars, Carson destroyed the compromise worked out so laboriously in the past three weeks. The bill he said was 'monstrous' 'The most cruel act ever attempted'. The army was losing trained veterans at the rate of 5,000 per month while unattested unmarried men were not even being called up. Those who had served their country were to be punished because the government feared to touch those who would not serve their country.[118] Carson was followed enthusiastically by a number of speakers of all parties, including, as all papers noted, Stephen Walsh, a Labour MP. Nearly all prefaced their remarks with the statement that they did not often agree with the Member for Dublin University. No one defended the bill.

Walter Long in desperation had obviously sent for the Prime Minister, who soon walked in symbolically holding up his hands in defeat. The bill, which in fact had not yet been introduced, he said would be withdrawn. He continued, virtually admitting that the bill had been offered as a ritual sacrifice:

> As an old Parliamentarian I always know what the House of Commons feels toward a Bill, and when the House feels as it does towards this Bill, it is not weakness but wisdom on the part of the Government to recognize the conditions of the case and to acquiesce in the determination of the House.[119]

This was a significant event. Asquith had made an error from which he would not recover. *The Times*, of course, was ecstatic. The paper referred to the 'humiliation' which would have 'broken' the government in normal times. 'Sir Edward Carson rent the stillborn Military Service Bill from top to bottom.' The Unionist War Committee which, one must remember, could have destroyed the government in an instant, 'would not look' at the proposal to keep time-expired men. 'How the Government came to propose such an impossible measure to the House, whose mood it had many opportunities for testing is a mystery.'[120] (The Unionist War Committee had met nearly every day during the previous week with an attendance of between 145 and 150. Beside it the so-called Liberal War Committee was insignificant.)

All of this could have been expected from the Northcliffe press, but the anger was apparent in other papers. More important for this discussion is that the fury of the Liberals at the humiliation of their revered leader was aimed at Lloyd George. In a way this may have been deserved. As was suggested at the beginning of this account Lloyd George intentionally may have led the Prime Minister astray by compromising, by agreeing not to resign and so allowing the Prime Minister to put before the House a measure that he, Lloyd George, knew perfectly well Carson and the Unionist War Committee would destroy. The two men may indeed have conferred on it. Lloyd George and Carson had met after all a number of times in the previous weeks when political conversation involved nothing but conscription. That he had deliberately led the government of which he was a member into a trap generally was the burden of Liberal criticism after the event. He had conspired to use conscription to weaken Asquith.

It is more likely, however, that Lloyd George in truth was not anxious to leave the Ministry of Munitions at that time and was unwilling entirely to part company with his Liberal followers. Hence he simply allowed an atrocious bill to go forward secure in the knowledge that its rejection would bring general compulsion anyway. Even if it were not rejected the measure could not possibly bring forward the number of men required and compulsion would come in six weeks. It was generally this reasoning that he conveyed to Scott and Miss Stevenson.[121]

What of Asquith? How could his astute political intuition have failed so badly? It was indeed a mystery, as *The Times* had said. One can only surmise that with his warnings that the government might break up, he was in fact attempting to repeat the miracle of the Bachelor's Bill, which had convinced his wife that God protected her husband at No. 10. First bring in an inadequate counterfeit measure, in this case the Military Finance Committee proposal being the equivalent of the Derby scheme proposals, with the warning that it could be followed by something harsher. Allow the measure to fail or be rejected meanwhile putting about warnings that if the problem were not solved the government would collapse. The real, or just, measure could then replace the unjust one. When the vote arrived the Unionists would support it because they wanted conscription and the Liberals because they wanted Asquith. Lytton Strachey wrote in May 1918 that Asquith had said precisely this to Maynard Keynes. 'The Conscriptionists were fools. . .He was giving them enough rope to hang themselves by.'[122] The initiative, the will, behind compulsion then would not have been his, but that of the House of Commons. Indeed Asquith's statement on 27 April, already quoted in part, betrays precisely this thinking. But he had not counted on the violence of Carson's attack. A measure he had expected to be held simply as inadequate was rejected with general contempt. Not one of the men who had fought general compulsion in the Cabinet and who had demanded compromise, dared to defend the bill in the House of Commons.

The Prime Minister knew he had been hurt. The old cockiness implicit in the statement about God Almighty was entirely absent in his first address to the House after 27 April, on 2 May when he announced that a new Military Service Bill would be put down the next day. He made an almost plaintive appeal for help. The government, he repeated in conclusion, must have the support of the House. If the House could find another Cabinet to administer affairs let it. But it must have trust.

> Let it [the House] find another body of men better qualified for the art of Government and for the practice of administration in these exacting days. I can say with perfect sincerity that there is not a man who sits on this Bench among my colleagues who is attached to his daily work by any other ties than a sense of duty and a love of his country. We cannot — I say it deliberately — carry the heaviest burden that had ever been laid upon the shoulders of British statesmen unless we can feel that we have not only the sympathy but the trust of our countrymen.[123]

In effect the battle for conscription was over. The *Daily News* lamented the loss in a bitter leading article entitled 'The Last Phase'. Compulsion would bring in no more than 200,000 in a volunteer army of 5,000,000. Suggesting that A.G. Gardiner also understood what had happened in the previous week, the article continued asserting that the real aim of the compulsionists was to destroy the Prime Minister. Asquith 'has been out-manoeuvred in this long and squalid battle by more supple intriguers.'[124] He named only Carson, but Carson's part had not been that of supple intriguer. He had merely sprung the trap. The hand that had set it may have been within the Cabinet.

On 3 May Asquith himself introduced the Military Service Bill providing for the compulsory enlistment of all physically fit men aged 18 to 41 not otherwise engaged in critical work, with a short, almost pallid, speech that suggested fatigue. The first reading passed without a division. The excitement arrived the following day, 4 May, in an attack by Llewelyn Williams upon Lloyd George, a cry of anger, frustration and pain. Williams began by saying that the House soon would hear 'the master's voice' like the dog sitting before the gramophone. 'Who?' asked someone. 'The Minister of Munitions', Williams replied.

> Today we are told that immediately after I sit down, we shall hear for the first time the greatest democratic leader this country has ever seen — and I say that in all sincerity — explaining in the House of Commons and to his countrymen the reasons which have made him, an old Pro-Boer, become a militarist, and the reasons which have induced him to impose his will in this matter upon a reluctant and mutinous Cabinet, on an indifferent and, until four months ago, a hostile House of Commons, and on a country that is bewildered at the change.

Williams's speech was devoted entirely to denunciation of Lloyd George and people under his control, Arthur Lee and Carson. They had forced the Prime Minister to bring forward the Bachelor's Bill by the threat of resignation, according to the *Daily Mail*, and had allowed the bill, as Williams reminded the House he had told it, to be 'whittled down' because he was aiming at the present measure. 'It is the greatest wrench of my life,' concluded Williams, 'to make a speech even purporting to be against any policy in which he is interested.'[125]

Lloyd George was not of the sort to allow the sheer sadness of Williams's words soften his reply. He taunted his former friend and revealed that Williams had recently convened a meeting of his constituents to support a resolution against conscription only to have them vote in its favor. After a time Williams could bear it no longer and began to interrupt. The address degenerated into a shouting match between the two men.[126] Lloyd George did not speak again on conscription, but the destruction of the old radical alliance was nearly complete. Universal compulsory military service became law on 25 May 1916.

Lloyd George had been scheduled for some weeks to make a speech in Conway, one of the six boroughs of Caernarvon District. Here on 6 May in the company of William Hughes, the new Prime Minister of Australia, he attempted to repair some of the damage to his Liberal credentials. He referred to his speech at Bangor on 28 February 1915 and reminded the audience that there too he had been talking of national mobilization, but then there were more men than munitions, now the problem was the reverse.

Generally the speech was a defense first of compulsion — there was no indignity in it, taxes, after all, were compulsory — but second, he defended vigorously his own Liberalism.

> I have been subjected to a very cloudy discharge of poison gas (laughter) and I am glad it has been done. These things have been

going on clandestinely and surreptitiously for months and I could not deal with them. My difficulty was that no self-respecting man or newspaper could be forced to give publicity to those attacks and therefore I could not answer them.

These attacks, by an unnamed man, 'an assassin', 'who invents conversations' impugned his loyalty to his party because he supported conscription. All but 28 Liberals in the House of Commons had voted for conscription, declared Lloyd George triumphantly, as if this proved beyond question his agreement with his colleagues.

Then there were stories of disloyalty to the Prime Minister. 'A war council cannot be run like a Sunday School tea party. You either make war or you do not.'

I have worked with him [Asquith] for ten years; I have served under him for eight. If we had not worked harmoniously — and we have — let me tell you here at once it would have been my fault and not his ...But we have had our differences. Good Heavens! What use would I have been if I had not differed? I should have been no use at all...

Freedom of speech is essential to everything, but there is one place where it is vital, and that is in the Council Chamber. The councillor who professes to agree with everything that falls from his leader betrays him.[127]

The *Daily News*, which by now could let no Lloyd George utterance go unchallenged, printed the speech but accompanied it with yet another open letter. Lloyd George had shown again his 'swift but shallow mind' which had made him contemptuous 'of more stable, more patient, more trustworthy minds,' presumably that of the Prime Minister, who somehow still trusted Lloyd George. Gardiner derided his enemy's defense of his relationship with Asquith as one of mutual good will and honest disagreement. If he were to pick Lord Rothschild's pocket, wrote Gardiner, it would not be a defense to say that he disagreed with him. Going back to the early days of the Ministry of Munitions the editor recalled the article in the *British Weekly*, already discussed, in which Robertson Nicoll had quoted Lloyd George as saying he would resign if he could not have his way with the new ministry. Even then he was undermining Asquith.

Inevitably Gardiner attacked Northcliffe as the fountainhead of anti-Liberal conspiracy, but the editor was no more certain than Riddell about the nature of the connection between the two men. 'If we inquire what is the link between you and Lord Northcliffe we shall find that it is in the common belief in the idea of dictatorship.' 'You cannot walk in step with Mr. Asquith and Lord Northcliffe at the same time,' he concluded.[128]

One must pause here and reflect again upon the Lloyd George-Northcliffe relationship. Did such a thing in fact exist? It may be likely that the invariable introduction of Northcliffe into attacks upon Lloyd George was simply the journalist's way of providing a motive for a conspiracy by Lloyd George against Asquith that the writer wished to assert but could not prove. Even if isolated in the Cabinet Lloyd George was a powerful and popular public figure. Attacking him directly was dangerous as several Liberal newspapermen would discover within the next several years. Northcliffe on the other hand was a generic villain of whom anything could be believed. No radical Liberal editor could hurt himself by denouncing the proprietor of the *Daily Mail.*

Yet there must have been more than the familiar newspaper weapon of guilt by association. Friends of Lloyd George, Addison and Riddell, had warned the minister frequently of the danger of the seeming alliance even while being unable to produce any evidence of collusion, conspiracy or even contact between the two men. Immediately after the introduction of the Military Service Bill, apparently in celebration of the victory, Riddell presented Lloyd George with the valuable lease to the Walton Heath house.[129] However, only a week later, as usual in sadness but this time tinged with anger, he wrote in his diary:

> There is no doubt that LG and Northcliffe are acting in close concert. . .LG and N. make a strong but dangerous combination. They are both apt to act hastily and to err on the side of innovation. N. is frequently very wide of the mark in his facts and sometimes forms very wild opinions notwithstanding his great powers of observations and his crafty cunning ways. N. is a wonderful man, but self-centered and unscrupulous. LG is growing to believe more and more every day that he (LG) is the only man to win the war. His attitude to the PM is changing rapidly. He is becoming more and more critical and antagonistic. It looks as if LG and Northcliffe are working to dethrone Mr. A.[130]

One has to believe that Riddell, who had concluded his entry on the gift of the Walton Heath house with the remark that Lloyd George's letter of thanks was a 'delightful souvenir of our friendship,' felt genuinely close to the man. There are not many such expressions of warmth in his diary. Yet he too hated and deplored the Northcliffe connection although, like Gardiner, he had no evidence, or at least recorded none, of what precisely it was. Lloyd George himself told him nothing. 'LG rarely mentions Northcliffe's name nowadays,' he wrote a few weeks later, 'and *never* mentions that he is in communication with him.'[131] Riddell had, of course, many private sources of information, but his many speculations never recorded evidence.

Gardiner's rage with Lloyd George continued and increased after the fall of Asquith. He became obsessed with the sinister influence of Northcliffe. His anger evidently reached a point where his denunciations could not be published in the United Kingdom.[132]

There is however a letter from Addison to Gardiner sent nearly two decades later which suggests that despite the tumult surrounding it there may not have been much to the infamous Northcliffe connection, as has been the contention of this study. Writing to Gardiner on 22 April 1934, Addison recalled the attack in the *Daily News* on 22 April 1916.

> Your article was remarkably definite in its suggestions that L.G., in concert with certain others, some of whom were named, was or had been taking a certain course of action. I was myself at that time in daily contact with what was going on and had participated, particularly in the crisis over recruiting, on several occasions in conversation with L.G. and others, and the line he was taking and the substance of conversations was quite different from what was suggested in your article; and,

although I myself have suffered at his hands, I felt then, knowing the facts as to the line he was taking, that the article was seriously unjust and on rereading it today I am still of the same opinion.[133]

III

On Easter Monday, 24 April 1916, the day before the secret session on conscription, the evening newspapers reported disorder in Dublin and the next day, Tuesday, 25 April, it was announced that martial law had been declared and that General Sir John Maxwell, a friend of Kitchener's from Egypt, had been appointed to take command. On the same Tuesday a German battle-cruiser squadron bombarded Lowestoft with considerable loss of life and escaped without injury. That evening London suffered its seventh and heaviest Zeppelin raid by ten airships. Then on Saturday, 29 April, the town of Kut in Mesopotamia under siege since the previous November was surrendered and 9,000 soldiers fell to the Turks. Finally, on Tuesday, 9 May, the steamer *Cymric* was sunk off the southwest coast of Ireland (by Kapitänleutnant Walther Schwieger of *Lusitania* fame) with an exceptionally valuable cargo of munitions and copper products: shell cases, fuses and projectile driving bands. Of far more importance, the *Cymric* carried also a year's production, 14,000 cases, of machine tools (largely from American Machine and Foundry). In general, it was not a prosperous fortnight for British arms.

Coming as this did in the midst of the public struggle over the purity of his Liberalism Lloyd George seems to have been more upset at the *Cymric*'s loss than at the preceding disasters. He directed his rage at the First Lord of the Admiralty, Arthur Balfour. He interrupted the Cabinet discussion of the Irish situation on the day of the sinking to announce the ship's loss and the next day an entire meeting of the War Committee was devoted to it.[134] The master of the *Cymric* had not waited for his sealed orders in New York and had not heeded a war warning issued from Queenstown on 7 May. Besides the critical harm to the war effort the cargo had been worth between 2 and 3 million pounds.[135]

The implications from the loss, as Lloyd George made clear in a strong letter to Balfour between the two meetings, were of Admiralty slackness. There was no protection for and indeed no real control of merchant shipping.[136] In the following years Balfour would participate fully in the adventure of Lloyd George's Prime Ministership and would serve him loyally; indeed by accepting the Foreign Office in December, 1916 he made service under Lloyd George respectable for Conservatives. Yet until the end of his days he wondered aloud why Lloyd George would not keep him at the Admiralty where he had been happy and was evidently popular. Admiralty slackness, as it was termed, not referring to the efficiency of the Fleet but to Admiralty administration, by this time was notorious.[137] The ominous question recurs in Marine Lieutenant Colonel Maurice Hankey's diary: 'Can the Army win this war before the Navy loses it?' But this was a situation that well antedated Balfour. The *Cymric* may provide a clue.

The Easter Rebellion remains for the historian of Britain as well as of Ireland one of the genuine monuments to change in the unhappy story of the relationship between the two islands. But for Lloyd George it was simply another intrusion by the other island into the political affairs of Britain, the sort of impudent preemption that he had known and resented since coming to the House of Commons. Again, 'Ireland blocks the way'. One may imagine that the impulse simply to remove Ireland from the center of British affairs so that the government could get on with the war, rather than the wish to achieve any lasting settlement, was a major reason for allowing himself to be pushed into the crisis.

On the other hand he rather admired the Irish Nationalist party leaders at Westminster, John Redmond, John Dillon, T.P. O'Connor who sat for the heavily Irish Scotland Division of Liverpool, and Joseph Devlin, MP for West Belfast, leader of the Ulster Nationalists.[138] All except Devlin, not yet in parliament, had been at his side in the bitter debates over the South African war and while he had fought with them over education he regarded the leaders of the party, if not the rank and file, as seasoned and responsible politicians, which clearly was not his view of the Labour party. And he knew, as he told C.P. Scott, that the Easter Rebellion marked the last opportunity to achieve Home Rule, the cause to which these excellent men had devoted their lives.[139]

The origins of the Easter Rising are not part of the life of Lloyd George. All that need be said perhaps is that the war, while on one hand bringing huge prosperity to the island, greater than it had ever known or would know again until the Second World War, had accelerated the process of decay in the machinery and influence of the Irish Nationalist party and the glamor of its cause. The simple reestablishment of Grattan's Parliament on College Green seemed no longer to mean a nation once again. The new goal was the old Fenian one, adopted by its terrorist successors, of total independence. The symptoms of the new temper never even hinted at in the British press and so far as one can discover even mentioned in either Cabinet or War Committee, was the almost total cessation of voluntary enlistment among Catholics in the south of Ireland after an auspicious but brief beginning in 1914.[140] All of this was exacerbated by Kitchener's thoughtless and shabby treatment of that portion of the Irish National Volunteers whom Redmond had induced to volunteer as a unit at the outbreak of the war. The problem was compounded in August 1915 by the sudden, almost total cessation of enlistment of Protestants — Asquith referred to it as a 'wave' — when a rumor swept over Ulster to the effect that men in the South were staying home in order to invade the North.[141]

Thus, by 1915 Ireland was a politically, one could say almost a culturally, divided nation. On the surface was the appearance of unexampled economic well being. The ancient curse of unemployment for the moment had disappeared. There was work in agriculture, in the shipyards and mills of Belfast and in England, all of which it may be presumed, itself militated against enlistment in the army. There was a growing Catholic commercial middle class, which itself many British politicians, including probably Lloyd George, believed would dilute Home Rule and radical sentiment.[142]

Yet below the surface was a small core of ferment and conspiracy. As the war brought prosperity it brought also opportunity. In October 1914, Sir Roger Casement, a retired member of the British consular service, of some fame as a humanitarian, had gone to Germany to raise an Irish Legion among prisoners of war. The Germans, it was hoped, would arm the force and transport it to Ireland while providing more arms for the men within the various secret militias already in the island.

At the center of this large untidy conspiracy was the small body of dedicated men of the Irish Republican Brotherhood and the political party of independence linked with it, Sinn Fein. The two were entirely separate organizations with different origins, but many men were members of both, and British newspapers regularly assigned the term Sinn Fein to the rebel command. But the only visible manifestations of revolutionary sentiment were the exhortations of Sinn Fein to young men not to enlist and the continued drilling of men in public. But as this had been going on before the war and was happening in Ulster as well, the authorities did nothing.

A rising, upon which the Irish leaders were by no means agreed, had been projected for Easter week of 1916 for some months. It was supposed to depend upon Casement's return from Germany with arms, and perhaps German advisors. But well before the beginning of the year Casement had come to despair of any substantial German help and determined to return to Ireland to stop the rising. Casement left Germany by submarine on 12 April. A series of misadventures and bad communications kept him from arriving on the Kerry coast at Tralee until Good Friday, 21 April. Meanwhile a supply ship carrying some 10,000 captured Russian rifles lost its way and was intercepted by the navy. Casement stumbled ashore with two comrades, frozen and half drowned, to be almost immediately captured. British naval intelligence for years had been intercepting his communications with Ireland which were sent via the German embassy in the United States.

Casement's arrest, and the news that there would be no German weapons, soon reported to Dublin, threw the leadership into more than usual disarray. (To some extent, this answers the question, frequently asked later, of why Dublin Castle intelligence had no warning of the rebellion. The answer is that the Irish did not know themselves.) Through Saturday and Sunday, 22 and 23 April, a debate raged on whether to cancel the uprising. Eoin MacNeill, commander of the Irish Volunteers, the only military force of any size with a semblance of training, was opposed to the waste of his men, while others insisted that at any cost a symbolic sacrifice was necessary. In the event the rising began at midday on 24 April.

As a military event the Easter Rebellion was unimportant. Although supposed to be a national upheaval, it was confined almost entirely to the center of Dublin and while it resulted in a good deal of damage in St. Stephen's Green and along Sackville (now O'Connell) Street not more than 1,500 rebels were involved and inhabitants of many parts of the city were unaffected by fighting. Resistance was largely over by Saturday, 29 April.

Asquith had spent Easter week-end at the Wharf preparing his speech for the secret session on Tuesday. On Monday Hankey appeared to help with the speech and in the afternoon the two men drove to London. There Hankey learned of the uprising and told the Prime Minister. 'Well that's really something' responded Asquith and went off to bed.[143]

Beyond the dispatch of General Sir John Maxwell with some troop reinforcements and the declaration of martial law, the government's response to the Dublin rising, even with the distraction of the conscription crisis, was remarkably slow. The Irish Secretary, who had held the post since the beginning of 1907, was Augustine Birrell. Birrell sent several letters during the fighting asking to resign, and warning of overreaction to a small event, but was not officially relieved until 1 May.[144] To run the Castle government, the Prime Minister sent Lloyd George's former Permanent Secretary, Sir Robert Chalmers, who quickly discovered he needed a political chief. Asquith responded on 11 May by going to Ireland himself to serve as interim Secretary of State and to investigate conditions.

He returned on 19 May evidently determined to send Lloyd George to handle the Irish government. In any case he wrote to the Minister of Munitions on 22 May:

> My dear Lloyd George,
>   I hope you may see your way to take up Ireland; at any rate for a short time. It is a *unique* opportunity and there is no one else who could do so much to bring about a permanent solution.
>   Yours very sincerely,
>   H.H. Asquith[145]

This recitation of the events leading to Lloyd George's attempt to solve the Irish problem by a new attempt at Home Rule has considerable importance in view of what followed and of Lloyd George's own story of the episode. But first of all it is clear that Asquith intended in the beginning to send Lloyd George to Ireland to pacify the country and to run and reform the government, which he was convinced had broken down. He had not thought, at this time, of altering Ireland's constitutional position by negotiations in London. He told one of his, by now several, female confidants, Kathleen, Lady Scott, widow of Captain Robert Scott, the Antarctic explorer, that he had suggested Lloyd George's going to Ireland as Chief Secretary. 'Bonar Law,' she wrote in her diary, 'upheld the suggestion.' Lady Scott continued:

> Ll.G. consulted the Irish leaders who agreed, but thought it should only be until the situation is settled. He would keep on his present position. The P.M. said in response to my many protests that he (Lloyd George) was an ambitious man, he'd stand or fall by the success he made. Couldn't grind any axe, etc.[146]

Ruby Carson, presumably reflecting her husband, was even less enthusiastic. 'They want to push Lloyd George into the Chief Secretaryship for Ireland,' she had written on the day of the invitation. 'They want to [bury?] him as he is too eager to get on with the war.'[147]

The burden of the evidence appears to show that what the Prime Minister had in mind on 22 May when he invited Lloyd George to 'take up' Ireland and what he consented to in the next three days, after Lloyd George had declined the Secretaryship but had agreed to try to solve the problem of the island's government, represent two substantially different projects. Lloyd George says nothing of this in his *War Memoirs* even though it is upon this difference that the Lloyd George agreement foundered.

The change seems to have been principally the work of Carson, whom Lloyd George saw at Arthur Lee's the next day, 23 May 1916, immediately after Asquith's invitation. Carson insisted that Lloyd George have nothing to do with the Irish Secretaryship. 'He said that he would support him and do everything he could to make his mission a success if he remained Minister of Munitions and acted simply as a conciliator and back him up with his own people,' Lloyd George told Addison,

> but he was vehement against his leaving the Ministry of Munitions and the War Council and running the risk of becoming involved in the difficulties of Irish Administration. Both LG and Lee told me afterwards that he became quite passionate on the subject. . .LG told me Wednesday morning [25 May] that he had definitely refused the Chief Secretaryship and that they had unanimously agreed to his appointment on the terms he mentioned, practically those suggested by Carson. On Monday he might have accepted the Chief Secretaryship if some of us had not done our best to put the brake on.[148]

Immediately upon his return from Ireland Asquith composed a substantial account of his experiences and reflections which the Cabinet saw on 21 May.[149] The section dealing with what should be done immediately to revive the gravely weakened Irish government began with the statement: 'It is clear that the Home Rule Act, however amended, cannot come into operation until the end of the war.' What then should be done in the meantime? First of all the Viceroyalty, 'a costly and futile anachronism,' should be abolished simply by not appointing a successor to Lord Wimborne. The King had agreed instead to take the court to Dublin annually.[150]

Far more important was the executive. 'With the disappearance of the Viceroyalty would disappear also the fiction of the Chief Secretary. There must be a single Minister controlling and responsible for Irish administration.' Asquith did not develop his ideas on this new post at any length except to say that the existing part-time executive who was also a member of the Cabinet in London, leaving effective administration in the hands of the under-secretary and the civil service, would end. This was the post the Unionists in the Cabinet believed they had invited Lloyd George to take.

There exists also a letter of 22 June, a month later, from Austen Chamberlain, at that time Secretary of State for India, to the Prime Minister, by which time the Unionists were convinced that Asquith and Lloyd George were smuggling in Home Rule under the pressure of the war emergency. Chamberlain outlined in painful detail how the stated goals of the government's solution to the Irish problem had changed since the Prime Minister arrived back from Ireland.

Asquith had returned, recalled Chamberlain, with the feeling that all Irishmen felt some good ought to come from the rebellion that would prevent renewal of struggle at the war's end. The time clearly had come for ending the Viceroyalty. Asquith had used '*in this connexion only*' the phrase 'Castle government has broken down'. He then offered the Chief Secretaryship to Lloyd George who refused it but agreed to try to find 'a solution to the Home Rule question which might relieve both countries of the incubus' of renewed civil war. But there was nothing in any of this to suggest that Lloyd George was authorized to establish 'any form of Home Rule *forthwith*'. Nor could he make proposals to the Irish parties without Cabinet consent. Lloyd George, wrote Chamberlain, was really supposed to see whether there was common ground, or whether the government could force some common ground, and then would report back for instructions on an agreement. None of this had happened and the first the Unionists knew of the negotiations for immediate Home Rule came with the news that Irish party leaders were summoning conferences to approve a pact that no one had ever seen.[151] The Unionists felt themselves betrayed.

One must conclude that the Irish negotiations of 1916 were the product of a private agreement between Lloyd George and the Prime Minister concluded between 22 and 25 May to give Ireland immediate Home Rule. Lloyd George himself had written to his brother on 22 May saying he had been asked by the Prime Minister and Bonar Law to 'take Ireland with full powers to effect a settlement. Rather interesting that when there is a special difficulty they always pick on me!'[152] Certainly both men knew, indeed Lloyd George had stated several times, that the Nationalist party had been gravely wounded by the rising. Only immediate Home Rule would save Irish parliamentarianism. He would get it if he could.[153] The two men had conspired in this way before, in the spring of 1915, on intervention in the Balkans.

Chamberlain's complaints about Unionist ignorance of Asquith and Lloyd George's intentions are confirmed by a letter from one of the most influential of the anti-Home Rulers, Walter Long, to Lloyd George on 23 May at a time Long evidently assumed Lloyd George would be Irish Secretary. He wrote cordially urging Lloyd George 'to go to Ireland'. There he could render a service to Britain and the Empire. 'I need not say,' he concluded,

> that my knowledge and experiences of Ireland, now extending over more than 50 years, and my influence with my friends will be at your service if you think they will be of use to you at any time.[154]

Long would become almost the first Unionist to realize that Lloyd George's aim was not unspecified reform of the Castle government, which nearly everyone could agree was desirable, but alteration of the constitutional settlement embodied in the Act of Union. And within a week he discovered that Carson was now prepared, as Long saw it, to abandon the southern Unionists. The story of Lloyd George's Irish negotiations of the summer of 1916 then is less an account of the framing of an agreement that both the Nationalists and Carson could accept, although that was a political miracle ambiguous as the agreement was, than of the growing conviction by a small but extremely powerful group of very senior Unionists, some but not all of them Irish peers, that they had been betrayed by Lloyd George with the connivance of Asquith. Under the excuse of war, to save a decaying Irish Nationalist political machine, Home Rule would be smuggled in and Ireland turned over to the rabble. Of Lloyd George such things could be expected; the anger turned toward the Prime Minister.

The Prime Minister announced Lloyd George's appointment in the House of Commons on 25 May. The statement became hugely controversial. In two columns of the *House of Commons Debates* he said almost nothing of what Lloyd George in fact was to do. He spoke early of an 'agreement' of the sort that had long been sought and of the Minister of Munitions's 'task' or mission and of the 'unanimous request' of the Cabinet that Lloyd George produce 'that [what?] result'.[155] There was general applause in the Unionist press.[156] Ruth Lee understood that her husband and Addison would manage the

Ministry of Munitions and indeed a few days later, in a typically Lloyd Georgean arrangement, Major General DuCane received a note from Frances Stevenson telling him that for the next week or two he would report to Lt. Col. Lee.[157]

Lloyd George was already at work. The next day, at Lee's home, No. 2 Abbey Garden, he lunched, not surprisingly, with the Ulster Unionist leaders, Carson and a new man who was emerging as the efficient party manager of Belfast, James Craig, MP for East Down, who in June 1921 became the first Prime Minister of Northern Ireland.[158] From this meeting came Lloyd George's plan for the settlement of Ireland. The Home Rule Act would be brought into immediate operation with an amending act passed as a war emergency measure to exclude the six most northeastern counties of Ulster, the four old plantation counties plus the whole of Fermanagh and Tyrone, a 'clean cut' as Carson insisted.[159] To emphasize the temporary nature of the settlement, the Irish delegation at Westminster would remain, for the duration of the war, at 103 who, with the exception of those from the excluded area, would constitute also the Irish House of Commons. There would be a nominated Senate and possibly, Lloyd George wrote later to Carson, a nominated contingent in the Dublin House of Commons representing Southern Unionists.

The critical question of the duration of Ulster exclusion was less clear. In the account in his memoirs Lloyd George postulated a grand imperial conference after the war which would look into many things, including perhaps the political status of the six counties. However, in the covering letter conveying the finished draft to Carson on 29 May he stated: 'We must make it clear that at the end of the provisional period Ulster does not, whether she wills it or not, merge in the rest of Ireland.'[160] Carson, in his reply, was more realistic, understanding, one may imagine, what Lloyd George in fact meant: everything would be considered again after the war. 'The six counties are to be excluded from the Government of Ireland Act and are not to be included unless at some future time the Imperial Parliament pass an Act for that purpose.'[161]

Here then was the crux of the Lloyd George plan and indeed the thrust of his political strategy. As always, everything was subject to change. Carson understood that the final settlement of Ulster was to be left to a general election after the war but personally Lloyd George had assured Carson that he would support the permanent exclusion of Ulster. However at the same time he could tell the Nationalists truthfully that everything would be reexamined. But Carson, by accepting this made a major concession. Lloyd George's plan differed only in detail, in that it specified the end of the war rather than six years, from the one he had laboriously worked out in the winter of 1913–14. Home Rule for 26 counties would be granted immediately with the position of the excluded six left to the judgment of parliament after an election. Ulster's final status thus would be determined in the last analysis by the voters. In the spring of 1914 Carson had contemptuously rejected this as a 'sentence of death with a six year stay of execution'. Now he accepted it. Negotiations were beginning where they had been left at the Buckingham Palace conference, he said repeatedly. The tortured discussions of an ethnic division of Fermanagh and Tyrone would be dropped in favor of a clean cut. If accepted by the respective parties Home Rule at last could be achieved, the Nationalist party saved, and the sacrifice at Easter given meaning. But, as he had declined to do in 1914, Carson now was abandoning the Southern Unionists. His foot soldiers, the Ulster Volunteers, were no longer available to coerce the government and save the Protestant Ascendancy.

Lloyd George's account of the breakdown of the Irish settlement states that he first became aware of discontent with his plan in an 'unexpected' letter of 11 June from a 'prominent Unionist member of the Cabinet'.[162] However, his papers show that he had plenty of warning of Southern Unionist unhappiness and that their response was immediate and forced upon his attention. One is inclined to wonder whether Carson himself, as he was entitled to do, had not told his Southern colleagues of the proposed constitutional changes in the government of their island. In any case on 27 May, the day after his meeting with Carson and Craig, Asquith passed to Lloyd George a letter he had received from Viscount Midleton (St. John Brodrick, at the War and India Offices from 1900 to 1905, an ancient and powerful County Cork landlord) on Carlton Club stationary, deploring the 'reopening' of the Home Rule question. He hoped the interests of Unionists outside Ulster would be considered and feared the question would be destructive of the party truce. The letter was signed by Midleton, however appended were the names of seven others, Irish Unionist peers and MPs, although the name of the greatest of all the Irish landlords, the Marquis of Lansdowne, did not appear.[163] Lloyd George evidently wrote immediately to Midleton inviting his group to a meeting for Midleton wrote again on 30 May declining a conference because they were not yet ready.[164]

Lloyd George did not take Midleton's intervention lightly. He quickly wrote to Carson warning him, as Carson had already anticipated, that Ulster's defection from the Unionist cause would bring trouble. Midleton, he said, was urging South Unionist friends to write, opposing the settlement, to Long, Bonar Law, Lansdowne, and probably Chamberlain. Long had sent these letters to Carson. '. . .in the innocence of his heart he thinks it all a spontaneous outburst of indignation.' It had occurred to him, he said to Carson, that it would be well to add representatives of the Protestant minority to the lower chamber of the provisional parliament as well as putting them in the Senate. 'The terrible disaster in the North Sea [the Battle of Jutland on 31 May] makes it more necessary than ever that we should get Ireland out of the way and press on with the war.'[165]

Clearly Carson also was receiving letters charging him with duplicity and bad faith. His replies were characteristically blunt. Since his return from Belfast he wrote to Sir Horace Plunkett, a moderate Dublin Unionist, he had been negotiating without 'any hint' that some colleagues in the Cabinet did not agree with Asquith's statement of 25 May. He would not withdraw now. The present settlement gave 'all that we could have achieved at the Buckingham Palace Conference.' To withdraw would mean weak government in Ireland and renewed hostilities at the end of the war.[166]

Midleton's complaints were underscored the day before by a letter to Lloyd George from the far more important Unionist, Walter Long, who though still as cordial as he had been six days earlier, nonetheless gave a warning. Long began by saying that he understood that the 'progress of your negotiations is all that we could desire' but he felt that he should remind Lloyd George of the cleavage between the Ulster Unionists and those of the South. Those of the South did not feel themselves represented 'or protected' by the Ulster people. '. . .neither Carson nor [Sir James] Campbell,' (Irish Attorney General since April, whom Carson had proposed for that post in May, 1915) represented the opinion of Dublin Unionists.[167]

In the next few days Lloyd George received several more worried communications from Long and angry ones from Midleton. Meanwhile he asked G.F. Stewart, head of a firm of Dublin property surveyors, former Governor of the Bank of Ireland, vice chairman of the Irish Unionist Alliance, and described by Long as a 'broadminded Dublin Unionist' to report on conditions in Dublin. Stewart's report was most unsatisfactory. Home Rule would simply justify a new Sinn Fein rebellion. It had worked once and would work again.[168] At the same time Lloyd George announced to the press that everything was going splendidly. He would soon have a statement to make.[169] Finally he corresponded with Carson about possible concessions to South Irish Unionists in the constitution of the Home Rule government. 'I think it is most important,' he wrote on 3 June

> that the Unionist minority should be adequately represented in the provisional Parliament at Dublin as well as in the Executive. I therefore suggest that instead of having a separate House during the Provisional period the Government nominees should sit in the first Chamber. [Under Lloyd George's original plan, it will be remembered, the Senate would be entirely nominated.] We might arrange that in the lower chamber there should be twenty or thirty, or even more, leading representatives of the minority and that in the Executive or Cabinet there should be at least two Protestant Unionists. This would be much more valuable than to pack those men into a separate Chamber. When the time comes to consider a permanent settlement all this can be readjusted; but I feel that the presence of a powerful minority in the Lower Chamber would give the Protestant Unionists the greater confidence at this period.[170]

This frantic activity, during a week when most of the nation was either dazed or jubilant over the Battle of Jutland, represents probably the nearest that Lloyd George was able to come to an Irish settlement. His enemy, it was becoming clear, was the Southern Unionists. Conscious that the Orange Card was no longer available and no doubt genuinely afraid that Home Rule's day had passed, Midleton and his followers, soon to be joined by important members of the Cabinet, were quite prepared to try to bring down the government to save the English connection. Power sharing, as it would now be called, was not enough.

Home Rule by the end of the first week in June was as dead as Queen Anne if it had not been before. On 26 May Lloyd George himself had received a letter from St. John Ervine saying that neither Carson nor Redmond had any influence in Ireland any longer and that Lloyd George should not 'look to them for guidance'. Redmond had 'not even visited Ireland since the Rebellion began, and his authority as a leader does not exist.' His photograph had appeared on the screen in a cinema recently and was widely booed. Ervine favored an Irish Council with Ulster excluded if necessary.[171] In effect even a decently representative Irish parliament made up of the existing parliamentary delegation from the 26 counties would be hardly more stable than the Castle.[172]

At the root of the crisis in negotiation that exploded in the first days of June was the British army's policy of repression. At the end of April when the rebellion was crushed the great majority of Irish people had been relieved. There were reports that columns of prisoners being escorted through the streets of Dublin were hooted at and jeered. A very little more than a month later the country was again in a ferment of conspiracy and rebellion. At the center of the problem were the indiscriminate and, one must say, clumsy, repressive tactics of the military commander in Ireland, who under martial law was the sole authority in the country, Major General Sir John G. Maxwell.

Maxwell, a Scot, always called 'Conky' Maxwell, was a highly decorated battlefield soldier, not a staff officer. He had commanded a unit at Omdurman and in South Africa, and had been military governor of Pretoria after its capture. Until almost the outbreak of the war he had commanded the Egyptian army under Kitchener who was High Commissioner, and at the time of his appointment to Dublin he was General Officer Commanding the Third Army Corps in France. One may presume that Kitchener, under whom he had served most of his life, recommended him for the post in Ireland.

The story of the military repression after the Easter rising has been told many times focusing generally on the outrage produced by the summary execution of thirteen of the Dublin rebel leaders (and a fourteenth in Cork). This act certainly contributed to popular fury, but it was at least an official decision authorized by the London government, which also specified for various reasons that certain individuals be spared. Upon reflection it seems that the more important charge against Maxwell lies in his failure to control his troops, allowing them to behave as if they were putting down a riot in a slum quarter of Cairo. A particular villain was Major I.H. Price, Director of Military Intelligence in Dublin, 'Maxwell's right hand man', wrote John Dillon on 11 June. He intended to destroy Home Rule. The irony of the situation was that by giving 'the soldiers and Price a free hand you are making yourselves the instrument of the enemies of your policy.'[173] There were mass arrests, with important municipal officials crowded into inadequate cells.[174] There were a number of indiscriminate shootings and most horrible of all the murder, on 26 April, by British soldiers, under the command of a deranged officer, of a fairly well-known journalist who had nothing to do with the rebellion, Francis Sheehy Skeffington, as well as two other men.[175]

The revival of Sinn Fein disastrously undermined Lloyd George's plans. Serious doubts began to appear among the Nationalists, whom after all the entire exercise was designed to save, about whether Home Rule was practicable under the present circumstances with the concessions Lloyd George had been forced to make. The most distrustful was John Dillon. Lloyd George refers to his problem with Dillon in his *War Memoirs* and assigns them generally to his difficult personality.[176] In fact there seems to have been real fear, shared by many besides Dillon, that Maxwell was making Ireland ungovernable except by soldiers.

On 9 June 1916 T.P. O'Connor, whom Lloyd George had known and liked since his entry into the House of Commons, wrote that Dillon objected to the presumed entirely Unionist composition of the Irish Senate, particularly if they would from time to time sit and vote with the Irish House of Commons. But there was something even more important.

Meantime, I would be glad if you would impress upon the Prime Minister that the real root of all this atmosphere of apparent irreconcilable hostility to any settlement among the Nationalists are [sic] the presence and proceedings of Sir John Maxwell. Unless he is withdrawn and military rule in Ireland brought to an end, I feel very despondent as to our ever being able to push the settlement through.

Maxwell should be replaced by another officer 'of greater capacity' and martial law withdrawn. D.O.R.A. could provide all the powers necessary.[177]

Lloyd George immediately wrote to Asquith enclosing O'Connor's letter. Everything he had heard from the Unionists confirmed its assertions. 'Maxwell is making agreement impossible.' (Dillon himself had written the day before saying that he understood Maxwell was about to arrest the Bishop of Limerick. Lloyd George denied this. Such an act was too stupid even for Maxwell.)[178] 'The country,' Lloyd George continued, 'is one seething mass of discontent. Sinn Feinism is for the moment right on top. The ghastly report of the Skeffington execution has roused the people to a pitch of fury.' Could something be done to restrain Maxwell?[179] Asquith replied characteristically that he had already told Maxwell of the necessity 'of going slow and of creating no "incidents"'. There were to be no more executions. He would write to Maxwell again.[180]

On that day, 10 June, apparently after writing to the Prime Minister, Lloyd George wrote to Dillon. The settlement was in danger and the alternative was chaos. He had heard from any number of sources that things were 'not very favourable'. Both the Irish Nationalists and the Carsonites were making trouble. If there were an agreement it would be grudging and Southern Unionists were working 'hard and skillfully against a settlement'. 'They are bringing unwanted pressure to bear upon the Unionist members of the Cabinet' and sending paragraphs to newspapers on Irish disloyalty. Lloyd George had been able to get some of them suppressed, but not in the *Morning Post*. The danger was that if a settlement were not achieved quickly there could not be one until after the war. 'Heaven knows, what will happen then!'

But the country had to be governed, Lloyd George continued to Dillon, and if there were no agreement among the Irish to govern it themselves there would have to be coercion. If it became too difficult England 'will get angry'.

The prospect is a horrible one; and as there are many people in your country — that I have discovered in the course of the recent negotiations — who whilst pretending to be Home Rulers, really detest it, you can never tell what will happen after a period of ruthless suppression.

Lloyd George referred to the generally recognized need to conciliate American opinion on Ireland (a threat he had been using constantly as a negotiating weapon). But, he said, people were already objecting to being bullied by the United States. He mentioned also that he had written the Prime Minister about Maxwell's 'fatuous administration'. He concluded on a note of hope.

No doubt if Dillon and Carson succeeded there would be a deadly struggle in the Cabinet. He did not believe Lansdowne would agree to any settlement and Long was 'sulky'. Nevertheless he was not greatly worried.

> If these men withdraw, the Prime Minister and I standing together could compel them to surrender. The British Government could govern Ireland by coercive means if both parties stand together; they cannot do so if we join forces with you. That I should do unhesitatingly if the Government refused to sanction an agreement and although I am not entitled to speak on behalf of the Prime Minister, I think I can say that he would do likewise.[181]

This long letter fairly describes the difficulties under which Lloyd George labored by early June after a hopeful beginning only two weeks earlier. Carson, before always the boulder in the path, had compromised quickly, at some sacrifice. The Southern Unionist grandees were as implacably hostile as ever, but they had lost the Orange Card, Carson's threat of civil war. However, in its place they had gained, as allies of sorts, unexpectedly, a large, growing and powerful but heterogeneous group of Southern Catholics who wanted Home Rule no more than they: the Sinn Feiners who wanted independence and the exploding number of moderate Nationalists who feared, under present conditions at least, that a restrained, constitutionally minded, Dublin parliament, made up largely of Nationalist MPs, could not govern.

The meaning of Lloyd George's concluding paragraph is obscure. Can one believe that Lloyd George really intended to resign should Home Rule be blocked by Cabinet Unionists? Likely this was his way of impressing his determination upon Dillon. But would Asquith finally press Home Rule to the point of breaking up the coalition? This seems most improbable. In the event he did not.

Dillon replied the same day in a letter of despair providing what would become the ordinary Irish Nationalist story of the failure of the 1916 negotiations. He agreed entirely with Lloyd George's analysis of the disastrous consequences of a failure to arrive at an agreement and concluded:

> Do you wonder now at the bitterness with [which] I spoke — when I came over fresh from observing the effect of the executions. When the fighting was over — and the Insurrection crushed — if there had been no executions the country would have been *solid* behind us — and we could have done what we liked with it.[182]

The harvest of bad news was not yet fully gathered in. On the same day Lloyd George received a letter from Walter Long partially quoted in the *War Memoirs* telling of Unionist anger. As has been noted Lloyd George refers to this letter as being 'unexpected'. This can be true only in the sense that it came from a popular, loyal, and influential Unionist leader who might have become party leader after Balfour's resignation in the autumn of 1911 and who had cordially supported what he had believed to be an attempt to reform Castle government sixteen days before.

'I enclose a brief statement of my views on the Irish Question,' the letter began, 'arrived at after long and anxious consideration.' Then followed a memorandum:

Information reaches me from both England and Ireland, that there is no disposition to come to a settlement, that the line taken by the leading Unionists...is that the Unionist Party in Ireland are being driven by the Prime Minister and Minister of Munitions into accepting a situation which they know to be morally wrong and wrong politically, that the Nationalist Party are sullen and hostile and have no intention of abandoning their policy and programme whatever may be the decision of their leaders.

At the same time I hear the gravest account of the condition of Ireland. If one half of what I have heard is true it seems to be quite clear that this is not the moment to embark upon any political experiment. The situation is very different from what I believed it to be when we first discussed the question, far graver and more serious, and unless I am wholly misinformed I don't think it would be possible for me to give my assent to any form of Home Rule...[183]

Lloyd George immediately wrote to Long in the tone of pain and sadness that came naturally to him when one of his plots was uncovered. He could not understand how Long could believe he had been deceived. 'It would have been fairer of you to a colleague who was undertaking a risky and a thankless task had you expressed the views now embodied in your Memo at the time I was chosen to negotiate.' Everything now was irretrievably lost. He would have to resign. '...in the face of your letter I have written to the PM withdrawing from the negotiations and from the Government. P.S. Sorry you have not been well.'[184]

Long replied saying he was 'really amazed' by charges of 'disloyalty'. How could he have objected at the time of Lloyd George's appointment, he asked reasonably enough, when he had no notion of what the plan was. He could not believe 'that you intend to base your resignation on this excuse.'[185]

At the same time Lloyd George wrote to Dillon telling him of Long's letter and saying that he had heard from Bonar Law that southern Unionists were 'moving Heaven and the other place' to thwart a settlement.[186] Irish difficulties were indeed great, but could have been overcome. However, he concluded, in this case: 'I replied promptly by saying that under these circumstances I placed my resignation in the hands of the Prime Minister, as I felt absolutely committed to these terms.'

Lloyd George obviously was discouraged by the clutch of bad news conveyed to him on 11 and 12 June. He sent Dillon's, O'Connor's and Long's letters to Asquith, but despite all the portentous threats, he did not resign. Clearly he thought about it and wrote a note of resignation concluding with the statement that 'without a united Government settlement is impossible'. However, this letter remains in his files carrying a pencilled notation in Frances Stevenson's manuscript, 'not sent'.[187] The chief problem lay in the decay of Nationalist vigor as would be amply proved within seven months by the beginning of a stunning succession of Sinn Fein by-election victories. No one in the South, it seemed, Nationalist, Unionist or terrorist wanted Home Rule. Only Carson remained committed to the settlement.[188]

Two days before, on 10 June, the Irish Nationalists, meeting in the Dublin Mansion House, had listened, unenthusiastically, to the Lloyd George proposals, which Redmond assured them were incomplete and temporary. They were, he said, only the basis of further negotiations, although they could reasonably be regarded as a proposal of the government. This statement apparently provoked Long's letter to Lloyd George. In a separate article entitled, significantly, 'The Nationalist Dilemma', *The Times'* Dublin correspondent stated that he believed most party members wanted to vote for the settlement but feared adverse opinion in the country.[189] The following day the same correspondent noted that of the four daily papers in Dublin, two Unionist and two Nationalist, only one, the official Nationalist organ, the *Freeman's Journal*, supported the Lloyd George scheme.[190] Two days later, on 12 June, the Ulster Unionist Council with similar apathy gave Carson their permission 'to continue negotiations' on the basis of a 'clean cut' of the six counties. In neither meeting had there been any published statements as to whether exclusion was permanent or temporary.

So far there had been much confused discontent entwined with suspicion of Lloyd George, but no action beyond the unhappy realization in both Belfast and Dublin that while the negotiations might be leading to a goal no one was sure he wanted, they could not be broken off. Carson's arguments to his followers turned upon several points: that Ulster had better take Home Rule with exclusion now, it would be impossible to raise rebellion after the war; that Britain was growing impatient with Irish problems; and above all that opinion in the United States demanded Home Rule. All of this was received in North Ireland with expressions of deep distrust of both Lloyd George and Asquith.[191] There was little beyond bare reports of meetings in the newspapers, despite the frantic private activity. After the Whitsun weekend, beginning on Monday, 5 June, the papers suddenly exploded with accounts of the Battle of Jutland, (apparently held up until the Germans announced a great naval victory) and the next day with stories of the greatness of Lord Kitchener.

The unravelling of the settlement began on 16 June with a letter to the Prime Minister from Lord Selborne. Selborne, an old Liberal Unionist who had disliked and distrusted Lloyd George for years, was not an Irishman but he was an important, high ranking, and influential peer and President of the Board of Agriculture in Asquith's huge coalition Cabinet. His anonymous biographer in the *Dictionary of National Biography* quite rightly assigns to him a leading place in resistance to the Lloyd George plan. He wrote that he had heard from Long that Lloyd George was putting it about that his scheme had been accepted by the Cabinet. He had understood, he said, that with the exception of the immediate passage of an act excluding Ulster from the operation of the existing Home Rule statute, nothing would be done until after the war. Not only had he never accepted anything more, but had never had the opportunity to do so. Unless this were repudiated he would resign. In his covering letter passing Selborne's letter to Lloyd George, Asquith remarked temperately that he did not suppose Lloyd George had made any such statement.[192] Lloyd George of course replied saying he had never told Redmond or Carson that his proposals had been accepted by the Cabinet. Only Asquith, who approved, Lansdowne who disapproved, and Long, had seen them. He had warned that it was 'quite in the cards' that the Unionists might reject the settlement, which would be, however, a repudiation of Asquith's authority.[193]

Lloyd George now showed uncharacteristic discouragement. The implications of Selborne's letter were clear. The prospects for the settlement were not bright at the moment, he wrote to Dillon. There was trouble in the Cabinet. 'The whole of the Unionist members are in a state of mutiny, and say they will not consent to any proposals to bring the Home Rule Act into operation during the war.' Nonetheless he stood by his settlement and had 'no doubt' the P.M. did. If the Ulster Unionists accepted the proposals the Cabinet Unionists would find opposition impossible.[194] (Selborne did not resign in fact until 25 June.[195] His statement to the House of Lords became the first public explanation of the Southern Unionist case: the Cabinet had been misled. Home Rule at this time was 'perilous'.)[196]

Perhaps it may be said that Lloyd George's mission was now impossible. His letter to Dillon suggests he thought so himself. Although attempts at a settlement were not abandoned until the end of the next month, Lloyd George no longer had room for maneuver and in any case decision-making was no longer in his hands, but in those of the Prime Minister. Lloyd George had done much. He had indeed achieved a settlement that could be put before the House of Commons. Whether Ulster's exclusion was to be permanent or temporary would rest with the electorate at some time after the war as, it must be emphasized, Carson himself understood. A new House of Commons could make the decision then. One has to believe that in Lloyd George's mind this issue was almost minor. That Carson had accepted a settlement, as he had not in 1914, was important. Lloyd George had handled negotiations in this way at least since 1907. The goal was never the achievement of perfect harmony, but of an agreement that would solve an immediate problem. Difficult points could be put off, delegated to a committee, a Royal Commission, or promised future legislation. Nothing was ever perfect, but nothing was ever finished. Politics was a matter of movement and initiative. A week, let alone years, was a long time. Many obstacles would remove themselves. In 1916 only one thing counted: getting on with the war.

In a way, therefore, Lloyd George had done his part. If his settlement were embodied in legislation twenty-six counties of Ireland would be governed by an Irish parliament made up of Irishmen. Even the devilish matter of power sharing had been accomplished. The difficulty, again, was that Home Rule's day had passed. In the month between the end of April and the end of May, General Maxwell's mindless overreaction had transformed an almost unplanned Dublin uprising into a national revolution. Augustine Birrell, a man of perception and sensitivity if not an ideal Irish Secretary, had written to the Prime Minister just as the uprising ended: 'It is not an Irish rebellion and it would be a pity if *ex post facto* it became one.'[197] Unhappily this prescient warning was forgotten.

And so the package that Lloyd George had put together was undeliverable. No one in Ireland beyond the old Nationalist leaders wanted it. (Ironically public opinion in Great Britain, distracted by many other things, seems generally to have supported the idea, if not the details, of a permanent Irish settlement. The country, thought *The Times*, was 'not ready to throw Ireland back into the melting pot.')[198]

Lloyd George had lost the initiative and control he always tried to maintain in negotiations. As he usually did, he had met each side separately with an already prepared plan. Necessary amendments were explained in differing terms to each side. Eventually there would have been the triumphant announcement of an agreement coupled with the statement of an unclear but desperate need for haste. Everything must be concluded immediately without further consultation. But this momentum was gone. The Southern Unionists, not party to the process, had nonetheless moved it to another level, the Cabinet. Moreover the Southern Unionists had a good moral case: they had been deceived by Lloyd George and the Prime Minister about the nature of the settlement Lloyd George would attempt and with conditions in Ireland as they were, Irish self government was not only dangerous but impossible. They were thus in a position at least as strong as Carson's had been in 1913 and 1914 when Ulster exclusion was dressed in the garb of British patriotism. However their goal was the same, not Home Rule with safeguards but no Home Rule.[199]

For the moment all of this was not entirely clear. The 'crucial test' of the settlement, everyone assumed, was the meeting of Ulster Nationalists on 23 June.[200] The representatives of the nearly 400,000 Catholics in the six counties, led by Joseph Devlin, would be invited to vote themselves out of the jurisdiction of a Dublin parliament. On the surface the meeting was a great success. 'Magnificent convention proposals carried by nearly two hundred majority' telegraphed Devlin whose irresistible oratory and sophisticated political cajolery, combined with a threat by Redmond to resign, carried the day.[201] But there were disturbing footnotes. For the first time the matter of Ulster exclusion had come into the open. The resolution so overwhelmingly approved had specified only that 'the proposals of Mr. Lloyd George for the temporary and provisional settlement' were a step toward 'a unified self-governing Ireland.' Indeed the resolutions contained no provision for action, only that the proposals seemed, as it were, to be a good idea.[202] Perhaps a worse omen was the revelation in *The Times* the next day that only about half of those eligible to attend the meeting had been present while a separate article revealed that the Unionist *Irish Times* had reported on the day of the meeting that Carson possessed a letter from Lloyd George saying that partition would be permanent.[203]

The Ulster Nationalist Conference was the last victory, if such is the proper term. Selborne announced his resignation two days later. Commenting on both, *The Times* judged that Devlin's victory helped but:

> If it were possible, perhaps, a good many moderate Nationalists would be glad to identify themselves with the new policy of the Southern Unionists which is quite willing to accept the decision of an Imperial Conference [the public provision, it may be recalled, in the Lloyd George settlement for the final determination of the status of the six counties], but regards the present scheme as dangerous and untimely.[204]

As if it sought to prove Selborne right and Devlin wrong the government allowed the trial for treason of Sir Roger Casement to begin on 26 June, the day Selborne's departure appeared in the papers. He was convicted on 30 June 1916 and sentenced to be hanged. F.E. Smith, in 1914 perhaps the most visible and enthusiastic British partisan of Ulster resistance, led for the prosecution.

All of this made the Cabinet meetings on Ireland of 27 and 28 June something of a fruitless exercise, at most an attempt to control damage. However the task was now the Prime Minister's. The leader of the opposition, until now in the background, was the Marquis of Lansdowne. Home Rule at this time, he argued, would be a 'concession to rebellion', an Irish parliament could not control the island and D.O.R.A. must remain in force. By the end of the meeting it was clear, at least to the Prime Minister and Lloyd George, that the settlement could cause the breakup of the government. On the suggestion of Lloyd George, Asquith appointed a new committee with himself and Lloyd George as members to investigate further safeguards for peace in Ireland, although General Maxwell, who was present, insisted that one division could guarantee Irish security.[205] At another meeting on Ireland on 5 July, the committee recommended seriously the dilution of the powers of a Home Rule government for the duration of the war. Lansdowne and Long agreed not to resign. The Prime Minister complacently reported to the King that he had won again.[206]

But Lansdowne was not yet finished. On 11 July he delivered an uncharacteristically pugnacious speech in the House of Lords announcing that the government intended to keep order in Ireland and that it had complete confidence in General Maxwell.[207] Lansdowne's statement seems to have completed the destruction of the Lloyd George settlement not because of any extreme position declared in it but because it grievously insulted the Irish Nationalists.[208] There would be no further concessions to them. Asquith had now to abandon the settlement if he were to save his government.

The dissolution of the Irish settlement began as a process by which Lloyd George chipped away bits of the agreement to be offered to the Southern Unionists as inducements to compromise, to be replaced when rejected by larger inducements. This process was now concluded. The end came on 22 July when Redmond, as he recounted to the House of Commons, was called to the War Office to be confronted by Lloyd George and Herbert Samuel who told him that the Cabinet had altered the draft amending bill. Exclusion would be permanent and the provision for full Nationalist membership in the House of Commons (Redmond's way of emphasizing the provisional nature of the settlement) would be dropped. When Redmond protested that he had received assurances from both Lloyd George and the Prime Minister that there would be no last minute changes of the sort he now had received he was told that the two men were acting only as 'messengers' and were not empowered to discuss their message.[209] On 31 July Asquith announced that 'for the moment' negotiations on an Irish settlement had broken down and that H.E. Duke would be appointed Irish Secretary.[210]

A large part of the history of parliamentary politics in any nation is that of individual disappointment and tragedy, of chances missed, of appointments not offered or of bills defeated for trivial or transient reasons. Few are sadder than Redmond's, a man of 65 in his thirty-fifth year in the House of Commons to which he was devoted, sick and soon to die, who saw his life's work destroyed on a Saturday morning in July 1916.

Lloyd George had also pronounced the epitaph, not the death sentence, of lawful Irish separatism. Obviously he knew this and tried continually, when he had the power to do so, to revive the corpse. He could not. Maxwell's work had been thorough. In a month he destroyed an 80 year tradition.

Lord Esher, the observer never the participant in the English political world, always detached yet usually correct, summed up what had happened in a letter to his wife just four days after Redmond received his heart-breaking news.

I should not be surprised if Asquith had to go and if little L.G. reigned in his stead. This Irish business has been so badly handled. Fancy getting an agreement between Redmond and Carson and then losing it. The agreement itself was a miracle. Of course the Irish are an impossible people — but still, in the middle of a war like this, it is criminal to go dabbling in Irish rows.[211]

9 The War Office.
The Military Moloch

At 7:40 p.m. on 5 June 1916 HMS *Hampshire*, about two hours out of the anchorage at Scapa Flow in the Orkney Islands, struck a mine just off Marwick Head on the northwest coast of the central island. The mine had been laid only a week before by a German submarine in anticipation of what would become the Battle of Jutland. A dozen men survived from a complement of 655. Among the casualties was Field Marshal Horatio Herbert, Earl Kitchener of Khartoum, Secretary of State for War. News of the loss was published in London in the early afternoon the next day.

Kitchener's journey to Russia had been a close secret and so the public reaction was of stunned horror. Could the war go on without him? Inevitably there was disbelief: stories that he had not been drowned, that he was on a secret mission, that he had been seen and would return.

Among politicians there were the usual conscience-clearing statements about Kitchener's sterling character and great patriotism, although Lloyd George told Riddell that the Field Marshal's reputation would suffer as the facts became known.[1] But the overriding political reality was that the War Office now lay vacant. Who would succeed him?

As was his custom the Prime Minister immediately occupied the War Office himself and informed the King that he would be in no hurry to appoint a successor.[2] Meanwhile, on the day news of Kitchener's death became public, Maurice Hankey enquired of General William Robertson whom he would like to take the office and learned that the Chief of the Imperial General Staff was 'very anxious not to have Lloyd George,' perhaps Austen Chamberlain.[3]

Lloyd George nonetheless was the obvious candidate and the only real competitor was the Unionist leader, Andrew Bonar Law. The question the historian must address concerns the motive that impelled Lloyd George to take the office, as he eventually did, with only the reduced powers Kitchener had possessed. For nearly two years he had consistently denounced the army and the Secretary of State for War for shortsightedness in ordering munitions, for inflexibility in strategy, and for unwillingness to adapt battlefield tactics to the new conditions of static warfare. He had fought to take from the War Office control over weapons, military operations, and strategy. He had deprived the Master General of the Ordnance of all his functions, had forced the Boulogne program upon an unwilling Kitchener, and had done as much as anyone to give Kitchener's control of operations to the admirable General Robertson. (Almost his last act in the War Office, on 29 November, was to force the retirement of the Master General, Stanley Von Donop. He was replaced by General W.T. Furse although the office now was practically without a function.) In his own mind, as he would repeat many times in the coming weeks, the Secretary of State's office was now an object of derision or pity. Yet in the end he took it, unenhanced.

Lloyd George is unclear about all of this in his *War Memoirs*. He did not care, he wrote, to 'work in fetters', and he leaves the impression that the alternatives were not the War Office or the Ministry of Munitions but rather the War Office or resignation. This last from contemporary evidence would seem to be quite true. As has been remarked, he had been talking of resignation since the autumn of 1915. He had consulted endlessly and would do so again. There was always a particular issue — munitions, Salonika, conscription (twice), yet the underlying contention was the general conduct of the war.

Kitchener's death occurred just as the Irish negotiations were approaching the impasse that they finally reached in the second week of June. During this time Lloyd George had been in constant touch with Edward Carson whom he had convinced that a quick settlement in the other island was absolutely imperative for the vigorous prosecution of the war. Either in office or out, Carson would be a powerful, if dangerous, ally.

On 3 June when, it must be remembered, Kitchener was still alive, Lloyd George expressed his worries in a letter to Carson.

> The management of the war on the part of the Allies is fortuitous and flabby, and unless something is done immediately the British Empire and civilization will sustain the greatest disaster since the days of Attila. I must therefore have a talk with you with a view to taking immediate action to force a decisive change in the control of the war. An appreciation of the situation by the general staff has just come into my hands. It fills me with gloomy forebodings. There is no time to lose. I must have a talk with you on Monday [5 June], not only about Ireland but about the whole position, before you leave for Belfast. Let us settle Ireland promptly...[4]

This letter has been introduced as additional support for the hypothesis that Lloyd George's interest in the War Office may have proceeded from his intention to do something about the army, a matter about which he felt so strongly that he was willing to take the post even without operational authority after having insisted to everyone that he was not interested in it without full control and responsibility for command appointments.[5] To accomplish revitalization of the army command he needed Unionist support. Carson, mistrusted by British and indeed Irish Unionist leaders since the beginning of the settlement negotiations, had nonetheless the loyalty of the war hawks on the Tory back benches and of H.A. Gwynne of the *Morning Post*. Carson despised the coalition government and its chief. No one could doubt his commitment to victory and he had resigned over the army command's failure to provide aid to Serbia. In the battle with the curious duality of enemies with which Lloyd George found himself faced — an inflexible, unimaginative and inept army command and a flabby government unable to force it to improve — Carson fitted perfectly.

In effect the alliance with Carson, already in the process of formation occurred less as a scheme to overthrow Asquith than to reform the army command, symbolized eventually by Robertson.[6] Nearly a year earlier, in the autumn of 1915, Lloyd George had proposed a small political war committee to supervise military operations. Asquith of course never objected to the formation of a committee; there had been three war committees since 1914. Each however had quickly grown into a reproduction of the Cabinet and indeed became a larger body when military advisors were added, meanwhile suffering the same disabilities of lack of information and of continuity and of the structural insecurity suffered by amateurs when confronted by professionals. The notion of an inner Cabinet, meeting daily, with its own military advice, which could talk to the military on equal terms, and presumably with its own sources of information, had been gestating for months. Lloyd George had evidently discussed it at least with Churchill as well as with the Prime Minister.[7] Such a body would make unimportant the formal monopoly possessed by Robertson under the Orders in Council of the provision of military advice to the Cabinet.

It is clear that Lloyd George without yet admitting it wanted to become Secretary of State for War. His first act therefore was the elimination of competition from Bonar Law. On Sunday 11 June, five days after Kitchener's death became known in London, he met Bonar Law at Cherkley Court, Max Aitken's home on the Thames. Aitken's well-known account of this meeting asserts that there was a good deal of rivalry and frostiness between the two men, which Lloyd George was at pains to allay and which suggests a contest for the vacant War Office.[8] One must question this estimate of the relationship between the two men. Lloyd George and Bonar Law by this time knew each other well and the latter, as he had indicated many times, did not, and could not, regard himself as a rival of Lloyd George. More important, with the troubles over the Irish settlement coming to a head at precisely this time, he was loyally supporting the Minister of Munitions in the Cabinet against the wishes of many influential men within his own party. Finally, Bonar Law's admiration for the Prime Minister would have made it difficult for him to demand Kitchener's chair for himself. Only a month before, Ruby Carson reported meeting at the House of Commons Bonar Law's sister, Mary Law, who lived with him and was the source of excellent political advice and who observed scornfully that her brother was 'entirely under Asquith's thumb'.[9]

In any event Bonar Law agreed that Lloyd George should be Secretary of State for War and agreed to convey word of his support to Asquith. Having been put off Sunday evening he and Aitken drove on Monday to The Wharf where after being asked again to wait Bonar Law insisted upon seeing the Prime Minister whom he found, according to Aitken, playing bridge with three ladies.[10] He now told the Prime Minister of the discussion with Lloyd George only to have the War Office offered to him. Bonar Law, according to Aitken, declined saying that it was too late. A few days before he would have taken it but he now supported Lloyd George.[11]

All of this, as Aitken tells it, is clear enough. Bonar Law had learned that Lloyd George wanted the War Office and was willing to stand aside. In other words Lloyd George would become Secretary of State for War. Aitken states flatly that the appointment was forced upon the Prime Minister and that it signalled the end of his administration.[12] Yet there are other accounts of the transactions of Sunday and Monday, 11 and 12 June and at least some confusion over important details. For example, one of the reasons that Bonar Law had insisted upon seeing the Prime Minister on Monday was that he and Aitken were leaving for Paris. There, at dinner on Thursday, he had told Lord Esher that Asquith had consulted him about the War Office and that he had recommended Lloyd George with the provision that if Lloyd George declined he, Bonar Law, was to get it.[13]

Bonar Law told yet another story to George Riddell on 4 May 1919. Confirming, generally, what Robertson had told Hankey about his preferences for the next incumbent of the War Office, the Conservative leader said to Riddell that the C.I.G.S. wanted someone 'plastic', perhaps Walter Long. Bonar Law continued that he had telephoned the Prime Minister and said that he must see him. When he did, he told Asquith that if Long were appointed he would resign. 'You must appoint L.G.,' he announced.

> He wants the job and you will have to give it to him. You had better do it with good grace. If you wanted to break him, perhaps at one time you might have done so, but now he is too strong for you. If you stand in his way he will probably crush you.[14]

A better source is Lloyd George's own account of the meeting at Aitken's given to George Riddell on Sunday evening 11 June 1916, before, indeed, Bonar Law had seen the Prime Minister. Lloyd George, Riddell understood, still was by no means certain that he wanted the War Office.

> Dined with LG. Found him very preoccupied. He said that he had dined with Max Aitken at his house, which is about three miles from Walton. Bonar Law was there. Bonar Law intends to resign unless LG is appointed Minister for War or he is appointed himself. LG is not disposed to take the office, and feels that the time has come when he can do greater service by resigning. He is very dissatisfied regarding the conduct of the war, and he thinks the situation in France very serious. . .He thinks our failures inexcusable, as we have men, guns and ammunition. He considers that we have no brains at the top, and that Haig is not an able man. He says that Asquith does not want a man at the War Office who will give him trouble. He is very dissatisfied with Mr. A and thinks him very tricky. Bonar Law agrees that LG is the most suitable man to go to the War Office. If he does Bonar Law would take over Munitions. LG thinks that the War Office is a difficult task. . .he might be met with insuperable difficulties. If he were leading the opposition he could accomplish more. . .He said, 'If I went out I should at once form a great Party organization. I have promises of all the money necessary. . .'[15]

Even though Lloyd George had professed to Riddell the greatest reluctance about the War Office he wrote to Arthur Lee that evening, in answer to a note from Lee urging him to take the post: '. . .it would be scarcely credible to anyone who does not know Asquith' but Lloyd George had not talked with him since Kitchener's death. Lloyd George confided that he inferred from press reports that 'he [Asquith] wants the W.O. himself. That being so there is nothing left to discuss.' He would talk to him tomorrow when he '*may* see A.'[16]

This letter conveys, if nothing more, some eagerness at least to be offered the War Office. Lloyd George, of course, did not know that Asquith would remain at The Wharf the next day, Whitsun Monday, 12 June. However on the following day, Tuesday, 13 June, he did see the Prime Minister and was asked evidently rather off-handedly whether he would like the critical office.[17] Specifically Asquith offered Lloyd George either the War Office with Kitchener's powers or the Vice Chairmanship of the War Council without Portfolio (whatever that might mean). Lloyd George believed the Prime Minister wanted him to leave Munitions so that he could offer it to Edwin Montagu, 'a special ally' (and Venetia Stanley's husband).[18] Lloyd George reserved his opinion.

By that time Lloyd George already had been with Edward Carson, evidently on 12 June. If Lloyd George's alternatives, as has been argued, were between resignation and the War Office, either decision would involve the Ulster leader. Here, for once, he was frank. He would take the appointment. 'Edward lunched with Col. Lee to meet Mr. Lloyd George,' wrote Ruby Carson. 'He is going to the war office, if he didn't Bonar Law would & that would be a disaster. How that man has changed [presumably Bonar Law], he is nothing but an office seeker & I hear rather up with ambition.'[19]

On the following day, Tuesday, 13 June, Lloyd George saw C.P. Scott to whom he gave the familiar litany of complaint: he would not take the office without power; 'no set of men more insolent than soldiers if they knew you had not power' and so on.[20] However, Scott's diary suggests that the pact with Bonar Law of which Beaverbrook evidently was so proud represented far less an accomplished fact than is suggested in *Politicians and the War*.[21] Lloyd George took the War Office in the end without power, because he wanted it and because, as he must have told Edward Carson, he did not want Bonar Law to have it and because he believed he could make something of it even without power.[22] The battle with the army, which had already begun as something of a private feud with Kitchener and Von Donop, would erupt in earnest during his period at the War Office. Caught in the crossfire was the Prime Minister.

Lloyd George's mind worked best in conversation. Although it may be accepted he now wanted the War Office, he wanted, reasonably, the fullest powers he could get. But he needed to know what would be the political impact of his acceptance of that office if it remained in the enfeebled condition in which Kitchener had left it. To this end he assembled at Riddell's on 15 June virtually the same group, with the exception that Christopher Addison was present in place of Lord Reading, that he had met there the previous October to discuss his future after Carson's resignation. Present were Lloyd George, Riddell, Addison, and, perhaps most important for Lloyd George, William Robertson Nicoll whom Lloyd George invariably consulted on political matters.

The conversation on this occasion is fully reported in Riddell's published diary and supplemented by a long account in Addison's diary. However it was here that Lloyd George discovered what he needed to know: that he was unlikely to get the powers he wanted but that he should, at last, take the office without them. Thus it deserves some attention.

That afternoon Riddell had seen Sir Reginald Brade, Permanent Secretary at the War Office, an astute political observer like most in his position. Brade feared trouble if any attempt were made to curb Robertson's powers.

> He said the Army would support R. . .LG had cracked many a tough nut, but would probably find the W.O. a tougher nut than any he had yet tackled and might break his teeth as others had done before him.[23]

All of this Riddell had evidently told Lloyd George before the others assembled.

After dinner Lloyd George announced not quite truthfully that the Prime Minister had formally offered him the War Office and that he had agreed to think about it while Asquith took a holiday in Scotland. He had consulted Northcliffe the previous day who had advised that acceptance would strengthen the government. 'I also saw Carson,' he continued,

> who said that he would be glad in one way if I came out. He would like to work with me and that together we might bring the Government down and replace it by a sounder more energetic body. He, however, thought I could render a more useful service by going to the War Office, but I must stipulate for full powers. I place great reliance on Carson's judgment. He goes to the heart of things. It was his judgment which made him such a success at the Bar. My own inclination is to resign. The Munitions Department is now in full swing, so that my mind would be easy on that score. The war is being sadly muddled.[24]

Lloyd George continued at some length on the familiar theme of the inept and feeble management of the war and concluded by saying he had long intended to resign but Kitchener's death had intervened. What now should he do? Nicoll replied:

> Mr. Minister, I think your position is quite clear. You must accept the offer. Do not haggle about powers; you will later get all the powers you want. Your appointment to the War Office will hearten the country and the Allies. The nation and the Army regard you as the only man capable of filling the position. If you refuse you will cause consternation and dismay. I implore you to accept the P.M.'s offer.

Nicoll was followed by Addison saying in one sentence that he agreed with Nicoll but that Lloyd George should insist upon full powers, and then by Riddell who reminded Lloyd George that Brade had said he would not get them. However, Riddell pointed out what was surely obvious to everyone present that the Prime Minister, while probably frightened of a fight with the military establishment, could not allow Lloyd George to resign. Lloyd George responded that Asquith would 'not mind a row with Robertson if someone else is to do the unpleasant work.' He believed however, that he could win Robertson. With his quickness of mind and facility of expression Lloyd George would enlarge, not diminish, Robertson's influence. The discussion of the War Office ended with Lloyd George saying that if he resigned Bonar Law would follow him and the government would break up. 'I think, however, it is my duty to take the office, subject to having reasonable powers. I shall see the P.M. upon his return.'[25] Lloyd George and Addison walked back to

Whitehall together. They discussed, as if the matter were settled, the disposition of the Ministry of Munitions. Ideally it should be combined with the War Office under Lloyd George with Addison and Arthur Lee in charge. However, Lloyd George believed that Asquith wished to give it to Edwin Montagu.[26]

Perhaps the most revealing facts to be derived from the conversation at Riddell's house were first the substance of Lloyd George's conversation with Carson three days earlier, that the Irish leader wanted Lloyd George to take the War Office. Second the conversation offers an unmistakable consensus that Lloyd George at the War Office would be in a position to direct military affairs even without the formal powers given to General Robertson by the Order in Council because of the man he was. Finally Lloyd George seemed to be convinced, as he remarked several times, that the alternative to himself, Bonar Law, could not handle the post, although he usually put it that the Conservative leader himself felt Lloyd George to be the better man. It must be remarked that Lloyd George surely had to expect, and so presumably wanted, the advice he received. Robertson's *British Weekly*, which Lloyd George never missed, had begun that morning, 15 June, a campaign for Lloyd George's translation to the War Office. After saying that the Secretary of State must be a civilian, the paper had said:

> We believe that a large majority are also of the opinion that the new Secretary must be a great figure, calculated to command the respect and indeed, the enthusiasm of all. In particular, he must be pleasing to the Allies and to the Army. These requirements would be supremely satisfied by the appointment of Mr. Lloyd George. It is not known, however, whether Mr. Lloyd George would accept the position with its new limitations and we believe that from the Munitions Department there come very impressive representations declaring that Mr. Lloyd George is absolutely essential for the mighty task he undertook a year ago. . .[27]

At this point one may assume that Lloyd George was determined to get operational authority if he could. But it is equally clear that Asquith, despite Lloyd George's remarks to the conclave on 15 June, was adamant that he should not have them. On 16 June Asquith wrote to Lady Scott, evidently sent from Scotland, saying that 'Lloyd George was behaving absurdly, & suggesting tremendous powers for himself at the W.O. — much more than K had had. Also he was suggesting leaving the Cabinet altogether, saying he could be more useful outside it.'[28] But Asquith may have had other thoughts. There is an interesting report in C.P. Scott's diary of a conversation occurring on the platform of Paddington Station, between Scott and Margot Asquith, evidently on 17 June. When asked by the Prime Minister's wife who Scott thought should succeed Kitchener, the editor had replied he believed Lloyd George to be the natural person. Mrs. Asquith then questioned Lloyd George's far too intimate relations with pressmen, particularly Northcliffe. Could not her husband continue in the office? '"There was very little in it now. Perhaps Mr. Lloyd George would not care for it on the Kitchener terms." I assured her he would not — a queer woman. She probably revealed the Prime

Minister's astute design.'[29] Scott immediately wrote to Lloyd George telling him of this encounter, remarking that Mrs. Asquith 'may have let the cat out of the bag' but adding that she had expressed 'great affection' for Lloyd George.[30]

Although Asquith's biographer, Roy Jenkins, who gave much space to the subject, argues the opposite, it seems certain that the Prime Minister, despite evident pressure, did not want Lloyd George at the War Office.[31] Very likely his personal preferences were for a lesser figure, Lord Derby, who was popular and who badly wanted the post, or Austen Chamberlain, as Robertson had suggested, with himself as the real decision maker. But this was impossible. One must believe he understood, as everyone did, that the alternatives for Lloyd George were between the War Office and resignation. And his fine instinct for self-preservation certainly told him also that if Lloyd George insisted upon the post, without increased power, it would have to be his. The appointment would be popular in the country, if not in the army command, and would strengthen the government. Everyone seems to have believed this, including Lloyd George himself who counted it as a reason for not taking the War Office.[32]

Two days after the meeting at Riddell's house, on Saturday, 17 June, Robert Donald's *Daily Chronicle*, an influential Liberal paper whose editor was generally friendly to Lloyd George while being also a near neighbor at Walton Heath, published a lead article attacking Lloyd George's pretension to glory and power at the War Office and inviting him to take a more modest view of himself. The Secretary of State for War should be content to 'shine in his own orbit, without infringing on the orbit of the Chief of the General Staff.'[33]

Lloyd George was furious. One must speculate whether he did not suspect Asquith of inspiring the article, although in truth he suggested this to no one and such an act would have been totally uncharacteristic of the Prime Minister. Yet Robertson Nicoll, always well informed, suspected J.A. Spender, the one close journalistic friend of Asquith.[34] Lloyd George did, however, suspect McKenna as he usually did. In any case on that day, 17 June, he wrote a letter to Asquith declining the War Office. 'As I told you in our interview I thought I should be of greater service in another sphere.' Lloyd George did not specify what this sphere was to be, but he added that he had recently taken up the project of soldiers' votes and wished to see it through. A new office would hinder action. 'It is better therefore from your point of view as well as mine that you should give no further thought to my appointment as War Minister. I thank you all the same for the offer.'

This letter is curious in several ways. The reference to Lloyd George's sudden interest in the military vote, rather made fun of by Jenkins, was not specious.[35] Indeed Addison had been working on just such a plan for some time.[36] Lloyd George was indeed popular in the ranks of the army and a wartime election, as a result of important resignations from the Cabinet, was not impossible. Finally, on behalf of this argument, when he became Prime Minister he insisted that the program be put into effect. The chief national department involved was the Local Government Board. The then President was forced to resign because of the failure of his ministry to perform its rather large tasks assigned under the plan. He was succeeded by Christopher Addison.

At issue more immediately is the fact that, although this letter from Lloyd George is in the Asquith papers, the typescript copy in the Lloyd George papers carries the clear pencilled inscription 'not sent', and indeed the movement of events leading to Lloyd George's appointment seem to have been entirely unaffected.[37] There was not the usual prompt Asquith reply pleading for delay. Within a few days Lloyd George was negotiating with Robertson about powers. The next day in fact with apparently no thought of resignation he was complaining to Riddell at Walton Heath that Donald's article had prejudiced his talks with Robertson. Nothing happened. What became of this letter? It is not mentioned in the *War Memoirs*.

However, on the same day, Saturday, 17 June, Lloyd George composed a much longer letter to the Prime Minister also not sent, but from which he quotes at length in the *War Memoirs*.[38] This document was at once an outright statement of resignation and an attack, without citing individuals, upon the army's conduct of the war. He insisted that the new Secretary of State for War should have power to control military appointments, referring, a bit ingenuously, to the repeated humiliation of 'poor Kitchener' in recent months. There was a critical need for effective civilian control. The British army because of its small size and minor place in affairs in peacetime simply did not attract men of the mental capacity to manage the projects upon which it was now embarked. Soldiers simply would not promote a brilliant man. 'A civilian on the other side would have no sense of the rivalries in military promotion and he would insist upon the best man being promoted.'

Similarly the War Committee should be able to supervise, although not take charge of, strategy with 'the common sense of a civilian'. 'The soldiers in this war have not been a conspicuous success. Up to the present there has not been a plan conceived and carried out by them which has not ended in bloody failure.' (The preliminary bombardment for the battle of the Somme would begin in precisely one week.)

Lloyd George insisted he had no personal interest in these questions, but

I have been profoundly dissatisfied for a long time with the progress and conduct of the War. I have expressed my dissatisfaction in writing and orally to you, the War Committee and the Cabinet. Had it not been for the fact that I had undertaken a task the carrying out of which was vital to the success of our Army, I should long ago have joined Carson, with whom I have been in the main in complete sympathy in his criticisms of the conduct of the War. But when there was trouble with labour, when the organisation which I had with the help of others created had not yet borne fruit, I felt as if I were running away from the post of difficulty. But now the Munitions Department has been an undoubted success. Ammunition is pouring in. When I came in we were manufacturing in this country 70,000 shells a week; that is about one-sixth of what we spend now in a single week of ordinary trench warfare activity. [In the seven days of 24 June–1 July 1916 British guns would fire 1,508,000 shells of all calibers on a single 14 mile front.[39]] The whole ammunition reserve was under 75,000, we produce more than twice that per day now. The guns are coming in by the hundreds. The policy for which I was mainly responsible in respect of heavy guns — a policy, by the way, which I heard described by one

of my colleagues as 'sheer lunacy,' and which has been consistently
opposed by him and by others for months — has now been
demonstrated by the facts of the war to be the only one that can
possibly achieve success. Our Army in France is now sending in a
requisition for hundreds more of heavy guns than had ever been
ordered by the War Office. Had it not been that I had in defiance of
all authority high and low made arrangements for the manufacture of
these guns, the requisition would be in vain.

This long passage is of considerable importance for what it reveals of Lloyd
George's state of mind after the unpleasant winter of 1915–16. As during the
South African War, he had been completely out of step with his party and
with a substantial portion of the voters in the country yet had been proven
right by events. But he had suffered, and now was angry, and would remain
bitter for years despite his repeated assertions that he did not care what
people thought of him. Asquith, of course, was perfectly aware of all of this,
including the success of the big gun program. Lloyd George may have written
the denunciation of his colleague, obviously McKenna, largely to relieve his
own feelings.

The final paragraphs carried out the threat implicit in the opening ones.

I. . .feel that my position in the Ministry is an anomalous one, as I am
completely out of sympathy with the spirit and the method of the war
direction. I feel we cannot win on these lines. We are undoubtedly
losing the war, and nothing can save us but the nation itself. The
people do not realize how grave the situation is. I feel they ought to
be told. . .I know you have always taken a more optimistic view of the
prospects, but I think up to the present my gloomy forebodings have
been realized. I hope to God I am wrong; but if I am not, I should
feel I had been guilty of a gross neglect of duty if in order to retain a
pleasant office I had chosen to muzzle myself and not warn them in
time of the danger impending their country.

All of this was no new or transient resolution. He had, he said, told Reading
of it many weeks ago. (Reading, Rufus Isaacs, the Lord Chief Justice, one
senses, was a regular, but unacknowledged, vehicle of communication between
Lloyd George and the Prime Minister at this time, trusted by both, clever,
discreet.) Finally, there came the threat. The government was dying. There
must be an election. Perhaps he would force one. There would be other
resignations.

It is with deep regret that from an overwhelming sense of public duty
I feel that I must sever my association with you with some of my other
colleagues who have shown me great kindness and goodwill, but I am
profoundly convinced that I can render better service to my country in
a very dark hour by standing outside and telling them what I know. I
believe the Government is rapidly losing the confidence of the nation.
It cannot retain it by artificially prolonging the life of Parliament. The
nation ought to have the opportunity of choosing its own policy and its
own representatives to expound it, and I specially feel that the men in
the trenches ought to have the opportunity of choosing Parliament and
the policy on which their lives depend. Here again I am conscious of

being out of touch with several of my colleagues [including the Prime
Minister] and I cannot help seeing that there is an attempt being made
to put off a decision on this important question until it is too late to act.

As to Ireland, as far as I am concerned it must be either through
or off in the course of the next few days; but I feel that outside the
Government I can be more helpful even in the settlement of that
question.

One may be content that the Prime Minister came to know of this letter.
There are many ways in British politics of threatening resignation. A politician
may write a letter and not send it, as this one was not, but he may instead
read, or show, the contents of the document to a man who, he is sure, will
convey the substance to the Prime Minister. Reading and Bonar Law, he
knew, were desperately anxious that he not resign. Lloyd George makes clear
in his *War Memoirs* that he spoke to both men about resignation, as well
as to Sir Edward Russell of the *Liverpool Post*. He admits sending the
memorandum to Russell, but says only that, after talking to Bonar Law, who
insisted that his own position would become impossible if Lloyd George
resigned and joined Carson, he decided to withhold the memorandum from
the Prime Minister.[40] With this he ends the story of the circumstances
surrounding his appointment.

It may be taken as certain that the Prime Minister was fully apprised of
Lloyd George's feelings about the War Office and indeed about the failings
of the military command; that he shared the belief Lloyd George's appointment would strengthen his administration; that Lloyd George's resignation
was a chance he dared not take and that Lloyd George's control of the War
Office would be little affected one way or the other by the infamous Order
in Council. Finally he was astute enough, as always, to calculate that Lloyd
George's strength emanated from his skill in Cabinet negotiations, not from
any formal powers attached to his post. Lloyd George, having said many
times he was not interested, probably wanted the War Office. Therefore
Asquith would have to put his own preferences aside. This assumption is re-
enforced by reports from Reginald Brade which show that Asquith made up
his mind in the week of 18 June. On that Sunday, Brade told Riddell, a man
who had spent the week-end with the Prime Minister had heard that 'under
no circumstance' would Lloyd George go to the War Office. Yet on 23 June,
the following Friday, Brade could assure Riddell that the appointment was
'fairly certain'.[41]

There is more than circumstantial evidence to confirm this. On 20 June,
Tuesday, Edwin Montagu wrote a now well-known letter to the Prime Minister
saying that he had seen Lloyd George at the home of Rufus Isaacs, Lord
Reading, the evening before. Lloyd George had talked much and excitedly
about Ireland and the War Office, which, one must comment, he never would
have done in Montagu's presence had he not intended his words to be
conveyed immediately to the Prime Minister. Supporting the idea that
Asquith's previous remarks about Lloyd George's taking the War Office had
been excessively casual, Montagu said that Lloyd George obviously believed
that he had been offered the post. He added that it was quite clear he would
take it without any change in 'status or [constitution?]' However he had said
'the War Office must wait till we're over [Ireland].'

345

Continuing, Montagu advised that so long as Lloyd George thought he had been offered it, it would be 'disastrous' for the Prime Minister to make any other arrangements for the War Office while Lloyd George was working on an Irish settlement. Finally, he concluded, perhaps Lloyd George ought to have the appointment.

> There would be many advantages to having LG at the War Office during the announcement of heavy casualties and a possibly unfruitful offensive. [The preliminary bombardment for the battle of the Somme would begin in three days.][42]

There was also the *Daily Chronicle* article. Lloyd George's fury at Robert Donald's effrontery surely came to the notice of the Prime Minister, perhaps through McKenna, who had also good connections in the press. If the Minister of Munitions did not care for the War Office, why should he be so angry? Lloyd George's anger at this time did not abate and became the origin of an important initiative in 1918: the purchase of the *Chronicle* and the summary discharge of Donald.

'Donald is not straight', he growled to Riddell on 18 June. 'He poses as a friend but stabs one in the back. He has done this before.' The article would prejudice an agreement with Robertson, which Lloyd George saw clearly as the only way the Prime Minister could be induced to restore powers to the Secretary of State for War. One often asks for more than one is willing to accept, observed Lloyd George. But now the opponent had been advised to grant nothing.[43] The next day he was still fuming about it. On Thursday, 22 June, when Riddell called at the Ministry of Munitions, Lloyd George had decided on a course of action and indeed made some preliminary enquiries. Riddell had suggested that he see Donald.

> LG said that he was treacherous and he did not feel inclined to see him. LG asked me to ascertain on what terms the 'Chronicle' could be bought and said that he could find the cash. I gathered that [Alfred] Mond and [Charles] Henry & Co. [wealthy Liberals. Henry's wife Julia was rumored to be one of Lloyd George's mistresses] are prepared to put up the money. LG said that he must have a Liberal paper. I suggested that it might be best to negotiate through Donald.
>
> LG: I can talk to Donald when I have got the paper.
>
> LG said that McKenna had been working hard to keep him from the W.O. and that he knew from Northcliffe that [Hedley] LeBas [managing director of the Caxton Press and McKenna's avenue to Fleet Street] had been round Fleet Street trying to get up agitation against LG. LeBas had said to Northcliffe that LG could not afford to resign because his means were not large enough. LG very indignant. He described LeBas [an enemy of Riddell also] as a contemptible jackal who did not understand that men were moved by other than sordid motives. As for money LG said he had been offered £5,000 by an American syndicate for three articles.[44]

The conversation continued two days later when, on Saturday, Riddell drove to Walton Heath with Lloyd George. He was 'still very angry' with Donald, noted Riddell. But by this time it was clear that the indirect communications of 17 June, via Reading, Montagu and no doubt Bonar Law, had done their work. Lloyd George would not be put off from the War Office. Riddell urged him to take it, 'questions as to the limitations of his authority will adjust themselves.' Lloyd George agreed that it would be impossible to amend the Order in Council but that he would insist on control of promotions. Lloyd George admitted that he now believed the Prime Minister realized that his appointment to the War Office was 'inevitable'. He had also heard from Douglas Haig offering 'good offices'.

The talk turned again to Donald, Riddell saying that he did not believe McKenna was behind the editor, rather that the article was only an example of Donald's 'heavy handed ways'. He warned Lloyd George yet another time against listening to Northcliffe who was 'a fair weather friend'.[45]

In the last week of June, indeed as it became clear that Lloyd George would be going to the War Office, he made a serious although brief attempt to arrive at an understanding with General Robertson. These exchanges included an apparently casual and inconclusive conversation between the two men, succeeded by three rather illuminating letters. Following the conversation Robertson wrote to Lloyd George on 24 June outlining the duties of the C.I.G.S. since 'last December': that he rather than the Secretary of State signed and sent the orders to the field commanders and advised the War Committee. Significantly, he quoted at length from the letter he had sent Kitchener offering to resign if the changes were not made.

Lloyd George replied on 26 June. On the whole he was conciliatory but he worried about his constitutional position unless he received complete information on everything, no doubt recalling his continual exasperation with Kitchener in the past two years. He cited at length the harmony between the First Lord and the First Sea Lord at the Admiralty even though the legal independence of the latter was greater than that of the C.I.G.S.

Lloyd George repeated that he must maintain control over command appointments. In this, he agreed, both the C.I.G.S. and the War Committee were involved, but the Secretary 'must bear the burden of convincing the War Committee and the Prime Minister where necessary, and of gaining the support of the submission which, in due course, it is for the Secretary of State to make to the King.' Here, he surely knew, he was making an argument Robertson would understand. Robertson, no more than Kitchener, could challenge Lloyd George's power in advocacy among politicians.

Robertson hastened to agree that consultation in everything was vital. The system as such amounted to very little; everything lay in the way it was carried out. There was no threat of resignation. Lloyd George could depend upon 'the loyal co-operation of myself and the whole of the General Staff.'[46]

By and large Lloyd George had what he wanted. Membership on the War Committee would give him control over appointments even if the War Office did not. And in fact it was not the problem of secrecy, which had so bedeviled relations with Kitchener, that caused the breach between Lloyd George and Robertson, but the General's single-minded, Lincolnshire stubbornness in his disinclination to examine any alternatives to the Western Front and, in a smaller degree, to Robertson's refusal to go to Russia to discuss first munitions and then support for Romania. Neither of these had much to do with Lloyd George's formal powers as Secretary of State. Kitchener's weakness, and certainly Lloyd George saw this, derived not from the deprivation of the command and advisory powers taken from the Field Marshal in the Order in Council in December 1915. In fact these made little difference. On the contrary, the reality was that in the Victorian political world, the glittering prizes, the War Office and the Admiralty, needed not a brave and experienced soldier but a seasoned and powerful politician with the confidence of the Prime Minister, a Cardwell or a Haldane. Despite his imposing presence, undoubted patriotism and devotion, Kitchener was not, and could not be, this man. It took a moment for the Cabinet to realize this but one may be sure that his momentous and solitary decision to build a mass army for France, taken a week after his appointment, would have occasioned more discussion six months later than it did in August, 1914.

Hence Lloyd George, although he would continue to talk of the humiliation of 'poor Kitchener', could take the War Office with reasonable confidence. One must imagine that he had known this from the beginning. Asquith would surely support him in military appointments and interfere only when a particular officer whom he disliked, H.H. Wilson or, for that matter, Churchill, was involved.[47] Lloyd George wrote to his brother on 28 June saying that he had 'decided to take the War Office',[48] His appointment was evidently held up by the Unionist revolution over the Irish settlement at the end of June, and by someone's sudden recollection that of the six Secretaries of State one, at least, had to be a peer. This was solved by making Edward Grey, whose eyesight was rapidly failing, a Viscount. The appointment finally was announced on 6 July 1916.

I

The move from the Ministry of Munitions caused distress in several quarters. Asquith had insisted that Lord Derby be named Under-Secretary, a post Arthur Lee had hoped would be his. Perhaps in anticipation of what was coming Lee had written to Lloyd George as early as 18 June urging Lloyd George to accept the offer of Vice Chairmanship of the War Committee, to try and stay at Munitions, and not to resign. He was bitterly disappointed when he discovered Lloyd George was leaving him and asked on 1 July to be sent to France. Lloyd George, unusually, took a week to reply. He advised Lee not to do anything rash. Lee would hear from him as soon as the War Office was 'sorted out'.[49] On 9 July Lee was appointed Personal Military Secretary to the Secretary of State for War. Addison remained as an Under-Secretary at Munitions.

Churchill was also wounded. With the lack of clarity that caused him endless political disappointment, that made him, as he once said of someone else, both indomitable and insufferable, he expected to be made Minister of Munitions. Evidently Lloyd George put this to the Prime Minister, with some urgency, at the time his own appointment was announced and received a flat refusal. The next day, 7 July, Riddell asked Churchill 'What happened regarding the Munitions Department? LG spoke very strongly in favour of your succeeding him.'

> Winston: Yes, both he and Bonar Law thought I should go. I did not want to join this Government, but felt I could have rendered useful service in that capacity. The PM. . .would not hear of it, and I am no

suppliant for office. The Government is rotten to the core. . .full of personal jealousies and intrigue. . .

The Prime Minister, Churchill concluded, wanted Munitions 'for one of his little doggies'.[50] Montagu's appointment was announced on 9 July.

Lloyd George's first weeks at the War Office were relatively placid. He seemed to have had no immediate reaction to the appalling casualties on the Somme and dwelt instead upon the successful Russian offensive in the East. Relations with other Cabinet members improved and, most important, he and Robertson cooperated amicably. On 7 August Robertson wrote to Haig complaining of unpleasant questions that were beginning to be raised by Churchill, French and other 'dégommé d' individuals about recent operations.[51] Lloyd George had defended the army stoutly. '*I believe Lloyd George is all right,*' Robertson concluded. '*He merely requires to be made a fuss over and put well into the limelight.*'[52] Lloyd George equally had fewer complaints. At dinner with Riddell on 30 July he remarked to Riddell that the Prime Minister

gets few cheers now-a-days. But the truth is that if you could get rid of McKenna the Government would not be a bad government. He is the bane of the whole thing. He is always wrong and allows personal jealousy and malice continually to influence his actions. I have just had a most unpleasant fight with him regarding the provision of Russian munitions for next year. [Earlier in the conversation Lloyd George had remarked upon how well the Russians were fighting.] I had to give undertakings to the Russians which made it impossible for McKenna to decline to perform them. He actually refused to furnish the Russians with munitions for next year.

The future of the war, Lloyd George concluded, depended upon the Russians.[53]

As it turned out, the problems of the Eastern Front, with the Czar's empire and subsequently with Romania, would dominate Lloyd George's short sojourn at the War Office and would appear behind both his breach with Robertson and with Asquith. At the beginning of June 1916 Russia had begun its only general offensive of the war on a huge 300 mile front between the Pripet River west of Pinsk and Romania, concentrating in Galicia, usually designated the Brusilov offensive. For nearly three months it was remarkably successful inflicting, to be sure at great cost, 700,000 casualties upon the Central Powers, more than any single operation of the war. Although designed partly to help the French at Verdun and particularly the Italians under pressure from Austria, the preparations for the Russian effort inevitably made even more critical that nation's munitions supply, increased their always frantic appeals for help, and caused an acrimonious competition with the French. Albert Thomas' mission to Russia where he had spent much of the month of May was one result.[54] On 2 June, Thomas, back in France, wrote Lloyd George a long letter stressing again French needs, but providing also a fascinating glimpse of the industrial situation in Russia on the eve of revolution by a well-informed, albeit prejudiced, observer. He had seen the Putilov factories. He was astonished at the profusion of modern machinery. Russia had greater industrial capacity than France. But nothing was working. Russia would do well to help herself rather than expending her energy clamoring for British aid which the

French army, now in crisis, needed itself. He feared Kitchener, about to leave for Russia, would encourage their demands. Could Lloyd George come to see him?[55]

Kitchener did not arrive in Russia, but Russia's pleas continued and Lloyd George remained convinced as he had been since the beginning of 1915 that in a war of attrition Britain and France alone simply did not have the manpower to defeat Germany and Austria. Of this the Russians were clearly aware.[56] In some way the Russian need for munitions would have to be satisfied but first someone would have to ascertain what those needs were. McKenna's complaint to the War Committee in May that the Russians ordered everything with abandon, were spending much money obtained on British credit in America where he was already borrowing nearly £2,000,000 per day, and were not to be trusted was, in spite of Lloyd George, perfectly justified. Of course Lloyd George understood this also. Another high level mission to Russia would have to be arranged.

A second series of complications directed attention to the Eastern Front at the end of August. Romania, after many weeks of negotiation culminating in a treaty signed on 17 August, declared war on Austria and Germany on 27 August. Then on 1 September Bulgaria declared war upon Romania. Romania's survival depended upon the success of the Russian offensive. But on 29 August General Eric von Falkenhayn, the architect of the Verdun offensive, was relieved of the German command in the West and replaced by Field Marshal Paul von Hindenburg, the hero of Tannenberg and at that time *Oberost*.

For the course of the war and, more important, for the British domestic politics of the next few months, these changes were momentous. As in the autumn of 1915, the Eastern Front was in danger of collapse. As Lloyd George himself saw, the disappearance of Falkenhayn would mean a winding down of the vast German effort at Verdun while the appearance of Hindenburg was likely to produce a renewed German concentration in the East. Brusilov's offensive had begun losing momentum at the end of August just as Romania entered the war and the Bulgarian declaration meant that Romania would now have to fight on two fronts, of which the southern was practically undefended. Without help Romania would go the way of Serbia. This brought up again Salonika.

On 4 September 1916 Lloyd George wrote what would come to be an important letter to Major General Frederick B. Maurice, the Director of Military Operations.

> I have just seen the telegram announcing the declaration of war by Bulgaria against Roumania. This is an additional ground for the anxiety which I expressed to you on Saturday as to the possibilities in the immediate future in the Balkans. I then expressed some apprehension that Hindenburg, who has strong Eastern proclivities and has always been opposed to the concentration of German forces in the West, would direct his attention to the crushing of Roumania and that we ought to be thinking out every practicable plan for giving effective support to Roumania in the event of her being heavily attacked. We cannot afford another Serbia tragedy. We were warned early in 1915 that the Germans meant, in confederation with the Bulgars, to wipe

Serbia out. In spite of the fact, when the attack came we had not purchased a single mule to aid the Serbians through Salonika. The result was when our troops landed there, owing to lack of equipment and transport, they could not go inland and Serbia was crushed.

I hope that we shall not allow the same catastrophe to befall Roumania through lack of timely forethought.

The rest of the letter was a remarkably accurate forecast of German dispositions. Hindenburg would abandon the 'foolish' Verdun attack, probably give ground on the Somme, and concentrate the relieved divisions in the East to crush Romania. Bulgaria would not have declared war without promises of substantial German help.[57]

Robertson was not concerned. 'I find L.G. has got the Servian fit again,' he wrote to Haig on 7 September,

and maintains we have been wrong & the French have been right, as shown by Rumania's coming in. He thinks Hindenburg will now go for Rumania a la Servia & therefore we ought to be ready to assist Rumania with *more* troops. Of course I have an answer to this talk if he makes it when I see him. But as you may see him before he comes back I send you this to let you know how his mind (?) is working.[58]

The day before this letter was written a combined Bulgar-Turkish force under German Field Marshal August von Mackensen had attacked the Romanians from the south and on 19 September Falkenhayn, with indeed some troops from Verdun, fell upon the invading Romanians in Transylvania. Romania's entry into the war spelled not only disaster for that nation but within three weeks had brought an end for all practical purposes to the Brusilov offensive.

Lloyd George's warnings in the letter of 4 September would remain in his mind. They would become an important cause of the political crisis that he forced at the beginning of December. He evidently carried a copy of the document with him which he produced occasionally.[59] Evidence of all of this appears in Addison's diary. On 23 November, the day as it happened German Field Marshal Mackensen crossed the Danube preparatory to the investment of Bucharest, Addison recorded

...Lloyd George told me an interesting piece of news in connection with the attacks which were made upon him early in October for trying to dictate to the General Staff. He was emphatic that assistance should be sent to Roumania. Robertson and the Staff, however, were against him on the ground that it was impossible for the Germans to get guns, etc., into Roumania over the passes at this time of the year...He gave me a copy of a letter which he wrote to Robertson [sic Maurice] on September 4. This week, as we know, the Germans have broken through into the Roumanian Plains, with what result we do not know at present...If the letter had been written this week, it could not have been better put. Nevertheless, with the geography as it is, it is difficult to see how we could have sent them much effective help.[60]

In his letter to General Haig of 4 September 1916, Robertson had referred to Lloyd George's presence in France. This visit, which lasted nearly two weeks, began on 4 September at Folkestone. The origins of this extended trip are unclear although he had gone briefly the previous month between 12 and 16 August to represent Britain in the Romanian negotiations and at that time had visited General Haig to discuss railway transportation in France.[61] Some weeks earlier Northcliffe, himself in Paris, had written to Arthur Lee urging him to tell Lloyd George to get to France at once. The new War Minister was regarded as a Seely or a Churchill and the view from the Ritz Hotel was that Lloyd George was not popular in the trenches. These letters seem to have shaken Lloyd George a good deal. Riddell was present in August when Arthur Lee brought in two letters from Northcliffe to Lee. He recorded Lee as saying: 'He is still friendly to you but the soldiers have got at him. There is a movement to undermine your influence. I can see it from several signs.' Although Riddell, for once, defended Northcliffe, 'LG would not have this and implied that N was taking part with his critics.'[62]

Lloyd George had a good deal of respect for Northcliffe's judgment on public opinion, but he may have been influenced also by the fact that two other new ministers in semi-military appointments, Montagu and Derby, not necessarily competitors to be sure but hardly supporters, were already in France. But finally, however, as he had done at the Ministry of Munitions, his way of learning about a new task was to travel, to talk to the people involved, to ask questions, to probe and reflect. Moreover, he needed to see Albert Thomas.

Lloyd George immediately went to Verdun, with Thomas and Arthur Lee, where, on 7 September, he watched French counterattacks upon the withdrawing Germans. The next day Lloyd George returned to Paris, giving interviews and being photographed emerging from an artillery dugout, still apparently with Thomas. On 10 September he was joined by Lord Reading who remained with him until 15 September.[63]

From Paris Lloyd George drove with Reading, Lee, evidently Albert Thomas, and several others to Amiens through, as he records, endless squadrons of cavalry jingling forward to exploit the expected breakthrough of the second Somme attack scheduled to begin on 15 September.[64] (It was in this attack, led by the Guards, that Raymond Asquith fell. Altogether the Guards lost 190 officers and 6,000 other ranks on that day noted Col. Repington, remarking characteristically: 'It is the first time since the early days of the war that Society has been hit so hard.')[65] At Amiens, he stayed at the Hotel du Rhin in the city and not at Haig's headquarters, since March 1916 at Montreuil. Here, in the afternoon of 11 September, he interviewed the French General Ferdinand Foch, at that time G.O.C. the French northern army.[66]

The talk with Foch, which became something of a scandal among British generals in the weeks that followed, eventually was leaked to the newspapers, and was certainly among the reasons for the rapid breakdown of relations between Lloyd George and Robertson that began in September.[67] So far the C.I.G.S. had been entirely content with his minister. As late as 29 August Robertson had written to Haig regarding the latter's resistance to demands from the French for renewed pressure on the Somme to relieve the situation at Verdun.

> I spoke to Lloyd George about this the other day, and he repeated what he has said many times lately that he thinks you are playing

exactly the right game, and doing your job in exactly the right way. You can attach any importance you choose to his opinion, but it will be satisfactory to you to know that he at any rate thinks you are doing the right thing.[68]

This letter, although it refers basically to relations with General Joffre rather than to the cruel losses in the first days of the Somme offensive, is worth noting as testimony that on the eve of his departure for France Lloyd George still approved of Haig. It is possible therefore that what came to be held as the infamous Foch interview was nothing more than an attempt by Lloyd George to gain information in the way he customarily did, and not, as became the general opinion, an attempt to elicit criticism of Haig.

As Foch told Haig on 15 September, Lloyd George, using Reading as an interpreter, had begun by saying that he had a right to be told the truth about the Somme offensive. Why had the British, who had gained no more ground, if as much, as the French, suffered so many more casualties. (The much smaller French attack on the British right had been remarkably successful and was halted only when the French commanders found themselves in danger of uncovering their flank.) Foch had replied carefully that the French had learned their lessons in 1914 and now were more cautious. He sometimes wished they were not. With artillery, he observed, the British had done wonders. (In fact it was well known that a large number of British projectiles, many produced by Lloyd George's Ministry of Munitions but with a good proportion of the smaller calibers manufactured in the United States, had not exploded.)

Finally Lloyd George asked about the quality of British generalship. He '"was sufficiently patriotic not to criticize the British Commander-in-Chief,"' Haig recorded Foch as saying, 'but he did not speak with confidence of other British Generals as a whole.'[69] (Evidently Foch had remarked also about Lloyd George's travelling about France with two Jews, 'an entourage from the Ghetto.' Lloyd George said nothing when he heard this, apparently from Churchill, except to say that Lee was not a Jew.)[70]

Haig was outraged by these revelations. 'Unless I had been told of the conversation personally by General Foch, I would not have believed that a British Minister could have been so ungentlemanly as to go to a foreigner and put such questions regarding his own subordinates,' he wrote. He immediately communicated with Robertson who was even more angry and announced he would have it out with the Secretary of State.[71] Haig urged caution and the confrontation never took place, but immense damage had been done and more would follow quickly.

Lloyd George would have been the last person to deny Haig's charge that he was not a gentleman in the English sense. He was, as he was fond of saying, only a Welsh country solicitor.[72] But nonetheless he was far too sensitive to have been unaware that the nature of his enquiries would cause offense and when the time came to get rid of Robertson he was far more skillful. Yet it remains likely that he was, in truth, looking only for information that he felt he could gain no other way. He genuinely admired French, indeed German, military expertise and deplored the clumsiness, while applauding the bravery, of the British army and had said so many times. But perhaps the most compelling evidence of the innocence of his question lies in the fact that two days after the conversation with Foch, on 13 September, Lloyd George, Reading and Arthur Lee turned up at the headquarters of the XVII Corps under the command of Henry Hughes Wilson. Wilson, hated and perhaps even feared by Asquith after the Curragh Mutiny, despised by Haig, was a close friend of Foch's and like Foch Wilson was an outsider in his nation's military establishment. Foch had communicated the substance of his conversation with Lloyd George to Wilson on 12 September even before he told Haig. Thus when Lloyd George and his party appeared Wilson was well prepared. He was asked the same questions and gave the same answers. The British had attacked in lines abreast because they were untrained for anything else. One could not, Wilson observed, increase an army from six divisions to sixty and expect its soldiers to behave like veterans.[73]

Haig does not appear to have discovered that Lloyd George had asked questions of Wilson as well as Foch. One may suspect that had he done so his fury would have been even greater. Wilson, the consummate political soldier as Haig saw him, could have said anything. However, Wilson was entirely discreet and Lloyd George dealt largely with operations, not personalities. Battlefield casualties, the carnage, the blood, the disfigurement had become an obsession with him, observable at least since his encounter with the Hinds boy at the beginning of February. If they could be avoided, as apparently the French were doing, it should be done. In the struggles with the generals in the ensuing two years, this inner rage needs to be borne in mind. If Britain's conduct of military operations was faulty not only might a battle be lost. Young men would be killed unnecessarily.

The interviews in France in mid-September 1916, certainly a lapse of military etiquette, left an enduring bad impression. Still they were probably innocent enough, simply a part of a thought process that invariably centered on the plight of the beleaguered individual rather than the mass: the workman of pre-war days begging for work was now the hideously wounded soldier.

II

On the return from France Lloyd George had to face again the problem of supply for Russia and through it for Romania. On 26 September, in London little more than a week, he suggested verbally to Asquith that Robertson and Reading be sent to Russia to confer with General Michael Alexeieff, nominally the Czar's Chief of Staff, but in fact the Russian commander in chief. He followed with a letter in the afternoon.[74] The letter emphasized less the matter of aid to Russia than the doubts, clearly abroad in the Russian government and army, about Western devotion to the position on the Eastern Front. The Russians, Lloyd George insisted, were unsure of the West, filled with suspicions of which pro-German influences were taking advantage. A delegation at the highest level, with power to make decisions, was needed to reassure them. Moreover they concentrated too much on their own front, as, indeed, Western generals did on theirs. 'It would be a good thing,' he concluded, 'for both General Robertson and General Alexeieff that they should interchange views, and the decision arrived at by those two great soldiers after such an interchange might very well be decisive.'

Lloyd George evidently had written to the Prime Minister before consulting

Robertson for a letter from the C.I.G.S. the next day indicates that he had seen both Lloyd George and Asquith that morning and was now pleading with the former that he not be ordered to go.[75] Lloyd George presents this letter as the conclusion of the discussion of Robertson's Russian trip which is not the case. The trip would come up again within weeks intertwined with the continuing plight of Romania. Britain could help Romania in two ways only: by pressing Russia to do more, the reason for Robertson's trip, or by reinforcing an alternative front which would preoccupy the Bulgarians: Salonika.

By the end of the first week of October it was obvious that the Allied attacks upon the Bulgarians in Serbia that had begun in support of Romania could go no further. At the War Committee on 9 October Lloyd George proposed that eight British and French divisions be sent to reinforce the Allied presence in Greece. He drew, according to Robertson, a 'lurid picture' of the consequences of the surrender of Romania. The argument between Lloyd George and Robertson, who maintained as always that Romania would be saved only by increased Allied activity in the West, became heated and after the meeting the C.I.G.S. confessed to Col. Repington that he could not go on under the circumstances. He produced a letter of resignation which he intended to send to Lloyd George.[76] As this letter, which is not in the *War Memoirs* nor in the Lloyd George papers, represents the documentary beginning of the feud between Robertson and Lloyd George, as well as of the breakdown of the intimacy between Lloyd George and Northcliffe, it must be given some attention.[77] One could note also that it confirms the argument that Lloyd George was justified in believing that he could control the War Office through his position on the War Committee, even without the revocation of the Order in Council.

Robertson felt that his position as military advisor to the government was being eroded. 'About a month ago,' he began,

I laid before the War Committee a memorandum regarding the probability of a heavy attack being made on Rumania, and the Committee agreed with my view that our best assistance would be the prosecution of the offensive on the Western Front combined with rigorous action by the Salonika forces.

I again brought the question before the Committee on the 9th instant and repeated the advice given before, and said that to attempt to assist Rumania by sending any further considerable body of troops to Salonika would be unsound and probably quite useless.

You felt it your duty to disagree with this advice and recommended certain action being taken by the Committee with the object of inducing France and Italy to combine with us in sending to Salonika a reinforcement of some 8 additional divisions for the purpose of undertaking extensive offensive operations, directed at Sofia.

He was directed, Robertson continued, to consult about all this with General Joffre. He was, in effect, to ask a Frenchman to approve an operation of which he, himself, disapproved. All of this showed want of confidence in his advice. It was essential for the war, he believed, that the C.I.G.S. should be able to count upon the support of the Secretary of State. And if the War

Committee were to decide to pursue this operation, upon the advice of General Joffre, he, Robertson, would be 'committed to a military plan which I have stated to the Committee is in my judgement unsound. I could not be responsible' he concluded, 'for conducting this very difficult war under these conditions, nor would it be in the Country's interest that I should attempt to do so.' He was sending a copy of the letter to the Prime Minister.

Upon seeing the letter Repington, a politician to his fingertips, urged Robertson to desist. Lloyd George would simply accept Robertson's resignation and that would be the end of it. At least Robertson should speak to the Prime Minister first. However Repington also told his employer Lord Northcliffe of the affair and recorded that he was 'much exercised'. Northcliffe had only that day seen a friend of the Prime Minister who had asked that *The Times* and *Daily Mail* show more support for Asquith's government. In Repington's presence he telephoned the man and told him that the politicians must not interfere with the soldiers. Finally Northcliffe reported to Repington two days later that he had personally seen Lloyd George at the War Office and 'had warned him in plain words not to interfere with the soldiers.'[78] Northcliffe in addition wrote to Robertson, who replied warmly. Robertson was also in touch with H.A. Gwynne of the *Morning Post*, which already was attacking Lloyd George. Clumsily, he was trying to build defenses.[79]

Lloyd George easily divined what Robertson was about. His reply to Robertson's letter was acid and threatening. He had, he said, talked with Robertson twice since the War Committee on Monday, 9 October and the latter had made no protest about Lloyd George's independent position on Romania-Salonika.

> Tonight's letter would therefore have caused me some surprise had not a leading newspaper proprietor given me the pith of its contents 8 hours before it was dispatched to me. He had clearly been taken into counsel by someone in your close confidence [Repington] & by him acquainted with matters so confidential in their nature that they have not yet been imparted to the Cabinet & so dangerous in their character that their publication would materially assist the enemy. This great journalist even threatened publication unless I withdraw immediately from the position I had taken up. Had he done so my only defence would have been the public disclosure of equally secret & equally dangerous material necessary to complete the story. Of course you could not have authorized such a breach of confidence & discipline. But unfortunately this kind of thing is of frequent occurrence in the service & must be stopped in the best interests of the Army.

Lloyd George continued on these lines for several paragraphs in a long letter, oblivious of the fact that in the past no one had been more accustomed than he to take secret Cabinet squabbles into the press when it suited him to do so.

He then reminded Robertson of the precise location of his authority. He had never questioned Robertson's powers under the Order in Council.

> But there seems to be some doubt I gather from your letter as to my position as a member of the War Council. It ought to be decided whether I have the same right — although I am War Secretary — to

express an independent view on the war in the discussions that take place as any other member of the War Council — or whether as long as I am War Secretary I must choose between the position of a dummy or a pure advocate of all opinions expressed by my military advisors.

Finally and above all there was the Balkans, Romania and Salonika.

You allude to the advice given by the General Staff about Salonika. They advised evacuation on the ground that the place could not be defended. Had not the War Committee overruled their advice Salonika would now have been German & the Bulgarians would have another 260,000 well equipped men available to crush Roumania.

I am perhaps overanxious that our prestige and honour should be saved in the East. The Servian blunder has damaged both badly. I know what will be said here if after bringing Roumania to aid us we look on whilst she is being butchered before our eyes without taking the most serious risks to rescue her.

Lloyd George concluded by reiterating that Robertson must not expect him to remain silent in the War Committee. He was not suited to being a dummy.[80]

'Nothing...did me so much harm with the Liberal Party as my relations with Northcliffe,' growled Lloyd George to Riddell three days later.

Donald tells me [wrote Riddell] that McKenna is saying LG will have to leave the War Office owing to the strong feeling against him by the soldiers. McKenna also says that LG complained to General Foch of the capacity of the English as compared with the French staff (I have recorded such a conversation) and that Foch when telephoning to Haig repeated the conversation adding 'We have interfering politicians but none would compare with this fellow.'[81]

Yet this was not the end of the struggle. As the Robertson-Lloyd George correspondence was taking place Romania's short, unhappy life as a belligerent power was approaching its end. In the second week of October 1916 her ill-considered advance to the west into Transylvania was turned back by the Germans and Austrians and in the south on 19 October Mackensen, at the head of a largely Bulgarian army defeated the Romanian-Russian force in the Dubrudja and occupied the port of Constansa closing the railway between Bucharest and the Black Sea. The collapse of Romania would allow the entire Bulgarian army to turn against Greece. Germany could dominate the Balkans.[82]

Lloyd George continued to support the concept of a Balkan front, but the only army that could save Romania at this juncture was Russia's. The next day he had lunch with Repington at the Carlton Club. He told Repington that he had proposed a force at Salonika in February 1915. Another division, practically two, were to be sent, but it was too late now. (In fact no more divisions seem to have gone to Greece in 1916 mainly because of the lack of shipping; the British contribution remained at six, numbers 10, 22, 26, 27, 28, and 60.) 'He was very much down on the soldiers, generally,' wrote Repington,

for not having made better plans when Romania entered the war, a point upon which I heartily agreed with him, saying that I supposed

Romania and Russia must have come to an arrangement on the subject, but he said he knew absolutely nothing of what had been arranged. We agreed that this was a most extraordinary manner of waging war.

The Romanian peril, one must interject, was the result of exactly the sort of gap in planning that Lloyd George's proposal to Asquith of a small full-time war committee of politicians was designed to close. This time it was in the Balkans, but the problem had bedeviled British fortunes before, most prominently in the Dardanelles operation, at that moment under the most intense investigation and occupying Churchill's energies to the exclusion of all else. Here had been a most useful and feasible proposal, the isolation and perhaps the neutralization of Turkey, the opening of a route to Russia and of an entry to the Balkans. It was frustrated by the inability of the politicians to force the cooperation necessary from the army to accomplish it. Now, in the summer of 1916 after months of negotiation, when an important diplomatic objective, the belligerence of Romania, had been obtained, the military not only were unwilling to exploit it but seemed to know nothing of it.[83] Russia, Lloyd George believed, was willing to help Romania, but without resources could not. Britain had the resources but was unwilling.

> LG said he was getting on well with Robertson but that he was very disappointed that R. would not go to Russia to visit Alexeieff [in September].

The whole trip could have been accomplished in a month. It would make Robertson more Eastern and Alexeieff more Western.

Toward the end of the conversation with Repington, which clearly lasted several hours, Lloyd George provided a hint, possibly a key to his behavior as Prime Minister: his misery at being engaged in the enterprise of war-making.

> He burst out once, and said that we were all asked to keep silent and bow the knee to this military Moloch, but that he was responsible, and as he would have to take the blame, he meant to have his own way. So the antagonism is even deeper than R. suspected, and I am not best pleased with the situation.[84]

Shortly before this conversation, and contributing to Lloyd George's depression, there had been a short, hastily arranged conference — at which nation's initiative is not clear — with the French on 19 and 20 October at Boulogne to discuss yet again options for the relief of Romania. Lloyd George by implying to the French that Edwin Montagu, now Minister of Munitions, would be present, had insured that Albert Thomas would accompany Briand. Beside Asquith and Lloyd George, Grey, Balfour and Robertson attended for Britain.[85]

Insofar as it accomplished anything for the beleaguered Romanians, the conference was a failure. Robertson repeated his now invariable formula that the only way to aid Romania, or indeed anyone else, was to increase pressure on the Germans on the Western Front. As Lloyd George reported to Miss Stevenson, Briand was afraid to press his case against a British delegation, hostile except for Lloyd George, as well as against his own, with support only from Thomas. The French Premier did produce, however, an epigram which

Lloyd George much admired, repeated many times, and which has become a part of the culture of military history: 'This war,' observed Briand, 'is too important to be left to military men.'[86]

Predictably the decisions, or the lack of them, of the Boulogne Conference were unacceptable to the French Left in the Chamber of Deputies. The Balkan Front had to be maintained. Accordingly three days after the conference, on 23 October, Thomas turned up in London to report that the Briand government was again in danger.[87]

In a sense the December 1916 crisis began at this moment. Lloyd George went to the War Committee the next day, as Miss Stevenson put it 'full of beans', to demand that two divisions be sent to Salonika, while admitting that they probably would not arrive in time. This elicited of course a general demand, Robertson not being present, that they indeed should be sent as a gesture of good faith.[88]

Evidently the clear inability to do anything for Romania by way of Salonika, or by coercion of the Bulgarians or some other way, revived in Lloyd George's mind the project of a delegation to Russia, headed by General Robertson. This time however he thought in terms of a full scale inter-Allied staff conference of the sort normally held at Chantilly in November after the end of active campaigning. What precisely the Russians would be encouraged to do was, and would remain, unclear but, as with most Lloyd George schemes, there was a narrow and a general purpose. In this case the immediate interest was to stimulate greater Russian effort on behalf of Romania and to allay Russian mistrust and defeatism.[89] The larger, the more important, was the construction of machinery to insure coordination of activity on all fronts. Potentially, this could be a huge Allied advantage of which the Germans were aware, but which so far had been almost entirely thrown away. In the remaining two years of the conflict he would return to the second idea repeatedly.

On 31 October 1916, with Robertson not invited and McKenna absent in France, Lloyd George revived the proposal of sending Robertson to Russia, apparently with the goal of attempting to excite Russian energy by a promise of an enhanced supply of munitions, particularly of heavy guns.[90] A few days earlier he had asked General Robertson to consider what would happen to the Salonika forces if the Germans disposed of Romania.[91] Robertson answered on 3 November in great detail, dealing with Salonika and generally giving his views on the course of the war, ending with the depressing conclusion that he could not see how the war could be won before the summer of 1918.[92]

Meanwhile, the date is not clear but before 3 November, Lloyd George entertained the Prime Minister, Crewe, Grey, Balfour, Curzon and Lansdowne at dinner to impress upon them the gravity of the military situation. Lloyd George records that Asquith was sympathetic and proposed that he bring the matter up at the next War Committee. At the same time Lloyd George was writing a long statement of his own on the war, which would later appear as a memorandum for the ministerial conference in Paris in the middle of November.[93]

Lloyd George was preparing for a major departure as he customarily did: by building a case, interviewing prospective jurors, and allowing potentially hostile witnesses, on this occasion the naive General Robertson, to provide evidence that would eventually be used against them. On the other hand there is no reason to believe that the Russian trip was a deception to remove the C.I.G.S. from London. Lloyd George honestly believed the war was going badly. The Somme was a disaster; Salonika, once Romania had gone the way of Serbia, could become a second Gallipoli. Submarine sinkings, even with shortening daylight and with warnings still given to victims, were increasing dangerously, promising a shipping shortage in 1917. And most ominously, the Russian army, despite its successes of the summer, was wounded and bleeding, while the government at Petrograd, amid a cloud of rumors of its pro-Germanism, presided over a chaotic and hungry empire. What if Russia left the war? (It should be noted that the 300 sixty pounders Lloyd George had sent to Russia in February 1916 had come into action at the front only within the last few days.)

These considerations Lloyd George put before the War Committee on 3 November with McKenna and Robertson again absent. How, he asked, is the war to be brought to an end? The Allied governments must take charge. He proposed that there should be held immediately a small conference of Allied leaders empowered to take decisions. This would be followed by a military conference in the East to be attended by the highest officers of all Allied countries.

There seems to have been general agreement that Lloyd George's presentation was effective and frightening.[94] The War Committee quickly agreed and telegrams went to Paris proposing a meeting for 14 November with the Generals' meeting at Chantilly to be postponed until afterwards. In one of those curious minor tangles which illustrated perfectly the hierarchy of priorities in both countries at this critical point in the war, the French replied that if the political conference were to precede the soldiers' discussion it must be held on Monday, 13 November because General Joffre was unwilling to delay his meeting. To this Asquith declared that Monday was impossible because he intended a Cabinet for that day. An earlier Cabinet would interfere with ministers' week-ends (including his own). (This data is from Maurice Hankey.)[95] Hence the ministers' conference would have to be held simultaneously with the Chantilly meeting and thus the soldiers' decisions could not be reviewed.

At this point Robertson was not aware of the revived Russian excursion. However at the War Committee on 7 November McKenna was present. He told Robertson immediately, and by speculating with Robertson on Lloyd George's motives took a long step toward destroying the government of which he was a part. After a terse meeting with Lloyd George, Robertson sent Haig a useful review of the War Secretary's activities which illustrate first the C.I.G.S.'s, admittedly innocent, knowledge of the divisions in the War Committee, but which describes perfectly the atmosphere of Asquith's dying administration.

> I am going to tell you some of my worries. But treat them as an entertainment. They do not generally trouble me.
> Did I tell you before that about 6 weeks ago L.G. tried to shove me over to Russia, saying I was such a splendid fellow to go & see Alexeieff & buck up Russia in general — about which we hear, still, rumours of a separate peace with Germany — which I *do* not believe.
> I told him I *could* not go. Also told the Prime Minister. The King

took up the matter strongly, & it was dropped. The idea was to let L.G. become top dog here & have his wicked way. Like he used to get rid of poor old K. I could not do the trip under a month, & he would keep me there for weeks more once he got me there. He has been a good deal with Winston & F.E. Smith, & [Field Marshal] French is also not far distant at times. Last Friday [3 November], in McKenna's absence (a friend of *ours*) he got up a War Committee at which there were no *naval or military experts*. He got together another yesterday [7 November]. Result was a telegram to Briand saying L.G. & Prime Minister would come over on Tuesday next [14 November] to discuss general matters & to arrange an Allied conference at *Russian* Headquarters, as the only useful way of securing real co-operation etc. etc. Also that Chantilly Conference should be postponed as it could not usefully meet until it had before it the decisions of the Tuesday (political) Conference. To represent *us* in Russia L.G. told me last night it was thought that Grey & *I* should go; France, Joffre (or Castelnau) & a minister; *Italy* Cadorna (or Poroo [Porro]). Of course *Italy* will send no one. France may refuse the whole thing. On the other hand Briand may be in on the plot. . .If he *agrees* to Russia, I imagine there will be no Chantilly Conference at all, as it will be superseded by the Russian one.

But I am not concerned except as regards myself. I have no intention of going. The idea is absurd. The Prime Minister ought to have said so. But he is very weak. It is a devilish clever plot & L.G. has misled the War Committee. I have seen McKenna & he says he will stick to me. I have *no* intention of going. But it is a nice mess! And takes so much of my time. Of course I have told the King, & he is lying low, on my advice, for the time being — like myself. Salonika is at the bottom of it all. L.G. is always saying the west is a failure & will be so. He is egged on by Winston & F.E. Smith. There will be no peace till we have a row.[96]

A few matters in this letter deserve brief comment. First is the obvious influence of McKenna. It is nearly incredible that Robertson could believe that the Chancellor of the Exchequer, anti-conscriptionist, opponent of the Boulogne program, and an advocate of limited war, was a friend of the army. To be sure, not all the soldiers were so trusting. H.H. Wilson and Haig knew better. Why McKenna had told Robertson that Lloyd George wished to send him to Russia to get rid of him as had been done to Kitchener needs little reflection. It suggests intense malevolence. That Robertson believed it, and wanted to fight about it, testifies to his innocence. Haig was always much more careful and maintained his social alliances. He cordially invited Lloyd George to his headquarters during the coming meeting in France.

Second, one should note Robertson's agreement that the Prime Minister was 'very weak', although weak of course because he supported Lloyd George. Yet there is little evidence that the C.I.G.S. was any more satisfied with the coalition government than Lloyd George himself. A good soldier, he wanted to trust authority. In the murky political world of intrigue in which personalities counted and the chain of command did not, Robertson was lost. 'The War Committee should give *orders*. . .London should have the same organization as there is in the field,' Robertson wrote to Lord Curzon on 28 November.[97]

One may note that he supported Lloyd George during the December 1916 crisis verbally and on 6 December, the day Lloyd George began the formation of his government, he wrote an entirely friendly and temperate letter full of good advice on Lord Derby and the composition of the new 'War Council'.[98]

Robertson's pugnacity, his inevitable desire to 'have a row' with Lloyd George was at once a source of his weakness and a danger to the government. He sensed a 'plot' against him; he would be replaced by Field Marshal French. Yet he was nearly as popular in the newspapers as Lord Kitchener had been, if without the semi-divine status accorded to the former War Secretary, and his clumsy efforts to capitalize on this through Repington and H.A. Gwynne carried the potential for much political harm. Probably at the behest of the Prime Minister, Hankey wrote to him pleading for reason and providing the historian with a valuable analysis of the growing desperation over the war that was dividing Asquith's decaying government.

After reassuring him of the War Committee's undiminished confidence in him and in Haig, Hankey warned that there was some disappointment with the Somme offensive. 'In the flush of early successes,' he observed, 'hopes were probably raised too high. Among some, but not all members there are doubts as to whether the enemy has lost as heavily as the Allies.'

> 3. There is general agreement (Ll.G. a possible dissentient, but I am not sure of this) that the offensive in the West must continue, both this winter, so far as is possible, and next year. But there is also a unanimous, or almost unanimous, feeling that this will not enable us to win the war in 1917 unless supplemented by greatly increased efforts elsewhere, and more especially in the east.

> 4. There is an intense desire to finish next year. This is due to a very real anxiety about the submarine danger, and a doubt as to after 1917 the shortage of shipping may not bring us to a stop. There is also felt grave doubt about the staying power of our finance after 1917.

Accordingly the War Committee thought it imperative that a complimentary offensive in the east be organized to support that in the west.

> 6. . . .I find no supporters of Ll.George's idea (if it is his idea) that additional divisions should be sent to Salonika. I believe it is recognized by everyone that an advance on Sofia is a chimera. . .

> 7. At the same time I believe that there is a strong inclination to think that, with more heavy guns and more technical equipment, the Russians would do a great deal more than they have done hitherto to supplement our offensive in the west. In fact we might get better value for our money by sending a larger proportion of our future output of heavy guns to the east.

Big guns were the blue chips of the war. No army could have too many. With them Russia could win for the Allies. (It is no wonder Lloyd George could never resist recalling in his letters to Asquith the vituperation he had suffered over the Boulogne program.) Hence:

> 9. There is a real and almost unanimous desire (McKenna is a possible but doubtful exception) that you should visit Alexeieff. Different

reasons for this are held by different members, but all the views may be summed up as follows —

(a) It is desirable that you should see the situation in the east and talk things over with Alexeieff in order that you should be in a position to advise the Committee with full local knowledge as to how much help we can expect from the east, and as to how far it is desirable to send guns &c there.

(b) It is essential that someone with real and great authority should explain to Alexeieff the limitations placed on the allied offensive from Salonika, especially by shipping, which Alexeieff is said not in the least to realize. (Grey and the Prime Minister are very strong on this.)

(c) It is essential to make a demonstration in Russia in order to improve the morale of the Russian people and to combat pro-German propaganda. The visit of a great General will have far more effect than that of any politician.

This is all very private of course and I have been absolutely frank about everything.[99]

This very important letter, which Robertson does not appear to have kept although Hankey fortunately retained a copy, is partially reproduced here because it provides, first of all, a remarkable summary of the problems that were facing Britain in the last weeks of Asquith's government: of the immense burden of supplying munitions to a Russia whose loyalty to the Allied cause was already suspect and even more ominously of the shipping shortage which stifled the utility of naval supremacy. Together these factors would soon end Lloyd George's clamor for a major front in Greece, although not for a search for some other alternative to the stalemate in France.

And it demonstrates again that the trip to Russia was not a Lloyd George trick, even if Robertson, simple and honest, believed McKenna's warning that such was the case. The entire Cabinet, excepting perhaps McKenna, desired that he go. Hankey, devoted to Asquith, was trying to avert the harm to the Liberal government that would follow Robertson's refusal enforced by the threat of his resignation as C.I.G.S.

Robertson replied to Hankey immediately repeating that he would not go to Russia and that he 'was out for a row without kid gloves on' as Hankey recorded in his diary.[100] Hankey, in desperation, wrote again the next day.

I burned your letter immediately. Lloyd George asked himself to lunch with me yesterday. I put it to him straight that his proposal that you should go to Russia was open to the suspicion of being a Lord K. dodge, particularly owing to the clandestine manner in which it had been manoeuvered. He at once disclaimed the remotest intention of anything of the kind. He spoke most warmly of you, and I don't think he could have simulated such evident sincerity. Finally he said he would be willing to go too in order to remove all possible suspicion. The rest of the War Committee would, I know, be no party to anything of the nature of the Lord K. dodge with you.

I would give almost anything to see you and he closer together. I believe that a permanent breach is an almost irremediable calamity just now. With all his faults Ll.G. does get things done — munitions, compulsory service &c. I believe he is the only man who is likely to bring about the re-awakening of national enthusiasm and effort which is now so necessary.

If the result of a row were for you to go, the effect on the army would be disastrous. If he were to go the political effect would be equally disastrous, for he would speak his mind openly, many people would rally to him, and the encouragement to the enemy would be prodigious. I suspect that [Albert] Thomas and his adherents and possibly [Leonida] Bissolati [Italian Commissioner for War Services] would do likewise.

Hankey concluded by remarking hopefully that although Lloyd George was 'desperately keen' on the trip it might fall through. Neither the French nor the Italians were interested. The coming conference in Paris might kill the project.[101]

Robertson concluded his quest for exemption with an almost hysterical letter to the Prime Minister on 13 November, not suggesting resignation, rather pleading to be allowed to stay in Britain — in winter he was at his busiest. He had no notion what he was to say to Alexeieff. (This letter is dated 13 November but was written on Hotel Crillon stationery. Evidently Robertson carried it to Paris.)[102] Asquith showed the letter to Hankey in Paris on 15 November, called in Lloyd George, and the three men agreed Robertson should not go, although Lloyd George announced grandly that he nonetheless would go to Russia himself, perhaps with Hankey.[103]

The McKenna treachery finally came into the open at a Cabinet meeting on 21 November after Robertson's trip had been dropped but only a week before the eruption of the crisis that ended the Asquith government. The real bitterness displayed at this time, coupled with Lloyd George's humiliation of McKenna before his colleagues cannot but have exacerbated the poisonous bad feeling that stifled all attempts at compromise and so contributed to Asquith's fall. On 21 November Lloyd George was able to force McKenna into admitting that he had given Robertson the impression that the Russian mission was a trick. Three weeks later on 10 December he described to Riddell what had happened, suggesting also that this was the event that drove him to conclude that Asquith had truly lost control of affairs.

McKenna has ruined the Prime Minister. He is responsible for all that has happened. [Lloyd George's government had been announced on the day of this conversation.] He is a contemptible creature — jealous, small-minded, malignant. We had a scene in the War Council [on 21 November]. I could not go on. I said at the Council 'I hear that one of my colleagues has said that I have been endeavouring to get rid of my Chief of Staff (Robertson) by sending him on a mission to Russia. That is a lie and the man who said it knows it to be so.' Curzon then said, 'I think out of fairness you ought to give the name.' I replied, 'It was the Chancellor of the Exchequer.' McKenna said, 'I?' I (LG) then said, 'Yes, you! Either you or another man is saying what is untrue and I know which I prefer to believe.' (The other man I (R) understood to be Robertson.) McKenna then collapsed. The P.M. did not rebuke him. Afterwards he said to me, 'I could not have believed it. It is almost unbelievable.' And yet the P.M. said not a word in public. That hardened me. I felt I could not go on with benefit to the nation under such circumstances. Bonar Law has been here today. He is very timid.[104]

The excusing of Robertson, it may be noted parenthetically was not the end of the Russian trip. On 26 November at Walton Heath, Lloyd George asked General Henry H. Wilson to undertake the journey. Grey and Castelnau would also be going. Better Wilson, Lloyd George added, than French.[105]

This project died with the change in government, but was immediately resurrected, then put off until after the great conference in Italy in January. Wilson finally arrived in Petrograd on 29 January 1917 and departed on 25 February. Ironically General Alexeieff, the object of so much discussion and concern, had suffered a heart attack in December and by the end of February the Czar's regime had only two weeks to live.

The conference in Paris in mid-November 1916, very much Lloyd George's project, was supposed to approve and plan an agenda for a full dress political-military meeting to be held, as Lloyd George hoped, at the Czar's head-quarters.[106] After the disagreements about the time of the meeting, it was scheduled for Wednesday, 15 November at the same time as the military council at Joffre's headquarters. In preparation Lloyd George drew up a long paper on the state of the war evidently along the lines of his statement to the War Committee which had approved the Paris meeting on 3 November. This statement is fully reproduced in the *War Memoirs* and need not be quoted here, although the document must be recognized, as Lloyd George probably intended it should be, as the manifesto of the rebellion that began at the end of the month.[107]

In it he condemned, deplored, the Allied war effort, using for statistics the figures supplied him by General Robertson two weeks before.[108] Generally he dwelt upon the familiar themes: Germany was not getting weaker but stronger and with Romanian oil and grain soon would become more formidable still (in the event the Romanian oil wells were pretty well destroyed before the Germans captured them); the Allies, particularly Britain, were becoming financially weak and spiritually weary and the growing shipping losses promised that these conditions would become worse; the loss of Serbia was both a moral outrage and a military disaster. Romania promised to be a repetition of Serbia.

'It is no exaggeration to say,' pronounced Lloyd George in a passage deleted by the Prime Minister,

> that Rumania may be the turning point of the campaign. If the Germans fail there it will be the greatest disaster inflicted upon them. Afterwards it will be only a question of time. But should Germany succeed I hesitate to think what the effect will be on the fortunes of the campaign. Eight hundred thousand men who constitute excellent fighting material if well equipped will have been thrown away. [This was from Robertson's figures.] The Germans' stores, much depleted, will be stocked with quantities of oil and corn, which will place the Central Powers above any anxiety in these two important respects — and yet no one seems to have thought it his particular duty to prepare a plan which would bring such triumph to the Allies if it succeeded, and which would avert a possible disaster of the first magnitude to

their cause. And this is the third year of a campaign which has seen many muddles of the same sort committed though this fatal lack of co-operation and forethought.[109]

The prayer at the end of this long brief was for an assembly of the military and political leaders of the four great powers in the east 'to discuss the situation and to formulate their policy or strategy.' The Central Powers did this constantly but the real leaders of Russia, of whom only the Czar and Alexeieff counted, had never engaged in five minutes' conversation with their counterparts in the west.[110] It may be noticed that the Prime Minister insisted upon cutting much of the discussion of the four power conference leaving only a single paragraph at the end saying without elaboration that such a conference was important.

Lloyd George recounts in detail the events, speeches and conversations of the next three days, during which the *nunc dimittis* as it were of the Asquith government, and indeed of the ancient congregation of British Liberalism, was pronounced.[111] On the morning of 15 November Asquith laid before Briand Lloyd George's much attenuated paper on the military situation. The French Premier, tired and upset from a mauling in the Senate Army Committee conducted by its chairman, Georges Clemenceau, gave Lloyd George's appeal for a conference only cursory, if polite, attention. That afternoon Briand made an eloquent and forceful speech asserting that governments not soldiers should control wars and that planning was always desirable, but proposing nothing. Asquith followed and loyally supported the idea of a conference in the east. But it quickly became apparent that neither the French military nor the Italians had any interest in the matter, even after Lloyd George himself had spoken at length. Then on the morning of 16 November the conclusions from the Chantilly conference arrived proposing major offensives in the west to be ready to begin by the middle of February of 1917. All military commanders, it announced, 'shall not cease to maintain close contact with each other' but there was no further reference to a meeting in the east. There was an extended discussion of what could, or should, be done to make the Salonika force operational. Nonetheless, there was nothing to do but approve the armies' recommendations.[112] The proposal for a large conference in the east was neither approved nor rejected. It was simply ignored.

Lloyd George records that after the politicians' meeting adjourned he, Hankey and the Prime Minister returned to the Hotel Crillon. After a short conversation Asquith retired for his usual pre-dinner nap.[113] Hankey and Lloyd George went for a walk. Lloyd George argued that if anything happened to Russia or Italy or if the rising submarine losses could not be contained the balance of advantage in the war would pass to the Central Powers. He felt he should resign. Hankey opposed this but agreed that some way of changing the political direction of the war should be found. As the two men passed the Vendôme Column Hankey proposed:

> You ought to insist on a small War Committee being set up for the day-to-day conduct of the war, with full powers. It must be independent of the Cabinet. It must keep in close touch with the P.M., but the Committee ought to be in continuous session, and the P.M. as Head

of the Government, could not manage that. He has a very heavy job in looking after the Cabinet and attending to Parliament and home affairs. He is a bit tired, too, after all he has gone through in the last two and a half years. The Chairman must be a man of unimpaired energy and great driving power.[114]

Both men agreed that Asquith should remain as Prime Minister. His great prestige and authority in the House of Commons were indispensible. Lloyd George suggests in his *War Memoirs*, although does not quite affirm, that Hankey understood that before placing the matter of a small war committee before the Prime Minister Lloyd George should discuss the proposition with Bonar Law, thus providing at least an inference, which Asquith would be quick to detect, of an inter-party conspiracy. From Paris that evening, Lloyd George sent a telegram to Max Aitken asking him to arrange a meeting with the Unionist leader for the following evening. So began the final chapter in the story of the decline of Liberalism and H.H. Asquith.[115]

III

There was a second theme in the decline in authority of Asquith's coalition, less easily defined than the dispute with the military and not identified so closely with the person of the Prime Minister himself, but which appears to have troubled Lloyd George and Carson nearly as much. This was the perceptible rising sentiment by the autumn of 1916 within the government, in politics at large, and indeed among some of Britain's friends abroad, that the war would have to be brought to an end soon by some sort of a compromise. It had become unwinnable. Lloyd George had long believed of course that some members of the Cabinet, here as usual McKenna was always mentioned, were, as he put it, 'soft on the Germans'. Lloyd George refers to this uneasiness, unspecifically, in a paragraph in his *War Memoirs,* as does Max Aitken, although neither man was clear about his evidence.[116] Nonetheless, for the historian, the autumn and winter of 1916 provide clearly a division in the course of the First World War. More to the point, many contemporary thinkers as well as the great suffering mass of Europe, saw events in the same way. The old expectations of a quick, and glorious, victory were long gone (although in Britain they had continued far too long). But so also at Verdun and the Somme had disappeared the new faiths in the ultimate power of artillery, 'artillery destroys, infantry occupies', and of the great wearing out battle. Russia and Austria-Hungary, one now knows, were dying. France and Italy, as the next year would show, were gravely wounded. How much of this Lloyd George understood in the months between September and December of 1916, that a great surge of the tide of history had begun (did he hear a roaring in his ears?) cannot be known. But he could sense such things. He had felt a climactic disaster approaching, albeit on a smaller or national scale, in 1910 with the impending menace of Home Rule that would appear after the Parliament Act. He had at that time tried to avert it.

On a narrower stage one cannot overestimate, any more than one can quantify, the shock of the losses on the Somme to Britain. In ten weeks, essentially between 1 July and 15 September 1916, the remote age of innocence and decadence that was Edwardianism was blown away. While the army uselessly covered itself with glory the nation drew back in horror. The railway platforms at Waterloo crowded with wounded, the daily eight column lists of officer casualties in *The Times*, and of course the promptly telegraphed news of family members dead, hurt, worst of all missing, followed by the awkward, mechanical, but anguished letter from the company commander, all became the British people's shared agony. The war at last had come home. Certainly Lloyd George, who was invariably driven to rage by human suffering, if by little else except attacks upon himself, felt all of this by instinct. And his mind would immediately translate his anger into political terms. As he made clear many times, he feared softness in the Cabinet and suspected that some of his colleagues would respond eagerly to any indication of a proposal for mediation from abroad.

This attitude must be reconciled with the cordiality he had shown toward Col. House at the beginning of the year. Then, it must be recalled, the proposals for a peace conference were linked to a promise, later diluted, that the United States would intervene if Germany resisted and made the conference a failure. But since then relations with the United States had cooled perceptibly. The large revisions in Britain's blockading strategy that came in the summer of 1916, particularly the enforcement of economic sanctions on American firms suspected of trading with Germany through neutrals, and the denial of bunker coal to American ships engaged in carrying such goods, styled the 'black list' in American newspapers, had caused a good deal of ill-feeling in the United States. So indeed had the harsh repression of the Easter Rebellion. Of course British impatience with America had risen accordingly, which would be evident in Lloyd George's own statements. In addition one must conclude his own estimate of his colleagues' sense of determination had changed.

In January and February 1916, House's mission had been dismissed as a cheap American political maneuver. But at that time the United States was unnecessary; the Allies would win without her. This over-optimism, so deplored by Lloyd George, was still apparent. However, seven months later it had been replaced by despondency. After 15 September the failure on the Somme was clear; the Russian offensive was stalled; Romania was in danger. To Lloyd George, no matter what the soldiers argued, Britain was no longer winning. Immediately his pugnacity took control. In such a situation a negotiated settlement was unthinkable and his nation would not welcome intervention. His colleagues, as well as the United States, needed to be warned, or reminded, that Britain would fight on to the end. The result was his statement to the American journalist Roy Howard on 27 September.

The Howard interview, as it came to be known, was therefore another very characteristic Lloyd George response to a political problem. Several have been cited before, although on this occasion his audience was also international. One is reminded in this case of the Queen's Hall speech of May, 1908, just before his trip to Germany, when he attempted to explain to Emperor William II that some Britons would be glad to see the end of the dreadnought competition.

The so-called interview evidently came about at the instigation of Lord Northcliffe who wrote to Lloyd George, just back from France, on 25 September, saying that he should see Mr. Roy Howard of the United Press Syndicate of the United States who had 'certain disquieting things to say'.[117]

What disturbing news Howard possessed did not become clear in the interview but may be inferred from Lloyd George's statement to C.P. Scott and others later that Germany was about to propose that the United States offer mediation and that President Wilson with an election approaching would be under strong pressure to agree.[118]

Howard himself confirmed this to E.M. House three months later. He was aware, he said, that Germany was trying to force an American mediation proposal. He went to Lloyd George and told him what was happening and that if the British objected what was needed was a good clear statement of the British position. The interview was this statement and it went around the world.[119]

Lloyd George saw Howard on 27 September, not on 28 September as he indicates in his *War Memoirs*. As he told Riddell three days later, he had told Howard that he 'would not give him an interview then'

> but I began to talk. When I had finished he said, 'I wish someone had been behind that map with a notebook!' He went away and wrote out what I had said. He showed it to Northcliffe who sent a message saying he wished I would allow the thing to be published. I asked to see it, and, after revising it, agreed to allow it to appear.[120]

The evidence that Lloyd George had seen, revised and initialled for publication Howard's recollection of his words is of major importance because the statement that appeared in the world's press on 29 September was remarkably blunt. In every way it was a total contradiction of the friendliness and goodwill with which Lloyd George had welcomed the House mission in January of 1916.

Generally Lloyd George, introduced as 'the man of the hour,' who 'looks and acts like an American businessman,' denied utterly that there was any sentiment in Britain for a compromise peace. Rather there was a

> popular suspicion toward America, a suspicion that did not exist a year ago. This feeling is directly attributable to the notion generally entertained by the men on the street that President Wilson might be induced to butt in for the purpose of stopping the European war.

The British nation had neither clock nor calendar for the war, announced Lloyd George. It would fight until it achieved victory. There was no concern about when the war would end — it had taken twenty years to defeat Napoleon — and no doubt about how it would end.

The proposal for mediation at this point was in itself an unneutral act.

> The whole world — including neutrals of the highest purposes and humanitarians with the best of motives — must know that there can be no outside interference at this stage. Britain asked no intervention when she was unprepared to fight. She will tolerate none now that she is prepared, until the Prussian military despotism is broken beyond repair. . .
>
> No man and no nation with the slightest understanding of the temper of the citizen army of Britons, which took its terrible hammering without a whine or a grumble, will attempt to call a halt now.

* * * *

Peace now or at any time before the final elimination of the menace [Prussianism] is unthinkable.

He concluded by paying his usual tribute to the 'magnificence, the nobility, the wonder of France' and, in an ironic forecast, that Russia 'will go through to the death'.[121]

Although London press response was almost uniformly favorable, on the day the article appeared Lloyd George received an admonitory letter from Grey. After explaining that Britain should do nothing to drive the United States and Germany closer and particularly now as the submarine threat was increasing, he reminded the War Secretary that it had always been his view that until the Allies were certain of victory 'the door should always be kept open for Wilson's mediation. [This had been his attitude in January and February.] It is now closed forever as far as we are concerned.'[122]

Lloyd George's instinct of course was precisely the opposite: as a crisis, military or political, became more desperate he grew increasingly pugnacious. He asked Grey whether he had seen the intelligence information on German intentions and explained what one must assume was the real reason for the statement to Howard.

> ...if Wilson's hand had been forced — and there is every indication that the Germans and Irish co-operation could do so — then we should be in a very tight place. Any cessation of hostilities now would be a disaster; and although we could always refuse or put up impossible terms, it is much better that we should not be placed in that predicament. *You* could not have warned off the United States without doing it formally. I could commit a serviceable indiscretion; you could not. It would ruin you. I am inoculated.
>
> You will find that it will work out all right. I know the American politician. He has no international conscience. He thinks of nothing but the ticket, and he has not given the least thought to the effect of his action upon European affairs.[123]

McKenna, as might be expected, also disapproved. Lloyd George's 'affront to America' was 'sheer lunacy', he told C.P. Scott a few days later. Nothing would happen because of profits being made in the United States, but still, he was not sure. 'I need not tell you,' Scott recorded McKenna saying, 'that for my department his action is most injurious. I am now in the position of borrowing from America two million pounds per day.' McKenna also assured Scott, quite accurately, that the entire statement, including Howard's printed interjections, had been written by Lloyd George himself.[124]

Lloyd George made no apologies for his statement in his *War Memoirs* and indeed concludes the chapter discussing it with the assertion that it 'steadied opinion' in the United States 'and helped to increase the sympathy felt with us in our desperate fight.'[125] Generally, in terms of British public opinion this may have been true. The British ambassador, Cecil Spring-Rice, whose opinions Grey tended to disregard, was probably correct in a letter of 6 October to the Foreign Secretary that the statement had had 'an immense and instantaneous effect in this country' and had 'put a stop to the peace rumours which for some time have been prevalent here.'[126] But within the Wilson administration the opposite was the case. In the White House there was real anger which led, at the end of November, to retaliatory action by the United States which, had not other events supervened, could have paralyzed much of Britain's war effort.

Lloyd George's statement was not the only factor. President Wilson's displeasure had been building at least since summer after the publication of the so-called black list on 18 July. In the next few days he considered asking Congress for power to prohibit loans and restrict exports to the Allies.[127] However, the Howard article seems to have been a turning point. Secretary of State Robert Lansing's covering note to the President transmitting a copy of the statement summarized it as 'unfriendly'.[128] In the next several weeks, in the face of attempts by Ambassador W.H. Page and E.M. House to remind the President that Lloyd George probably represented British opinion, and despite Roy Howard's own statement that Lloyd George believed he was helping Wilson in the election, his anger grew.[129] One must note, in passing, that Ambassador Spring-Rice, as disregarded in the Foreign Office as was W.H. Page by Wilson, and with all his problems of pique and sensitivity, remained nonetheless an astute observer of underlying American opinion whose comments might well have been heeded by Grey and, indeed, by Lloyd George. Three weeks after the Howard statement he wrote again to Grey:

> Many people will say to you: 'your course is so just that Americans must sympathise with it: they speak your language, they are of your race, you are fighting for their ideals.' Please remember that for instance, in the State of New York less than 20 percent of the inhabitants are children of English-speaking parents. Remember that during the American Civil War the English and American peoples were far more of one blood than they are now. The cause of the North was the cause of freedom, and the cause of the South was the cause of slavery. But in spite of the common blood, the sympathies of a large part of the British nation were against the Union. . .I do not think therefore, we would be wise to count either on the sympathy or the common blood in this country. . . There is a very strong, active, and powerful element opposed to the Allies and irrevocably hostile to England.[130]

Lloyd George would continually assert in the years to come that the American President did not understand the politics of Europe. This was of course quite true. But neither did Lloyd George comprehend the equally complex realities of United States affairs. Despite his confident assertions to the contrary, he never realized that Wilson did not see Britain's cause as the cause of all mankind.

The climax arrived in November 1916. With the election over, Wilson determined to make on his own initiative a bid for peace. He would use the best weapon at hand to get attention, financial pressure. On 24 November, the day before he began to compose his peace notes, he learned that Kuhn and Loeb, private bankers, were about to buy bonds from a number of German cities. On his personal typewriter he wrote a series of instructions to E.M. House. House was to inform Kuhn and Loeb through Jacob Schiff that they were not to make the loan. House was then to inform Viscount Grey 'in the strongest terms' that the United States 'would go to any length to promote a League for peace'

> and that her people were growing more and more impatient with the intolerable conditions of neutrality, their feeling as hot against Great Britain as it was first against Germany and likely to grow hotter still against an indefinite continuation of the war if no greater progress can be shown than now appears either for the Allies or the Central Powers.

Further Grey was to be made to understand that Ambassador Page 'no longer represents the feelings or point of view' of the United States any more than did any other American resident in London.[131]

This was a remarkably stiff note even if suitably couched in the terms of diplomacy. Whether Wilson described accurately the attitudes of the American people in November 1916 toward the Allies, the historian must question, but there can be no mistaking the undertone of real anger on the President's part.[132] And within hours Wilson had the opportunity to make his fury effective.

Of the £5,000,000 that the British Treasury needed each day for the prosecution of the war by the autumn of 1916, about £2,000,000, as McKenna reiterated, had to be found in the United States. Since the previous year Britain had been raising secured loans in the United States from a consortium of New York banks led by Morgan's. Between the loans, bills were paid by an overdraft at the Morgan bank. However, it was becoming clear that the capacity of the New York banking community to absorb the ever-growing flood of British, and other Allied, placements was coming to an end. In October the Anglo-French Financial Committee of the Treasury, with the approval of H.P. Davison of Morgan's, began to consider plans to sell short term, unsecured, British Treasury bills directly to banks in the midwest and the far west. It was in these regions, after all, more than in New York, that the huge proceeds of the New York loans were being spent and the money was being deposited there. Accordingly the financial institutions were more liquid. The notes, unsecured direct obligations of the British and French governments, would be constantly renewed until the end of the war. There were estimates that $1,000,000,000 could be quickly raised in this way. Morgan's would act only as a broker. In effect Britain would begin to tap the almost unlimited investment potential of the entire United States, now at the peak of war-time prosperity, by borrowing back its own money, by tapping the retail money market. In planning, the assumption was that the program would begin in January 1917.[133]

However, Britain needed $175,000,000 to finance its overdraft at Morgan's in December and so plans were made in November for the first installment of unsecured Treasury notes to be marketed to banks, or indeed to individuals through banks, in the Chicago financial community, the nation's second money center. Davison, although he was not required to do so, consulted as a courtesy the Federal Reserve Board of Governors, although clearly he expected no opposition. Nonetheless on 24 November, on the day Wilson wrote to E.M. House the message he was to convey to Grey, the Board determined to publish a warning to American banks against investing too heavily in short term foreign securities. W.P. Harding of the Board took the circular to Wilson evidently on 25 November. Wilson now had at hand the weapon he needed and, most important, one that did not require congressional approval. He demanded that the Board strengthen the warning, not on the financial basis that so huge an issue of notes constantly renewed would be essentially illiquid, but rather on the basis of foreign policy. So large a holding of foreign securities by Americans, either banks or individuals, could become embarrassing in the event of a change in international relations. The Board made the required changes and banks were informed on 27 November. The circular appeared in the press on the front page of the *New York Times* on 28 November.[134] It carefully specified that the Board desired 'to declaim any intention of discussing the finances or of reflecting upon the financial stability of any country.' Britain was not mentioned. The core of Wilson's changes appeared in the first and last sentences of the conclusion; the issue was not the financial, but the national, welfare of the United States. At the beginning: 'The Board deems it, therefore, its duty to caution the member banks that it does not regard it in the interest of the country at this time that they invest in foreign Treasury bills of this character.' And at the end: banks must remain liquid because at the end of the war 'we shall wish to do our full share of the work of international reconstruction and development which will then be asked of us. . .'[135]

For a moment Morgan's, solidly pro-British and Republican, wished to disregard the notice and sell the notes anyway.[136] (The Board's powers were still somewhat unclear; the Federal Reserve Bank had come into existence only in 1914.) McKenna, however, prudently ordered the issue withdrawn, publishing a note saying the British government would show 'every regard' for the wishes of the Federal Reserve Board.[137] But at the same time new munitions orders in America were briefly suspended.

The chaos in British-American financial markets fortunately was obscured in Britain by the growing Cabinet crisis, but Lloyd George had to respond. In the United States Britain was bankrupt. The first meeting of Lloyd George's War Cabinet, on 9 December was devoted, not to the war, but to the exchange crisis. Britain no longer could pay its bills. Sir Robert Chalmers, recalled from Ceylon, provided an admirable summary of the deterioration of Britain's position. Morgan's was nervous 'as we had in the summer got beyond the point where British credit could carry a loan without collateral.' The cost of maintaining the pound had risen in the current week to 76 million from 12 million in September. It had been hoped that a straight loan (without collateral) would be possible in January when credit would be easier, but 'suddenly the whole situation was changed by the issue of the Federal Reserve Board's announcement to banks.' The War Cabinet agreed to restrict imports from the United States.[138] At the same time Morgan's had to buy pounds frantically to support the exchange thus further increasing its overdraft and the Treasury was forced into a variety of unprecedented, perhaps humiliating, expedients which continued well into the next year when a carefully secured loan was placed in New York. It hastily borrowed $50,000,000 in Japan, announced on 2 December, and persuaded Bethlehem Steel to accept payment in Treasury notes.[139] In a very real sense the turmoil caused by Wilson's order did not end until the United States entered the war in April 1917 when the United States government purchased the British obligations from Morgan's.[140]

The question must be addressed of how much blame for Wilson's trouble making may be assigned to Lloyd George's statement. The author of the latest, excellent, book on the topic, much used in the composition of this account, concludes that there was no doubt that Wilson was still angry over the statement to Roy Howard. He therefore seized the opportunity offered by the Federal Reserve Board's desire to warn American banks against securities they might not be able to sell easily and used it for the diplomatic purpose of bringing pressure on what Lloyd George had shown to be the most intransigent of the Allied governments. The Fed's circular was even more useful because the President's intervention could be suspected, but was unclear. Ambassador Spring-Rice had no doubt that the Reserve Board Circular was motivated by diplomacy, not finance. Although he named neither Wilson nor Lloyd George, he suspected the State Department which, he wrote to Grey on 29 November, was organizing a movement 'to bring pressure on the Allies to entertain proposals of peace which, it is suspected, the President may contemplate submitting. . .'[141] However Wilson refused, a few days later, to modify his stand even when the Comptroller of the Currency assured him, contrary to the point of the Fed circular, that there was plenty of money in regional banking centers.[142]

In addition, Lloyd George's outburst seems to have had serious effects among Britain's other Allies and, as will be seen, within the closest circle of British politicians. At the end of October the Ambassador to Russia, George Buchanan, wrote to the permanent under-secretary at the Foreign Office, Lord Hardinge that 'never since the war began have I felt so depressed about the situation here and more especially about the future of Anglo-Russian relations.' Rapidly increasing German influence portrayed Britain, with her new armies, as determined to continue the war and so to dominate the world.

> Mr. Lloyd George's statement to a representative of the Press, which I personally had hoped would have been welcomed and admired, as it ought to be by all our Allies, has been used against us. It is Great Britain, German agents keep on repeating, who is forcing Russia to continue the war and forbidding her to accept favourable terms of peace which Germany has offered her, and it is Great Britain who is responsible for the privations which the scarcity of all necessities of life is imposing on everyone and especially on the poorer classes.

Russia, the argument concluded, has nothing to gain from continuing the war; Great Britain does.[143]

Reaction to the Howard statement in France was mixed. H. LeRoy-Lewis, Military Attaché in Paris and an important source of information for Lloyd George on French affairs, reported that the Howard statement was widely reported and approved in the French capital.[144] There were, on the other hand, reports in British newspapers suggesting otherwise.[145]

Prime Minister Asquith has no recorded reaction to the Howard statement although shortly afterward he solicited from members of the Cabinet opinions upon which a peace might be concluded. Following this request Lord Lansdowne, Unionist leader in the Lords and Minister Without Portfolio, submitted a memorandum to the Cabinet, dated 13 November, not proposing peace, as is sometimes asserted, but rather questioning whether Britain was any longer in a position to dictate terms of a settlement and, more to the point, questioning whether, for example in another year, the British position would be better. In this sense after close reading, the Lansdowne Memorandum was strongly defeatist. But more important, after beginning with the same arguments that Lloyd George had used so frequently in the Cabinet — that Britain was not winning but losing the war — it came to precisely the opposite conclusion. It was in fact a direct answer to the Howard statement.

Lord Crewe in his account of the fall of the first coalition written only two weeks after the Prime Minister's resignation described Lansdowne's memorandum as the true inner cause of the fall of Asquith's government, an assertion mildly questioned, but not directly contradicted by Lansdowne's biographer.[146] What the Lansdowne paper did accomplish was the establishment of a clear intellectual division, which could be grasped by anyone, between the possible solutions to the Allied dilemma in the autumn of 1916.[147] The nation either could fight harder or it could negotiate a peace. There were no other alternatives. If Britain were to consider negotiation a venue might soon be forthcoming. 'As time goes on,' Lansdowne wrote, 'the neutrals', he mentioned Sweden and the United States, 'are likely to become more and more restive and intolerant of the belligerents, whose right to go on disturbing the peace of the civilized world they will refuse to admit.' The alternative, Lloyd George had said, was to make war more effectively. But, he continued, this was impossible under the present system. Lansdowne invited the Cabinet to make a choice. As would become plain within two weeks, the decision had to be, in effect, Lloyd George or peace by negotiation. Lansdowne's memorandum, terse and hard-minded, clarified the intellectual atmosphere.

Although couched in the language of an experienced Foreign Secretary, Lansdowne made the alternatives described above clear in the last paragraph of his memorandum. After noting the movements toward peace abroad and applauding recent statements by the Prime Minister and Grey, which in fact had discussed generally the sort of peace Britain could not accept, but who had at least alluded to the subject of negotiation, he concluded by discussing Lloyd George's statement to Roy Howard:

But it is unfortunate that, in spite of these utterances [by Asquith and Grey] it should be possible to represent us and our Allies as committed to a policy partly vindictive and partly selfish, and so irreconcilably committed to that policy [of continued war, as Lloyd George had put it a 'knock-out blow'] that we should regard as unfriendly any attempt, however sincere, to extricate us from the impasse. The interview given by the Secretary of State for War in September last to an American correspondent has produced an impression which will not be easy to efface. There may have been circumstances of which I am unaware, connected perhaps with the American Presidential election, which made it necessary to announce that at the particular moment any intervention, however well meant, would be distasteful to us or inopportune. He said, indeed, that 'the world must know that there can be no interference at this stage' — a momentous limitation. For surely it cannot be our intention, no matter how long the War lasts, no matter what the strain on our resources, to maintain this attitude, or to declare as M. Briand declared about the same time, that for us too 'the word peace is a sacrilege'. Let our naval, military, and economic advisors tell us frankly that they are satisfied that the knock-out blow can and will be delivered. The Secretary of State's formula holds the field, and will do so until something else is put in its place. Whether it is to hold the field, and, if not, what that something else should be, ought surely to depend upon their answer, and that again upon the result of careful stocktaking, domestic and international, which, I hope, is already taking place.

L.[148]

Historically the Lansdowne memorandum of 1916 has been obscured by the far more famous letter to the *Daily Telegraph* that appeared just a year later on 29 November 1917. The public letter, as Lansdowne's biographer observes, took much courage, which no one doubted for a moment Lansdowne possessed, but was probably less important politically than the confidential note to his Cabinet colleagues of 13 November 1916, although the arguments it contained were identical.[149] For purposes of the present story, it may be concluded that Lansdowne provided an honorable rallying point for those who wished to see the war ended and accordingly was seen as a mortal danger to the proponents of Lloyd George's 'knock-out blow'.

In his long discussion of the matter in his *War Memoirs*, Lloyd George prints many extracts from papers submitted to the Cabinet in response to Asquith's invitation for comments, from Grey, Lord Robert Cecil and Robertson, as well as an earlier memorandum on the possible European territorial settlement after the war, written by Balfour on 4 October. Lloyd George agrees that Asquith after considering the submissions formally rejected the notion of peace proposals, however disguised, at the Cabinet meeting on 22 November, which he mentioned also in a letter to his brother.[150] Yet Lloyd George himself avoided condemning the Lansdowne memorandum or indeed expressing any opinion upon it in his *War Memoirs*. But one can hardly question that at the time he recognized the threat it contained. Of course a peace without victory and devastation at the end of 1916 might have appeared to the world as something other than a disaster in the less than sanguine days of the early 1930s when he was writing his *War Memoirs*. It must be repeated, however, that he was himself as pessimistic as Lansdowne about the future course of the war and that he had described his fears in the Cabinet only a few days earlier. He mentioned the memorandum only to Frances Stevenson, leaving her, at least, with the impression that Lansdowne ought to resign.[151] He was far more forthright with General Haig three days later. Saying goodbye to the commander of the B.E.F., he warned him, wrote Haig, that the 'political situation was serious. Lord Lansdowne had written a terrible paper urging that we make peace now, if the Naval, Military and Financial and other Heads of Departments could "not be certain of victory by next autumn."'[152]

Lord Beaverbrook states that Lansdowne's memorandum was aimed at the Prime Minister and that the Unionist leader believed he could convince Asquith of the necessity of peace by negotiation. He suggests further, which may be more important, that a number of powerful Tory leaders — Beaverbrook cites Chamberlain, Lord Curzon and particularly Lord Robert

Cecil, who had written a powerful reply to Lansdowne's paper — were driven to join Lloyd George's government because of the fear of weakness among Asquith and his followers. These men had only slight admiration, and no love, for Lloyd George.[153] Lansdowne may indeed have made the Lloyd George coalition possible.

Whether Lloyd George saw any such sequence of events proceeding from his statement to Roy Howard cannot be known, but it is certainly clear that he had long feared a lack of determination among some of his colleagues. One can hardly question that the violence of his pronouncement was calculated to force a division between the hard line and the soft. Lansdowne, as his final paragraph demonstrates, simply took up the challenge. The conclusion, then, must be that while Lansdowne probably did not force the breakdown of Asquith's administration, his statement made possible the appearance of leading Tories in Lloyd George's coalition.

A part of this effect, as a second point, hinted at by Beaverbrook, is that the letter drove a wedge between the Prime Minister and Bonar Law. Beaverbrook devotes, perhaps unnecessarily, a chapter to the Nigeria debate on 8 November when Bonar Law was humiliated by Carson and rebuffed by his own party in the defense of a government motion to allow world wide, instead of only British, sales of German property in that colony.[154] Sixty-five Unionists supported Carson against the government, and just seventy-three heeded the party whips. The Nigeria debate reminded Bonar Law again of Carson's strength among the Unionist back bench and of the party's contempt for his manifest admiration of the Prime Minister. But by November 1916 these menaces could not have been a surprise to Bonar Law. He was fully aware of his weak position. Then, just a week after the Nigeria debate, Lansdowne's memorandum appeared. Whatever were Bonar Law's weaknesses as a determined and forceful party leader, he was unshakable in his conviction that Britain must push forward in the war to complete victory. And, he could reflect, there were any number of men in the administration, some with much influence on the Prime Minister, who felt, like Lansdowne, that the conflict with Germany no longer could be concluded with full success. Therefore if a compromise peace were to be avoided, reasoned Bonar Law, he would have to join the campaign for a more vigorous prosecution of the war. This meant a painful break with Asquith and, perhaps distastefully, an alliance with Carson and Lloyd George. Lansdowne in Beaverbrook's phrase had 'belled the cat'.[155]

Bonar Law's estrangement from Asquith and his agreement to join Lloyd George and Carson, in the face of a clear lack of enthusiasm for these men among many other leaders of his party, was obviously important for many reasons, but perhaps the most significant of them generally has been forgotten. Of course he was party leader, but on the other hand, he was a pale and fugitive shadow beside the incandescent figure of Edward Carson. To be sure he commanded nominal party loyalty, not an insignificant matter among Tories, but little of the personal devotion lavished upon Carson. Nothing if not a realist, he had been aware of this for at least two years. However, of supreme importance for the events that lay ahead, he controlled the party organization. Here was real power. Had he remained loyal to Asquith and had the two men chosen to meet the challenge of Lloyd George and Carson with a dissolution and with an agreed coalition ticket, what would have been for practical purposes a Coupon Election in 1916, Carson and his hot-blooded followers and the anti-Asquith Liberals, would have been wiped out.[156] '. . .it was this special combination of the Tory and Liberal machine' wrote Beaverbrook, 'which made the power of dissolution such a deadly one in the joint hands of Asquith and Bonar Law.'[157] Therefore the most important result of Lansdowne's slogan of 'Peace Without Victory' was to detach Bonar Law from Asquith. Single-handedly Bonar Law could not have destroyed Asquith, but he could have ruined Lloyd George forever.

IV

Before embarking upon the discussion of the climactic event in Lloyd George's political career, his succession of H.H. Asquith as Prime Minister, a few matters concerned with his tenure at the War Office, unrelated to Westminster politics but illuminating for the study of his life, should be noted.

Lloyd George speaks in his *War Memoirs*, with some pride, of his employment of Eric Geddes to solve the tangled problem of the near breakdown of internal railway transportation behind the British lines in France.[158] This self congratulation, a humor that came easily to Lloyd George, in this case is undoubtedly justified. Nonetheless the historian must remark that Geddes's appointment reflects equally well upon Haig, who found little enthusiasm within the army for the employment of a civilian upon a task belonging so clearly to the military.

Much earlier, while at the Ministry of Munitions, Lloyd George had learned that even though production, particularly of artillery ammunition, had risen hugely, slow delivery from French ports caused guns at the front to continue to be rationed on daily firing assignments and that stockpiling for the Somme battle was being delayed. He had spoken to Kitchener of this stricture in the flow of British supplies, suggesting an investigation, but found the great man unwilling to permit a civilian intrusion into such an exclusively military matter.[159] After becoming Secretary of State for War Lloyd George immediately sent Derby, who was popular with the soldiers, to enquire again, but Derby also was rebuffed. Finally when in mid-August he visited France to represent Britain at the negotiations on Romania's entrance into the war at the suggestion of the ubiquitous Lord Esher, he saw Haig and procured his assent to an interview from Geddes who, it will be recalled, was, among other things, an expert in railway construction and operation. Geddes arrived quickly, on 24 August. 'A most pleasant and capable man,' wrote Haig, who clearly did not know much about him, to Lady Haig. 'He is afraid that the I.G.C. [Inspector General of Communications, General F.T. Clayton, of whom Geddes had a poor opinion[160]] resents his visit. I said that I was glad to have practical hints from anyone capable of advising.'[161]

Geddes was of course a Scot, and nominally, unlike Haig, a member of the Church of Scotland. He would attend, reluctantly or not, many church services with the Commanding General of the B.E.F. in the months to come. But he appears to have commended himself to Haig principally by convincing the general that he was not in France to spy for Lloyd George but to help win the war. In any case, he established an easy relationship with the general, who invited Geddes to make a complete survey of military transportation and depot requirements. Lloyd George provided a staff, largely taken from the Ministry of Munitions and the North Eastern Railway, and the report was completed within weeks. When Geddes returned to Britain in the third week of September, Lloyd George appointed him Director General of Military Railways in Great Britain and Haig responded immediately by making him Director General of Transportation in France while abolishing the old military appointment of Inspector General of Communications. By holding the two posts simultaneously Geddes controlled all transportation from the tip of Scotland to the Somme battlefield.[162]

All of this occasioned a minor revolt in the Army Council, which Lloyd George put down firmly, but which was accompanied by the usual leaks to newspapers.[163] The *Morning Post* article of 28 September 1916, already noted, on Lloyd George's interference with the military cited, unspecifically, the imposition of Geddes as well as the conversation with General Foch. Meanwhile Geddes became also the cause of what C.P. Scott referred to as a 'useful rupture' between Lloyd George and Northcliffe.[164]

The fact remains that imposition of Geddes as commander of all transport in Europe, and also the superintendent of the reception and dispatch of military supplies, over the heads of thousands of army officers would have been impossible without the absolute cooperation of Douglas Haig. General Haig had also to suppress a revolt within his own command. His Director of Movements, Major General R.M. Stuart-Wortley, resigned refusing to work under Geddes, who was not an easy man to serve in the best of circumstances. Several others threatened departure. This involved, as army politics frequently did, the King.[165] However Haig was nothing if not stubborn, as Lloyd George would soon discover. He paid no attention to gossip within his own headquarters and recorded nothing but praise of Geddes in his diary. In one of the few references to the subject, a passage that reveals much about the general, and one with which Lloyd George would have entirely agreed, Haig wrote on 27 October.

> There has been a good deal of criticism apparently being made at the appointment of a civilian like Geddes to an important post on the Headquarters of an Army in the Field. Those critics fail to realize the size of this Army, and the amount of work which the Army requires of a civilian nature. The working of the railways, the upkeep of the roads, even the baking of bread, and a thousand other industries go on in peace as well as in war. So with the whole nation at war, our object should be to employ men on the same work in war as they are accustomed to do in peace. Acting on this principle, I have got Geddes at the head of all railways and transportation, with the best practical civil and military engineers under him. . .To put soldiers who have no practical experience of these matters into such positions, merely because they are generals and colonels, must result in utter failure.[166]

Haig may have been an unimaginative tactician but he was a meticulous, and broad minded, administrator. Geddes was in fact quickly commissioned a Major General although he rarely wore his uniform.

Without question, Geddes saved British military transport in France from collapse. His greatest contribution perhaps was the construction in nine months of a huge network of over 1,000 miles of light railways webbed behind a front of less than 100 miles providing for the distribution and lateral transfer of men and supplies, from butter to bombs. The huge British army, now nearly sixty divisions, remained prosperous.

Geddes seems to have enjoyed this work more than any other in his life. For once he was engaged in pure construction and operation of railways unencumbered by any problems of finance or difficulties with labor. (Workers were largely prisoners of war or Chinese, or West Indians, whose use the trade unions resolutely forbad in Britain.)[167] Geddes remained in France at his headquarters at Monthoues, soon nicknamed 'Geddesburg', until May, 1917 when Lloyd George called him to London to become Admiralty Controller, which meant he was to oversee construction of ships. So began his political career.

Geddes's very success in France nevertheless increased the strain on French railways. By mid-November the French, specifically General Joffre, were insisting that the movement of British supplies to France be curtailed. He demanded a meeting.[168] This meeting, put off by the change of administration in Britain and the simultaneous fall of Joffre in France, then by a large inter-Allied conference in Italy, finally occurred on 26 and 27 February 1917 at Calais.[169] The Calais conference dealt with decisions of far greater moment than railway transportation, but the original motive for it had been the French complaints. Afterwards Lloyd George would be charged with subterfuge. He had used transportation as a cloak for the virtual assassination of Haig. On this occasion the critics were wrong. In fact, he had told the truth.

Two other matters must be examined very briefly. The first is the removal of General Maxwell from Ireland. Characteristically, Lloyd George put this off until his last weeks at the War Office, and then, presumably, remembered it. That he waited until the end of October to relieve both Von Donop, as has been already mentioned, and Maxwell, whom he had so frequently denounced in May and June, suggest that he began to realize well before his resignation letter of 5 December that, one way or another, he soon would be leaving the War Office. Lloyd George wrote to Field Marshal French, Commander in Chief of the Home Forces since leaving the B.E.F., on 26 October 1916 asking him to assign the General to York, the headquarters of the Northern Command. Maxwell, Lloyd George wrote temperately, deserved the 'highest praise' but he was 'irrevocably associated in the public mind with stern measures taken to repress rebellion'. A 'popular Irishman' should take his place, perhaps Bryan Mahon (the friend of Carson).[170] Two days later French agreed unenthusiastically to order the transfer. He evidently notified Maxwell immediately for on 30 October Lloyd George received a note from Asquith saying that Maxwell felt he was being demoted. Could Lloyd George make of the Northern a First Class Command?[171] Lloyd George certainly had no desire to reward Maxwell, but the status of the Northern Command was improved nonetheless. The General was consoled, in addition, with the Grand Cross of the Bath and the Irish Privy Council.

The reassignment of Major General Maxwell took place smoothly and quickly. It was gazetted on 16 November. Well decorated, he went without fuss. The story of the attempted transfer of an obscure, newly commissioned Second Lieutenant, Patrick Barrett, became a delicious society scandal, involving a well-known hostess, a friend many years earlier of Edward VII and patroness of Lillie Langtry, the Army Council and the Quartermaster General, and, most difficult for Lloyd George, North Wales county politics.[172]

The events leading up to the Barrett case occurred during the autumn, winter and spring of 1915–16 during Lloyd George's time at the Ministry of Munitions, but he inherited the problem when he entered the War Office. The first question on it was asked by his old friend Sir Arthur Markham, ill with cancer and to die five weeks later, on 28 June just as Lloyd George's appointment was decided, although it remained unannounced. The affair should be noted here for several reasons in addition to its interest as a remarkable example of the continuing vigor of the patronage network of the pre-war British army — 'a social institution,' as H.O. Arnold-Foster, Balfour's war secretary, styled it, 'prepared for every emergency except that of war.'[173]

The Barrett case became the occasion for Lloyd George to put his last measure, the Army Act (Amendment) Bill of 1916, through parliament. Of perhaps more general historical importance, many people at the time and since have assumed that the woman at the center of the delightful gossip, 'Mrs. Cornwallis West' was Jennie Jerome, Winston Churchill's mother.[174] This was not true. The lady at issue was Mary 'Patsy' Cornwallis West, briefly Lady Randolph's mother-in-law. Far more important for Lloyd George, Patsy was the wife of Col. William Cornwallis West, owner of Ruthin Castle and 10,000 acres, and for 43 years Lord Lieutenant of Denbighshire. Col. Cornwallis West had been allied closely with Thomas Gee, Lloyd George's political godfather. Gee's paper had helped to put Cornwallis West into the House of Commons for West Denbighshire in 1885 at the same time that it was supporting the young solicitor Lloyd George for Caernarvon District. And Cornwallis West was at that time, like Lloyd George, a Liberal Unionist. The two men served together in the House of Commons for two years, until 1892 when Cornwallis West was defeated. In the small world of North Wales he was altogether a very considerable man and it is almost inconceivable that Lloyd George and he had not known each other.

As if this were not enough, another figure in the case was Hon. Brigadier General Owen Thomas of Anglesey whom Lloyd George, as he recounts, had first introduced to Kitchener in the winter of 1914–15 and who had been the highly successful chief recruiter for the Welsh division in North Wales. (He also gave the army two of his sons, who were killed in action.)[175] Thomas had expected to command the Welsh division, but was superseded by Ivor Philipps and was by 1916 commanding the reserve battalions of the Royal Welch Fusiliers to one of which Paul Barrett was assigned in 1915.

The Barrett affair provides a story, unrelentingly sad, as old as the Book of Genesis. Sergeant Patrick Barrett, age 26, Irish and a devout Roman Catholic, invalided home from France for exhaustion and shell-shock, was sent to recuperate on the estate of Col. Cornwallis West. There Mrs. Cornwallis West, age 63, took, in the words of the official report, 'an extraordinary interest' in him.[176] Her infatuation caused her to pursue an officer's commission for Sergeant Barrett. Through her connections in the Royal Welch and her friendship with the Quartermaster General, Major General John Cowans, she attracted support from General Thomas and from Barrett's commanding officer, Lt. Col. Delmé Radcliffe. Barrett's commission was dated 24 December 1915.

Evidently after this date Mrs. Cornwallis West pressed Barrett for recognition of her services leading to a letter of anguished remonstrance from the young man on 14 February 1916. He did not, he said, care to join her world. He wanted only to serve 'my God and King'.[177] Barrett's letter caused the affair. Mrs. Cornwallis West sent it to Barrett's commanding officer, Lt. Col. Delmé Radcliffe who rebuked the new subaltern in the presence of the adjutant without giving him the opportunity to reply. He announced in addition that he would transfer Barrett from the locality, although not back to France as was assumed by society gossip.[178] General Owen Thomas was informed and Mrs. Cornwallis West wrote also a series of increasingly hysterical letters to General Cowans denouncing Barrett and demanding action.

Such was the state of the case when it came to the attention of Sir Arthur Markham, Liberal for Nottinghamshire, Mansfield, and a friend of Lloyd George's since the days of national insurance. On 28 June Markham and J.H. Roberts, also a friend and the man who had defeated Col. Cornwallis West for West Denbighshire in 1892, raised a question in the House of Commons, not indeed about Barrett but about the alleged inefficiency of General Owen Thomas.[179] Within the next month Markham, who now knew he was dying, had seen Lloyd George privately, evidently several times. C.P. Scott writes of a breakfast with Lloyd George on 27 July with Reading and the Adjutant General, Neville Macready, on the Barrett case. Markham came with Scott but became too ill to stay.[180] Markham quickly elicited a promise that as Secretary of State Lloyd George would pursue the matter.[181] Lloyd George went to work immediately for on 29 July Col. Repington recorded that General Cowans knew there was to be an official investigation and was 'very sick' about it.[182]

The first, necessary, step was a bill to amend the Army Act sections on courts of enquiry to permit military courts to examine civilian witnesses and to include civilians as members. (Courts martial could question civilians, courts of enquiry could not.) Lloyd George introduced the Army Act (Amendment) Bill, referred to in the press without explanation as the 'Barrett Bill' on 7 August, just two days after Markham's death.[183] The measure passed all its stages in a single day and became law immediately. The court, headed by Field Marshal Lord William Nicholson, C.I.G.S. until the war, and including also a rising Liberal MP for Peebles and Selkirkshire, Donald Maclean, began work within days. Its report was in Lloyd George's hand by mid-November.

The nature of the court's findings have been indicated. An early determination, one suspects insisted upon by Lloyd George, was an interim report, dated 29 September and immediately communicated to Lt. Barrett, assuring the wretched young man that no blame whatever was attached to him.[184]

Exonerating young Barrett was easy, what to do with the figures condemned in the report troubled Lloyd George for six weeks after 16 November. Although the court denounced in measured terms the behavior of Patsy Cornwallis West and deplored the fact that so unbalanced a woman should be allowed to participate in good works affecting soldiers, there was in fact little they could recommend. The court criticized Owen Thomas and Lt. General Henry Mackinnon, retired, who had also been induced to write supporting Barrett for a commission, for injecting themselves into matters that were none of their business. It strongly condemned Delmé Radcliffe, Barrett's immediate commanding officer who should have protected him rather than insulting him. Delmé Radcliffe was removed from his command in the Royal Welch Fusiliers. The great problem was Major General John Cowans with whom Mrs. Cornwallis West was clearly well acquainted. He was a busy and efficient man. He often complained of her importunities, but usually he had done what she asked. The court noted his injudicious behavior but recommended nothing.

Lloyd George received the report upon his return from the Paris meeting that had been called to arrange the conference in Russia. As the days passed he became fully involved in conversations aimed at forcing Asquith to appoint a new, small, full-time war committee, all of which led, on 1 December, to the Cabinet crisis. Meanwhile, in the face of persistent questions in the House of Commons, he put off any statement on the report. Lloyd George's inclination, obviously, was to remove Cowans. He told both Miss Stevenson, who rather sympathized with the General, and C.P. Scott, who probably did not, that a man who abused his influence as Cowans had done could not remain on the Army Council.[185] As usual he was groping toward a decision by conversation. He was enraged to have passed to him by Reginald Brade, Permanent Secretary at the War Office, a note from Stamfordham saying that the King believed Cowans should be retained.[186] For a moment he seemed to have made up his mind. 'Cowans has got to disappear,' wrote Miss Stevenson on 30 November, 'though I think D. is rather sorry for this.'

> The King, however, ventured to send a message that in his opinion Cowans had done nothing to justify being dismissed, which made D. very angry, as he said the King has no right to try & use his influence in that way.

Cowans would have to go, therefore, to show the King that he should not meddle in affairs of this kind. But there was another more characteristic reason.

> I am sorry for Cowans, but he is being made Q.M.G. in France. D. says that those dismissals will make the soldiers more afraid of him. It will show them that he has the power to enforce his will.[187]

These were strong words. But six days after Miss Stevenson inscribed them Lloyd George was Prime Minister. The realization of great office, like the knowledge that one soon is to be hanged, concentrates the mind. Perspectives change. Big problems become small, and perhaps the opposite also occurs. Lloyd George needed no longer to impress the soldiers, or indeed the King, that he meant business. But he needed efficient servants around him and no one questioned Cowans's ability as a military administrator. The excellent housekeeping arrangement of the British army in France, often remarked upon here, reflected upon him as well as Haig.[188] And so Cowans did not go to France. On 22 December the new Under-Secretary of State for War, James Macpherson, announced that Major General John Cowans would be retained as Quartermaster General and a member of the Army Council.[189] He was simply too valuable. Soon he was promoted to Lt. General. On the other hand, Col. and Mrs. Cornwallis West disappeared from *Who's Who*.

10 A Week is a Long Time in Politics

The circumstances surrounding the fall of the first coalition government and the appointment of Lloyd George as Herbert Asquith's successor as Prime Minister, most of which occurred in a single week between Friday, 1 December and Thursday, 6 December of 1916, have been written about and analyzed many times. There is little unpublished material. Most accounts are founded upon the highly detailed story compiled by Lord Beaverbrook who, as Max Aitken, was a participant in these affairs as a back-bench Unionist MP and as an advisor to Bonar Law. Beaverbrook began to collect material for his history immediately after the events he set out to describe. Lloyd George stated in his *War Memoirs* that he found Beaverbrook's account quite impartial, lacking in any bias between himself and Asquith, although he remarked that it was inevitably written from Bonar Law's point of view.[1]

One could add that Beaverbrook wrote, as he had to, from his own position as a Unionist. Accordingly the attitudes and reactions of that political interest were assigned major importance, perhaps more than the facts warranted. In any case a biography of Lloyd George must tell the story from a different perspective.

There are several major considerations to be borne in mind in any account of the fall of Asquith. Certainly none is new, but each is obscured if the researcher allows himself to become preoccupied with the detail of meetings, letters and whispered conversations that dominate the immense scholarly writing on the affair. First, from Lloyd George's point of view, the chain of events did not begin with an attempt to remove the Prime Minister, but with a proposal to strengthen the political direction of the war, to give the government an agency that could force the army to heed political priorities. Lloyd George had been demanding such a body long before he came to the War Office. Probably Robertson's refusal to go to Russia was the symbol of military intransigence, but not more than that, and the immediate trigger was the impending fall of Romania. (One wonders whether Lloyd George found some bleak satisfaction in the news that Bucharest surrendered on 6 December, the day the King invited him to form a government.) But if control of the army began the crisis, Asquith, with the curious stubbornness that sometimes invaded his customary political dexterity, deliberately made his person the center of it by insisting that he be the active chairman, not the absentee reporting authority, of any full-time war directorate. Thus the hitherto peaceful reformers were faced with a murderous choice: in order to invigorate the war effort, Asquith had to go.

This question leads then to a second: why did Asquith behave as he did? What did he hope to accomplish when he tendered his resignation on Tuesday, 5 December? Did he feel Lloyd George had defeated him or did he hope to teach Lloyd George a lesson, as it were, in parliamentary infighting. The assumption that Asquith felt himself defeated, which began, apparently, with Roy Jenkins, constitutes a major dispute among historians of the 1916 crisis.[2] This study will attempt to show that at least on the evening of the first Tuesday in December Asquith was perfectly confident that he would have to return. The evidence for this assertion will appear, but the core of it must be that Asquith's long tenure as Prime Minister, longer than any other for nearly a century, of which he was demonstrably proud, had convinced him that his control of the members of the Liberal party in the House of Commons, no matter what newspapers might say of him, was unshakable. Everyone agreed on this, including Lloyd George who had remarked upon it many times.

In this connection there is a third point, the impact of the public press. Historians have written at length on the power of newspapers in the fall of Asquith, one of the great print journalism stories of this century.[3] Did Northcliffe, who controlled half the newspaper circulation of London, bring down Asquith, as he himself liked to think? On December 11, the day after Lloyd George's government was announced, Northcliffe printed an incredible article, signed by himself, in *The Times*. Everything Lloyd George had done, Northcliffe agreed, had badly needed doing but Lloyd George had been fortunate to have Northcliffe at his elbow for advice. There were still, thought Northcliffe, too many 'has beens' and 'fossils' in the government.[4] Asquith indeed came to believe that he was the victim of a Unionist newspaper conspiracy. Yet, as always, there is more. The fact is that the coalition government, and not only the person of the Prime Minister, was under severe attack by Liberal as well as Unionist papers in the last weeks of November for a variety of sins unconnected with the control of the army and strategic direction of the war. There was a litany of complaints: the proposed air board, food control, manpower, pensions. These examples are from the *Westminster Gazette* on 29 November, edited by Asquith's friend and biographer, J.A. Spender. Here were complicated, but straightforward, administrative decisions. The Cabinet for some reason could not make them. The Unionist papers to be sure were a part of this chorus and so the general effect upon ordinary readers, and voters, had to be that the government apparently had come to a stop.[5] Members of Parliament, if they read the newspapers, or their post, were surely concerned. Lloyd George everyone knew was the man of action. He 'delivered the goods.' Lloyd George was not a man of detail who applied added force to the principles of sanction and audit like Peel, wrote Lord Esher, the quintessential insider, to Lord Murray (formerly Alec Murray, Liberal Whip) on 28 November 1916. But 'he can get things done where other men cannot. On manpower he must do what Asquith did to him at Munitions or what he himself did to Geddes on railways. Find a man, back him, to solve the problem.'[6]

From this perception may have proceeded the Liberal support for Lloyd George in the House of Commons upon which hitherto Asquith himself had counted. Equally, Unionists were unhappy about their association with a do-nothing government and wanted action. Curzon had been demanding angrily for weeks a decision on an air board. He did not love Lloyd George but he intended to win the war. Similarly Walter Long, certainly no friend of Lloyd George and one of the senior Unionists involved in the collapse of the Home Rule plan the previous summer, told Laurance Lyon, proprietor of the *Outlook*, evidently on 23 November, that he was disgusted with the war leadership. Lloyd George would be an alternative if he could get support in the House of Commons.[7] Did not the press, one has to wonder, as it often does, reflect, rather than create, the public mood?

There were also the simple arithmetical politics of a war-time change of government. Here, although it was not immediately apparent either to Asquith or Lloyd George, both the statistical facts (always in the absence of a general election) and the normal self-serving considerations of career building, militated toward a new administration. According to the *Pall Mall Gazette* of 6 December, the 670 members of the House of Commons included 260 Liberals and 37 Labourites, 287 Unionists, 75 Irish Nationalists, 9 O'Brienites, and 2 Independents. The nominal dependable Liberal majority even with unlikely total Labour support therefore was only ten, a considerable erosion from the figures of December 1910. But the trusty radical Christopher Addison, who, it may be recalled, had taken a poll of Lloyd George's Liberal support at the time of the second conscription debates in April and May, had begun again in December to sound preference for Lloyd George among his colleagues. He discovered that Lloyd George could count upon 49 Liberal MPs who would follow him unconditionally and another 126, in all well over half the Liberal presence in the House and far more than half the back bench, who would maintain a Lloyd George government.[8] These numbers, one must conclude, would have shocked Asquith had he known them.

There was also the shift of allegiance among Unionist Cabinet members, which occurred early enough in the Friday to Thursday affair to affect the Prime Minister's decisions. These defections were a blow. In the opinion of those historians who argue that he became discouraged, it was the departure of Unionist Cabinet members, above all Balfour, which caused him finally to resign his own office on 5 December. The behavior of the Unionists was the unstable element in the events about to be described. The volatility of Bonar Law's party, if it is proper to use the possessive in reference to him, made the displacement of Asquith less a conspiracy than an accident.

But finally the unpredictable behavior of the Unionists made December 1916 unusual in terms of Lloyd George's career up to that point, in that he could not control events. This time he seems to have been unable to see how the affair would end. For comparison one should recall the letters to his brother or his wife during earlier crises announcing that he could see his way through it now. He knew what he needed to do to bring a resolution. As an instance he and Bonar Law had decided within hours of Fisher's resignation in May 1915 that coalition was the proper response. All they needed to do was to convince Asquith, which turned out to be easy.

On this occasion circumstances were different. Lloyd George's only real initiative was the first memorandum to the Prime Minister on 1 December proposing the independent war committee without Asquith. The long chain of events that prompted this step have been recounted. It certainly was not the result of sudden impulse. But it is hard to believe that he genuinely intended to make it a cause for his resignation, even though he told Miss Stevenson on 27 November that he would soon leave the Cabinet. The impending fall of Bucharest could provide the reason.[9] But however important, these events would have had no meaning for the public even if they could have been revealed. And it is clear in his remonstrances to the Prime Minister on Monday, 4 December, after the plan for an independent war committee had been rejected, that he was not anxious to resign. It was totally unlike Lloyd George to force a decision on a resolution of this sort. Yet the next day he had in fact resigned. Thereafter he was swept along by events and he was alone. On the other hand, Asquith had at his summons the solace and counsel provided by the Liberal members of the Cabinet, whom he called upon repeatedly during the first week of December. Even if their advice was bad, they afforded comfort. Lloyd George had none of the customary meetings with Riddell, Reading and Robertson Nicoll, who by now were dubbed Lloyd George's three Rs. Except for Addison and Arthur Lee, he was for practical purposes without confidential advice. He communicated regularly, to be sure, with Carson and Bonar Law, but they were as isolated as he. The senior Unionist Cabinet members, Curzon, Lord Robert Cecil, Austen Chamberlain, to whom Beaverbrook refers as the three Cs, Walter Long and above all Balfour, operated independently, wrote and talked to the Prime Minister, and took, and changed, positions during the crisis without reference to Bonar Law. They doubted the judgment of their party chief and uniformly they mistrusted Lloyd George and Carson.

I

After his conversation in the shadow of the Vendôme Column with Hankey about a small independent war committee, as Lloyd George told it in his *War Memoirs*, he telegraphed Max Aitken from Paris asking him to arrange a meeting with Bonar Law. But Aitken himself records that he had already wired Lloyd George in Paris urging him to return.[10] This is a minor point but it illustrates the disparity in orientation of the source material with which the historian must contend in dealing with a highly personal, and in reality painful, event such as the overthrow of Asquith. Some men, Aitken and Northcliffe, for example, wanted credit for it. Others tried to avoid responsibility. Among the latter was Lloyd George.

Lloyd George's dinner with Bonar Law, which was to have taken place on 18 November, the day after Lloyd George's return from Paris, did not occur. Aitken explains that Bonar Law was dining with General H.H. Wilson that evening, and that Wilson did not like Lloyd George — he hated only Asquith more — and that Bonar Law was unwilling to postpone his engagement with the general.[11] This may have been true, but Wilson was also the most political and most accommodating of soldiers. (C.R.M.F. Cruttwell recalls that the word among junior officers was that General Wilson fell into a state of sexual excitement — not perhaps the term in fact used — at the mere approach of a politician.)[12] Wilson's diary shows he was happy to see Lloyd George overthrow the Prime Minister and a few days later was quite willing to make the Russian trip for the War Secretary.[13]

The real problem, as Lloyd George was well aware, was that Bonar Law was entirely under the Prime Minister's influence and was either unwilling or perhaps afraid to enter a conspiracy against him.[14] The facts seem to be that even with Max Aitken's energetic and well-recorded maneuvers to try and bring Bonar Law and Lloyd George together, despite Carson's public threats, and despite the rising sense in the press of an impending crisis, in the first week after the Paris conference there was really no conspiracy. Indeed when Carson, Bonar Law and Lloyd George finally convened on Monday evening, 20 November in Aitken's rooms in the Hyde Park Hotel, the talk was inconclusive and on that day Lloyd George announced rather off-handedly to Miss Stevenson that he was thinking of a tour of the Empire to arouse war spirit, upon which she would accompany him. Clearly there was no matter afoot to keep him in Britain.[15] More illustrative of the distance between Bonar Law and Lloyd George is the former's action in taking immediately to the Prime Minister Lloyd George's plan for an independent war committee to be made up of himself, Carson and Lloyd George. This was the design which Lloyd George had confided to Aitken on 18 November. Although Asquith did not seem exercised, Aitken was angry at this breach of trust.[16] So far Bonar Law's loyalty to Asquith remained the paramount determinant of his action.

This firmness began to dissolve after the Cabinet of 22 November, when Lansdowne's memorandum was discussed. Causality here cannot be established, but Aitken noticed the alteration of mood three days later on 25 November. On that day Lloyd George, Carson, Bonar Law and Aitken agreed to present to the Prime Minister a draft plan drawn up by Aitken for a war committee of not three but four. Its members would have no portfolios and would devote themselves entirely to the day to day management of the war. The plan specified no individual members except, notably, that Asquith would be president and in his absence Lloyd George would preside as chairman. This curious amendment to the original plan, missed in some accounts, may have been intended by Aitken to calm Asquith's fears of a conspiracy, but also it could have been Aitken's way of bringing along Bonar Law. Aitken did not, it would appear, know of the Lansdowne memorandum at this time, but he took the occasion to record that the agreement upon his document 'marked a decisive step in the negotiations, and also a primal definite. . .step forward to the fall of the first Coalition Government.'[17] Bonar Law had said during the discussion, with such firmness that Aitken remembered it, that the Prime Minister either would accept this plan perhaps with some changes or in the end he would have to resign.[18] Bonar Law now understood that he was participating in a plan that could cause Asquith's downfall.

Lloyd George, on the other hand, was by no means sure on 25 November, or for several more days, that the Unionist leader had the inner strength to oppose the Prime Minister face to face. Bonar Law did take Aitken's memorandum to Asquith in the evening of 25 November. Although not rejecting it outright the Prime Minister had declined even to think of bringing Carson into the Cabinet, a contingency not mentioned in the document, but admitted by Bonar Law as being part of the scheme.[19] The interview clearly had shaken Bonar Law. Asquith had appealed for loyalty, had practically wept to him, Lloyd George recounted to Miss Stevenson a few days later, 'telling him how much affection he had for him & how much he relied upon his help in this great struggle.'[20] Aitken had heard much the same account from Bonar Law by telephone on the evening of the interview. He thought the news serious enough to drive the next day, Sunday, 26 November, from Cherkley to Walton Heath to convey the somewhat disturbing information to Lloyd George. Lloyd George was certain that McKenna would be consulted and would advise against any compromise.[21] Among other things, Asquith had belittled to Bonar Law Lloyd George's prestige both in the party and in the country. Bonar Law had been impressed. All of this suggested to Aitken, and evidently also to Lloyd George, the frightening prospect that the Unionist leader might, even at this time, defect to and link himself with the Prime Minister in a general election. Such a treason among revolutionaries would have been disaster. Lloyd George was more optimistic even though he also expected it to happen. '. . .on the contrary,' recorded Aitken, 'in prophesying a rupture he [Lloyd George] dwelt on his influence with the rank and file at Westminster and enlarged on the weight he would carry in the constituencies if Asquith persuaded Bonar Law to join in an appeal to the country.'[22] One must wonder how confident Lloyd George could have been. He knew the power of the party organization. He had tried, years before in Wales, to organize one and had failed. His inability to construct a machine, at a time when he was Prime Minister, would be a large part of the story of his final political defeat.

Asquith responded predictably to the proposal of 25 November in a letter written on Sunday, 26 November, and delivered the next day, with copies to Lloyd George and Carson. His objections basically were two: first, a lawyer's point, that no war committee could function without the presence of the service ministers, and second, probably nearer his innermost opinions, that he could not appoint Carson to such an exalted post. It would mean passing over Balfour, Curzon and, of course, McKenna, whom he named. He did not believe Carson was suitable for general Cabinet work. 'As to Lloyd George,' wrote Asquith, 'you know as well as I do both his qualities and his defects. He has many qualities that would fit him for the first place, but he lacks one thing needful — he does not inspire trust. . .' The new arrangement was designed to accomplish only one thing: 'as soon as a fitting pretext could be found, of his displacing me.'[23] Clearly among those who did not trust Lloyd George was the Prime Minister, although the un-Asquithlike bluntness of the last sentence suggests consultation with McKenna.

This was uncompromising rejection. There might be a new war committee, the fourth since November 1914, Asquith had said, but its personnel would vary little from the body it replaced. In effect nothing would be changed. The four men held a discouraged meeting in the afternoon of Monday, 27 November, and determined that Lloyd George should talk to the Prime Minister alone, a meeting for which Bonar Law prepared the way by seeing Asquith himself and warning of the unpopularity of his government.[24] Lloyd George's interview took place on the morning of Friday, 1 December before the War Committee meeting at noon. With it, even though the conversation was inconclusive, the final crisis began.

Probably at the meeting in the afternoon of Monday, 27 November, after Asquith's rejection of their first proposal, the four men had determined to insist upon going back to a war committee of three, not four, two of whom now would be the service ministers under a chairman without portfolio, Lloyd George, Bonar Law and Carson, although names again were not mentioned. Of vital importance in view of what followed was that although the new body would remain under the final authority of the Cabinet, the Prime Minister would not be a member. Such an arrangement had been in Lloyd George's mind from the beginning. He could work with the Prime Minister, he had said many times, but the Prime Minister, with McKenna at his elbow, declined to work with him. If Asquith were present nothing would be done.[25] Here was a direct challenge to Asquith's leadership. One can imagine that Carson and Aitken hoped the Prime Minister would not accept it, while Lloyd George hoped that he would. The provision for making two of the members the service ministers was inserted in this account. Names again were not included, but Lloyd George was determined that Carson should come into the government and that Balfour should not remain at the Admiralty.[26]

Whether the new proposals were written or simply agreed upon on 27 November is not clear. What is certain is that Bonar Law felt he was now outrunning his party and on 30 November called a meeting of the Unionist Cabinet members to tell them of the proposal for an independent war committee without Asquith. He encountered unanimous disapproval. Whatever they thought of the present conduct of the war, his colleagues were unwilling to be dragged into an intrigue to forward the career of Lloyd George. Fortunately Carson's name did not come up. Walter Long and Lansdowne wrote sharp letters afterwards, from different points of view but equally critical.[27]

Even with Bonar Law almost totally cut off from his party, Lloyd George intended to push ahead alone if necessary. He had an appointment to see Asquith on Friday morning, 1 December. He poured out his anger to Addison the day before. 'He had taken the bit in his teeth' wrote Addison in his diary on 4 December.

> and was determined to make a finish of it so far as he was concerned. Of course the Roumanian business was, so to say the last straw with him. There is the same toleration and indecision over shipping and innumerable Board of Trade matters. He had apparently been discussing the matter with Carson and others. He says he is not keen to be P.M. but is determined there shall be a small War Committee entirely emancipated from departmental committees which could drive along and get decisions made.[28]

This is an admirable summary of Lloyd George's thinking on the eve of the crisis by one who knew his mind well and who sensed his former chief's feeling of isolation. To be noted again is the fact that the sense of outrage and frustration apparent in Lloyd George's words was little different than the feelings he had expressed more than a year earlier when Serbia was being overrun, the calamity that had brought him and Carson into line with each other. The strength of that partnership was already apparent in the newspapers.

On 23 November, the *Morning Post* suddenly announced that Lloyd George would be the saviour of the nation. He was 'a force to which the nation may adhere, a power...for victory, which the nation may follow.'[29] This article caused something of a sensation. H.A. Gwynne, the paper's editor, was a close, indeed devoted, friend of Carson and rarely published an issue without some complimentary reference to the Ulster Unionist champion. But Lloyd George, after the unfortunate interview with General Foch in September when he had asked the French officer about the incapacity of British commanders and after the now well-known attempt to send Robertson to Russia, was routinely criticized for interference with the military. He had been specifically denounced in a lead article as recently as 28 September. Now Lloyd George and Carson were heroes.[30]

The following week saw a growing chorus of press criticism of the government. This was not, it should be noted, directed at the conduct of military operations, but rather at what seemed to be a perception by all journals, Liberal and Conservative, of a near breakdown of decision-making in the Cabinet. Most remarkable is that the items in the list of actions not taken were, in all papers, nearly identical: the proposed manpower board, an air board, a Pension Bill, a food controller, martial law for Ireland, the introduction of colored labor. The 'government discloses half-baked schemes before it is ready to act on them' concluded the *Westminster Gazette*.[31] *The Times* of course had been hammering at the government for months. On 29 November it provided the same list of unsolved problems, adding significant slackness at the Admiralty and the failure to come to grips with the growing submarine menace.[32] This uniformity of press comment may not have been fortuitous. Max Aitken, fearing that Bonar Law's fidelity to the Prime Minister might somehow lead to compromise, began a secret campaign among newspaper editors to attack the government.[33] One of the early results was an article in the *Daily Chronicle* on 29 December calling for 'a War Council' of four, which caused a sensation.[34]

There was then a sense in the political world of growing tension, real but undefined, when Lloyd George saw Asquith on Friday morning, 1 December. What passed between them is unclear. Lloyd George records in his *War Memoirs* that he gave the Prime Minister the memorandum describing the war committee of three drawn up by himself after consultation with Bonar Law, Carson and Aitken and explained the motives that had led to it. He said that he had shown it to Lord Derby, who entirely approved. Although he does not say so in his *War Memoirs*, he told Addison three days later that he had insisted that the Prime Minister accept the changes outlined. Should he decline, Lloyd George would resign.[35] The Prime Minister took the document and agreed to compose a reply later that day.[36] In view of what he would say later it must be noted that Lloyd George had lunch that day with Northcliffe at Arthur Lee's house and according to Ruth Lee's diary seems to have told him of the plan for an independent war committee of three.[37] He saw the publisher again at the War Office later in the afternoon.[38]

That evening Lloyd George received the Prime Minister's reply. Asquith agreed that the present War Committee should be reconstituted. It was too large, often lacked important information, was overwhelmed by detail and hence slow to make decisions, although it had done much good work. However:

In my opinion whatever changes are made in the composition or function of the War Committee, the Prime Minister must be its Chairman. He cannot be relegated to the position of an arbiter in the background or a referee in the Cabinet.

The absence of the Prime Minister from the new war committee became, it should be repeated, the core of the dispute. With this new stipulation, which had not appeared in the first proposal presented by Bonar Law on 25 November, the dispute over the control of the army became a dispute over the leadership of H.H. Asquith. He himself saw it in precisely these terms. If he were not fit to run the war committee he was not fit to be Prime Minister, he muttered to Maurice Hankey the next day, Saturday, when, unperturbed by the rising political storm, he left Downing Street for Walmer Castle.[39]

The rest of Asquith's letter professed agreement with the new plan although he began to add new members to the proposed committee: the Minister of Munitions and another without portfolio. He was turning it again into an executive body rather than a directorate. The directorate would remain the Cabinet. Then he added, no doubt seeing it as a further gesture of conciliation: 'I purposely do not in this letter discuss the delicate and difficult question of personnel.' As war committee membership had been the gravamen of his objection to the first war cabinet proposal — Carson could not come into the government — he offered a distinct concession.[40]

In Asquith's defense it needs to be remembered again that there were other pressures on him. The anti-Lloyd George ministers were always at his elbow and clearly aware of the contest with Lloyd George. The next day George Riddell recorded that he had heard from Robert Donald, editor of the *Daily Chronicle*, that McKenna's man in Fleet Street, Hedley LeBas, had a letter from the Chancellor of the Exchequer saying that he would resign if he were not included in any new war committee.[41]

Clearly Asquith's reply left Lloyd George furious. That night, more likely the following morning, Saturday, 2 December, he composed a bitter letter to the Prime Minister. He repeated his often expressed frustration at the delays and hesitations in the management of the war. 'The latest illustration is our lamentable [changed in manuscript from 'inexcusable'] failure to give timely support to Roumania.' He had argued and objected at every stage and asked permission to publish his warnings if challenged. He now felt that he must leave the government 'in order to inform the people of the real condition of our affairs' before it was too late. He had remained in the government only at Asquith's 'urgent personal request'.[42]

This letter of course was not sent. As was becoming his custom Lloyd George was using pen and paper to relieve his feelings, but it provides ample evidence of the depth of his outrage, and he intended that the Prime Minister should know of it. Moreover, and this is entirely supposition, as he had done the previous July when negotiating for the War Office, he may have communicated its substance to certain friendly newspaper editors. This speculation proceeds from articles which appeared in *Reynold's News* on Sunday, 3 December, whose editor and proprietor was his old friend Sir Henry Dalziel, and on Thursday, 7 December in the *British Weekly* belonging to the ubiquitous Robertson Nicoll. The two articles were remarkably similar, each resembled an interview written in the third person and each contained information that was not yet public. The *British Weekly* article, which could have been written no later than Wednesday, 6 December, sounds as if it were quoting the letter.

> It is well known that Mr. Lloyd George was not anxious to accept the office of War Secretary. He believed he could render greater service out of office as an understanding critic of the Government.

The situation was even more precarious now.

> ...under the present system, under which everything has to be referred to the Cabinet, he was continually thwarted. Remonstrances and memoranda were ignored. The war went from bad to worse. Every day brought its story of humiliation, of indecision, and of disaster. Mr. Lloyd George became convinced that we are not winning the war, and that with present methods we never should win it.[43]

These were the first public indications, circumlocutory but clear, that Lloyd George would resign if he did not get his way. In the event, by the time the *British Weekly* appeared the entire government had disappeared. In this connection it is important to note that the papers on Saturday, 2 December which mentioned the crisis — and some, for example A.G. Gardiner's *Daily News*, did not — assumed that the rumored new war committee would include four or five ministers, Lloyd George as War Secretary, Balfour at the Admiralty, another person, presumably Bonar Law, perhaps Carson, and the Prime Minister.[44] *The Times* manifested little to suggest that its proprietor had spent several hours with Lloyd George the day before except to say that the country needed an 'inner Cabinet' of men so far as possible exempt from departmental duties.[45]

Lloyd George records that he had seen Bonar Law on Friday evening and the two had agreed to push forward with their plan, whatever the consequences.[46] This clearly was before he had received Asquith's firm rejection of any war committee of which he was not a member, for Saturday morning, as he composed his unsent letter of resignation, he wrote also to the Unionist leader a two sentence note: 'My dear Bonar, I enclose copy of P.M.'s letter. The life of the country depends upon resolute action by you now.'[47]

Asquith meanwhile was departing for Walmer Castle. Carson's biographer surmises that the Prime Minister chose the Lord Warden's residence in Kent near Deal rather than the more hospitable and nearer Wharf on the Thames in Oxfordshire, to which he usually repaired, because Walmer Castle was within easy reach of Carson's country retreat at Birchington. Perhaps he could see Carson alone. There may be something in this. Carson had remained in London all day on Friday in case Lloyd George needed him but received no call and Friday evening drove to Kent. Then Saturday morning Lloyd George, perplexed and angry, had telephoned. He felt deserted. Would Carson return to London? Immediately after he left, Ruby Carson recorded in her diary, Margot Asquith called and asked for her husband. Upon being told he had gone back to London the Prime Minister's wife exclaimed: 'London. Why has he gone to London?' and hung up.[48]

According to Hankey, Reading, as usual commissioned by Asquith to do so, saw Lloyd George at the War Office.[49] Equally in character, Lloyd George summoned Montagu in the afternoon, no doubt talked gravely to him, and showed him his letter of resignation as, it may be suspected, he had already shown it to several others. 'He says he knows,' wrote Miss Stevenson, 'that anything he shows or tells Montagu will go straight to the Prime Minister!'[50] Lloyd George's belief in the sure and certain forwarding of his discontents was well founded. Montagu had no sooner returned to Queen Anne's Gate than he wrote an almost hysterical note to the Prime Minister.

> The situation is irretrievably serious. I have just come from Ll.G., with whom I have spent an hour of hard fighting, but it seems to me to be of no avail, and I fear he has committed himself, though there is always a chance. . .
>
> He regards it as essential that the small War Committee should sit so frequently and act with such rapidity that the P.M., whoever he were, ought not to have a place upon it, but he is loud in his assertions that you are the right Prime Minister in the right place [one can hear Lloyd George speaking].'

Lloyd George would go, warned Montagu, and Derby with him. This would make it impossible for Bonar Law to stay. The government would break up. There would be an election on the 'situation in Rumania, Serbia, etc.' with Lloyd George supported by 'the soldiers who have been suborning the Press.'

Montagu was at a loss for advice. He knew what Margot and McKenna believed: that everything in the press was attributable to Lloyd George. But yet the press (on Saturday) did not know the plan for a three member war committee.

'I remain of the opinion. . .' Montagu concluded, 'that there is no conceivable Prime Minister but you. I remain of opinion that Lloyd George is an invaluable asset to any government. . .' Asquith should come to London immediately. 'It is all a nightmare to me.'[51]

Asquith's biographers agreed with varying emphases that this letter was the catalyst. The Prime Minister now had to act. Indeed in his account of actions to Liberal MPs at the Reform Club on Friday, 8 December, Asquith dwelt at some length on the unpleasant necessity of breaking his weekend.[52] In the early afternoon on Sunday, 3 December, he returned to London, evidently with Maurice Bonham Carter, who had delivered Montagu's letter.

Bonar Law responded to Lloyd George's short note of the previous day by calling a meeting of Unionist Cabinet members at his home in Kensington on Sunday morning, 3 December. This gathering has received much attention in Beaverbrook's account of the December crisis and in most subsequent writing.[53] But Beaverbrook, then still Max Aitken, did not attend the meeting. Rather he waited, indeed hid, in a room upstairs. Other recollections are available in Curzon's letter to Lansdowne, written that evening and Austen Chamberlain's story in his memoir taken largely from a contemporary letter to Lord Chelmsford, Indian Viceroy.[54] An important weakness of all of these histories lies in the fact that each author confines himself to summarizing the results of the conference rather than attempting to tell what his colleagues had said. Recently however, has appeared the most useful diary of David Lindsay, Earl of Crawford and Balcarres, President of the Board of Agriculture since Selborne's resignation, which makes available an extended contemporary account by a participant.[55] It contains also the most extended recitation available, except for Beaverbrook's, of the conversation at Bonar Law's famous meeting with the Prime Minister on Sunday afternoon when he did, or did not, tell Asquith that the Unionist ministers advised him to resign. The Prime Minister, far from being frightened as Bonar Law suggests in his own account of the event, evidently defended himself with some vigor and Bonar Law, as always, was impressed.[56]

However, from Lloyd George's point of view, the mishandled attempt by the Unionists to inject themselves into the battle between Lloyd George and Asquith was for the moment important only for its effect upon the Prime Minister. Lloyd George did not know of the meeting he declares in his *War Memoirs*, and learned generally what had happened only when he read Beaverbrook's *Politicians and the War*.[57]

In any case, at the Sunday morning meeting in Kensington the eight Unionist leaders listened to Bonar Law's account, evidently explained unclearly, of the struggle between Lloyd George and Asquith, which concluded with the statement that Bonar Law felt he must himself resign. There followed nearly an hour's conversation filled with criticisms of Asquith for 'invincible indecisiveness' and denunciations of Lloyd George for trafficking with newspapers, with the interesting addition by Walter Long that Lloyd George's intrigues were being conducted by Max Aitken in luncheon rooms at hotels where there were eavesdroppers.[58] In the end the group determined that instead of Bonar Law resigning alone, all of them would leave the Cabinet together unless the Prime Minister agreed to dissolve the government by resigning himself. The publicity given to Lloyd George's threat of resignation made internal reconstruction impossible. This would perhaps mean that Lloyd George would be commissioned to attempt to form a government, but that would be a problem for him to work out with Asquith. As Crawford put it: 'The country and the press don't want a reshuffling of the cards, they want a new pack!'[59] Bonar Law would convey this decision to the Prime Minister.

Bonar Law took a written statement of the Unionist ministers' position to Asquith in mid-afternoon. He reported afterwards to the men, reassembled at his house, that the Prime Minister seemed shocked that anyone believed things were not going well.[60] He was prepared to justify everything he had done. He refused to consider any subordinate post in an alternative government but said that no government could survive that did not include both himself and Lloyd George. He asked Bonar Law not to give him the text of the Unionist resolutions, containing the resignations, but told him that he would be asking soon for the resignations of the entire Cabinet. He intended to reconstruct the government while remaining Prime Minister, as he had done in May, 1915, in effect discharging all its members except himself. 'We said reconstruction was no longer possible — Asquith proposes to reconstruct,' wrote Crawford ironically.[61]

The Unionists' fulminations may have had one effect nonetheless. Asquith determined to see Lloyd George and try to make an arrangement about the independent war committee. Lloyd George had gone to Walton Heath on Saturday. Thence he had invited C.P. Scott who arrived for lunch on Sunday. At some point there was a telephone message from Bonham Carter asking Lloyd George to come to London. Indeed the timing of the call, not long after lunch, admittedly unclear, suggests that Asquith may have determined, even before hearing of the Unionist ultimatum from Bonar Law, that he would talk with Lloyd George that afternoon. While Scott and Lloyd George rode back together, the latter recounted the story of the affair and showed Scott his letter of resignation, which apparently he carried about in his pocket.[62]

Evidently Lloyd George was asked to go to the War Office and there await a summons from the Prime Minister. He had already arranged to meet Aitken there. The two discussed the situation, while Lloyd George smoked a cigar. With his political career in jeopardy, not to mention the Liberal government and the war, he was absolutely calm and detached. 'I have never seen any man exhibit so much moral courage in the face of such great events,' wrote Beaverbrook, who bestowed superlatives carefully.

> He considered that what he had to avoid was a settlement which was not really a decision. He would not be duped into accepting a position which gave the competent man no final and complete control of the conduct of the war. He must know how he stood in this matter before he left Downing street. If this control was refused, events must take their course. He finished his cigar quietly and left for Downing street.[63]

What transpired at the critical meeting in the gloomy late afternoon of Sunday, 3 December can be reported from only two sources: the subsequent correspondence between Lloyd George and the Prime Minister and Beaverbrook's account of what he was told later by Bonar Law. There is not much disagreement. Asquith was willing to compromise. There would be a war committee of three, although Asquith urged the inclusion of a Labour member, probably Arthur Henderson. But of critical importance he accepted the provision that the Prime Minister would not be a member. However:

> The agenda of the War Committee will be submitted to him; its Chairman will report to him daily; he can direct it to consider particular topics or proposals; and all its conclusions will be subject to his approval or veto. He can, of course, at his own discretion attend meetings of the Committee.[64]

There was no discussion of personnel although Asquith's account of the meeting to Bonar Law who came in as the discussion was ending, seemed to indicate that this would be no problem. What had become of his objections to Carson, so decisive before, it is impossible to guess.[65] Bonar Law then returned to the third meeting of his colleagues, now gathered at F.E. Smith's house in Westminster, where he announced a compromise had been reached. The statement on the government's reconstruction would go to the newspapers that evening.[66]

Lloyd George briefly went back to the War Office. In view of what subsequently occurred it should be noted that he conferred there again with Lord Northcliffe, generally, but not exclusively, about an appointment to write some political articles in the not unlikely event that he would soon need another source of income.[67] Tom Clarke, who worked for the publisher, adds some circumstantial detail. Northcliffe had spent Sunday at his mother's home in Hertfordshire and had returned to see Lloyd George at seven o'clock.

After the interview he had gone to *The Times* office and had written a two column political article on the crisis.[68]

It was now nearly 8 p.m. Lloyd George apparently remained in London that evening in a flat that David Davies had rented for him in St. James Court. He had moved out of No. 11 under the pressure of war-time taxation. As he retired he could reflect that he had achieved most of what he wanted. The war committee was not entirely independent. Asquith could indeed attend as he wished, but would he? There was his indolence.

Others had more doubts about Lloyd George's plan. Churchill wrote later that the war committee could not work simply because of the man Herbert Asquith was. Every decision to which the Prime Minister was not a party, no matter how trivial, would be debated again in Cabinet. Decision making would not be accelerated, but delayed.[69] Carson as well did not like the independent war committee. His biographer recalls that afterwards he used to say that Asquith 'had got all he required; that if the Prime Minister cared to attend and preside over every sitting no one could have prevented him.' But then he made the mistake of telling McKenna who said: 'Have nothing to do with it; you are indispensible.'[70] To be sure this is a simplification of what happened in the next three days, but in its essence Carson's description of Asquith's mistake was correct. If Asquith was to be destroyed the independent war committee by itself was too weak an instrument for this purpose.

The next morning, Monday, 4 December 1916, Carson, Derby and Lloyd George breakfasted together, evidently at Carson's house for Ruby Carson reported some of the conversation. The announcement that Asquith would reconstruct the government, handed in just before midnight on Sunday, was in the morning papers and so was a long leading article and a second two column story by the 'Parliamentary Correspondent' recounting in some detail the history of the previous 24 hours' events. In both articles Lloyd George was identified for the first time as the man behind the crisis and both articles stressed his close association with Carson and Derby. Most of all the sense was that the independent war committee had been accepted.[71] *The Times'* leading article has become the famous turning point in the story of the collapse of the Asquith coalition, not, so far as one can see, because of the revelation of political secrets, except for the proposed inclusion of Henderson on the war committee — and even the *Manchester Guardian* on the same day had mentioned this, adding also that the country had better be prepared to think new and kindlier thoughts about Carson — but because of the ironic way it told what it knew. Asquith quickly saw he was being mocked. He was 'never slow to note political tendencies when they became inevitable,' said *The Times.* His qualities 'are better fitted, as others are fond of saying, to "preserve the unity of the nation"... than to force the pace of the War Council.'

The 'Political Correspondent', on the other hand, knew of the previous afternoon's meeting at No. 10 between Lloyd George, Bonar Law and the Prime Minister. But he did not know that the new war committee would be only three, not four, which had been the substance of Friday's demand. For a production of Northcliffe's own hand, the political article was remarkably uninflammatory.[72]

The accepted story seems to be that the leading article was written by *The Times* editor, Geoffrey Robinson (who changed his name nine months later to Dawson), who had visited Cliveden during the week-end, had talked to the house's owner and proprietor of the *Observer*, Waldorf Astor, also to Lord Milner, another guest, and to Sir Edward Carson. On the rest he made informed guesses, like a good journalist.[73]

At the breakfast on Monday, 4 December Lloyd George, Carson and Derby seem to have been unaware that anything had happened. The three men placidly discussed Carson's impending appointment to the Admiralty.[74] Then sometime during the morning arrived a letter from the Prime Minister, the man who never read newspapers, complaining about the leader in *The Times*.

> My dear Lloyd George:
>   Such production as the first leading article in today's *Times* showing the infinite possibilities for misunderstanding and misrepresentation of such an arrangement as we considered yesterday made me at least doubtful as to its feasibility. Unless the impression is at once corrected that I am being relegated to the position of an irresponsible spectator of the War, I cannot go on.

The Prime Minister then recited, as quoted earlier, the terms of the 'suggested arrangement'.[75]

Two points should be noted in this letter. First it was not a declaration breaking the agreement. No doubt Asquith did believe Lloyd George had communicated their conversation of the evening of 3 December to the press. One can say with certainty that if he did not believe it on the morning of 4 December he became convinced of it soon afterwards and remained so for the rest of his life. But second, the tone is of wounded feelings, as much as anger. He had found the leader insulting, as indeed it was. The wrong impression given by the article had to be corrected. Presumably Lloyd George was to do this, perhaps by a statement to the press. To some extent he was asking for help. The only ominous part of the letter lay in the Prime Minister's reference to a '*suggested* arrangement'. Lloyd George believed the two had come to an agreement. Unfortunately he had failed to get a written copy of it.

Lloyd George records in his *War Memoirs* that he found in the letter a complete change of mood from the previous evening. There was none of Asquith's usual cordiality and friendliness. To the historian the tone is of hurt, wounded *amour propre*. Certainly Lloyd George answered in that sense: It was all a mistake and the Prime Minister should pay less attention to the views of Northcliffe.

'I have not seen the *Times* article,' wrote Lloyd George, the man who never missed a newspaper, 'but I hope you will not attach undue importance to these effusions.

> I have had these misrepresentations to put up with for months. Northcliffe frankly wants a smash. Derby and I do not. Northcliffe would like to make this and any other arrangement under your Premiership impossible. Derby and I attach great importance to your retaining your present position — effectively. I cannot restrain, or, I

fear, influence Northcliffe. I fully accept and in spirit your summary of the suggested arrangement — subject of course, to personnel.[76]

Following this letter Lloyd George spent much of the mid-day trying to arrange a meeting with Asquith. Both Frances Stevenson and J.T. Davies called at No. 10, only to be put off. Finally the Prime Minister agreed to see his War Secretary at 6 p.m. But this was cancelled by a note from Bonham Carter saying that Asquith would not meet Lloyd George but would write instead.[77]

Clearly the Prime Minister had had second thoughts. What, the biographer must ask, caused him to withdraw an arrangement clearly so full of holes that any politician one quarter as deft as he could have destroyed it in a moment whenever he chose. Rather one feels that when his temporary panic following Bonar Law's badly handled mission subsided, he began to count the assets that were piling up in the vestibule at No.10 after the announcement that all ministers were to return their seals. He realized that he did not need to compromise on the war committee. His position, in fact, was much stronger than he had believed it to be 24 hours earlier.

The comings and goings at No. 10 on 4 and 5 December, who saw Asquith in those days and when, are the stuff of detective novels. Did Chamberlain, Curzon and Cecil see him once or twice was a matter of great concern to Lord Beaverbrook and Austen Chamberlain. This writer believes they saw him once, on 5 December. But what may have been more reassuring was the parade of younger Liberals, some in the government and some who were not, who communicated with the Prime Minister by post or telephone pledging loyalty. On 6 December the *Westminster Gazette* would announce that the number of Lloyd George supporters in the House of Commons stood at 20.[78] This estimate, obviously made no later than 5 December, the day the Prime Minister finally resigned, by a good friend and a journalist whom he trusted, cannot have been unknown to him.[79]

No doubt Bonar Law's clumsy handling of an overly subtle commission (in effect: 'We Unionists insist that you resign your office, but do not think that we dislike you. We are really trying to help.') had needlessly frightened him. He had rushed into what had seemed to be to him a workable compromise: Lloyd George could have the appearance of an independent war committee, without any power. The Prime Minister could destroy, temporarily or permanently, any of its policies or decisions whenever he chose. Both Carson and Churchill, each of whom loathed Asquith, disliked intensely the new war committee. It would do no job that needed doing. It could neither run the war nor emasculate the Prime Minister. Asquith did not know, of course, of Carson's or Churchill's opinions, but he had his own set of well used and trusted political rules: like follows like, an uncovered hole is dangerous at night no matter which party is in power. These would have led to the same conclusions. But nevertheless on Monday morning the Prime Minister discovered in *The Times* that influential people believed he had allowed himself to be made a political eunuch. *Roi fainéant* was the phrase he would use. Even if its assumptions were incorrect, *The Times* leader was far worse than a hurt. It was an embarrassment.

This was H.H. Asquith in December 1916 at age 64. Soon he would have been in office, he could recall, for nine years. On Monday, things began to change. There were rumors from Unionists — from motivations one need not speculate upon — that he had entirely misunderstood the purport of the Sunday letter. Certain individuals were anxious he should know that they would never serve under Lloyd George. One of these was George Curzon.

At about 5 p.m. on Monday evening Lord Lansdowne, apparently at the urging of Curzon but unquestionably with reasons of his own, came to see the Prime Minister. The interview could not have lasted long for much other business was transacted that evening. Moreover No. 10 was crowded with junior and senior Liberals clamoring to meet their leader, as Bonar Law had discovered when he went there an hour or two earlier.[80] Among other things, Lansdowne, who was beyond office-seeking for himself, was to convey that Curzon's '[threat of] resignation yesterday' had no 'sinister import,' all of which Curzon in a subsequent letter to Asquith, was frantic that the Prime Minister should understand.[81] Lansdowne's interview is remarkable, not because of Curzon, who had announced regularly during the meetings on Sunday that he would never serve under a Lloyd George dictatorship, but because of Lansdowne's report afterwards to his colleagues who had met almost continuously through that afternoon. He stated then that he had gathered at No. 10 that Asquith 'would come to terms with Ll.G.' The 'Prime Minister,' Lansdowne continued, according to Crawford's diary, 'says that the new war committee must submit to him the agenda and the minutes, and he will attend it.'[82] As support for the argument of this account — Asquith threw over an easily destroyable and badly thought out plan for an independent war committee not because he felt *The Times* leader had insulted him but because he felt himself strong enough to force the resignation of Lloyd George — Lansdowne's short conversation with him and the time of day it occurred is of great importance. Asquith had been at No. 10 for the entire Monday, 4 December, except for an hour or two when he went to Buckingham Palace to turn in his ministers' resignations and then to the House of Commons in his last appearance there as Prime Minister to adjourn the House until 7 December. Otherwise he had spent his hours listening to assurances by politicians of their loyalty. He had, or soon would have, J.A. Spender's assurance, already noted, that only 20 members of the House of Commons supported Lloyd George. (Three weeks later, discussing the crisis, as they did constantly, Lloyd George observed to Riddell: 'Three men helped bring Mr. A. down — McKenna, Gulland [the Chief Whip, who apparently was unable to count Liberal heads] and Spender. They have ruined him.')[83] In the morning he had written Lloyd George the carefully qualified letter, already discussed, demanding that Lloyd George make the world understand that he, the Prime Minister, was still in charge. But then he had carefully avoided seeing his offending War Secretary. Nonetheless at the end of the day Lansdowne believed that the Prime Minister was still prepared to honor the accommodation worked out with Lloyd George. So far nothing had changed.

Available evidence then and Asquith's own story given five days later both affirm that the decisive rejection of the Sunday compromise, taken in the late evening of Monday, 4 December, was the result of the advice of the Liberal Cabinet members. At the Reform Club meeting, Asquith was unclear about the hours but not the sequence of events. Several men present at that time, for example McKenna, had been with him most of the day. Any one of them could have testified that the appearance of *The Times* leader and the determination to push on without Lloyd George were separated by nearly twelve hours.[84] At the Reform Club, Asquith said simply that after receiving Lloyd George's reply to his complaint about *The Times*, he decided to consult his colleagues. When he had done this, he wrote to Lloyd George again.[85] But one event occurred in the morning, the other in the evening.

The meeting at No. 10 on Monday evening was close to being a formal Cabinet, not a round table discussion. One of the few unpublished sources available on the events of the first week of December 1916 is a note from Herbert Samuel to J.A. Spender, written the following day, telling what he had seen. He went to No. 10 in the evening, not to find out what was happening as others had done, but because he was summoned by the Prime Minister. Present were Grey, Harcourt, Runciman, and McKenna [Montagu?]. Each man was asked to tell what he thought of Lloyd George's proposals. Each found them unacceptable but each thought the country wished to see both Asquith and Lloyd George in office. Evidently in response to the question of whether he, Asquith, should resign himself, there was a unanimous response that he should, to throw upon Lloyd George the burden of forming a government, which Lloyd George could not do. This advice was precisely what had come from the Unionists the preceding night, but a fact which the Liberals presumably did not know. Samuel records that he dissented by saying that possibly Lloyd George could form a government, but that it would not last. At this point Arthur Henderson also appeared. Few men in Britain could read the tea leaves of political opinion more accurately than this plain spoken Glaswegian ironfounder. He announced that Lloyd George not only could form a government but that at least some Unionists would support it. Asquith's only response appears to have been that he feared a Lloyd George-Carson government would stimulate pacifism.[86]

Thus it was late in the evening when Asquith sat down to write again to Lloyd George. Evidently the consultations of the day had affected his plans only to the extent that he had become more convinced of the strength of his position. He need not resign. If his colleagues believed that only he could form a government, why resign to teach Lloyd George a lesson? He would begin again to move toward reconstruction taking the steps that had been interrupted twenty-four hours earlier. He would rebuild the government from the inside. There would be a new, smaller, war committee, but Carson would not enter the government and Balfour would remain at the Admiralty. Above all he, Asquith, would be chairman of the war committee. One has to assume that the Prime Minister pondered the effect of these decisions on Lloyd George. No doubt he would resign, but perhaps upon reflection he would return.

The letter he wrote largely restated the position taken in his first letter of 1 December, rejecting the original war committee proposed by Lloyd George the previous Friday. He began by announcing that the King that day had accepted the resignations of all the members of the government tendered by him and had asked him to form a new government. No one now had an office from which to resign.

He then took up bluntly the vexed question of the constitution and personnel of the new war committee, specifically repudiating all previous agreements. 'I have come decidedly to the conclusion that it is not possible that such a Committee would be made workable without the Prime Minister as its Chairman.' Although there might occasionally be other calls on his time 'I am satisfied, on reflection, that any other arrangement (such, for instance, as the one indicated to you in my letter of to-day) would be found in experience impracticable, and incompatible with the retention of the Prime Minister's final and supreme control.'

That was clear enough. The rest was no more conciliatory.

The other question, which you have raised, relates to the personnel of the committee. Here again, after deliberate consideration, I find myself unable to agree with some of your suggestions.

Specifically, the First Lord of the Admiralty must be a member of the war committee and A.J. Balfour must remain First Lord. He would not hear of any suggestion to the contrary.

I must add that Sir Edward Carson (for whom personally and in every other way I have the greatest regard) is not, from the only point of view which is significant to me (namely, the effective prosecution of the war), the man best qualified among my colleagues, present and past, to be a member of the War Committee.

The question of personnel, Asquith concluded 'I reserve for myself to decide.'[87]

In the almost unfriendly directness of its language this letter appears to have been designed to force Lloyd George's departure and there is indeed testimony that the dismissal of the War Secretary was the primary goal of the Liberal ministers surrounding Asquith. Christopher Addison's diary contains a long passage which must be quoted. Unquestionably its information was retailed by Montagu, Addison's chief at the Ministry of Munitions, and to whose house in Queen Anne's Gate the Prime Minister had repaired for dinner on Monday after a long day.

After *The Times* leader, wrote Addison, Asquith had written to Lloyd George that he could not continue, that he must resign. *The Times* leader

however, was not the real reason. The fact was that on Monday morning McKenna, Harcourt and Simon [the latter two not mentioned elsewhere] immediately busied themselves endeavouring to upset the arrangement come to on Sunday evening. They got together their colleagues at No. 10 and represented the whole thing was an affront to Asquith. LG is to Harcourt and McKenna a chronic source of irritation, and McKenna is often intent upon damaging LG. It was due to their pressure on Asquith — and Montagu confirmed it to me with lamentations and despair that his letter was sent to Lloyd George and the breakdown was caused.

There was also this further calculation which they did not conceal — that, with all of them standing out, neither Bonar Law nor LG would be able to form a Government. Asquith would have to be sent for by the end of the week, so that after LG on Monday had refused the PM's withdrawal of the arrangement of Sunday night and sent in his resignation their object was achieved.[88]

Lloyd George took breakfast on Tuesday, 5 December with Derby, Bonar Law, and Carson, as he had done the day before, this time at Derby House.[89] He had not yet seen the Prime Minister's letter, which was waiting for him at the War Office, although Ruby Carson records that 'B.L. is strong for Edward now!' as if some momentous news had come to them.[90] When he read Asquith's letter, Lloyd George appears truly to have been surprised by the quick unravelling of the Sunday agreement. The tone of his reply suggests it, although one can never be sure how much of the wounded outrage is genuine.

In his reply, after saying he had not expected such a letter, he went over at some length the course of his dealing with the Prime Minister since the previous Friday, recalling in every sentence his concern that Asquith should always retain supreme power and responsibility. Asquith, he argued, had accepted the arrangement in his letter of Monday complaining of *The Times* leader. But: 'Today [Tuesday, 5 December 1916] you have gone back on your own proposals.'

There followed a lengthy disquisition on the familiar subject of the mismanagement of the war, much of it taken from the most recent addition to his growing file of unsent but well advertised resignation documents, the by now widely circulated letter of 2 December.[91] The list of mistakes culminating in the assertion 'The latest illustration is our lamentable failure to give timely support to Roumania,' was taken from the 2 December letter without the alteration of a word.

He reminded the Prime Minister of the many times he had offered to resign. He had remained at Asquith's 'urgent personal request,' but now, he felt, the country was faced with disaster. New methods of prosecuting the conflict were necessary. 'As all delay is fatal in war, I place my office without further parley at your disposal.' He had already asked the Prime Minister's permission to publish his correspondence and memoranda warning of impending disasters.[92]

Asquith's reply to a letter one has to believe he had expected was as terse as Lloyd George's had been emotional. He had read Lloyd George's letter 'with much regret', but there were none of the usual requests for delay and consultation. Instead he said simply that the former War Minister should not publish any part of their correspondence and that Lloyd George, in his long letter, had omitted any reference to the 'first and most material part of my letter of yesterday.'[93] This phrase is unclear. Asquith had sent two letters, but probably he referred to the earlier one, the complaint about *The Times* leader. He himself made no mention of this matter in the second letter rejecting compromise, confining himself, as has been seen, to the substantial and important questions of war committee powers and personnel. Correspondence between the two continued throughout the day of Tuesday, 5 December, Lloyd George contending that he must be able to give reasons for his resignation and Asquith replying that public interest forbade it. The letter writing ended only in late afternoon when Asquith told Lloyd George that he had tendered his own resignation. The period of maneuver and negotiation now ended. The public action began.[94]

Perhaps no single act in the December crisis has fascinated historians as much as Asquith's resignation as Prime Minister in the late afternoon of

Tuesday, 5 December. Was it a challenge or despair? Asquith's letter to Lloyd George on Monday evening was clearly written from what he considered to be a position of strength. Then he had some reasons to believe that even if the more prominent Unionists, obviously Curzon, were divided about their course of action, they would not cooperate in a government dominated by Carson and Lloyd George with Bonar Law in attendance. And he had the comforting assurance that his own Liberal colleagues supported him to a man, as did nearly all the House of Commons Liberals. He did not need even to give Lloyd George the opportunity to try to form a government. He would reconstruct from the inside as in May, 1915. Yet by 5 p.m. the next day he had changed his mind.

According to Roy Jenkins, Asquith received Lloyd George's reply at about noon on Tuesday. It contained presumably what he had expected, but soon afterwards he opened an entirely unexpected and unwelcome note from A.J. Balfour written from Carlton Gardens where the First Lord lay ill. While Balfour's letter suggests that he may not have been entirely in touch with the latest facts in the rapidly unfolding drama of the new war committee, its message was clear: the Prime Minister need no longer consider him a candidate for the Admiralty in any reconstructed Cabinet. If Lloyd George did not want him at the Admiralty he would not take the office. 'I am quite clear,' wrote Balfour, 'that the new system should have a trial under the most favourable circumstances; and the mere fact that the new Chairman of the War Council *did* prefer, and, so far as I know, *still* prefers, a different arrangement is, to my mind quite conclusive, and leaves me in no doubt as to the manner in which I can best assist the Government which I desire to support.'[95]

This obviously was a blow even though Asquith's biographer suggests that the Prime Minister may not have understood immediately how important was this defection.[96] In any case, soon afterward Asquith asked Curzon, Chamberlain and Lord Robert Cecil to come to Downing Street. This mission of 'the three Cs', as Beaverbrook styles them, has assumed a good deal of importance in all accounts of the crisis. Were the three senior Unionists, together with Walter Long, trying to undermine Bonar Law's position? Bonar Law himself clearly believed this to be true, at least for a time.[97] Austen Chamberlain's clear and circumstantial account of his own and his colleagues' activities, written six days after the events described — Chamberlain being a man that even Beaverbrook admitted to be honest — shows such sinister intent to have been unlikely, even though Chamberlain had many misgivings about his party leader's intelligence and judgment. In the event, the visit of the three Cs cannot have told Asquith much that he did not already know, nor to have confirmed for him any course of action. The bungled message of Sunday, they insisted, was not directed at him but was intended to force Lloyd George to sound the depth of his own support. Chamberlain states the Prime Minister had not understood this before, but surely there had been several men, indeed Curzon was one, affirming this meaning. One should add here that the Liberal ministers, as Addison's diary shows, had urged after all the same course of action upon their chief on Monday evening, and for the same reason. Perhaps Asquith's more crucial question to the three was would they serve under him should Lloyd George and Bonar Law refuse office? Conversely, would they serve in a Lloyd George administration? Their response to these alternatives was the same: they sought only the strongest possible government to prosecute the war. Chamberlain believed that these unhelpful responses rather shook the Prime Minister, but one is bound to ask what answer he expected.[98] The only decision, to which unwillingly he was being driven, was the necessity of a trial of conclusions with Lloyd George in the House of Commons. Here the three Cs were even less secure than he. Carson's mutinous Praetorians on the Unionist War Committee might easily turn all of them out. That was what the Nigerian debate had shown. Asquith, on the other hand, still controlled, presumably, the Liberal back bench. Addison's fatal numbers were unknown to Asquith, and perhaps not yet to Lloyd George.

After meeting Asquith, the three Cs returned to still another Unionist meeting at the Colonial Office, a venue upon which Bonar Law had insisted after a tiff over the question of his leadership.[99] Lord Crawford has left a full account of this meeting which would be of great value for historians attempting to revise Beaverbrook's story. What is important in this study is that the Unionists discovered at this time that Balfour, who was absent, had given up his office. Asquith had not told the three Cs of this important defection and there was some consternation at such bad form. Balfour, obviously unknown to Asquith, had sent a copy of his letter to the Prime Minister to Bonar Law. (One wonders why so astute a man as the Prime Minister had not anticipated a courtesy note of this sort?) However what finally came from the meeting was a second note to Asquith, signed and written by Bonar Law, but composed by the Unionist ministers generally, saying unequivocally that he must resign. It was delivered, not by Bonar Law, but by Curzon.[100] The sense of the letter conveyed quite accurately the sense of the meeting: the Unionists had not changed their position since Sunday afternoon; Asquith had to resign. The constitutional process must begin.

The Unionist note, signed only by Bonar Law, evidently caused Asquith's decision to resign. He did so immediately. The contention of this researcher is that he did so with confidence; he deplored fights, trouble, unpleasantness. Had he not believed he would soon be invited back on his own terms he might have waited upon events.

Asquith saw the King at about 7 p.m. on Tuesday, 5 December after a second meeting with his colleagues, who argued now that with the resignation of Bonar Law and Lloyd George and without the assurance of any Unionist support, there was no alternative.[101] Yet this conclusion does not necessarily confirm desperation. There is no record by Asquith of his thoughts on the resolution of the crisis but there are some useful clues. Evidently the Prime Minister, who generally disliked the company of newsmen, had asked Robert Donald, editor of the *Daily Chronicle*, a Liberal but never a clear supporter of Lloyd George, to come and see him on Sunday, 3 December. Donald reported this to George Riddell and expressed surprise. He had never met the Prime Minister on political business before.[102] The Sunday meeting did not take place. Asquith was fully occupied with Bonar Law and Lloyd George that day but Donald did see Asquith at some time later in the week, evidently after he had resigned, but before Lloyd George had formed a government, presumably

Wednesday, 6 December.[103] He told the story of this conversation to Riddell and Lloyd George a month later.

Riddell wrote that Donald was sure that Asquith believed Bonar Law could not form a government unless he himself took office in it. Hence he refused. In this Donald agreed the Prime Minister was quite correct. On Lloyd George

> Asquith was convinced that you [Lloyd George, now Prime Minister] would be unable to form a Government and the King would have to recall him. Asquith confirmed this when I saw him, and when I inquired what would happen regarding you, Mr. P.M., he said, striking his hand upon the table, "He will have to come in on my terms!"
> L.G.: Yes, I think that is a correct historical statement.[104]

(At some point during the week Donald, according to Riddell, was offered a knighthood, which he refused. Asquith then proposed a baronetcy, and was refused again.)[105]

There is a second, more personal glimpse of Asquith at this moment, which suggests anything but despair. In his account, Lord Crewe states that he dined at No. 10 with Asquith after the Prime Minister's resignation. One has the vision of the two statesmen sitting alone together in morose silence, each pondering, but unable to discuss, the coming of the end of the world.[106] In fact Lord and Lady Crewe were part of a large, and evidently impromptu, party. Lady Cynthia Asquith, summoned at the last minute, was seated at her father-in-law's right. '. . .he was too darling — rubicund, serene, puffing a guinea cigar (a gift from Maud Cunard), and talking of going to Honolulu . . .He was so serene and dignified.' Asquith, of course, was quite capable of such detachment. It was part of his strength. But when the ladies withdrew Cynthia learned, apparently from Lady Crewe, until she was interrupted to join the inevitable bridge game, that 'before dinner, Mr. Asquith had said that he thought there was quite a chance of Lloyd George failing to form a Government at all. The Tories — in urging him to resign — had predicted such a failure. In any case, most people seem to think that any Government he could succeed in forming would be only very short-lived.'[107]

The last observation, that Lloyd George might form a government, but could not maintain it, seems to represent a consensus, even, as will be seen, among Lloyd George supporters.[108] In this assumption lies the importance of the Maurice Debate. The *Westminster Gazette* the next day speculated loyally that Asquith would have to return. The *Daily Chronicle* feared a general election. Even *The Times* on both 6 and 7 December spoke not of Lloyd George's success but of the disaster that would ensue should Asquith return.

While Asquith was enjoying bridge on Tuesday evening, Addison received a summons from J.T. Davies to come to the War Office. There he found Bonar Law and Carson with Lloyd George. He surmised that Lloyd George was feeling rather alone, surrounded by Unionists. Bonar Law, he learned, had been asked to form a government and would try. The four would meet again at Carson's house at 10 p.m. Carson, Addison observed, had grown weak on the Irish settlement, which Lloyd George was still determined to put into effect, but had agreed that Irish internees should be released. Beaverbrook records that in the interval, while Bonar Law was gone, Lloyd George went to dinner with himself and Churchill at F.E. Smith's residence. However, Addison states that Lloyd George remained at the War Office to discuss Ireland with Carson. Although Beaverbrook's account is highly circumstantial, Addison's diary, written only three days later, should be accepted. Also, there was hardly enough time for a dinner in the interval between Bonar Law's departure and return.[109]

Bonar Law returned at 11 p.m. The Unionist leader had seen Asquith. He would not join a Bonar Law government.[110] At this time evolved the suggestion of a general conference of all leaders, Asquith, Bonar Law, Balfour, Lloyd George and Henderson, in the presence of the King.[111] The King, it was assumed, would be enthusiastic.[112]

Bonar Law, Carson told Arthur Lee the next day, was shaken by the enormity of the task he was trying to accomplish and after Asquith's rejection of office 'was in a complete funk' when the men had met at midnight. Asquith of course, concluded Carson, was trying to make impossible the formation of any government but his own.[113]

The next morning, Wednesday, 6 December, Lloyd George and Bonar Law went to see Balfour, still ill, in Carlton Gardens. One can sense that the two men felt the pace was slowing. Asquith's intransigence might indeed have accomplished what he intended it should.[114] Bonar Law's sister, Mary, an astute politician in her own right, had received a letter that morning from Bonar Law's private secretary at the Colonial Office, J.C.C. Davidson, warning her that Asquith would win and that her brother and Lloyd George would be pulled down together.[115] In many ways Balfour was the key that could unlock Unionist hostility. Probably his letter to Asquith had finally forced the Prime Minister's resignation. His adherence to a new administration would bring others flocking in. Indeed so it proved.

As always Balfour was cordial, but also non-committal. He made no promises. Everything would have to wait upon the meeting at Buckingham Palace.

Formally the King's conference, which began that afternoon at 3 p.m., was a meeting of His Majesty's advisors who were constitutionally bound to find a way of maintaining the governance of the realm. But in its essence, the meeting represented an attempt not to name a Prime Minister, but rather to ascertain whether there was any government other than one of his own in which Herbert Asquith would serve. And historically it may have been the last opportunity, certainly the last but one, for Asquith to avoid a crushing division of the great Liberal party.

Present, besides the King and clearly Stamfordham were Asquith, Balfour, who left his sick bed to attend upon what he knew to be, perhaps more surely than anyone else, a great matter of state, Lloyd George, Bonar Law, and Arthur Henderson. Given its charge the conference had to become a series of dialogues between Asquith and everyone else, Balfour acting as chairman. Each leader in turn sought a means to satisfy the former Liberal leader. His presence and Lloyd George's in any ministry, Balfour insisted, was vital. Henderson added that Labour could not serve in any ministry that did not include Asquith. Bonar Law announced with an assurance that remains mysterious, that no Unionist could serve with Asquith as Prime Minister.

Asquith's response indicated his confidence. He could help the war effort better on the outside. The crisis was the result of press machinations, but his hold on the Liberals in the House of Commons and in the party would ensure that there were no conspiracies in the future.

Asquith's intractibility, of course, provided a perfect atmosphere for Lloyd George to appear as the voice of sweet reason. He sought no office. He would support any government, even one formed by Asquith, and even though he might be excluded.[116] He insisted only upon the establishment of a strong and independent war committee, whether or not he was himself a member.

This was heavy fire. One has to wonder whether toward the end of the conversation Asquith's resolution did not begin to weaken. Bonar Law reported as much to Max Aitken, and evidently Lloyd George did the same to Addison.[117] Beaverbrook himself, however, felt the opposite was true, that the conference only confirmed Asquith in the belief that he was indispensible.[118] In any case Asquith began to fall back upon the pallid, overworked arguments that there really was no crisis; the present War Committee was less a failure than it seemed to be. By the time the conference adjourned at 4:40 p.m. Asquith had agreed to a course of action put before the conference by Balfour. He would consult the Liberal ministers again about joining a Bonar Law government in a subordinate capacity, presumably as Lord Chancellor. It will be recalled he had refused any post only the evening before. Should Asquith stand out Bonar Law would give up the attempt and Lloyd George would try to form a government.[119]

On Asquith's momentary hesitation, the historian has to speculate upon the evidence of Asquith's domestic circumstances. Men also live by bread and Asquith was nearly penniless, not much richer than Lloyd George who certainly wondered continually how he would survive if he left office. Carson had sneered about Asquith's poverty several times. The bar was a gamble. It produced millionaires and paupers. Carson himself was an example of one, Asquith of the other, and he betrayed the anxieties of a poor man in the management of his office. 'Every day I feel greater contempt for Asquith,' Carson had written to Lady Londonderry in March, 1912, three weeks before the Home Rule bill was introduced. 'He has so many chances, just look at the time of the naval scare. . .I imagine he suffers from indolence and also from the consciousness of his lack of means should he have to retire.'[120] These were observations of one who had beaten Asquith once and expected to do so soon again. Yet Asquith's problem was real. Margot's substantial inheritance seemed to be gone, probably long since capitalized and spent. He was clearly giving allowances to his married children. He had £5,000 as First Lord of the Treasury and the not inconsiderable visible and invisible perquisites that came with the Prime Ministership. Most telling were the closing lines in Cynthia Asquith's diary for the entry of 5 December in which she had described the resignation dinner at No. 10. She fully expected the detestable intrigue against her father-in-law to fail, but should it not 'what will happen to all our finances I daren't think! Certainly it is a most painfully interesting situation. . .'[121]

Unquestionably the financial implications of resignation were in Asquith's own mind as he considered the Woolsack. The £10,000 per year and the £5,000 pension belonging to the Lord High Chancellor cannot have escaped him. In what may have been the beginnings of a review of the first of the many money-earning books written in the last decade of Asquith's life,

Occasional Addresses, Lytton Strachey wrote in May, 1918 that he gathered from Maynard Keynes, who had it on 'the best authority' that Asquith 'was willing and in fact anxious' to become Lord Chancellor in December 1916.[122] Even though Strachey condemned this behavior as a weakness and Asquith was indeed a Sybarite, Asquith would have been a magnificent Lord Chancellor. And so perhaps in the failing light of the late afternoon of 6 December 1916, as he left Buckingham Palace, he may have considered it. As an afterthought, he might have kept alive, also, the Liberal party.

The Liberal ministers, perhaps forewarned, met immediately at No. 10. Lord Crewe's extended account of their discussion indicates that Asquith offered little resistance to the inevitable advice that he stand aside. In fact one detects in Crewe's description of the conversation the assumption by Asquith that his support in the House of Commons was so great that were he to join a government any disagreement over policy by himself would provoke a second crisis, which would be a disaster.[123] He was, in effect, too powerful to join a ministry in a subordinate capacity.

As a second point, Crewe wrote: 'Mr. Asquith's influence, though now so powerful and pervading, would melt away if he were to accept office.' There would be resentment both in parliament and in the country. Far better, thought apparently everyone except Henderson and Montagu, for him to keep his party intact, create a responsible opposition, criticize when necessary, and 'in the last resort [offer] an alternative administration.'[124] Clearly Asquith expected to return and when he sailed back he would want to be aboard a well-found ship with a full crew.

It is easy to question the wisdom or even the political perspicacity of these observations, particularly within the terms of facts as they were already known. Crewe wrote, after all, ten days after Lloyd George had announced his government. But emphatically they are not the lamentations of participants in a lost cause. Lloyd George's government could not last and Asquith would be in a better position to overthrow it from the outside. The Liberals would now depart, but not in peace. So they thought.

Asquith immediately wrote to Bonar Law saying that he could not join an administration headed by him, and by 7 p.m. Bonar Law had informed the Palace that he could not form a government. Immediately Lloyd George went to see the King.

Considering the array of forces against it, the formation of the Lloyd George government came easily and, most surprisingly, in only twenty-four hours. As the whole body of Liberal ministers, with the possible exception of Montagu, was totally loyal to Asquith, a Lloyd George administration would have to come entirely from the Unionists. This was taken for granted, but it meant also that much of the negotiation, cajolery, or intimidation, would have to be undertaken by Bonar Law.

In all this the central figure, as Bonar Law and Lloyd George had understood for days, was A.J. Balfour. He would be offered the Foreign Office. Upon leaving Buckingham Palace in the evening of Wednesday, 6 December Bonar Law proposed that he see Balfour immediately. With Lloyd George's approval he went off to Carlton Gardens. According to Bonar Law's account the conversation between the two men was short and Bonar Law asked the critical question with his usual bluntness: "'Of course you understand that I have come from Lloyd George to ask you on his behalf to become Foreign Minister." Mr. Balfour rose from his seat and without a moment's hesitation said: "That is indeed putting a pistol to my head, but I at once say, yes."'[125]

That appears to have been all. The dam of Unionist intransigence was broken. The rest of the Unionist appointments came easily enough the next day. Lloyd George acknowledged two days later in a letter to H.A. Gwynne the importance of Balfour's acceptance of office. The editor of the *Morning Post* wrote on 8 December, before the new government was announced, saying that he had heard Balfour would go to the Foreign Office. He was not forceful enough for that post, thought Gwynne, and he was, in addition, in the pocket of Lord Robert Cecil, 'No friend of yours.' Lloyd George responded immediately, not disputing these points, but saying that he would be involved in foreign affairs himself. On the other hand: 'There are many things to consider in the formation of a Government, and the placing of Balfour at the Foreign Office was of incalculable assistance to me throughout. After Bonar Law and Carson, he was the first man to come to my aid.'[126]

In the evening of 6 December, while Bonar Law was closeted with Balfour, Lloyd George stopped for supper at Riddell's house in Queen Anne's Gate. Also present was Edward Levy Lawson, Lord Burnham, the proprietor of the *Daily Telegraph*. Riddell thought Lloyd George looked tired. The conversation turned generally on the conference at Buckingham Palace and what seemed to all to be Asquith's inexplicable behavior, first in denying that he had arrived at any settlement with Lloyd George the previous Sunday — Lloyd George wondered whether he was losing his memory — and second in declining to take office in a Bonar Law government. Burnham reported that he had seen Asquith that day, presumably before the conference (Asquith belatedly had discovered the utility of newspapermen). He had urged the Prime Minister to serve under Bonar Law and had come away believing he would do so. Lloyd George said flatly that Asquith was persuaded to decline by McKenna, Runciman, and Margot Asquith. Finally the three men spoke of Curzon, whose adherence to the new government became the important event of the next day and whom Lloyd George admitted was extremely valuable. (Lloyd George regarded Curzon rather as Winnie the Pooh saw Rabbit: 'He *will* talk but he knows things.')[127]

Lloyd George refused to eat more than a plate of soup and soon hurried off. Riddell wished him good luck. 'I shall do my best,' Lloyd George replied. 'The belief of these fellows that I shall fail will be an additional incentive.'[128]

Lloyd George returned to the War Office where he was awaited by Bonar Law, Carson, Addison, and Edmund Talbot, the Unionist whip. (Addison himself had dined that evening at the Reform Club, the ordinary resort for younger Liberals after the government took over the National Liberal Club. He found general rejoicing at the imminent humbling of Lloyd George.)[129] It appears that Addison now reported to Lloyd George the results of the canvass of Liberals which showed that should Lloyd George form a government he could expect the support of a good majority of the back-bench Liberals in the House of Commons. The bedrock of Asquith's assumption about his position, the loyalty of the parliamentary party, had crumbled.

After Balfour's defection, if such is the proper word, the solid Unionist front broke up quickly. After seeing Balfour, Bonar Law had approached the three Cs and Long without success and declined to do so again.[130] On Thursday, 7 December Lloyd George offered a post to Long, who refused. But, then he proposed to Curzon that he join the war council (soon to be styled the War Cabinet). This was more than Curzon, who had proclaimed repeatedly to his colleagues that he would never serve a Lloyd George dictatorship, could bring himself to refuse. He neglected even to consult the other Conservative Cabinet members.[131]

The rest of the Unionists came quickly. In the late afternoon Lloyd George and Bonar Law met the three Cs and Long at the War Office. Lord Beaverbrook provided a transcript summarizing the agreement that came from this negotiation. It must be examined briefly here not only for its importance in the formation of the new coalition, which is obvious. It provides also the political platform, almost the charter, of the Lloyd George administration. It answers a good many questions about the form and personnel of the emerging government.

Lloyd George was first asked about Liberal support. There would be no former Liberal ministers at present, he replied, but he had promises of support from 136 Liberal MPs and believed this number would grow. In the event of serious opposition he would not shrink from a general election and expected no resistance on this from the King. Similarly he had met the Labour party earlier in the afternoon and expected support from a large majority of this group.

In response to a question about promises given to Labour: Arthur Henderson would have a seat on the new war committee, there would be a ministry of labor, Labour would hold one other important portfolio and several minor offices. The coalfields in the rest of the country would be taken over by the government as had been those in South Wales in June 1915. He had discussed with the Labour party he admitted, but made no commitments on the matters of nationalization of shipping nor on industrial conscription.

There was a long discussion of the constitutional position of the new small war committee. It was agreed that the war committee would be the Cabinet, not a sub-committee of the larger body. It would consist of four members all without portfolios: Lloyd George, Curzon, Carson and Henderson. However Bonar Law, who was to be Chancellor of the Exchequer, could attend when he chose and would be kept informed of its proceedings. When required, Balfour as Foreign Secretary would attend. So would the First Lord of the Admiralty, a post for which the Unionists strongly pressed Lord Milner. However, the War Office would be represented by Sir William Robertson, not the new Secretary of State, Lord Derby. (Six months of argument over the position of the Secretary of State for War was forgotten in minutes.)

Other ministers would manage their departments as before and could attend the war committee when called upon, but would not be members nor in constitutional terms would they be collectively responsible to parliament for acts of the government. Among these men Walter Long would replace Bonar Law as Colonial Secretary. Chamberlain, Cecil, F.E. Smith and H.E. Duke, the Irish Secretary, would retain their offices. Sir Robert Finlay, a decent 74 year old Scottish Unionist MP who had been Salisbury's and Balfour's Attorney General, would take the exalted post of Lord Chancellor. (Apparently he was to be *locum tenens* either for George Cave, who became

Home Secretary, following Herbert Samuel, or, in the back of Lloyd George's mind, Asquith. Finlay had agreed with Lloyd George not to claim the pension. Asquith, indeed, was offered and declined the Chancellorship in May 1917, through Lords Murray and Reading.)[132]

Lloyd George reiterated, in the face of many questions on both sides of the issue, that he intended to do nothing to control the press. But while proclaiming he had no immediate plans on Home Rule, he declined to promise that the matter might not come up in the future in connection with conscription for Ireland. On the army command, similarly, he had no plans for changes. Sir Douglas Haig would retain his post because Lloyd George knew of no officer better qualified. He avoided answers on franchise reform. The business of his government, he said, was to make war. Finally as the conference moved to the level of personalities and pure politics, 'Mr. Lloyd George stated that he had no intention of asking Mr. W. Churchill or Lord Northcliffe to join the Administration. . .'

> After these explanations, the Unionist ex-members stated their
> willingness to accept office under Mr. Lloyd George, and the latter
> expressed his intention to inform the King without delay that he
> was now in a position definitely to accept the duty of forming an
> Administration.[133]

According to Frances Stevenson Lloyd George had been sure, even before meeting the Unionist ministers, that he had won. After several anxious days he was again in high spirits. Wrote Miss Stevenson: "'I think I shall be Prime Minister before 7 o'clock," he said to me. And he was.'[134]

Conferring with the Unionists Lloyd George had spoken of his meeting and agreements with the Labour party. He regarded the adherence of Labour as vital and said so to Riddell three days later adding as usual that he had given the best speech he ever made.[135] Nonetheless in purely political terms, it is hard to see where Labour's importance lay. He did not need the party's votes in the House of Commons and in no case would he get all of them. The Labour party was badly split on the war. The pacifist wing was talented and influential if small. No doubt Lloyd George believed — as have Labour politicians ever since and, despite his experiences in Glasgow at Christmas in 1915 — that former working men who had risen to prominence in Westminster still could control trade union affairs.

Addison, who served as the emissary to the left as Bonar Law did to the right, already had been in touch with union leaders. On Wednesday, 6 December Addison had seen J.H. Thomas, General Secretary of the National Union of Railwaymen, who was regarded at that time as one of the most influential men in the labor movement. Later, he and Frederick Kellaway, Liberal for Bedford who had helped Addison with the canvass of Liberal MPs, had dined with John Hodge of the Steel Smelters. On Thursday morning Thomas came to breakfast with Lloyd George in David Davies' flat.[136]

After these embassies, Lloyd George, with Derby, met the Parliamentary Labour party, including some men, Sidney Webb and Ernest Bevin for example, who were not MPs, at noon at the War Office. The speech according to all accounts, as well as Lloyd George's own of course, was indeed extraordinarily effective.[137] He made two points: the war was going badly; Bucharest at that moment was falling and so Germany had broken the navy's block-ade. And second, the King's government had to be carried on. He, as it hap-pened, had been asked to form a government — he regretted Asquith would not help — but he was trying to accomplish this task. He needed Labour's support.

He made the promises reported to the Unionists and evaded many more. There would be a ministry of labor and of pensions. Mines, food and shipping would be controlled. He had never considered introducing black labor into Britain but it was being used in France. One of the leading pacifists, Philip Snowden (Labour's Chancellor of the Exchequer in 1924 and from 1929 to 1931) asked him, he reported to Riddell 'whether I was in favour of this terrible slaughter.' To which he replied, 'Mr. Snowden must know there are men in this room who have sons fighting in the war.'[138] And he joked that he might have to put Ramsay MacDonald in jail but he hoped that MacDonald would come and have breakfast with him on the day he was released. It was, in short, a remarkable feat of salesmanship. The Labour MPs agreed 18 to 12 to support him.[139]

One must reflect on the dissimilarities between Lloyd George's dramatic performance before Labour and his treaty negotiation, for it was nothing less, with the Unionists. Labour was concerned with the recognition of itself as a free-standing party, which it received.[140] This, for Lloyd George, was not a trivial matter. His attitude towards Labour before the war, already discussed at length, had been that he perceived no difference between Labour and the radical wing of his own party among whom, when engaged in a peroration on topics of this sort, he invariably included himself. If Liberalism did its duty, he always declared, there was no need for a Labour party. But now Labour, at some risk to itself, one must comment — there would be no more electoral agreements on constituencies — was bringing this accommodation to an end. It was abandoning the protecting, but stultifying, shade of the Liberal umbrella. It may be assumed that not all the men present understood this. Many were clearly dazzled by Lloyd George's oratory. But the effects were clear in 1918.

On Lloyd George's part, if he believed that by obtaining the support of the Labour party, he was insuring the good behavior of the trade unions — and there was little reason for the concessions otherwise — he made a bad bargain. The first year of his administration saw unprecedented discontent among workers not only over economic matters as on the Clyde in 1915, but over political and pacifist issues as well. Moreover his relations with the party's leaders with whom he was associated, above all the honest Arthur Henderson, grew not better but worse.

Labour, in 1916, had been concerned with symbols, most important of which indeed was the Ministry of Labour.[141] The Unionists, on the other hand, were severely practical. Not to put too fine a point on it, what men would get offices, and of course who would be excluded? More critical, what precisely did Lloyd George, almost uniformly mistrusted, intend to do? His agreement with this group then provides an outline of his domestic political initiatives for the next two years. Nearly every item in what would become the Prime Minister's grand program of war-time national reconstruction, from franchise reform to Home Rule, barring only Fisher's rebuilding of the school system, was touched upon on the afternoon of 7 December. The historian seldom is given so accurate a statement of things to come.

As has been seen, Lloyd George had promised the Unionists that among those not to be given office under any circumstances was Winston Churchill, who was still totally occupied by his battles with Asquith over the details of the Dardanelles Inquiry. Lord Beaverbrook gives a frequently cited and detailed account of his warning to Churchill that he would not get the post he expected in a Lloyd George government in his story of the dinner at F.E. Smith's house on 5 December. He, Lloyd George, and Churchill were the guests. After dinner Beaverbrook (then Aitken) had driven Lloyd George back to the War Office. During this journey Lloyd George asked that Churchill be given a hint that he should not expect, as he obviously did, an appointment. When he returned Aitken did as he was told, without any superfluous tact. When he realized the meaning of what he heard, Churchill picked up his coat and hat and strode from the house into the night.[142]

It would appear that this dinner could not have taken place with Lloyd George present on 5 December. On the other hand, Aitken must have known by that date that Churchill would receive no office. Days earlier Lloyd George had promised this to Bonar Law and the latter surely told his friend, as he did everything. So most of the story could well be accurate. Finally, after the government was announced on 10 December, Lloyd George asked Riddell to explain to Churchill the reasons for his exclusion. The following day he did so.[143]

Churchill received the news, which could hardly have been a surprise, with some painful anger. Afterwards Riddell confided to his diary, apparently not telling Lloyd George:

> Winston made me a little speech. He told me that for 12 years he
> and Lloyd George had acted in concert and that he (W) had almost
> invariably subordinated his views to those of LG, the exception being
> the dispute on the naval estimates in 1913. At the Marconi time he
> (W) had stood loyally by LG and had debased himself to Northcliffe in
> order to secure his neutrality. LG had repaid him by bringing about
> his downfall when the Coalition was established, and now he had
> passed him by. Winston had determined on the first occasion never to
> speak to LG again, but had succumbed to his advances. Mrs. Winston
> remarked that LG had said in her presence that he would do his bit to
> atone for what was done.

Churchill began his peroration with a threat.

> I am still a member of the Liberal party, and an event may happen at
> any moment which will lead me to alter my position. I will take any
> position which will enable me to serve my country but I have had
> enough of soft soap and can only judge by actions. Had he stood by
> me he would have had a loyal and capable colleague whom he could
> trust. Instead he has allied himself with associates who are not really in
> sympathy with him, and who, when he has served their purposes, will
> desert him without compunction.[144]

After the interview Riddell reported to Lloyd George that Churchill had demanded to know who had objected to his inclusion in the government.

Riddell had replied that he did not know, reasoning later that no matter what he said Churchill would believe no one opposed him except Lloyd George. Lloyd George became somewhat angry after hearing Riddell's account. Churchill had no right to ask. He was 'unreasonable'.[145]

There was some nervousness among senior ministers in the months to come over the unlikely possibility that Churchill would find a way to conspire with Asquith. On the other hand Lloyd George showed no sign he found passing over Churchill a difficult decision. That it was a political necessity, for Lloyd George, was enough. The Unionist leadership simply would not have him and among the back bench of both parties he remained the most dispensable man in politics. The Unionist papers remarked with their customary pleasure at his most recent humiliation, but in fact there was little comment. The *British Weekly*, which, as Lloyd George began to realize how far he was moving from his old constituency, became an increasingly valuable channel of communication, commented mildly on 14 December:

> It is a strange and painful fact that Mr. Winston Churchill's name has
> hardly been mentioned in connection with the construction of the
> new Government. It is clear that, even if the Prime Minister had
> been disposed to give him office, it would have been impossible to do
> so. . .His best friends counsel him to go back to the front and do his
> part as a soldier.[146]

Churchill remained in purgatory for seven more months. When he was redeemed, the blameless Christopher Addison served as the ritual sacrifice.

There was another matter of personnel in the government as finally announced that seemed at the time to be a good deal more important than the exclusion of Churchill. This was the appointment of Alfred, Viscount Milner, not to the Admiralty as had been stipulated to the Unionists on the afternoon of 7 December, but to what was already being styled the War Cabinet. And Carson, whose presence beside him directing the war Lloyd George had always insisted upon as a vital component of his plan for the independent war committee, went to the Admiralty.

Milner, to many politicians and certainly to the public, was a figure from the past, and so must be accounted for. He never sat in the House of Commons, but after a brilliant career at Balliol and a brief excursion in journalism, he had entered government service as an administrator. He was remarkably successful. By 1892, at age 38, he was Chairman of the Board of Inland Revenue. However, Milner made his name as Governor and High Commissioner in South Africa between 1897 and 1905 as a ruthlessly efficient, autocratic administrator. As such he had been endlessly attacked by Lloyd George and many others during the South African War as the engine of ruthless Anglo-Saxon aggression. But at the same time he gathered around him a talented group of young men, civil servants and, after the Boer rebellion had begun, journalists, who looked upon him as the oracle of a new, efficient, social reforming, economically effective, British Empire. After the Boer war these members of what was styled 'Milner's Kindergarten', Leopold Amery, John Buchan, Philip Kerr, Lionel Curtis, and perhaps most important in 1916, Geoffrey Robinson, editor of *The Times*, all of whom continued to regard Milner as a minor deity, carried his gospel into journalism and politics where many were quite successful. Inevitably they and those they influenced were Chamberlainite tariff reformers, anti-Home Rulers, and since 1916, members or journalistic supporters of Carson's Unionist War Committee.

Milner resigned his posts in South Africa in February 1905 and returned to Britain a highly controversial figure, either the savior of the Empire or the promoter of Chinese slavery in the Transvaal. He was abused by the Liberals, particularly by Churchill, after the party came to power in December and went into semi-retirement. Nonetheless he did not give up politics, published a book of his speeches in 1913, and attended the House of Lords, more frequently after the coming of the war.[147] And in 1916 he continued to be the center of a modest but influential group of followers from both politics and journalism who were contemptuous of Asquith (who had in fact supported Milner during the South African War), and who were dedicated to victory in Europe at all costs.[148]

Such a man was valuable. Indeed he apparently was offered a place in the Cabinet on 28 November 1916 by Asquith himself, who possibly by that date had felt the earth trembling slightly under his feet. It was quickly refused.[149] One cannot be sure that Lloyd George knew of this approach, although for him Milner's refusal alone would have been a recommendation for office. But probably above all Lloyd George saw in Milner a man who would give his government validity, a seal of approval among the hard line Tories, and yet who would remain loyal to him as Prime Minister. Milner had no independent political ambitions. He would be trustworthy and hugely efficient, the perfect functionary.[150] Lloyd George, who had not known Milner well, soon came to admire him greatly. '. . .I think that Milner and I stand for very much the same things,' he declared to Riddell in February, 1917. 'He is a poor man, and so am I. He does not represent the landed or the capitalist classes any more than I do. He is keen on social reform, and so am I.'[151]

The logic of putting Carson at the Admiralty was less clear. One of the central areas of Lloyd George's contention with Asquith had been, of course, that Balfour should leave that post and that Carson should come on to the independent war committee as First Lord. But Lloyd George had changed position several times on the matter of whether or not the service ministers should sit on the committee as regular members. A conversation with Riddell in April 1917 gives a clue about Carson's surprising absence from what was now the War Cabinet and his equally unexpected appointment to the Admiralty, a decision Lloyd George himself was by that time beginning to question.

Like many others the determination on Carson's place clearly had been made hastily and to solve a particular problem. The problem was the need to find an office grand enough to satisfy the Marquess of Curzon who was after Balfour the most important Unionist recruit to the Lloyd George government. As Lloyd George related to Riddell he had just seen Beaverbrook's manuscript account of the Cabinet crisis — 'very good it is' — and Carson came out well in it. 'He must have been disappointed not to be on the War Cabinet' said Riddell.

LG: It was a question whether he should be on the Cabinet without a department or whether he should go to the Admiralty. Curzon would not. He [Curzon] is essentially an office man. Very keen on routine. That is not what you want at the Admiralty.[152]

Despite the self serving last sentences, one can gather from this that in Lloyd George's mind Curzon was destined for the Admiralty but found it *infra dignitatem*. As Lloyd George had already determined that War Cabinet members (Bonar Law excepted) would be without portfolio, Curzon then was offered Carson's seat in the Cabinet and Carson went to the Admiralty.

The important Liberal appointments in addition to Addison as Minister of Munitions, were the historian H.A.L. Fisher as President of the Board of Education, with Lloyd George's old friend, J.H. Lewis, as Parliamentary Secretary and, like Fisher also on Addison's nomination, D.A. Thomas, now Baron Rhondda, to replace Long at the Local Government Board. Lloyd George naturally was desperate to bring into the government as many Liberals as possible.[153] He clearly pondered some unlikely appointments. 'What a fool Sam Evans [Welsh Liberal MP for Mid Glamorgan from 1890 to 1910, whom Lloyd George had never liked and who was in 1916 President of Probate, Divorce and Admiralty] was to quarrel with me,' he observed to Riddell on 10 December.

He would have had the Woolsack. We wanted a Liberal and would, in default of better, have appointed Loreburn if he had not been a pacifist.[154]

Lloyd George had gone to the Palace shortly before 7 p.m. on Thursday, 7 December and returned to the War Office after about a half an hour, holding the King's appointment as his Prime Minister with the commission to form a government. He called Addison to his room and was congratulated. Lloyd George suggested some supper. A messenger appeared, laid a cloth at the end of the long table, and then produced some cold ham, parts of a chicken, then a fish and two bowls of soup and finally a bottle of champagne. It was his first ministerial dinner, joked Lloyd George.[155]

Before going to the Palace, Lloyd George had determined to sound out some Asquithian Liberals. Montagu had been spoken to and had dithered. During the supper at the War Office Herbert Samuel arrived. Addison retired but Lloyd George told him later he had proposed that Samuel remain at the Home Office. (An offer to George Cave had been deferred.) Samuel declined immediately citing his loyalty to Asquith but adding he did not believe the new government would last. He was, Lloyd George reported, in a 'superior mood'. Lloyd George, according to the account given Addison, then enticed Samuel into asking who had already accepted office. He was told and taken aback by the news that both Long and Balfour had agreed to serve.[156] The Liberal front still was holding firm, but Lloyd George now was Prime Minister. It was the end of a long day.

Two other matters of government construction must be noted. In the crowded days of December 1916 Lloyd George appears to have ignored entirely Arthur Lee, except to award him, with many others, a K.C.B. Carson wrote to the Prime Minister on 26 December urging him to see the former colleague who thinks 'he has been quite forgotten even without a "good-bye" and I know that was not your intention.'[157]

This letter evidently had no effect for at the end of January, 1917 Ruby Carson remarked in her diary

> Sir Arthur Lee came to luncheon, really Lloyd George has treated him awfully badly, never said or wrote one word to him since he became Prime Minister & Sir Arthur was absolutely his standby before all this upset. Ll.G. has some very bad traits & I do think not standing by one's friends the worst that can be.[158]

Finally, in February, Lee became Director-General of Food Production.

Lee's difficulties were personal, illustrating nothing except Lloyd George's callousness toward those most loyal to him, of which there were already many examples. However, in the same busy days he tried to strengthen his ties with the Liberal MPs in the House of Commons whom Addison had uncovered for him. On the day after the government was announced he addressed a letter to — it is unclear how many — Liberal MPs, formally asking for support. He had been entrusted with the task of forming a government and had hoped to make a statement on 12 December but could not.

> The predominant task before the Government is the vigorous prosecution of the War to a triumphant conclusion and I feel confident that I can rely on your support as long as they devote their energies efficiently to that end.[159]

On the day after Lloyd George's appointment as Prime Minister, Friday, 8 December, Margaret Lloyd George received a letter from Margot Asquith, which Lloyd George showed to Riddell the next day, asking that she and her husband be allowed to remain in No. 10 for two weeks. They had to find a house. It would be a small one, Margot remarked acidly. She recalled how 'Puffin' (Arthur Asquith), born in 1902, and Megan, born the same year, had played together as children in the garden of No. 10. It was an 'oily letter and insincere', observed Riddell.[160] Lloyd George immediately responded cordially on Saturday, 9 December saying to Asquith that he could remain at No. 10 as long as was convenient. He himself would live in No. 11.[161] Nonetheless, Friday was Asquith's last night in Downing Street and on Saturday as he had done the Saturday before under more congenial circumstances, Asquith motored down the familiar road to Walmer Castle. A week, he could have reflected, is a long time in politics.

Conclusion

In the months that followed his succession to the Prime Ministership Lloyd George reflected often, as men have done since governments began, on the chances and accidents that had given him the supreme power. Lloyd George, Riddell wrote, had told him on 31 July 1917,

> that strangely he never thought he would become P.M. He thought that Asquith would continue for some years and that jealousies would rob him, LG, of the office when it became vacant. He thinks he would have led a happier life had he kept out of politics. It is a harassing pursuit with never ending trials and anxieties.[1]

But more fascinating to both men was the decline of Asquith. What had happened to this man, the great impervious rock, the Olympian? A few days after the conversation above while the two drove to a house Riddell had taken at Great Walstead, Lindfield, Sussex, Riddell, as he had done many times before, observed that the Prime Minister — significantly both men usually referred to Asquith by that title — made a mistake thinking only he could form a government.

> LG: Yes, I shall never forget his face when he went to see the King. [Presumably this refers to Asquith's own resignation in the evening of Tuesday, 5 December. However, Lloyd George did not see Asquith between Sunday, 3 December and Wednesday, 6 December at the Palace.] He thought at last his chance had arrived. Now he would be able to get rid of Lloyd George. He had often been advised to do so, but his courage had failed him.[2]

This conversation continued a few weeks later in mid-August, 1917 as the two were walking on Beachy Head. Riddell asked the same question: what had gone wrong with the Prime Minister? He had lost the power of making decisions, Lloyd George replied. Later Riddell noted in his diary upon a Lloyd George remark, made earlier, that the last decision Asquith had made was the decision for war.

Riddell replied that Philip Kerr, a member of the Prime Minister's new secretariat — a devout Christian Scientist and a man of whom Lloyd George would see a great deal in the next few years — had described Asquith 'as having become a sensualist, bent entirely on his own enjoyment, wine, women and cards.'

> LG: Yes. It is only true in a sense. He had become self indulgent. He hated to make himself disagreeable. He hated to have to do unpleasant things. He hated to decide differences of opinion. He disliked to have to take action.

All of this, one could remark, made Asquith's Cabinet so successful in peace-time. He would support absolutely men of action, Haldane, Churchill, or Lloyd George. His political moderation and his good judgment forwarded their schemes and certified them as sensible. Asquith's real pleasure, and power, Lloyd George observed, was in parliament.

> Speaking in the House of Commons is a different thing. There is a sensuous pleasure in speaking under conditions which the speaker loves. Applause is gratifying.[3]

The villain of the story, Iago to the honorable but weak Asquith, was always McKenna. Within a year Lloyd George's story became the one he told for the rest of his life. At breakfast just after Christmas in 1917, he recited it to C.P. Scott and Lord Buckmaster, who had been Asquith's Lord Chancellor and whom Scott at the time was pushing forward to effect Liberal reconciliation. The presence of McKenna, Lloyd George said, made Asquith impossible to deal with.

> McKenna was a man of narrow mind, very competent and efficient within his limits, with very strong likes and dislikes and completely dominated by these feelings. He was a very small man and yet by his persistence and his faculty for intrigue exercised a great and unfortunate influence. . .It was he who, working directly on Asquith and then indirectly through Grey and Harcourt had upset the arrangement which he, Lloyd George, had made with Asquith before the change of Government and with which Asquith was perfectly happy. 'Believe me,' he said, 'there was not the least intention of displacing Asquith and that this took place was due entirely to his having been persuaded to go back on the agreement he had made.' McKenna persuaded him that he (Lloyd George) could not form a Ministry and that he would have to come back on his own terms.[4]

With the help of McKenna's fatal advice, Lloyd George had defeated Asquith, an achievement which at the time seems to have surprised him.

But he continued to fear the pernicious influence of the men surrounding Asquith. When Lloyd George became Prime Minister a pressing political decision to be made involved the matter of whether to publish the Report of the Dardanelles Commission, which had been appointed as an alternative to a Select Committee in July 1916 to take and evaluate evidence secretly on the unhappy Gallipoli campaign. Asquith was severely criticized in the report and had put off releasing it while Prime Minister, but Lloyd George determined to publish it immediately. He quickly received a letter of protest from the former Prime Minister. This angered Lloyd George. Asquith he observed to Riddell in mid-February 1917 was already the center of what was becoming a hero cult. On 16 February 1917, George Riddell noted in his diary:

> LG says that there is an organized attempt to re-establish the Asquith legend and that if necessary certain things will have to be said in public. Mr A is posing as a high-minded, magnanimous statesman, while McKenna, Runciman, Geoffrey Howard and Co are spreading all sorts of malicious falsehoods. Carson told LG that having known Mr A for years he has no doubt as to the policy he is pursuing. He is playing

a deep game and at the right moment will endeavour to strike and regain his office.

After discussing Gallipoli further, wrote Riddell, Lloyd George stated

> with great emphasis: If the truth were told and if we lived in other times there is no doubt that Asquith would be shot or beheaded. It is a serious statement to make but a true one. If you examine the actual conduct of affairs you cannot point to one thing that Mr A did for the war.[5]

The preliminary report of the Dardanelles Commission appeared, with some excisions, on 8 March 1917.[6]

Asquith, Lloyd George had concluded, had lost the will to command and as a result was entirely the creature of the lesser men around him. Lloyd George had observed this of course and had remarked upon it as recorded in these pages since at least the spring of 1915. It was only with a spasm of energy that he had saved himself in May of that year with a coalition.

Occasionally Lloyd George made fun of the former Prime Minister, imitating his mannerisms in Cabinet — rubbing his stomach with the palm of his hand and then peering about over his shoulder toward the clock on the mantle behind him below the picture of Bacon, to see how close it was to dinner time. But he did not hate Asquith, as, for example, did Carson. The *War Memoirs* show little rancor.

To this writer the story of men in political office is one of inevitable tragedy. After victory, defeat eventually will come. The lucky ones die in office. The rest suffer lingering suffocation as did both Asquith and Lloyd George. What might have happened to the great man had Lloyd George been absent, remaining say a prosperous solicitor and Alderman in Caernarvonshire, is not for the historian to say. Yet still Asquith, the bastion and fortress of Liberalism, contrived his own demise, not for tiring of, but for loving too well, the office he held. When confronted with a man who would do anything to win a desperate war he was helpless. In retrospect, one must conclude Lloyd George destroyed him easily. Perhaps Asquith's future monument might display not an arm holding an upraised sword, but a question mark.

However, it was not certain in December 1916 that Asquith's defeat was Lloyd George's victory. Many political observers, not only the optimistic Liberal partisans of the former Prime Minister, saw Lloyd George's succession not as a solution to a problem but simply as a phase in a crisis that would continue to unfold. The end was unclear, but to some the portents were ominous. Britain might soon be faced with a choice between the abandonment of its unique heritage of parliamentary government and defeat in war. Perhaps even the army would have to take part. Lloyd George might not be able to save the nation. Perhaps the force was not in him.

In Paris Lord Esher, the last courtier and the quintessential insider, profoundly conservative but, like many, a reluctant admirer of Lloyd George summed it up well. He feared what might come next. On 4 December, the day Lloyd George resigned, he wrote to General Douglas Haig:

> In view of Lansdowne's memorandum and of the reluctance of Asquith to give a decision on man power, food, etc., I think Lloyd George was

more than justified in resigning. I suppose you heard that, after much deliberation, this plan was decided upon as the only way on bringing the question of "reconstruction" to a head.

Now everything will depend upon L.G.'s determination and persistence. It is hoped by his friends that he will become Prime Minister. It is realised that Asquith would lead an Opposition, and that in less than two months L.G. would be beaten in the House of Commons and we should have a General Election. That is the prognostic, according to the fomenters of "our present discontents". It may be the only method of extricating ourselves from an inertia that is going to lose the war.

If L.G. does become Prime Minister, then his only chance of success is to govern for a time as Cromwell governed. Otherwise Parliamentarianism (what a word!) will be the net in which his every effort will become entangled. It is of no use to make a *coup d'état* unless you are ready with the whiff of grapeshot.

The organizing of our resources is the objective of Lloyd Georgeism. If he gets the power into his hands and does not use it because of hide-bound tradition, you will remain stuck in our present line, and we shall lose the war. If L.G. sweeps away all the old instruments and abolishes red-tape — that is to say, Ministries, Bureaux, Ambassadors and Treasury control, until such a time as the Boche is back on the Rhine, we shall come into our own. I cannot believe that he will have the courage to tell the truth to the nation. This, of course, must be his first step. We shall see.[7]

References

Introduction, pp. 17–24

1. Lady Olwen Carey Evans, *Lloyd George Was My Father*, Llandysul, 1985, p. 68.

2. A.J.P. Taylor, ed., *Lloyd George, A Diary by Frances Stevenson*, London, 1971, p. 23, 21 January 1915.

3. Arnold Bennett, *Lord Raingo*, New York, 1926, p. 33. This is a very early public reference to Miss Stevenson. Bennett, in the Ministry of Information, working for Lord Beaverbrook, clearly had visited No. 10. Certainly Lord Beaverbrook, with whom Bennett consulted on the political nuances of the novel, knew Miss Stevenson well and admired her. See his remarks to A.J.P. Taylor in the introduction of the Lloyd George-Stevenson letters. (A.J.P. Taylor, ed., *My Darling Pussy, The Letters of Lloyd George and Frances Stevenson, 1913–1941*, London, 1971, p. viii.)

   Raingo's parliamentary career and his relationship with the Prime Minister, although not his personality, are clearly modelled on the political life of D.A. Thomas.

Chapter 1, pp. 25–79

1. Henry W. Massingham, 'The Position of Mr. Lloyd George,' *Nation*, 6 January 1912.

2. See Masterman's observations in George, Lord Riddell, *More Pages From My Diary*, London, 1934, p. 65, 28 May 1912.

3. Public Record Office, Cab. 41/33/37, H.H. Asquith to Geroge V, 21 February 1912.

4. See for example Almeric Fitzroy, *Memoirs* (London: n.d. [1925]), II, 480–1, 6 March 1912. The occasion was the loss by 600 of the South Manchester seat in which the Liberals had been unopposed in December 1910.

5. Gainford Papers, Nuffield College, Box 38, J.A. Pease Diary, 16 March 1912.

6. Austen Chamberlain, *Politics From Inside*, New Haven, 1937, p. 414, 14 February 1912.

7. Riddell, *More Pages*, p. 54, 27 April 1912.

8. J.H. Lewis Papers, National Library of Wales, 10/231, 26 March 1912.

9. Bonar Law Papers, House of Lords Record Office, 26/1/76, 'Reports by Walter Long on the State of the Party,' n.d. 'Private and Confidential.' In 1913 Lloyd George ordered an informal survey of the effect of the super tax on British taxpayer compliance based upon the reduction in declared dividend income. The report showed a substantial movement to foreign countries of investments belonging to a number of distinguished men, among whom inevitably was the Duke of Westminster, but which included also some important Liberal supporters. Lloyd George Papers, House of Lords Record Office, C/14/1/11, 'Appendix to Memorandum dated 31/1/14 on the Avoidance of Income Tax by Accumulation of Interest Abroad.'

10. Lucy Masterman, *C.F.G. Masterman*, London, 1939, p. 235.

11. See: Willoughby De Broke, 'National Toryism,' *National Review*, LIX (May 1912), 413–27.

12. BLP, 24/3/7, LG to ABL, 13 November 1911.

13. See: 'The Spoils System,' *Nation*, 24 February 1912; on this speech see also: Robert Blake, *Unrepentant Tory, The Life and Times of Andrew Bonar Law, 1858–1923*, New York, 1956, pp. 94–5.

14. The speech is reprinted in Herbert DuParcq, *The Life of David Lloyd George* (London: 1913), IV, 802–16.

15. See: lead article, *The Times*, 29 November 1911.

16. James Marchant, *Dr. John Clifford*, London, 1924, pp. 133–4.

17. Bernard M. Allen, *Sir Robert Morant: A Great Public Servant*, London, 1934, pp. 248–9.

18. Lloyd George Papers, National Library of Wales, 20431C/1400, LG to MLG, 30 December 1911.

19. BLP, 25/2/21, Arthur Pole Nicholson to ABL, 19 February 1912. Nicholson was lobby correspondent of *The Times*.

20. The phrase 'the Lloyd George' was evidently current by 1913 and remained common until the end of the war. *National Insurance Gazette*, 11 October 1913.

21. Alfred Cox, *Among the Doctors*, London, 1950, pp. 94–5. Cox, who greatly admired Smith Whitaker, succeeded him as Medical Secretary.

22. *The Times*, 26 December 1911.

23. Stenographic notes of Brighton Conference, 18–19 February 1911, Braithwaite Papers, British Library of Political and Economic Science, Part I, 'Memoirs, 1910–12,' Part 3, TS.

24. The best source for the story of the establishment of the health insurance administration is: *Parliamentary Papers, 1913, Cd. 6907*, 'Report for 1912–13 of the Administration of the National Insurance Act, Part I.'

25. *PP, 1912, Cd. 6305*, 'Existing Conditions in respect of Medical Attendance and Remuneration in Certain Towns.'

26. Masterman, *Masterman*, p. 242; Alfred Cox, 'Seven Years of National Health Insurance in England,' *Journal of the American Medical Association*, 7 May 1921, p. 1310.

27. BLP, 25/2/12, A. Carson Roberts to ABL, 11 February 1912.

28. BLP, 33/4/46, ABL to A.St.G. Hammerseley, 26 June 1912.

29. BLP, 27/4/46, A. Steel Maitland to ABL, 20 November 1912.

30. LGP, NLW, 20431C/1437, LG to MLG, 14 August 1912.

31. 'Medical Supplement,' *Nation*, 3 August 1912.

32. 'X,' 'The Allocation of the Medical Benefit,' *Nation*, 10 August 1912. The evidence for Lloyd George's authorship of this letter appears in LGP, NLW, 20431C/1429, LG to MLG, 30 July 1912.

33. PRO Cab. 41/33/65, HHA to George V, 23 October 1912; PRO Cab. 37/112/115, 'Proposed Increase of Medical Remuneration,' 21 October 1912.

34. This speech was later printed in *The National Insurance Year Book*, 1913, pp. 289–300. It was at this time that Lloyd George suggested he had made a survey in Caernarvon District along the lines of the Plender Report, pp. 298–9.

35. Cox, *Doctors*, pp. 97–8.

36. Asquith Papers, Bodleian Library, Vol. XIII, LG to HHA, 28 December 1912.

37. Riddell, *More Pages*, p. 111, 29 December 1912.

38. Speech, 2 January 1913, *National Insurance Gazette*, 11 January 1913. In a report at the end of October Bradbury had estimated that a salaried service would cost about

£170 per thousand patients as opposed to £350 per thousand at a 7s capitation fee. LGP, H of L, C/18/8/2 'J.B.' (untitled typescript) dated 18/10.

39. *National Insurance Gazette*, 11 January 1913.

40. J.H. Lewis Papers, 10/231, J.H. Lewis to Ruth Lewis, 5 January 1913. Christopher Addison's recollection of events leading up to the beginning of the medical benefit is simply incorrect. Christopher Addison, *Politics From Within* (London: 1924), I, 23–5.

41. In November 1912, a number of newspapers published a ballot provided by the 'Proportional Representation Society' showing how p.r. would work in a constituency returning seven members with six transferable votes. Twelve leading politicans were listed as candidates. Of the more than 47,800 ballots returned, Lloyd George was named first choice on 22,778, almost exactly twice the vote of his runner up, Bonar Law. *Spectator*, 7 December 1912. It should be noted that Asquith was not on this ballot. This vote deserves more study. A beginning has been made in Martin Pugh, 'New Light on Edwardian Voters: The Model Elections of 1906–12,' *Bulletin of the Institute of Historical Research*, May 1978, LI, 103–10.

42. LGP, H of L, C/7/6/2, 3, Edward Russell to LG, 29 May 1913; Robert Donovan (Russell's secretary) to LG, 30 May 1913.

43. BLP, 29/4/14, Northcliffe to ABL., 21 May 1913.

44. Alfred George Gardiner, *Pillars of Society*, London, 1913, p. 280–2. Gardiner began with one of the most familiar stories about Lloyd George: a villager who had rescued a man from the local pond because he seemed to be drowning was asked what he had done. It was nothing he responded, 'I simply turned him over to be sure he wasn't Lloyd George and pulled him out.'

45. Frances Donaldson, *The Marconi Scandal*, London, 1962.

46. A recent example is A.J.P. Taylor's bewilderment that Lloyd George should have summoned Frances Stevenson from Scotland at the end of December 1912 because of terrible news that had come to him. Frances L. Stevenson, *The Years That Are Past*, London, 1967, p. 55. Taylor observes that nothing was happening in the Marconi affair at that time. A.J.P. Taylor, ed., *My Darling Pussy, The Letters of Lloyd George and Frances Stevenson, 1913–1941*, London, 1975, p. 2.

47. For example, BLP, 25/2/36, 37, J. Kebty-Fletcher to ABL, 19 February; Arthur Back to ABL, 19 February 1912. Kebty-Fletcher's letter concerns a patronage appointment by Lloyd George, but Beck asks: 'Would it interest' Bonar Law to know that Lloyd George has not paid his election agent since 1906 and instead has found him a sinecure post? What is important here is that Beck was not an obscure, outraged, Tory but private secretary to H.J. Tennant, who was financial secretary at the War Office and Asquith's brother-in-law.

48. *The Times*, 8 March 1912; The Marquess of Reading, *Rufus Isaacs, First Marquess of Reading* (London: 1942), I, 227–9; Herbert, Viscount Samuel, *Memoirs*, London, 1945, 75. The tender, contract and other relevant documents, were published in the *National Review*, LXI (May 1913) 576–96.

49. *The Times*, 23 April 1912, 'Marconi Finance,' Finance, Commerce and Shipping Supplement.

50. By far the best source on the American negotiations by no means new but unconsulted is Reading, *Isaacs*, I, 252–5.

51. In fact he was dealing in options to buy, warrants in the United States. No stock could be issued until the directors approved. The suggestion frequently made that Lloyd George and Isaacs had bought stock not otherwise available to the public is unwarranted.

52. *Financial World*, New York and Chicago, 6, 13 April 1912. By autumn American financial journals carried notices that Western Union would accept and deliver 'Marconigrams,' fifteen cents per word.

53. Reading, *Isaacs*, I, 236–7.

54. This was not, as it has been termed, a 'relatively low price.' Anyone in London could have done the same.

55. Before the select committee that investigated the Marconi contract he began by insisting that he had not heard of the opportunity before the date on which he made his purchase, only to be told that Isaacs had told the committee a few days earlier that he had talked to Lloyd George and Murray several times between the 9th and the 17th of April. *PP*, 'Report and Special Report from the Select Committee on Marconi's Wireless Telegraphy Company Ltd. Agreement,' VII, 1913, p. 91, 28 March 1913.

56. LGP, NLW, 20431C/1417, 1420, 1422, LG to MLG, 12, 15, 19 April 1912.

57. *PP*, 1913, 'Select Committee,' VII, p. 92, 28 March 1913.

58. *Ibid.*, p. 94, 31 March 1913.

59. *New York Times*, 22, 23 April 1912.

60. *The Times*, 29 July 1912.

61. *Outlook*, XXX, 20 July, 3, 17, 24 August 1912.

62. *Outlook*, 17, 31 August, 14 September 1912. *The Times*, 'Political Note' 7 August 1912.

63. Poem, 'Our Arithmetical Problem,' *Eye-Witness*, 4 July 1912. Lloyd George was identified as 'David Erasmus Jacks, MP, the People's Champion' and Isaacs as 'Sir Josephus Hafiz Saul.'

64. *Eye-Witness*, 8, 15 August 1912.

65. Reading, *Isaacs*, I, 240–42. Samuel's statement in his memoirs that he had told the Prime Minister of Lloyd George's and Murray's purchases and that the Prime Minister had said 'our colleagues could not have done a more foolish thing,' simply cannot be corroborated. On 26 March 1913 when asked by Major Archer-Shee what he knew of his ministers' dealing in American Marconi shares before the debate of 11 October Asquith said only that he had been told by Murray at the end of July and subsequently by Isaacs at the beginning of August that the three had purchased shares in the American Marconi company. *Official Report, House of Commons Debates*, Series Five, L (26 March 1913), cols. 1629–30.

66. *National Review*, LX (September 1912), 126–8; *Spectator*, 19 October 1912. Lawson continually pointed out that he was carrying the fight alone. *Outlook*, 5 October 1912.

67. *Outlook*, 12 October 1912.

68. *PP*, 1913, 'Select Committee,' VII, p. 87, 28 March 1913.

69. *H of C Deb*, XLII (11 October 1912), cols. 667–750.

70. *Ibid.*, col. 712.

71. *Ibid.*, col. 714.

72. *Ibid.*, col. 717.

73. See for example: John Grigg, *Lloyd George, From Peace to War*, Berkeley, 1985, p. 52. Grigg mentions only 'an unnecessarily heated exchange' with Lansbury. Peter Rowland, *David Lloyd George, A Biography*, New York, 1975, pp. 263–64, provides a better account.

74. Robert Speaight, *The Life of Hilaire Belloc*, New York, 1957, pp. 309–10. This letter is misdated '1911'.

75. *National Review*, LX (November 1912), 363.

76. Quoted in John A. Hutcheson, 'Leopold Maxse and the *National Review*, 1893–1914,' unp. Ph.D. dissertation, University of North Carolina at Chapel Hill, 1974, p. 478.

77. Stevenson, *Years*, p. 52.

78. *Ibid.*, pp. 52–55.

79. A.J.P. Taylor, ed., *Lloyd George, A Diary by Frances Stevenson*, London, 1971, p. 23, 21 January 1915.

80. Asquith stated in the House of Commons that he had become aware that Lloyd George and Murray had purchased 3,000 additional shares of American Marconis, a fact which was certainly part of Lloyd George's confession at this time, either at the end of the previous year or at the beginning of this one. *H of C Deb*, LI (9 April 1913), col. 374.

81. Michael and Eleanor Brock, eds., *H.H. Asquith, Letters to Venetia Stanley*, Oxford, 1982, p. 24. HHA to VS, 7 January 1913.

82. Gainford Papers, Nuffield College, J.A. Pease diary, 8 January 1913. On 15 January 1913 Godfrey Isaacs wrote to the Post Office asking to be relieved from the Imperial Wireless tender even though the company had spent much money putting together a large staff to carry out the government's work. LGP, H of L, C/24/2/5. Godfrey Isaacs to Post Office, 15 January 1913. The tender finally was cancelled in April.

In June, in a Cabinet on Marconi, Asquith remarked that when he was Chancellor of the Exchequer 'it had never occurred to him that he was not free to buy Govt. or any other stocks...' Edward David, ed., *Inside Asquith's Cabinet, From the Diaries of Charles Hobhouse*, London, 1977, 22 June 1913. (This cannot be the correct date.)

83. *National Review*, LX (February 1913), 904–8.

84. Masterman Papers, University of Birmingham, Lucy Masterman TS diaries, Chapter 12, page 3, 'dictated 18 June 1913.' The quoted paragraph was scratched out of the typescript. Mrs. Masterman had an unfortunate habit of filling out her diary entries from memory. No one could have anticipated the *Matin* trial in early February.

85. *PP*, 1912–13, 'Select Committee,' VIII, pp. 944–5.

86. *Spectator*, 15 February 1913.

87. British Library, Add MS 62972, Riddell diaries, 19 March 1913.

88. 'Daylight in the Marconi Mystery,' *National Review*, LXI (April 1913), 279–80.

89. *Spectator*, 22 March 1913.

90. BL Add MS 62972, Riddell diaries, 22 March 1913.

91. Masterman, *Masterman*, p. 255. In this connection it must be emphasized that neither Lloyd George nor Masterman had more than the most rudimentary knowledge of finance. Riddell records a dinner table conversation about two weeks later with Lloyd George, Masterman and Isaacs in which the discussion turned to some bonds recently stolen from the Bank of England. It developed that neither the Chancellor of the Exchequer nor the Financial Secretary to the Treasury had ever seen a bond, nor did they know the coupon method of paying interest. Riddell and Isaacs had to explain it. BL Add MS 62972, Riddell diaries, 12 April 1913.

92. *PP*, 1913, 'Select Committee,' VII, pp. 83–100, 28, 31 March 1913.

93. BL Add MS 62972, Riddell diaries, 28 March, 30 March, 13 April 1913.

94. *National Review*, LXI (April 1913), 307.

95. Masterman Papers, Lucy Masterman TS diary, Chapter XII, p. 10. Dictated 23 June 1913.

96. *The Times*, 3 May 1913.

97. BLP, 29/5/12, A. Locker Lampson to ABL, 9 June 1913.

98. See for example Northcliffe to Churchill, 6 June 1913 in Randolph S. Churchill, *Winston Churchill* (Boston: 1967), II Companion volume 3, 1747. H.W. Massingham, in the *Nation* was particularly virulent about government duplicity, ruining his relations with Lloyd George forever. *Nation*, 14 June 1913.

99. BL Add MS 62972, Riddell diaries, 8 June 1913.

100. LGP, H of L, C/1/1/3, HP Hamilton to LG, 19 May 1913. Separately and much earlier, well before the *Matin* trial, Isaacs had told Falconer and F. Handel Booth, another Liberal partisan, about the American transactions in order to help them in questioning journalists. Nothing came of this but the result was a squabble on the committee and a resignation. Reading, *Isaacs*, I, 255.

101. The two reports are printed in Donaldson, *Marconi*, appendix B and C.

102. Fitzroy, *Memoirs*, II, 514, 6 June 1913.

103. Riddell noted that Bonar Law was not attending inter-party social gatherings any longer. BL Add MS 62972, Riddell diaries, 8 June 1913. It should be recalled that the man who had given Bonar Law his oportunity to become leader of the Unionist party and who was his strongest journalistic supporter was Leopold Maxse.

104. Ibid.

105. Gainford Papers, J.A. Pease diary, 8 June 1913; Asquith papers, VII, HHA to George V, 7 June 1913.

106. Masterman Papers, Lucy Masterman TS diary, Chap. XIII, pp. 5–7.

107. Ibid.

108. *The Times*, 18 June 1913.

109. LGP, H of L, C/6/11/13, HHA to LG, 16 June 1913; India Office Library, Reading Papers, Eur. F118/1, HHA to Isaacs, 16 June 1913.

110. See also Reading Papers, Eur. F118/62, Margot Asquith to Isaacs, 13 June 1913.

111. *H of C Deb*, LIV (18 June 1913) cols. 448–9.

112. Masterman Papers, Lucy Masterman TS diary, Chap. XIII, p. 4, 18 June 1913.

113. British Library, Add MS 46335, John Burns Papers, vol. LV, diary, 18 June 1913; see also David, ed., *Hobhouse Diaries*, p. 139, 22 June 1913. Hobhouse, like Burns, was impressed by neither speech.

114. *H of C Deb*, LIV (19 June 1913), cols. 548–60.

115. Asquith never admitted hearing anything about the affair from Samuel.

116. *H of C Deb*, LIV (19 June 1913), col. 559.

117. *Ibid.*, col. 629.

118. *Ibid.*, cols. 560–72.

119. *The Times*, 20 June 1913.

120. Masterman Papers, Lucy Masterman TS diary, Chap. XIII, p. 5, 23 June 1913.

121. Ibid.

122. *H of C Deb*, LIV (19 June 1913), cols. 663–70. The Adkins amendment then passed without a division.

123. Kenneth Young, ed., *The Diaries of Robert Bruce Lockhart*, London, 1973, p. 308, 10 October 1934.

124. Churchill, *Churchill*, II, 536.

125. See Blake, *Unrepentant Tory*, pp. 145–8.

126. J.A. Spender and Cyril S. Asquith, *The Life of Herbert Henry Asquith, Lord Oxford and Asquith* (London: 1932), I, 365.

127. Reading papers, Eur. F, 118/62, Margot Asquith to Reading, 5 a.m., 4th July.

128. Masterman Papers, Lucy Masterman TS diary, Chap. XIII, p. 2, 23 June 1913.

129. BL Add MS, 46335, vol. LV, Burns diary, 11 July 1913.

130. In his confession to the House of Lords, Murray said that he had told no one of the party's ownership of these shares except the Liberal party solicitor. *Official Report, House of Lords Debates*, XV (17 February 1914), col. 222. In all this, a recently published letter from Riddell to Robertson Nicoll must be noted. Writing on 10 August 1912, Riddell told Nicoll that he had interviewed Murray two days earlier about his resignation as Chief Whip. He was leaving with regret and only because of his health, the need to make some money, and a third, personal reason that he did not divulge. This could have been Marconi, but it is most unlikely. As it happened, the first *Eye-Witness* article appeared only that day and he had been considering resignation and discussing it with Asquith for weeks. Moreover, Murray said that he had told Asquith the third reason, which unless both men were dishonest in their discussion of the Liberal party shares in parliament, could not have included this matter. Riddell to W. Robertson Nicoll, 10 August 1912 in J.M. McEwen, ed., *The Riddell Diaries, 1908–1923*, London, 1986, pp. 417–18.

131. See for example Kipling's poem, written in the fall of 1913 after Isaacs was made Lord Chief Justice but not published until 1915, entitled 'Gehazi,' comparing him to the covetous servant of Elisha in Kings II who in his master's name obtained a gift from Naaman after he was stricken with leprosy. See also G.K. Chesterton's open letter to Isaacs in 1931 when he became Foreign Secretary. Donaldson, *Marconi*, pp. 256–9.

132. DuParcq, *LG*, IV, 818–9.

133. *National Review*, LXI (August 1913), 1046–66.

134. Mr. J.M. McEwen has done the profession a favor with excellent detective work on this elusive man. See: McEwen, ed., *Riddell Diaries*, pp. 1–18.

135. For example during the coal strike in the spring of 1912 he provided a 'jackal,' a former trade union secretary now in the pay of the Newspaper Proprietors Association, who could give the government information on union secrets. LGP, H of L, C/7/4/1, Riddell to LG, 25 April 1912.

136. Stevenson, *Years*, pp. 58–9.

137. W. Watkin Davies, *Lloyd George, 1863–1914*, London, 1939, pp. 448–50.

138. Colin Cross, ed., *Life With Lloyd George: The Diary of A.J. Sylvester, 1931–1945*, London, 1975, p. 115.

139. See 'A Pleasure House,' *National Review*, LXI, (March 1913), 35–8.

140. On the Irish point of view see Trevor Wilson, ed., *The Political Diaries of C.P. Scott, 1911–1928*, Ithaca, 1970, pp. 64–7, 15, 16 January 1913.

141. BLP, 24/5/153, F.E. Smith to ABL, 27 December 1911.

142. See his statement to Alec Murray, evidently in the summer of 1912. Arthur C. Murray, *Master and Brother, The Murrays of Elibank*, London, 1945, pp. 101–2 and Riddell, *More Pages*, p. 36, 6 February 1912.

143. Spender and Asquith, *Asquith*, I, 359; Asquith Papers, Vol. VII, HHA to George V, 25 January 1913; James Lowther, Viscount Ullswater, *A Speaker's Commentaries* (London: 1925), II, 136; Brocks, eds. *Stanley Letters*, p. 27, 27 January 1913.

144. *Nation*, 22 January 1913.

145. LGP, H of L, C/10/2/25, anon. to LG, 12 November 1913.

146. LGP, H of L, C/9/4/85, 85a /5/8a, 11; /11/68; /1/72/74, Catherine E. Marshall to LG, 26, 28 July, 6, 10 August 1913; 11, 17, 22 July 1914; E. Sylvia Pankhurst to LG, 21 July 1914; C/5/12/9, LG to McKenna, 6 July 1914.

147. Ibid., Sylvia Pankhurst to LG, 21 July 1914.

148. W.R.P. George, *The Making of Lloyd George*, London, 1976, p. 113.

149. British Library, Add MS 62971, Riddell diaries, 7 July 1912.

150. PRO Cab 37/98/45 'Land Value Tax,' 16 March 1909; see also Riddell, *More Pages*, p. 65, 27 May 1912.

151. *PP Cd 7315*, 'Departmental Committee on Local Taxation,' 1914.

152. *Westminster Gazette, The Times*, 25 November 1911.

153. *Nation*, 6 January 1912.

154. The signatories were: H.W. Massingham, Joseph Rowntree, J.A. Hobson, L.T. Hobhouse, Percy Alden, B.S. Rowntree, E. Richard Cross and Arnold Rowntree. See LGP, H of L, C/21/1/17.

155. B.S. Rowntree to Oscar Rowntree, 26 June 1912, quoted in Asa Briggs, *Social Thought and Social Action: A Study of the Work of Seebohm Rowntree*, London, 1961, p. 64.

156. Riddell, *More Pages*, pp. 63, 64, 27 May 1912.

157. McEwen, ed., *Riddell Diaries*, p. 45, 19 June 1912.

158. *Ibid.*, p. 71, 19 June 1912.

159. Briggs, *Rowntree*, p. 70.

160. Asquith makes no mention of this in his letters to the King. See Gainford Papers, J.A. Pease diary, 23 July 1912.

161. See: BLP, 27/1/50, A.R.M. Lockwood to ABL, 22 August 1912, Hotel Stern, Marienbad. Colonel Mark Lockwood was a prominent Unionist MP. He reported a long interview with Lloyd George in which the Chancellor, after demanding solemn promises of secrecy, had described his land program and his thinking on Ulster. Clearly Lloyd George had intended these remarks to be passed on, as they were.

162. BLP, 26/5/32, Lord Hugh Cecil to ABL, 20 July 1912.

163. LGP, H of L, C/2/1/12,13, J.S. Scott (President of the Newcastle Liberal Club) to J.St.G. Heath, 16 August; E. Richard Cross to LG, 21 August 1912.

164. *H of C Deb*, XLII (15 October 1912), col. 1191.

165. LGP, NLW, 20431C/1452, LG to MLG, 16 October 1912.

166. LGP, H of L, C/2/3/15, Rowntree to LG, 4 October 1913.

167. Lloyd George and Churchill sponsored him for the Reform Club, but even as a Liberal Member of Parliament his application was blackballed. Consequently the two men resigned. *Nation*, 8 February 1913. By this time Lloyd George was a member of the Athenaeum.

168. Wilson, ed., *Scott Diaries*, pp. 68–9, 16 January 1913. Nonetheless in July he took the trouble to ask Haldane about his proposals. LGP, H of L, C/4/17/3, 'Report of Interview with Haldane,' 23 July 1913.

169. LGP, H of L, C/9/4/10, Nicoll to LG, 13 March 1913.

170. See Riddell's note on a dinner at his house on 9 July. Riddell, *More Pages*, pp. 168–9. Nicoll recorded his impressions of the same gathering. Stephen Koss, *Nonconformity in Modern British Politics*, Hamden, Conn., 1975, p. 122.

171. PRO Cab 37/116/56, 'Land,' 'Secret' 21 August 1913, 9pp.

172. PRO Cab 37/116/66, 'C.H.,' 'The Land Question,' n.d. (printer's mark, 6 October 1913).

173. LGP, H of L, C/2/2/44, LG to Rowntree, 25 August 1913.

174. David, ed., *Hobhouse Diaries*, p. 146, 19 August.

175. This statement evoked an angry letter from the General Secretary of the Caernarvonshire Constitutional Association followed by a warning note from William George advising his brother not to go into details. LGP, H of L, C/10/1/33, W.H. Wright to LG, 13 October 1913; I/2/2/20, W. George to LG, 16 October 1913.

176. *The Times*, 13 October 1913. Pheasants and mangolds became the joke of the land campaign. They provided the cartoonist Strube, drawing at that time for the *Standard*, with an enduring symbol for Lloyd George.

177. Although he took all his speeches seriously, the composition of this one occupied nearly a week. On 7 October he declaimed it for Masterman, Isaacs, and the Land Committee. See LGP, NLW, 20432C/1492, LG to MLG, 7 October 1913.

178. See LGP, H of L, C/8/1/9, LG to C.P. Scott, 4 September 1913; Riddell, *More Pages*, p. 79, 6 September 1913. Masterman Papers, Lucy Masterman TS diary, Chap. 15, pp. 3–5.

179. Riddell, *More Pages*, p. 181, 16 October 1913.

180. LGP, H of L, C/10/1/40, Hodder and Stoughton to LG, 15 October 1913.

181. LGP, H of L, C/10/1/58, W.H. Lever to LG, 22 October 1913.

182. See: Maxse Papers, West Sussex Record Office, 468, Maxse to LG, 10 October 1913.

183. LGP, H of L, C/3/7/2, LG to F.E. Smith, 6 October 1913.

184. David, ed., *Hobhouse Diaries*, p. 148, 17 October 1913.

185. Masterman Papers, Lucy Masterman TS diary, Chap. 15, pp. 3–5, dictated 2 December 1913; BL Add MS 46335, John Burns papers, Vol. LV, Burns diary, 11 October 1913.

186. Gainford Papers, J.A. Pease diary, 14 October 1913.

187. Asquith Papers, Vol. VII, HHA to George V, 18 October 1913.

188. Riddell, *More Pages*, p. 181, 17 October 1913.

189. *The Times*, 23 October 1913.

190. Lloyd George's announcement at Swindon that national health insurance funds would be invested in agricultural laborers' cottages had hurt. There were reports of huge posters: 'Reading Electors? Do you want your Insurance taxes fooled away on wild-cat country cottage schemes?' *National Insurance Gazette*, 22 November 1913; see also Frank Eyck, *G.P. Gooch*, London, 1982, pp. 182–4.

191. LGP, H of L, C/14/1/10, 'Notes of a dinner at Eleven Downing Street,' 12 November 1913.

192. LGP, H of L, C/9/4/82, 'Petition from Caernarvon on Leasehold Enfranchisement,' 23 July 1913.

193. LGP, H of L, C/10/2/32, R.L. Outhwaite to LG, 13 November 1913; C/2/4/11, P. Wilson Raffin to LG, 17 December 1913. Outhwaite, spokesman for the land value tax in the House of Commons, was responsible, it should be noted, for the only new seat the Liberals had won in the two years, 1911–12, and he had taken it from Labour.

194. See: E.V. Emy, 'The Land Campaign,' in A.J.P Taylor, ed., *Lloyd George Twelve Essays*, New York, 1971, p. 59.

195. *PP Cd 7315*, 'Departmental Committee on Local Taxation, Final Report,' 1914, p. iv, LG to Sir John A. Kempe, 13 November 1912.

196. The arguments are set out in detail in PRO Cab, 37/117/92, 'Part I, The Rating of Site Values; Part II, A National Site Value Tax,' D.Ll.G., 13 December 1913. Lloyd George was at pains to point out in this paper that separate site value rating had 'no connection whatever with a single tax.'

197. LGP, H of L, C/2/4/1/, LG to P.W. Raffin, 1 January 1914.

198. *British Weekly*, 22 January 1914.

199. The best, almost a classical, description of pre-war naval strategy, heavily used by Asquith in his discussions in *The Genesis of the War* is found in Churchill's speech to the Committee of Imperial Defense on 11 July 1912. See: Churchill, *Churchill*, II, Comp. Vol. 3, pp. 1595–1607.

200. These vessels had been part of the naval scare of 1909. See: McKenna Papers, Churchill College 3/3/7, McKenna to Winston Churchill, 12 April 1909. This referred to newspaper reports of new construction, eventually denied by the Austrian Ministry of Marine. But in 1910 Admiralty intelligence had discovered that two dreadnoughts were secretly under construction without any parliamentary sanction. David, ed., *Hobhouse Diaries*, p. 85, 4 February 1910.

201. Minutes for Asquith and Grey, 23 August 1912, in Winston S. Churchill, *The World Crisis, 1916–1918* (New York: 1924), I, 115–6.

202. H.H. Asquith, *The Genesis of the War*, New York, 1923, p. 133.

203. Churchill, *Churchill*, II, Comp. Vol. 3, C. I. D. Minutes, p. 1607.

204. Gainford Papers, J.A. Pease diaries, 16 July 1912.

205. LGP, NLW, 20431C/1433, LG to MLG, 7 August 1912. 'Had a most interesting hour's chat with Borden.'

206. Stephen Leacock, 'The Canadian Senate and the Naval Bill,' *National Review*, LXI (July 1913), 986–98.

207. David, ed., *Hobhouse Diaries*, p. 137, 6 June 1913 for the Cabinet of 4 June.

208. Asquith Papers, Vol. VII, HHA to George V, 5 June 1913.

209. See: WSC, 'Naval Estimates, 1914–15,' 10 January 1914; LGP, H of L, C/24/3/27, 'The Canadian Dreadnoughts,' n.d. (printer's mark, 30 January 1914); Ibid., C/24/3/33.

210. Asquith Papers, Vol, VII, HHA to George V, 18 November 1913, Cabinets 14, 15, 16 October.

211. LGP, H of L, C24/3/21, 'Navy Estimates, 1914–15,' 5 December 1913.

212. See: LGP, H of L, C/24/3/29, 'Cost of. . .New Programmes. . .in the Nine Years of the Dreadnought Era,' 16 January 1914.

213. Asquith Papers, Vol. VII, HHA to George V, 11, 20 December 1913, Cabinets 8, 11, 15, 16, 17, 19 December 1913.

214. LGP, NLW, 20432C/1479, LG to MLG, 13 September 1913.

215. BL Add MS 62973, Riddell diaries, 31 October, 1 November 1913. (Underlining in original.) In conversation with Riddell on 2 November Isaacs confirmed that support of Churchill by Lloyd George 'will be very unpopular.' Ibid.

216. Churchill, *Churchill*, II, 642.

217. David, ed., *Hobhouse Diaries*, p. 154, 20 December 1913.

218. BL Add MS 46355, John Burns Papers, Vol. LV, Diaries, 1913, Tuesday, 16 December 1913.

219. Quoted in Churchill, *Crisis*, I, 183.

220. BL Add MS 62973, Riddell diaries, 16 November 1913.

221. Riddell, *More Pages*, pp. 189–90, 14 December 1913.

222. *Ibid.*, pp. 190–1, 18 December 1913.

223. This Cabinet paper, Cab. 37/117/97 was written by R.G. Hawtrey, at that time a junior Treasury clerk who had entered the civil service at the Admiralty. Lloyd George kept him at his side throughout his period in office. Eventually he became Director of Financial Enquiries at the Treasury.

224. PRO Cab 37/117/97, 'Navy Estimates, 1914–15,' 24 December 1913, covering letter, p. 11.

225. LGP, H of L, C/24/3/27, 'Naval Estimates, 1914–15,' 19 pages.

226. Churchill, *Churchill*, II, Comp. Vol. 3, p. 1814, Borden to WSC, 31 December 1913.

227. *Ibid.*, p. 1815.

228. *Ibid.*, pp. 1841–2.

229. Brocks, eds., *Stanley Letters*, p. 40, HHA to VS, 6 January 1914.

230. George M. Trevelyan, *Grey of Fallodon*, Boston, 1937, pp. 271–3.

231. *Daily Chronicle*, 1 January 1914. The circumstances of this interview are not clear. The conversation took place in Criccieth to which Lloyd George had gone on 20 December. But by the time the interview appeared in print Lloyd George was in Algiers for his winter holiday. See: LGP, NLW, 20433C/1494, LG to MLG, 'Sunday,' (probably 4 January 1914).

232. *The Times*, 13 July 1912; 12 July 1913.

233. Balfour to Selborne, 7 January 1914, quoted in Arthur Marder, *From the Dreadnought to Scapa Flow* (London: 1961), I, 319.

234. See for example: LGP, H of L, C/4/12/4, Charles Trevelyan to LG, 6 January 1914.

235. *The Times*, 18 July 1914.

236. *H of C Deb*, LXV (23 July 1914), cols. 666–70.

237. *Ibid.*, cols. 726–29.

238. He insisted to Riddell that the *Daily Chronicle* interview contained nothing that he had not said many times before, which was true, and that anyway he had given it only as a favor to the *Chronicle* reporter who called three times upon him in Criccieth before he agreed to talk. Riddell, *More Pages*, p. 196, 17 January 1914.

239. Churchill, *Churchill*, II, Comp. Vol 3, p. 1835.

240. David, ed., *Hobhouse Diaries*, p. 155, 25 January 1914; Wilson, ed., *Scott Diaries*, p. 75, 18 January 1914.

241. Kenneth Morgan, ed., *Lloyd George Family Letters*, Cardiff, 1973, pp. 165–6, 15 January 1914.

242. LGP, NLW, 20433C/1499, LG to MLG, 17 January 1914.

243. LGP, H of L, C/3/16/1, WSC to LG, n.d. (January 1914) 'Private and Personal.' The Canadian Speech from the Throne, which as Borden had warned contained no reference to battleships, came on 14 January, 15 January in Great Britain.

244. Churchill recapitulated the substance of this conversation in a draft of a letter on 18 January to the Chancellor, a copy of which was transmitted to Asquith when the latter returned. Churchill, *Churchill*, II, Comp. Vol. 3, pp. 1849–50, WSC to LG,

18 January 1914. The account of the estimates struggle of 1914 given here differs substantially from that to be found in Randolph Churchill's biography of his father.

245. *Ibid.*, pp. 1850, 1852, WSC to HHA, 19, 23 January 1914.

246. *Ibid.*, pp. 1850, 1851, WSC to LG, 19 January; LG to WSC, 20 January 1914.

247. Wilson, ed., *Scott Diaries*, p. 75–77, 21 January 1914.

248. Spender and Asquith, *Asquith*, II, 76.

249. See Lloyd George's letter to C.P. Scott on the alternatives. LGP, H of L, C/8/1/14, LG to C.P. Scott, 23 January 1914. This long and important letter does not appear in Wilson, ed., *Scott Diaries*.

250. Riddell, *More Pages*, p. 198, 23 January 1914.

251. Churchill, *Crisis*, I, 188.

252. Wilson, ed., *Scott Diaries*, pp. 78–9, 25 January 1914.

253. Spender and Asquith, *Asquith*, II, 76.

254. See: David, ed., *Hobhouse Diaries*, p. 156, 23 January, 1914; Riddell, *More Pages*, p. 198, 23 January 1914; Wilson, ed., *Scott Diaries*, p. 78, 23 January 1914.

255. See: David, ed., *Hobhouse Diaries*, p. 157–8, 26 January 1914; LGP, H of L, C/8/3/6, Simon to LG, 26 January 1914; see also McKenna's account of the meeting to C.P. Scott. Wilson, ed., *Scott Diaries*, p. 80, 6 February 1914.

256. The mental depression that his physician noted during the Second World War, 'the black dog' as Churchill called it, was clearly already upon him. See Riddell, *More Pages*, p. 199–200, 25 January 1914.

257. David, ed., *Hobhouse Diaries*, p. 158, 27 January 1914.

258. Churchill, *Churchill*, II, Comp. Vol. 3, p. 1856.

259. David, ed., *Hobhouse Diaries*, p. 158, 27 January 1914.

260. *Ibid.*

261. Wilson, ed., *Scott Diaries*, p. 80, 6 February 1914.

262. Riddell, *More Pages*, p. 201, 26 February 1914.

263. Ironically after the outbreak of the war two of the four battleships projected under the 1914 budget were dropped in favor of construction of smaller craft. LGP, H of L, C/24/3/39, Cabinet Memorandum, 'New Construction Since the Outbreak of War,' WSC, 14 December 1914.

264. HHA to VS, 7 March 1914. This note is not among the published letters.

265. Churchill, *Churchill*, II, 662. Randolph Churchill reports that in 1962 Megan Lloyd George confirmed this conversation. On the other hand, Lucy Masterman records that Churchill was 'one of Mrs. George's fixed aversions.' She hissed with contempt whenever his name was mentioned. Masterman Papers, Lucy Masterman TS diary, Chap. 9, p. 22. In any case during the critical weeks of January, Maggie was in Criccieth.

Chapter 2, p. 81–120

1. *Parliamentary Papers, Cd. 7315*, 'Departmental Committee on Local Taxation,' 1914, p. 102.

2. Central Land and Housing Council, 'Speech Delivered by the Rt. Honourable David Lloyd George, M.P. at Glasgow on February 4th, 1914.'

3. *Official Report, House of Commons Debates*, Series Five, LVIII (10 February 1914) cols. 52–3; Lloyd George Papers, House of Lords, C/2/3/49, Rowntree to LG, 23 November 1913.

4. *H of C Deb.*, LVIII (27 February 1914) cols. 2102–4.

5. Michael and Eleanor Brock, eds., *H.H. Asquith, Letters to Venetia Stanley*, Oxford, 1982, p. 66, 18 April 1914.

6. William George, *My Brother and I*, London, 1958, p. 248. This letter, an example of the aggravation of the latter portions of W. George's book, is clearly misdated 11 March, and in fact appears to combine portions of two letters. The first paragraph discusses the Cabinet's approval of an agreement with Redmond for excluding some counties of Ulster from Home Rule, which action the Cabinet took on 4 March. In the letter as printed, Lloyd George mentions a Monday dinner but on the Monday before 11 March (i.e. 10 March) Lloyd George was in the House of Commons trouncing F.E. Smith whose party had moved a vote of censure against him. His letter to Maggie suggests what he was thinking about the next day. Kenneth Morgan, ed., *Lloyd George Family Letters*, Cardiff, 1973, p. 166, LG to MLG, 11 March 1914. 'I pounded them flat,' he bragged. It was of course the best speech he ever made. Asquith also refers to a dinner with Lloyd George to discuss the budget in late April. Brocks, eds., *Stanley Letters*, p. 67, HHA to VS, 22 April 1914.

7. Gainford Papers, Nuffield College, J.A. Pease diary, 24 April 1914.

8. George, Lord Riddell, *More Pages From My Diary*, London, 1934, p. 210, 25 April 1914.

9. Asquith Papers, Bodleian Library, Vol. VII, HHA to George V, 30 April 1914. This letter does not appear in the List and Index Society Calendar of Cabinet letters at Windsor.

10. The best exposition of the rate relief plan appears in, *PP 1914*, Vol. L, Accounts and Papers, House of Commons Paper No. 212, E.S. Montagu, 'Financial Statement, 1914–15,' 5 May 1914.

11. British Library, Add MS 46336, John Burns papers, LVI, J.B. diary, 30 April 1914.

12. *H of C Deb*, LXII (4 May 1914), cols. 56–94.

13. Trevor Wilson, ed., *The Political Diaries of C.P. Scott, 1911–1928*, Ithaca, 1970, p. 85.

14. *H of C Deb*, LXII (4 May 1914), col. 93.

15. *Ibid.*, cols. 69–70.

16. *Ibid.*, col. 72.

17. *Ibid.*, col. 68. Bernard Mallet described it charitably as being 'notable for a lack of clarity.' Bernard Mallet and C. Oswald George, *British Budgets, 1913–14 to 1920–21*, London, 1929, p. 29.

18. Brocks, eds., *Stanley Letters*, p. 70, 5 May 1914.

19. *H of C Deb.*, LXII (7 May 1914) cols. 460–1.

20. *Ibid.*, col. 462.

21. *Nation*, 23 May 1914.

22. *Nation*, 16 May 1914.

23. LGP, H of L, C/2/4//22, G. Wallace Carter to LG, 28 May 1914. The second volume of the land enquiry report, on urban areas, had been published in March and received little notice.

24. Ibid., C/2/4/16, B.S. Rowntree to LG, 12 May 1914.

25. Ibid., C/2/4/20, 21, Rowntree to LG, Rowntree to F.L. Stevenson, 25, 28 May 1914.

26. Arthur Ponsonby Papers, Bodleian Library, Eng. Hist., C660, ff9–11, Masterman to Ponsonby, 30 May 1914.

27. Brocks, eds., *Stanley Letters*, p. 74, 24 May 1914.

28. See for example, *Saturday Review*, 30 May 1914.

29. India Office Library, Reading Papers, Eur. F, 118/53, Lucy Masterman to Isaacs, n.d. [evidently February 1915].

30. Walter, Viscount Long, *Memories*, London, 1923, p. 205.

31. Riddell, *More Pages*, pp. 212–4, 24 May, 19 June 1914.

32. Ponsonby Papers, Eng. Hist., C660, ff9–11, Masterman to Ponsonby, 30 May 1914.

33. Edward David, ed., *Inside Asquith's Cabinet, From the Diaries of Charles Hobhouse*, London, 1977, p. 170, 22 May 1914.

34. British Library Add MS 62974, Riddell diaries, 13 June 1914.

35. LGP, H of L, C/11/1/49, Violet Mond to LG, 25 May 1914. Evidently Mond had solicited office in 1910 and had been fobbed off with a baronetcy. Hector Bolitho, *Alfred Mond*, London, 1933, p. 155. Mond was MP for Swanseatown and Sir John Brunner's business partner.

36. LGP, H of L, C/6/11/15, LG to PM, 5 June 1914.

37. Brocks, eds., *Stanley Letters*, pp. 77–8, HHA to VS, 7 June 1914.

38. LGP, H of L, C/6/11/16, HHA to LG, 7 June 1914.

39. On Illingworth's reaction see: George, Lord Riddell, *War Diary, 1914–1918*, London, 1933, pp. 49–50, 9 January 1915.

40. LGP, H of L, C/11/1/58, Report by G. Ward Humphrey, n.d., covering note, 7 June 1914.

41. *The Times*, 1, 3 June 1914.

42. Neither the Lloyd George papers nor the Cabinet papers contain material on this change. The only historian who appears to have understood what actually happened in this complicated episode, even though he did not pursue it, is, as might be expected, Elie Halévy. See: *The Rule of Democracy* (University Paperback Edition) New York, 1961, p. 349n.

43. *The Times*, 18 June 1914.

44. Brocks, eds., *Stanley Letters*, p. 89, 18 June 1914.

45. *The Times*, 19 June 1914.

46. On the Cabinet of 22 June see *The Times*, 23 June 1914.

47. Almeric Fitzroy, *Memoirs* (London: n.d. [1925]), II, 553, 23 June 1914.

48. David, ed., *Hobhouse Diaries*, p. 172, 22 June 1914.

49. *H of C Deb*, LXIII (22 June 1914) cols. 1589–90. For the changes in the bill see: *PP*, Vol. L, 1914, House of Commons Paper 293, E.S. Montagu, 'Copy of Revised Estimates of Revenue and Expenditure for the year 1914–15 with an Explanatory Memorandum,' 23 June 1914.

50. *New Statesman*, 27 June 1914.

51. 'Mr. Speaker's Ruling,' *Saturday Review*, 27 June 1914.

52. Runciman to Chalmers, 24 June 1914, in Cameron Hazlehurst, *Politicians at War, July 1914 to May 1915*, London, 1971, pp. 106–7.

53. Riddell, *More Pages*, p. 218.

54. Public Record Office Cab. 37/120/75, 'Ministry of Land,' 25 June 1914; Christopher Addison, *Politics From Within, 1911–1918* (London: 1924), I, 32, Diary, 3 July 1914.

55. Gainford Papers, J.A. Pease diary, 15 July 1914.

56. David, ed., *Hobhouse Diaries*, pp. 111, 11 February 1912. See also Asquith's explanation to the King in: Roy Jenkins, *Asquith*, London, 1964, pp. 276–7. He was supported in this by Asquith, Churchill and Haldane.

57. J.H. Lewis Papers, National Library of Wales, 10/231, diary, 18 February 1912.

58. Riddell, *More Pages*, p. 252–3, 14 March 1912.

59. Long, *Memories*, p. 212–3.

60. LGP, NLW, 20431C/1416, 11 April 1912.

61. That this was on the minds of the Unionists see Carson's statement to Bonar Law, 20 September 1913, quoted in John D. Fair, *British Interparty Conferences*, Oxford, 1980, p. 103.

62. Bonar Law Papers, House of Lords Record Office, 27/1/50, A.R.M. Lockwood to ABL, 22 August 1912.

63. See J.M. McEwen, ed. *The Riddell Diaries, 1908–1923*, London, 1986, pp. 40–41, 14 April 1912. But see also, for example: BLP, 33/5/57, Bonar Law to Carson, 18 September 1913, insisting that any settlement on Ulster must have the agreement of the Unionists in the South and West. This portion of this letter is not printed in Robert Blake, *Unrepentant Tory, the Life and Times of Andrew Bonar Law, 1858–1923*, New York, 1956. See also: BLP, 30/2/14, 27, Lansdowne to Bonar Law, 20, 26. September 1913 declaring that Southern Unionists were in no way committed by negotiations with Carson. See also: BLP, 30/3/16, Lansdowne to LG, 10 October 1913 reminding the Chancellor that Bonar Law had stated publically that he would not approve exclusion 'unless it commanded a large measure' of Southern support. See also: BLP, 32/4/16, Midleton to Bonar Law, 16 June 1914. Even the King was upset by the 'inevitable abandonment of the Unionists in the South.' BLP, 32/2/34, Stamfordham to Bonar Law, 15 April 1914.

64. On the rejection of Carson's exclusion amendment in December see: David, ed., *Hobhouse Diaries*, pp. 126–7, 31 December 1912.

65. Harold Nicholson, *King George the Fifth*, London, 1952, pp. 223–4.

66. Morgan, ed., *Family Letters*, p. 165.

67. BLP, 30/2/35, F. Harcourt Kitchin to Bonar Law, 30 September 1913.

68. BLP, 30/3/31, Lansdowne to Bonar Law, 16 October 1913.

69. BLP, 33/6/93, Bonar Law to Balfour, 7 November 1913. For Asquith's own account of this interview see: Jenkins, *Asquith*, pp. 290–91.

70. BLP, 33/6/94, Bonar Law to Long, 7 November 1913.

71. LGP, H of L, C/14/1/10, 'Notes of a dinner at 11 Downing Street, 12 November 1913.' This account differs somewhat from the excellent and highly detailed study provided by Pat Jalland, *The Liberals and Ireland*, New York, 1980, p. 145–170, which questions from Asquith's own account of the 6 November meeting that an offer of temporary exclusion was ever made, hence the proposal at the Downing Street dinner was Lloyd George's own. On the other hand, although Lloyd George had discussed exclusion with Churchill, F.E. Smith and others in September and early October, he was at this time busy with the land campaign and unlikely to bring it up himself. Second, Asquith clearly tried, on 11 November, the day before the dinner to prepare the full Cabinet for a dilution of Home Rule by describing at length, but unclearly, his conversations with Bonar Law. Finally, Bonar Law firmly stated to two correspondents that the Prime Minister had proposed, albeit hypothetically, temporary exclusion, had offered to present it to the Cabinet and the Nationalists, and had asked for nothing in return. Asquith's and Bonar Law's accounts are not irreconcilable. See: David, ed., *Hobhouse Diaries*, pp. 149–50, 11 November 1913; Jenkins, *Asquith*, p. 292.

72. Riddell, *More Pages*, p. 185, 15 November 1913.

73. Asquith Papers, Vol. VII, HHA to George V, 14 November 1913.

74. LGP, H of L, C/20/2/4, 'Report of Interviews between Lloyd George and John Dillon at 11 Downing Street, 17 November 1913', MS. See also: F.S.L. Lyons, *John Dillon, A Biography*, London, 1968, pp. 338–40; Denis Gwynn, *The Life of John Redmond*, London, 1932, pp. 234–6.

75. David, ed., *Hobhouse Diaries*, pp. 151–2, 25 November 1913; Gwynn, *Redmond*, pp. 236–7.

76. See: Lyons, *Dillon*, pp. 341–2; Gwynn, *Redmond*, pp. 237–8.

77. Quoted in Lyons, *Dillon*, p. 343.

78. Rupert Hart-Davis, ed., *Siegfried Sassoon Diaries, 1915–1918*, London, 1983, p. 278, 4 August 1918.

79. *H of C Deb*, XXXVII (29 April 1912) cols. 1265–86.

80. Eluned E. Owen, *The Later Life of Bishop Owen* (Llandysul: 1961), II, 188; *North Wales Observer*, 24 May 1912 in LGP, H of L, C/35/2/8. For the parliamentary story of the fourth Disestablishment Bill see: Kenneth Morgan, *Wales in British Politics*, Cardiff, 1970, pp. 262–74.

81. Blake, *Unrepentant Tory*, p. 161n.

82. W. Watkin Davies, *Lloyd George, 1863–1914*, London, 1939, p. 410.

83. M.Q. Sale, 'The Problems of Wales,' *National Review*, LXII (November 1913), 507–18.

84. Owen, *Owen*, p. 203–4.

85. See: Lloyd George to McKenna on concessions to the Church. McKenna Papers, Churchill College, 4/4/25, LG to McKenna, 18 April 1914.

86. 'Viator Cambrensis,' *The Rise and Decline of Welsh Nonconformity*, London, 1912 (paperback pamphlet, 85pp.), p. 26.

87. O'Connor to Dillon, 13 January 1914 in Lyons, *Dillon*, p. 345.

88. Riddell, *More Pages*, p. 202, 6 March 1914.

89. Reading Papers, Eur. F. 118–1, Cynthia Asquith to Isaacs, 20 June 1933, asking if this was true. Christopher Adisson confirms this estimate of the Prime Minister by Carson. Addison, *Politics*, I, 36.

90. This TS paper initialed 'D Ll G' undated, appears in LGP, H of L, C/20/2/7 and is printed in Gwynn, *Redmond*, p. 260–61.

91. LGP, H of L, C/20/2/6, undated, unsigned, in C of E envelope marked 'Mr. Devlin, Confidential.'

92. LGP, H of L, C/20/2/7. 'D.Ll.G,' (untitled, udated), (dated in pencil '23–2–14').

93. David, ed., *Hobhouse Diaries*, pp. 161–2, 25 February 1914.

94. LGP, H of L, C/20/2/5, 'Letter to the Cabinet from the Irish Party, *Secret*,' TS, undated, unsigned. See: Gwynn, *Redmond*, pp. 267–9.

95. Gwynn, *Redmond*, p. 264.

96. Asquith Papers, Vol. VII, HHA to George V, 5 March 1914.

97. W. George, *Brother*, p. 248. This letter is misdated 11 March.

98. *H of C Deb*, LIX (9 March 1914) cols. 906–934.

99. The King told Lord Esher in November 1913 that the Army was 'honeycombed' by 'orangism.' Esher had heard the same and Sir Henry Wilson noted similar rumors

in his diary a few weeks later. Maurice V. Brett, ed., *Journals and Letters of Reginald, Viscount Esher* (London: 1934), III, 145, 18 November 1913; C.E. Callwell, *Field Marshal Sir Henry Wilson* (London: 1927), I, 134, 2 December 1913.

100. Brett, ed., *Esher Journals*, III, 169, 23 May 1914.

101. David, ed., *Hobhouse Diaries*, p. 171, 22 May 1914.

102. Gwynn, *Redmond*, pp. 328–9.

103. See: Gainford Papers, J.A. Pease diary, 15 July 1914.

104. Callwell, *Wilson*, I, 148, 3 July 1914.

105. Public Record Office, Northern Ireland, Edward Carson Papers, D. 1507/A/6/40, Lord Milner to Carson, 21 July 1914.

106. Asquith Papers, Vol. VII, HHA to George V, 17 July 1914.

107. Brocks, eds., *Stanley Letters*, p. 106, 17 July 1914.

108. LGP, H of L, C/6/11/18, Mark Bonham Carter to LG, 17 July 1914.

109. Gainford Papers, J.A. Pease diary, 22 July 1914.

110. Ibid., 24 July 1914.

111. Brocks, eds., *Stanley Letters*, p. 122, 24 July 1914. Neither Lyons's nor Gwynn's excellent biographies of Dillon and Redmond refer to this monumental if temporary change of position by the Irish leaders.

112. Asquith Papers, Vol. VII, HHA to George V, 25 June 1914.

113. Wilson, ed., *Scott Diaries*, p. 91, 27 July 1914.

114. Brocks, eds., *Stanley Letters*, p. 125, 26 July 1914.

115. Asquith Papers, Vol. VII, HHA to George V, 25 July 1914. Except for a brief remark on 17 July this represents the first notice in the Cabinet letters to be taken of the Austro-Serbian conflict. Ibid., 17 July 1914.

116. David Lloyd George, *War Memoirs* (Boston: 1933), I, 66.

117. A.J.P. Taylor's characteristically dogmatic statement: 'no one, anywhere, foresaw the massive German invasion of Belgium' simply is not true. A.J.P. Taylor, *Politics in Wartime*, London, 1964, p. 88.

118. Esher, *Journals*, III, 174; David, ed., *Hobhouse Diaries*, p. 179, 'August' 1914. 'Lloyd George's combative nature and combative instincts, will keep him in office and lead him on from battlefield to battlefield,' wrote Esher later. 'In his heart he hates the German temper, that is so unlike his, and he cares nothing for the Kultur that appeals to some of his colleagues.'

119. Frances L. Stevenson, *The Years That Are Past*, London, 1967, pp. 73–4.

120. Wilson, ed., *Scott Diaries*, p. 86, 6 May 1914.

121. *Ibid.*, p. 91, 27 July 1914. This statement, often quoted as evidence of Lloyd George's pacifism, needs to be read in terms of the progress of events when it was made. Austria had not yet declared war on Serbia and Grey that day publicly proposed an international conference to settle the dispute.

122. Ponsonby Papers, MS. Eng. Hist., C660/50, Ponsonby to Asquith, 30 July 1914; Brocks, eds., *Stanley Letters*, p. 146, 2 August 1914.

123. Morgan, ed., *Family Letters*, 27, 28, 29, 30 July 1914, pp. 166–7. It is important to remember that Belgium was not popular in Britain in the years before the war. Roger Casement's reports on the horrible conditions in the Congo had filled Liberal newspapers in 1912 and 1913. Moreover King Leopold II, responsible for the atrocities, was of German extraction and had died only in December 1909.

124. For example, Hazlehurst, *Politicians at War*, pp. 66–76.

125. Edward, Viscount Grey, *Twenty-five Years 1892–1916* (New York: 1925), I, 327–8.

126. Riddell, *War Diary*, p. 6, 2 August 1914.

127. LGP, H of L, C/13.

128. Samuel Papers, House of Lords Record Office, A/157/697, Herbert to Beatrice Samuel, 2 August 1914.

129. Ibid., A/45/1, 'The Cabinet in the Days Preceding the War,' Typescript, n.d.

130. Brocks, eds., *Stanley Letters*, p. 140, 1 August 1914.

131. Gainford Papers, J.A. Pease diary, 2 August 1914.

132. Samuel Papers, H of L, A/157/697, Herbert to Beatrice Samuel, 2 August 1914.

133. John, Lord Morley, *Memorandum on Resignation*, London, 1928, pp. 14–5.

134. 'At three PM a note came to Douglas from Squiff ordering the Precautionary Period.' H.H. Wilson diaries, Imperial War Museum, 29 July 1914.

135. Riddell, *War Diary*, p. 5.

136. David Marquand, *Ramsay MacDonald*, London, 1977, p. 164.

137. Arthur Murray records that Grey received the news of the German ultimatum at about 9:00 p.m. on 2 August. This would have been after the Cabinet adjourned but Lloyd George could have learned of it before he departed for Riddell's house. *Master and Brother, The Murrays of Elibank*, London, 1945, p. 122.

138. McEwen, ed., *Riddell Diaries*, p. 52, 29 December 1912.

139. *British Weekly*, 30 July 1914.

140. Riddell, *War Diary*, pp. 6–7.

141. Morgan, *Letters*, p. 167, LG to MLG, 3 August 1914.

142. Samuel Papers, A/157/698, Herbert to Beatrice Samuel, 3 August 1914, 5:30 p.m.

143. Wilson, ed., *Scott Diaries*, pp. 96–7, 4 August 1914.

144. Lloyd George's own account of the City crisis in *War Memoirs*, I, 90–105, even though written apparently by E.D. Swinton of the Treasury, in consultation with Bradbury and R.G. Hawtrey, and corrected by Isaacs, is not entirely satisfactory. Reading Papers, Eur. F., 118–84, Swinton to Isaacs, 13 July 1925. By far the best summary of the onset of the crisis, lucid and well-informed, is: J.M. Keynes, 'War and the Financial System, August 1914,' *Economic Journal*, XXIV (September 1914), 460–86. For documents see: *PP*, 1914, L, House of Commons Papers 457, 'Return of Papers Relating to the Assistance Rendered by the Treasury to Banks and Discount Houses Since the Outbreak of War...' 27 August 1914; see also: *PP*, 1914–16, LV, *Cd. 7684*, 'Further Papers relating to the Measures taken by His Majesty's Government for sustaining credit and facilitating Business.' n.d. (end of November 1914).

145. The three discount companies, whose figures were public, were holding on 30 June 1914, £58,200,000 in bills, although their total capital and resources was £3,600,000. Keynes 'War and Finance,' 468n.

146. Economists since the war have questioned whether there really would have been a gold crisis had not clearing banks insisted upon paying out notes instead of gold to customers withdrawing money for the holiday weekend. A.W. Kirkaldy, ed., *British Finance During and After the War*, London, 1921, pp. 1–22.

147. See Cunliffe to LG, 31 July 1914, *Ibid.*, p. 1.

148. Brocks, eds., *Stanley Letters*, p. 139, 1 August 1914.

149. *H of C Deb*, LXV (3 August 1914), cols 1805–9.

150. *Ibid.*, (5 August 1914), cols. 1991–2000.

151. LGP, H of L, C/1/1/20–25, 7 August 1914.

152. Morgan, ed., *Family Letters*, p. 163, LG to MLG, 7 August 1914.

153. Keynes, 'War and Finance,' p. 469n.

154. H of C Paper, 457, 27 August 1914, p. 4.

155. Gainford Papers, J.A. Pease diary, 13 August 1914.

156. This small group of about 12 became, and remains, the famous, or infamous, London Accepting House Committee, the core of the City's invisible power network. It continues to hold direct access to the Bank of England. Presumably no member can be allowed to fail.

157. Asquith Papers, Vol. VII, HHA to George V, 2 September 1914, Cabinets 1 and 2 September.

158. David, ed., *Hobhouse Diaries*, p. 182, 21 August 1914. This point was seconded by another non-admirer, Wilfred Lawson, the publicist of the Marconi scandal, in an excellent book on the first fiscal year of the war. Wilfred R. Lawson, *British War Finance*, London, 1915, p. 9.

159. W. George, *Brother*, pp. 248–9, 13 August 1914. See: LGP, H of L, C/11/2/2, N.A. Rothschild to LG, 13 August 1914.

160. Keynes, 'War and Finance,' pp. 460, 484.

161. Churchill, who had boasted earlier in the spring that not a day went by without a few minutes conversation with Lloyd George, noted to his surprise on 24 August that he had not seen his friend except at Cabinets since 2 August. Winston Churchill, *The World Crisis 1916–1918* (London: 1924), I, 219–20.

162. See: LGP, H of L, C/7/3/11, Redmond to LG, 4 August 1914; C/6/10/10, O'Connor to LG, 21 August 1914; Brocks, eds., *Stanley Letters*, p. 163, 10 August 1914. Home Rule finally became law on 18 September.

163. Gainford Papers, J.A. Pease diary, 25 August 1914.

164. Asquith Papers, Vol. VII, HHA to George V, 31 August 1914.

165. Morgan, ed., *Family Letters*, p. 169, 174, LG to MLG, 11 August 1914, 30 October 1914.

166. Riddell, *War Diary*, p. 14.

167. Morgan, ed., *Family Letters*, p. 172, LG to MLG, 10 September 1914.

168. See: Lloyd George's letter to Sir Henry (not J.H.) Lewis on the second stage of the campaign, to be conducted in Wales. LGP, H of L, C/11/2/60, LG to Lewis, 7 October 1914.

169. Morgan, ed., *Family Letters*, p. 173, LG to MLG, 19 September 1914.

170. See his remarks to Frances Stevenson after the speech. A.J.P. Taylor, ed., *Lloyd George, A Diary by Frances Stevenson*, London, 1971, p. 2, 21 September 1914.

171. Riddell, *War Diary*, p. 32, 18, 19 September 1914.

172. 'For all we have and are,' 1914.

173. D.R. Daniel Memoir, National Library of Wales, III, pp. 10–11.

174. *The Times*, 21 September 1914.

175. Taylor, ed., *Stevenson Diary*, pp. 2–3, 21 September 1914.

176. LGP, H of L, C/11/2/69, E. Hodder Williams to LG, 17 November 1914.

177. *British Weekly*, 24 September 1914.

178. LGP, H of L, C/11/1/60, LG to Sir Henry Lewis, 7 October 1914.

179. The *British Weekly*, among other papers, remarked upon how the attacks on Lloyd George, so recent, had been thrust out of memory by later events. *British Weekly*, 24 September 1914.

Chapter 3, pp. 121–150

1. Edward David, ed., *Inside Asquith's Cabinet, From the Diaries of Charles Hobhouse*, London, 1977, p. 207, 25 November 1914.

2. Lloyd George Papers, House of Lords, C/8/4/13, 'A Few Notes on the Economic Position. A New Factor. The Action of Governments.' n.d., 10 pp. (Covering letter dated 12 December 1914.)

3. Reginald, Viscount Esher, *The Tragedy of Lord Kitchener*, New York, 1921, pp. 9–10. This book, published and reviewed nearly twenty years before the appearance of Esher's diaries which show his great admiration for the Field Marshal, has been wrongly condemned as an attack upon Kitchener.

4. In the autumn of 1915, by which time he had begun to realize the exasperation, almost the contempt in which he was held by some of his colleagues, Kitchener confided pathetically to Edward Carson, 'I don't know Europe; I don't know England and I don't know the British Army.' Ian Colvin, *The Life of Lord Carson* (London: 1936), III, 79. See also: Philip Magnus, *Kitchener*, New York, 1959, p. 279.

5. The tales about Kitchener were innumerable. His single interest beyond the army was the reconstruction and decoration of his seat, Broome Park in Kent, which he had purchased in 1910. For the embellishment of this estate he would buy or borrow or steal all over the world objects which took his fancy: two rifles, for example, borrowed and not returned from Lord Derby. He boasted of having traded an Indian prince two counterfeit vases for two ancient swords. Lloyd George discovered later, as he told Frances Stevenson, that the swords were also faked. A.J.P. Taylor, ed., *Lloyd George, A Diary by Frances Stevenson*, London, 1971, pp. 227–8, 25 January 1915.

A bachelor whose adult life had been spent largely in the tropics, he knew nothing of women. In January 1915, as the labor shortage was beginning to appear, he startled the Cabinet by proposing that women be employed on the docks in Britain. It was done in Zanzibar he said, with excellent results. Michael and Eleanor Brock, eds., *H.H. Asquith, Letters to Venetia Stanley*, Oxford, 1982, p. 372. 12 January 1915.

6. For a recent investigation of this see: David French, 'The Meaning of Attrition, 1914–1916,' *English Historical Review*, CIII (April, 1988), 385–405.

7. Kitchener, as nearly his first act as Secretary of State for War, had called, on 7 August, for 100,000 men and parliament had sanctioned increasing the army by 500,000. But this was all most men expected. Francis Hirst, editor of the *Economist*, wrote to Charles Trevelyan on 14 August that he was sure people were opposed to 'the infinite and unlimited export of British troops to the continent.' Hirst to Trevelyan, 14 August 1914, quoted in Cameron Hazlehurst, *Politicians at War, July, 1914 to May, 1915*, London, 1971, p. 125.

8. Winston S. Churchill, *The World Crisis 1916–1918* (New York: 1924), I, 253–4; Edward, Viscount Grey, *Twenty-five Years, 1892–1916* (New York: 1925), II, 71.

9. Public Record Office, Cab 41/35/27, HHA to George V, 11 August 1914.

10. Both Churchill and Grey assert, albeit years afterwards, that this would have been the time to introduce military conscription. Churchill, *Crisis*, I, 253–4; Grey, *Twenty-five Years*, II, 71.

11. Before the war the standard maintainable ammunition reserve had been 1,500 rounds per gun for 18 pounders and 1,000 for 60 pounders. This assumed of course

a mobile war. There would be extended periods of maneuver when guns would not be firing and ammunition could be accumulated and was based upon a small army. However in May 1915 French reported to Lloyd George that at Neuve Chapelle the field guns had fired 120 rounds per day and the larger calibers proportionally less. Moreover by May there were 22 divisions in France and four in Egypt. He requested 24 rounds per day per gun of which 50 percent would be high explosive, although there was really no limit to the amount of ammunition that would be useful. 'History of the Ministry of Munitions,' Vol. I, 'Industrial Mobilization,' 1914–15, Part 1, 'Munitions Supply,' 1922, pp. 12–25.

12. See Grey, *Twenty-five Years*, II, 233.

13. David, ed., *Hobhouse Diaries*, p. 196, 8 October 1914.

14. *Ibid.*, p. 197, 9 October 1914. However, only three weeks later he was asking, rather humbly, to borrow artillery and ammunition from the French. Raymond Poincaré, *The Memoirs of Raymond Poincaré, 1914*, New York, 1929, p. 222, 1 November 1914.

15. David Lloyd George, *War Memoirs* (Boston: 1933), I, 132. See also: British Library, Add MS 62974, Riddell diaries, TS, 11 October 1914.

16. Evidently Lloyd George had not told the Cabinet in advance of his trip to France. J.A. Pease noted in his diary on 20 October 1914 that Lloyd George, Reading, and Simon were in France on Sunday and that Lloyd George had met Foch and Castelnau and liked them both. Gainford Papers, Nuffield College, J.A. Pease diary, 20 October 1914.

17. Castelnau was an unusual figure among French commanders, an anti-Dreyfusard, a staunch Roman Catholic, and a member of an aristocratic military family going back to Napoleon. He had already lost a son in the war. For an appreciation see: Maurice Baring, *Flying Corps Headquarters, 1914–1918*, London, 1985 (first published 1920), p. 273–4.

18. David, ed., *Hobhouse Diaries*, p. 199, 20 October 1914.

19. Lloyd George, *War Memoirs*, I, 140–41.

20. *Official Report, House of Commons Debates*, LXXI (21 April 1915) cols. 311–14.

21. For example, Lloyd George received a box of cigars from Edward Montagu on 24 December 1914 as payment for a bet that the Germans would be out of Belgium and France by Christmastime. LGP, H of L, C/1/1/36, Montagu to LG, 24 December 1914.

The German army was deteriorating General H.H. Wilson told Almeric Fitzroy in January 1915. He 'speaks with confidence of the future.' Almeric Fitzroy, *Memoirs* (London: n.d. [1925]), II, 579, 19 January 1915. And on 29 January 1915 Edward Carson's wife recorded being told categorically by the Director General of the Territorial Forces, Lieutenant General Edward Bethune, that the war would be over in three months. Public Record Office Northern Ireland, Edward Carson Papers, D.1507/C/1, Ruby Carson diary, 29 January 1915. Still later, at the end of March 1915, after the failure of the naval attack in the Dardanelles, Asquith predicted to Venetia Stanley that the war would be over in three months. Brocks, eds., *Stanley Letters*, p. 530, 30 March 1915.

This misapprehension, as will be seen, would persist among British soldiers and politicians alike until well into the spring of the following year. Part of it may be ascribed to the euphoria following the Battle of the Marne when even the far more realistic French were talking of peace terms. (Poincaré, *Memoirs*, p. 177, 19 September 1914.) In Britain however there is the fact that even the Cabinet through September knew little about what was happening in France as Hobhouse's and Pease's diaries amply show. The frustration of the Schlieffen Plan was by no means clear. More likely the optimism derived from the poor performance of the German infantry, particularly the reserve formations. In effect the Germans were not supermen after all. They had not walked through the French 'like partridges' as Kitchener had predicted. At the same time British small arms fire, 'musketry' as it was then styled, practiced intensely in the BEF since 1909, had been devastating even in retreat. The great German advantage lay in her employment of hugely superior artillery, especially in the use of large calibers as field guns. Traditionally the British had considered their 4.7 inch cannon almost too large for the field while the Germans from the first were using a 5.9 inch howitzer as a field gun.

22. LGP, H of L, C/1/1/30, Edward C. Grenfell to J.P. Morgan & Company, 5 November 1914.

23. LGP, H of L, C/5/7/6, Von Donop to LG, 12 November 1914. Von Donop, who would become for Lloyd George the perfect example of everything that was wrong at the War Office, was nevertheless a professional artillery expert of great distinction who had been a close colleague of Haldane during the reform of the army. Haldane defended him publicly in the spring of 1915 when Lloyd George began a newspaper quarrel with the War Office. F.B. Maurice, *Haldane*, reprinted (Westport, Connecticut: 1970), II, 4. Apparently Von Donop was not aware that Grenfell and Morgan were a single company.

Von Donop on 5 October had asked the United States military attaché, Lt. Col. George O. Squier, about buying 100 or 150 thousand United States army Springfield rifles and 5,000,000 rounds of ammunition. He was quickly rebuffed and afterwards turned toward contracting with manufacturers. Burton J. Hendrick, *The Life and Letters of Walter H . Page* (New York: 1925), III, 157–61, Page to Woodrow Wilson, 6 October 1914.

24. LGP, H of L, C/1/1/33, Grenfell to LG, 13 November 1914. Grenfell included the angry cable from New York describing events there and remarking that it had been held up by British censors for six hours. Ibid., J. Pierpont Morgan to E.C. Grenfell, 12 November 1914.

25. LGP, H of L, C/5/7/8, Von Donop to Reading, 14 November 1914; LG to Von Donop, 23 November 1914. See also: Lloyd George, *War Memoirs*, I, 146–7.

26. LGP, H of L, C/1/1/34,35, Grenfell to Morgan, Morgan to Grenfell, 26 November 1914.

27. Thomas W. Lamont, *Henry P. Davison: The Record of a Useful Life*, New York, 1933, p. 189. It has been suggested that Morgan's was not the inevitable choice as British agent in the United States. The National City Bank was also interested. This would have been possible, but as an organizer of syndicated loans Morgan's, the bankers' banker, was in those days unrivalled. Robert A. Dayer, 'Strange Bedfellows: J.P. Morgan & Company, Whitehall and the Wilson Administration During World War I,' *Business History*, XVIII (July 1976), 2, 127–51.

28. LGP, H of L, C/1/2/7. Morgan's later was always at pains to emphasize that the initiative for these increasingly profitable contracts had come from Britain through Davison. In the beginning the banking house had assumed they were only to be part time advisors. See B.C. Forbes's interview with Edward R. Stettinius: 'The Biggest Buyer in the World,' *American Magazine*, LXXXIV (September, 1917), 3, 15–82.

29. Taylor, ed., *Stevenson Diary*, p. 3–4, 28 September 1914.

30. Gainford Papers, MS 39, J.A. Pease diary, 23 October 1914; MS 42, J.A. Pease to Ethel Pease, 23 October 1914. Christopher Addison, a member of the committee, recorded that the War Office proposals for entertainment consisted of 'putting up a few huts' for military lectures in the evening. Christopher Addison, *Politics From Within, 1911–1918* (London: 1924), I, 42–3.

31. LGP, H of L, C/5/7/1, Lieutenant General E.C. Bethune to LG, 23 October 1914.

32. LGP, H of L, C/5/7/2, LG to Kitchener, 27 October 1914. Kitchener evidently had a low opinion of Welsh soldiers. No Welsh regiment was to be trusted, he told Asquith. They were 'always wild & insubordinate & ought to be stiffened by a strong infusion of English or Scotch.' Brocks, eds., *Stanley Letters*, p. 298, HHA to VS, 30 October 1914.

33. David, ed., *Hobhouse Diaries*, pp. 203–4, 28 October 1914. According to Lloyd George's account to Frances Stevenson Kitchener suggested at one point that perhaps the Chancellor would like to take over the War Office himself and Lloyd George replied that he would not hesitate to criticize Kitchener in the House of Commons if War Office policies were not mended. Taylor, ed., *Stevenson Diary*, p. 7, 30 October 1914.

34. Brocks, eds., *Stanley Letters*, p. 299, HHA to VS, 30 October 1914.

35. Gainford Papers, J.A. Pease diary, 30 October 1914.

36. George, Lord Riddell, *War Diary, 1914–1918*, London, 1933, pp. 37–8, 31 October 1914.

37. LGP, H of L, C/7/1/9, 10, Philipps to LG, 19, 20 January 1915.
   For a recent account of the somewhat unhappy history of the 38th (Welsh) Division and the effects of its political association with Lloyd George see: Clive Hughes, 'The New Armies' in I.F.W. Beckett and Keith Simpson, eds., *A Nation in Arms, A social study of the British army in the First World War*, Manchester, 1985, pp. 114–22.

38. Margot Asquith diary in Martin Gilbert, *Winston S. Churchill* (London: 1971), III, Comp. Vol. 3, Part 1, 400, 10 January 1915.

39. Examples from Hobhouse's diary in the fall of 1914 include a retort by Churchill during a Cabinet discussion on the licensing of trawlers that Hobhouse's 'opinion was of no value' and Churchill's untruthful defense of an incident in Lerwick where Vice Admiral S.C.J. Colville on 6 November had locked up under war powers the entire staff of the local post office on the grounds that his mail had been opened. When it finally transpired that the Admiral had mistakenly done this himself Churchill refused to admit the error or pay compensation until Hobhouse threatened to cut off all postal and telegraphic services to the Admiralty and fleet. 'He behaved like an untruthful and spoilt schoolboy, which leavened by a genius for speech he really is,' concluded Hobhouse. David, ed., *Hobhouse Diaries*, pp. 188, 206, 3 September, 13 November 1914.

40. BL Add MS, 62974, Riddell diaries, TS, 21 September 1914. This statement was recorded after dinner at Lloyd George's with Margaret Lloyd George, Megan and Charles Masterman present. It is not clear from the text whether the statement by McKenna was made to Lloyd George or to Riddell.

41. Churchill himself wrote in the *World Crisis* that he noticed a 'turning point' in the public attitudes toward him after this disaster. Churchill, *Crisis*, I, 3433. He was referring here however to newspapers, which were becoming fiercely critical. He never seems to have sensed the antagonism of his colleagues.
   A longer lasting result of this tragedy appeared in the almost pathological fear of the naval leadership, particularly John Jellicoe, about the vulnerability of warships to submarine torpedoes. Again and again British naval activity at the Dardanelles, and at Jutland, would be modified by this conviction.

42. In fact the Seventh Division was aimed at Ostend. See Lloyd George's account of the operation to Frances Stevenson and to C.P. Scott. Taylor, ed., *Stevenson Diaries*, p. 4, 9 October 1914; Trevor Wilson, ed., *The Political Diaries of C.P. Scott, 1911–1928*, Ithaca, 1970, pp. 111–2, 24 November 1914.

43. BL Add MS, 62974, Riddell diaries, TS, October 1914.

44. Brocks, eds., *Stanley Letters*, p. 275, HHA to VS, 13 October 1914. Martin Gilbert prints this letter although he leaves the impression that only newspapers, mainly Tory, disapproved of the First Lord's Antwerp adventure. Gilbert, *Churchill*, III, 96–134. This dislike did not abate. Margot Asquith recorded in her diary on 7 March 1915 that her husband had told her that Churchill was 'far the most disliked man in the Cabinet.' 'He is intolerable!. . .Noisy, long-winded, full of perorations.' Quoted in: Gilbert, *Churchill*, III, 329–30.

45. Brocks, eds., *Stanley Letters*, pp. 262–3, 266–7, 5, 7 October 1914.

46. Taylor, ed., *Stevenson Diary*, pp. 19, 21, 23, 23 December 1914, 17, 21 January 1915; Wilson, ed., *Scott Diaries*, pp. 111–2, 27 November 1914. BL Add MS 62974, Riddell diaries, 5 December 1914.

47. See the account in David, ed., *Hobhouse Diaries*, pp. 206–7, 13 November 1914. Lloyd George accused the Admiralty of undermining the authority of Stanley Buckmaster who was in charge of censorship and who had refused to suppress newspaper criticisms of Churchill. Churchill denounced the Chancellor's 'insolence.' Lloyd George was perhaps the only man in the Cabinet who could hold his own in a shouting match with Churchill. It could be noted that in May 1915, when Churchill lost the Admiralty, Buckmaster became Lord Chancellor. See also Taylor, ed., *Stevenson Diary*, p. 42, 8 April 1915.

48. His letters show no trace of a sense of isolation and Violet Bonham Carter, who saw him frequently at this time states flatly that 'he had not suffered. . .in the eyes of his colleagues.' Violet Bonham Carter, *Winston Churchill, An Intimate Portrait*, New York, 1965, p. 279.

49. The Conservative leader, Andrew Bonar Law, wrote on 14 October 1914 that he thought Churchill's mind was 'unbalanced.' Robert Blake, *The Unknown Prime Minister*, London, 1955, p. 234.

50. Taylor, ed., *Stevenson Diary*, p. 44, 18 April 1915.

51. Colin Cross, ed., *Life With Lloyd George: The Diary of A.J. Sylvester, 1931–1945*, London, 1975, pp. 223–4. 10 January 1939.

52. BL Add MS 62974, Riddell diaries, 1 November, 4 December 1914.

53. Ibid., 6 December 1914.

54. Taylor, ed., *Stevenson Diary*, p. 22, 17 January 1915.

55. *The Times*, 17 December 1914.

56. *Ibid.*, 26 December 1914.

57. BL Add MS 62974, Riddell diaries, 20 December 1914.

58. Robert Blake, *Unrepentant Tory, The Life and Times of Andrew Bonar Law, 1858–1923*, New York, 1956, pp. 237–38.

59. LGP, H of L, C/4/12/8, J.A. Pease to LG, 1 January 1915.

60. *The Times*, 24 December 1914.

61. BL Add MS 62975, Riddell diaries, 14 January 1915.

62. Ibid., 17 January 1915; Taylor, ed., *Stevenson Diary*, p. 22, 17 January 1915. Years later Lloyd George would attribute the break-up of the Liberal party to Illingworth's death from eating an oyster from which the Chief Whip had caught typhoid fever. Illingworth, thought Lloyd George, could have healed the breach between himself and Asquith. Taylor, ed., *Stevenson Diary*, p. 320, 17 November 1935.

63. Brocks, eds., *Stanley Letters*, p. 393, HHA to VS, 24 January 1915.

64. BL Add MS 62975, Riddell diaries, 13 January 1915.

65. Brocks, eds., *Stanley Letters*, pp. 404–5, HHA to VS, 28 January 1915; BL Add MS 62975, Riddell diaries, 7 February 1915.

66. Ibid.

67. Ibid., 13 February 1915.

68. *H of C Deb*, LXVIII (17 November 1915), cols. 348–77.

69. LGP, H of L, C/7/2/10, Reading to LG, 24 November 1915.

70. *H of C Deb*, LXVIII (17 November 1915), cols. 372–4.

71. See the note by Richard Vassar Vassar–Smith, Chairman of Lloyds Bank, congratulating Lloyd George on the fact that part of his bank's commitment would not be needed: '...one of the greatest — if not the greatest — achievements that have ever been recorded in the financial history of the Nations.' LGP, H of L, C/11/2/74, Richard Vassar Vassar-Smith to LG, 26 November 1915.

72. LGP, H of L, C/3/14/5, 6, Austen Chamberlain to LG, 9, 18 November 1914.

73. LGP, H of L, C/6/11/22, HHA to LG, 24 November 1914.

74. Churchill had indeed proposed in Cabinet on 3 September 1914 that Britain seize the Gallipoli peninsula, before the Turks, with German help, could arm the forts. This was nearly two months before Turkey declared war. David, ed., *Hobhouse Diaries*, p. 187, 3 September 1914.

75. Lloyd George, in his *War Memoirs*, is unfair about Grey's apprehension of the Bulgarian threat by suggesting that 'a more virile and understanding treatment of the Balkan situation' could have changed the course of the war. Lloyd George, *War Memoirs*, I, 339. On 4 December Asquith told the King: 'The Serbian army is in sore straits and unless help is quickly forthcoming cannot avoid defeat. It is, therefore, of great importance that Greek troops, of which 80,000 are available, should be at once sent to its assistance. This is impossible unless the cooperation, or at least the neutrality, of Bulgaria is assured.' Asquith Papers, Vol. VII, HHA to George V, 4 December 1914. The problem was that although the Bulgarians to be sure hated the Turks, the territory they coveted was held by Serbia.

76. Samuel Roskill, *Hankey, Man of Secrets* (New York: 1970), I, 219–20.

77. Asquith Papers, Vol. VII, HHA to George V, 20 August 1914.

78. Noel Buxton had traveled extensively in the Balkans and had written on the area and so counted as something of an expert.

79. LGP, H of L, C/6/7/1a, N. Buxton to Grey, 5 October 1914. On the origins of the mission see: Ibid, C/6/7/1, N. Buxton to LG, 26 August 1914. This letter seems to contradict the assertion of the most recent scholar to write on the subject of the Buxton mission: that the mission was entirely unofficial. Christos Theodoulou, *Greece and the Entente, August 1, 1914–September 25, 1916*, Thessaloniki, 1971, p. 71.

80. See for example: LGP, H of L, C/6/7/1–10; C/6/7/3, 'Notes on the Balkan States, Jan, 1915' printed report, covering letter dated 28 January 1915; C/6/7/4, 'Notes on the Balkan States II,' covering note dated 16 February 1915.

81. Asquith Papers, Vol. VII, HHA to George V, meeting, 2 November 1914.

82. Brocks, eds., *Stanley Letters*, p. 341, HHA to VS, 27 December 1914.

83. This was the first meeting of the so-called 'War Council', a small group, which steadily grew larger, which was Asquith's way of taking the detailed discussion of military strategy from the disorderliness of the Cabinet. Part, although not all of Hankey's minutes of the first meeting of the War Council are printed in, Gilbert, *Churchill*, III, Comp. Vol. 3, Part 1, 278–80.

84. George H. Cassar, *The French and the Dardanelles, A Study of Failure in the Conduct of War*, London, 1971, pp. 35–6.

85. Lloyd George, *War Memoirs*, I, 322–30.

86. Brocks, eds., *Stanley Letters*, p. 357, 1 January 1915; Gilbert, *Churchill*, III, Comp. Vol. 3, Part 1, 347–9, 31 December 1914.

87. Gilbert, *Churchill*, III, Comp. Vol. 3, Part 1, 384–90, 391–6, 7, 8 January 1915.

88. *Ibid.*, p. 411.

89. See for example *Ibid*, 573, meeting 26 February 1915.

90. There is an oblique reference to the meeting in Frances Stevenson's diary, Taylor, ed., *Stevenson Diary*, p. 23, 21 January 1915. Hankey's diary also mentions the meeting and includes Grey. Roskill, *Hankey*, I, 154.

91. LGP, H of L, C/8/7/1, 'Greek Minister' to Venizelos, 21 January 1915.

92. For the official attitude as expressed in the Council see: Gilbert, *Churchill*, III, Comp. Vol. 3, Part 1, p. 470. Minutes of the War Council, 28 January 1915, conclusion 2.

93. Lloyd George, *War Memoirs*, I, 352; on this conversation see also: Brocks, eds., *Stanley Letters*, p. 391, HHA to VS, 22 January 1915.

94. Poincaré, *Memoirs*, pp. 179–210.

95. See Lloyd George speech, *H of C Deb*, LXIX (15 February 1915), cols. 209–18. A Russian subscription for a £10,000,000 credit had closed at noon that day. *Ibid.*, col. 916. So, with the Morgan contract a month before, began the enormous post-Armistice problem of war debts.

96. Gainford Papers, J.A. Pease diary, 10 February 1915. At least in the first year the lack of Belgian enthusiasm for the war was a major problem for the Allies. Pease referred to it several times as the big secret of the war. Their unmilitary behavior at Antwerp had angered many members of the British government, including Lloyd George.

97. Taylor, ed., *Stevenson Diary*, p. 26, 28 January 1915.

98. *Ibid.*, pp. 30–31, 32; 11, 23 February 1915.
    Murray's note said: 'My old Tory Catholic Solicitor Philip Witham is *delighted* with your achievement in Paris.
    I value his opinion as he moves in vy good business circles.' LGP, H of L, C/6/5/23A, Murray to LG, 9 February 1915, 'Tear up.'

99. BL Add MS 62975, Riddell diaries, 13 February 1915.

100. Oliver, Viscount Esher, *Journals and Letters of Reginald, Viscount Esher* (London: 1938), IV, 22, 6 May 1916.

101. LGP, H of L, C/3/6/2, Report by Francis Bertie of a conversation between Lloyd George and the President of the Republic, 3 February 1915.

102. Lloyd George, *War Memoirs*, I, 354–58. Italics in the original letter.

103. Six months later driving to Walton with Riddell, Lloyd George commented upon this untoward publicity. He remarked that the Dardanelles had become an 'obsession' with Churchill. He feared that its failure would ruin his career. Riddell recorded:

> LG says that Winston did not act straight when the operation was commenced. He suggested to the Cabinet that the attempt should be made by the Navy and that if it failed it should be treated as a mere demonstration. The Cabinet agreed on the condition that nothing be published. Winston disregarded this stipulation and made a public announcement which altered the whole situation. BL Add MS 62976, Riddell diaries, 2 October 1915.

104. PRO, Cab. 42/1/34, 'Some Further Considerations on the Conduct of the War,' 22 February 1915, 8 pp. Parts of this document are printed in Gilbert, *Churchill*, III, Comp. Vol. 3, Part 1, 544–7 and Lloyd George, *War Memoirs*, I, 566–73.

105. Lloyd George, *War Memoirs*, I, 374, 375–8.

106. LGP, H of L, C/16/1/9, 'M.P.A.H.,' 'After the Dardanelles. The Next Steps,' 1 March 1915.

107. Asquith Papers, Vol. VIII, HHA to George V, 2 March 1915.

108. Brocks, eds., *Stanley Letters*, p. 456, HHA to VC, 1 March 1915.

109. George M. Trevelyan, *Grey of Fallodon*, Boston, 1937, p. 321.

110. David, ed., *Hobhouse Diaries*, p. 226, 4 March 1915.

111. Brocks, eds., *Stanley Letters*, p. 460, HHA to VS, 6 March 1915.

112. On the Russian intervention see: Churchill, *Crisis*, II, 202–3. Lloyd George does not mention the Russian veto of Greek participation and contents himself with attacking Grey for lack of vigor in pursuing the Balkan option while being careful to disassociate himself from the Dardanelles operation. Lloyd George, *War Memoirs*, I, 338–363. This is particularly unfair in view of his proposal to Maurice Hankey, over lunch on 14 March, according to a letter from Hankey to Lord Esher, that Britain could now 'chuck Greece over and bring Bulgaria into the war' with a promise of territory. Roskill, *Hankey*, I, 168.

113. A Turkish official report, quoted in Stephen Roskill's biography of Maurice Hankey states that 'up to the 25th of February it would have been possible to effect a landing at any point on the Peninsula and the capture of the Straits would have been comparatively easy.' Roskill, *Hankey*, I, 156. Ironically the first British landings occurred precisely two months later, on 25 April.

The German commander of the Turkish forces, Liman Von Sanders, recorded in his memoirs that 'the British gave me four full weeks before their great landing' in which to prepare resistance and '...that was just sufficient time to complete the essential arrangements.' Quoted in Trevor Wilson, *The Myriad Faces of War*, Oxford, 1986, p. 132n.

Chapter 4, pp. 151–178

1. See William Maxwell Aitken, Lord Beaverbrook, *Politicians and the War, 1914–1916*, London, 1960, pp. 65–70.

2. Asquith Papers, Bodleian Library, Vol. VIII, HHA to George V, 24 February 1915. This represents the first reference to labor problems in the Cabinet letters.

3. Cameron Hazlehurst, *Politicians at War, July 1914 to May, 1915*, London, 1971, pp. 210–12. Lloyd George himself has contributed to this misunderstanding by suggesting in his memoirs that the Bangor speech was devoted to the question of temperance. David Lloyd George, *War Memoirs* (Boston: 1933), I, 284–85.

4. See: James Hinton, 'The Clyde Workers' Committee and the Dilution Struggle,' in Asa Briggs and John Saville, eds., *Essays in Labour History, 1886–1923*, Hamden, Conn., 1971, pp. 158–60.

5. *The Times*, 1 March 1915.

6. *Observer*, 7, 14 March 1915.

7. Asquith Papers, Vol. XIV, G.R. Askwith to HHA, 10 March 1915.

8. See Lloyd George's comments. *War Memoirs*, I, 262–3.

9. Charles Hobhouse recorded in his diary that Walter Runciman has told him that he had seen a printed dossier showing that the War Office had dealt with only 27 large contractors at the beginning of the conflict. By July of 1915 there were 279 and 3,000 subcontractors. Edward David, ed., *Inside Asquith's Cabinet, From the Diaries of Charles Hobhouse*, London, 1977, p. 250, 25 July 1915.

10. Asquith Papers, VIII, HHA to George V, 24, 26 February 1915. The 24 February Cabinet letter provided the first indication that weapons shortages existed. Hitherto Asquith had always reported that Lord Kitchener had assured his colleagues that supply problems were well in hand.

11. Lloyd George, *War Memoirs*, I, 258.

12. Lloyd George Papers, House of Lords, C/14/3/2, 'Minutes of a Conference held at Ten Downing Street on Friday, March 5, 1915 at 12 noon.' 'Most Secret'.

13. Lloyd George, *War Memoirs*, I, 153–58.

14. *Ibid.*, pp. 156–58.

15. LGP, H of L, C/14/3/2, 'Minutes at a Conference.'

16. Lloyd George, *War Memoirs*, I, 157.

17. George, Lord Riddell, *War Diary, 1914–1918*, London, 1933, p. 68, 13 March 1915. Sir John Simon, the Attorney General, within whose field the Bill technically belonged, had told Riddell in January that amendment of D.O.R.A. would be difficult. *Ibid.*, 54, 25 January 1915. Lloyd George boasted to Frances Stevenson that Asquith had said that if the Bill were to go through only Lloyd George could accomplish it. A.J.P. Taylor, ed., *Lloyd George, A Diary by Frances Stevenson*, London, 1971, p. 35, 25 March 1915.

18. *Official Report, House of Commons Debates*, Series Five, LXX (9 March 1915), col. 1277.

19. Gainford Papers, Nuffield College, VIII, J.A. Pease diary, 11 March 1915.

20. Asquith Papers, HHA to George V, 16 March 1915 (Meeting of 15 March). See also Edward David, ed., *Inside Asquith's Cabinet, From the Diaries of Charles Hobhouse*, London, 1977, p. 228, 16 March 1915.

21. The 'Cabinet forced me to take this job [labor negotiation] in hand. I wish I could come down instead as I need a week's rest.' Kenneth Morgan, ed., *Lloyd George Family Letters*, Cardiff, 1973, p. 176, LG to MLG, 12 March 1915.

22. The newspapers in the first weeks of March carried columns of letters with sensational stories about the evils of alcohol.

23. Michael and Eleanor Brock, eds., *H.H. Asquith, Letters to Venetia Stanley*, Oxford, 1982, p. 488, 18 March 1915.

24. Taylor, ed., *Stevenson Diary*, pp. 36, 26 March 1915.

25. *The Times*, 18 March 1915.

26. Riddell, *War Diary*, p. 69–70, 21 March 1915.

27. W.H. Beveridge, *Power and Influence*, New York, 1955, p. 123; *The Times*, 20 March 1915.

28. See: Taylor, ed., *Stevenson Diary*, p. 33, 25 March 1915; Lloyd George, *War Memoirs*, I, 258–63; José Harris, *William Beveridge, A Biography*, Oxford, 1977, p. 205.

29. *The Times*, 19 March 1915.

30. Brocks, eds., *Stanley Letters*, pp. 502, 520, HHA to VS, 23, 30 March 1915. On the 13th Riddell had recorded for the first time criticism by Lloyd George of the Prime Minister's indolence. Riddell, *War Diary*, p. 68, 13 March 1915.

31. PRO Cab/42/1/20.

32. Quoted in David French, 'The Meaning of Attrition, 1914–1916,' *English Historical Review*, CIII (April, 1988), 390–91.

33. Asquith Papers, VIII, HHA to George V, 17 February 1915.

34. *Official Report, House of Lords Debates*, XVIII (9 March 1914), cols. 614–16.

35. See the letter from Llewelyn Williams, *The Times*, 13 March 1915, and from the Bishop of St. Asaph, *The Times*, 16 March 1915.

36. See the speech of J.H. Roberts of Denbighshire West who had succeeded Brynmor Jones as Leader, *H of C Deb*, LXX (15 March 1915), col. 1801.

37. *H of C Deb*, LXX (15 March 1915), cols. 1814–19.

38. Taylor, ed., *Stevenson Diary*, p. 42, 4 April 1915.

39. Morgan, ed., *Family Letters*, p. 176, LG to MLG, 15 March, 14 April 1915.

40. *The Times*, 15 March 1915; Brocks, eds., *Stanley Letters*, p. 481, HHA to VS, 15 March 1915.

41. Gainford Papers, J.A. Pease diary, [Sunday], 20 March 1915?.

42. Taylor, ed., *Stevenson Diary*, p. 40, 4 April 1915.

43. Brocks, eds., *Stanley Letters*, p. 41, HHA to VS, 15 March 1915.

44. LGP, H of L, C/11/3/25/26, 29, Birmingham to LG, 16 March; E. Cornwall Jones to LG, 16 March; 'A Welsh Bishop' to LG, 17 March 1915.

45. Trevor Wilson, ed., *The Political Diaries of C.P. Scott, 1911–1928*, Ithaca, 1970, p. 119, Diary, 15 March 1915.

46. Riddell, *War Diary*, p. 68, 10 March 1915; LG to Robertson Nicoll, 16 March 1915, quoted in Morgan, ed., *Family Letters*, p. 176n.

47. Lloyd George connected the issues of disestablishment and drink in an open letter to the Rev. Evan Jones of Moriah Chapel, Caernarvon, with whom he had first battled over disestablishment while still a parliamentary candidate in 1890. Jones had recently denounced Lloyd George publicly, for the hundredth time, for weakness in the pursuit of the destruction of the Welsh Church. Referring to Jones' 'courageous interview' attacking himself, and after briefly defending postponement, Lloyd George invited the venerable pastor to join 'a greater task' the war on drink. *Daily Chronicle*, 25 March 1915.

48. Kitchener did not suggest, as would be charged later, that the reason for the failure of Neuve Chapelle was the lack of artillery support.

49. What employers Lloyd George had seen was not clear. The Treasury conference with the unions had ended only that day.

50. Public Record Office Cab. 22/1/20, 'Secretaries' Note of a Meeting,' M.P.A.H., 'Secret', 19 March 1915. Pub hours in those relaxed days were at the discretion of the local authority and usually generous, 6 a.m. to 9 p.m. most frequently but to 11p.m. in Liverpool and 10:30 a.m. to 10 p.m. in Manchester.

51. See the appeal of the Archbishop of Canterbury and by leaders of the four major sects in Ireland, *The Times*, 18 March 1915. All mentioned the Bangor speech and the examples of Russia and France, even of Germany. See also 'When Will the Government Act?', *Daily Chronicle*, 24 March 1915; 'Lure of Drink,' *Daily News*, 27 March 1915.

52. Cammell Laird reported that drink cost them 20 percent of their men's time and mentioned the 'truculence' of their workers and of the men's 'indifference to the welfare of the country.' Armstrong Whitworth advised total national prohibition or at least split pub hours. All reports dilated upon the surliness of the men caused by drink. LGP, H of L, C/3/2/2, 3.

53. Lloyd George, *War Memoirs*, I, 285–87; LGP, H of L, C/21/2/18, Cabinet Memorandum, 'Deputation from the Shipbuilding Employers' Federation to the Chancellor of the Exchequer,' 29 March 1915, stenographic transcript.

54. *The Times*, 31 March 1915. In his Cabinet memorandum cited above, this became the better known 'we are fighting Germany, Austria and drink' and 'the greatest of all these deadly foes is drink.'

55. LGP, H of L, C/21/2/18, Cabinet Memorandum, 29 March 1915.

56. *The Times*, 31 March 1915.

57. Gainford Papers, J.A. Pease diary, 30 March 1915.

58. Asquith Papers, Vol. VIII, HHA to George V, 30 March 1915.

59. LGP, H of L, C/5/6/12, Stamfordham to LG, 30 March 1915.

60. British Library, Add MS 62975, Riddell diaries, TS, 13 March 1915.

61. Lloyd George, *War Memoirs*, I, 287; William George, My *Brother and I*, London, 1958, p. 249.

62. LGP, H of L, C/5/6/11, LG to Stamfordham, 29 March 1915.

63. LGP, H of L, C/5/6/13, LG to Stamfordham, 30 March 1915.

64. See for example *Daily Chronicle*, 1 April 1915.

65. LGP, H of L, C/5/6/15, LG to Stamfordham, 1 April 1915.

66. *Daily Chronicle*, 2 April 1915. However Kitchener was himself active, independently of Lloyd George, in early March attempting to do something about drink. See Stanley Salvidge, *Salvidge of Liverpool*, London, 1934, pp. 137–42.

67. Arthur, Viscount Lee of Fareham, 'A Good Innings,' privately printed, 1939, Lee of Fareham Papers, House of Lords, II, 661, Ruth Lee diary, 12 July 1916.

68. *Daily Chronicle, The Times*, 31 March 1915. There were also letters of congratulation. One came immediately from St. Loe Strachey of the *Spectator*, one of Lloyd George's most implacable enemies during the Marconi episode, who, after admitting he could not drink because of gout, declared himself no teetotaler but in favor of national prohibition. LGP, H of L, C/11/3/41, Strachey to LG, 30 March 1915. In the following weeks there were more letters of encouragement from such varied sources as George Lansbury and William Jennings Bryan, the American Secretary of State.

69. PRO Cab. 37/127/23, 'Drinking in the Shipbuilding Trades,' Reginald McKenna, 'April, 1915' (printer's mark April 14). This report of twelve pages provides an untouched mine of information on the obscure and complicated union regulations and social habits that governed pre-war British shipbuilding, theoretically the most efficient in the world.

70. The report emphasized that the drinking problem was much smaller among the engineers, the other large union in the shipyards. Many of the Amalgamated Society of Engineers were teetotalers.

71. By the end of the first week of April evidence on the effect of drink requested by Lloyd George on 29 March was pouring in from arms and shipbuilding firms. For example 'a Director of Cammell Laird,' presumably G.J. Carter, reported that in March there was not a day in which fewer than 2,000 of his 11,000 men did not lose at least one quarter of the work turn and of those, between 1,000 and 1,500 were out the entire day. LGP, H of L, C/11/1/48. 'Director of Cammell Laird' to LG, 8 April 1915. An Admiralty return showed that during the month of April 35 ships sailed from Avonmouth with one or more crewmen short because of drunkenness. In addition, even when a full complement was on board, some men were too drunk to work. LGP, H of L, Admiralty return for April, 30 April 1915. A letter from Frank Beadnell, Master of the *Cymric* to Captain Hubert Stansburry, Naval Transport Officer of Southampton, 24 October 1914, complained of having to sail to Havre with 1,000 men, 600 horses and a drunken crew. This letter reached Lloyd George on 1 May 1915. LGP, H of L, C/3/16/35.

72. Riddell, *War Diary*, p. 73, 2 April 1915.

73. LGP, H of L, C/8/1/21, Scott to LG, 6 April 1915.

74. LGP, H of L, C/11/3/43, 'Breweries', Sir William Plender, 30, 31 March 1915. On the Plender Report see Lloyd George, *War Memoirs*, I, 389–91.

75. BL Add MS 62975, Riddell diaries, 10 April 1915.

76. Salvidge, *Salvidge*, p. 143.

77. *Ibid.*

78. On 15 April Lloyd George wrote to Lord Northcliffe asking for help. LGP, H of L, C/6/8/2.

79. *Daily Chronicle*, 14 April 1915, news article and leading article.

80. Plender's report had been submitted to the Cabinet and two committees had been appointed, one under Thomas McKinnon-Wood, Secretary of State for Scotland who with Lloyd George had received the shipbuilders' deputation, to compare prohibition and purchase and a second under Herbert Samuel, president of the Local Government Board, to consider the cost of purchase based on Plender's findings.

81. St. Loe Strachey Papers, House of Lords, S/9/13/3, LG to Strachey, 15 April 1916.

82. LGP, H of L, C/11/3/49, Strachey to LG, 17 April 1915.

83. Ibid., C/8/11/3, George Younger to LG, 19 April 1915.

84. Robert Blake, *Unrepentant Tory, The Life and Times of Andrew Bonar Law, 1858–1923*, New York, 1956, p. 239.

85. *Ibid.* He would discover soon that his generous accommodation would have to be modified.

86. Gainford Papers, J.A. Pease diary, 19 April 1915; see also Asquith Papers, Vol. VIII, HHA to George V, 19 April 1915.

87. Brocks, eds., *Stanley Letters*, p. 553, HHA to VS, 19 April 1915.

88. *Ibid.*

89. David, ed., *Hobhouse Diary*, pp. 238–39, 22 April 1915; Gainford Papers, J.A. Pease diary, 22 April 1915.

90. Asquith Papers, VIII, HHA to George V, 28 April 1915 (Cabinet of 26 April).

91. Riddell, *War Diary*, pp. 77–78, 18 April 1915.

92. Plender had estimated that the simple land value of the public houses alone in England, Scotland and Wales, without allowance for the capital value of an established business or of good will, was £250 million. LGP, H of L, C/11/3/43, 'Breweries,' 30, 31 March 1915.

93. See: Wilson, ed., *Scott Diaries*, p. 122, Scott to L.T. Hobhouse, 23 April 1915.

94. *H of C Deb*, LXXI (20 April 1915), cols. 864–96.

95. *Ibid.*, cols. 1912–13.

96. *Ibid.*, cols. 930–32.

97. *Parliamentary Papers*, 1914–16, Vol. LV, pp. 947–67.

98. *Daily Telegraph*, 3 May 1915.

99. For conflicting reports of this conversation, both with Lloyd George as a source, see: Brocks, eds., *Stanley Letters*, p. 582, HHA to VS, 3 May 1915; Taylor, ed., *Stevenson Diary*, p. 47, 6 May 1915.

100. *H of C Deb.*, LXXI (4 May 1915), cols. 1036–37. Lloyd George had already seen the resolution, sent to him that day by Richard Hazelton, a former Nationalist MP and temperance advocate. LGP, H of L, C/11/3/62.

101. Taylor, ed., *Stevenson Diary*, p. 48, 6 May 1915. He did not however make clear to Miss Stevenson the fact of his defeat. On the conversations with the brewers see: Asquith Papers, VIII, HHA to George V, 7 May 1915.

102. *Daily Telegraph*, 'A Futile Policy,' 7 May 1915.

103. BL Add MS 62975, Riddell diaries, 7 May 1915.

104. Harold Spender, *Fire of Life*, London, 1926, pp. 280–81.

105. Lloyd George, *War Memoirs*, I, 290.

106. *The Times*, 30 November 1973.

107. The *War Memoirs* carry the entire text of a long memorandum from Edwin Montagu, almost without explanation, attacking control of drink. Lloyd George, *War Memoirs*, I, 291–94.

108. See Thos. P. Whittaker, 'The Drink Trade and State Purchase,' *Contemporary Review*, CVIII (June 1915), 695–704. See also LGP, H of L, C/11/3/53, 71, T.P. Whittaker to LG, 21 April, 14 May 1915.

109. A national prohibition would 'lead to a universal strike' and state purchase would 'ruin our finances & create a vast engine of possible corruption' thought Asquith. Brocks, eds., *Stanley Letters*, p. 525, HHA to VS, 31 March 1915.

110. Lloyd George, *War Memoirs*, I, 296.

111. J.M. McEwen, ed., *The Riddell Diaries, 1908–1923*, London, 1986, pp. 183–4, 27 January 1917.

112. *H of C Deb* LXXI (4 May 1915), col. 1002.

113. *Ibid.*, col. 1011.

114. *Ibid.*, cols. 1024–29. This speech, made on 20 April, outraged both the opposition and the newspapers. It is discussed in the next chapter.

115. Brocks, eds., *Stanley Letters*, pp. 497–8, HHA to VS, 22 March 1915.

116. HHA to LG, 22 March 1915 in Lloyd George, *War Memoirs*, I, 161.

117. LGP, H of L, C/6/11/37, Kitchener to HHA, 25 March 1915.

118. Ibid., C/5/7/18, LG to Kitchener, 25 March 1915.

119. Ibid., C/3/16/20, Kitchener to LG, 26 March 1915.

120. Ibid., C/3/16/20, LG to WSC, 26 March 1915.

121. Ibid., C/3/3/3, A.J. Balfour to LG. 27 March 1915.

122. See Brocks, eds., *Stanley Letters*, p. 514, HHA to VS, 28 March 1915. The issues in the argument, an advisory or an executive committee, were made clear in an undated memorandum sent by Montagu to Asquith, evidently after the meeting of 28 March. Lloyd George, *War Memoirs*, I, 162–5.

123. *H of C Deb*, LXXI (15 April 1915), col. 39.

124. *Punch*, 21 April 1915. This cartoon is usually associated mistakenly with the Ministry of Munitions.

125. See *The Times*, 14 April 1915, leading article 'A Committee with Full Powers.' This was accompanied by a long news article which assumed the committee would also attack the drink problem.

126. Lloyd George, *War Memoirs*, I, 166.

127. *Ibid.*

128. LGP, H of L, C/14/2/1, 'Munitions of War Committee, Minutes of First Meeting,' 12 April 1915.

129. W.H. Beveridge, *Power and Influence*, New York, 1955, p. 124.

130. LGP, H of L, C/5/7/25, 'Statement prepared by the Master General of the ordinance for "Treasury War Munitions Committee,"' 13 April 1915.

131. LGP, H of L, C/14/2/4, 'Memorandum on the Provision of High Explosive,' Lord Moulton, 13 April 1915. In the copy of the document in the Lloyd George Papers the phrase 'No one is keeping his contract even approximately' was underlined in pencil.

132. LGP, H of L, C/5/7/25, 'Statement by the M.G.O.,' 13 April 1915.

133. Beaverbrook, *Politicians*, pp. 62–3.

134. David, ed., *Hobhouse Diaries*, pp. 235–37, 16 April 1915.

135. Brocks, eds., *Stanley Letters*, p. 544, HHA to VS, 16 April 1915. The Prime Minister avoided the matter entirely in his letter to the King.

136. Taylor, ed., *Stevenson Diary*, p. 45, 25 April 1915. This passage illustrates a general weakness of the Stevenson diary: Miss Stevenson's tendency to wait several days after a conversation with Lloyd George before recording it, thus sacrificing accuracy and detail. The Cabinet was not on Monday, as she writes, but on Thursday, and did not break up after the argument with Kitchener.

137. *H of C Deb*, LXXI (21 April 1915), cols. 311–24.

138. *Ibid.*, col. 313.

139. *Ibid.*, cols. 319–20.

140. Taylor, ed., *Stevenson Diary*, p. 45.

141. See Lloyd George, *War Memoirs*, I, 176–77.

142. LGP, H of L, C/18/6/1, C.aC. Repington to LG, 17 May 1915.

143. Lloyd George, *War Memoirs*, I, 179–81.

Chapter 5, pp. 179–207

1. 'Winston reasoned like this,' Lloyd George told George Riddell at dinner on 11 April 1915, after saying that the Gallipoli operation was not going well despite Churchill's assertions to the contrary. 'The operations of the Germans and Belgians prove the superiority of modern guns over fortifications. I have better and larger guns than the Germans. The Turkish forts are worse than the Belgian forts and the Turkish forts are manned by Turks. Therefore I must be able to demolish them. He would not take into account the different conditions. He would not give due weight to the fact that our guns are on ships necessarily operating within narrow limits and which if seriously hit are necessarily destroyed because the ship goes to the bottom. A battery of guns is not out of action when the men or the guns are hit. The earth is not like a ship.' British Library, Add. MS. 62975, Riddell diaries, TS, 11 April 1915.

2. He was aware to the day, as he made clear many times, how long he had sat in the Prime Minister's chair in the Cabinet room at No. 10.

3. That he was in town on Saturday, 15 May, was itself unusual. Evidently he was at Geoffrey Howard's wedding and was about to leave when Fisher arrived at No. 10. According to Lloyd George the Prime Minister had a queer liking for weddings and funerals and never missed one. David Lloyd George, *War Memoirs* (Boston: 1933), I, 199.

4. British casualties in the first nine months of the war, although heavy as a proportion of men engaged, were small in terms of what would come later, about 200,000, and many of these were regular troops of the B.E.F. More to the point from the civilian point of view, the submarine menace, despite the fears of the navy about its warships, had hardly touched the merchant marine. Official published figures through 24 March showed only 35 merchant ships sunk by submarines since the beginning of

the war, fewer than one per week, even though the Germans had declared unrestricted submarine warfare on 8 February. Far more, 54, had been sunk by surface raiders. *Sunday Times*, 28 March 1915. This accounts for the popular horror at the loss of the *Lusitania* on 7 May.

5. Even so loyal an Asquithian as C.P. Scott, angered at the Cabinet's failure to approve Lloyd George's national purchase scheme, could write to L.T. Hobhouse on 23 April: 'Really Asquith gets worse as he gets older and it is time he were dead and buried — politically.' Trevor Wilson, ed., *The Political Diaries of C.P. Scott, 1911–1928*, Ithaca, 1970, p. 122, 23 April 1915.

6. For many years, until the opening of the Lloyd George papers, the only copy of the 1910 coalition proposal available to the public was printed in an appendix to Sir Charles Petrie's biography of Austen Chamberlain. Lloyd George obviously believed none existed other than his own when he wrote his *War Memoirs*.

7. Lloyd George Papers, House of Lords, C/3/14/8. Notes by Austen Chamberlain of a meeting with Bonar Law and Lloyd George on 26 January 1915, dated 29 January 1915.

8. See Ian Colvin, *The Life of Lord Carson* (London: 1936), III, 45–47.

9. Michael and Eleanor Brock, eds., *H.H. Asquith, Letters to Venetia Stanley*, Oxford, 1982, p. 469, HHA to VS, 10 March 1915.

10. William Maxwell Aitken, Lord Beaverbrook, *Politicians and the War, 1914–1916*, London, 1960, pp. 13–14; Winston S. Churchill, *The World Crisis* (New York: 1924), II, 199–200.

11. *Observer*, 21 March 1915.

12. George, Lord Riddell, *War Diary, 1914–1918*, London, 1933, p. 68, 13 March 1915.

13. Brocks, eds., *Stanley Letters*, p. 495, HHA to VS, 21 March 1915.

14. *Ibid.*, p. 508, HHA to VS, 25 March 1915.

15. R.J.Q. Adams and Philip Poirier, *The Conscription Controversy in Great Britain, 1900–1918*, Columbus, Ohio, 1987, pp. 72–73.

16. *Observer*, 28 March 1915.

17. *Morning Post*, 29 March 1915.

18. *Daily Chronicle*, 29 March 1915.

19. Riddell, *War Diary*, p. 70, 20 March 1915.

20. BL Add MS 62975, Riddell diaries, 29 March 1915.

21. He charged also Alec Murray with his loss of the Admiralty. See Brocks, eds., *Stanley Letters*, p. 410, HHA to VS, 30 January 1915.

22. BL Add MS 62974, Riddell diaries, 31 October 1914. A few weeks later Riddell noted that Pamela McKenna was 'very pro-German'. Ibid., 14 November 1914.

23. Ibid., 20 November 1914.

24. Brocks, eds., *Stanley Letters*, p. 517, HHA to VS, 29 March 1915, 3pm.

25. *Ibid.*, p. 519, HHA to VS, 29 March 1915, 7pm.

26. *Daily Chronicle*, 30 March 1915.

27. Brocks, eds., *Stanley Letters*, pp. 522, 523–4, HHA to VS, 30 March 1915, 6pm; 30 March 1915, 'nearly 1am'.

28. *Daily News*, 30 March 1915.

29. BL Add MS 62975, Riddell diaries, 3 April 1915.

30. Gainford Papers, Nuffield College, MS 40, J.A. Pease diary, 3 May 1915.

31. BL Add MS 62975, Riddell diaries, 6 April 1915.

32. Part of this quotation is to be found in Riddell, *War Diary*, pp. 82–83, 29 April 1915. See also BL Add MS 62975, Riddell diaries, 29 April, 1 May 1915.

33. See Asquith's labored defense of his handling of the munitions problem in a speech at the Connaught Rooms on 2 June 1919 after the publication of John French's memoir, *1914.* J.A. Spender and Cyril S. Asquith, *The Life of Herbert Henry Asquith, Lord Oxford and Asquith* (London: 1932), II, 144–51.

34. Brocks, eds., *Stanley Letters*, p. 540, HHA to VS, 14 April 1915.

35. *Ibid.*

36. Quoted in Brocks, eds., *Stanley Letters*, p. 558.

37. *Ibid.*, Stephen Koss, *Asquith*, New York, 1976, pp. 181–82.

38. What George Sherston (Siegfried Sassoon) would observe of the troops moving up the Somme the next year, Lord Esher remarked upon in July 1915 when the shell scandal was at its peak. The British army simply was prosperous. He contrasted the British soldiers with the French. The French were 'bedraggled,' 'dirty,' with 'poor shapeless horses,' 'but dauntless.' The British looked 'so "rich": men, fine looking fellows (1/2 London), with clean well shaved faces, all in waterproof cloaks and really fine well-groomed horses. A curious contrast.' Maurice V. Brett, ed., *Journals and Letters of Reginald, Viscount Esher* (London: 1934), III, 254, 17 July 1915. The French themselves were continually amazed at the depth and richness of British logistical support. See for example: Raymond Poincaré, *The Memoirs of Raymond Poincaré, 1914*, New York, 1929, p. 199.

39. 'Mr Asquith's Omissions,' *The Times*, 22 April 1915.

40. 'The Voice from the Trenches: When are you going to make war?' *Daily Mail*, 23 April 1915.

41. Edward David, ed., *Inside Asquith's Cabinet, From the Diaries of Charles Hobhouse*, London, 1977, p. 237, 21 April 1915.

42. Riddell, *War Diary*, p. 81, 24 April 1915. The Riddell TS diaries offer no elaboration of this. Lord Esher described a version of the same plot to his diary on 19 May after dinner with Lord Kitchener although he does not make clear that Kitchener had been his informant. Oliver, Viscount Esher, *Journals and Letters of Reginald, Viscount Esher* (London: 1938), III, 240, 19 May 1915.

   For some months Riddell had been convinced that there was some sort of secret understanding between Lloyd George and Northcliffe. Lloyd George was not anxious to attack him. As early as 7 November 1914 the publisher had mused in his diary that Northcliffe had done 'a clever thing' with Lloyd George over Marconi. 'Then again I have little doubt that LG gave the "Times" the information as to the Home Rule Conference [of July 1914]. I have not forgotten the secret meeting at the Mansion House on the night of the Bankers' Dinner. My suspicions.' Lloyd George and Northcliffe had met privately in an upstairs room after the Mansion House speech on the eve of the war. BL Add MS 62974, Riddell diaries, 7 November 1914. There is no indication of any such conspiracy in the papers of either man.

43. See *Daily Chronicle*, 22 April 1915.

44. *Observer*, 9 May 1915. Early in the year Garvin had written to Lloyd George evidently to congratulate him on the Queen's Hall speech: '. . .to my mind the greatest democratic speech in wartime since Abraham Lincoln.' Then he continued 'you know very well that [party] loyalty with me is and will be unflinchingly subordinate to the winning of the war; and to the people on our side and everybody else I have never made the least concealment of my belief that the man we have always to look at at the last is you as the only leader of [popular?] genius we have. The soul of the

people wants stirring...' LGP, H of L, C/4/13/4, J.L. Garvin to LG, 3 January 1915.

45. *Daily Telegraph*, 11 May 1915. On that day the Home Office began the internment of all Germans of military age, naturalized or not, on ships and in 'concentration camps' on the Isle of Man.

46. BL Add MS 62975, Riddell diaries, 11 May 1915.

47. By way of comparison, at the end of September in 1918, in preparation for his attack on the Hindenburg Line, admittedly a larger operation although on a relatively narrow front, Douglas Haig fired one and a quarter million rounds, many of large caliber, in forty-eight hours.

48. George H. Cassar, *The Tragedy of Sir John French*, Newark, Delaware, 1985, p. 240.

49. *The Times*, 14 May 1915.

50. Lt. Col. Charles aCourt Repington, *The First World War, 1914–1918* (Boston: 1920), I, 36–37.

51. *Official Report, House of Commons Debates*, Series Five, LXXI (12 May 1915) col. 1642.

52. A.J.P. Taylor, ed., *Lloyd George, A Diary by Frances Stevenson*, London, 1971, p. 51, 18 May 1915. Taylor points out, that except for Lloyd George's own statement to Miss Stevenson there is no independent evidence that the Unionists wished Lloyd George to be Prime Minister. This is not precisely true. Lloyd George told Riddell the same and Riddell, unlike Miss Stevenson, had sources of information of his own. Riddell, *War Diary*, p. 94, 23 May 1915.

53. Stamfordham to George V, 19 May 1915, in Martin Gilbert, *Churchill*, III, Comp. Vol. (London: 1972), III, Part 2, p. 911.

54. Riddell, *War Diary*, p. 93, 23 May 1915.

55. On Sunday, J.L. Garvin added his powerful voice to the denunciation of the government.

> We must have more shells and still more shells and still more shells and shells wihout end. We must have more men and still more men until we are able to sustain the West. British armies twice or even thrice as large as now so that the enemy, pressed at many points simultaneously, and, no longer able with effect to manipulate his admirable railway facilities for the transfer of reinforcements to successive points in turn, may be the sooner shattered and routed.

Observer, 16 May 1915.

56. Taylor, ed., *Stevenson Diary*, p. 50, 15 May 1915.

57. Churchill, *World Cirisis*, II, 379–80.

58. *Ibid.*

59. Gilbert, *Churchill*, III, 441–42. Fisher to McKenna, 16 May 1915. How McKenna avoided seeing Churchill is unclear.

60. Evidently the two newspaper proprietors also had a discussion of the Repington article which had appeared the previous Friday, for Riddell recorded that evening: 'Lord Murray has been the medium of communication with Northcliffe. No doubt he is in N's pay. N told me he had found him very useful in communicating with French and Joffre and he has done similar jobs before.' BL Add MS 62975, Riddell diaries, 16 May 1915.

61. Ibid., 17 May 1915.

62. For a recent statement of the Lloyd George conspiracy thesis see: Peter Fraser, 'British War Policy and the Crisis of Liberalism,' *Journal of Modern History*, LIV (March

1982), 1–26. Fraser does not mention Asquith's fulsome letter of thanks to Lloyd George after the crisis was over.

63. LGP, H of L, C/18/6/1, CaC Repington to LG, 17 May 1915.

64. Beaverbrook, *Politicans*, pp. 160–7; Lloyd George, *War Memoirs*, I, 200–01.

65. See the covering note to Lloyd George's copy of the letter in: Lloyd George, *War Memoirs*, I, 202. The letter is in LGP, H of L, C/5/8/5, A. Bonar Law to Asquith, 17 May 1915.

66. Nothing in either account suggests that Bonar Law pressed Lloyd George to become Prime Minister as Lloyd George told Riddell in his account of the interview six days later. He had said nothing to Asquith of this proposal, he related, as he thought it might 'unnerve him.' Riddell, *War Diary*, p. 94, 23 May 1915.

67. Gilbert, *Churchill*, III, Comp. Vol. III, Part 2, 901–2, Cabinet Memorandum, H.H. Asquith, 17 May 1915; *Ibid.*, 911–14, Stamfordham to Geo. V, 19 May 1915.

68. Robert Blake, *The Unknown Prime Minister*, London, 1955, pp. 246–7.

69. David, ed., *Hobhouse Diaries*, p. 243, 17 May 1915.

70. BL Add MS 62975, Riddell diaries, 19 May 1915.

71. Ibid.

72. Asquith Papers, Bodleian Library, Vol. XIV, WSC to HHA, 17 May 1915.

73. The Liberal papers were much slower to recognize, or admit, the crisis. The next day the *Daily News* noted simply that the report of Fisher's resignation was 'not denied' and only on the 20th were there leading articles on the subject. *Daily News*, 19, 20 May 1915. Even George Riddell did not know anything unusual until 18 May. Riddell, *War Diary*, p. 88, 18 May 1915.

74. Asquith Papers, Vol. XIV, WSC to HHA, 18 May 1915. This letter is printed in Gilbert, *Churchill*, III, 450–1.

75. *Pall Mall Gazette*, 18 May 1915.

76. Maurice, Lord Hankey, *The Supreme Command, 1914–1918* (London: 1961), I, 316. See also Fisher's account of the visit: Blake, *Unknown Prime Minister*, p. 245 (misdated, 17 May).

77. BL Add MS 62975, Riddell diaries, 20 May 1915. Part of this quotation is to be found in Riddell, *War Diary*, pp. 89–90. See also Churchill's statement to J.A. Pease saying that Lloyd George had wrecked the Liberal government in order to obtain the War Office. Gainford Papers, Nuffield College, MS 40, J.A. Pease diary, n. d. [June].

78. Koss, *Asquith*, p. 187.

79. See the excellent history of the background of the crisis by Garvin: *Pall Mall Gazette*, 18, 19 May 1915.

80. *Daily News*, 19 May 1915.

81. Public Record Office, Northern Ireland, D. 1507/C/1, Carson Papers, Ruby Carson diary, 17, 18, 20 May 1915.

82. Churchill, *World Crisis*, II, 381.

83. Ruby Carson understood that the 'Rads', for whom one may read the Nationalists and their Liberal sympathizers, would not have him as Lord Chancellor. PRONI D. 1507/C/1, Ruby Carson diary, 21 May 1915.

84. LGP, H of L, D/18/6/1, 2, Repington to LG, 17, 20 May 1915.

85. Taylor, ed., *Stevenson Diary*, p. 51, 18 May 1915.

86. Riddell, *War Diary*, p. 89, 17 May 1915.

87. LGP, H of L, D/18/6/2, Repington to LG, 20 May 1915.

88. Asquith Papers, Vol. XIV, LG to HHA, 19 May 1915. This letter is printed in Lloyd George, *War Memoirs*, I, 179–81, without an indication of the political climate in which it was written.

89. Riddell, *War Diary*, p. 87, 17 May 1915.

90. Taylor, ed., *Stevenson Diary*, p. 53, 24 May 1915.

91. *The Times*, 18 May 1915.

92. *The Times*, *Daily Mail*, 21 May 1915.

93. *The Times*, 21 May 1915.

94. Kenneth Morgan, ed., *Lloyd George Family Letters*, Cardiff, 1973, p. 177, LG to MLG, 20 May 1915.

95. Riddell, *War Diary*, pp. 90–1, 20, 21 May 1915.

96. Taylor, ed., *Stevenson Diary*, p. 53, 24 May 1915. It is difficult to imagine Lord Cunliffe in tears.

97. *Ibid.*

98. Blake, *Unknown Prime Minister*, pp. 248–52.

99. Morgan, ed., *Family Letters*, p. 176, LG to MLG, 24 May 1915.

100. Asquith Papers, Vol. XIV, John Bradbury to HHA, 20 May 1915, 'Personal.'

101. David, ed., *Hobhouse Diaries*, p. 246, 23 May 1915.

102. Morgan Grenfell to Morgan, New York, 19 February, 1915, *United States Senate Documents*, 74th Congress, Second Session, 1936, 'Special Committee on the Investigation of the Munitions Industry,' III, 169, Document No. 68. See also: Charles Hobhouse, 'The Financial Situation,' *Contemporary Review*, CVIII (August 1915), 137–45. This does not mention Lloyd George, but represents an informed and critical analysis of Britain's growing financial desperation by a man who, to be sure, had an interest. City liquidity was about gone. Foreign borrowing was the only answer.

103. It may be of interest that once Lloyd George left the Treasury he reversed all his thinking about broadening the base of taxation. In the Cabinet in the middle of September, Asquith reported, he 'raised the question of exacting a much larger contribution from the working class.' Asquith Papers, Vol. 8, HHA to Geo V, 16 September (Cabinets 14, 16 September) 1915. The next month he wrote to Sir Leo Chiozza Money, one of the economic experts in the House of Commons, asking him to work out the figures for a national income levy of 50%, one half in tax, one half in a compulsory loan to be assessed against all but the poorest, those with 20 or 25 shillings a week. He had already proposed it to the Cabinet where it had 'received a considerable measure of acceptance.' LGP, H of L, D/3/2/14, LG to Chiozza Money, 27 October 1915.

104. LGP, H of L, D/12/11/11, Morgan Grenfell (no name) to LG, 14 August 1915. Why this letter came to Lloyd George and not McKenna is unclear.

105. 'J.P. Morgan and Co., Principal Sources of Dollar Income of the British Treasury, Quarterly, 1915 to 1921 Inclusive,' British Government Treasury Accounts. *United States Senate Documents*, 1936, 'Investigation of the Munitions Industry,' IV, 154.

106. Taylor, ed., *Stevenson Diary*, p. 54, 24 May 1915.

107. This may be the reason that Churchill did not receive the Colonies which Lloyd George had suggested for him.

108. It appears in full in Blake, *Unknown Prime Minister*, p. 251.

109. *Ibid.*, p. 250–1. For the original printing of the Asquith memorandum see Spender and Asquith, *Asquith*, II, 171. Lloyd George's account of what he had said to

Bonar Law, but not what it meant, appears in the clearest possible terms in Morgan, *Family Letters*, p. 178, LG to MLG, 25 May 1915.

110. BL Add MS 62975, Riddell diaries, 22 May 1915.

111. E.M. Horsley, ed., *Lady Cynthia Asquith, Diaries, 1915–1918*, New York, 1969, p. 25, 21 May 1915.

112. *Ibid.*, p. 28, 22 May 1915.

113. Riddell, *War Diary*, p. 96, 25 May 1915. Lloyd George himself had not mentioned seeing Northcliffe.

114. *Ibid.*, p. 25, 21, 22 May 1915.

115. BL Add MS 62975, Riddell diaries, 23 May 1915.

116. LGP, H of L, C/11/3/80, St. L. Strachey to LG, 21 May 1915 suggesting that the government revive the old post of Commander in Chief for Kitchener.

117. BL Add MS 62975, Riddell diaries, 23 May 1915. Part of this quotation appears in: Riddell, *War Diary*, pp. 93–4, 23 May 1915. The fiction of Lloyd George's remaining at the Treasury was not composed until the following day, although it is hard to believe the Chancellor had not thought of it by Sunday.

118. LGP, H of L, D/18/2/1, IIIA to LG, 25 May 1915. This letter also appears in full in Morgan, ed., *Family Letters*, pp. 178–9.

119. David, ed., *Hobhouse Diaries*, p. 247, 17 June 1915.

120. BL Add MS 62975, Riddell diaries, 26 May 1915. There were others, good Liberals, who felt Northcliffe was justified. See F.E. Guest's letter to Rufus, Lord Reading. The shell shortage was real. India Office Library, Reading Papers, Eur F/18/27, Guest to Reading, 24 May 1915.

121. BL Add MS 62975, Riddell diaries, 26 May 1915. Two days later Churchill's cousin and friend, F.E. Guest, had written to Lord Reading to say that Lloyd George was doing everything he could to obtain a better place for Churchill and had gone to him to tell him so. He was unable to see Churchill but had talked to his long-time personal secretary Edward Marsh. Marsh agreed that if Churchill knew this 'it would make all the difference in his feelings toward LG.' Evidently Marsh did not tell him. Reading papers, Eur. F. 118/27, Guest to Reading, 28 May 1915, '26 Park Lane'.

Chapter 6, pp. 209–250

1. Charles Seymour, ed., *The Intimate Papers of Colonel House*, London, 1926, p. 468. House found Lloyd George 'an American type politician.'

2. Lloyd George Papers, House of Lords, C/7/5/21, 22, H. Ll. Smith to LG, 21, 22 May 1915.

3. Christopher Addison, *Politics From Within, 1911–1918* (London: 1924), I, 64.

4. Lawrence R. Buchanan, 'The Governmental Career of Eric Campbell Geddes,' unp. Ph.D. dissertation, University of Virginia, 1979.

5. Addison, *Politics*, pp. 65–67. Geddes, like many others, found Lloyd George difficult to serve. To protect himself he developed what came to be called his 'Charter Book' in which he wrote down all of Lloyd George's instructions and which he required the minister, to his fury, to sign. No one but Geddes, recalled George Booth, had the courage to do such a thing. Duncan Crow, *A Man of Push and Go, The Life of George Macaulay Booth*, London, 1965, pp. 117, 125.

6. LGP, H of L, D/1/2/13, 14, 16, 17, 18. A file of correspondence between Lloyd George and Girouard, 22 June–24 July 1915.

7. Christopher Addison, *Four and a Half Years* (London: 1934), I, 108, diary, 22 July 1915.

8. *Official Report, House of Commons Debates*, Series Five, LXXII (23 June 1915), col. 1188.

9. LGP, H of L, D/18/2/4, M. Bonham Carter to LG, 3 August 1915.

10. David Lloyd George, *War Memoirs* (Boston: 1933), I, 220.

11. Crow, *Booth*, p. 116.

12. R.J.Q. Adams, *Arms and the Wizard, Lloyd George and the Ministry of Munitions, 1915–1916*, College Station, Texas, 1978, pp. 45–6. See also: 'History of the Ministry of Munitions,' Vol. II, Part I, Appendix II, 'Departmental Organization on 1 July 1915. Lloyd George states in his *War Memoirs*, I, 231, that this history was composed long after he left the government, but these unpublished pamphlets covering the early period of the ministry carry the date 1921, and W.H. Beveridge states in his memoirs that the first draft of the history was before him for comment in February 1919. W.H. Beveridge, *Power and Influence*, New York, 1955, p. 131n. Indeed the history was first projected by Christopher Addison in 1916. He appointed W.G.S. Adams to begin it. Addison, *Four and a Half Years*, I, 237, 4 August 1916.

13. See for example: LGP, H of L, C/1/2/9, E.C. Grenfell to LG, 8 March 1915.

14. LGP, H of L, D/12/1/1, 2, LG to D.A. Thomas, 8 June, Thomas to LG, 12 June 1915. Thomas's daughter's memoir records that he met Lloyd George in the street in Cardiff and was asked to undertake his mission at that time. The meeting may well have occurred, Lloyd George was in Cardiff on 11 June, but Thomas already had been asked. Viscountess Rhondda, *D.A. Thomas, Viscount Rhondda*, London, 1921, p. 201.

15. 'History of the Ministry of Munitions,' Vol. II, General Organization for Munitions Supply, Part 3, 'Munitions Organization in the United States of America,' 1921, p. 43–44.

16. See for example: Addison Papers, Bodleian Library, Box 15, Addison to LG, 18 June 1915.

17. 'History of the M of M,' Vol. II, Part 3, p. 10.

18. *H of C Deb*, LXXII (23 June 1915), col. 1204.

19. 'History of the M of M,' Vol. II, Part 3, p. 8.

20. LGP, H of L, D/12/2/22, 'Report of Mr. D.A. Thomas to the Minister of Munitions on his mission to Canada and the United States,' 9 December 1915, 'Confidential,' p. 4. This may not have been so generous as it seemed. Morgan's profit from the British connection came not so much from the Export Department as from its participation in the vast syndicated loans it organized and from the interest on the huge overdraft it was carrying. Nonetheless by April 1917, when the United States government took over purchasing, the Treasury had paid Morgan's, for its services alone, £4,000,000. 'History of the M of M,' Vol. II, Part 3, p. 12. Renegotiation of the contract was referred to the Cabinet in November but Asquith postponed discussion and finally let the matter drop. Ibid.

21. Thomas Report, p. 4. Lloyd George had already come to the same conclusion about British contractors.

22. Thomas Report, pp. 7–8.
Even though much effort was made to keep the Moir Organization inconspicuous it evidently caused some unhappiness at Morgan's particularly as Moir began to purchase also. See J.D. Forbes, *Stettinius Sr., Portrait of a Morgan Partner*, Charlottesville, Virginia, 1974, p. 59. In early March 1916 J.P. Morgan and Stettinius appeared in London and offered to give up their contract. Cecil Spring-Rice, the British Ambassador in Washington, had written in January that Morgan's were 'absolutely vital. We can't get along without them.' LGP, H of L, D/12/1/23, Spring-Rice to E. Grey, 28 January

1916. While Spring-Rice was barely taken seriously in London by this time, his advice on this occasion appears to have been heeded. Morgan was quickly reassured, evidently with many expressions of good will. 'History of the M of M,' Vol. II, Part 3, pp. 46–7.

23. LGP, H of L, D/17/11/6, covering letter Long to LG, 23 September 1915.

24. Ibid., D/17/11/7, LG to Long, 24 September 1915.

25. Thomas Report, p. 10. The history of the Ministry of Munitions noted wryly that these generous terms made it possible for Canadian firms to buy arms in the United States and resell them to the British. 'History of the M of M,' Vol. II, Part 3, pp. 49–50.

26. *H of C Deb*, LXXII (7 June 1915), col. 113.

27. 'History of the M of M, Vol. II, General Organization for Munitions Supply, Part I, Administration and Policy Organization,' 1921, p. 191.

28. Lloyd George, *War Memoirs*, I, 231.

29. LGP, H of L, D/17/6/5, 'H. Ll. S. to War Office,' 5 June 1915.

30. Lloyd George, *War Memoirs*, II, 18.

31. See the remark of Christopher Addison, himself later Minister of Munitions, and, by the time he wrote his memoirs, no friend of Lloyd George. Addison, *Politics*, I, 92.

32. The Army Council attempted to hold on to a remnant of the munitions procurement by the establishment of a testing facility at the School of Musketry at Hythe. Lloyd George quickly stifled this symbolic challenge to his authority with a War Committee memorandum of 3 February 1916 which laid down the rule that weapons testing would by conducted by his ministry, with army participation, and that there would be no appeal of decisions thus arrived at to some higher authority within the army itself. Lloyd George, *War Memoirs*, II, 94–5.

33. Edward David, ed., *Inside Asquith's Cabinet, From the Diaries of Charles Hobhouse*, London, 1977, p. 250, 25 July 1915. Hobhouse heard this from Walter Runciman who had dined with Kitchener and had seen the official file on subcontracting.

34. *The Times*, 4, 5, 12, 14 June 1915.

35. *Ibid.*, 12 June 1915.

36. Lloyd George, *War Memoirs*, I, 137–8.

37. *Ibid.*, p. 138.

38. *H of C Deb*, LXXII (23 June 1915), col. 1188.

39. *Ibid.*, col. 1189.

40. David Daiches, *Scotch Whisky*, London, 1969, p. 90.

41. See Lloyd George's description of the ministry's structure in his account of the first six months of its work to the House of Commons. *H of C Deb*, LXXVII (20 December 1915), cols. 106–10.

42. 'History of the M of M,' Vol. II, Part 2, p. 20.

43. David Hubback, *No Ordinary Press Baron, A Life of Walter Layton*, London, 1985, p. 36.

44. Lloyd George, *War Memoirs*, II, 32–8.

45. LGP, H of L, D/10/2/2, Moulton to LG, 16 June 1915. See also: Lloyd George, *War Memoirs*, II, 42–44.

46. Lloyd George notes in his *War Memoirs* the only useful consequence of the Battle of Loos, in late September, was the transfer of Woolwich to the ministry. This is incorrect. Woolwich was transferred in August. The only useful consequence of the

Battle of Loos was the teaching of some British politicians that the war would not be over in three months, and the dismissal of Field Marshal French.

Christopher Addison records in his memoirs that in July 1915 British shell production had just reached 150,000 rounds per week. The best intelligence information available reported that German and Austrian production at that time amounted to 250,000 rounds per day. Addison, *Politics*, I, 94.

47. About half the letters were from Catherine Marshall, the handsome former secretary of the Women's Social and Political Union, whom Lloyd George had known for years, and who now was secretary of the 'Women's War Interests Committee'. LGP, H of L, D/11/2/1–28.

48. See Lloyd George's proud account of his work in his foreword to a survey of wartime welfare activities published by the London School of Economics after he became Secretary of State for War. 'These lessons,' he concluded, 'must not be allowed to slip away.' Dorthea Proud, *Welfare Work*, London, 1916. *The Times*, 1 August 1916. See also his statement in his *War Memoirs*, I, 301–08. In his farewell speech on 1 August, Lloyd George suggested that the history of the ministry be entitled 'Advancement, Social Welfare, New Ideas, Improved Conditions of the Workers, New Discoveries.' Addison, *Four and a Half Years*, I, 247.

49. In May 1916 Addison recorded in his diary that at the Battle of Loos at the end of September 1915 the British fired off 600,000 rounds of ammunition which had been accumulated by three months hard saving. 'Last week' alone (i.e. May, 1916), he continued, the Ministry of Munitions had delivered 690,000 rounds. 'They have more than 5,000,000 in stock in France and have notified us that all of their depots are full.' Addison, *Four and a Half Years*, I, 209, 15 May 1916. 'We might be alive to the fact that our political future might be buried under an accumulation of unused 18 pdr. shells,' he wrote to Lloyd George on 20 April 1916. Addison Papers, Box 59, Addison to LG.

50. Lloyd George in his *War Memoirs*, II, 35, refers to this first offer as coming from Leeds, but other evidence indicates that Leicester is the proper location. See George M. Booth to Lloyd George, 8 April 1915, quoted in Adams, *Arms*, p. 59.

51. Crow, *Booth*, p. 111.

52. See Lloyd George, *War Memoirs*, II, 34. Steel helmets, one of the earliest innovations of the ministry, were first issued in October 1915.

53. Addison, *Politics*, I, 74; Lloyd George, *War Memoirs*, I, 200.

54. LGP, H of L, D/17/6/2, K to LG, 26 May 1915.

55. Ibid.

56. British Library, Add MS 62976, Riddell diaries, TS, 26 June 1915. Three days later he told Reginald Brade, Permanent Secretary at the War Office, of the feeling against Von Donop. Brade said he would tell Kitchener, but nothing happened.

57. Ibid., Riddell diaries, 2, 3, 4 July 1915. Parts of this quotation are printed in Riddell, *War Diary*, pp. 108–9. Italics in original document.

58. Ibid., 20 August 1915. One would like to have known Pamela McKenna. Only two months earlier, on 5 June, Cynthia Asquith noted in her diary that Reginald McKenna had thrown from his house, having found him holding hands with Pamela, unbelievably, J.A. Pease. E.M. Horsley, ed., *Lady Cynthia Asquith, Diaries, 1915–1918*, New York, 1969, p. 38, 5 June 1915.

59. LGP, H of L, D/19/6/1, Thomas to LG, 30 May 1915.

60. Bertus Willam Schaper, *Albert Thomas, trente ans de reformisme social*, Assen, Netherlands, 1959, p. 110. Unfortunately in this book most of the information about Thomas's

contact with Lloyd George comes from the Lloyd George Papers. Thomas's own papers are in Geneva and cover his work at the International Labor Office.

61. LGP, H of L, D/19/6/4, Thomas to LG, 1 September 1915.

62. Lloyd George, *War Memoirs*, II, 21.

63. LGP, H of L, D/23/1/7, 'Supply of Heavy Guns to the Army, Memorandum by the Secretary of State' 6 October 1915, 'Secret,' Appendix C, 'Meeting of Ministers of Munitions at Boulogne, June 19th and 20th' John Philip DuCane, p. 5.

64. 'History of the M of M, Vol. II, General Organization for Munitions Supply, Part I, Administrative Policy and Organization,' n.d. [after 31 May 1921], p. 21.

65. Kitchener memorandum, Appendix C, DuCane Notes, p. 6.

66. 'History of the M of M,' Vol. II, Part I, p. 21.

67. Kitchener memorandum, Appendix C, DuCane Notes, p. 6

68. Lloyd George, *War Memoirs*, I, 22.

69. Kitchener memorandum, Appendix C, DuCane Notes, p. 6.

70. Ibid.

71. Lloyd George, *War Memoirs*, II, 24.

72. LGP, H of L, D/17/6/14, French to War Office, 25 June 1915.

73. Those attending besides Kitchener were Asquith, Balfour and Lord Crewe.

74. LGP, H of L, D/22/4, Papers of the Committee of Imperial Defence 'Statement made by Mr. Lloyd George at a Meeting of the War Policy Cabinet Committee,' 16 August 1915, 'Secret,' 8pp. That evening he wrote to his wife: 'Just been giving an a/c of Munitions to a Cabinet Committee. They were appalled at the War Office delay.' Kenneth Morgan, ed., *Lloyd George Family Letters*, Cardiff, 1973, p. 179, LG to MLG, 16 August 1915.

75. *H of C Deb*, LXXVII, (20 December 1915), cols. 96–7.

76. See Adams, *Arms*, p. 166.

77. LGP, H of L, D/3/3/20, 'Cabinet Committee Meeting, Mr. Lloyd George's Evidence,' 18 August 1915, 'Secret' TS. A part of this quotation appears in Lloyd George, *War Memoirs*, II, 166.

78. He had referred to it even at the Eisteddfod at Bangor on the day Warsaw fell. See his warning to the Trades Union Congress at Bristol on 9 September. Russia was in danger. Only Britain could help her. *The Times*, 10 September 1915.

79. See Adams, *Arms*, p. 167.

80. Lloyd George, *War Memoirs*, II, 165.

81. Lloyd George states in his *War Memoirs* that Britain at the end of the war had 89 divisions in all theaters, admitting however that this included Dominion (and no doubt also Indian) divisions. Lloyd George, *War Memoirs*, II, 166n. What he does not say is that all of these were seriously under strength. Nor does he mention that in January 1918 he had imposed a nine battalion division on the British army based precisely upon the tactical doctrine discussed here: that the new machines of war so enhanced firepower that men could be removed without loss of battlefield potential.

82. *The Times*, 13 September 1915.

83. A.J.P. Taylor, ed., *Lloyd George, A Diary by Frances Stevenson*, London, 1971, p. 59, 13 September 1915.

84. Riddell, *War Diary*, p. 129, 13 September 1915.

85. *The Times*, 20 September 1915.

86. Lloyd George, *War Memoirs*, II, 25–31.

87. *Ibid.*, 26.

88. LGP, H of L, D/23/1/7 'Supply of Heavy Guns to the Army'.

89. See, among many examples, Lloyd George's attack upon McKenna, recorded by Frances Stevenson, over the latter's complaints about the cost of big guns. Taylor, ed., *Stevenson Diary*, p. 63, diary, 5 October 1915.

90. Lloyd George, *War Memoirs*, II, 28.

91. Again and again decades later, Lloyd George would recall the abuse he suffered at the Ministry of Munitions from the Cabinet radicals as the worst time of his life. See for example Colin Cross, ed., *Life with Lloyd George: The Diary of A.J. Sylvester, 1931–1945*, London, 1975, pp. 59, 167, 202, 19 November 1931; 6 January 1937; 13 March 1938; Lloyd George, *War Memoirs*, II, 185, 187.

92. Addison, *Four and a Half Years*, I, 264–65, 22 November 1916.

93. Lloyd George, *War Memoirs*, II, 62–68.

94. B.I. Gudmondsson, *Storm Troop Tactics*, New York, 1989, p. 93 and n.

95. For a recent discussion see: Timothy H.E Travers, *The Killing Ground: The British Army, The Western Front and the Emergence of Modern Warfare, 1900–18*, London, 1987, pp. 62–71.

96. D.A. Thomas Report, p. 9.

97. Lloyd George acknowledged this in his long account of the work of the Ministry of Munitions to the House of Commons in December 1915. Asquith assented audibly. *H of C Deb*, LXXVII (20 December 1915), col. 111.

98. Lloyd George, *War Memoirs*, II, 67.

99. Crow, *Booth*, pp. 128–9.

100. Public Record Office, Cab 22/3/5, 'Memorandum by Mr. Lloyd George on Machine Guns Read at the Meeting of the War Committee, 13th November 1915,' TS. Part of this memorandum appears in Lloyd George, *War Memoirs*, II, 72–3.

101. Lloyd George, *War Memoirs*, II, 48. Lee states in his memoirs that Philipps had been fired from the ministry. Lee of Fareham Papers, House of Lords Record Office, Arthur, Viscount Lee of Fareham, 'A Good Innings' (privately printed, 1939), II, 621.

102. Robert Blake, ed., *The Private Papers of Douglas Haig, 1914–1919*, London, 1952, p. 100, 1 August 1915.

103. See for example at Manchester on 3 June, *The Times*, 4 June 1915.

104. Stephen Koss, *The Rise and Fall of the Political Press in Britain* (London: 1984), II, 275–6.

105. Balfour described it in the Cabinet as a measure 'for guiding voluntary enlistment.' Asquith papers, Bodleian Library, Vol. 8, HHA to Geo. V, 24 June (Cabinet 23 June) 1915.
    There is much evidence that recruiting officers simply ignored the starring exemption and continued to press skilled workers to enlist until the advent of conscription. The strongest argument was that if a man did not enlist immediately, when conscription came he would be sent straight to the front. LGP, H of L, D/11/3/5, file of letters forwarded to S.G. Tallent by LG, 10 December 1915.

106. *The Times*, 4 June 1915.

107. *Ibid.*

108. See Addison Papers, Box 70; C.J. Wrigley, *David Lloyd George and the British Labour Movement*, Hassocks, 1976, pp. 118–20.

109. LGP, H of L, D/2/4/4, 'Min of Mun Memo No. 4' 'Supply of Rifles and Recruiting' C. Addison, 31 May 1915.

110. Trevor Wilson, ed., *The Political Diaries of C.P. Scott. 1911–1928*, Ithaca, pp. 127–8, diary 16 June 1915.

111. *H of C Deb*, LXXII (23 June 1915), col. 1201.

112. *Official Report, House of Lords Debates*, XIX (2 July 1915), col. 213.

113. Addison, *Four and a Half Years*, p. 103, 6 July 1915.

114. LGP, H of L, D/11/3/2, J.T. Davies to LG, 26 July 1915.

115. Addison, *Politics*, I, 178–9.

116. LGP, H of L, C/14/2/13, 6 May 1915, MC-13, 'The Effect of Recruiting on the Supply of Armament Labour,' H.Ll.Sm.

117. J.M. McEwen, ed., *The Riddell Diaries, 1908–1923*, London, 1986, p. 129, 12, 14 August 1915.

118. Quoted in Adams, *Arms*, p. 97.

119. For a discussion see: *Ibid.*, pp. 96–8.

120. *H of C Deb*, LXXII (23 June 1915), cols.

121. *H of L Deb*, Vol. XIX (2 July 1915), col. 206.

122. Beveridge, *Power and Influence*, p. 131. Section 7, as it became, was repealed by an amendment bill of the Lloyd George government in August 1917 during labor's summer of discontent.

123. *H of C Deb*, LXXII (28 June 1915), cols. 1553–63.

124. Despite his general sympathy for the miners Lloyd George had declared in 1912 that the concession of a minimum wage would destroy the Liberal party. George, Lord Riddell, *More Pages From My Diary*, London, 1934, p. 42, 2 March 1912.

125. The best accounts of the unbelievable complications of the South Wales coal dispute are to be found in George, Lord Askwith, *Industrial Problems and Disputes*, London, 1920, pp. 390–5 and 'History of the Ministry of Munitions, Vol IV, The Supply and Control of Labour, Part 2, Labour Regulation and the Munitions of War (Amendment) Act, 1916,' pp. 5–9.

126. Askwith, *Industrial Problems*, p. 393.

127. 'History of the M of M, Vol. IV, Part 2,' p. 8.

128. Asquith papers, Vol. 8, HHA to Geo V, 19 July 1915.

129. LGP, H of L, D/18/7/2, 3, Riddell to LG, 19, 20 July 1915.

130. Riddell, *War Diary*, pp. 114, 18, 21 July 1915.

131. Asquith papers, Vol. 8, HHA to Geo V, 24 July 1915.

132. Askwith, *Industrial Problems*, p. 395. Like a number of other memoir writers cited here Askwith detested Lloyd George by the time he composed his recollections.

133. See Addison, *Politics*, I, 185–7.

134. See for example Isaac Mitchell to the Ministry of Munitions, 21 February 1916, quoted in Wrigley, *Lloyd George and Labour*, p. 161.

135. See Vickers' account of itself. J.D. Scott, *Vickers, A History*, London, 1962, p. 99.

136. Wrigley, *Lloyd George and Labour*, p. 136.

137. *The Times*, 10 September 1915. See Lloyd George's own comments on his speech, Lloyd George, *War Memoirs*, I, 271–3.

138. *The Times*, 13 September 1915.

139. *H of C Deb*, LXXVII (20 December 1915), col. 123, speech by J.H. Thomas.

140. See Addison Papers, Box 70, transcript of A.S.E. delegation to Lloyd George, TS, 32pp, 17 September 1915. See also Addison, *Politics*, I, 180–4.

141. *The Times*, 18 September 1915.

142. Addison Papers, Box 70, transcript of meeting, 17 September 1915. 'History of the M of M,' Vol. IV, 'The Supply and Control of Labour,' Part 4, 'The Progress of Dilution,' pp. 98–9.

143. This account of Lang's attempt at dilution is taken largely from 'History of the M of M,' Vol. IV, Part 4, 98–101.

144. James Hinton, 'The Clyde Workers' Committee and the Dilution Struggle' in Asa Briggs and John Saville, eds., *Essays in Labour History, 1886–1923*, Hamden, Conn., 1971, pp. 161–2.

145. 'History of the M of M,' Vol. IV, Part 4, p. 101.

146. LGP, H of L, D/3/2/23, LG to Walter Layton, 29 November 1915.

147. See 'History of the M of M,' Vol. IV, Part 4, p. 101.

148. Taylor, ed., *Stevenson Diary*, p. 87, 29 December 1915. The troubles on the Clyde were probably the cause of the formation of an intelligence service within the Ministry of Munitions, which evolved finally into the short-lived Directorate of Intelligence when Lloyd George was Prime Minister.

149. *Forward*, 1 January 1916, quoted in 'History of M of M,' Vol. IV, Part 4, p. 102.

150. *Ibid.*, p. 102.

151. *Ibid.*

152. *Ibid.*, pp. 103–4. Lloyd George does not mention this meeting in his *War Memoirs*.

153. Lloyd George, *War Memoirs*, I, 276.

154. For example James Hinton's excellent 'The Clyde Workers' Committee and the Dilution Struggle' in Briggs and Saville, eds., *Essays in Labour History*, pp. 152–184 leaves one with the impression that the Minister of Munitions was moved by some hatred of the Clyde Workers' Committee while scarcely mentioning the visit to Glasgow.

155. Appendix XIX, 'History of the M of M,' Vol. IV, Part 4.

156. Taylor, ed., *Stevenson Diary*, p. 87, 29 December 1915; Lloyd George, *War Memoirs*, I, 277.

157. 'History of the M of M,' Vol. IV, Part 4, pp. 111–12.

158. LG to Layton, 29 December 1915, quoted in José Harris, *William Beveridge, A Biography*, Oxford, 1977, p. 214.

159. Taylor, ed., *Stevenson Diary*, p. 88, 21 January 1916. This is one of the more obvious examples of Lloyd George's tendency to be less than liberal with the truth when reporting his accomplishments to Miss Stevenson and indicates the care with which her diary must be used.

160. Beveridge, *Power and Influence*, p. 133. Lloyd George says nothing about the matter in his memoirs.

161. *H of C Deb*, LXXVII (4 January 1916), cols 801–04.

162. *Ibid.* (10 January 1916), cols 1402–15.

163. Beveridge, *Power and Influence*, p. 133.

164. See Addison's frantic telegrams to Lloyd George in Paris at the end of March. Addison Papers, Box 59, Addison to LG, LG to Addison, 28 March 1916.

165. 'History of the M of M,' Vol. IV, Part 4, p. 135.

166. *The Times*, 14 July 1916.

Chapter 7, pp. 251–286

1. Robert Blake, *Unrepentant Tory, The Life and Times of Andrew Bonar Law, 1858–1923*, New York, 1956, p. 297.

2. Very early in his work at munitions Lloyd George had subscribed to a clipping service, Durrant's Press Cuttings. These files show that by November, when he was under public attack, he was busily planting articles in newspapers: 'The Birth of Big Guns', *Standard*, 11 November, 'Prodigy of Organization', *Ibid.*, 12 November, 'The Energy of Mr. Lloyd George', *Evening News*, 15 November 1915. All of these are soft news, not connected with any events. Sometimes the same story, line for line, but over different by-lines, appeared on the same day in competing newspapers. For example 'Munitions Making, Progress in the North, Delivering the Goods' by W.T. Massey in the *Daily Telegraph* on 15 November and 'The Making of Munitions, Supply Problem Nearly Solved' by 'Our Special Correspondent' in the *Morning Post* on the same date, are identical, word for word. Lloyd George Papers, House of Lords, D/5/2/14.

3. Frances L. Stevenson, *The Years That Are Past*, London, 1967, pp. 80, 83.

4. Oliver, Viscount Esher, ed., *Journals and Letters of Reginald, Viscount Esher* (London: 1938), III, 247, Esher to M.V. Brett, 6 June 1915.

5. *Ibid.*, 248, 11 June 1915.

6. British Library, Add MS 62976, Riddell diaries, 11 June 1915. Evidently Northcliffe also had placed a man in the Treasury, a journalist, Headley LeBas, whom he had recommended to McKenna to handle publicity for the first public war loan. British Library, Add MS 62157, Northcliffe Papers, McKenna to Northcliffe, 25 June 1915.

7. BL Add MS 62976, Riddell diaries, 5 June 1915. A part of this conversation appears in George, Lord Riddell, *War Diary*, London, 1933, p. 99, 5 June 1915.

8. BL Add MS 62976, Riddell diaries, 5 June 1915.

9. Ibid., 6 June 1915.

10. Ibid. More than occasionally Lloyd George was less than frank even with Riddell. The War Council (now the Dardanelles Committee) minutes show that Lloyd George attended no meetings after his appointment as Minister of Munitions until 17 June 1915.

11. Northcliffe could not refrain from broadcasting whom he had seen and what he knew. Esher's already cited letter to his son, it should be remarked, had been written on the same Sunday, 6 June.

12. BL Add MS 62976, Riddell diaries, 9, 10 June 1915.

13. *British Weekly*, 10 June 1915. Evidently Robert Donald, editor of the *Chronicle*, was also present at Lloyd George's interview with Nicoll, and came away with the impression that the minister had literally dictated the *British Weekly* article. See his comments: Edward David, ed., *Inside Asquith's Cabinet, From the Diaries of Charles Hobhouse*, London, 1977, p. 249, 22 June 1915.

14. *The Times*, 11 June 1915.

15. BL Add MS 62976, Riddell diaries, 10 June 1915.

16. Ibid., 19 June 1915.

17. Kathleen Burk, *Britain, America and the Sinews of War, 1914–1918*, Winchester, Mass., 1985, p. 62–3.

18. LGP, H of L, D/12/1/11, Morgan Grenfell to LG, 14 August 1915. Morgan's apparently paid this by an overdraft. For a discussion of the August crisis see: Kathleen

Burk, *Morgan Grenfell, 1838–1988, The Biography of a Merchant Bank*, Oxford, 1989, pp. 130–31.

19. HHA to McKenna, 25 July 1915, quoted in Stephen McKenna, *Reginald McKenna*, London, 1948, p. 237.

20. The story of these negotiations is well told in Burk, *Sinews*, pp. 67–73. For a fuller account see: Marquess of Reading, *Rufus Isaacs, First Marquess of Reading* (London: 1945), II, 31–50.

21. Trevor Wilson, ed., *The Political Diaries of C.P. Scott, 1911–1928*, Ithaca, 1970, p. 137, L.T. Hobhouse to Scott, 24 September 1915. This was no transient notion. McKenna gave the same lecture to Scott three weeks later. *Ibid.*, pp. 144–45, 14–15 October 1915, and conveyed it at much greater length a year later to Col. Repington. Lt. Col. Charles aCourt Repington, *The First World War, 1914–1918* (Boston: 1920), I, 348–52, 29 September 1916.

22. Wilson, ed., *Scott Diaries*, p. 157, 13–15 November 1915.

23. BL Add MS 62976, Riddell diaries, 9 November 1915. Part of this quotation is printed in Riddell, *War Diary*, pp. 136–7, 9 November 1915.

24. See Stephen Koss, *Fleet Street Radical, A.G. Gardiner and the Daily News*, Hampden, Conn., 1973, p. 173.

25. David Lloyd George, *War Memoirs* (Boston: 1933), I, 415–17.

26. *Daily News*, 18 September 1915.

27. *Ibid.*, 22 April 1916.

28. *Ibid.*, 23 September 1915.

29. *Ibid.*, 6 May 1916.

30. BL Add MS 62976, Riddell diaries, 28 November 1915.

31. *Daily News*, 18 September 1915.

32. BL Add MS 62976, Riddell diaries, 14 November 1915.

33. A.J.P. Taylor, ed., *Lloyd George, A Diary by Frances Stevenson*, London, 1971, p. 72, 15 November 1915.

34. Asquith Papers, Bodleian Library, Vol. VIII, HHA to Geo V, 4 October 1915; Stephen Roskill, *Hankey, Man of Secrets* (New York: 1970), I, 232.

35. Randolph S. Churchill, *Lord Derby, King of Lancashire*, London, 1959, pp. 185–87.

36. LGP, H of L, D/17/12/11, Smith to LG, n.d [probably about 9 August].

37. See the excellent discussion of this episode in R.J.Q. Adams and Philip Poirier, *The Conscription Controversy in Great Britain, 1900–1918*, Columbus, Ohio, 1987, pp. 102–3, 111.

38. Taylor, ed., *Stevenson Diary*, p. 56, 2 September 1915.

39. Roskill, *Hankey*, I, 227, 228.

40. Taylor, ed., *Stevenson Diary*, p. 63, 5 October 1915. This lunch may have been the result of a squalid minor controversy, typical of the poisoned atmosphere in Asquith's Cabinet in this period, over the deputy leadership of the House, which office Lloyd George had held since 1908. Perhaps to separate Lloyd George and Bonar Law, Asquith asked, or may have been persuaded to ask, Bonar Law to take the post, without consulting Lloyd George. This led to some angry exchanges among the three men ending with Bonar Law's admission that he did not know Lloyd George had not been consulted, that he was not trying to compete with him and 'could not compete' with him. LGP, H of L, D/17/8/7, ABL to LG, 15 September 1915; Blake, *Unrepentant Tory*, p. 264, LG to ABL, 15 September 1915; Taylor, ed., *Stevenson Diary*, pp. 60–61, 17 September 1915.

41. BL Add MS 62976, Riddell diaries, 7 November 1915.

42. LGP, H of L, D/22/4 (CID.G25), Murdoch to Andrew Fisher, 23 September 1915, 'Secret' (A covering note, 25 September says that Lloyd George had suggested that a copy be sent to Asquith).

43. Public Record Office, Cab. 22/2/12, Dardanelles Committee, 23 September 1915.

44. Ibid., Cab. 22/2/5, 5 July 1915.

45. Asquith Papers, Vol. VIII, HHA to Geo V, 30 June 1915.

46. Ibid., HHA to Geo V, 2 October 1915 (Cabinets 28 September, 1 October 1915).

47. Taylor, ed., *Stevenson Diary*, p. 62, 5 October 1915.

48. See: Jere Clemens King, *Generals and Politicians, Conflict Between France's High Command, Parliament and Government, 1914–1918*, Berkeley, 1951, pp. 68–81; George H. Cassar, *The French and the Dardanelles, A Study of Failure in the Conduct of War*, London, 1971, p. 196–209.

49. The British Tenth Division under Lieutenant General Bryan Mahon and the French 156th Division landed at Salonika on 5 October. Within a few days there were 35,000 French and 13,000 British troops in the city.

50. PRO, Cab. 22/2/12, Dardanelles Committee, 22 September 1915. See also Ibid., 22/2/5, 5 July 1915.

51. Ibid., 22/2/19, 11 October 1915.

52. Lloyd George, *War Memoirs*, I, 427–30.

53. *Ibid.*, p. 430.

54. LGP, H of L, D/23/4/17 (untitled), 12 October 1915.

55. Lloyd George, *War Memoirs*, I, 432–38.

56. At first the Germans scoffed at the Salonika force. It was, they said, their largest concentration camp, an enemy army, prisoner of itself.

57. LGP, H of L, D/23/5/1, K to LG, 13 October 1915; Grey's letter appears in full in Lloyd George, *War Memoirs*, I, 439.

58. Ian Colvin, *The Life of Lord Carson* (London: 1936), III, 82–5. Carson's London papers were destroyed during the Second World War. Hence for English political correspondence Colvin's biography has become a primary source.

59. *Ibid.*, III, 85–7, LGP, H of L, D/17/8/8, LG to Carson, 25 September 1915.

60. LGP, H of L, D/17/8/8, LG to Bonar Law, 25 September 1915. One may speculate in this connection, that the source for many of Murdoch's military opinions was General Mahon who no doubt also directed the journalist to see Carson first when he came to London.

61. *Official Report, House of Commons Debates*, Series Five, LXXIV (28 September 1915), col. 732.

62. G.M. Trevelyan, *Grey of Fallodon*, Boston, 1937, p. 318.

63. Lloyd George, *War Memoirs*, I, 423–4; Colvin, *Carson*, III, 93, 95.

64. Edward, Viscount Grey, *Twenty-five Years, 1892–1916* (New York: 1925), II, 224.

65. PRO, Cab 22/2/19 Dardanelles Committee, 11 October 1915. Asquith had allowed the Dardanelles Committee to grow. By October it included most of the Cabinet.

66. Derby recorded in his diary that he had obtained from the Prime Minister a signed statement agreeing to conscription if recruitment did not revive. Churchill, *Derby*, p. 192.

67. Taylor, ed., *Stevenson Diary*, pp. 67–8, 12 October 1915; see also, Asquith Papers, Vol. VIII, HHA to Geo V, 12 October 1915.

68. Colvin, *Carson*, II, 97.

69. Bonar Law could not 'have looked with equanimity upon the presence of such a formidable member of his party standing outside the government, a focus for all the discontents inevitable in time of war,' commented Robert Blake dryly. Blake, *Unrepentant Tory*, p. 268.

70. Colvin, *Carson*, II, 126.

71. See Taylor, ed., *Stevenson Diary*, p. 68, 12 October 1915; see also Esher, *Esher Journal*, I, 263, 12 October 1915.

72. See Margot Asquith's frantic letter to Hankey, 15 October 1915, Roskill, *Hankey*, I, 228.

73. Taylor, ed., *Stevenson Diary*, p. 69, 19 October 1915; Wilson, ed., *Scott Diaries*, p. 143, 14–15 October 1915.

74. Colvin, *Carson*, II, 104–5. One should note in regard to the Prime Minister's illness that Cynthia Asquith dined at No. 10 that evening. There was a large family gathering held for the Prime Minister's eldest son Raymond, who was leaving for France. Nothing was amiss. E.M. Horsley, ed., *Lady Cynthia Asquith, Diaries, 1915–1918*, New York, 1969, p. 89, 18 October 1915.

75. *The Times*, 19 October 1915.

76. *Ibid.*, 20 October 1915.

77. He was saying it two decades later. Lloyd George, *War Memoirs*, I, 441.

78. *Ibid.*

79. *H of C Deb*, LXXIV (20 October 1915), cols. 812–13.

80. *Ibid.*, LXXV (2 November 1915), cols. 533–7.

81. Riddell, *War Diary*, p. 128, 23 October 1915.

82. *Ibid.*, pp. 130–1, 29 October 1915; see also: J.M. McEwen, ed., *The Riddell Diaries, 1908–1923*, London, 1986, p. 135, 29 October 1915.

83. Lloyd George, *War Memoirs*, I, 442.

84. LGP, H of L, D/18/2/11, LG to HHA, 31 October 1915, pencil. This letter is printed with some small changes in Lloyd George, *War Memoirs*, I, 442–5. It is misdated in the calendar of Lloyd George papers. Spender and Asquith put it 'towards the end of September,' which complicates the discussion of the October crisis. J.A. Spender and Cyril S. Asquith, *The Life of Herbert Henry Asquith, Lord Oxford and Asquith* (London: 1932), II, 195.

85. LGP, H of L, D/18/2/12, HHA to LG, 3 November 1915.

86. Roy Jenkins, *Asquith*, London, 1964, p. 380.

87. This letter is printed in Lloyd George, *War Memoirs*, I, 446–7.

88. LGP, H of L, D/7/8/9, ABL to LG, 1 November 1915.

89. Ibid., D/18/2/13, LG to HHA, n.d. [November, 1915].

90. Quoted in Stephen Koss, *The Rise and Fall of the Political Press in Britain* (London: 1984), II, 285.

91. LGP, H of L, D/22/1, War Committee 1, 12 November 1915, 'Very Secret.'

92. *Ibid.*, WC 5, 17 November 1915.

93. *Ibid.*, WC 8, 20 November 1915.

94. Asquith Papers, Vol. VIII, HHA to Geo V, 3 December 1915.

95. LGP, H of L, D/25/3, 'Report of a Visit to Greece by Mr. J.J. Stavridi,' 26 November 1915.

96. A few days later Lloyd George reported that the parliamentary wits were referring to Asquith and Balfour as 'Boozle and Foozle.' BL Add MS 62976, Riddell diaries, 11 December 1915.

97. Cassar, *The French and the Dardanelles*, pp. 230–5.

98. PRO Cab 22/3/16, War Committee, 6 December 1915. Asquith's *Memories and Reflections* provide an account of the Calais meeting. The Earl of Oxford and Asquith, *Memories and Reflections, 1852–1927* (Boston: 1928), II, pp. 132–3.

99. Taylor, ed., *Stevenson Diary*, p. 85, 6 December 1915. See also PRO Cab 22/13/16, War Committee, 6 December 1915, although this outburst is not recorded.

100. W.R. Nicoll to Dr. James Moffatt, 29 October 1918, quoted in T.H. Darlow, *William Robertson Nicoll, His Life and Letters*, London, 1925, p. 278.

101. Bertus Willem Schaper, *Albert Thomas, trente ans de reformisme social*, Assen, Netherlands, 1959, pp. 127–8. Schaper records that this letter was in the hands of Thomas's widow.
The importance to the Allied victory of the Salonika force has been contested by military thinkers since the war as violently as was its lodgment during the conflict. But one must note that General Eric von Ludendorff saw the attack up the Vardar valley from Salonika on 15 September 1918 and the subsequent rout of the Bulgarians at Krivolac in Serbia as the beginning of the rot throughout the entire eastern front, not only in the Balkans — a new front in Serbia — but in Turkey. It began indeed the German withdrawal from Russia. Eric von Ludendorff, *Ludendorff's Own Story* (New York: 1919), II, 365–69, 370–71.

102. Taylor, ed., *Stevenson Diary*, p. 86, 29 December 1915.

103. Grey, *Twenty-five Years*, II, 231–2. The best recent discussion of the politics surrounding the Salonika crisis is: D.J. Dutton, 'The Calais Conference of December, 1915,' *Historical Journal*, XXI (March, 1978), 143–56.

104. Lloyd George, *War Memoirs*, II, 334–35.

105. PRO, Cab 37/139/4.

106. Asquith, *Memories and Reflections*, II, 134–5. Derby's figures are unclear. Only those who had attested were given physical examinations where it could be noted that far more, nearly one quarter, of the single men than married men were found unfit. As the single cohort was younger than the married, one is led to wonder whether many single men who knew they were unfit attested. Bonar Law believed this. See ABL to C.P. Scott, Wilson, ed., *Scott Diaries*, p. 167, 4 January 1916. But the total number remaining available, officially 2,182,178, was thus surely unrealistic. None had been examined and the final rejection rate under National Service, even under the relentless manpower demands of 1917 and 1918, was nearly fifty percent. For the figures see Adams, *Conscription*, pp. 135–35. After Derby's report was published *The Times* concluded that after mistakes in exemption and medical rejections there would be 343,286 physically fit single men available and 487,676 married men. *The Times*, 4 January 1916.

107. *H of C Deb*, LXXVII (20 December 1915), col. 121.

108. Riddell, *War Diary*, p. 144, 31 December 1915; Taylor, ed., *Stevenson Diary*, p. 87, 29 December 1915.

109. Taylor, ed., *Stevenson Diary*, p. 89, 31 January 1916.

110. See McKenna's and Dillon's remarks, Wilson, ed., *Scott Diaries*, pp. 165–6, 169, 30 December 1915, 10–11 January 1916.

111. Kenneth Morgan, ed., *Lloyd George Family Letters*, Cardiff, 1973, p. 180, 27 December 1915. As additional evidence, the next day Lloyd George received from Arthur

Lee a note saying that Lee had heard Lloyd George had threatened to resign. If the 'break comes today' and Lloyd George left, Lee would go too. LGP, H of L, D/1/1/11, Arthur Lee to LG, 28 December 1915.

112. Morgan, ed., *Family Letters*, p. 181, 28 December 1915.

113. Asquith Papers, Vol. VIII, HHA to Geo V, 28 December 1915.

114. *Manchester Guardian*, 8 January 1916.

115. Wilson, ed., *Scott Diaries*, p. 169, 7 January 1916.

116. Roskill, *Hankey*, I, 266, 2 May 1916.

117. *Ibid.*, pp. 169–174, 10, 11 January 1916.

118. *H of C Deb*, LXXVII (5 January 1916), col. 1035.

119. *The Times*, 7 January 1916.

120. *H of C Deb*, LXXVII (5 January 1916), cols. 1034–35.

121. *Ibid.*

122. Gainford Papers, Nuffield College, J.A. Pease diary, 21 September 1915.

123. See: Michael Frieden, *Liberalism Divided, A Study in British Political Thought, 1914–1939*, Oxford, 1986.

124. *The Times*, 11 January 1915.

Chapter 8, pp. 287–334

1. William Maxwell Aitken, Lord Beaverbrook, *Politicians and the War, 1914–1916*, London, 1960, p. 195; Stephen Roskill, *Hankey, Man of Secrets* (New York: 1970), I, 237.

2. British Library, Add MS 62971, Riddell diaries, 25 July 1912.

3. George, Lord Riddell, *War Diary, 1914–1918*, London, 1933, p. 36, 25 October 1914.

4. *Ibid.*, p. 61, 7 February 1915.

5. A.J.P. Taylor, ed., *Lloyd George, A Diary by Frances Stevenson*, London, 1971, p. 29, 8 February 1915.

6. Robert Blake, ed., *The Private Papers of Douglas Haig, 1914–1919*, London, 1952, p. 113, 14 November 1915.

7. See: Roskill, *Hankey*, I, 237, 8 December 1915; Victor Bonham Carter, *Soldier True, The Life and Times of Field Marshal Sir William Robertson*, London, 1963, pp. 137–38 for the text of the agreement.

8. Taylor, ed., *Stevenson Diary*, p. 91, 31 January 1916.

9. On these doubts of victory see also Edward, Viscount Grey, *Twenty-five Years, 1892–1916* (New York: 1925), II, 128–9.

10. See the memorandum by Lloyd George (untitled) 4 November 1915, Addison Papers, Bodleian Library, Box 9.

11. Lloyd George Papers, House of Lords, D/18/8/3, Lloyd George to William Robertson, 6 January 1916.

12. LGP, H of L, D/19/6/27, Thomas to LG, 25 April 1916.

13. Ibid., War Committee, WC 39, Appendix to minutes, 'Very Secret,' 2 May 1916.

14. David Lloyd George, *War Memoirs* (Boston: 1933), II, 148–49.

15. Roskill, *Hankey*, I, 268–69.

16. LGP, H of L, D/19/16/12, George Buchanan to Westminster, 11 May 1916.

17. See Lloyd George's discussion in *War Memoirs*, II, 133–6.

18. LGP, H of L, D/16/7/4, A. Chamberlain to LG, 8 January 1916; see also Public Record Office, Cab. 37/142/11, Maurice Hankey, Report, 4 February 1916. The committee deserves further investigation.

19. Lloyd George, *War Memoirs*, II, 135–6.

20. LGP, H of L, D/2/2/25, 'Minutes of the Eighteenth Meeting of the War Committee held at 10 Downing Street on Friday April 7th, 1916.'

21. Charles Seymour, ed., *The Intimate Papers of Colonel House* (Boston: 1926), II, 124.

22. Arthur S. Link, *Wilson* (Princeton: 1964), IV, 101–17. Sir Edward Grey seems also to believe this. Grey, *Twenty-five Years*, II, 125–6.

23. Roskill, *Hankey*, II, 247–8. One must remark, however, that in House's dispatches to the President there are absolutely no references to politics.

24. Arthur S. Link, ed., *The Papers of Woodrow Wilson* (Princeton: 1980), XXXV, 484–6, House to Wilson, 15 January 1916.

25. Seymour, ed., *House Papers*, II, 126–9, 14 January 1916.

26. Roskill, *Hankey*, I, 247, 1 February 1916.

27. Link, ed., *Wilson Papers*, XXXV, 484–6.

28. Seymour, ed., *House Papers*, II, 130, 15 January 1916.

29. *Ibid.*, p. 131, 19 January 1916. He had been told this by others also. See *Ibid.*, p. 125, 16 January 1916.

30. This was Grey's view as well. Angry mobs, he predicted, would break the windows of his house when it became public. Grey, *Twenty-five Years*, II, 183–4, 15 February 1916.

31. *Ibid.*, 170, 176, 188–9.

32. Lloyd George, *War Memoirs*, II, 137.

33. *Ibid.*

34. Seymour, ed., *House Papers*, II, 183–4, 16 February 1916.

35. Link, *Wilson*, IV, 137.

36. Seymour, ed., *House Papers*, II, 182–3, 15 February 1916; see also Roskill, *Hankey*, I, 248, 16 March 1916.

37. Grey, *Twenty-five Years*, II, 124.

38. Link, *Wilson*, IV, 138.

39. *Ibid.*, Grey, *Twenty-five Years*, II, 127.

40. Taylor, ed., *Stevenson Diary*, p. 101, 21 February 1916.

41. LG to William George, 1 February 1916, in William George, *My Brother and I*, London, 1958, p. 253.

42. Riddell, *War Diary*, p. 154, 11 February 1916; Taylor, ed., *Stevenson Diary*, p. 93, 1 February 1916, see also LG to Haig, 8 February 1916, Blake, ed., *Haig Papers*, p. 128.

43. BL Add MS 62978, Riddell diaries, 1 August 1916.

44. Martin Gilbert, *Winston S. Churchill* (London: 1971), III, 697.

45. Taylor, ed., *Stevenson Diary*, p. 92, 1 February 1916.

46. *Ibid.*, p. 93; see also W. George, *Brother*, p. 253, 1 February 1916.

47. Public Record Office, Northern Ireland, D. 1507/C/2, Carson Papers, Ruby Carson diary, 10 February 1916.

48. Almeric Fitzroy, *Memoirs* (London: n.d. [1925]), II, 612, 12 November 1915.

49. Taylor, ed., *Stevenson Diary*, p. 96, 8 February 1916.

50. *Ibid.*, p. 94, 3 February 1916.

51. Trevor Wilson, ed., *The Political Diaries of C.P. Scott, 1911–1928*, Ithaca, 1970, p. 180, 7 February 1916.

52. See R.J.Q. Adams and Philip Poirier, *The Conscription Controversy in Great Britain, 1900–1918*, Columbus, Ohio, 1987, p. 148.

53. See, for example, Wilson, ed., *Scott Diaries*, p. 200, 17 April 1916.

54. Ian Colvin, *The Life of Lord Carson* (London: 1936), III, 142.

55. PRONI, D. 1507/6/2, Ruby Carson diary, 6 March 1916.

56. Ibid., 25 March 1916.

57. David Woodward, ed., *The Military Correspondence of Field-Marshal Sir William Robertson, Chief of the Imperial General Staff, December 1915–February 1918*, London, 1989, No. 19, Robertson to Haig, 22 March 1916.

58. Wilson, ed., *Scott Diaries*, p. 199, 17 April 1916.

59. British Library, Add MS 46388, Spender Papers, Vol. III, TS, 15 March 1916, unsigned, untitled. In pencil 'conversation with Bonar Law' 'Redmond.'

60. Roskill, *Hankey*, I, 258.

61. Taylor, ed., *Stevenson Diary*, p. 105, 27 March 1916. Miss Stevenson assumes the initiative came from France.

62. WSC to Clementine Churchill, 19 March 1916, quoted in Gilbert, *Churchill*, III, 740–1.

63. PRONI, D. 1507/C/1, Ruby Carson diary, 12 May 1915.

64. Wilson, ed., *Scott Diaries*, p. 187, 6 March 1915.

65. Violet Bonham Carter, *Winston Churchill, An Intimate Portrait*, New York, 1965, p. 368.

66. *Official Report, House of Commons Debates*, Series 5, LXXX (7 March 1916), cols. 1420–30.

67. Riddell, *War Diary*, p. 163, 10 March 1916.

68. Bonham Carter, *Churchill*, p. 368.

69. Wilson, ed., *Scott Diaries*, p. 191, 8 March 1916.

70. Bonham Carter, *Churchill*, p. 373.

71. One must recall his injunction in old age to the boys at Harrow: 'Never give in! Never give in! Never, Never, Never — in nothing great or small, large or petty!'

72. Gilbert, *Churchill*, III, 738.

73. PRONI, D. 1507/C/1, Ruby Carson diary, 13 March 1916.

74. Wilson, ed., *Scott Diaries*, p. 192, 22 March 1916.

75. Gilbert, *Churchill*, III, 743.

76. PRONI, D. 1507/C/1, Ruby Carson diary, 24 April 1916.

77. The boycott of Churchill continued for a year: he was ignored in the House, he said, his speeches were not reported in the press. See his complaints to C.P. Scott, Wilson, ed., *Scott Diaries*, pp. 234–5, 20 November 1916.

78. Colvin, *Carson*, III, 142.

79. British Library Add MS 62977, Riddell diaries, 21 May 1916.

80. Arthur, Viscount Lee of Fareham, 'A Good Innings' (privately printed, 1939, Lee of Fareham Papers, House of Lords), II, 632–3.

81. Colvin, *Carson*, III, 144.

82. Riddell, *War Diary*, p. 168, 1 April 1916.

83. *Ibid.*

84. Christopher Addison, *Four and a Half Years* (London: 1934), I, 189–90, 7 April 1916.

85. Lee, 'Innings,' II, 638. Ibid., II, 639, Ruth Lee diary; Addison, *Four and a Half Years*, I, 191. Lloyd George reported precisely such an offer to C.P. Scott on 17 April. Wilson, ed., *Scott Diaries*, p. 200.

86. Lee, 'Innings,' II, 639, Ruth Lee diary; Addison, *Four and A Half Years*, I, 191.

87. See: Beaverbrook, *Politicians*, p. 401.

88. Lee, 'Innings,' II, 828–9, Ruth Lee diary, 12 March 1921.

89. *The Times*, 29 March 1916.

90. Addison, *Four and a Half Years*, I, 191, 7 April 1916; see also Blake, ed., *Haig Papers*, p. 139, 15 April 1916. Hankey, himself opposed to general compulsion, wrote bitterly on 2 May after the crisis was over that at the moment the army was not, in fact, short of men.

> The only real military case for [universal conscription] is the great offensive. For an ordinary campaign there are heaps of men. That is to say we could fight the whole summer [of 1916] and lose men on the same scale we lost them last year, which included Gallipoli, Neuve Chapelle, Loos and Festubert, and still have 50,000 men up our sleeve at the end of the year. But the Army want a regular orgy of slaughter this summer, and it is for this that they demand the extra men.

Roskill, *Hankey*, I, 266, 2 May 1916.

91. LGP, H of L, D/2/2/25, 'Minutes of the Eighteenth Meeting of the War Committee held at 10 Downing Street on Friday April 7th 1916.'

92. Colvin, *Carson*, III, 148–9.

93. Wilson, ed., *Scott Diaries*, p. 197, 13 April 1916.

94. 'Mr. Bonar Law came to luncheon,' recorded Ruby Carson on 27 March. 'I really believe he is hypnotised by Asquith, he thinks it will be difficult to find anyone to do better.' PRONI, D 1507/C/2, Ruby Carson diary.

95. Addison, *Four and A Half Years*, I, 191, 13 April 1916.

96. Wilson, ed., *Scott Diaries*, p. 197, 14 April 1916.

97. This was not strictly true. The Cabinet met to approve a report by the Military Finance Committee (essentially the old Committee for the Co-ordination of the War Effort, Asquith, McKenna and Chamberlain, but with Lord Lansdowne added) which in fact had not recommended general compulsion. Lloyd George had insisted that the Army Council see and accept the report, which he knew it would not. He was supported by Bonar Law. Roskill, *Hankey*, I, 264, diary, 14 April 1916.

98. Riddell, *War Diary*, pp. 170–72, 13 (i.e. 14) April 1916. To add to the confusion of dates the biography of Nicoll places this meeting on Wednesday 12 April. T.H. Darlow, *William Robertson Nicoll, His Life and Letters*, London, 1925, p. 255.

99. Wilson, ed., *Scott Diaries*, pp. 197–98, 14 April 1916.

100. BL Add MS 62977, Riddell diaries, 14 [15] April 1915. 15 April, a Saturday, always saw Lloyd George at Walton Heath.

101. Wilson, ed., *Scott Diaries*, p. 198, 16 April 1916.

102. Taylor, ed., *Stevenson Diary*, p. 106, 17 April 1916. Riddell, in a rare mistake, assumes that Stamfordham came to Walton Heath.

103. Wilson, ed., *Scott Diaries*, p. 198, 16 April 1916.

104. Clearly in writing his *War Memoirs*, in which he never admits a change of policy, Lloyd George cleared out his papers on this topic.

105. Wilson, ed., *Scott Diaries*, pp. 199–200, 20 April; Taylor, ed., *Stevenson Diary*, pp. 106–7, 18 April 1916.

106. *Ibid.*; Riddell, *War Diary*, p. 176, 20 April; W. George, *Brother*, p. 254, 20 April 1916.

107. For the reports see: Adams, *Conscription*, pp. 156–7.

108. Conveniently *The Times* obtained (one wonders how) and printed during the week of 15–22 April an almost complete account of Cabinet proceedings, far fuller than those sent by Asquith to the King.

109. *The Times*, 20 April 1916.

110. No man since Joseph Chamberlain of the turn of the century could inspire such terror, particularly among younger members of the House of Commons. A few weeks later Carson literally froze hapless Herbert Samuel into petrified silence on a government motion to refer the Registration of Voters Bill, a favorite of Lloyd George's, to a Select Committee. Asquith had to intervene. See *The Times*, 20 July 1916. In normal times this could have brought down the government, thought the paper.

111. *Manchester Guardian*, 20 April 1916. This political note brought an angry letter from Lloyd George and a disavowal from Scott. Wilson, ed., *Scott Diaries*, 20 April 1916.

112. *Daily News*, 22 April, 1916.

113. Riddell, *War Diary*, p. 179, 28 April 1916. Bonar Law himself had described it as 'vicious and uncalled for.' *Ibid.*, pp. 176, 24 April 1916.

114. Christopher Addison, *Politics from Within, 1911–1918* (London: 1924), I, 251, 28 April 1916.

115. *The Times*, 20, 21 April 1916.

116. Roskill, *Hankey*, I, 265.

117. 'Official Announcement on the Secret Session' *The Times*, 26 April 1916.

118. *H of C Deb*, LXXXI (27 April 1916), cols. 2537–41.

119. *Ibid.*, col. 2560.

120. *The Times*, 28 April 1916.

121. Wilson, ed., *Scott Diaries*, pp. 199–200, 17 April 1916; Taylor, ed., *Stevenson Diary*, p. 106, 17 April 1916.

122. 'Asquith by Strachey,' *The Times*, 15 January 1972.

123. *H of C Deb*, LXXXI (2 May 1916), col. 2616.

124. *Daily News*, 3 May 1916.

125. *H of C Deb*, LXXXII (4 May 1916), cols. 166–69.

126. *Ibid.*, cols. 175–84.

127. *The Times*, 8 May 1916.

128. *Daily News*, 8 May 1916.

129. BL Add MS 62977, Riddell diaries, 13 May 1916.

130. *Ibid.*, 21 May 1916.

131. *Ibid.*, 11 June 1916.

132. See his violent article: 'A British Observer,' 'Lloyd George and the Coup D'Etat,' *Atlantic Monthly*, CXIX (March, 1917), 392–401.

133. Addison to Gardiner, 2 February 1934, Gardiner papers quoted in Stephen Koss, *Fleet Street Radical, A.G. Gardiner and the Daily News*, Hampden, Conn., 1973, p. 191.

134. Asquith Papers, Vol. VIII, HHA to Geo. V, 9 May 1916.

135. LGP, H of L, D/29/1, War Committee Minutes, WC 40, 10 May 1916.

136. LGP, H of L, D/5/1/8, LG to Balfour, 9 May 1916.

137. For a recent discussion of the problem see: Jon T. Sumida, 'British Naval Administration and Policy in the Age of Fisher,' paper presented before the Midwest Consortium on Military History, University of Chicago, October 1988.

138. See his comments on Redmond at this time. Riddell, *War Diary*, p. 184, 27 May 1916.

139. Wilson, ed., *Scott Diaries*, p. 207, 26 May 1916.

140. Although ignored in Britain, in Ireland the recruitment boycott is celebrated in song and story. See for example: 'Sergeant William Bailey' and 'The Recruiting Sergeant' who stood at 'Murphy's corner' for typical mockery.

Redmond asserted in the House of Commons in October, 1916 that the total number of Irish in the army including those serving when war broke out was 157,000. Lloyd George, then Secretary of State for War replied that the number enlisted since the war began was 105,000 and that 50,000 others had been rejected on medical grounds. This was 2½% of the population, he added, far less than the effort in Great Britain and the Dominions. *H of C Deb*, LCCCIV (18 October 1916), cols. 651–2.

Statistics separating enlistments in the various Catholic and Protestant areas and leaving out the very large number of Irishmen in the army at the outbreak of the war are seldom available, but there are a few. During the four years and three months of the war, according to a return evidently demanded by Lloyd George as Prime Minister, the intake at Belfast was 48,000. In Dublin, a city in the 1911 census of almost exactly equal size, it was 26,000. In Cork, about a third as large as the other two, it was 11,100. The figures represent only men passing though the military depots in those towns. Many Irishmen, the report specifies, enlisted in Liverpool and Glasgow. LGP, H of L, F/180/3/1, 'Enlistments in Ireland,' 4 August 1914–11 November 1918, George Murray, War Office, 14 May 1919, MS.

141. See Asquith's fascinating report of his trip to Ireland in May 1916 in John D. Fair, *British Interparty Conferences, A Study of the Procedure of Conciliation in British Politics, 1867–1921*, Oxford, 1980, in Appendix V, pp. 294–98, Selborne Papers. This document does not appear in the PRO handbook: *List of Cabinet Papers, 1915 and 1915*, London, 1966.

142. See the resolution against a Home Rule parliament without an 'adequate nominated element representing property and trade' sent to Lloyd George by the Dublin Chamber of Commerce. LGP, H of L, D/14/2/19, 8 June 1916. There are other letters in this file conveying the same message. The word 'rabble' appears. English government, it was held, was at least settled government.

143. Roskill, *Hankey*, I, 265.

144. Birrell had written immediately protesting the general declaration of martial law. The War Committee responded tartly on 28 April saying that they intended a general declaration and that it would stand. LGP, H of L, D/29/1, War Committee minutes, WC 37, 'Very Secret,' 28 April 1916.

145. Lloyd George, *War Memoirs*, II, 149. LGP, H of L, D/14/1/5. The *War Memoirs* contain a photographic reproduction of this letter. Asquith's letter was followed by the usual incredible letter to Lloyd George from Margot. A person with wit and humor such as he would 'enjoy Ireland, trying as the Irish are.' *Ibid.*, D/14/1/7.

146. Quoted in Roy Jenkins, *Asquith*, London, 1964, p. 399, Lady Scott diary, 24 May 1916.

147. PRONI, D.1507/C/2, Ruby Carson diary, 22 May 1916.

148. Addison, *Politics*, I, 254, diary, 28 May 1916.

149. Quoted in Fair, *Interparty Conferences*, Appendix V, p. 298.

150. This accounts for the peculiar dismissal and reappointment of Lord Wimborne, Churchill's cousin, Ivor Guest. Wimborne fought fiercely to keep his post and then after virtually being ordered to resign in mid-May was back at the Lodge by mid-August.

151. LGP, H of L, D/14/3/34, Chamberlain to HHA, 22 June 1916. Lloyd George immediately wrote to Asquith saying he had consulted with both Walter Long and Lord Lansdowne before submitting terms to Carson and Redmond. Neither had said anything about the Cabinet. Asquith Papers, Vol. XIV, LG to HHA, 23 June 1915 [sic 1916].

152. George, *Brother*, p. 254, 22 May 1916.

153. See T.P. O'Connor's report to Dillon on a conversation with Lloyd George about intervening in Ireland, 19 May 1916 in F.S.L. Lyons, *John Dillon, A Biography*, London, 1968, pp. 383–5.

154. LGP, H of L, D/14/9, Long to LG, 23 May 1916.

155. *H of C Deb*, LXXXII (25 May 1916), cols. 2310–11.

156. 'Negotiating. Hard at it,' he wrote to his brother on 26 May. 'Resuming tomorrow. Daily Mail very funny. Great headlines WHEN IN TROUBLE SEND FOR LLOYD GEORGE.' George, *Brother*, p. 254.

157. Lee, 'Innings', II, 646, Ruth Lee diary, 25 May; LGP, H of L, D/3/2/74, unsigned [F.L.S.] to DuCane, 30 May.

158. Lee, 'Innings', II, 646, Ruth Lee diary, 26 May 1916. See also: PRONI, D.1507/C/2, Ruby Carson diary, 26 May 1916.

159. Colvin, *Carson*, III, 166. See also Lloyd George, *War Memoirs*, II, 151.

160. Colvin, *Carson*, III, 166.

161. *Ibid.*, 167.

162. Lloyd George, *War Memoirs*, II, 152.

163. LGP, H of L, D/141/26, covering letter, David Davies to LG, 27 May 1916. Davies, MP for Carmarthenshire, was Lloyd George's new Parliamentary Secretary. As there were many Davies, Lloyd George often refers to him in letters in the Welsh way as 'Davies Llandinam,' his birthplace.

164. Ibid., D/14/1/40, Midleton to LG, 30 May 1916.

165. PRONI, D.1507/A/17/7, Carson Papers, LG to Carson, 3 June 1916. Colvin's generally excellent biography of Carson omits all references to the Southern Unionists. It reproduces only the latter part of this letter. Colvin, *Carson*, III, 167. Jutland was hardly a victory, but no disaster. This was typical Lloyd George hyperbole.

166. PRONI, D.1507/A/17/8, Carson Papers, Carson to Plunkett, 5 June 1916.

167. LGP H of L, D/14/1/37, Long to LG, 29 May 1916.

168. See Ibid., D/14/1/45, G.F. Stewart to Long, 31 May; Ibid., D/14/2/4, Midleton to LG, 2 June 1916.

169. *The Times*, 31 May 1916.

170. Colvin, *Carson*, III, 167.

171. LGP, H of L, D/14/1/14, St. John Ervine to LG, 26 May 1916, Abby Theatre.

172. In the Lloyd George papers is a letter dated 16 May 1916 from the Bishop of Tuam to the Archbishop of Dublin, probably intercepted by Royal Irish Constabulary intelligence, asking to be excused from the forthcoming bishop's meeting in the capitol. The West was in 'great trouble.' His train had been attacked with gunfire the previous Saturday, 13 May. Rebels were well-armed and people were 'now aiding them in their efforts at evading the police.' Redmond might not be able to hold the people in control and the bishop's place was with his people and clergy. LGP, H of L, D/14/1/45, Benjamin J. Plunket, Bishop of Tuam to William J. Walsh, Archbishop of Dublin, 16 May 1916, TS.

173. See Ibid., D/14/2/27, Dillon to LG, 11 June 1916.

174. Charles Tennant reported on 21 June that there had been about 3,000 arrests. This is twice the number of men involved in the uprising, and there were many arrests outside Dublin. *The Times*, 22 June 1916.

175. *Cd. 8376*, 'Royal Commission on the Arrest and Subsequent Treatment of Mr. Francis Sheehy Skeffington, Mr. Thomas Dickson and Mr. Patrick Jones McIntyre,' 1916. After Sheehy Skeffington was shot, on 26 April, the officer responsible, Captain J.C. Bowen-Colthurst of the Royal Irish Rifles, invaded his house and held his widow and seven year old son at gun-point while soldiers ransacked the place in the hope of finding some evidence to justify the execution.

176. Lloyd George, *War Memoirs*, II, 150.

177. LGP, H of L, D/14/2/23, T.P. O'Connor to LG, 9 June 1916.

178. Ibid., D/14/2/20, LG to Dillon, 9 June 1916.

179. Ibid., D/14/2/22, 10 June 1916.

180. Ibid., D/14/2/23, Asquith to LG, 10 June 1916.

181. Ibid., D/14/2/24, LG to Dillon, 10 June 1916. Part of this letter appears in Lyons, *Dillon*, pp. 390–91.

182. Ibid., D/14/2/25, Dillon to LG, 11 June 1916. Lloyd George received also a long gloomy letter from O'Connor saying the same. Negotiations were breaking down. Ibid., D/14/2/27, O'Connor to LG.

183. Ibid., D/14/2/28, Long to LG, 11 June 1916. Part of this message appears in Lloyd George, *War Memoirs*, II, 152.

184. Ibid., D/14/2/22, LG to Long, 12 June 1916.

185. Ibid., D/14/2/33, Long to LG, 12 June 1916.

186. Indeed the Bonar Law papers for this period are chiefly letters threatening various reprisals if the party leader continued to support the Prime Minister and Lloyd George. See A. Bonar Law Papers, H of L, 53/3/2, 3, 4, 7, 19–26 June 1916, Long, Midleton, St. Audries, Lord Hugh Cecil to Bonar Law.

187. LGP, H of L, D/14/2/29, 12 June 1916.

188. On 19 June Ruby Carson reflected in her diary:

The whole Cabinet is at daggers drawn over the Ulster Settlement & pretend they know nothing, at least the Unionist part & Walter Long is going to resign & says Lloyd George has tricked E[dward]...*He* [Walter Long] would be much better hoeing turnips than in the Cabinet.

And on 20 June: Edward 'now finds himself on the side of Bonar Law, Lloyd George & Asquith over the Ulster settlement, a funny world this is,' PRONI, D.1507/C/2, Ruby Carson diary, 19, 20 June 1916.

189. *The Times*, 12 June 1916.

190. *Ibid.*, 13 June 1916.

191. See the letters of Hugh de Fellenberg Montgomery to his constituents in Co. Tyrone, PRONI, D.627/429/39, 42, 44, de Fellenberg Montgomery to 'Stewart,' 17, 19, 22 June 1916.

192. LGP, H of L, D/14/3/9, HHA to LG, 16 June 1916, TS. Selborne wrote a similar, even more angry, letter to Carson virtually accusing him of disloyalty. PRONI, D.1507/A/17/20, Carson Papers, Selborne to Carson, 17 June 1916. Carson told C.P. Scott some months later that by going as far as he did with Lloyd George he 'lost half his friends' and would have to leave Dublin University and seek a new seat in Belfast. Wilson, ed., *Scott Diaries*, p. 277, 19 April 1917.

193. LGP, H of L, D/14/2/30, LG to HHA [17 June 1916] misdated 12 June.

194. Ibid., D/14/3/11, LG to Dillon, 17 June 1916.

195. *The Times*, 26 June 1916.

196. *Official Report, House of Lords Debates*, XXII (27 June 1916), cols. 387–89. *The Times* leader on Selborne's resignation so precisely reflected the view Lloyd George had conveyed to Dillon — by himself Selborne was not important; everything depended upon Carson — that one must wonder whether Riddell's suspicions of a Lloyd George-Northcliffe axis had not some basis. *The Times*, 27 June 1916. In the early years of the war *The Times* was even more than usually well-informed.

197. J.A. Spender and Cyril S. Asquith, *The Life of Herbert Henry Asquith, Lord Oxford and Asquith* (London: 1932), II, 214–15. '"Before the executions,"' raged T.P. O'Connor to C.P. Scott on 7 June,

> "99 percent of Nationalist Ireland was Redmondite; since the executions 99 percent is Sinn Fein." He could find no words strong enough with which to denounce the folly of the whole proceeding and Maxwell himself he described as a wooden-headed soldier full of stupid little airs who had been sent back from Egypt because he had neglected to make trenches.

Wilson, ed., *Scott Diaries*, pp. 217–8, 7 June 1916.

198. See *The Times*, 20, 28 June 1916. The long article on 20 June, 'The Cabinet and Ireland', provides an excellent summary of political events following 23 May.

199. See the statement of 50 Irish Unionists who saw Bonar Law at the Colonial Office on 27 June. *The Times*, 27 June 1916.

200. *The Times*, 24 June 1916.

201. LGP, H of L, D/14/3/36, Devlin to LG, 23 June 1916.

202. Ibid., D/15/1/15, 'Journal and Minutes of the Ulster Nationalist Conference held Friday, June 23, 1916.' The vote, in fact was 475 to 265. This document carries a note estimating that about 100 of the negative votes were priests.

203. *The Times*, 24 June 1916. The tenor of Devlin's speech had been that when the benefits of Home Rule became apparent, Ulster would soon clamor to join the rest of Ireland.

204. *The Times*, 26 June 1916.

205. Asquith Papers, Vol. VIII, HHA to Geo V, 28 June 1916. For a summary of Lansdowne's objections see Lloyd George, *War Memoirs*, II, 153–4, Lansdowne to HHA, 28 June 1916. This appears in LGP, H of L, D/14/3/43. There are extended quotations from Asquith's long letter to the King in Jenkins, *Asquith*, pp. 400–1 and in Spender and Asquith, *Asquith*, II, 219–21.

206. Asquith Papers, Vol. VIII, HHA to Geo V, 5 July 1916.

207. *H of L Deb*, XXII (11 July 1916), cols. 645–52. As a barometer of Southern Unionist feeling Midleton's speech preceding Lansdowne's may have been more

revealing if less important. The government was going to turn Ireland over to murderers and cast the Southern Unionists aside. *Ibid.*, cols. 635–41.

Lord Newton's biography of Lansdowne carries no discussion of any kind of the 1916 rising or his subject's part in the attempted settlement after it.

208. See Asquith's letter to Lord Crewe the next day quoted in Spender and Asquith, *Asquith*, II, 222, 12 July 1916.

209. *H of C Deb*, LXXXIV (24 July 1916), col. 1433.

210. *Ibid.* (31 July 1916), cols. 2134–9.

211. Esher, *Esher Journal*, Esher to L.B., 26 July 1916.

Chapter 9, pp. 335–383

1. George, Lord Riddell, *War Diary, 1914–1918*, London, 1933, p. 189, 11 June 1916.

2. The King, it may be noted, had told Hankey he was not enthusiastic about Lloyd George. Stephen Roskill, *Hankey, Man of Secrets* (New York: 1970), I, 283, 10 June 1916. Reginald Brade, Permanent Secretary at the War Office, warned George Riddell some weeks later, after it became apparent that Lloyd George would be appointed, that the latter would do well to pay some attention to His Majesty 'who is a great power in the Army.' He did not interfere but without his 'good will matters may be awkward.' British Library, Add MS 62977, Riddell diaries, 30 June 1916.

3. Roskill, *Hankey*, I, 280, 6 June 1916.

4. Public Record Office, Northern Ireland, D.1507/A/17/7, Carson papers, LG to Carson, 3 June 1916. This letter, another part of which has been cited before in connection with the Irish negotiations, is partly printed in Ian Colvin, *The Life of Lord Carson* (London: 1936), III, 167–68.

5. See his long oration to C.P. Scott on Tuesday afternoon, 6 June, hours after the sinking of the *Hampshire* was announced: '. . .he would not dream of taking the post without power,' the soldiers would treat him 'with contempt,' and so on. Trevor Wilson, ed., *The Political Diaries of C.P. Scott, 1911–1928*, Ithaca, 1970, p. 217, 6–8 June 1916.

6. This suggestion is in some ways parallel to the theme of David Woodward's excellent chapter on Lloyd George at the War Office in his recent book *Lloyd George and the Generals*, although Professor Woodward believes that the process began later in the year. David R. Woodward, *Lloyd George and the Generals*, Newark, Delaware, 1983, pp. 121, 122–3. Apparently the idea came first from A.J.P. Taylor. A.J.P. Taylor, *Beaverbrook*, London, 1972, p. 109.

7. See A.J.P. Taylor, ed., *Lloyd George, A Diary by Frances Stevenson*, London, 1971, p. 63, 5 October 1915; Wilson, ed., *Scott Diaries*, p. 142, 1 October 1915.

8. William Maxwell Aitken, Lord Beaverbrook, *Politicians and the War, 1914–1916*, London, 1960, pp. 207–9.

9. PRONI, D.1507/C/2, Ruby Carson diary, 11 May 1916. The Carsons already had seen evidence of this.

10. Robert Blake, *Unrepentant Tory, The Life and Times of Andrew Bonar Law, 1858–1923*, New York, 1956, pp. 289–90. This last point has been contested by Violet Bonham Carter who has written that according to the guest book there were not three bridge playing ladies at The Wharf on Whitsun weekend in 1916 and that her father never played bridge before dinner.

11. Beaverbrook, *Politicians*, pp. 207–9.

12. *Ibid.*, p. 212.

13. Oliver, Viscount Esher, *Journals and Letters of Reginald, Viscount Esher* (London: 1938), II, 34, 15 June 1916.

14. Riddell, *War Diary*, pp. 234–35, appended to entry of 25 December 1916.

15. J.M. McEwen, ed., *The Riddell Diaries, 1908–1923*, London, 1986, pp. 158–9, 11 June 1916. Riddell notes that after dinner Aitken drove the short distance from Cherkley Court to talk again with Lloyd George but that he did not stay to hear about it.
    The rich men were three Liberals who would back him without reservation and two Unionists, he grandly announced to C.P. Scott and Churchill three days later. Wilson, ed., *Scott Diaries*, p. 220, 13–17 June 1916.

16. Arthur, Viscount Lee of Fareham, Lee of Fareham Papers, House of Lords, Lloyd George file, unsorted, LG to Lee, 'Sunday' [11 June 1916].

17. Roy Jenkins, *Asquith*, London, 1964, p. 407.

18. Arthur, Viscount Lee of Fareham, 'A Good Innings', privately printed, 1939, II, 655, in Lee of Fareham Papers, Ruth Lee diary, 13 June 1916. This seems to be the original source for the conversation with the Prime Minister.

19. PRONI, D.1507/C/2, Carson Papers, Ruby Carson diary, 13 June 1916.

20. Despite the date, one must assume Lloyd George's luncheon with Carson took place on Monday, 12 June and that Mrs. Carson recorded it the next day, for C.P. Scott's diary shows that Lloyd George telegraphed him late on the 12th to come to London and that Lloyd George, Churchill and Scott had lunched on 13 June. Wilson, ed., *Scott Diaries*, p. 218–9, 13–17 June 1916.

21. *Ibid.*

22. One must remark that the infamous Orders in Council which gave Robertson his enhanced authority were not reversed when Lloyd George became Prime Minister. Robertson remained military advisor to the War Cabinet to which the Secretary of State, Lord Derby, frequently was not invited.

23. Riddell, *War Diary*, pp. 189–90, 15 June 1916.

24. *Ibid.*

25. *Ibid.*, p. 192.

26. Christopher Addison, *Politics From Within, 1911–1918* (London: 1924), I, 262, 16 June 1916.

27. *British Weekly*, 15 June 1916.

28. Quoted in Jenkins, *Asquith*, p. 407.

29. Wilson, ed., *Scott Diaries*, p. 221, n.d. [17 June 1916].

30. Lloyd George Papers, House of Lords, D/18/15/2, Scott to LG, 17 June 1916.

31. Jenkins, *Asquith*, pp. 408–9. Reginald Brade told Riddell, after indeed Asquith had decided to appoint Lloyd George, that the Prime Minister had said on Sunday, 18 June that 'under no circumstances' would Lloyd George go to the War Office. His informant had spent that day with Asquith. BL Add MS 62977, Riddell diaries, 23 June 1916.

32. See Lloyd George's conversation with Riddell on 24 June. Riddell, *War Diary*, p. 195. Margot Asquith's famous entry in her diary after the appointment was made: 'We are out: It can only be a question of time now when we shall have to leave Downing Street' voiced a sentiment shared by no one and was as little in accord with visible political realities as had been her statement about her husband's invulnerability five months earlier. Margot Asquith, *An Autobiography* (New York: 1922), II, 245. Asquith was indeed growing weaker, and had been doing so for a year, but Lloyd George's appointment, by itself, was not one of the causes.

33. *Daily Chronicle*, 17 June 1916.

34. McEwen, ed., *Riddell Diaries*, p. 161, 21 June 1916.

35. Jenkins, *Asquith*, pp. 407–8.

36. Addison, *Politics*, I, 254, also Appendix X.

37. LGP, H of L, D/18/2/18, LG to Asquith, 17 June 1916, MS and TS; Asquith Papers, Bodleian Library, Vol. VII, LG to Asquith, 17 June 1916.

38. David Lloyd George, *War Memoirs* (Boston: 1933), II, 204–8; LGP, H of L, D/18/2/19, LG to Asquith, 17 June 1916, TS.

39. Martin Middlebrook, *First Day on the Somme*, New York, 1972, p. 86.

40. Lloyd George, *War Memoirs*, II, 208–9.

41. BL Add MS 62977, Riddell diaries, 23 June 1916.

42. LGP, H of L, D/17/16/5, E.S. Montagu to PM, 20 June 1916, MS note (corrections in ESM MS). There is a note in the file in the Lloyd George Papers at the House of Lords dated September, 1938 stating that this letter had been found by J.T. Davies, Lloyd George's secretary, in a drawer in 10 Downing Street in 1918 and given to Elizabeth Bowdidge who was in 1938 sending it to Frances Stevenson. However Arthur Lee records that Lloyd George received a carbon copy of the TS from a typist within days after it was written. Lee, 'Innings', II, 654. He adds that Lloyd George was unwilling to take any action in this treachery. He had, he said, sympathy for criminals as he was close to being one himself.

Evidently Montagu also sent the Prime Minister another memo, undated, saying that LG before the war was discredited, 'an ill advised Budget' but 'the war had rehabilitated him'. Now he was most popular. Therefore he ought to be appointed to the War Office. The post was not important any longer. Somehow Asquith had given the memorandum to J.T. Davies. Davies told Lloyd George but said he had not kept a copy of the memorandum. Lloyd George mentioned this letter both to Riddell and to Frances Stevenson. BL Add MS 62978, Riddell diaries, 2 August; Taylor, ed., *Stevenson Diary*, pp. 109–10, 26 July 1916.

43. McEwen, ed., *Riddell Diaries*, p. 161; Riddell, *War Diary*, p. 193, 18 June 1916.

44. BL Add MS 62977, Riddell diaries, 22 June 1916.

45. Ibid., 24 June 1916. On 26 June Reginald Brade called Riddell to say that Lloyd George's appointment was 'definitely settled' but that 'provision must be made' for Lord Derby. Would Riddell tell Lloyd George? Ibid., 26 June 1916.

46. LGP, H of L, D/18/8/18, 19, 20, Robertson to LG, 24, 26 June, 1916. Portions of these letters appear in Victor Bonham Carter, *The Strategy of Victory, 1914–1918, The Life and Times of the Master Strategist of World War I: Field-Marshal Sir William Robertson*, New York, 1964, pp. 279–81.

47. For a totally uncharacteristic, bitter, public, denunciation of General Wilson see Asquith's remarks in: The Earl of Oxford and Asquith, *Memories and Reflections, 1852–1927* (Boston: 1928), II, 184–85 and n.

48. William George, *My Brother and I*, London, 1958, p. 255, 28 June 1916. Characteristically, in an important letter he enquired after the health of Richard Lloyd, now 82 years old, and recommended that William urge his uncle to take Benger's Patent Food twice a day. He took it constantly himself.

49. LGP, H of L, D/1/1/21/23, 18 June, 1, 7 July 1916.

50. BL Add MS 62978, Riddell diaries, 7 July 1916.

51. 'Dégomméd,' literally 'unstuck,' was fashionable army slang of the first war to describe the fate of military grandees who had been relieved of their duties.

52. David R. Woodward, ed., *The Military Correspondence of Field-Marshal Sir William Robertson, Chief of the Imperial General Staff, December 1915–February 1918*, London, 1989, No. 48, Robertson to Haig, 7 August 1916, TS (underlining in original letter).

53. BL Add MS 62978, Riddell diaries, 30 July 1916. See also Lloyd George's flattering comments to Col. Charles Repington on Robertson made at lunch on 19 July. Repington was military correspondent for *The Times* and knew Robertson well. The remarks would be passed on. Lt. Col. Charles aCourt Repington, *The First World War, 1914–1918* (Boston: 1920), I, 283–87, 19 July 1916.

54. See LGP, H of L, D/19/6/22, 23, 25–28, A. Thomas to LG, 2 Feb, 20, 26 May 1916.

55. Ibid., D/19/6/29, A. Thomas to LG, 2 June 1916, TS.

56. Taylor, ed., *Stevenson Diary*, p. 110, 26 July 1916.

57. Lloyd George, *War Memoirs*, II, 14–5. In his memoirs Lloyd George states that this letter was sent to Robertson although the copy in the Lloyd George papers shows clearly it was addressed to General Maurice. LGP, H of L, E/1/5/6, LG to D.M.O., 4 September 1916.

58. Woodward, ed., *Robertson Correspondence*, No. 55, Robertson to Haig, 7 September 1916. Robertson denied in his memoirs that he ever saw Lloyd George's letter although his communication to Haig, cited here, would suggest otherwise. Sir William Robertson, *Soldiers and Statesmen* (London: 1926), II, 127. He adds to the confusion by saying it was directed to the Prime Minister. Moreover he spoke to the military correspondent of *The Times* about it on 7 September. Repington, *World War*, I, 323, 7 September 1916.

59. See: Riddell, *War Diary*, p. 216, 29 October 1916; Wilson, ed., *Scott Diaries*, p. 238, 20–22 November 1916.

60. Addison, *Politics*, I, 266–7, 23 November 1916.

61. See J.A. Spender and Cyril S. Asquith, *The Life of Herbert Henry Asquith, Lord Oxford and Asquith* (London: 1932), II, 238; *The Times*, 12, 16 August 1916. On the visit to Haig see: Lloyd George, *War Memoirs*, II, 225–26.

62. LGP, H of L, E/1/2/3, Northcliffe to Lee, Ritz Hotel, n.d.; BL Add MS 62978, Riddell diaries, 9 August 1916.

63. Lloyd George's itinerary, upon which he is vague, perhaps deliberately, in his *War Memoirs* can be partially reconstructed from his telegrams to William Sutherland, his confidential, mainly press and patronage, secretary who clearly was instructed to keep Miss Stevenson informed of his whereabouts. He had no schedule and apparently no fixed date for a return to Britain. Unusually Frances Stevenson, on a vacation, says nothing of this trip in her diary. LGP, H of L, E/1/4/3–6, Sutherland to FLS, 6–9 September 1916.

64. Lloyd George, *War Memoirs*, II, 12.

65. Repington, *World War*, I, 345, 25 September 1916. The slaughter of the Brigade of Guards, a tragedy far less celebrated than the murderous holocaust on 1 July, remained engraved on the minds of two participants in the attack, both future Prime Ministers, when as old men they wrote their memoirs.

66. Haig's diary suggests that Lloyd George was expected at British Headquarters that evening. The meeting with Foch may have been fortuitous. Robert Blake, ed., *The Private Papers of Douglas Haig, 1914–1919*, London, 1952, p. 165, 11 September 1916.

67. See *Morning Post*, 28 September 1916.

68. Woodward, ed., *Robertson Correspondence*, No. 54, Robertson to Haig, 29 August 1916.

69. Blake, ed., *Haig Papers*, p. 167, 15 September 1916.

70. BL Add MS 62978, Riddell diaries, 29 October 1916.

71. Bonham Carter, *Strategy of Victory*, p. 188.

72. See for example: Edward David, ed., *Inside Asquith's Cabinet, From The Diaries of Charles Hobhouse*, London, 1977, p. 98, 30 October 1910.

73. C.E. Callwell, *Field Marshal Sir Henry Wilson* (London: 1927), I, 292. (Foreword by Ferdinand Foch.)

74. Lloyd George, *War Memoirs*, II, 211–12, 26 September 1916.

75. *Ibid.*, p. 213, Robertson to LG, 27 September 1916.

76. Repington, *World War*, I, 358–59, 10 October 1916.

77. Woodward, ed., *Robertson Correspondence*, No. 60, Robertson to LG, 11 October 1916. A.J.P. Taylor reports that because of the marks of a paperclip in the diary at the point at which Miss Stevenson records having a copy of the letter that it was once in the Stevenson diary but had disappeared. Taylor, ed., *Stevenson Diary*, p. 116 and n., 12 October 1916.

78. Repington, *World War*, I, 358–59, 361, 10, 13 October 1916. According to Miss Stevenson Northcliffe, in fact, did not see Lloyd George who was away and so the shower of denunciation fell upon David Davies. Taylor, ed., *Stevenson Diary*, p. 115, 12 October 1916.

79. Woodward, ed., *Robertson Correspondence*, Nos. 61, 62, Robertson to Northcliffe, Gwynne to Robertson, 11 October 1916.

80. *Ibid.*, No. 65, LG to Robertson, 11 October 1916.

81. BL Add MS 62978, Riddell diaries, 14 October 1916.

82. See: Taylor, ed., *Stevenson Diary*, p. 119, 24 October 1916.

83. On the matter of the failure of coordination at the top, and the pernicious effect of the separation between military strategy and diplomacy, Robertson fully agreed. See his extremely important letter to Edward Grey on 29 November 1916 evidently after the news arrived that the Germans had pushed through the passes in the Transylvanian Alps, as the story goes just 12 hours before the snows, and that in the south Mackensen and the Bulgarians had crossed the Danube. Bucharest was lost. (It would fall on 6 December.) Military preparations and diplomacy were 'out of step' insisted Robertson. Neither knew what the other was doing. In a fascinating example, Robertson brought up the British commitment to France before 1914 when all officers knew that military preparations were inadequate. While simplifying an extremely complicated question, Robertson was at least partly right. Lloyd George would have agreed. Woodward, ed., *Robertson Correspondence*, No. 85, Robertson to Grey, 29 November 1916. See also his letter to Col. Repington, *Ibid.*, No. 70, Robertson to C.A. Repington, 30 October 1916.

84. Repington, *World War*, I, 374, 25 October 1916.

85. See Roskill, *Hankey*, I, 308–9.

86. Taylor, ed., *Stevenson Diary*, p. 118, 23 October 1916.

87. *Ibid.*, p. 119, 24 October 1916.

88. See Robertson's comments on this decision to Haig, and, more illuminating, General B.F. Milne's letter to Robertson. Woodward, ed., *Robertson Correspondence*, Nos. 68, 69, Robertson to Haig, 25 October; Milne to Robertson, 27 October 1916. Milne was British G.O.C. in Salonika and himself opposed to reinforcements.

89. The origins of these ideas are not clear; the most obvious source would be Thomas.

90. On Lloyd George's report of the meeting see: Taylor, ed., *Stevenson Diary*, p. 120, 31 October 1916.

91. LGP, H of L, E/1/5/4, LG to Robertson, 29 October 1916.

92. Ibid., WRR, War Office to the Secretary of State, 3 November 1916, 9 pp. TS. Lloyd George prints a portion of this memorandum in his *War Memoirs*, II, 323–25.

93. Lloyd George, *War Memoirs*, II, 330–43.

94. On this meeting see Woodward, *Lloyd George and the Generals*, pp. 118–19.

95. Maurice, Lord Hankey, *The Supreme Command, 1914–1918* (London: 1961), II, 557, diary, 10 November, 1916.

96. Woodward, ed., *Robertson Correspondence*, No. 73, Robertson to Haig, 8 November 1916.

97. *Ibid.*, No. 82, Robertson to Curzon, 28 November 1916. On his view of the old War Committee see also, Bonham Carter, *Strategy of Victory*, p. 192.

98. Frances Stevenson noted Robertson had told Lloyd George after his resignation: 'Stick to it! You are all right!' Lloyd George was comforted. Taylor, ed., *Stevenson Diary*, p. 132, 5 December 1916. Woodward, ed., *Robertson Correspondence*, No. 91, Robertson to LG, 6 December 1916.

99. Woodward, ed., *Robertson Correspondence*, No. 75, Hankey to Robertson, 9 November 1916, *'Secret and Personal'*.

100. Roskill, *Hankey*, I, 317, 9 November 1916.

101. Woodward, ed., *Robertson Correspondence*, No. 76, Hankey to Robertson, 10 November 1916, 'Secret and Personal'. Hankey, literally, was in despair. See his account of the conversations with Lloyd George: Hankey, *Command*, II, 557–58, 7, 9, 10, 11, 12 November 1916.

102. Woodward, ed., *Robertson Correspondence*, No. 81, Robertson to HHA, 13 November 1916.

103. Hankey, *Command*, II, 560, 15 November 1916.

104. BL Add MS 62978, Riddell diaries, 10 December 1916. See also his less circumstantial account to Frances Stevenson: Taylor, ed., *Stevenson Diary*, p. 126, 21 November 1916.

105. Callwell, *Wilson*, I, 299, 26 November 1916.

106. Lloyd George, *War Memoirs*, II, 328–9.

107. *Ibid.*, 330–43.

108. See for example Robertson's estimate of the available German and Allied reserves. *Ibid.*, pp. 321, 331.

109. *Ibid.*, 335–36.

110. *Ibid.*, 341.

111. *Ibid.*, 343.

112. Lloyd George prints most of the transcripts of the 15–16 November meetings to which Hankey, for some hours, was not invited. *Ibid.*, II, 345–69.

113. On Asquith's pre-dinner naps, Roy Jenkins states that he did not sleep but merely wished for some time alone to read or reflect. Lloyd George would not have understood this. Jenkins, *Asquith*, p. 420n.

114. The Prime Minister's weakening physical condition, remarked upon by Hankey, is confirmed by the extremely useful newly published diary of the Earl of Crawford and Balcarres, who had succeeded Selborne at Agriculture. Asquith's hands shook, his face drooped. He never expressed an opinion. His response to any request for guidance was for a memorandum. Crawford already had sent many. John Vincent, ed., *The Crawford Papers, The Journals of David Lindsay twenty-seventh Earl of Crawford and tenth Earl of Balcarres, 1892–1940*, Manchester, 1984, pp. 356–64, 12 July–17 November

1916. This condition seems to have become particularly apparent after the death of his son in mid-September.

115. Hankey generally concurs in his own memoirs with Lloyd George's account of the evening conversation on 16 November. He did not, he admits, record it in his diary, but it corresponds with his recollection and with other evidence. One must remember however that *The Supreme Command* was written long after the publication of the *War Memoirs* and that Hankey himself had participated closely in the compilation of Lloyd George's account. Hankey, *Command*, II, 563.

116. Lloyd George, *War Memoirs*, II, 278–79; Beaverbrook, *Politicians*, p. 314. McKenna evidently was aware that he was under suspicion. Riddell notes on 8 July, just after the beginning of the Battle of the Somme, in the presence of Henri Franklin-Bouillon, a French politician, that McKenna spoke in 'unctuous terms' of British ferocity against the Germans. He was

> glad they are killing all the prisoners, etc., etc. [Apparently there was in fact an order passed at battalion level on the first day for units to refrain from escorting prisoners back to the British lines.] I think he over did it and was anxious to counteract the impression that he was pro-German. When he had gone Franklin-Bouillon remarked, 'That man is a humbug. I do not trust him. He was trying to remove the impression created by what he said to me on my last visit. He then told me that the Allies were virtually defeated.'

BL Add MS 62978, Riddell diaries, 8 July 1916.

117. LGP, H of L, E/2/21/2, Northcliffe to LG, 25 September 1916.

118. Wilson, ed., *Scott Diaries*, p. 236, 20–22 November 1916. These rumors were of course perfectly correct. Germany had been planning an initiative for weeks. The literature on United States diplomacy during the war is immense but one may find a summary of what the United States knew of German diplomatic maneuvers in early autumn 1916 in a memorandum from Irwin Laughlin, First Secretary of the American Embassy in London, to Ambassador Walter Hines Page who was at the time in Washington. Laughlin's information, he said, came from the Admiralty, clearly the office of the Director of Naval Intelligence, the famous 'Room 40,' which was at that time reading all German diplomatic traffic. Burton J. Hendrick, *The Life and Letters of Walter H. Page* (New York: 1922), II, 180–82, Laughlin to Page, 30 August 1916. By this time relations between Ambassador Page and Captain Reginald Hall of the Office of Naval Intelligence were exceptionally close. Patrick Beesly, *Room 40: British Naval Intelligence 1914–18*, New York, 1982, pp. 225–51.

119. Arthur S. Link, ed., *The Papers of Woodrow Wilson* (Princeton: 1982), XL, 345–6. Roy Howard to E.M. House, 26 December 1916.

120. Riddell, *War Diary*, p. 212, 1 October 1916. Northcliffe's letter referred to here urging publication of the statement and saying that he personally would see that it received the widest possible distribution, appears in LGP, H of L, E/2/21/3, Northcliffe to LG, 27 September 1916.

121. *New York Times*, 29 September 1916.

122. LGP, H of L, E/2/13/5, Grey to LG, 29 September 1916.

123. LGP, H of L, E/2/13/5, 6, Grey to LG, 29 September, LG to Grey, 2 October 1916. The greater part of these two letters appears in Lloyd George, *War Memoirs*, II, 282–84, although Lloyd George prudently deleted the final paragraph of his message to Grey.

124. Wilson, ed., *Scott Diaries*, p. 228, 2–3 October 1916.

125. Lloyd George, *War Memoirs*, II, 286.

126. LGP, H of L, E/3/28/2, Spring-Rice to Grey, 6 October 1916.

127. Donald R. Schwartz, 'From Rapprochement to Appeasement: Domestic Determinants of Anglo-American Relations Under Lloyd George and Wilson,' unp. Ph.D. dissertation, New York University, 1977, p. 50.

128. Link, ed., *Wilson Papers*, XXXVIII, 313, Lansing to Wilson, 30 September 1916.

129. *Ibid.*, 392, 496, 619, Page to Wilson, 11 October, House to Wilson, 20 October, House to Wilson, 6 November 1916.

130. Schwartz, 'Relations Under Lloyd George and Wilson,' pp. 21–2, Spring-Rice to Grey, 20 October 1916.

131. *United States Senate Documents*, 74th Congress, Second Session, 1936, Special Committee on the Investigation of the Munitions Industry, Vol. III, 169, Document 119, p. 212, Wilson to House, 24 November 1916.

132. See Arthur S. Link, *Wilson* (Princeton: 1964), V, 196–97.

133. Kathleen Burk, *Britain, America and the Sinews of War, 1914–1918*, Winchester, Mass., 1985, pp. 81–3.

134. *Ibid.*, pp. 83–4.

135. *New York Times*, 28 November 1916.

136. See: Kathleen Burk, *Morgan Grenfell, 1838–1988, The Biography of a Merchant Bank*, Oxford, 1989, p. 131.

137. *Westminster Gazette*, 2 December 1916. The *New York Times* named Britain as the target of the circular only on 2 December. The decision to withdraw was 'wise' but Britain's credit facilities were huge.

138. LGP, H of L, F/103, War Cabinet Papers, War Cab. 1, 9 December 1916, printed, 'Secret.'

139. Burk, *Sinews*, p. 91. *New York Times*, 2 December 1916.

140. On 2 April 1917, the new Chancellor of the Exchequer, Andrew Bonar Law, reported that the overdraft at Morgan's was $345,000,000 (ten times their capitalization). Against this Britain had $490,000,000 worth of securities in the United States and $87,000,000 in gold, leaving visible assets in New York of $232,000,000, but with claims on uncompleted contracts amounting to $75,000,000 per week. See Burk, *Sinews*, p. 95.

There were in effect about three weeks' resources. Both France and Russia possessed a good supply of gold, the amount of which neither nation would truthfully disclose. McKenna had forced the Russians to disgorge some of hers, part of which still lies at the bottom of the Arctic Sea, but for practical purposes, despite what the business section of the *New York Times* was saying, Britain was in April, 1917, as she was in December, 1940, without negotiable foreign tender.

141. Spring-Rice to Grey, 29 November 1916, quoted in Schwartz, 'Relations Under Lloyd George and Wilson,' p. 60; see also *Ibid.*, Spring-Rice to Grey, 5 December 1916.

142. Burk, *Sinews*, p. 88.

143. LGP, H of L, E/3/23/3, George Buchanan to Charles Hardinge, 28 October 1916.

144. LGP, H of L, E/3/14/13, 14, LeRoy-Lewis to LG, 29 September, 2 October 1916.

145. See also Wilson, ed., *Scott Diaries*, pp. 228–31 for an extended series of letters between Lloyd George and Scott disputing the *Guardian*'s reports of French criticism.

146. R.A.O. Crewe-Milne, Marquis of Crewe, 'The Breakup of the First Coalition,' in Asquith, *Memories*, II, 152–164; Thomas W. Legh, Lord Newton, *Lord Lansdowne*, London, 1929, pp. 449–52.

147. It should be remembered that Lloyd George's lecture to the Cabinet on Britain's missed opportunities and failing leadership, admired indeed by Asquith himself, had been made only ten days earlier, on 3 November. On the statement see Asquith's comments to Hankey reported by Lloyd George to Riddell. Riddell, *War Diary*, p. 219, 5 November 1916. Hankey, it should be noted, made no record of the Prime Minister's statement in his diary.

148. The Lansdowne memorandum has been frequently reprinted: in Lloyd George, *War Memoirs*, II, 288–96 and in Asquith, *Memories*, II, 165–175. It appears in LGP, H of L, E/8/4/2, with a covering MS note from Arthur Lee, 13 November 1916, saying that it was the 'most nakedly pessimistic document' to come from outside the UDC (Union for Democratic Control). It was 'the wail of a tired old man.' Would Lloyd George note the 'scarcely veiled hostility' at the end.

The memorandum appears to have retained a confidentiality singular for secret documents in the chaotic government of late 1916. Riddell evidently did not hear of it at the time, nor Scott, nor Hankey, although it should be remembered that Lansdowne submitted it only to the Cabinet, not to the War Committee, and Hankey had no access to Cabinet documents until after Lloyd George became Prime Minister.

149. Newton, *Lansdowne*, p. 463.

150. W. George, *Brother*, p. 256, 22 November 1916. Lloyd George, *War Memoirs*, II, 296–316.

151. Taylor, ed., *Stevenson Diary*, p. 127, 22 November 1916.

152. Blake, ed., *Haig Papers*, p. 182, 25 November 1916.

153. Beaverbrook, *Politicians*, pp. 372–5.

154. *Ibid.*, pp. 287–300.

155. Beaverbrook, *Politicians*, pp. 378–79. Austen Chamberlain reports that the Lansdowne memorandum had precisely this effect upon him also. Austen Chamberlain, *Down the Years*, London, 1936, pp. 112–13. See Lord Beaverbrook's account of his discussion with Bonar Law after an unpleasant meeting of the Unionist Cabinet members on 28 November 1916 at which Lansdowne had spoken vigorously for his plan. Beaverbrook, *Politicians*, pp. 377–80.

156. See Lord Beaverbrook's comments upon this. Beaverbrook, *Politicians*, pp. 308–09.

157. *Ibid.*, p. 309.

158. Lloyd George, *War Memoirs*, II, 209–10.

159. *Ibid.*, 223–24.

160. LGP, H of L, E/1/1/3, Derby to Lloyd George, 30 August 1916.

161. Blake, ed., *Haig Papers*, p. 161, Haig to Doris Haig, 23 August 1916.

162. See Lloyd George, *War Memoirs*, II, 229–30, Haig to Geddes, 22 September; *Ibid.*, 230–31, Lloyd George to Haig, 27 September, Haig to Lloyd George, 1 October 1916.

163. See Lloyd George's account: *Ibid.*, 227–28; Riddell, *War Diary*, p. 211, 19 September 1916.

164. Wilson, ed., *Scott Diaries*, p. 237, 20–22 November 1916. See also the rather incorrect version of events transcribed by Frances Stevenson. Taylor, ed., *Stevenson Diary*, p. 115, 12 October 1916.

165. LGP, H of L, E/1/1/6, Derby to Lloyd George, 15 September; Ibid., E/2/16/3, Stamfordham to LG, 5 October 1916. Stuart-Wortley was finally relieved in January 1917, but he received a field command.

166. Blake, ed., *Haig Papers*, pp. 173–4, 27 October 1916.

167. Lawrence R. Buchanan, 'The Governmental Career of Sir Eric Campbell Geddes,' unp. Ph.D. dissertation, University of Virginia, 1979, pp. 24–26.

168. See: LGP, H of L, E/1/5/16, Geddes to Lloyd George, 19 November 1916.

169. See: Hankey, *Command*, II, 615.

170. LGP, H of L, E/1/6/10, LG to French, 26 October 1916.

171. Ibid., E/2/23/7, PM to LG, 30 October 1916.

172. King George V, to whom Lloyd George explained the Barrett affair on 8 August, said of Mrs. Cornwallis West 'My father often told me that she was the most beautiful girl he had ever met.' Taylor, ed., *Stevenson Diary*, p. 113, 8 August 1916.

173. Quoted in: Byron Farwell, *Mr. Kipling's Army*, New York, 1987, p. 11.

174. See for example: E.M. Horsley, ed., *Lady Cynthia Asquith, Diaries, 1915–1918*, New York, 1969, pp. 201–02, 8 August 1916.

175. See Lloyd George, *War Memoirs*, II, 196–97.

176. *Parliamentary Papers*, 1917–18, IV, *Cd. 8435*, 'Reports of the Courts of Enquiry into the cases of 2nd Lt. Patrick Barrett and Hon. Lt. Col. Owen Thomas,' 327, 16 November 1916.

177. The full report of the Barrett enquiry appears in: LGP, H of L, E/6/3/2, 16 November 1916, 76pp. Its chief interest lies in some fascinating letters.

178. *PP., Cd. 8435*, 'Barrett case.'

179. Wilson, ed., *Scott Diaries*, p. 223, 27 July 1916.

180. *Ibid.*

181. Taylor, ed., *Stevenson Diary*, p. 113, 8 August 1916.

182. Repington, *World War*, I, 293, 29 July 1916. Like a true old army man Repington found the complaints 'trivial and idiotic.'

183. *Official Report, House of Commons Debates*, Series Five, LXXXV (7 August 1916), cols. 701–757.

184. See Lloyd George's statement on this: *Ibid.*, LXXXVII (21 November 1916), cols. 1200–01.

185. Taylor, ed., *Stevenson Diary*, pp. 125–26, 20 November; Wilson, ed., *Scott Diaries*, pp. 238–39, 20–22 November 1916.

186. LGP, H of L, E/2/16/5, Stamfordham to Brade, 23 November 1916.

187. Taylor, ed., *Stevenson Diary*, p. 130, 30 November 1916.

188. See Lloyd George's praise of Cowans in *War Memoirs*, II, 260–62. After the war Hankey received a note from Asquith saying he and the King agreed that Britain's success was attributable to him and Cowans. Roskill, *Hankey*, I, 631, 15 November 1918.

189. *H of C Deb.*, LXXXVIII (22 December 1916), cols. 1124–28.

Chapter 10, pp. 385–419

1. David Lloyd George, *War Memoirs* (Boston: 1933), II, 387.

2. Roy Jenkins, *Asquith*, London, 1964, p. 454.

3. See for example J.M. McEwen, 'The Press and the Fall of Asquith', *Historical Journal*, XXI (December, 1978), 4, 863–83; 'Northcliffe and Lloyd George at War, 1914–1918,' *Ibid.*, XXIV (September, 1981), 3, 651–72. Stephen Koss, *The Rise and Fall of the Political Press in Britain* (London: 1984), II, 274–306.

4. *The Times*, 11 December 1916.

5. See the essay by Robertson Nicoll in the *British Weekly*, 14 December 1916, on Northcliffe, Asquith and the press.

6. Oliver, Viscount Esher, *Journals and Letters of Reginald, Viscount Esher* (London: 1938), II, 68–9, Esher to Elibank, 28 November 1916.

7. Anon. [Laurence Lyon], *The Pomp of Power*, New York, 1922, pp. 115–120. Lyon was a Unionist MP from 1918 to 1921 and later proprietor of the *Outlook*.

8. Christopher Addison, *Politics From Within, 1911–1918* (London: 1924), I, 271.

9. A.J.P. Taylor, ed., *Lloyd George, A Diary by Frances Stevenson*, London, 1971, p. 129, 27 November 1916.

10. William Maxwell Aitken, Lord Beaverbrook, *Politicians and the War, 1914–1916*, London, 1960, pp. 335–36.

11. *Ibid.*, pp. 336–37.

12. C.R.M.F. Cruttwell, *A History of the Great War*, Oxford, 1936, p. 501.

13. C.E. Callwell, *Field Marshal Sir Henry Wilson* (London: 1927), I, 299, 27 November 1916.

14. See Lloyd George's comments to Aitken on the morning of 18 November, Beaverbrook, *Politicians*, p. 337; see also Bonar Law's statement to Aitken on 20 November, *Ibid.*, p. 340; Taylor, ed., *Stevenson Diary*, pp. 128, 129, 27, 30 November 1916.

15. Taylor, ed., *Stevenson Diary*, p. 125, 20 November 1916. Evidently it would be an official visit. On the meeting see Beaverbrook, *Politicians*, p. 342.

16. Beaverbrook, *Politicians*, p. 340, 20 November 1916.

17. *Ibid.*, p. 349, 25 November 1916.

18. *Ibid.*

19. Bonar Law's account of the meeting appears in Robert Blake, *Unrepentant Tory, The Life and Times of Andrew Bonar Law, 1858–1923*, New York, 1956, p. 306.

20. Taylor, ed., *Stevenson Diary*, p. 129, 27 November 1916.

21. In the years that followed, press gossip generally took it for granted that McKenna had destroyed the agreement worked out by Lloyd George and Asquith on Sunday, 3 December. See for example, Anon. [Lyon], *Power*, p. 119.

22. Beaverbrook, *Politicians*, p. 114, 26 November 1916.

23. *Ibid.*, pp. 355–57, Asquith to Bonar Law, 26 November 1916.

24. Blake, *Unrepentant Tory*, p. 308. See also Beaverbrook, *Politicians*, p. 358, 'Monday afternoon.'

25. Beaverbrook, *Politicians*, pp. 344, 349.

26. See Taylor, ed., *Stevenson Diary*, p. 126, 22 November 1916. Balfour wondered to the end of his life why Lloyd George would not have him at the Admiralty. Frances Stevenson records that he asked Lloyd George about it years later and was told that he was needed at the Foreign Office, which may have been true but was not an answer to the question asked. Frances L. Stevenson, *The Years That Are Past*, London, 1967, p. 95. Closer to the truth no doubt was Lloyd George's description of Balfour to A.J. Sylvester. 'He would get up at 10:30.' 'He did not go to the Admiralty before he came to Cabinet. He would see his First Sea Lord for the first time at Cabinet.' One could not run a war that way. Colin Cross, ed., *Life With Lloyd George: The Diary of A.J. Sylvester, 1931–1945*, London 1975, p. 177, 27 March 1937.

27. Blake, *Unrepentant Tory*, pp. 308–09; Beaverbrook, *Politicians*, pp. 362–384.

28. Addison, *Politics*, I, 268, 4 December 1916.

29. *Morning Post*, 23 November 1916.

30. See McEwen, 'Press and Asquith,' *Historical Journal* (December, 1978), 869. Even Lloyd George attributed it to the 'Young Tories,' in effect the Unionist War Committee. Carson was unpopular among the leadership but he controlled the back bench. J.M. McEwen, ed., *The Riddell Diaries, 1908–1923*, London, 1986, p. 174, 26 November 1916.

31. *Westminster Gazette*, 29 November 1916. See also: *Daily Chronicle*, which added that there should be a small 'War Council of four, the Prime Minister, Balfour, Bonar Law and Lloyd George.' The *Daily News* noted a resolution of the Labour party against colored labor on 'moral, social, industrial and economic' grounds. *Daily News*, 30 November.

32. *The Times*, 28, 29 November 1916.

33. A.J.P. Taylor, *Beaverbrook*, London, 1972, pp. 112–13.

34. *Daily Chronicle*, 29, 30 November. Riddell told Lloyd George on 26 November, the day that Asquith had rejected the first proposal for a war committee of four including himself, that he had urged Robert Donald, editor of the *Chronicle*, to see Asquith and propose such a body. George, Lord Riddell, *War Diary, 1914–1918*, London, 1933, p. 222, November 26. McEwen, 'Press and Asquith,' *Historical Journal* (December, 1978), 872.

35. Addison, *Politics*, I, 268, 4 December 1916.

36. Lloyd George, *War Memoirs*, II, 388–89. This memorandum appears in Lloyd George Papers, House of Lords Record Office, E/2/23/9, 'Memo. to Prime Minister, December 1st, 1916.'

37. Arthur, Viscount Lee of Fareham, 'A Good Innings', privately printed, 1939, Vol. II, p. 676 in Lee of Fareham Papers, House of Lords Record Office, Ruth Lee diary, 1 December 1916.

38. McEwen, 'Northcliffe and Lloyd George,' *Historical Journal* (September, 1981), 663.

39. Stephen Roskill, *Hankey, Man of Secrets* (New York: 1970), I, 324, 2 December 1916.

40. Lloyd George, *War Memoirs*, II, 389–90; LGP, H of L, E/2/23/10, Asquith to LG, 1 December 1916.

41. British Library, Add MS 62978, Riddell diaries, 3 December 1916.

42. LGP, H of L, E/2/23/11, LG to Asquith, 2 December 1916. TS with MS corrections. This letter does not appear in the *War Memoirs*.

43. *British Weekly*, 7 December 1916. See also, McEwen, 'Press and Asquith,' *Historical Journal* (December, 1978), 879–80.

44. *Daily Chronicle*, 2 December 1916. The *Daily News* said virtually the same thing on Monday. *Daily News*, 4 December 1916.

45. *The Times*, 2 December 1916.

46. Aitken discusses this interview in some detail. Lloyd George was dining at the Berkeley Hotel with Reading, Montagu and Walter, Lord Cunliffe, Governor of the Bank of England. Bonar Law, evidently having an attack of nerves, insisted that Aitken call Lloyd George from the dinner so that the two could talk. Beaverbrook, *Politicians*, pp. 391–95.

47. Lloyd George, *War Memoirs*, II, 391.

48. Ian Colvin, *The Life of Lord Carson* (London: 1936), III, 206–7. Jenkins says that Asquith indeed had told Reading that he intended to see Carson at Birchington. However, Jenkins continued, the Prime Minister was misinformed about Carson's

whereabouts. Carson had not left London. In fact he had. Jenkins, *Asquith*, pp. 433–4.

49. Roskill, *Hankey*, I, 324, 2 December 1916.

50. Taylor, ed., *Stevenson Diary*, p. 131, 2 December 1916.

51. J.A. Spender and Cyril S. Asquith, *The Life of Herbert Henry Asquith, Lord Oxford and Asquith* (London: 1932), II, 254. Jenkins's biography reproduces another portion of the same letter. Jenkins, *Asquith*, p. 434. Montagu to Asquith, 2 December 1916.

52. *Daily Chronicle*, 9 December 1916. See also his letter written on Sunday evening, 3 December, to, not surprisingly, Pamela McKenna. Beaverbrook, *Politicians*, p. 435. It was a '"Crisis" — this time with a very big C'. As an interesting social note, among the guests that week-end at Walmer Castle was Quartermaster General Sir John Cowans, still, at this time, in danger of losing his assignment.

53. Beaverbrook, *Politicians*, pp. 410–24.

54. Thomas W. Legh, Lord Newton, *Lord Lansdowne*, London, 1929, pp. 452–53, Curzon to Lansdowne, 3 December 1916; Austen Chamberlain, *Down the Years*, London, 1936, pp. 115–29.

55. John Vincent, ed., *The Crawford Papers, The Journals of David Lindsay twenty-seventh Earl of Crawford and tenth Earl of Balcarres, 1892–1940*, Manchester, 1984, pp. 369–372, 3 December 1916.

56. Blake, *Unrepentant Tory*, pp. 318, 320.

57. Lloyd George, *War Memoirs*, II, 391.

58. Vincent, ed., *Crawford Papers*, p. 372, 3 December 1916.

59. *Ibid.*

60. The text of the Unionist resolution appears in Spender and Asquith, *Asquith*, II, 257.

61. Vincent, ed., *Crawford Papers*, p. 371.

62. Trevor Wilson, ed., *The Political Diaries of C.P. Scott, 1911–1928*, Ithaca, 1970, p. 243, 2–5 December 1916.

63. Beaverbrook, *Politicians*, p. 430.

64. Asquith to Lloyd George, 4 December 1916, in Lloyd George, *War Memoirs*, II, 392–93.

65. Beaverbrook, *Politicians*, p. 431.

66. Vincent, ed., *Crawford Papers*, p. 371, 3 December 1916.

67. Koss, *The Political Press in Britain*, II, 305.

68. Tom Clarke, *My Northcliffe Diary*, New York, 1931, p. 95. Diary, 3, 4 December 1916. Clarke seems to have been certain. He repeated the story in an entry the next day.

69. Winston S. Churchill, *The World Crisis, 1916–1918* (New York: 1924), I, 256.

70. Colvin, *Carson*, III, 209. See also his letter to Bonar Law of 4 December. *Ibid.*, p. 210.

71. *The Times*, 4 December 1916, Lead Article 'Reconstruction,' and the political article 'Mr. Lloyd George's Stand.'

72. *Ibid.*

73. Koss, *The Political Press in Britain*, II, 304–6. See also H. Montgomery Hyde, *Carson*, New York, 1974, p. 410.

74. Colvin, *Carson*, III, 209, Ruby Carson diary, 4 December 1916.

75. Lloyd George, *War Memoirs*, II, 392, Asquith to LG, 4 December 1916.

76. *Ibid.*, 193, LG to PM, 4 December 1916.

77. *Ibid.*, 394.

78. *Westminster Gazette*, 6 December 1916.

79. It will be recalled that Christopher Addison had reported on Wednesday evening, 6 December, as Lloyd George was preparing to try to form a government, that Lloyd George had 49 unconditional Liberal supporters in the House of Commons and another 126 who would support a Lloyd George government if formed. Addison, *Politics*, I, 271–72, 9 December 1916. This canvass must have been underway at least since the beginning of the week.

80. Blake, *Unrepentant Tory*, p. 330–31.

81. See Curzon to Asquith, 4 December 1916, in Spender and Asquith, *Asquith*, II, 260.

82. The reports of Curzon's apparently repeated outbursts on 3 December and of Lansdowne's brief account of his meeting with the PM the following day are found in Vincent, ed., *Crawford Papers*, pp. 372–3, Diary, 3, 4 December 1916. Beyond the passing reference in Curzon's letter to Lansdowne this seems to be the only solid evidence that Asquith saw any Unionists on Monday, 4 December.

83. McEwen, ed., *Riddell Diaries*, p. 180, 25 December 1916.

84. Roy Jenkins speculates about this matter at some length. Jenkins, *Asquith*, pp. 444–48.

85. *Daily Chronicle*, 9 December 1916.

86. British Library, Add MS 46392, J.A. Spender papers, Vol. VII, Samuel to Spender, 5 December 1916, 'Home Office' TS. As the *Westminster Gazette* had announced only that day that the crisis was practically over, Spender may have begun to feel, reasonably, that his sources of information were less than perfect. Hence the solicitation of this letter, which does not seem to have been used in the biography of Asquith.

87. HHA to LG, 4 December 1916, quoted in Lloyd George, *War Memoirs*, II, 304–06.

88. Christopher Addison, *Four and a Half Years* (London: 1934), I, 271, dictated 9–10 December 1916.

89. Randolph S. Churchill, *Lord Derby, King of Lancashire*, London, 1959, p. 237.

90. Colvin, *Carson*, III, 211, Ruby Carson diary, 5 December 1916.

91. LGP, H of L, E/2/23/11, LG to PM, 2 December 1916.

92. Lloyd George, *War Memoirs*, II, 397–98, LG to HHA, 5 December 1916.

93. *Ibid.*, 399, HHA to LG, 5 December 1916.

94. The resolution of the publication of the letters controversy should be given here. The Asquith-Lloyd George correspondence and a number of Lloyd George's memoranda warning of military disasters, including the one of which Lloyd George was particularly proud, the warning to Robertson on the fall of Romania, appeared in the *Atlantic Monthly* of February, 1919. ('Anon.' [Ellery Sedgwick], 'Unwritten History,' *Atlantic Monthly*, CXXIII (February, 1919), 145–56.) The article provided a decent story of the December crisis along Beaverbrook lines, emphasizing the Prime Minister's discussions with his colleagues at all stages and including everyone's assumption that Lloyd George would be unable to form a government or that it would not last if he did. All the papers already had been privately printed and circulated, said the article. On the whole, the tone was unfriendly to Lloyd George. Its appearance caused

something of a refreshing minor scandal. (See Almeric Fitzroy, *Memoirs* (London: n.d. [1925]), II, 694, 4 February 1919.)

The footprints here seem to lead to Lord Beaverbrook who at the end of the war was Minister of Information and through him to Arnold Bennett. For nearly two years Beaverbrook had been collecting documents for *Politicians and the War*. He employed at the Ministry of Information, among other excellent artists, Bennett, a friend of Ellery Sedgwick. Sedgwick at the end of the war was in London researching an article on British politics. See Newman Flower, ed., The *Journal of Arnold Bennett*, New York, 1933, p. 668, 12 October 1918. Probably this was it.

95. Quoted in Jenkins, *Asquith*, p. 453.

96. *Ibid.*

97. See Blake, *Unrepentant Tory*, p. 333.

98. Chamberlain, *Years*, p. 124.

99. Blake, *Unrepentant Tory*, pp. 333–34.

100. Vincent, ed., *Crawford Papers*, pp. 373–75, 5 December 1916. For the letter see: Blake, *Unrepentant Tory*, p. 334.

101. Addison, *Four and a Half Years*, I, 271.

102. Riddell, *War Diary*, p. 226, 2 December 1916.

103. *Ibid.*, p. 229, 8 December 1916.

104. *Ibid.*, p. 238, 14 January 1917.

105. McEwen, ed., *Riddell Diaries*, p. 180, 28 December 1916.

106. Crewe, 'First Coalition,' in: The Earl of Oxford and Asquith, *Memories and Reflections, 1852–1927* (Boston: 1928), II, 159–60.

107. E.M. Horsley, ed., *Lady Cynthia Asquith, Diaries, 1915–1918*, New York, 1969, pp. 241–42, 5 December 1916.

108. See for example Leo Maxse, no friend of Lloyd George to be sure, but a supporter of Bonar Law and the new government. *National Review*, LXVII (January, 1917), 596.

109. Beaverbrook, *Politicians*, pp. 488–90. Addison, *Politics*, I, 270.

110. See Crewe, 'First Coalition,' in Asquith, *Memories*, II, 160. Cynthia Asquith does not mention Bonar Law's appearance at No. 10.

111. Addison, *Four and a Half Years*, I, 271–72, 9–10 December 1916.

112. That evening at No. 10 Cynthia Asquith had heard that the King had declared 'I shall resign if Asquith does.' Horsley, ed., *Cynthia Asquith Diaries*, p. 242, 5 December 1916.

113. Lee, 'Innings,' II, 681, Ruth Lee diary, 6 December 1916.

114. Beaverbrook, *Politicians*, p. 494.

115. Robert Rhodes James, ed., *J.C.C. Davidson's Memoirs and Papers*, London, 1969. Davidson would remain close to Bonar Law, was his confidential secretary as Prime Minister and became eventually Chairman of the Conservative party.

116. The two basic sources on the conference are a note by Balfour in Blanche E.C. Dugdale, *Arthur James Balfour* (London: 1936), II, 178–80; and, much fuller, Stamfordham's memorandum for the King in Harold Nicolson, *King George the Fifth*, New York, 1953, pp. 290–91.

117. Beaverbrook, *Politicians*, p. 495. Addison, *Politics*, I, 270.

118. Beaverbrook, *Politicians*, p. 496.

119. The best, most recent, and extended account of the King's conference appears in John D. Fair, *British Interparty Conferences, A Study of the Procedure of Conciliation in*

British Politics, 1867–1921, Oxford, 1980, pp. 155–56. Blake, *Unrepentant Tory*, says that Lloyd George declined to serve under Asquith. No other account gives any evidence of this.

120. Public Record Office, Northern Ireland, D.2846/1/1/85, Theresa, Lady Londonderry papers, Carson to Lady Londonderry, 12 March 1912.

121. Horsley, ed., *Cynthia Asquith Diaries*, p. 243, 5 December 1916. When Asquith died a little more than a decade later his estate was valued at £9,000. Ramsay MacDonald had left more than twice as much. W.D. Rubenstein, *Men of Property*, New Brunswick, N.J., 1981, p. 175, n. 43.

122. 'Asquith by Strachey,' *The Times*, 15 January 1972. On this article see: Michael Holroyd, *Lytton Strachey* (London: 1968), II, 258, 331–2. Holroyd discussed the review and used it extensively in his biography.

123. Crewe, 'Coalition,' in Asquith, *Memories*, II, 162.

124. *Ibid.*, p. 163.

125. Quoted in Blake, *Unrepentant Tory*, p. 340.

126. LGP, H of L, F/22/4/1, Gwynne to LG, 8 December; Ibid., F/22/4/2, LG to Gwynne, 8 December 1916.

127. Riddell, *War Diary*, pp. 229–30, 6, 10 December 1916. Imitating Curzon's affected accent, he told Riddell, 'I could sit and listen to him for hours.' Lloyd George could have added that Curzon knew both things that were important and things that were not, and was ready to expound on either at length. Addison found him a bore.

128. BL Add MS 62978, Riddell diaries, 6 December 1916. Most, although not all, of this passage appears in Riddell, *War Diary*, pp. 227–29, 6 December 1916. Lloyd George denied vigorously to Riddell and Burnham that he had seen anything of Northcliffe for months until the previous day, or Monday (when *The Times* leader had appeared). He had forgotten which. This was patently untrue but it became the official story. He said the same to C.P. Scott eight months later. Wilson, ed., *Scott Diaries*, pp. 297–98, 10 August 1917.

129. Addison, *Politics*, I, 270.

130. Beaverbrook, *Politicians*, p. 516.

131. *Ibid.* Blake, *Unrepentant Tory*, p. 340. Much has been written of Curzon's unseemly pursuit of office. Yet there are some things to be said in his defense. He was president of the Air Board. He was under intense pressure from General Hugh Trenchard, Commander of the Royal Flying Corps, who in fact did not like him, for supplies, new aircraft designs, and for definition of the place of the navy. Among the circumstantial, as opposed to the political, charges against Asquith's government in the press, the Air Board always appeared. Curzon's posturing and vanity were objectionable as everyone knew including Trenchard. But perhaps also he wanted to win the war. Andrew Boyle, *Trenchard*, New York, 1962, pp. 191–93.

132. Riddell, *War Diary*, p. 232, 10 December 1916; Jenkins, *Asquith*, pp. 466–67.

133. 'Memorandum of Conversation between Mr. Lloyd George and certain Unionist ex-Ministers,' December 7, 1916 in Beaverbrook, *Politicians*, pp. 520–27.

134. Taylor, ed., *Stevenson Diary*, p. 134, 7 December 1916.

135. Riddell, *War Diary*, p. 230, 10 December 1916.

136. Addison, *Politics*, I, 271–72, 9 December 1916.

137. Nearly the entire speech and the discussion following is printed in: David Lloyd George, *War Memoirs* (Boston: 1934), III, 12–22.

138. Riddell, *War Diary*, p. 230, 10 December 1916.

139. On the meeting see: Norman and Jeanne MacKenzie, eds., *The Diary of Beatrice Webb* (Cambridge, Mass.: 1984), III, 270–71, 8 December 1916. Mrs. Webb was disgusted by Labour's capitulation.

140. *Ibid.*

141. This office, as its historian admits, remained in political Siberia through the interwar period, although in 1940, under a truly powerful minister and with control of national service, it suddenly emerged as the most important and visible of the home departments. For Lloyd George its usefulness ended once it had been founded. It barely escaped elimination in the Geddes economy drive in 1921 and did not become permanent, in the jargon 'established,' until 1923. See: Rodney Lowe, *Adjusting to Democracy, The Role of the Ministry of Labour in British Politics, 1916–1939*, Oxford, 1986, pp. 36–37.

142. Beaverbrook, *Politicians*, pp. 488–91.

143. Riddell, *War Diary*, p. 232, 10, 11 December 1916.

144. McEwen, ed., *Riddell Diaries*, p. 179, 11 December 1916.

145. BL Add MS 62978, Riddell diaries, 12 December 1916.

146. *British Weekly*, 14 December 1916.

147. Alfred, Viscount Milner, *The Nation and Empire*, London, 1913.

148. Alfred Gollin, *Proconsul in Politics, A Study of Alfred, Lord Milner in Opposition and Power*, London, 1964, p. 324.

149. Roskill, *Hankey*, I, 322.

150. See: Gollin, *Milner*, pp. 370–75.

151. Riddell, *War Diary*, p. 243 18 February 1917.

152. BL Add MS 62979, Riddell diaries, 1 April 1917.

153. See Addison Papers, Bodleian Library, Box 59, Addison to LG, 8, 11 December 1916.

154. BL Add MS 62978, Riddell diaries, 10 December 1916.

155. Addison, *Politics*, II, 273, 9 December 1916.

156. *Ibid.*, 274.

157. LGP, H of L, F/6/2/5, Carson to LG, 26 December 1916.

158. PRONI, D.1507/C/3, Carson papers, Ruby Carson diary, 31 January 1917.

159. John Herbert Lewis Papers, National Library of Wales, Group 10, Folder 230, unsorted, MS, LG to 'Sir,' 11 December 1916. Lewis of course already had an appointment, announced the previous day.

160. BL Add MS 62978, Riddell diaries, 10 December 1916.

161. LGP, H of L, F/42/5/1, LG to Asquith, 9 December 1916.

Consclusion, pp. 421–424

1. British Library, Add MS 62980, Riddell diaries, 2 August 1917.

2. Ibid.

3. Ibid., 19 August 1917.

4. Trevor Wilson, ed., *The Political Diaries of C.P. Scott, 1911–1928*, Ithaca, 1970, p. 326, 28 December 1917.

5. BL Add MS 62979, Riddell diaries, 16 February 1917.

6. *Parliamentary Papers, 1917–1918, Cd. 8490, 8502*, 'Dardanelles Commission, Preliminary Report and Supplement.' The fuller account did not appear until after the war: *P.P. 1919, Cmd. 371*, 'Dardanelles Commission, Final Report,' Part II.

7. Oliver, Viscount Esher, ed., *Journals and Letters of Reginald, Viscount Esher* (London: 1938), IV, 71–2, Esher to Haig, 4 December 1916.

Bibliography

Primary Sources

1. Letters and Manuscript Collections

   Christopher Addison Papers, Bodleian Library

   H.H. Asquith Papers, Bodleian Library

   Andrew Bonar Law Papers, House of Lords Record Office

   William John Braithwaite Papers, British Library of Political and Economic Science

   John Burns papers, vol. LV, diary, British Library

   Edward Carson Papers, Public Record Office Northern Ireland

   D.R. Daniel Memoir, National Library of Wales

   Gainford Papers, J.A. Pease diary, Nuffield College

   Arthur, Viscount Lee of Fareham, 'A Good Innings,' privately printed, 1939, Lee of Fareham Papers, House of Lords Record Office

   Arthur, Viscount Lee of Fareham Papers, House of Lords Record Office

   John Herbert Lewis Papers, National Library of Wales

   David Lloyd George Papers, House of Lords Record Office

   David Lloyd George Papers, National Library of Wales

   Londonderry Papers, Letters of Theresa, Lady Londonderry, Public Record Office Northern Ireland

   Masterman Papers, Lucy Masterman TS diaries, University of Birmingham

   Leopold Maxse Papers, West Sussex Record Office

   Reginald McKenna Papers, Churchill College, Cambridge University

   Montgomery Family Papers, Letters of Hugh de Fellenberg Montgomery, Five Mile Town, Co. Tyrone, Public Record Office Northern Ireland

   Alfred, Lord Northcliffe Papers, British Library

   Arthur Ponsonby Papers, Bodleian Library

   Rufus, Lord Reading Papers, India Office Library

   George, Lord Riddell diaries, British Library

   St. Loe Strachey Papers, House of Lords Record Office

   Herbert Samuel Papers, House of Lords Record Office

   J.A. Spender Papers, British Library

   Henry H. Wilson Papers, Imperial War Museum

2. Unpublished official documents

   History of the Ministry of Munitions

   Public Record Office, Cabinet Papers

3. Published documents

    Official Report, House of Commons Debates, Series Five

    Official Report, House of Lords Debates

    Parliamentary Papers

    United States Senate Documents, 74th Congress, Second Session, 1936

4. Newspapers and periodicals

American Magazine	*Manchester Guardian*
Atlantic Monthly	*Morning Post*
British Medical Journal	*Nation*
British Weekly	*National Insurance Gazette*
Business History	*National Review*
Contemporary Review	*New Statesman*
Daily Chronicle	*New York Times*
Daily Mail	*North Wales Observer*
Daily News	*Observer*
Daily Telegraph	*Outlook*
Economic Journal	*Pall Mall Gazette*
Evening News	*Punch*
Eye-Witness	*Reynolds News*
Financial World	*Saturday Review*
Financier	*Spectator*
Historical Magazine of the Protestant Episcopal Church	*Standard*
	Sunday Times
Journal of the American Medical Association	*The Times*
	Westminster Gazette

5. Contemporary pamphlets, polemical material and personal sketches, speeches

    Gardiner, Alfred George, *Pillars of Society,* London, 1913

    Milner, Alfred, Viscount, *The Nation and Empire,* London, 1913

    Proud, Dorthea, *Welfare Work,* London, 1916

    'Viator Cambrensis,' *The Rise and Decline of Welsh Nonconformity,* London, 1912

6. Published letter collections and diaries

    Addison, Christopher, *Four and a Half Years* (London: 1934)

    (Essentially Addison's diary at the Bodleian)

    ——, *Politics From Within, 1911–1918* (London: 1924), Foreword by Edward Carson

    Baring, Maurice, *Flying Corps Headquarters, 1914–1918,* London, 1985

    Blake, Robert, ed., *The Private Papers of Douglas Haig, 1914–1919,* London, 1952

    Brock, Michael and Eleanor, eds., *H.H. Asquith, Letters to Venetia Stanley,* Oxford, 1982

    Chamberlain, Austen, *Down the Years,* London, 1936

    ——, *Politics From Inside,* New Haven, 1937

    Clarke, Tom, *My Northcliffe Diary,* New York, 1931

Cross, Colin, ed., *Life With Lloyd George: The Diary of A.J. Sylvester 1931–1945*, London, 1975

David, Edward, ed., *Inside Asquith's Cabinet, From the Diaries of Charles Hobhouse*, London, 1977

Esher, Oliver, Viscount, *Journals and Letters of Reginald, Viscount Esher* (London: 1938), IV

Fitzroy, Almeric, *Memoirs* (London: n.d. [1925])

Flower, Newman, ed., *The Journal of Arnold Bennett*, Garden City, New York, 1932

Hankey, Maurice, Lord, *The Supreme Command, 1914–1918* (London: 1961), I

Hart-Davis, Rupert, ed., *Siegfried Sassoon Diaries, 1915–1918*, London, 1983

Horsley, E.M., ed., *Lady Cynthia Asquith, Diaries, 1915–1918*, New York, 1969

Link, Arthur S., ed., *The Papers of Woodrow Wilson* (Princeton: 1980, 1982)

MacKenzie, Norman and Jeanne, eds., *The Diary of Beatrice Webb* (Cambridge, Mass.: 1984)

Masterman, Lucy, *C.F.G. Masterman*, London, 1939

McEwen, J.M., ed., *The Riddell Diaries, 1908–1923*, London, 1986

Morgan, Kenneth, ed., *Lloyd George Family Letters*, Cardiff, 1973

Repington, Lt. Col. Charles aCourt, *The First World War, 1914–1918* (Boston: 1920), I

Riddell, George, Lord, *More Pages From My Diary*, London, 1934

——, *War Diary, 1914-1918*, London, 1933

Seymour, Charles, ed., *The Intimate Papers of Colonel House* (Boston: 1926)

Taylor, A.J.P., ed., *Lloyd George, A Diary by Frances Stevenson*, London, 1971

——, ed., *My Darling Pussy, The Letters of Lloyd George and Frances Stevenson, 1913–41*, London, 1975

Vaughan, Edwin Campion, *Some Desperate Glory: The World War I diary of a British officer, 1917*, New York, 1981

Vincent, John, ed., *The Crawford Papers, The Journals of David Lindsay twenty-seventh Earl of Crawford and tenth Earl of Balcarres, 1892–1940*, Manchester, 1984

Wilson, Trevor, ed., *The Political Diaries of C.P. Scott, 1911–1928*, Ithaca, 1970

Woodward, David R., ed., *The Military Correspondence of Field-Marshal Sir William Robertson, Chief of the Imperial General Staff, December 1915–February 1918*, London, 1989

Young, Kenneth, ed., *The Diaries of Robert Bruce Lockhart*, London, 1973

Selected secondary sources

1. Significant Lloyd George biographies and memoirs

Carey Evans, Olwen, *Lloyd George Was My Father*, Llandysul, 1985

Davies, W. Watkin, *Lloyd George, 1863–1914*, London, 1939

DuParcq, Herbert, *The Life of David Lloyd George* (London: 1913)

Evans, Beriah G., *The Life Romance of David Lloyd George*, London, 1916

George, William, *My Brother and I*, London, 1958

George, W.R.P., *The Making of Lloyd George*, London, 1976

Grigg, John, *Lloyd George, From Peace to War*, Berkeley, 1985

Lloyd George, David, *War Memoirs* (Boston: 1933–7), I, II, III

Lloyd George, Richard, *My Father, Lloyd George,* New York, 1961

Mills, J. Saxon, *David Lloyd George, War Minister,* London, 1924

Rowland, Peter, *David Lloyd George, A Biography,* New York, 1975

Spender, Harold, *The Prime Minister,* New York, 1920

2. Other useful biographies

Allen, Bernard M., *Sir Robert Morant: A Great Public Servant,* London, 1934

Blake, Robert, *The Unknown Prime Minister,* London, 1955

——, *Unrepentant Tory, The Life and Times of Andrew Bonar Law, 1858–1923,* New York, 1956 (American edition of *Unknown Prime Minister*)

Bolitho, Hector, *Alfred Mond,* London, 1933

Bonham Carter, Victor, *Soldier True, The Life and Times of Field Marshal Sir William Robertson,* London, 1963

——, *The Strategy of Victory, 1914-1918, The Life and Times of the Master Strategist of World War I: Field-Marshal Sir William Robertson,* New York, 1964 (American edition of *Soldier True*)

Bonham Carter, Violet, *Winston Churchill, An Intimate Portrait,* New York, 1965

Boyle, Andrew, *Trenchard,* New York, 1962

Briggs, Asa, *Social Thought and Social Action: A Study of the Work of Seebohm Rowntree,* London, 1961

Callwell, C.E., *Field Marshal Sir Henry Wilson* (London: 1927), 2 vols. Foreword by Ferdinand Foch

Cassar, George H., *The Tragedy of Sir John French,* Newark, Delaware, 1985

Churchill, Randolph S., *Lord Derby, King of Lancashire,* London, 1959

——, *Winston Churchill* (Boston: 1967), II

Colvin, Ian, *The Life of Lord Carson* (London: 1936), II, III

Crow, Duncan, *A Man of Push and Go, The Life of George Macaulay Booth,* London, 1965

Darlow, T.H., *William Robertson Nicoll, His Life and Letters,* London, 1925

Dugdale, Blanche E.C., *Arthur James Balfour* (London: 1936)

Esher, Reginald, Viscount, *The Tragedy of Lord Kitchener,* New York, 1921

Eyck, Frank, *G.P. Gooch,* London, 1982

Farrar-Hockley, Anthony, *Goughie, The Life of General Sir Hubert Gough,* London, 1975

Forbes, J.D., *Stettinius, Sr., Portrait of a Morgan Partner,* Charlottesville, Virginia, 1974

Gilbert, Martin, *Winston S. Churchill* (London: 1971), III

Gollin, Alfred, *Proconsul in Politics, A Study of Alfred, Lord Milner in Opposition and Power,* London, 1964

Gwynn, Denis, *The Life of John Redmond,* London, 1932

Hancock, W.C., *Smuts* (Cambridge: 1962)

Harris, José, *William Beveridge, A Biography,* Oxford, 1977

Hendrick, Burton J., *The Life and Letters of Walter H. Page* (New York: 1925), II, III

Holroyd, Michael, *Lytton Strachey* (London: 1968), II

Hubback, David, *No Ordinary Press Baron, A Life of Walter Layton*, London, 1985

Hyde, H. Montgomery, *Carson*, New York, 1974 (reprint)

Jenkins, Roy, *Asquith*, London, 1964

Koss, Stephen, *Asquith*, New York, 1976

——, *Fleet Street Radical, A.G. Gardiner and the Daily News*, Hampden, Conn., 1973

——, *Lord Haldane, Scapegoat for Liberalism*, New York, 1969

Lamont, Thomas W., *Henry P. Davison: The Record of a Useful Life*, New York, 1933 (reprint, 1975)

Link, Arthur S., *Wilson* (Princeton: 1964)

Lyons, F.S.L., *John Dillon, A Biography*, London, 1968

Magnus, Philip, *Kitchener*, New York, 1959

Marchant, James, *Dr. John Clifford*, London, 1924

Marquand, David, *Ramsay MacDonald*, London, 1977

Maurice, F.B., *Haldane*, reprinted (Westport, Connecticut: 1970), II

McKenna, Stephen, *Reginald McKenna*, London, 1948

Morgan, Kenneth and Jane, *Portrait of a Progressive: The Political Career of Christopher, Viscount Addison*, Oxford, 1980

Newton, Thomas W. Legh, Lord, *Lord Lansdowne*, London, 1929

Nicholson, Harold, *King George the Fifth*, London, 1952

Owen, Eluned E., *The Later Life of Bishop Owen* (Llandysul: 1961)

Reading, The Marquess of, *Rufus Isaacs, First Marquess of Reading* (London: 1942, 1945)

Rhondda, Viscountess, *D.A. Thomas, Viscount Rhondda*, London, 1921

Roskill, Stephen, *Hankey, Man of Secrets* (New York: 1970), I

Ryan, W. Michael, *Lieutenant-Colonel Charles á Court Repington, A Study in the Interaction of Personality, the Press and Power*, New York, 1987

Salvidge, Stanley, *Salvidge of Liverpool*, London, 1934

Schaper, Bertus Willam, *Albert Thomas, trente ans de reformisme social*, Assen, Netherlands, 1959

Speaight, Robert, *The Life of Hilaire Belloc*, New York, 1957

Spender, J.A. and Cyril S. Asquith, *The Life of Herbert Henry Asquith, Lord Oxford and Asquith* (London: 1932), II

Taylor, A.J.P., *Beaverbrook*, London, 1972

Terraine, John, *Douglas Haig, The Educated Soldier*, London, 1963

Trevelyan, George M., *Grey of Fallodon*, Boston, 1937

3. Studies of special political issues, events or topics

Adams, R.J.Q., *Arms and the Wizard, Lloyd George and the Ministry of Munitions, 1915–1916*, College Station, Texas, 1978

—— and Philip Poirier, *The Conscription Controversy in Great Britain, 1900–1918*, Columbus, Ohio, 1987

Asquith, H.H., *The Genesis of the War*, New York, 1923

Beaverbrook, William Maxwell Aitken, Lord, *Men and Power*, London, 1959

——, *Politicians and the War, 1914–1916*, London, 1960

Beckett, I.F.W. and Keith Simpson, eds., *A Nation in Arms, A social study of the British army in the First World War*, Manchester, 1985

Beesly, Patrick, *Room 40: British Naval Intelligence 1914–18*, New York, 1982

Briggs, Asa and John Saville, eds., *Essays in Labour History, 1886–1923*, Hamden, Conn., 1971

Burk, Kathleen, *Britain, America and the Sinews of War, 1914–1918*, Winchester, Mass., 1985

——, *Morgan Grenfell, 1838–1988, The Biography of a Merchant Bank*, Oxford, 1989

Cassar, George H., *The French and the Dardanelles, A Study of Failure in the Conduct of War*, London, 1971

Cruttwell, C.R.M.F., *A History of the Great War*, Oxford, 1936

Daiches, David, *Scotch Whisky*, London, 1969

Donaldson, Frances, *The Marconi Scandal*, London, 1962

Fair, John D., *British Interparty Conferences, A Study of the Procedure of Conciliation in British Politics, 1867–1921*, Oxford, 1980

Farwell, Byron, *Mr. Kipling's Army*, New York, 1987

French, David, *British Economic and Strategic Planning*, London, 1982

Frieden, Michael, *Liberalism Divided, A Study in British Political Thought, 1914–1939*, Oxford, 1986

Fry, Michael, *Lloyd George and Foreign Policy* (Montreal: 1977)

Gilbert, Bentley Brinkerhoff, *British Social Policy, 1914–1939*, London, 1970

——, *The Evolution of National Insurance, The Origins of the Welfare State*, London, 1966

Gudmondsson, B.I., *Storm Troop Tactics*, New York, 1989

Guinn, Paul, *British Strategy and Politics, 1914–1918*, Oxford, 1965

Halévy, Elie, *The Rule of Democracy* (University Paperback Edition) New York, 1961

Hazlehurst, Cameron, *Politicians at War, July, 1914 to May, 1915*, London, 1971

Jalland, Patricia, *The Liberals and Ireland*, New York, 1980

King, Jere Clemens, *Generals and Politicians, Conflict Between France's High Command, Parliament and Government, 1914–1918*, Berkeley, 1951

Kirkaldy, A.W., ed., *British Finance During and After the War*, London, 1921

Koss, Stephen, *Nonconformity in Modern British Politics*, Hamden, Conn., 1975

——, *The Rise and Fall of the Political Press in Britain* (London: 1984), II

Lawson, Wilfred R., *British War Finance*, London, 1915

Anon. [Laurance Lyon] *The Pomp of Power*, New York, 1922

Mallet, Bernard and C. Oswald George, *British Budgets, 1913–14 to 1920–21*, London, 1929

Marder, Arthur, *From the Dreadnought to Scapa Flow* (London: 1961), I, II

Middlebrook, Martin, *First Day on the Somme*, New York, 1972

Morgan, Kenneth, *Wales in British Politics*, Cardiff, 1970

Rubenstein, W.D., *Men of Property*, New Brunswick, N.J., 1981

Sayers, R.S., *The Bank of England, 1891–1944*, Cambridge, 1976

Scally, Robert J., *The Origins of the Lloyd George Coalition: The Politics of Social-Imperialism, 1900–1918*, Princeton, 1975

Scott, J.D., *Vickers, A History*, London, 1962

Taylor, A.J.P., ed., *Lloyd George Twelve Essays*, New York, 1971

——, *Politics in Wartime*, London, 1964

Theodoulou, Christos, *Greece and the Entente, August 1, 1914–September 25, 1916*, Thessaloniki, 1971

Travers, Timothy H.E., *The Killing Ground: The British Army, The Western Front and the Emergence of Modern Warfare, 1900–18*, London, 1987

Webb, Sidney and Beatrice, *English Poor Law History: Part II: The Last Hundred Years* (London: 1929), II

Wilson, Trevor, *The Myriad Faces of War*, Oxford, 1986

Woodward, David R., *Lloyd George and the Generals*, Newark, Delaware, 1983

Wrigley, C.J., *David Lloyd George and the British Labour Movement*, Hassocks, 1976

4. Memoirs and autobiographies

Askwith, George, Lord, *Industrial Problems and Disputes*, London, 1920

Asquith, Margot, *An Autobiography* (New York: 1922), III

Beveridge, W.H., *Power and Influence*, New York, 1955

Churchill, Winston S., *The World Crisis* (New York: 1924–7), I, II

Cox, Alfred, *Among the Doctors*, London, 1950

Grey, Edward, Viscount, *Twenty-five Years, 1892–1916* (New York: 1925), II

James, Robert Rhodes, ed., *J.C.C. Davidson's Memoirs and Papers*, London, 1969

Long, Walter, Viscount, *Memories*, London, 1923

von Ludendorff, Eric, *Ludendorff's Own Story* (New York: 1919)

Morley, John, Lord, *Memorandum on Resignation*, London, 1928

Murray, Arthur C., *Master and Brother, The Murrays of Elibank*, London, 1945

Oxford and Asquith, Earl of, *Memories and Reflections, 1852–1927* (Boston: 1928), II

Poincaré, Raymond, *The Memoirs of Raymond Poincaré, 1914*, New York, 1929

Robertson, Sir William, *Soldiers and Statesmen* (London: 1926)

Samuel, Herbert, Viscount, *Memoirs*, London, 1945

Spender, Harold, *Fire of Life*, London, 1926

Stevenson, Frances L., *The Years That Are Past*, London, 1967

Swinton, Ernest D., *Eyewitness*, New York, 1933

Thomson, Basil, *The Scene Changes*, New York, 1937

Ullswater, James Lowther, Viscount, *A Speaker's Commentaries* (London: 1925)

Steed, Henry Wickham, *Through Thirty Years* (London: 1924)

5. Scholarly journals

Albion

Bulletin of the Institute of Historical Research (now *Historical Research*)

Historical Journal

Journal of American History

Journal of Business History
Journal of Modern History

6. Unpublished dissertations and conference papers

Buchanan, Lawrence R., 'The Governmental Career of Sir Eric Campbell Geddes,' unp. Ph.D. dissertation, University of Virginia, 1979

Hutcheson, John A., 'Leopold Maxse and the *National Review*, 1893–1914,' unp. Ph.D. dissertation, University of North Carolina at Chapel Hill, 1974

Schwartz, Donald R., 'From Rapprochement to Appeasement: Domestic Determinants of Anglo-American Relations Under Lloyd George and Wilson,' unp. Ph.D. dissertation, New York University, 1977

Sumida, Jon T., 'British Naval Administration and Policy in the Age of Fisher,' paper presented before the Midwest Consortium on Military History, University of Chicago, October 1988

7. Novels

Bennett, Arnold, *Lord Raingo*, New York, 1926

Sassoon, Siegfried, *Memoirs of an Infantry Officer* (paperback reprint), London, 1983

Wells, H.G., *Ann Veronica*, New York, 1909

Index